BUSINESS POLICIES and
CENTRAL MANAGEMENT

FIFTH EDITION

BY

WILLIAM H. NEWMAN
Samuel Bronfman Professor
of Democratic Business Enterprise
Graduate School of Business
Columbia University

and

JAMES P. LOGAN
Associate Professor of Management
Graduate School of Business
Columbia University

Published by

SOUTH-WESTERN PUBLISHING CO.

Cincinnati   Chicago   Dallas

New Rochelle, N. Y.   Burlingame, Calif.

G46

Library of Congress Catalog Card No. 65-19821

H165
Printed in the United States of America

TO
SAMUEL BRONFMAN
able exponent of free enterprise

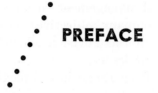 **PREFACE**

A shift is occurring in the study of business policies. More attention is being given to an analytical framework for sifting and relating the numerous elements involved in sensing a whole company and its environment; less reliance is being placed on only an intuitive grasp. To be sure, formal "model" building has a long way to go before it can begin to embrace the complexities of a total, dynamic enterprise; but some structure in our thinking is highly beneficial.

The growing use of this book in business policy courses undoubtedly reflects this trend. The book combines (a) a general framework for company analysis, explained and illustrated in the chapters, with (b) an array of cases for developing skill and understanding in the practical application of the framework. The proposed analytical structure—when used with discretion appropriate to all such guides for rational thought—is especially valuable to executives in making mental transitions from a rapidly changing environment to concrete management decisions.

A business enterprise can be analyzed in many ways. Choice of a way, which is necessary because we become confused if we try to follow many approaches, is a matter of usefulness. The approach outlined in this book has been successfully applied to a wide variety of enterprises by business executives, management consultants, and teachers. Not only the major parts, but also the subdivisions, have proven useful. With experience, refinements have been made; the basic viewpoint and sequence of analysis, however, was developed by Mr. James O. McKinsey—a leading management consultant and senior executive—to diagnose overall company situations.

Recent management concepts have been woven into the basic analytical framework in this edition of the book. The place of PERT, discounted cash flow, and long-range programming, for example, in a comprehensive framework is shown. Sections or chapters have been added on central-management organization, mergers, and acquisitions. Major company objectives now are examined prior to policies. Throughout this revision added focus has been placed on *central-management* issues.

A majority of the cases are new. They range in complexity so that the professor can select cases suited to the aims of his course and the background of his students. (1) Cases at the end of each chapter deal with concrete problems as parts of the total management complex. (2) Integrating cases for groups of chapters cut across conventional boundaries and bring out interrelationships. (3) Comprehensive cases at the end of the book cover the entire range of business operations.

Just as a senior executive faces problems varying in scope and deals with them from an overall company viewpoint, all these cases can contribute to a sensing of total company operations. Coupled with the framework provided in the chapters, the cases enable the student to develop an effective, operational grasp of central management.

An early draft of the text was prepared in collaboration with Mr. McKinsey for an executive development course in Marshall Field & Company. Many individuals have contributed to this revision. Businessmen have been generous with their time in providing data and ideas for cases, but for obvious reasons they must remain anonymous. Many professors have made helpful suggestions. Professor R. S. Alexander of Columbia University, Professor A. H. Keally of the University of Tennessee, and Dr. E. H. Curcuru of the Life Office Management Association supplied excellent case material. Also, the Executive Programs of the Graduate School of Business, Columbia University, generously permitted us to draw upon cases prepared for their use.

We gratefully acknowledge the competent and cheerful assistance of Camilla Koch in transforming our illegible notes to typed drafts and revised drafts to final manuscript.

WILLIAM H. NEWMAN
JAMES P. LOGAN

CONTENTS

Chapter   Page

Part 1 · Establishing Company Goals

1   Approach to Central-Management Problems 3
2   Dynamic Setting of Business 21
3   Appraising the Outlook for a Company 48
4   Basic Company Objectives 81

Part 2 · Defining Major Policies

5   Sales Policies—Products 113
6   Sales Policies—Customers 133
7   Sales Policies—Pricing 155
8   Sales Policies—Sales Promotion 177

Integrating Cases—Sales Policies 196

9   Production and Purchasing Policies 209
10 Production and Purchasing Policies (Concluded) 231
11 Personnel Policies—Selection and Training 253
12 Personnel Policies—Compensation and Arrangements
    for Work 278
13 Personnel Policies—Employee Services and Industrial
    Relations 301

Integrating Cases—Production and Personnel Policies . 325

14 Financial Policies—Uses of Capital 338
15 Financial Policies—Sources of Capital 367
16 Financial Policies—Protection of Capital and Distribu-
    tion of Earnings 396

Integrating Cases—Financial Policies 418

Chapter   Page

Part 3 • Organizing for Action

17 Grouping Activities for Effective Operations 431
18 Organizational Relationships 455
19 Balancing the Organization Structure 477
20 Board of Directors and Central-Management Organization 500

Integrating Cases—Organization 522

Part 4 • Developing Major Resources

21 Executive Personnel 541
22 Facilities 570

Integrating Cases—Resources 598

Part 5 • Guiding the Execution of Plans

23 Short- and Long-Range Programming 613
24 Activating 639
25 Controlling Operations 663
26 Budgetary Control 685

Integrating Cases—Execution 713

Part 6 • Synthesis

27 Company-Wide, Integrated Approach to Central Management 735

Part 7 • Comprehensive Cases

Case

1 Norris Paper Company 749
2 Robbins Lawn Mower Company, Inc. 777
3 Barber Ice Cream Company 787
4 Jones Joints, Incorporated 823
5 Rocklyn Corporation 844
6 Eastern States Iron and Steel Company 864
7 Novins Wallpaper Company 888
8 Frederick & Frank 914

Selected Bibliography 930

Index 937

LIST OF CASES
End of Chapter—Integrating—
Comprehensive

Firm Name	Nature of Case	Page
A.B.C. Corporation	Organization problems of a multiline food company	497
Andersen Starch Company	Pricing a new product	173
Auberge Hotels, Inc.	Evaluating the control system of a hotel chain	678
Automatic Lathe Company	Design change related to source of supply and procurement of a lathe base	250
Barber Ice Cream Company	Comprehensive case; financial, marketing, and facilities problems of a street-vending division of a regional dairy products manufacturer	787
William E. Berry Company	Programming construction and operation of a new plant	635
Blair Plastic Company	New plant versus addition to present plant to take care of overcrowding	595
Blakeman Textiles, Inc.	Training executives and choosing a president	565
Blends Woven Label Company	Personnel policies and labor relations policies of resolving a strike of a small textile manufacturer	320
Blue Island Plating Co.	Personnel policies of hiring and training in a small manufacturing company	274
Central Wire Company	Integrating case; financial and purchasing policy problems of a wire and cable manufacturing company	423
Eastern States Iron and Steel Company	Comprehensive case; central management problems and policies of an integrated steel producer	864
J. Findlager & Sons, Inc.	Integrating case; personnel and facilities policies of a lumber wholesaler	329
Frederick & Frank	Comprehensive case; overall policies of a management consulting firm	914
Hargrove, O'Donnell and Co.	Integrating case; marketing policies of a small investment banking firm	202

Firm Name	Nature of Case	Page
The Hoopes Ribbon Company	Integrating case; sales and other questions of expansion into a new market	196
The I.C.L.A. Construction Company	Organization problems of a diversified regional construction firm	471
Industrial Scale Company	Sources of capital to finance growth	391
Island Creek Coal Company	Forecasting the future of energy supply and relating company product policy to this forecast	70
Jones Joints, Inc.	Comprehensive case; management problems of a manufacturer of pipe joints	823
Koch Electronics, Inc.	Problems of the board of directors' composition and duties	517
Major Spectacle Corporation	Personnel policies of compensation and working conditions for a manufacturer of eyeglass frames	296
Metzger Chemical Company	Marketing decision on taking on a major new product	127
Middle States Steel Corporation	New equipment and balance of facilities at operation stages in an integrated steel company	227
National Lumber and Plywood Corporation	Long-run forecast of general economic conditions related to this firm's resource needs	41
National Sponge Rubber Division of Nation-Wide Rubber and Chemical Corporation	Integrating case; organization problems of a division of a major rubber and chemical firm	533
Norris Paper Company	Comprehensive case; overall problems of managing a wholesale paper and folding box manufacturing firm	749
Novins Wallpaper Company	Comprehensive case; sales and financial problems of a wallpaper company	888
The Silas Oates Company	Issues facing president and central management of a company making specialized castings	13
Orient Magnetics Company	Integrating case; personnel and procurement policies for a manufacturer of metal products	325
Parker Gear Company	Integrating case; overall control problems of a gear manufacturing company	721
Phoenix Company	Distribution channels for a manufacturer of hand tools	149
Premier Paper Company	Financial policies on protection of capital and distribution of earnings	414

Firm Name	Nature of Case	Page
Prometheus Steel Corporation	Alternative sales promotion policies for a specialized steel producer	193
Quality Watch Company	Financial policies relating to sources of funds	359
Robbins Lawn Mower Company, Inc.	Comprehensive case; what to do about a newly developed power mower	777
Rocklyn Corporation	Comprehensive case; a small company in the automotive replacement parts business	844
St. Louis Blues, Inc.	Organization of a major league baseball team	453
Service Drug Wholesale, Inc.	Supervision by a new branch manager	656
Solie Bakeries, Inc.	Integrating case; control of a firm with many branches	713
State Telephone Company	Evaluation of a consultant's proposal for revising the budgeting structure of an independent telephone company	702
The Textron Mills at Nashua	Decision of the board of directors in light of public repercussions	101
Town Shirt Company	Integrating case; adapting organization structure to changes in policies	522
Triboro Textile Equipment Company	Integrating case; adequacy of facilities and executive personnel	598
Western Nadir Markets, Inc.	Integrating case; facilities problems of a supermarket chain	606
Western Plywood Mills, Inc.	Integrating case; sources and uses of capital	418

PART

1 · ESTABLISHING COMPANY GOALS

Ch. 1 · Approach to Central-Management Problems

Ch. 2 · Dynamic Setting of Business

Ch. 3 · Appraising the Outlook for a Company

Ch. 4 · Basic Company Objectives

CHAPTER 1

APPROACH TO CENTRAL-MANAGEMENT PROBLEMS

Need for analytical framework. The top—or "central"—executives of every company face a special set of issues. They must think of their company as a totality—a whole, integrated enterprise.

Central-management issues include: identifying key factors for the survival and growth of the company and devising basic objectives, policies, and programs for dealing with these factors; being sensitive to the interdependence of the numerous actions taken by the company and maintaining a strategic balance in these actions; and keeping an eye on how current activities of the company will mesh with predicted changes—social, political, technological, economic, and competitive—and adapting company plans to the anticipated environment.

Even this terse and incomplete list of problems indicates that the task of central management is complex. And, as with any complex situation, a tested approach for dealing with it can be very helpful. The approach outlined in this book is basically a framework for thinking about central-management issues. It expedites analysis and it assists in forming a synthesis of action to be taken.

Of course, any single approach must be adapted and amplified to fit the peculiarities of a specific company. In a small importing firm, for instance, organization may be relatively unimportant whereas political outlook is crucial. On the other hand, the senior executives in a young electronics company may be predominantly concerned about technology and additional sources of capital.

Most useful is an approach that draws attention to a limited (comprehensible) number of basic issues in a systematic arrangement and that at the same time is reasonably complete in the potential trouble spots it flags or suggests. A way of thinking about central-management problems is more important than an exhaustive listing of all possible difficulties.

3

An understanding of the nature of central-management problems is important to subordinate executives and employees as well as to the top executive himself. If an employee wishes to understand the "why" of his job as well as the "how," he must appreciate the significance of the activities of his senior executives. Moreover, by taking the point of view of central management, an employee is able to secure a perspective over the operations of the entire business that will enable him to cooperate more effectively with his fellow workers.

Major divisions of management job. For orderly thinking about the diverse issues confronting senior executives of a company, a division into basic aspects is needed. A very practical approach is to recognize that every central manager must:

1. Determine *policies* and *objectives* which will focus and guide the activities of the company. These plans give purpose and direction to the work of all employees, and they indicate the broad limits within which action is to be taken.

2. Set up an *organization* to carry out the objectives and policies. Responsibility for the many activities which are necessary to execute the policies must be assigned to different employees, and relationships among the jobs should be clarified.

3. Develop *resources* needed to put the plans into effect. Executives and other key employees must be obtained to staff the organization; buildings and equipment of various kinds will be required in every division.

4. Guide the *execution* of plans through the organization with the resources assembled. This calls for programming, activating, and controlling the operations.

Since this division of the tasks of central management will be used throughout the book, the nature of each section should be recognized from the start. Two examples, a simple case of a drugstore and the more complex activities of a steel company, will help give meaning to these basic problems.

Managing a small business. The manager of a small business faces many of the same issues as the president of a large concern. For instance, the manager of a corner drugstore must first decide that he wants to go into the retailing trade for himself on small— or large—scale at a given location. And even before he opens his doors for business he faces policy questions:

Shall he sell prescriptions as well as prepared drugs; cosmetics and candy; newspapers and cameras; banana splits and hot soup?

Shall he deliver goods if customers request him to do so?

Shall he price his products below competitors, or try to build up his business on the basis of quality and service?

Shall he sell for cash only, or shall he also sell on credit?

Shall he pay his employees a fixed salary, or shall he pay them a percentage of sales?

In making decisions of this nature, the manager is establishing *policies* for his business. While the objectives and the policies are subject to revision, usually they will be followed for quite a period of time. They will be referred to again and again in day-to-day activities, and they will serve as major guides to what action should be taken.

At first, the druggist may attempt to do all the work at the store himself, but if the store prospers he will soon need additional people to help him. When this happens, he will have to *organize* the work. One or more people will be assigned to wait on customers, and one man may be given full responsibility to run the soda fountain. Perhaps a job will be set up for a registered pharmacist who will do nothing but fill prescriptions. The cashier-bookkeeping duties may be set off as another job. Still a different position may be created for delivery, janitor, and other manual work.

Of course, if several new stores are added so that a drug chain is established, further organization problems will arise. There will be questions as to the desirability of central units for buying, inventory control, sales promotion, warehousing, and even simple manufacturing. The relationships between such central units and the managers of each store will call for special definitions of responsibility.

Whether there be one store or many, the manager will have to bring together the *resources* he needs for operations. Qualified people to fit the positions in the organization will have to be recruited and trained. The store building and also showcases, counters, shelves, soda fountains, and other equipment must be obtained and properly laid out. These fixed assets involve significant investments of capital and must be selected with an eye to their effect on total profits.

Following all these preparations will come the day-by-day *execution*. Specific plans for window displays, special sales, purchasing, and many other activities will be needed. Even with a few employees some time will have to be devoted to supervision; and a variety of controls on inventory, service, quality of prescriptions, and other matters will be necessary. No matter how large the enterprise becomes, every executive will have to spend some time on "make happen" duties.

Central-management problems of a steel company. *Objectives and policies.* This same method of approach—objectives and policies, organization, resources, and execution—may also be illustrated by key problems facing a large steel company. A steel company, like the corner drugstore, must decide what products it will handle. At one time, most big companies made rails for railroads. With a shift in demand to lighter-weight alloy products now, many companies do not enter the rail market at all. A few firms fabricate their steel into consumer products—nails, fences, even kitchen pans. But this raises the delicate problem of competing with important customers of wire, sheet, or other semifinished steel. There are hundreds of specialty products, such as seamless steel tubing used primarily in the manufacture of airplanes, and management must frequently consider whether to add new products or to drop old ones. These decisions on product policy have a direct impact on research activities, personnel requirements, capital investment, facilities, and other aspects of the business.

A steel company, like many other companies, has a major problem in deciding whether to produce its own raw materials or to purchase them from an outside company. The desire of major firms is to mine most if not all of the iron ore they use, and with dwindling United States deposits, companies must decide whether to invest millions of dollars in new properties in Labrador, Venezuela, or other foreign countries. Risk of interruption of vital supplies as well as costs are factors in establishing such a policy.

If a steel company produces its raw materials, it must provide for their transportation from the mines to the steel plant. Here a choice must be made between use of public carriers or investing in one's own shipping company.

Many other production plans must be made before the desired products can be manufactured. For example, technology is changing. In making steel from pig iron, the company must decide whether the electric furnace or the open-hearth process will be used and the extent to which continuous casting or oxygen inverters are feasible. Decisions of this type involve tremendous sums of capital. In addition, large sums are needed for inventories and to finance sales to customers. Such funds may be obtained from the sale of stocks or bonds, or if the need appears to be temporary, money may be borrowed from a bank. The steel company problems discussed thus far illustrate broad issues of objectives and policies. As in the case of the corner drugstore, these broad plans determine the scope and the nature of activities that will be undertaken.

Organization. The manager of a steel company has another major type of problem that requires careful attention. He must organize the numerous activities so that each employee can concentrate on his particular duties and at the same time coordinate his efforts with those of other executives and operators. The manager of a sales branch, for example, should know how much freedom he has to set prices, make delivery promises, and agree to unusual product specifications. With greater freedom he can better meet local competition; but what he does directly affects the production department and may have repercussions in other sales offices and even in the antitrust division in Washington.

A continuing difficulty, especially in very large firms, is to sustain the initiative and the resourcefulness of key executives. For this purpose, central managements often establish decentralized operating divisions. Steel companies often organize their mines or shipping companies in this fashion; but there is serious question as to how far this organization concept may be carried because steel technology does not lend itself to small, semiautonomous units.

These examples indicate that the form of organization can have a marked influence on the success of a company.

Resources. Men of widely differing skills will be needed. Metallurgists, mechanical engineers, accountants, and other men with specialized training will be recruited. The source of junior executives is not so clear because men with technical training may not make as good supervisors as those "up from the ranks."

The executive personnel problem is only partly solved, however, by initial recruitment. More important is training on the job and careful selection for promotion within the company. A continuing problem is to help men who move into the higher executive positions to broaden their perspective and to develop judgment in areas outside of their technical specialty.

The location and the design of equipment is a recurring problem for all steel companies that wish to maintain their position in the industry. In steelmaking, there are significant economies in large-scale plants, yet there are offsetting advantages in a location close to customers and in tapping a new labor supply. In addition to technical considerations such as heat balance and continuous operation, executives must predict future growth in markets for various types of steel. For instance, the outlook for sale of steel sheets for automobile bodies differs significantly from the outlook for rails. Consequently, central management must exercise considerable judgment in deciding how much or what kind of plant to build where.

Neither the chief executive of a steel company nor the corner druggist needs to be an expert on the technical features of the facilities he acquires. Each of these men will rely on advice from technical experts. Nevertheless, they must decide the directions in which their respective enterprises ar going, make sure that any new facilities are in balance with other phases of their business, and weigh the relative strategic value of each proposed investment.

Execution. The central management of a large company typically spends less time on execution than the manager of a small firm because in a large enterprise much more of the detailed planning and supervision can be delegated to middle tiers of executives. The final stage in the management cycle is nonetheless vital.

Numerous actions must be taken if the steel company is to succeed, and the chief executive will influence the timing of many of these actions. He may push in one direction, and hold back in another. He probably will use long-range and short-range programs to reflect these timing decisions. Moreover, top executives have to provide inspiration and drive—directly to their own subordinates and indirectly throughout the company. And attention must be given to designing and using controls—the feedback flow of information on both good and bad results.

This review has indicated how central-management problems of a steel company may be classified in terms of objectives and policies, organization, resources, and execution. Although the particular subjects faced by executives of department stores, banks, railroads, and other firms will have their distinctive content, nevertheless the basic problems will fall into the same classifications. In other words, the nature of administration is similar in all enterprises, and there are certain common, underlying problems that can very profitably be studied.

Interdependence of objectives and policies, organization, resources, and execution. Each of the types of problems we have discussed is dependent on each of the others. Objectives and policies should be considered when an organization is established, for otherwise the form of organization may not be suitable to carrying out the basic plans effectively. For example, a company planning to sell its products in foreign markets by means of traveling representatives may need to establish a different form of organization than that used in a domestic market. If it uses specialty salesmen who handle only one line of products in several countries, its sales may be curtailed in those countries where the salesmen do not speak the local language fluently. The steel company that plans to sell its products within a radius of 200 miles of its plant will not need branch sales offices that might be required if it followed a policy of selling throughout the United States.

On the other hand, if it is not practical to change rapidly the organization of an established company, the limitations of this organization must be considered in adopting new policies. For example, a company producing machine tools experienced a substantial reduction in the volume of its sales at the beginning of a business depression. The management found it would be possible to manufacture sun-ray lamps in its factory and proceeded to produce a substantial quantity of them. It then discovered that its former sales organization was unable to sell the new product. The sun-ray lamps had to be sold to electrical equipment retailers and not to the manufacturers who purchased the machine tools. The cost of rebuilding its sales organization was so large that the company became bankrupt even though it had succeeded in producing a desirable product.

If a company owns substantial facilities of a certain type, changes in policy and organization may have to be restricted to the limitations of this equipment. To cite a specific example, a carpet company that had a large investment in 27-inch looms could not suddenly decide to sell only broadloom carpets. The company lacked sufficient capital to buy new equipment, and consequently it could not establish a policy of selling products that the present equipment was not capable of producing. In the same way a company should not establish a sales organization for selling specialties if its equipment will produce only staples. Thus a textile company equipped to produce standard cotton piece goods should not create a selling organization capable of handling fancy weaves of silk, wool, and cotton mixture.

Policies, organization, and resources will naturally be considered in execution. Many elaborate systems of accounting, production, and statistical control have broken down because the ability of those responsible for their enforcement was not considered when the systems were designed. Contrariwise, when a particular production or selling division is unusually efficient, the facilities and even the policies may be adjusted to make possible the use of this distinctive capability.

This interdependence of objectives, policies, organization, resources, and execution should be kept in mind when dealing with an actual problem. Decisions in one area are almost sure to have effects in other areas; consequently, it is only prudent to check all angles before taking action.

Intangibles in administration. One other aspect of general management should be stressed in this introductory chapter. Most of the problems faced by senior executives have so many intangible factors that the use of fixed rules and formulas is impractical.

Throughout business activities will be found human reactions and human behavior. While we know something about typical behavior patterns and average responses, any single case is likely to be different. The administrator is usually dealing with a specific case, and consequently he must use his judgment about the human factors present in that situation. Throughout this book frequent reference is made to human behavior, but this can serve only as a reminder that we are dealing with problems which are more or less intangible.

A second reason why business administration cannot be treated like engineering is the ever shifting business environment. The future volume of sales and the level of costs are often unknown when major decisions must be made. Time and time again, the executive has to make the best forecast he can of business conditions in his industry and then set his course on the basis of this forecast; but here again much of the basis for action rests on judgment of intangibles.

While these intangible factors make management difficult, their existence also requires that we get all the help we can from an orderly and logical approach to the management of an enterprise.

SUMMARY AND ORGANIZATION OF BOOK

Although each company is distinct in many respects, there is a common core of problems faced by the central management of every business concern. These basic problems include (1) establishing company objectives and determining major policies, (2) setting up an organization, (3) developing necessary resources, and (4) guiding execution of plans.

A separate part of this book will be devoted to each of these major administrative tasks. Problems faced in most, if not all, companies will be discussed in logical order. In this way, a comprehensive view of company management will be developed.

Since forecasting affects so many business decisions, special chapters on appraising the outlook for a company are introduced before objectives and policies are examined.

An understanding of company management requires both (a) a familiarity with the various problems that will be encountered and (b) a recognition of the relationships between these problems. This book contains an analysis of central-management views common to most business firms; and consequently it should (a) give the reader familiarity with key management problems and (b) provide help with the relationships. The arrangement of material in logical sequence immediately suggests relationships; throughout the discussion and questions, relationships are often stressed; and integrating and comprehensive cases provide opportunity to study relationships in realistic situations.

In using the book, then, each chapter should be studied for new ideas, and at the same time the ideas presented should be related to those in other chapters. If this is done, the structure of the book can become a useful tool of analysis and of integration.

QUESTIONS FOR CLASS DISCUSSION

1. Companies in the pharmaceutical manufacturing and chemical manufacturing industries typically have a policy of spending a considerably larger portion of their revenues on research and development work than do firms in many other industries. Among other things, this means a rapid introduction of new products. What else does such a policy mean to a pharmaceutical or chemical company? How does it affect resource requirements, for example?

2. Give illustrations of policies, organization, resources, and execution for each of the following organizations:

- (a) A bank.
- (b) A company operating chain stores.
- (c) A manufacturer of farm implements.
- (d) A railroad.
- (e) A labor union.
- (f) A university.

3. In a search for markets and supplies of oil, major United States-based oil companies have expanded operations around the world. What problems of policy, organization, resources, and execution does such a company face in its expansion phase? Do these problems differ from those of (a) multinational firms engaged in the machinery business and (b) rapidly growing United States discounters of food and general merchandise?

4. Some firms in the electrical goods industries and in the machinery industries make only a limited line of products and specialize in higher-grade, higher-priced items while others manufacture and sell products across the entire spectrum of quality and price. How do these differences in policy relate to the resources needed and the organization used?

5. The products, the location and facilities, the individuals involved, the size and financial strength, and the traditions of one company will all be more or less different from those of every other company. For these reasons, some executives contend that business training should take place on-the-job in each individual firm. How would you justify to such an executive your study of business administration in college?

6. Suppose the administrator of one steel company thought steel sales were going up 5% per year for at least five years, but the administrator of a second steel company thought sales would be lower. How would this difference in outlook affect decisions these men would be likely to make regarding the various problems described on pages 6 to 9?

7. This chapter has considered primarily the problems of the top executive of a company, because we want to take a company-wide view of business activities. Do you think the division of management problems into policies, organization, resources, and operations has any useful application to the work of a departmental executive such as a sales manager or a production manager? That is, can a departmental executive apply these same concepts *within* his department? Explain.

8. (a) It has been said that the difference between the study of economics and business is only a matter of viewpoint; economics takes the view of society as a whole, whereas business looks at the same facts from a view of a company. This means that business administration is applied economics. Do you agree? (b) How do you reconcile this suggestion with a concept of administration as a social process necessary to all cooperative endeavor—be it business, government, or military?

9. The John Smith Shoe Company decided to move to Missouri from upstate New York because its taxes would be reduced; a modern, low-cost plant was available; and there was a plentiful supply of unskilled and semiskilled labor. Sales of the company's rather old-fashioned women's walking shoes had been declining and a line of children's shoes was proposed. What basic problems of administration did the executive committee need to face in connection with the move?

CASE I

The Silas Oates Company

Executives of The Silas Oates Company are appraising the present position and planning the future course of the company.

The firm was first organized to exploit the skills and know-how in making metal castings that Mr. Silas Oates had developed while a graduate student and instructor at Pennsylvania State College. It started operations in an old auto repair shop on the outskirts of the town of State College, Pennsylvania. Early sales were manly to defense contractors. Sales grew and then fluctuated with changes in the government's defense program.

Mr. Oates says, "Our business is making castings that require engineering and tooling that others in the industry are unable to or don't want to do. Their castings often lack smoothness of surface, precision of dimension, and uniformity of quality. In addition, certain alloys require careful processing while casting. It is often difficult to make certain shapes from them. To do so requires not only a high degree of skill in techniques, but enginering ability in tool and mold design to obtain desirable and maximum properties."

The Silas Oates Company specializes in making castings from aluminum alloys. By using patented processes and special mold compositions developed by Silas Oates's brother, John, a metallurgical engineer, the company can make castings within very narrow dimensional and quality tolerances. Also, these castings will take a high polish and are very uniform from lot to lot. Several years ago, the research group, under John's leadership, developed a process for making ductile iron castings that possess similar characteristics.

The firm operates two plants: one is a modern building with specially built machinery, several miles outside State College, which specializes in aluminum alloy castings; the other, in Houserville about 10 miles away, is equipped to produce castings of ductile iron. The firm employs between 300 and 400 persons, approximately 80% in the State College plant and the balance in Houserville. The capacity of each plant has been increased during the past year to meet peak production requirements. Each plant has operated close to capacity during occasional rush periods over the past year. At present there is unused space available in each plant amounting to about one third of the square footage. During peak periods this space is used for raw materials and work in process inventory storage and for an extension of the pouring floor. (Considerable space is needed to lay out the molds so that the hot metal can be poured into them.)

Many of the company's assets are intangible. They include a high degree of skill and experience in research and in the development of casting methods, a large fund of know-how throughout the executive and working force in making intricate and difficult castings, a spirit of insistence on precision and accuracy that pervades all ranks of the personnel, and a willingness to try new things.

Another intangible asset of the firm is its relations with its employees. It provides vacations with pay and a retirement fund based on contributions by both company and employees. It operates an employee stock ownership plan in which about half of the employees participate. They own over 50% of the common stock. In addition, The Silas Oates Company maintains a profit-sharing plan. Almost one third of the profits before interest charges are paid to employees. Part of this is used to build the retirement fund; the balance is paid as a cash profit share. The books of the company, aside from confidential figures on classified government orders, are open to the employees.

Employees take an active personal interest in the affairs of the firm and appear to prize highly their close personal relationships with the management. Some years ago, a strenuous effort was made to unionize the plant. The employes defeated it, preferring their existing relationship. The management has been careful to avoid any paternalistic relationship and believes strongly in the development of the individual. Communications between central management and men in the shop are considerably better than is common in industry today.

Appendixes I and II on pages 19 and 20 show certain financial statistics of The Silas Oates Company in recent years.

The company's main product, accounting for a third to a half of its total volume, is tire molds. The Silas Oates Company supplies castings for 60% to 70% of all passenger tire molds made in this country. Rubber companies change their tire designs about every two or three years. During the period of six months to a year when a tire company is developing new designs, its purchases of molds of the old design shrink drastically; then when it begins to retool for the new design, its demand for molds expands tremendously. This effect is multiplied by competitive pressures. Redesigning and retooling activities of the different companies tend to coincide rather than be staggered so as to offset each other. This demand behavior causes wide fluctuations of sales from year to year with consequent fluctuations in the number of workers needed. This, in turn, affects the firm's personnel policy and requires very rapid adjustment by management.

In their off-the-road tire business (tractors, farm equipment, construction equipment, etc.) the rubber companies follow a different pattern of behavior. Design changes are less frequent. Their timing tends to be staggered among the several companies. Molds used to make off-the-road tires do not require quite the same accuracy and precision as do those used to make passenger car and truck tires. The Silas Oates Company can and does make these molds and has recently improved its position through better tooling and introduction of large ductile iron castings that, for some applications, are more suitable than aluminum alloys.

Tire molds are also needed in the retread business. The Silas Oates Company has not made a serious effort to sell such molds for several reasons. First, firms supplying the retread service do not require molds of the precision and overall quality needed for original tire manufacture. To seek heavy volume in this business, therefore, the company would have to use cheaper production methods that would still meet the quality requirements for retread molds. By producing retread molds of a different quality, the company might also dilute its habit of precision and accuracy.

Second, many of the firms doing retread work are small establishments needing only one or two molds. They are also widely scattered geographically. This means a difficult task in getting retread molds distributed. One competitor, the Sampson Company, has been successful in making retread molds and distributing them. The Sampson Company sells some of its molds, leases some of them to firms doing retread work, and uses some of them in an extensive retread business it conducts itself. It also produces a wide variety of tire building equipment, including steam boilers and other products not suited to the facilities of The Silas Oates Company. The Sampson Company, the largest firm in the industry, has sales approximately double the volume of The Silas Oates Company.

Several of the major rubber companies, to improve the quality of their retread molds, have recently purchased castings from The Silas Oates Company. They intend to lease or sell these castings to their new tire dealers who wish to offer a retread service.

About one half to two thirds of the sales of The Silas Oates Company are usually of other kinds of specialty castings. During one year the sale of such castings exceeded 85% of the output of the company. Some of these sales arise from defense contracts, some from civilian business. Oates castings can be used wherever high-speed rotating parts are required as compressors or special pumps. Executives of the company are convinced that Oates castings could be substituted for parts or assemblies now produced by other processes by many equipment manufacturing firms. By such substitution, substantial savings have often resulted as well as improved product performance for the company using such castings. This more diversified market has not been extensively explored by The Silas Oates Company, partly because of marketing difficulties and partly because of research and production considerations.

Tire mold contracts of The Silas Oates Company are handled by Mr. Soames, the tire mold sales manager, and two sales engineers. Mr. Soames is a very capable young man in his early thirties who has been with the firm since he returned from services in the Navy. Miscellaneous or specialty casting sales are handled by a force of five salesmen under the direction of Mr. Rogers, who is also in his early thirties. Since Mr. Rogers' background before coming with the company about three years ago was in the advertising business, he also is the advertising manager. Both of these men are responsible to Mr. Upton, a man about 40 years of age, who has been with the company from its beginning. The present sales force is about as big as the volume of the company can support. Total marketing expenses run somewhat under 5% of sales.

Mr. Upton states that The Silas Oates Company has not more than scratched the surface of the specialty, nontire mold castings business. He also says that most of the work of selling the miscellaneous or specialty castings is "bird-dogging"; that is, the salesman visits a prospect in the hope of being able to learn enough about his operations to uncover some part or assembly in which Oates castings can be used profitably to the customer. This is very expensive and time-consuming. With the sales force available, not as much of it has been done as seems desirable.

Mr. Upton wishes some way could be developed by which the sales force could "call its shots." Some attempt has been made by advertising in several engineering publications. Thought has also been given to trying direct mail to a prospect list culled from the *Thomas Register*. The executives wonder whether advertisements in *Business Week* or *Fortune* might not be worthwhile, since these journals are read extensively by production executives who are concerned with the kind of components problems the Oates Company is equipped to solve.

Mr. John Oates, head of research, and Mr. Mountain, the manager of the State College factory, point out that such selling is apt to be very expensive from a factory point of view. Many inquiries received from advertising or uncovered by "bird-dogging" are for only one or two castings. Many of them also require extensive research and factory experimentation to develop precisely the casting the requirements specify. In such a situation, a run of less than 100 castings results in a net loss.

Mr. John Oates and Mr. Mountain also point out that many of the miscellaneous or specialty inquiries involve considerable research and production planning to produce experimental models, which must be tested by the customer and may or may not result in volume orders. About two or three in every five experimental models result in orders of sufficient volume to make them pay. Usually six months to a year or two must elapse after the model is supplied to the customer before an order is received.

All the executives agree that there are many situations in which Oates castings could be used. Their discovery and exploitation would add greatly to sales and would help stabilize volume from year to year. The executives are not all in agreement as to the best way to locate these situations. They do not entirely accept the notion that the firm must put out a lot of seed corn over a long period of time before it can expect much of a harvest. Mr. Silas Oates is an exception to this general attitude.

The salesmen are technical men. Most of them have had experience in the factory. They are not assigned specific territories, but their assignments are to customers or prospective customers. In most cases, a salesman is assigned the prospects he asks for, provided no other salesman also wants them—in which case the sales manager adjudicates the matter. The sales manager also makes specific assignments of leads received by mail from advertising.

When a salesman finds a customer who seems to be able to use a specialty casting, he collects all the necessary information about it. He then brings the data to the factory and spends whatever time is necessary with the research and production people to make sure that they understand the problem involved. When they come up with a casting or a plan for making one, the salesman prepares a proposal for the customer and transmits it either in person or by mail. A proposal may be supplying a test sample or a contract to supply the casting in quantity. The average salesman spends from a third to a half of his time in the factory office.

The executives of The Silas Oates Company are convinced that there are many manufacturing firms which would profit from using the company's research skills and knowledge and its production know-how to develop specifications for castings that would later be bought on an open-bid basis. This is particularly true of government subcontracts. In fact, the company has been asked a number of times to work on a development contract under which it would be paid a fee for the development work and then might bid or refrain from bidding on the contract to supply the castings developed. The executives have discouraged such arrangements on the theory that they might drain off research talent and interest from projects that would be more likely to result in castings sales for the firm.

There appear to be promising opportunities opening up in special castings of steel, titanium, zirconium, and their alloys. To enter this field would mean broadening research interest and knowledge and developing new techniques and skills in production. The demand for castings of the latter two metals is still in the initial stages.

Mr. Silas Oates, founder and president, is about 50 years of age. He is very pleasant to work with. He usually issues requests rather than orders to subordinates, and he freely tolerates—even welcomes—their expression of opinions contrary to his. Under his genial manner, however, are a firmness and a drive that enable him to play concurrently the somewhat contradictory roles of spark plug and balance wheel of the company.

Mr. Silas Oates is gratified by the history of his company and is pleased with its current profit performance. He wonders, however, it perhaps there may be in it elements of weakness for the future. Next week he plans to hold a meeting of his management group to canvass the present situation and the probable future of the firm to the end of pinpointing the areas needing attention and the order of priority among problems.

REQUIRED: (a) From the data in the case, give examples of problems relating to (1) objectives and policies, (2) organization, (3) resources, and (4) execution of plans.

(b) Do you think the firm should now bend its efforts toward new ventures, such as tire molds for the retread business or special castings of new alloys?

(c) What problems are the most important for Mr. Siles Oates to take up with his management group at next week's meeting? What priorities would you assign to these problems?

Appendix I

The Silas Oates Company
Balance Sheet Statistics

Assets	Last Year (Year End)	Current (6 months)
Cash	$ 138,542	$ 562,293
Accounts receivable	421,644	348,429
Inventory—materials	267,718	328,556
Inventory—in process	158,346	223,080
Total current assets	$ 986,250	$1,462,358
Land and improvements	$ 97,907	$ 97,907
Buildings	619,492	593,223
Machinery and equipment	964,884	930,391
Other fixed asets	——	97,026
Total fixed assets	$1,682,283	$1,718,547
Accumulated depreciation	838,886	928,841
Net fixed assets	$ 843,397	$ 789,706
Deferred charges	$ 20,370	$ 12,347
Total assets	$1,850,017	$2,264,411

Liabilities

	Last Year (Year End)	Current (6 months)
Accounts payable	$ 106,740	$ 103,264
Mortgage payable	18,174	——
Accrued items, including payroll tax deductions	143,594	222,852
Federal income tax	66,994	200,707
Total current liabilities	$ 335,502	$ 526,823
5% notes payable:		
Due in 10 years	$ 45,000	$ 45,000
Due in 12 years	90,000	83,070
Due in 18 years	38,610	45,630
Mortgage payable	126,116	135,316
Total long-term debt	$ 299,726	$ 309,016
Total liabilities	$ 635,228	$ 835,839

Capital

	Last Year (Year End)	Current (6 months)
Capital stock [1]	$ 515,950	$ 535,612
Premium on sale of stock	61,181	85,552
Reserve for contingencies	21,897	21,897
Earnings reinvested	615,761	785,511
Total capital	$1,214,789	$1,428,572
Total liabilities and capital	$1,850,017	$2,264,411

[1] Authorized, 24,000 shares, $25 par; issued, 23,103 shares; treasury stock, 172 shares.

Appendix II

The Silas Oates Company
Operating Statistics

	Past Years			*Current Year* [1]
Net sales	$2,411,737	$5,368,628	$2,817,625	$2,309,094
All operating costs .	2,058,659	4,307,215	2,606,249	1,704,655
Operating income ..	$ 353,078	$1,061,413	$ 211,376	$ 604,439
Other income	1,819	2,127	4,030	2,998
Total income	$ 354,897	$1,063,540	$ 215,406	$ 607,437
Charges against income:				
Employees' profit .	$ 88,733	$ 257,305	$ 63,254	$ 197,856
Interest	20,882	27,569	15,822	7,868
Total charges	$ 109,615	$ 284,874	$ 79,076	$ 205,724 [2]
Net income before income tax	$ 245,282	$ 778,666	$ 136,330	$ 401,713
Federal income tax .	119,061	400,922	66,994	200,707
Net income	$ 126,221	$ 377,744	$ 69,336	$ 201,006

[1] Six months.
[2] Includes contribution to employees' retirement fund.

DYNAMIC SETTING OF BUSINESS

Change. The automobile is not merely a substitute for the horse and buggy. It mobilizes labor, opens remote vacation areas, fosters suburban shopping centers, disperses social and community relations, spells downfall to streetcar manufacturers—to mention only a few of its ramifications.

Similarly, the rise of independent nations in Africa is much more than a local political matter. World sources of raw materials are jeopardized; potential new markets for such items as radios and pharmaceuticals are created; fair-employment practices in, say, Detroit, become even more crucial in foreign diplomacy; added strain is placed on United States foreign aid.

These examples of change illustrate a major problem for the modern executive: adapting the direction and the operation of his enterprise to shifts in the social, economic, and political climate of the United States and the world. Change is the one sure thing business managers know will occur.

This chapter indicates some of the major long-term changes that are taking place in our economy and then discusses a way of thinking about changes—a way of organizing thoughts that may be useful to executives in grasping what is occurring in the world outside a particular company or industry. The purpose of this discussion is an understanding of the general setting in which company objectives and policies are established.

LONG-TERM CHANGES IN AMERICAN AFFAIRS

Social changes. *Population.* The United States now has a population of close to 200 million. This is about twice as many people as in 1915 and is an increase of over 50 million since the close of World War II. At present growth rates, the population may increase another 100 million in the next 35 years. Population growth, looked at in total, means more consumers and more workers—more people who buy and more people who can turn out goods and services needed.

In recent years the number of consumers has increased faster than the labor force. Why? This has to do with the age distribution of the population. Because of a jump in the birthrate—from less than 18 per thousand of population in the 1930's to 24 per thousand after 1947—we now have an unusual number of youngsters below working age. The effects of this bumper baby crop and well known to school boards—and to companies that sell school equipment.

Migration. These 200 million people do not stay put. They move from farm to city and from city to suburb. They also move from East to West and from South to North. The drift from rural to urban centers of population has been going on for a long time. During the current century, the proportion of people living in rural territory (places of less than 2,500 population) has dropped from 60% to 30%. No longer can we assume that our labor force will have attitudes toward work and self-reliance engendered by a farm background.

More striking in recent years has been the move from downtown areas to the suburbs. In fact, in our largest population areas (those with over 2 million people) the population of the central cities actually decreased in the decade between 1950 and 1960. Only Los Angeles with its exuberant city limits reported a growth. Declines occurred in Boston, Chicago, Detroit, New York, Philadelphia, Pittsburgh, San Francisco, and Washington. At the same time, the suburbs of most of these cities grew 50% to 80%. This move to the outskirts not only helped to boom housing and the construction industry, but it also revolutionized retail selling.

The continued westward movement of the country's center of population—now halfway across Illinois—was largely due to the influence of California, which grew faster than the rest of the country. During the last half century its average growth per decade has been 47%. At the bottom of the growth scale are a group of southern and prairie states, which have increased very slowly, if at all. Arkansas, Mississippi, North Dakota, Oklahoma, and West Virginia, by migration, lost population between 1940 and 1960.

Education. More people are spending more time in school. The increase in youngsters 5 to 15 years old is tied directly to population growth. For the older groups the key factor has been a jump in the percentage attending school. Only 8% of the 20-year olds went to school in 1920, for example; by 1950 this figure was 18% and in 1960 it was 24%. The increase in total education is also reflected by the growth in college graduates—49,000 in 1920 and 392,000 in 1960. Since the large postwar baby crop is now reaching college age, the total enrollment in college and professional schools is expected to double in the next 15 years.

These educational changes are significant for business in several ways. A better educated population means better skills available in the work force. Many of these skills are needed for the highly mechanized production; but people with college educations can no longer be regarded as exceptional individuals, and problems may be encountered in matching skills and aspirations to the work available. The corollary is that workers for dirty, boring, back-breaking jobs will become more difficult to find and more restive about their assigned tasks. Still another issue is the extent to which business firms should help finance higher education. This is no small question in light of the colleges' desperate need for funds.

Economic changes. *Total incomes.* Not just more people, but more people with money, which they are willing to spend—this is the story of the market. In 1929, the first year for which Department of Commerce statistics are available, disposable personal income amounted to $83 billion. This looks small indeed from the lofty heights of 1964 when people had $420 billion available to spend or to save. With all effects of price changes removed to indicate real income and on a per capita basis so that population increases are washed out, the additions to income still look impressive. In 1947 dollars, per capita disposable personal income was: 1929, $927; 1940, $981; 1950, $1,280; 1963, $1,580.

Income distribution. An outstanding economic fact and a major factor in keeping the economy in high gear is the redistribution of income, especially the upgrading of the lower-income classes. In 1929 only 8% of American families had incomes of over $5,000 per year. Some 60% had incomes of less than $2,000. Today 57% have incomes of more than $5,000 and only 13% have less than $2,000 to spend. Now one family in six has income of over $10,000. The "middle class" bracket has grown enormously. This is the

CHANGES IN INCOME CLASSES

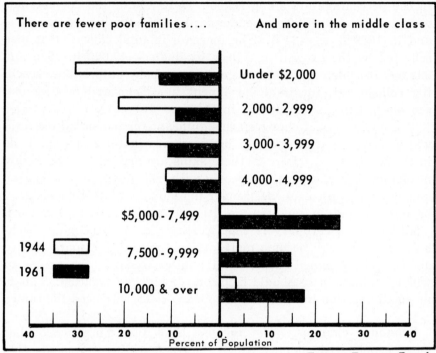

Federal Reserve Board

group that now has "discretionary" spending power and that has been using its discretion to create a continuing demand for all kinds of goods that make ordinary living easier, more comfortable, and more luxurious and that make leisure more varied. This is the group that upgrades luxuries into necessities and buys huge quantities of old and new consumer durables—refrigerators, TV sets, automatic washers, air conditioners, and medium-priced cars.

Total output. As population grows, so does production—but only over the long-term, not every year. Industrial production, according to its most comprehensive measure, the Federal Reserve Board Index, by 1964 was 25% above its 1957-59 average. And the 1957-59 level was two and a half times the production in 1929, the year of the Big Crash and the peak of prosperity up to that time. More people mean more workers; but obviously the total of goods turned out has climbed far faster than the labor force. How has this come about? There are two answers to this that go hand in glove: technological change and individual productivity.

Technological change. The work of Frederick W. Taylor and other pioneers in the scientific management movement early in the twentieth century meant an irreversible change in business habits of thinking. From that time on, no good manager has omitted thinking about new ways and better methods to get the work done. Added to this in the 1910's was Henry Ford's great contribution to organization production—the assembly line.

The obvious extension of an assembly line using many people on simple tasks is mechanization of these tasks. This mechanization has been a dominant development of the past 25 years. In a few cases, such as chemicals, petroleum-refining, and some foods, factories are fully automatic. The new technology hits everywhere— in more automatic handling of materials and in automatic feeding, loading, machining, waste disposal, and inspection. For example, a company that used to manufacture scales for weighing wheat now finds that to stay in business it must add materials-handling equipment before and after the weighing equipment, must do the weighing automatically, and must add electronic controls over the flow of materials.

The other major contribution to technological change is the alliance of science and industry. A constant stream of new products —nylon, tranquilizers, color TV tubes, communication satellites— all result from and reinforce the businessman's belief in scientific research and development. Private industry has increased its expenditures for research and development from $100 million in 1929 to $5,000 million currently, and the federal government is spending an additional $10,000 million annually.

Individual productivity. The new processes call for a large increase in investment in machinery and much higher use of electric power per worker. Hence the amount paid for electric power by commercial and industrial establishments has risen three and a half times since 1950.

Another significant factor underlying productivity changes needs to be looked at. This is the finding of human relations research since the 1930's that the supervisory atmosphere, the interrelations among groups of workers, and the organization of supervisory practices have tremendous effect on production and output. The Western Electric researches of Mayo and Roethlisberger [1] demon-

---

1 See F. J. Roethlisberger and W. J. Dickson, *Management and the Worker*, Harvard University Press, 1939.

strated that production of switchboard parts was affected as much as 50% with changes in these factors. Work and the drive to work appear to be fundamental characteristics of human behavior. This can be hindered or helped by the way supervision and the organization of work is carried out.

These effects on individual output can be expressed in terms of output per man-hour, or productivity. Productivity measurements are key factors in explanations of what has happened to our economy over the long run, as well as in projections into the future. The most striking increase has occurred in agriculture, where the hourly productivity expressed in constant (1960) dollars rose from $.62 in 1940 to $1.59 in 1960, an average annual increase of 4.8%. In private nonagricultural employment, productivity rose from $2.71 to $4.15 per hour during the same period. The average annual increase here was 2.3%. The future prosperity of our country depends, to a large degree, upon continud increases in productivity. The interplay of commercial research, managerial skill, and favorable economic and social conditions will determine our progress in the future.

One factor cutting down the long-run increase in total output is the decrease in average hours worked per week. The trend here is downward. The average dropped from 60 hours per week in 1890 to 40 hours in 1931 and has fluctuated around 40 ever since.

Political changes. *Big government.* For the last four years of the nineteenth century, the total national government expenditures amounted to about $450 million a year. They are now more than $500 million every two days. This is the story of the federal government as a single massive consumer, initiating and buying huge quantities of the total output year after year.

In 1929 purchases of goods and services by the federal government came to slightly over 1% of the gross national product. In recent years the federal take has been nearly 15%. The percentages naturally vary sharply from war to nonwar years, but there is no question that the government as a consumer will be an important part of the economic picture for a very long time to come.

Defense requirements alone will see to this—defense not only of our own shores, but, to a very large extent, of the whole free world. The United States is now in a position of world leadership, both in peace and war. World leadership means world commit-

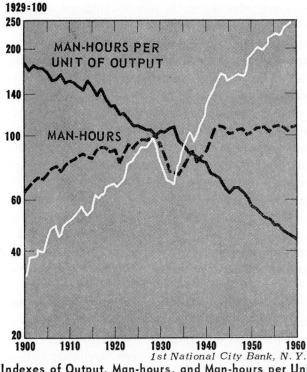

1929=100

Indexes of Output, Man-hours, and Man-hours per Unit
of Output in the Private Economy, 1900-60

1st National City Bank, N. Y.

ments for military aid, economic aid, technical aid. And this means big—and expensive—government.

This country now has what amounts to a permanent arsenal industry. A defense products division is commonplace in many of today's large industrial concerns. Some companies would not exist at all if it were not for government loans, government purchase contracts, and government tax privileges.

New philosophy. Behind this great economic power stands a new philosophy of government. This is a way of thinking about the role of government in the everyday lives of its citizens and the responsibilities of government for their welfare, which one author has called an evolution not "toward socialism, but past socialism." This philosophy, which has deep historic roots and which received its major impetus in the days of the New Deal, was finally nailed down by the Employment Act of 1946. The Act spelled out specifically the principle that an enlightened government has responsibility to its citizens in peace as well as war, and that the responsibility includes using its powers to tame the business cycle and to maintain an expanding economy with "maximum employment, production, and purchasing power."

The Employment Act made the principle of government responsibility official. In carrying out that responsibility, there is a long list of powers gradually developed over many years. To cope with recessions: guaranteed purchasing power for the farmer through price supports on major crops; higher purchasing power for labor through the minimum wage, unemployment compensation, and social security; aids to housing; loans to business; public works. To curb excesses as business moves up: margin requirements for buying stocks; restriction and regulation of the stock market. For general regulation and assistance of the economy: controls on mortgage terms; controls on banking—manipulation of reserve requirements and rediscount rates for easy money or hard money; management of the public debt and of the powers of taxation and spending.

Federal responsibility is not only for economic growth and stability but also for regulation of the institution of business. Measures toward this end include the well-known anti-trust laws, labor relations act, minimum wage laws, and Fair Labor Standards Act. The principle involved, agreed to by the vast majority of Americans, is that the government should supervise and regulate business to *some* extent, that it should subsidize and guarantee various groups to some extent, but that it should keep intervention limited and should let the great bulk of business remain under private management.

Institutional changes. *Labor.* Until 1932 organized labor had little or no support outside its own ranks. Before the Norris-LaGuardia Anti-Injunction Act and the Wagner Act such laws as seemed to authorize collective bargaining were frequently nullified by the courts. These legal handicaps plus general prosperity during the 1920's caused unionism to languish. Total trade union membership in the United States dwindled from over 5 million in 1920 to less than 3⅓ million in 1931.

With the clear and specific authorizations to organize in the 1932 and 1933 laws, there was a rush to join unions. By 1940 the unions were 12 million members strong. These great new institutions wielded vast economic powers and were operating in mass-employing, mass-producing industries. After 1940, when recognition was no longer a battle, the unions centered attention on getting "union security"—union shops and closed shops. They also worked for repeated wage increases. Shortly after World War II a widespread series of strikes on these issues established a towering new record for amount of work time lost. Public reaction to this paved the way for the Taft-Hartley Act. This act did not completely reverse the Wagner Act's encouragement of collective bargaining nor was it a return to an earlier period of passive toleration. It had two practical effects: 1. Union efforts to organize and penetrate new areas became more difficult. 2. Unions had a heavier legal responsibility for their action.

With unions well established and the cost-of-living contracts taking care of the demands to keep wages in pace with the cost of living, union demands shifted to a whole series of "fringe benefits." Items such as paid vacations, fifteen-minute rest periods, paid differentials between shifts, life and health insurance, pension plans, and supplementary unemployment benefits (popularly known as the guaranteed annual wage) became matters for collective bargaining. This means that there has been a basic change in the process by which a large number of business policy decisions are made. Labor must now be given a voice in the wage-making and employment policies of individual enterprises and must be considered in introducing technological change.

The business corporation as an institution. The American Telephone and Telegraph Company, which in 1900 had 7,535 stockholders, today has more than a million. What is more, it boasts of this and makes constant efforts to increase the number. No major steel company in the middle of the twentieth century has its ownership concentrated in one man's holdings, as did Carnegie Steel Corporation—owned 58½% by its founder, Andrew Carnegie. Fifty years ago there were certainly no companies advertising, as does General Motors today, that it is not just a single firm but an alliance with 30,000 suppliers.

Corporations, then, have spread out. They are not, cannot, and do not want to be considered as isolated entities. They wrap themselves in the mantle of public participation and are deeply woven into the economic fabric of the world. This development of the corporation, the primary legal instrument of management, into a quasi-public institution has at least three implications for the managers—the personal responsibility of executives, operations carried on in a goldfish bowl, and adjustment of management methods to the size that goes along with big corporations doing big economic jobs.

When a company has hundreds of thousands of stockholders, and many major companies today do, it does not subscribe to the statement of John D. Archbold, successor to John D. Rockefeller as active head of the old Standard Oil Company: "Private corporations should not be required to make public items of receipts and expenditures, profits and losses. A statement of assets and liabilities is all that can benefit the public. Items of receipts and expenditures, profits and losses can only benefit the competitors." Reporting to the public by press releases, open-houses, sponsored trips of students, as well as useful and revealing annual reports on slick paper with pretty pictures and simplifying cartoons is, of course, not entirely voluntary on businesses' part. The government is everywhere—and is always looking over the management man's shoulder. Many essentials of a company's operations come out in reports to the Securities and Exchange Commission. The ever-watchful eyes of the Federal Trade Commission and the Department of Justice, as well as the Food and Drug Administration or the Federal Power Commission supervising specific industries, keep constant vigil. Add to this the possibility of a Congressional investigation into a particular company—General Motors and its dealers perhaps.

Individual businesses and the markets they serve have become so big, the scope of management responsibilities so broad, and the tools of management so varied that the executive job is out of the hands of a single decision-maker and administrator. Methods of long-range planning, various structures of organization, and professional techniques of control pervade business enterprises and are constant subjects of study.

Stress and strain. Change, the theme of this chapter so far, produces stress in any individual or organization that goes through it. Pouring new wine into old bottles builds pressure that must be planned for beforehand or mopped up after the explosion takes place.

The turret-lathe operator who must develop new skills when electronic controls are added to his machine, the company which must change its organization structure when new products are added or sales growth makes the old relationship among executives inefficient, the woolen-worsted company which finds its existence threatened by the growth of synthetic fabrics, and the stock brokerage firm which loses clients to the mutual funds—all must plan for some adaptation in their way of operating or find it more and more difficult to continue.

These stresses do not come only from changes within the business system. The uncertainties from war and depression and from the changes in government policy necessary in a changing political world bring from time to time to the minds of many Americans a feeling of uneasy tension combined often with one of frustration —a feeling that unmanageable forces might be taking one toward some impending disaster and that there is nothing one can do about it. Psychiatrists occasionally call this an Age of Anxiety.

Management has the never-ending task of providing enough stability and continuity of action to permit efficient performance, and at the same time adjusting company operations to the array of changes reviewed in the preceding pages. Objectives, policies, organization, programs, and other devices explored in this book are tools modern management uses to achieve this balance.

FORECASTING CHANGES IN ENVIRONMENT

The manager should regard changes in the business environment as opportunities—opportunities to make his own activities more useful and more profitable. To take full advantage of these opportunities, however, he needs to anticipate them. The company which hopes to gain from, say, the growth in the purchasing power of people past 65 years of age should forecast carefully when and where such purchasing power is likely to arise.

Forecasting business conditions is no simple matter. The range of things to consider is great, and fitting all these elements into predictions which will be helpful in making business decisions requires much skill. One of the best ways to think about the numerous forces at work is to analyze:

1. The general, overall economic outlook.
2. The outlook for the particular industry.
3. The position of the company in that industry.

A framework of this sort, going from the general toward the specific, helps the business executive see how anticipated changes may affect his own bailiwick. Consequently, the rest of this chapter will be devoted to a brief discussion of forecasting general business conditions. The next chapter gives suggestions for appraising the outlook for an industry and the position of a company in its industry. An analysis of the business environment along these lines will provide the executive with an excellent background for dealing with policies and other phases of administration.

An approach to the economic outlook. The total economy of the United States includes so many facets it is difficult to know where to begin in making a forecast. Also troublesome is how to relate the several different parts. One approach, now widely used, is to relate the various facets to the gross national product.

Since an analysis in terms of the gross national product is the best way anyone has yet devised to summarize changes in general business conditions, we shall take a look at what is included in this concept and then briefly indicate how it can be used to make long-range and short-range forecasts.

Gross national product (GNP). To use Department of Commerce terminology, "The gross national product measures the Nation's output of goods and services in terms of its market value.' We have, then, a sum of the market prices times quantities sold of all the goods and services produced in the country in one year. Fully as important to the businessman are the components which add up to the grand total.

Two views: total sales and total costs. There are two different ways of measuring total output. Since they are essentially two aspects of the same thing, they will have to add up to the same amount. First, gross national product is the sum of costs incurred in producing all the goods and services made during the year. Let's look at the table on the opposite page.

On the left-hand side we find amounts paid to those who contributed toward making the gross national product. These are the costs of output. Included here are the wages of workers, net rents and royalties, net interest on capital loans and securities, business taxes and depreciation, corporate profits, and income of unincorporated enterprises and farms.

National Income and Product Accounts

1st Quarter, 1964

(Annual rate, in billions of current dollars)

Costs of Output		Sales (or Uses) of Output	
Compensation of employees .	$352	Personal consumption expenditures	$390
Rentals paid to persons	12		
Net interest	26	Government purchases of goods and services	125
Business taxes and depreciation	111	Private investment in U.S. ..	86
Corporate profits	57	Net exports	8
Income of unincorporated firms	51		
Gross national product ...	$609	Gross national product ...	$609

In the example given in the table, the total costs incurred in producing final goods in the economy was measured at an annual rate of $609 billion. In passing we may note that all these costs, except business taxes and depreciation charges, reflect a flow of earned income. This income was available for personal expenditures, income tax, or investment.

The right-hand side of the table shows the uses made of the total output of goods and services. For direct and immediate consumption, people were buying at the rate of $390 billion, or almost two thirds of the total. Government bodies—federal, state, and local—used 21% of the total. Investment in private houses, plant and equipment, inventories, and the like used 14%.

One important thing to note about the gross national product is that it is a *measure* expressed in dollars. Having such a measure, subject to statistical manipulations, is a great advantage in trying to estimate the significance of changes in economic, political, and social affairs, since it enables us to avoid the confusion of merely saying "more" or "less." With gross national product statistics, we can answer the question, "How much?" We can also chart the movements of a country from depression to prosperity or its steady long-term rate of economic development.

Use of GNP in long-run forecasting. Often business policies must be established on the basis of forecasted conditions five, ten, or twenty years hence. The impact, for instance, of adding a new product line or leasing branch plants is likely to be greatest at least ten years after the original decision is made. Clearly, many of the dynamic factors discussed in the first part of this chapter will have a bearing on that future business environment. Can the gross national product concept be helpful in forming a sharper picture of the future and thereby aid in the setting of policies?

A few examples from a forecast of 1980 will show how the gross national product idea may be used for this purpose. Among the changes discussed earlier in this chapter were rising population, shorter hours of work, and increasing output per man-hour. These facts can be used to estimate the GNP for 1980 as follows:

> Since the people who will be in the 1980 work force are already living, we can come pretty close in estimating the number of workers at that time. Assuming that the increase in the proportion of housewives and older people working will offset an increase in the number of adults in school, we can be reasonably sure that the work force in 1980 will be about 102 million.
>
> The output per man-hour has shown an annual increase during the past half-century and the last decade of 2.5%. However, the rate of increase has been slowing down in the last few years, so that a projected increase of 2% per annum is more conservative.
>
> Applying the 2% annual increase to the gross national product per worker in 1960 ($6,900), we arrive at a 1980 output per worker of $10,400.
>
> Now, the forecast of gross national product in 1980 is easy. Multiplying the output per worker by the number in the labor force, the impressive result is $1,060 billion. And, this estimate makes no allowance for an increase in the general price level.

The important point in this example is not the specific figures but the way knowledge about several diverse factors can be combined to give us a prediction of the total volume of business which is likely to be done several years hence. In a similar manner subparts of gross national product may be forecast. The private investment sector can serve as an illustration.

> Private investment in the United States is expected to total $167 billion in 1980, and the major part, about $106 billion, will be due to business expenditures on plants and equipment. This implies a rapid annual rate of modernization of productive facilities both to keep up with and to make possible technological change. Inventory investment is assumed to rise to keep pace with the total growth in output. Most of the rest of the $167 billion will be in investment in private homes. To achieve a stock of housing for a total of 73 million households, residential construction is expected to be $51 billion in 1980.

Note that this estimate took into consideration such factors as technological change, growth and age distribution of population, and general volume of business. Of course as new facts become available they must be weighed, and revisions of the forecast made if necessary. Yet the gross national product framework can serve as a summation device, much as a profit and loss statement summarizes the results of a wide variety of activities within a company.

Application of long-range forecasts. A company supplying lumber for crates takes a hopeful view toward the future despite a variety of unfavorable developments. Virtually all consumer durable goods and many lighter producers' goods are now shipped in heavy corrugated paper containers. As a result, lumber for boxes and crating dropped from 4.3 to 4.1 billion board feet between 1950 and 1960. However, wood is used almost entirely for packing export shipments and for heavy industrial equipment. Consequently, the company predicts that sales in its particular industry will be tied to the production of durable goods. On the basis of past trends, it predicts that the ratio betwen durable goods output and lumber used for boxes will continue to decline—perhaps 15% between 1960 and 1980. Nevertheless, when this conservative ratio is applied to the substantial increase in output of durable goods predicted for 1980—from $97 billion in 1960 to $229 billion in 1980—the projected demand for box lumber rises from 4.1 to 6.6 billion board feet in 1980. In other words, the prediction is that the rapid growth in the end use will more than offset the displacement by other kinds of packaging materials.

This is an illustration of long-range planning, something an increasing number of companies are undertaking. This long-run planning is a process in which management tries to decide what the world will be like ten or even twenty years ahead. It attempts to gain this understanding by carefully analyzing political, social, cultural, and economic trends and estimating in what fashion they will continue. Next, management looks at itself to analyze how the particular company can best adapt to the trends it sees. Finally, it sets long-range goals for the company accordingly.

Forecasts of this kind obviously may prove to be wrong. A classic example is that of Montgomery Ward and Company under Sewell Avery's jurisdiction. Montgomery Ward policy in the late

1940's and early '50's was based upon expectations of a primary post-war depression. Therefore, the company hoarded cash, and did not build new retail stores. It soon slipped far behind Sears Roebuck, which forecast economic growth and was expanding its retail outlets rapidly.

These illustrations do not exhaust the possibilities of long-range planning nor do they begin to explore the means by which planning studies are carried out and planning decisions made within the company. We leave this to future sections of the book. They do suggest the kind of thinking a business executive should do in order to deal effectively with long-range changes.

Short-range forecasts of general economic conditions. The manager must keep his eye on short-range changes in the general business situation, as well as on the long-run outlook just discussed. As in mountain climbing, the trend may be clearly rising (or falling) but typically there are many ups and downs along the way. Some business plans extend for only a few months or a few years, and for these the shorter forecast is paramount. Also, the *timing* of major changes is often speeded up or slowed down on the basis of immediate prospects. For example, the sale of bonds or the building of a new plant may be delayed a year because the manager believes "the market" will be better, even though the action is part of a definite long-range program.

The process of forecasting short-range conditions differs from long-range forecasting in at least one important respect. Trends known to exist in the past are quite useful in long-range predictions. They are far from fully reliable, yet they are among the best guides we have. For short-range fluctuations, trends are of much less help. The man with an excess inventory of Christmas trees beside a new highway finds little aid in knowing that "the trend is to the suburbs."

The usual approach to short-range forecasting is (a) to analyze at what stage events now are and then (b) to forecast where they may be going. This is sometimes called the "lost horse" technique. How do you find a lost horse? You do it by going to where the horse was last seen and asking yourself where you would go from there if you were a horse.

This is no simple assignment. Many aspects of business need to be considered even to decide where you now are—industrial production, prices, bank loans, employment, construction, foreign trade, retail sales; each reflects only part of the total picture. Here, again, the framework of the gross national product accounts is useful in relating and summarizing the diverse elements. By expressing the effect of each element in terms of one or more of the GNP accounts, we can get a composite picture and can readily compare this picture with similar summaries for earlier periods.

Predicting "where we go from here" is even more difficult. At this point business cycle theory can often be applied. There is no single, simple key to short-run expansions and contractions of business, but the various theories do suggest what to watch. If, for example, you believe business cycles are greatly influenced by credit, then you will analyze the likelihood of increases or decreases in the use of bank credit. Or, you may believe that construction of plant and equipment is a vital factor, and give close attention to prospects in that area.

Because of the many dynamic aspects of life in the United States—already reviewed in this chapter—there are multiple forces operating in each business cycle. In addition, the combination of forces varies from clcle to cycle. Therefore, the procedure of a good forecaster is not to follow just one or two of the forces alleged to be the primary cause of cycles, but to determine the combination of forces predominant at the time of the forecast and to assess their probable effects upon future business. If an analysis has already been made of the present in terms of gross national product accounts, then the predicted changes can also be summarized in these same terms.

The role of a forecast. A forecast is not a formulation of policy. Ultimately, every businessman must make his own management decisions. But his decisions should be based upon his own final forecasts. The automobile executive, for example, who finds out from his economist that the increase in the number of middle-income receivers is still continuing and that consumer disposable income will likely rise 5% during the next year has only some guidance. He must decide for himself (a) whether these and other facts clearly point to greater salability of deluxe cars, and (b) on the basis of this premise, along with data regarding costs, competition, engineering, and similar considerations, whether a policy to upgrade his cars is warranted.

SUMMARY

Change dominates the world of today. The environment in which business operates is dynamic, and the manager should be always alert to adapt the operations of his company to the opportunities and challenges which these changes create.

Social changes include the growth in population, the movement from farms to urban communities and migration westward, and the increase in educational levels. In economic activity, long-run changes are the growth in total incomes, the shift in the distribution of incomes from a combination of a few wealthy people and many poor people to the huge majority of middle-income people, the growth in total output, and the constant increase in productivity resulting from technological change. Long-run changes in political affairs involve the rise of big government and the philosophy of a partly controlled, partly free economy. Institutional changes include the growth in numbers and power of labor unions and their influence on business policies as well as the development of the corporation as a quasi-public institution, operating well within the public eye.

The manager can deal more effectively with these and other shifts if he has a framework to help organize his thinking. The first broad division suggested for this purpose is consideration of (a) the general, overall economic outlook, (b) the outlook for his particular industry, and (c) the position of his company in that industry.

An important aid to summarizing and forecasting general economic conditions is the concept of gross national product and its components. Comprehensive in scope and expressed in numbers, this set of accounts is helpful in making both long-range and short-range projections.

The procedure for developing a satisfactory economic forecast is complex and is based upon sound reasoning and the use of data covering all segments of the economy. The executive who uses such a forecast needs to check the reasoning behind it, the assumptions on which it is based, and the exactness by which it is stated. After he has accepted the forecast or modified it according to his own judgment, he must still formulate his own plans. Economic forecasting is necessary, but it is no substitute for effective planning nor is it all that goes into a set of plans.

Overall economic conditions provide the general background for policy decisions. Additional pertinent data will come from an analysis of industry and company outlook—discussed in the next chapter.

QUESTIONS FOR CLASS DISCUSSION

1. The chairman of Consolidated Foods reports: "Back in colonial times 85% of our population was required to produce the nation's food supply; now the task is accomplished by less than 15% . . . Thirty years ago a grocery store handled less than 1,000 different food items; today's supermarkets carry from 4,500 to 6,000 . . . Today processed or semiprocessed foods are 80% of all groceries." Do you believe these trends will continue? What significance do these trends have for grocery stores, vegetable canneries, mail-order houses, and kitchen equipment manufacturers?

2. The treatment of management as a *profession* is becoming more widespread. How have the major changes discussed in this chapter contributed to this view of management, e.g., income distribution, concept of the corporation, education, complex technology, big government, etc.?

3. "The rates of increase in population in the United States vary at times but the overall trend has been clear—a continual growth." Do changing rates of increase have a different effect on businesses than does the underlying trend? Explain the significance of your answer for a manufacturer of children's shoes, a telephone operating company, a dairy, and a textile producer of gray cloth (a basic fabric used in many different kinds of garments and other textile products).

4. The hypothesis of "Megalopolis" envisions eventually a continual city in the eastern United States from Boston to Norfolk, Virginia. Should business executives be concerned with such an idea in the course of their business responsibilities or do the possible problems belong to state, local and federal governments and to the businessman in his off-hours as a citizen? What kind of business firms will be affected? In what way?

5. Why do the major automobile companies have both economics departments and market research departments? What kind of questions would the two departments focus on and what kinds of information would they use? From the standpoint of central management, what is the usefulness of having varying approaches to the analysis of economic events external to the firm—if indeed the approaches do vary?

6. "Forecasting economic and social events external to the firm is more difficult than predicting what is likely to happen in the future within the company. First, the relevant facts are less readily apparent and available. Second, there is less available experience with the events and happenings upon which to base sound opinions and judgments." Do you agree with this statement? If you do, what is its significance for central management? For example, who should make the official economic forecasts to be used in short-and long-range programming?

7. A consulting service offered forecasts of general economic conditions to a selected group of business firms. One forecast read as follows: "The major depressant of the economy has been the decline in demand for inventories. Later in the year, net foreign investment is likely to decrease. The major portion of the national expenditure will probably continue to increase at least for the next two quarters. Consumer demand for nondurables will probably continue to increase under the pressure of expanding wage rates and personal income. In the investment sector, recent surveys show the business community intends to expand its capital outlays for new plants and equipment in the near future. Total new construction expenditure will probably remain fairly steady. Finally, most economists agree that federal, state, and local government expenditures will increase over the next year. Such a rise should further stimulate the expansion." Appraise the usefulness of this forecast. Does it tell you all you need to know to understand what may happen to gross national product?

8. "The outstanding single fact of recent economic history is the relative elevation of low-income groups and the high-level consumption that goes along with this." Explain what facts lie behind this quotation and explain its implications for a retail grocery firm, a major appliance manufacturer, and a jewelry store.

9. A very famous statistician and economist has listed as one of the major changes affecting the economy of the United States over the last half century "an irreversible trend toward a steadily expanding government debt with inflation as a continuing characteristic of the economy." Summarize the implications of this change for a company with which you are familiar. What bearing does it have on the planning of this company and on the operating problems that face its executives?

CASE II

National Lumber and Plywood Corporation

Our forecast is for a land 'deficit' of about 50 million acres by the year 2000. This assumes the use of every last square foot of mountain, desert and swampland in the continental United States. Based on our projection of trends, the total land area of 1,904 million acres will be insufficient to support, by the end of the century, all land demands for cropland, grazing land, commercial forest land, recreation, urban, transportation, wildlife refuge, and reservoirs. Our forecast is conservative since it does *not* provide for any increased acreage of commercial forest land above the 484 million acres in use in the mid-1960's.

Had we merely projected trends of (a) the present rate of substitution of other materials for lumber, (b) the present rate of improvement of technology in using forest products, and (c) the current level of skill in the management of forests and lands, the prediction would have been much different. It would then have called for as much as an additional 300 million acres to be put into forest use by the year 2000. It would also mean a saturation of land use in the continental United States by 1980—including an expansion of commercial forest land by 60 million acres (12.5% above the current average). Since the outcome of such a prediction is not reasonable (that is, adding 300 million acres to forest lands in light of all other needs for land by the year 2000), we have settled on a conservative forecast as stated—expansion of total demand for land to use all the acreage in the continental United States with *no* increase in commercial forest lands.

The forecast and the conclusions stated above were serious enough to warrant a review by the executive committee of National Lumber and Plywood Corporation. The group was to appraise the consultant's conclusions, make an independent long-range estimate of the demand for lumber products and the supply of forest land, and then decide if the results of the estimates called for any action by the company.

National Lumber and Plywood Corporation is one of the ten largest firms in an industry of over 30,000 producers. These ten companies together produce about one eighth of estimated industry output. The corporation's latest annual report indicated:

Sales	$275,000,000
Total Assets	$320,000,000
Invested Capital	$230,000,000
Net Profit	$ 15,000,000
Employees	14,280

Plants and Products:

Washington .... Dressed Lumber, Kraft Pulp, Corrugated Liner Board

Oregon .... Fir Plywood

Tennessee .... Lumber, Flooring, Windows, Doors

Georgia .... Hardwood Lumber and Plywood

W. Virginia .... Hardwood Lumber

Demand for forest products. There were several ways for the committee to arrive at its estimate of future demand. On what was called the "macro-level," the simplest of projections was to forecast United States population and relate this to per capita trends in the use of the company's traditional products—lumber and plywood—to develop an overall idea about possible expansion. The statistics relevant to production and consumption were:

TABLE 1

PRODUCTION AND CONSUMPTION

	Lumber			Plywood	
Year	*U.S. Production (million board feet)*	*Net Imports (million board feet)*	*Per Capita Consumption (board feet)*	*U.S. Consumption Veneer Logs (million feet, log scale)*	*Per Capita Consumption (log feet)*
1899	35,077		456		
1910	40,018		466		
1920	29,878		324		
1930	26,051	(1,133)[1]	196	n.a.[2]	n.a.[2]
1940	28,934	(232)[1]	224	n.a.[2]	n.a.[2]
1950	38,902	2,914	274	1,157	7.6
1955	37,858	2,753	249	2,431	14.5
1960	34,737	3,060	209	3,446	19.1
1962	33,174	4,140	200	4,158	22.3
1963	34,584	4,464	204	4,449	23.5
1964	35,600	5,482	215	n.a.[2]	26.0

[1] Net Exports in 1930 and 1940.
[2] Not available.
Sources: Bureau of the Census, Current Industrial Reports, Series M24H.
U.S. Forest Service, *Lumber Distribution and Consumption.*
National Lumber Manufacturers Association, *Lumber Industry Facts.*

The raw statistics reflected various changes in the market for lumber and plywood. Over the entire period, three fourths of lumber consumption had been in construction. The balance was about equally divided between wooden containers and other manufacturing uses (including furniture). Wooden containers, by 1964, were obsolescent; their use was slowly declining in absolute amount. Wood remained the most popular building material in the United States. However, its inherent weakness as an organic material and its comparative lack of versatility from the design standpoint contributed to the relative rise of substitute products— steel and concrete in large building construction, aluminum and sandwich panels or brick veneer for surfacing, metal for roof trusses and plaster lath, plastic tiles for finished flooring. Thus, lumber's position in its various uses was, by the mid-1960's, still strong (as the data on U. S. production indicates), but, relatively, it certainly was not expanding at the expense of other materials.

Plywood's picture differed, as can be seen from the data. Its applications in both rough and finished construction and in furniture was expanding.

A second macro-level approach to estimating future demand for lumber and plywood was to relate output and expenditures for these to projections of gross national product or its components. As an indication, Americans had, with the exception of major depression and war years, spent a reasonably stable percentage of gross national product dollars on new construction. The relevant indicators were:

TABLE 2

GROSS NATIONAL PRODUCT, NEW CONSTRUCTION, AND LUMBER AND PLYWOOD CONSUMPTION

Year	Gross National Product (billions of 1954 dollars)	New Construction (billions of 1954 dollars)	New Construction Percentage of GNP	U.S. Lumber Consumption per 1000's of New Construction Dollars (board feet)	Plywood Veneer Log Use per 1000's of Construction Dollars (log feet)
1930	164.5	15.4	9.3	1,620	
1935	152.9	6.7	4.4	2,780	
1940	205.8	13.6	6.6	2,110	
1945	314.0	6.6	2.1	4,350	
1948	243.1	22.7	7.8	1,610	
1950-4 avg.	349.1	27.3	7.8	1,510	66
1955-9 avg.	406.4	32.7	8.0	1,200	90
1960	439.9	34.4	7.8	1,100	100
1962	476.4	36.7	7.7	1,020	113
1963	492.6	37.9	7.7	1,030	118
1964	516.0	38.9	7.5	1,060	n.a.[1]

[1] Not available

Land supply. The executive committee's interest in the consultant's forecast of acreage available for commercial forests stemmed from its knowledge that forest products was the only extractive sector of the economy that gave any sign of long-term scarcity. Trends in the ratio of employment to output and in deflated prices indicated increasing scarcity of logs and timber.[1]

[1] Barnett and Morse, *Scarcity and Growth* (Baltimore: Johns Hopkins Press, 1962).

The key to expected land shortages was in the projected demand for land for recreation. All other uses required increases in acreage by the year 2000 that were small or relatively insignificant in total over uses in 1950 and 1960. Recreation, however, was projected to demand 134 million acres in 2000 as against 42 and 44 million acres used in 1950 and 1960 respectively. This forecast was a source of concern to the committee. Were population, incomes, leisure time, mobility, and the proportions of the very young and the aged in the population going to increase enough to press so strongly on outdoor recreation? Could changes be made in land usage? (At present very little commercial forest land was used for outdoor recreation and vice versa.)

TABLE 3

VISITS TO RECREATIONAL AREAS
(per thousand population)

Year	National Park System	National Forests	State Parks
1920	9	n.a.[1]	n.a.[1]
1930	32	65	n.a.[1]
1940	114	122	n.a.[1]
1950	240	180	753
1960	439	516	1,439
1963	542	665	1,520 (1962)

[1] Not available.
Source: Clawson, Marion, *Statistics on Outdoor Recreation* (Washington, Resources for the Future, Inc., 1958).
Statistical Abstract of the United States.

TABLE 4

VISITS TO RECREATIONAL AREAS PER ACRE (1960)

Mt. McKinley National Park . .	.011	New York State Parks . . .	14
Yellowstone National Park . . .	.65	Virginia State Parks	42
Grand Canyon National Park .	1.8	Washington State Parks . .	91
Shenandoah National Park . . .	9.2	Oregon State Parks	181
Badlands National Monument .	8.5	Wisconsin State Parks	282

Possible acquisition of commercial forest land by the company depended not only on total demand and supply but also on regional shifts in these. In general, regional trends in income and in population were the important points to forecast. The committee was already well acquainted with the regional distribution of timber.

United States wood imports had been increasing since 1950 and were now about 12% of total consumption (80 to 85% of the imports came from Canada). The committee did not expect import ratios to change significantly in the near or long-term future for various reasons that the committee had reviewed extensively. A final possibility for increasing supply was better technological practice or research and development work on wood products. The situation currently was mixed but not particularly hopeful.

In the East, about 58 million acres were poorly stocked with commercial-grade trees (less than 40% of their potential) and 35 million acres had no commercial trees. For the United States as a whole, the Forest Service estimated over ten years ago that placing all forest land in each region under management equal in quality to that of the best practice in that region would double the total volume of annual growth. No such increase has taken place. Annual sawtimber growth in the early 1960's was 9% more than it was twenty years before then. As another example, the certified Tree Farm Program covered about 65 million acres (less than 15% of total commercial forest lands) in the middle 1960's and was growing at less than 1% of the total acreage per year. With 60% of commercial forest land owned by farmers, fishermen, housewives, professional people and businessmen not in the forest products industry and with their holdings averaging well under 500 acres, the spread of better management practices was a challenge, to say the least.

TABLE 5

RESEARCH AND DEVELOPMENT EXPENDITURES
BY ALL SOURCES, GOVERNMENT & PRIVATE
(millions of dollars)

Year	Total	Lumber and Wood Products	Paper and Allied Products
1953-54	$ 5,150	$ 7 [1]	$18 [2]
1958-59	11,130	10	42
1961-62	14,740	9	60

[1] Industry laboratories spent 70%, government laboratories, 30% (1953 est.).
[2] Industry laboratories spent 90%, government laboratories, 10% (1953 est.).
Source: Statistical Abstract of the United States.

The opportunity to increase returns and yields can be seen in one experience of a major plywood, paper, and chemical manufacturer. It bought 146,000 acres of timberland in Oregon from which a sawmill and a plywood plant had used 150 million feet of timber annually. The old sawmill was closed, the plywood plant was modernized, a new plywood plant and a new particle board plant were constructed, and a new sawmill was installed to utilize small logs formerly left in the woods. Timber requirements dropped to 130 million feet annually, while sales and net returns went up over 60% in total. Finally, wood chips were produced for a pulp and paper plant from wood scrap formerly considered waste.

TABLE 6

STAND-SIZE CLASSES ON COMMERCIAL FOREST LAND

(thousand acres)

Region and State	Total Commercial Forest Area	Sawtimber Stands			Pole Timber Stands	Seedling and Sapling Stands	Non-stocked and Other Areas
		Total	Old Growth [1]	Young Growth			
New England ..	30,658	10,302	.....	10,302	14,501	4,969	886
Maine	16,601	5,869	.....	5,869	8,494	1,811	427
Middle Atlantic .	42,225	15,002	.....	15,002	16,991	8,842	1,390
New York ...	12,002	5,029	.....	5,029	4,276	2,406	291
Pennsylvania .	15,108	3,279	.....	3,279	7,481	3,730	618
Lake (Michigan, Minnesota, Wisc.)	53,272	6,457	.....	6,457	16,010	20,370	10,435
Central	42,394	14,486	.....	14,486	15,722	8,957	3,229
Kentucky	11,446	4,964	.....	4,964	4,040	1,830	612
Missouri	15,064	2,033	.....	2,033	6,477	4,778	1,776
Plains	5,492	1,475	25	1,450	2,289	1,053	675
South	193,288	60,502	.....	60,502	78,376	38,338	16,072
Alabama	20,756	6,091	.....	6,091	10,912	3,503	250
Georgia	23,969	6,355	.....	6,355	8,814	7,200	1,600
Douglas Fir	25,455	14,611	7,468	7,143	4,542	4,260	2,042
Oregon (West)	14,512	9,080	4,655	4,425	1,934	2,200	1,298
Washington (West)	10,943	5,531	2,813	2,718	2,608	2,060	744
Western Pine ..	91,556	55,781	38,562	17,219	20,977	7,920	6,878
(including Redwood Region) California ...	17,317	14,038	11,240	2,798	1,122	44	2,113
Idaho	13,372	6,922	3,695	3,227	3,610	1,453	1,387
Montana	15,727	5,683	3,943	1,740	6,330	2,402	1,312
Oregon (East)	11,363	8,874	6,926	1,948	2,012	334	143
Washington (East)	8,547	5,191	2,984	2,207	1,956	893	507
Total United States	484,340	178,616	46,055	132,561	169,408	94,709	41,607

[1] Because of scattered occurrence and very limited area, no estimates have been made of old-growth sawtimber in the Eastern regions, except for eastern South Dakota.
Source: Forest Service, U.S. Department of Agriculture, *Timber Resources Review.*

One of National Lumber and Plywood Corporation's plants in Washington produces Kraft pulp and corrugated liner board, which is sold to manufacturers of corrugated shipping containers. The recent history of the pulp and paper industry seems to indicate that demand for such products is likely to be substantially greater than that for lumber. If this is true, then possibly the corporation should begin to appraise a policy of integrating forward into paper manufacturing as well as backward into the acquisition of additional forest lands.

TABLE 7

PAPER AND PAPERBOARD PRODUCTION AND UTILIZATION

Year	Production, Paper and Paperboard, All Types (million tons)	Paper and Paperboard, Tons per Thousand Population	Paper and Paperboard Tons per Million Dollars, Disposable Personal Income (1954 dollars)	Estimate of Capacity Utilization, Paper and Paperboard Production (per cent)
1929	11.14	92	82.5	
1946	19.26	136	93	
1950	24.38	160	105	
1955	30.14	182	112	90
1957	30.7		105	80
1959	34.05		110	85
1961	35.6	197	108	83
1962	37.6	202	110	88
1963	39.1	206	110	90

Sources: Survey of Current Business; Statistical Abstract of the United States.

REQUIRED: (a) Estimate the demand for lumber and plywood in the United States in 1980 and 2000. How much expansion over current domestic production does your estimate call for?

(b) Explain the bases of your estimate and the factors you took into account.

(c) Estimate the supply of land needed to produce the timber product needs you forsee in 1980 and 2000. Does this call for increased commercial forest acreage?

(d) Appraise the consultant's forecast of a land shortage. Explain why you agree or disagree.

(e) Explain in what regions National Lumber and Plywood Corporation should acquire more land if you think such acquisition is warranted. What is your estimate of regional trends in income, population, and timber supply?

(f) From the data given, does there appear to be a reasonable opportunity for forward integration into the paper and paperboard industry by National Lumber and Plywood Corporation?

CHAPTER

3

:·: **APPRAISING THE OUTLOOK**

FOR A COMPANY

Chapter 2 was concerned with forecasting activity in the entire economy. Now, in focusing on the specific needs of company management, this general forecast must be translated into the outlook for one industry and then into the outlook for a company.

The predicted outlook for a company has a direct bearing on most objective and policy decisions. A decision to construct a new plant calls for considering the future volume of business, the kinds of products that will be manufactured, methods of transportation to and from the plant, the size and nature of packages that must be handled within the warehouse, and numerous other issues that depend upon future conditions in the industry. A forecast of rising labor costs may call for a shift in product emphasis to those which can be made primarily by machine; personnel policies may also be changed to reduce the number of high-paid craftsmen in the plant.

Outlook must also be considered in studying administrative organization. Is competition increasing in one field so that we should add a specialized force? Will sales quadruple and the president's job become so important to the community that we should add a public relations department to help him with speeches?

The inevitability of change has already been amply demonstrated in Chapter 2. Now such changes need to be related to a particular company.

Approach to forecasting problem. The previous chapter shows a way to organize thinking about general economic trends. This chapter explains an outline that will help assemble ideas about the outlook for an industry and a company and that will provide a way to sift and classify these ideas, determine their relationships, and weigh their relative importance. The key topics of this outline are:

I. Outlook for the Industry
  A. Demand for Products or Services of the Industry
    1. Usefulness and desire for products
    2. Stability of desire for products
    3. Ability of customers to pay for products
  B. Supply of Products or Services
    1. Capacity of the industry
    2. Labor costs
    3. Material costs
    4. Taxes and other operating costs
  C. Competitive Conditions in the Industry
    1. Nature of companies
    2. Organization of the industry
    3. Government regulation

II. Position of the Company in the Industry
  A. Market Position of the Company
    1. Relation of company sales to those of industry and leading competitors
    2. Standing of company products
    3. Reputation of company in major markets
  B. Cost Position of the Company
    1. Comparative location
    2. Relative efficiency of equipment
    3. Unique cost advantages
  C. Special Competitive Considerations
    1. Relative financial strength
    2. Ability of company management

The nature and importance of each of these topics will be examined in the following pages. All subheadings may not be significant for a particular company, but the list as a whole suggests a range of factors that should be considered.

DEMAND FOR PRODUCTS OR SERVICES OF THE INDUSTRY

Usefulness and desire for products. In many cases it is necessary to consider the varied uses of the products of an industry to understand fully the demand picture. For example, in addition to heating homes, bituminous coal is used in tremendous quantities for at least three other major purposes—generation of electric power, manufacture of coke and gas, and production of industrial power and heat. Total demand must be appraised in terms of the likely growth or decline of all of these uses.

Occasionally the possible uses for a product are not fully known. This is illustrated by vermiculite, a mineral that expands greatly upon being heated and has unusual insulation properties. Possible uses for vermiculite are as a wall-fill insulation, a plaster base, a filter material, and also as the basic material for a light fireproof tile. In determining the demand for such a product, its probable effectiveness for these and other uses should be explored thoroughly.

Still another question arising in connection with different uses is that of joint products. Here the different uses arise from the fact that two or more commodities are produced from a single raw material. The cotton farmer, for example, has no choice but to raise both cotton fibre and cottonseed; the meat packer secures numerous by-products from a hog. Consequently, demand for raw cotton or live hogs is not simply a matter of a single product.

After the possible uses of a product or service of an industry have been explored, it is often desirable to classify potential customers by type and area. Thus the customers for passenger automobiles may be grouped as private and commercial, and may be further divided among states, regions, and foreign markets. This information will be useful in determining the probable demand in the future; it will also provide a basis for sound sales policies.

Stability of desire for products. A second step in exploring the demand for a product is considering the stability of desire for the product. Stability may be affected by the following factors.

Substitutes. The desire for the "utility" or satisfaction rendered by a product may be reasonably stable, yet the demand for the product itself may be quite unstable because of increased or decreased use of substitutes that render this same satisfaction. In recent years, for instance, oil and natural gas have been replacing coal as a domestic fuel. Thus, in considering the demand for coal as a domestic fuel, the possible increased or decreased substitution of oil and natural gas must be appraised. Automobiles and trucks have proved effective competition for railroads (see table on following page), and their expansion has resulted in the virtual elimination of electric interurbans. In the machinery industry the development of the steel stampings and the welding process has resulted in an effective substitution for heavy iron castings. Chain stores have tended to replace independent stores in some lines;

and television has reduced the demand for radios. In each case the problem has been not so much a decline in the demand for the service as the substitution of one product for another.

FLUCTUATIONS IN DEMAND FOR DIFFERENT KINDS OF PRODUCTS

(Index numbers of physical volume, 1929 = 100)

	Wheat Flour	Motor Trucks	Railroad Freight Service (carloadings)	New Freight Cars
1929 (prosperity)	100	100	100	100
1932 (depression)	87	31	53	1
1939 (recovery)	92	89	64	27
1944 (war period)	105	96	82	87
1950 (prosperity)	100	173	74	47
1954 (recession)	99	133	64	41
1962 (prosperity)	117	161	55	39

Technological and social changes. Technological and social changes that will sooner or later materially expand or contract the desire for a given product may be occurring. The blacksmith shop has virtually disappeared, but in its place we have ubiquitous filling stations and garages. Due to technological and social changes, fresh fruits and vegetables have become a year-round part of our diet and the distribution of frozen foods has made rapid strides in the last few years. Changes in style and habits of living have resulted in a sharp decline for wool piece goods for women's clothing. Such changes as these usually do not occur overnight, but they may be sufficiently rapid to upset a prediction for a five- or ten-year period.

Durability of products. Durable products have wider fluctuations in demand than do the more transient products. Houses, highways, and washing machines once constructed render services over a period of time, and consequently the demand for such products is more active during periods of original construction than during periods when existing facilities are merely being replaced. Also, the replacement of durable goods can often be postponed for a substantial period of time. For these reasons the demand for durable products tends to fluctuate over wider ranges than does the demand for such things as food, clothing, travel, and entertainment, which must be replenished to render additional services. Speculation may play a part in fluctuations of demand for almost any product; however, the more durable the product, the more lasting the maladjustment that may result from the unwarranted speculation.

Nature of use of products. Necessities, such as food and clothing and other products that people have come to regard as essential to their well being, will probably enjoy a more stable demand than products that are regarded as luxuries and are purchased only at times when people have funds over and above what is necessary for the purchase of the first class of goods. Sometimes a product is a necessity in one of its uses or for one group of customers, whereas it is regarded as a luxury by another group of customers.

The demand for new machines and equipment used to produce other goods or services almost always fluctuates widely. Not only are such 'capital goods" durable and hence subject to shifting dates of replacement; they also depend upon the demand for the goods they produce, and if this demand changes, the existing plant capacity may be too large or too small. We can see from the table on page 51, for example, that the fluctuations in demand for freight service have caused much greater shifts in demand for new freight cars.

The federal government is a large buyer of some products. These purchases go primarily to the armed services, but from time to time, purchases for foreign aid, stockpiling, atomic research, and the like, assume large proportions. Here again, the demand is likely to change sharply, and it is difficult to predict because it depends on national and international politics fully as much as economic factors.

These influences, along with other special reasons for instability in the desire for a particular product, should be carefully studied when forecasting demand.

Ability to pay for products or services. A given product may be useful and desired by potential customers, but if these customers do not have funds available to spend on the product it will be of little advantage. In exploring the potential demand for products, therefore, it is necessary to consider the probable availability of funds to spend for this purpose. If the demand for the product can be directly associated with ultimate consumers, the purchasing power of each type of consumer should be predicted. Moreover, the purchasing power in different areas of the country, or in foreign countries, will be significant in an analysis made on an area basis.

The products of many industries are sold primarily to business concerns for further fabrication. In such cases the ability to pay for products depends primarily upon the activity in the consuming industry. For example, the amount of effective demand for steel depends largely upon the activity in the automobile industry, the construction industry, the machinery industry, and the container industry. The forecast of the demand for steel must include some prediction regarding the activity in each of these major consuming industries.

It is particularly in connection with "ability to pay" that business cycles affect the demand for the products of an industry.

SUPPLY OF PRODUCTS OR SERVICES

The outlook for profitable operations in an industry depends not only upon the demand for the commodities and services which that industry produces, but also upon the available supply and the cost of bringing such products on to the market. This leads to questions of capacity and changes in costs of production.

Capacity of the industry. In a dynamic business system such as that of the United States, some industries are likely to have excess capacity while others have inadequate capacity. Commercial laundries, for instance, have capacity far in excess of demand because of the great increase in home washing machines and driers. The aircraft and shipbuilding industries are so dependent on war demand that overcapacity is a chronic condition in peacetime. In addition to such drops in demand, excess capacity may result from overexpansion. Sometimes a field of business looks so attractive that too many firms enter it. Thus, there may be an excess of resort hotels or office buildings in a given locality because promoters expanded their facilities too fast.

Undercapacity is common in any expanding industry. If a new product like orlon meets with wide public acceptance, the original plants will probably not be able to fill the demand. Or, a rapid increase in demand, such as that caused by the erection of the huge Fairless steel works north of Philadelphia, may make local housing and shopping facilities quite inadequate.

Significance of undercapacity. When capacity of an industry is scarcely adequate to meet demand, most companies will enjoy profitable operations. Products will find a ready market, prices will be firm, and a high level of operation will permit spreading overhead costs over many units.

There are, however, several modifying influences that may affect the outlook for an industry with undercapacity. Often old or otherwise inefficient equipment can be called back into production if selling prices are high enough. For example, there are many old beehive coke ovens that can be put into operation if the capacity of the more efficient by-product coke ovens is inadequate to meet demand. In other instances capacity may be expanded through changes in quality. Specifications for strip steel to be used for tin plate, for instance, became so exacting that for a time the capacity of the older Welsh mills was unusable; however, when demand became very strong, customers were again willing to accept the products of these mills. Thus, "capacity" in many industries is somewhat elastic and must be considered in terms of price and specifications. It is for this reason, as well as matters of multiple shifts and shutdowns, that statistics on capacity are difficult to interpret.

The significance of undercapacity also depends upon the ease of entering the industry. If a new concern can be established with comparatively small capital and within a reasonably short period of time, undercapacity will probably be a temporary matter. The production of baking powder, for example, requires little more than a machine to mix the ingredients and a canning machine; consequently, the capacity of a plant making this type of product can be easily expanded to meet demand. In contrast, virgin copper production requires an expensive plant and access to satisfactory ore deposits, with the result that few firms enter the business.

The possibility of expansion or contraction of imports from foreign countries must be taken into account for some commodities. The importation of sugar from the Philippines has long been a crucial factor in the outlook for the domestic sugar industry. Similarly, domestic paper producers must consider imports from Canada and Scandinavian countries. The extent of imports is, of course, strongly influenced by tariffs and foreign exchange, which may entirely prevent foreign goods from entering local markets or allow only certain types of goods to enter at competitive prices. Since the United States has become the principal creditor nation of the world and we sponsor, at least for others, the idea of world trade, it is reasonable to anticipate significant changes in the extent to which foreign productive capacity affects United States industry.

Effect of excess capacity. Excess capacity will have a depressing influence on the outlook for an industry, for it may lead to low prices, low rates of operation, and a high proportion of sales expense.

The seriousness of excess capacity depends, in part, upon how large depreciation, interest, and other expenses connected with the facilities are in relation to total costs. If, as in the cement industry, these overhead charges are a high percent of total expenses, the individual companies may cut prices to low levels in an attempt to secure volume and at least some contribution above out-of-pocket expenses toward the fixed burden. On the other hand, if the bulk of expense goes for materials and labor, the excess capacity will have much less effect on supply and price because the relation between out-of-pocket costs and prices will be the controlling influence—whether the plant is busy or not.

Durability of the excess capacity is also important. In the silk and rayon weaving business, for instance, excess looms and other equipment were available for many years. The failure of a particular company did not remove this capacity, for the equipment was merely sold—usually at a low price—to another firm and again placed in operation. A similar condition prevailed in other branches of the textile industry, with the result that profitable operations in these lines were very difficult. Scrapping of existing facilities must sometimes be considered when overcapacity exists, although the usual pattern is the development of more efficient methods and machinery which make operation of the old facilities impossible at competing prices.

Labor costs. Labor costs loom large in the outlook for many industries, and on this point it is necessary to predict both the trend in costs and the extent to which increased payroll may be passed on to the consumer.

The success of a few industries has depended upon a ready supply of immigrant or southern mountain labor. For such industries future governmental action on minimum wages and on immigration will be of paramount importance. Most industries, however, will be primarily concerned with trends in union activities. Governmental sponsorship of collective bargaining along with a fundamental change in social attitude toward organized labor makes past experience in this connection of limited value. The point at issue is not so much a general rise in wages, for this has been the trend for decades, but whether unions will force changes in wages and hours and introduce the inflexibilities in personnel relations to which a given industry cannot adjust. Perhaps of equal importance is the question of whether the unions and the managements in the industry have developed a reasonable working understanding that may go a long way toward minimizing strikes and unbearable increases in labor costs.

In many industries it has been possible to pass the additional labor cost on to the consumer, and in some instances the contention that the additional labor cost can be offset by technological improvements is justified. On the other hand, a particular industry that is facing competitive substitution of other products or that produces an article for which the demand is comparatively elastic may not be able to pass on additional labor costs. In such instances the prediction regarding labor costs may be vital to a conclusion regarding general profitability of the industry.

Material costs. The sheer existence of an adequate supply of raw materials may be a factor in the outlook of a few industries, notably those depending upon a natural resource such as timber, crude oil, iron ore, or other minerals. In most cases, however, the problem is the price at which the materials can be obtained.

Changes in raw material prices have varying effects on different industries. For example, some industries have a product the selling price of which is comparatively stable; this is true not only of the classic example of chewing gum, but also of other food products. As a consequence, a fall in raw material prices increases the gross margin, and rising prices decrease the profit margin. In other industries, such as textiles or containers, the selling price is comparatively flexible and may be adjusted as material prices go up or down. Fluctuations in the total volume of sales, operating efficiency, and the relative importance of fixed costs become prime considerations under such conditions.

A forecast of prices of the major raw materials of an industry requires at least a brief study of the history and present conditions in the raw material producing industry. Past prices should be reviewed for the purpose of determining any general trend or the typical behavior of the commodity price. Some raw materials show sharp seasonal fluctuations, others are characterized by very wide and rapid changes in price, while still others are typically stable or sluggish in their movements. Prices of finished steel products, for example, reveal considerable rigidity; on the other hand, a product such as raw cotton or leather fluctuates over a wide range. Generally speaking, then, the problem with respect to material costs is to predict the way fluctuations in both raw material prices and finished goods prices will affect the *margin* between the two.

Occasionally changes of raw material prices are less important because of the possibility of using substitutes. In the production of some steel products, for example, the proportion of scrap iron to pig iron can be varied in accordance with relative prices and availability of supply. Synthetic fibers have almost completely replaced raw silk in the piece goods and hosiery industries. Insofar as such substitution is practical, the availability of either raw material at low prices will be favorable factor in the outlook of the consuming industry.

Taxes and other costs. Taxes make a heavy drain on all profitable industries, but the burden falls more heavily on some than on others. The major question, from the viewpoint of industry outlook, is whether the particular industry being studied is subjected to unusually heavy taxes such as the excise tax on alcoholic beverages or a processing tax on agricultural commodities. When such special taxes are found, it is then necessary to explore (a) whether the amount of the tax can be added to selling prices and thereby passed on to the consumer, and (b) if it is passed on, whether the increase in selling price will be large enough to cut sales volume.

It should also be recognized that taxes are now being used by various governmental bodies as a device for enforcing certain regulations rather than for the purpose of raising revenue. This, then, becomes more a question of governmental regulation than of cost of operation.

Other costs such as rents or interest may influence the prospects for an industry. The heavy interest and retirement charges incurred by the airlines in their rush to fly jet planes, for instance, casts a pall upon the entire industry. Usually it is a specific company that is in a particularly favorable or unfavorable position because of "other costs" rather than an industry as a whole, and consequently these other costs will generally have only a minor bearing on the outlook for the industry.

COMPETITIVE CONDITIONS IN THE INDUSTRY

The outline thus far has suggested that the outlook for an industry will be determined by the balance of the various forces affecting demand and supply of the products of the industry. Competitive conditions within the industry will often affect the manner and the rapidity with which these forces work themselves out.

Nature of companies in the industry. Some industries are dominated by a few large companies, the actions of which are of major importance to the future profitability of the entire industry. For example, the Federal Trade Commission has alleged that profits in the farm machinery industry have been abnormally high due, in part, to the fact that this industry was dominated by two or three large companies. Likewise, the United States Steel Corporation is reputed to have "held the umbrella" over the price structure of the steel industry for a long period of years. In contrast, other industries are characterized by atomistic competition, in which each small firm seeks to adjust the current condition as rapidly as possible. The weaving of dress goods and numerous other branches of the textile industry typify this type of competition.

Companies in an industry also vary as to stability and financial strength. An industry characterized by firms of great instability and comparative financial weakness is illustrated by the women's ready-to-wear industry. Here firms are organized, operate for a limited period of time, and then pass out of the picture so rapidly that widespread goodwill among customers or reputation for dependability is rarely established. In other branches of the clothing industry, such as the men's shoe industry, several of the leading firms have been in operation for two or more generations and have a stability and financial backing that tend to make competitive conditions less chaotic and unpredictable.

The attitude of the management of companies in an industry may also affect the outlook. The typical managements in some industries are sharp and irresponsible and take only a short-run point of view. They are likely to engage in activities that may give them an immediate benefit irrespective of the future repercussions of their actions. In contrast, the typical managements in other industries tend to adhere strictly to an accepted code of business ethics and are inclined to take a long-run industry viewpoint in their action. Leadership in an industry may also be characterized as aggressive and alert, as in the container industry. This is in contrast to unimaginative leadership, which with some qualifications was said to characterize the ice industry during the period when domestic electric refrigeration was first becoming established.

These particular characteristics of companies in an industry are very likely to affect the way in which adjustment is made to changes in either demand or supply, and consequently such characteristics must not be overlooked.

Organization of the industry. Organized cooperative effort has a significant effect upon the outlook for some industries. There are literally hundreds of trade associations, which are the central agencies for such voluntary action. Many of these associations do little more than sponsor an annual convention and perhaps a trade paper. Others carry on a much more extensive program that may include research and compilation of information of interest to its members, lobbying in national or state legislatures, conducting a public relations campaign, and promotion of fair trade practices. Some of the trade associations play an active role in governmental price and production controls. While the scope of such government-industry cooperation is in a state of flux, it is likely that the trade association will assume increasing importance in this regard. In any event, it is already clear that an intelligently run trade association can contribute significantly to the stability, public relations, and government relations of an industry.

Government regulation of industry. Even the most ardent advocates of "American individualism" will admit that the forces of supply and demand should not be given free sway in the contemporary business world. There are, however, wide differences of opinion regarding the extent to which government should seek to restrict and regulate these forces. During recent years government regulation has been extended on many fronts, and it appears likely that this tendency will continue. Consequently, in formulating an opinion of the outlook for an industry it is necessary to appraise the possible effects of government regulation of the industry.

Federal and state governments have for some time regulated in considerable detail the activities of utilities and railroads. There is much discussion as to the desirabiltiy of extendng this utility concept to other industries such as coal or even all industries vital to public welfare. If for a given industry any action in this direction seems likely, it is highly important to study the nature and effects of the regulations that might be imposed.

The government often provides special advantages to particular industries. Our merchant marine is heavily subsidized; many other industries are protected from foreign competition by tariffs; more recently agricultural products have been granted large subsidies. In order to qualify for such special advantages, it is often necessary for any industry to conform with stipulations and regulations of the government. This is particularly true in the agricultural industries where the whole program of subsidies is associated with a plan for controlled production and marketing.

Governmental bodies are exercising influence over general trade practices. The Federal Trade Commission Act has been strengthened so that the commission may more effectively regulate what it considers unfair methods of competition; at the same time special powers were granted over advertising of foods, drugs, health devices, and cosmetics. It is quite probable that additional statutes regulating trade practices will be enacted from time to time.

Such governmental action is frankly and deliberately designed to modify the underlying forces of demand and supply. It is part of the composite picture of the outlook for any industry.

MARKET POSITION OF THE COMPANY

An analysis of the outlook for an industry, such as suggested in the preceding pages, will indicate the setting in which a specific company must carry on its operations. An appreciation of these general forces at work is vital to intelligent management decisions. It is highly desirable, however, to pursue the analysis one step further to ascertain how the specific firm is likely to fare within its industry. Will the company get its share of new markets; is it fortified against impending hazards; does it enjoy a favorable or unfavorable cost position as compared with its competitors; will its management make it a leader in the industry? Such factors as these will determine whether a specific enterprise will get along better or worse than the industry as a whole, and they will point to the particular problems to which the administrators should give special attention.

First, what of the market position of the company?

Relation of company sales to those of the industry and leading companies. The ups and downs of a total industry often obscure how well a specific company is being managed. A revealing way to screen out such external influences is to watch company sales as a percentage of its total industry and its major competitors.

A classic case of when this simple guide was not heeded is Baldwin Locomotive Company. For years a "blue chip" firm and a leader in its industry, Baldwin's record during the period of its decline is shown in the following table. Viewed alone, the sales increase from 5 locomotives in 1932 to 303 in 1941 looked good. Actually, the company was at best swimming with the tide, and by 1945 its share of industry sales had dropped to 15%. This was a clear sign that something fundamental was wrong—a warning that complete elimination from its chosen field and bankruptcy lay ahead.

LOCOMOTIVES ORDERED

	From Total Industry	*From Baldwin Locomotive Company*	*Baldwin % of Industry*
1932	12	5	42%
1935	97	28	24
1937	354	81	23
1939	400	80	20
1941*	1,268	303	24
1943*	1,048	234	22
1945	845	129	15
1947	2,229	282	13
1949	1,805	178	10
1951	4,107	426**	10**
1954	1,050	44	4
1956	1,311	0	0

* Excludes U. S. Government orders.
** Includes Lima and Hamilton locomotives because companies were merged.

Comparisons of a company's sales with those of its industry are usually possible in one form or another. The United States Department of Commerce and other government agencies publish vast quantities of valuable statistics; trade associations often compile figures on volume of activity; sometimes trade papers assemble data and publish indexes of activity; or occasionally a special source, such as F. W. Dodge Corporation (construction industry) or the A. C. Nielsen Company (retail grocery and drug sales), is available to subscribers. In spite of statistical weaknesses that often exist in such comparisons, some measure of the trend in a company's position is highly valuable.

Standing of company products. The market position of a company is strongly influenced by the quality and distinctiveness of its products. The automobile that has distinctive engineering features, the restaurant that serves good food, the hospital equipment that has dependability and durability, or the brand of women's hose that has style—is the product that will improve its position on the market. In the case of each type of product, the important characteristics from the consumer's point of view should be determined and a company's products appraised in terms of these characteristics. In this process it is necessary to distinguish between various price ranges because the controlling characteristics may not be the same for, say, low-priced shoes and high-priced shoes.

A failure to keep attuned to customer requirements was the source of Baldwin Locomotive Company's undoing. This company for many years manufactured steam locomotives. When diesel-electric engines were introduced for light hauls and switching, Baldwin executives clung to the tradition that steam engines would continue to be used for heavy freight and passenger runs. In fact, the 1940's witnessed a drastic technological change. By 1956 almost 90% of the locomotive power was provided by diesels; *all* new locomotives purchased by United States railroads were diesels. In contrast, Electro-Motive division of General Motors Corporation pioneered in diesel development; and because its product required less servicing, had lower maintenance costs, needed a shorter time "getting up steam," and enjoyed other operating economies, Electro-Motive's position in the industry moved from 14% in 1935 to 76% in 1956.

Sometimes the past success of a company is attributable to a single product, whereas future success in the industry must be built upon a more complete line of products. For example, the Mead

Johnson Company has enjoyed very large sales of its prepared baby cereal "Pablum," but possible substitutes or changes in ideas regarding child feeding make this single product an inadequate base for maintenance of a leading position in the industry. This company, fully recognizing the danger, developed a wide line of baby foods and then hit upon another winner—Metrecal.

Reputation of company in major markets. A company's position in its industry is also affected by its reputation in major markets. For instance, some piston ring manufacturers have carefully nurtured their reputation with garages and auto repairmen while their competitors have been primarily interested in relations with automobile producers. The former group prefer the replacement market because there is little risk that the decision of one or two buyers will seriously affect total volume. In the hosiery industry, to cite another example, a field survey revealed that one company was particularly well regarded by managers of small-town stores, while the large stores in big cities thought of this concern as just another manufacturer. The strength of this hosiery company's market position depended, therefore, primarily upon the outlook for sales through small-town stores.

Often the reputation of a firm varies by area as well as by type of customer. This is illustrated by different brands of coffee. Many local brands exist that are known in only one metropolitan area or perhaps one region; even the nationally advertised brands experience substantial differences in consumer acceptance in different sections of the country. In the same way, a particular manufacturer of farm machinery may be generally and favorably known in the corn-belt states but have comparatively little standing in the cotton states.

Reputation is an intangible thing including, in addition to being known, a prominence for giving service, for offering a good buy in terms of product and price, and for fair dealings. Many companies, as already indicated, have a strong reputation in a particular area or with certain types of customers; in a sense they have a niche in the industry where they are outstanding. For purposes of forecasting, the problem is to identify those areas or types of trade from which a company will obtain its business and then consider the prospects for such groups on the basis of the outlook for the general industry.

Determination of the market position of a company, then, requires a thorough analysis of available statistics regarding trends in general sales—sales by products and sales in important markets—and, in addition, an appraisal of such things as leadership in product design, adaptability of product line to anticipated conditions in the industry, and reputation with the trade.

COST POSITION OF THE COMPANY

The position of a firm in its industry depends upon its ability to deal with supply factors as well as with demand or market factors. Its relative cost position influences the extent and direction of company expansion and may be the key to survival itself.

Comparative location. Ready and inexpensive access to raw materials is a major asset for companies using bulky products. The newsprint mills of Canada, for instance, now have a controlling advantage over their former competitors in Wisconsin, Michigan, or the New England states because the virgin timber in the latter areas has been cut off and logs—or pulp—must be transported long distances to the mills. In fact, most of the remaining mills in these areas have turned to specialty paper products to counteract the disadvantage of their location.

Steel companies are likewise concerned with accessibility of raw materials; only here three products are needed, iron ore, coal, and limestone. The desirable location is one to which all three products may be cheaply transported. Thus, the mills on the Great Lakes, which can use water transportation for Minnesota ore and a short rail movement for coal, had a cost advantage over many inland plants, and at the same time were adjacent to large markets. Largely for this reason, many "furnaces" along the Ohio River were closed down. However, with the supply of high grade ore in Minnesota running low, East Coast locations where foreign ores can be brought in may prove to be the most economical in the future.

Location with respect to labor is sometimes a definite advantage or disadvantage to a company. Minimum wage legislation and union activity have greatly reduced geographic differentials in wage rates, however, and the advantage in labor cost such as the southern textile mills formerly enjoyed over their northern competitors has now largely disappeared. Occasionally a company located in a rural area is at a disadvantage if expansion requires that skilled workers must be induced to move from the cities, although the importance of this depends upon the level of unemployment and the living conditions surrounding the plant.

In some industries, location close to markets is crucial. This is obvious for retail stores for which buyer traffic may mean the difference between success or failure. A Canadian steel mill at Sault Ste. Marie had a favorable location while transcontinental railroads were being constructed; but when this business diminished, it found its shipping expenses to distant industrial markets a barrier to expansion. Aside from reduced shipping expense, a location close to market facilitates contacts with customers and eases delivery problems.

Relative efficiency of equipment. The production facilities of a company may have an important bearing on its future success. A prime consideration is whether the plant and machinery can make products suited to the trends in demand. Pharmaceutical companies, a few years ago, found their capacity to make sulfa drugs far in excess of demand because newer antibiotics had been discovered.

Often such outmoded facilities are doubly disadvantageous because other companies are also likely to have excess equipment for the declining products; therefore, profit margins tend to be very narrow, especially in contrast with margins on the expanding products which may be in short supply.

A second consideration is the operating costs of the equipment. This is illustrated in the printing industry where one-color, hand-fed presses can be used for three- or four-color work by running the paper through the presses a separate time for each color. However, an automatic, multi-color press can do the entire printing job in one operation with a single pressman. Except for special jobs a firm with only one-color, hand-fed presses cannot compete for multi-color work because its costs are too high.

Flexibility of equipment is often a factor in operating costs. For example, large jet planes such as the Boeing 707 are efficient for transatlantic and cross-continental flights, but they are expensive and hard to handle on short runs where traffic is lighter. Consequently, new equipment is smaller and more flexible. Such flexible equipment costs more to operate per passenger mile than a 707 when the latter is fully loaded on a long flight, but it has decided advantages in filling varying needs. Again, the crucial point is having equipment suited to the market the company wants to serve.

Unique cost advantages. In practice, firms often achieve cost advantages in a variety of other ways that may not be available to their competitors. The following examples are merely suggestive of these possibilities. Sometimes a patented or secret process gives a firm unusually low operating costs. In other cases a long-term contract or lease may be particularly beneficial. Some companies, through affiliations with other operating units or by virtue of their own size, are able to buy materials at lower prices because of the large quantities taken.

A concern may enjoy for a time low depreciation expense because its facilities are carried on the books at substantially less than replacement costs. This usually occurs when equipment or even an entire plant is bought secondhand at a distress sale, or the assets may have been written down in connection with a financial reorganization. On the other hand, the assets may be overvalued in terms of present replacement costs and the firm may be trying to cover depreciation charges that are substantially higher than those of its competitors.

Whatever the reason, the basic problem is to attempt to discover any significant reasons why the company in question is in a better, or worse, position than its competitors in supplying goods that are in demand.

SPECIAL COMPETITIVE CONSIDERATIONS

These are at least two further considerations, in addition to market and supply factors, that influence the ability of an enterprise to do as well as or better than its industry as a whole; namely financial strength and competence of the company executives.

Relative financial strength. Adequate capital provides one of the necessary means to put plans of the business administrator into action. A company may enjoy a distinctive product, an unusually low cost, or some other advantage over its competitors, but virtually every type of expansion requires additional capital for inventory and accounts receivable if not also for fixed assets. Moreover, if a firm is to maintain its position it must have sufficient financial strength to withstand depressions and aggressive drives by competitors for choice markets. Competition may force a company to expand the variety of products offered for sale, to establish district warehouses and local sales organizations, or to buy new equipment, and this requires capital.

The simplest way for a company to meet these capital requirements is from its own cash balances, which may be larger than necessary for day-to-day operations. Most concerns, however, do not carry large amounts of idle cash (or nonoperating assets readily convertible into cash such as government securities), in which case financial strength is primarily a question of ability to borrow new capital or to secure it from stockholders. Ability to raise new capital will reflect not only past and probable future earnings, but also the existing debt structure and fixed charges of the company. So, the entire financial structure of the company should be examined, particularly if there are likely to be major readjustments in industry operations.

Ability of company management. The most important single factor influencing the position of a company in its industry is the ability of its executives. The executives of a business turn potential sales into actual sales, keep costs in line, and face the endless stream of new and unanticipated problems.

The qualities desired for executives are numerous and vary to some extent for different types of companies; for example, a women's hat manufacturer needs a style sense, whereas the producer of electronic equipment benefits more from a thorough understanding of electrical engineering. No single executive should be expected to have all the talents required, but within the management group there should be vision, creativeness, supervisory ability, human understanding, diligence, perseverance, and other qualities essential to the planning, direction, and control of the enterprise.

In predicting the future of a business it is also necessary to consider the extent to which success is dependent upon a few individuals and the provision that has been made for a succession of capable leadership. This is a crucial factor in the outlook for a small "one-man company."

SUMMARY

The outlook for the volume of business and the profitability of a company depends upon (a) conditions in the economy where the company operates, (b) the prospects for its industry generally, and (c) its position in that industry. A systematic analysis of each of these aspects should be made frequently by the top executives of the company. In studying the industry outlook, a continuing review is desirable of the demand for the products of the industry, the factors affecting supply, and the competitive conditions. Similarly, analysis of company position calls for appraisal of the relative standing of the company in markets and in costs, and also review of its competitive strength.

Clearly a great many facts and forecasts bear on a company outlook. Some device is needed to put these data into systematic relationship. The outlines in Chapters 2 and 3 provide a method of putting the array of data into meaningful order.

Such an analysis is far from a mechanical or routine matter, however. Keen judgment is especially vital in attaching *relative importance* to the numerous factors that have some influence on the outlook. A general outline, such as the one discussed in the last two chapters, suggests possibilities but cannot decide which are the key considerations for a specific company. To identify the key factors, ask: (1) What influences or elements are probably going to determine which companies in the industry will enjoy outstanding success and which will decline? (2) How do the strengths and the weaknesses of Company X match against the crucial factors identified in answer to question (1)?

QUESTIONS FOR CLASS DISCUSSION

1. One expert in retail distribution claims that a "distribution revolution" has been needed to keep up with consumers who (a) have increased mobility with new cars and new highways, (b) are better educated and more conscious of price than they were twenty years ago, and (c) have moved from farms and out of cities to the suburbs." In light of this analysis, should the automobile industry continue to emphasize dealerships that offer a complete package of new car sales, used car sales, and authorized service and that, on the average, sell 96 new cars a year (less than one every three days). Can the dealership package of service be adjusted to changing consumer desires?

2. "Over the past ten years average hourly earnings in the steel industry have increased 54% while average steel mill product prices have gone up only 30%." This quotation implies that all wage increases for steel companies cannot be passed along in the form of higher prices. A young accountant, noting this, forecast increasing labor costs in the future as unions demanded wage increases and decided that profit margins would go down steadily since prices could not be increased as rapidly as wages; therefore, he decided that he should quit the steel business. Do you agree?

3. Changes in the level of business activity are often classified as (a) seasonal fluctuations, (b) cyclical fluctuations, (c) long-term trends, and (d) random changes. What is meant by each of these terms? Which type of change is easiest to forecast? Why has most attention of forecasters been devoted to predicting cyclical fluctuations?

4. "For at least a decade, the world has had an oversupply of crude oil. During the last four years, options taken by oil companies on new land for exploration have declined." What is the significance of these events for an oil-refining firm that uses crude oil as its major raw material?

5. (a) Using the outline given in this chapter insofar as it is applicable, appraise the outlook for a specific laundry serving your college community. (b) Do the same for your college bookstore.

6. Small steel companies were the first to introduce both oxygen converters and continuous casting into the United States. These have been the two most recent of a very few major technological changes in the steel industry in the past fifty years. They meant substantial process cost reductions for the firms who first utilized them. Explain why several small firms, rather than the giants of the industry, were the first to undertake these new processes.

7. "Competitive conditions in the industry will often affect the manner and the rapidity with which the forces of demand and supply work themselves out." What is meant by competitive conditions in this statement? Explain how each of these conditions modify the influences of supply and demand.

8. Explain how (a) a favorable and (b) an unfavorable outlook for a furniture manufacturing concern might affect its wage policy, dividend policy, advertising policy, inventory policy, establishment of branch offices, and installation of automatic machinery.

9. Select a company close to your college (or a nationally known company familiar to most members of your class) and explain how its outlook would probably be affected if the United States became involved in another world war. It is suggested that you consider, systematically, each point in the outline of this chapter and decide, point by point, how the selected company would be affected, if at all, by a war; then consolidate your opinions on the several points to form your overall conclusion.

CASE III

Island Creek Coal Company

COMPANY HISTORY

The Island Creek Coal Company was founded in the early 1900's when immigrants straight from Ellis Island were brought to Logan County, Kentucky, to mine coal by pick and shovel. The Hatfields fought the McCoys over land on which the company later built roads, towns, stores, and schools to help provide modern living conditions for the miners and their families.

As the firm grew toward becoming a major producer of bituminous coal, it opened more mines in West Virginia, eastern Kentucky, and western Virginia. Returns were high for the stockholders. Every year after 1916 (except 1932) profits exceeded one million dollars.

In the early days, labor relations were turbulent. John L. Lewis was blocked in 1921 in his first organizing attempts when Island Creek and local operators under the tough personage of Sheriff Don Chafin manned the passes along the Logan line. They repulsed an armed force of 5,000 miners. Before the fighting stopped, 47 men were killed.

Conditions have changed over the years. Many of the mines are highly mechanized, using the most modern equipment available for underground mining. Labor organization has become well established, and aside from relatively minor strikes, generally stable labor relations have been maintained between the company and the United Mine Workers since 1950. The number of employees has declined substantially, while unemployment in the area has become a matter of national concern.

Island Creek Coal Company has been a profitable venture. Up through 1954 (before a series of mergers), the company had net earnings of about $100,000,000 and had paid cash dividends to common stockholders in excess of $80,000,000.

From 1954 to 1962, the company went through six mergers and formed two new joint ventures with large steel companies. These combinations increased the number of mines operated and the reserves—some to replace mines abandoned because of high operating costs. Reserves, by 1962, exceeded one billion tons of bituminous coal. They were mainly low-volatile coals, particularly well suited for metallurgical purposes.

The company's history of profits and return on investment for recent years preceding 1962 should be examined and then thought of in light of predictions about supply and demand in the coal industry and about a potential cost squeeze.

Exhibit 1

ISLAND CREEK COAL COMPANY AND SUBSIDIARIES
(dollar figures in thousands)

Year	Net Sales	Net Income	Dividends	Shareowner's Equity	Property Additions	Number of Employees
1953	63,921	2,995	3,588	45,384	2,726	6,358
1956	117,879	8,793	4,444	61,811	14,579	6,994
1957	121,531	9,382	4,485	67,833	8,375	6,239
1958	90,317	4,688	4,488	67,732	3,165	5,298
1959	99,122	3,402	4,473	66,672	18,200	6,027
1960	86,545	3,231	3,894	64,108	4,427	4,118
1961	79,778	3,091	3,239	63,960	6,050	4,534
1962	80,884	2,722 [1]	3,241	65,664	3,849	3,784

[1] In addition, there was a capital gain of $2,201,000 from the sale of mines and equipment to a subsidiary of National Steel Corporation. Island Creek manages the new company and receives royalties from the coal mined.

BITUMINOUS COAL INDUSTRY

Production and forecasts

The problem is shown in perspective in Exhibit 2. Bituminous coal has not only lost its relative position in supplying energy, but there has also been an absolute decrease in its total consumption, especially since 1950. Use of coal by railroads and ocean vessels has virtually ceased, its use for domestic fuel has sharply declined, and both oil and gas have made sharp inroads into its industrial markets.

Studies of the future of the energy market, however, indicate that the outlook for coal is not so dismal as the preceding data suggests. A national fuels and energy study group, in its 1962 report to the United States Senate, predicted that total United States energy requirements would be double by 1980 and that coal would play a substantial role in this dramatic expansion. The study group noted that various experts differed on how much the consumption of coal would increase—the estimates for 1980 range from 550 to 960 million tons, compared with the present rate of 400 million—but there is considerable evidence that bituminous coal consumption will increase.

The conclusions of the study group for 1980 were, in summary:

1. Total energy needs—nearly double the consumption in 1960.
2. Total electrical energy—three and one-half times that generated in 1960, or about 2,700 billion kilowatt-hours.
3. Coal—roughly double that of 1960, or over 800 million tons.
4. Gas—somewhat less than double the consumption in 1960.
5. Oil—about two thirds as much again as in 1960, or about 5.7 billion barrels.

Exhibit 2

U. S. PRODUCTION OF MINERAL FUELS AND WATER POWER, 1900-1961

Year	(MILLIONS OF BITUMINOUS COAL EQUIVALENT TONS)					(PERCENTAGE ON A BTU BASIS)				
	Bituminous Coal and Lignite	Anthracite Coal	Crude Petroleum	Natural Gas	Water Power	Bituminous Coal and Lignite	Anthracite Coal	Crude Petroleum	Natural Gas	Water Power
1900	212	56	14	10	10	70.5	18.4	4.7	3.2	3.2
1910	417	82	46	21	21	71.1	14.0	7.9	3.5	3.5
1920	569	87	98	34	28	69.7	10.7	12.0	4.1	3.5
1930	468	67	199	82	28	55.4	8.0	23.5	9.7	3.4
1940	461	50	300	114	34	48.1	5.2	31.3	11.9	3.5
1950	516	43	437	261	60	39.2	3.2	33.2	19.8	4.6
1961	400	17	580	531	67	25.1	1.1	36.4	33.2	4.2

6. Hydropower portion—down to 2½%.
7. Nuclear power—about the same portion as hydropower, but there should be no surprise if nuclear power should insinuate itself into the energy economy of the country at a much faster rate.[1]

Another forecast of bituminous coal requirements is shown in Exhibit 3.

Exhibit 3

FORECAST OF U. S. BITUMINOUS COAL CONSUMPTION, 1960-1980 *

Report of Panel on the Impact of the Peaceful Uses of Atomic Energy, submitted to the 84th Congress, January 1956, Vol. 2, p. 78.

(millions of tons)

	1960	*1965*	*1970*	*1975*	*1980*
Electric power	159	183	220	364	459
Coke	130	140	150	160	170
Steel and cement plants (other than coke)	15	15	15	15	15
Other industrial uses	85	75	70	60	60
Retail	45	35	30	25	20
Exports	30	35	40	50	60
Total	464	483	525	674	784

* This table is derived on the assumptions that (a) atomic energy will not be a significant source of energy prior to 1980, and (b) electric generating capacity will increase about 4.9% annually—a Federal Power Commission forecast. If forecasts of the *Electrical World* prevail— 7.3% annual increase in generating capacity until 1970 and 6.5% from 1970 to 1980—the electric power consumption of coal would be 845 million tons by 1980 and the total estimated consumption 1,170 million tons.

Exports from United States

Export sales are the most difficult to predict. Europe will undoubtedly have to increase its import of energy fuels substantially during the next decade. According to an article in *Fortune* (December, 1962), there is a potential billion dollar coal market, and U. S. production costs are so much below those in Europe that U. S. coal probably can be delivered at competitive prices to European ports. (European prices now are often $15 per ton.) However, for U. S. companies to capture a major part of this potential, a concerted effort will have to be made to overcome difficulties with import restrictions, dollar exchange, and uncertainties about the cost of ocean transport (shipping rates have varied from $3 to $17 per ton during the past 10 years). Oil imports and other sources of energy will also compete for the market.

[1] *Report of the National Fuels and Energy Study Group on An Assessment of Available Information on Energy in the United States*, to the Committee on Interior and Insular Affairs, United States Senate, September 21, 1962, pp. 40-41.

On the other hand, competition in the metallurgical field is less severe. The United States is the best world source for coking coal. As the steel industry expands in Japan, Latin America, Europe, and elsewhere, there is a good prospect that U. S. metallurgical coals will find foreign markets. The projected increase in Exhibit 3 presumes that most U. S. exports will be metallurgical coal.

Metallurgical use

In this field, bituminous coal faces less competition from oil and gas than in the energy field. Most metallurgical coal is converted into coke, and most of this coke is used by the steel industry in blast furnaces.

Exhibit 4

INDEXES OF INDUSTRIAL AND STEEL PRODUCTION AND TONS OF COKE PER TON OF PIG IRON

Year	Federal Reserve Board Index of Industrial Production (1957-9 = 100)	Index of Steel Production (1957-9 = 100)	Tons of Coke Used to Produce One Ton of Pig Iron
1929	38	54.8	
1939	38	46.8	
1949	64	80.3	.935
1955	96	120.5	.873
1957	100	116	.808
1959	105	96.2	.785
1960	108	101.9	.749
1961	109	100.9	.708
1962	118	101.2	.690
1963	124	111	n.a.[1]

[1] Not available.

Technological developments reduce the amount of coke needed for each ton of iron produced in a blast furnace. If natural gas, fuel oil, or even pulverized coal is used as a supplementary fuel, coke requirements can be reduced by 15%. The supplementary fuels are much less expensive than coke, which for most of the U. S. steel industry costs between $16 and $22 per ton. Also, experiments have been conducted on the direct reduction of iron ore, which would replace the blast furnace process entirely. The capital investment appears to be very high, however, and the process appears likely to be used only in new locations where coking coal is not readily available.

Only certain grades of bituminous coal are usable for making coke. Low ash, low sulphur, low moisture coal with a high degree of uniformity is desired. In contrast, the public utilities are looking primarily for Btu's and are unwilling to pay a premium for quality, such as low sulphur or uniformity.

Utility market

Coal provides two thirds of the energy for heat-generated electricity (excluding hydropower) in the United States; the remaining one third comes from fuel oil and gas. Federal Power Commission statistics show a marked increase in efficiency in electric utility plants. The 3 pounds of coal used to generate 1 kilowatt-hour of electricity in 1920 has been reduced steadily to .86 pounds per kwh in 1961. Gains in efficiency applied as much to oil and gas plants as to coal plants. Competition between types of fuels for utility use is extremely keen. Reduction of both (a) transportation costs and (b) mining costs are vital if coal is to maintain its share of this expanding market.

(a) Transportation costs

The cost of moving coal from the mine to many of its markets is as high as the mining cost itself. Island Creek has an unfavorable transportation differential of about $1.52 per ton compared with Pennsylvania coalfields in serving the northeastern states. Transportation costs explain why coal fuels 96% of the steam electricity plants in the east north central portion of the country but none at all on the Pacific coast and in the west south central section.

Several technological developments are modifying the transportation picture. A coal pipeline was, for a while, successfully operated from southern Ohio to Cleveland.

Generation of electricity close to the mines and transportation of the electricity over superhigh tension lines is being tried in western Pennsylvania to serve the Philadelphia market. The technical feasibility of such a "mine mouth" plant is yet to be ascertained.

The railroad's answer is a unitized train, whereby trainloads of coal are assembled at a given loading point for delivery to a single customer. Unitized trains have supplanted the coal pipeline in Ohio because of their flexibility in increasing capacity and because of a substantial reduction in rail freight rates.

(b) Mining costs

Production costs in U. S. bituminous mines have been cut by (a) a dramatic mechanization of all types of mines and (b) increasing emphasis on strip mining. The resulting increase in productivity has enabled coal producers to actually reduce the average at-the-mine price per ton from $4.99 in 1948 to $4.65 in 1961.

Hand labor has virtually disappeared in the larger U. S. mines. Recently, continuous mining machines, some capable of producing up to 8 tons per hour, have been replacing earlier machine cutting equipment.

Even more spectacular is the mining equipment now used for surface operations in strip mining. Output per man day of strip mines is over twice that of underground mines. (See Exhibit 5.) More efficient yet is auger mining, which works horizontally into the side of a hill; but the number of locations suitable for this kind of equipment is limited.

Exhibit 5

OUTPUT PER MAN DAY—TONS

	1940	*1950*	*1960*
United States			
Underground mines	4.86	5.75	10.64
Strip mines	15.63	15.66	22.93
Auger mines	....	....	31.36
Average	5.19	6.77	12.83
United Kingdom	1.62	1.78	1.99
Germany and Saar	1.71	1.60	2.26
U.S.S.R.	1.45	1.43	2.08

Strip mining has expanded threefold between 1940 and 1960, whereas total production from underground mines declined over 30% during the same period. There are, of course, only a limited number of deposits suitable for strip mining, and the quality of coal from them is rarely suitable for metallurgical purposes. Most of the coal from strip mines goes to electric generating plants.

Along with the mechanization of mining itself has come comparable improvements in the preparation plants that remove rock from the coal (about 20% of the raw coal tonnage), screen, pulverize, or otherwise prepare the coal for the market.

All this mechanization does, of course, require substantial investment of capital. A big modern continuous mining machine and its collateral equipment cost more than $250,000; investment in a large stripping shovel is over $3.5 million dollars. Competitive pressure in the industry is such that firms which fail to install the cost-reducing equipment will have a difficult time surviving.

Labor

Increased productivity coupled with the reduction in total output has reduced the number of men employed by the bituminous coal industry. Between 1950 and 1960 the decline was drastic, from 415,000 to 169,000 men, or about 60%. Such a decline has, of course, created severe unemployment problems in mining communities.

Exhibit 6

EMPLOYMENT, EARNINGS, AND SAFETY IN U. S. BITUMINOUS COAL MINES

	1930	*1940*	*1950*	*1960*
Average number of men employed	493,202	439,075	415,582	169,400
Average hourly earnings ...	$ .68	$ .88	$ 2.01	$ 3.15
Average yearly earnings ...	$ 1,155	$ 1,285	$ 3,658	$ 5,600 (est.)
Fatalities per million man hours	1.90	....	.93	1.13

A remarkable aspect of the coal industry is that this decrease in employment has occurred with relatively minor labor difficulties. There has been no major national strike during the past 12 years.

There are no clear indications that the recent trend in the labor picture will be modified in the future, although it is obvious that the percentage decrease in employment and the increase in productivity that occurred in the past decade cannot continue indefinitely.

Fuel oil imports and nuclear power

Imported residual fuel oil poses a threat to coal sales, especially to generating plants along the coast. Domestically produced residual fuel oil is a low value part of the output of an oil refinery, and its supply is expected to increase approximately in proportion to the total demand for petroleum products in the United States.

On the other hand, there are substantial quantities of residual fuel oil available from the Caribbean oil refineries. It could be imported to coastal points at prices that would displace coal. To protect the coal industry, the United States Government has established import quotas on residual fuel oil. Conceivably, conditions in the world fuel market might change so that such imports no longer threaten the sale of coal. In the meantime, coal sales to utilities along the east coast are dependent upon this form of government protection.

The economic feasibility of using nuclear energy as a source of electric power is still uncertain. A statement by the chairman of the Atomic Energy Commission sought to reassure the coal industry that there was no immediate threat—see Appendix A. A later statement somewhat modified his views—see Appendix B.

POSITION OF ISLAND CREEK COAL COMPANY IN THE BITUMINOUS COAL INDUSTRY

Although Island Creek was one of the largest companies in this industry, its total sales accounted for only around 3% of total production. (See Exhibit 7 for a comparison with other large producers.)

Exhibit 7

COMPARISONS OF FOUR LEADING COAL COMPANIES: 1961

	Consolidated Coal Company	Eastern Gas & Fuel Associates	Peabody Coal Company	Island Creek Coal Company
Sales (in millions)	241	147	119	80
Assets (in millions)	380	234	172	75
Net Profits (in millions) .	23.4	8.3	13.5	3.1
Invested Capital (in millions)	322	119	116	64
Profit as a % of Sales ...	9.7	5.7	11.4	3.9
Profit as a % of Invested Capital	7.3	7.0	11.6	4.8
Number of Employees ...	7900	7600	3800	4500

Source: Fortune survey of 500 largest U.S. industrial corporations.

Both Consolidated Coal and Peabody Coal make large sales to utilities. They operate substantial strip mines. The comparison with Eastern Gas & Fuel Associates is perhaps less significant because this company runs a large gas utility company in the Boston area as well as its mining operations.

A more specific view of the type of customers served by Island Creek is given in Exhibit 8. The "Lake" customers are those located on the Great Lakes and typically served by water transportation; most of these customers fall into industrial categories.

Island Creek lays considerable stress on classifying its coal according to different specifications. One of its advertising slogans is "Precisioneered Coals." Many customers in the metallurgical and industrial markets have quite specific requirements, and Island Creek feels that it has a competitive market advantage by selling coal to specifications. Also, quality control enables Island Creek to get higher prices for some of its output; for example, its f.o.b. mine price for metallurgical coal is around $5.70 per ton, whereas its industrial coal sells for about $1 less. All of its mines and most of its coal reserves are within a radius of about 100 miles of the junction of West Virginia, Kentucky, and Virginia.

Island Creek has also given considerable attention to reducing production costs and spends millions of dollars each year in modernizing its equipment. Continuous mining machines have been installed where such equipment can operate most effectively.

The company's general focus in 1962 seems quite clear. A company executive, in talking of the future, once said:

> Our problem is not going to be so much sales, as it is developing production and productive capacity. Our sales organization believes,

Exhibit 8

MARKETS SERVED BY ISLAND CREEK

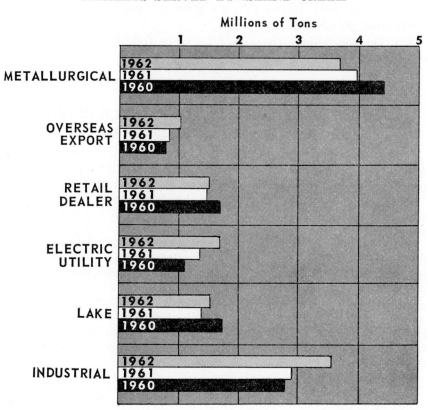

Millions of Tons

and we all tend to agree, that we will be able to sell pretty much anything we can produce. Our problems are those of growth. We will have problems in keeping up our production and, especially, in keeping our production competitively *efficient*. We will also have some real problems if we are to maintain our position in the industry. It's going to grow, and most of us hope to do more than just that. We would like to grow faster than the industry as a whole. . . .

Of course, there is the alternative of deciding *not* to try to maintain our share of industry production. Perhaps, also, we could decide *not* to try to keep up on mechanization. I don't think, however, that either of those two alternatives appeals to anybody in the management, nor to any of the directors.

A slogan appearing upon many of the company documents is, "A career company . . . dedicated to coal."

REQUIRED: (a) What are the crucial factors for long-run success in the bituminous coal industry?

(b) What were Island Creek's reserves, marketing, labor, and operations policies in late 1962?

(c) Do you believe these policies were following a wise course considering the outlook you foresee?

APPENDIX A

POTENTIAL COMPETITION FROM NUCLEAR POWER
(*New York Times,* June 18, 1963, page 49)

Glenn T. Seaborg, chairman of the Atomic Energy Commission, told coal dealers today that development of civilian nuclear power poses no immediate competitive threat to their industry.

Coal men are known to view the development of nuclear power with some misgivings. Mr. Seaborg sought to assure them on several fronts.

Looking to the years ahead, Mr. Seaborg said that by 1980 it is likely than 40,000 megawatts of nuclear power will have been installed. This, he said, is likely to displace 50,000,000 to 70,000,-000 tons of coal. However, he added, "If you keep your portion—about 65 per cent of the very substantial steam-electric market which is left after deducting our estimates of nuclear power—then the domestic market for coal should increase by more than $2\frac{1}{2}$ times by 1980 from 385,000,000 tons in 1962 to about 1,000,000,000 tons."

APPENDIX B

THE AGE OF NUCLEAR POWER HAS BEGUN
(*New York Times,* August 30, 1964)

Dr. Seaborg told reporters:

By 1975 the atom will be the source of at least half of all the additional electric power needed by the expanding American economy.

The United States expects to produce electric power directly from atomic fission during the next decade. Direct conversion will make possible substantial reductions in the cost of nuclear power.

By 1980 the United States will have nuclear-power capacity of 70,000 megawatts. (A megawatt is one million watts.)

4 BASIC COMPANY OBJECTIVES

Forecasting the outlook of a company and setting its objectives require sharply different thinking. The forecaster is objective and passive; he simply predicts what he thinks will happen. The executive setting objectives assumes that he can influence company behavior; he decides where he would like to be, and he takes actions to get there. The distinction is similar to weather forecaster versus sailor, or stockbroker versus company treasurer.

Of course the wise executive considers the outlook when he sets his objectives. He wants to be aware of obstacles and opportunities. For this reason we devoted the preceding chapters to appraising the social and economic setting in which a company will operate. Now, and in the rest of the book, we take the viewpoint of a top executive who is making choices that guide company actions. Judgments regarding outlook are vital data to be used in the active process of directing the company.

Role of objectives. For the concept of objectives to be most useful to a manager, the function of objectives in the total management process should be clear.

Significance of basic objectives. The need for basic objectives has long been recognized by military leaders who insist that good planning and administration must begin with a clear statement of "the mission." In business, the objectives may not be formally stated in writing, as they are in military operations, but they are no less important for effective management.

A manufacturer of pharmaceuticals, for instance, should decide whether he wants to be known as "an ethical drug house" which will be regarded favorably by doctors, or whether he is going to feature the sale of proprietary and "patent" medicines. Such a choice of objectives will influence almost every phase of the manufacturer's activities.

Recognition of objectives is an important first step in planning. Objectives serve as guides in the determination of policy, in selecting resources, and in setting up programs. Moreover, well recognized objectives are useful in guiding the day-to-day execution because they help to avoid getting off on a sidetrack, and actions taken by different individuals and at different times are more likely to be consistent rather than working at cross purposes. Finally, the objectives serve as a useful standard when an executive is appraising the accomplishment of a department or enterprise.

Relation of objectives to policies. The term "business policy" is often used to cover both the objectives and the general rules of action for an enterprise. In a strict sense, however, an objective is a goal or an end to be sought, whereas a policy is a general rule of action. The objective sets a long-range target; a policy provides guides which will assist the company in reaching this target.

This distinction between objective and policy becomes more important when a company seeks several different objectives at the same time. There is nothing strange about having several objectives, for, as individuals, we often seek a large income, security, fun in our work, a sense of performing a worthwhile service, and probably still other aims. Similarly, a business firm may have several objectives. When two or more objectives are sought, as is almost always the case, the business administrator must work out a single plan of action which he believes will lead as near to the goals as is practical.

Often all the goals cannot be achieved, at least within a limited period of time. Consequently the policies, organization, and programs an executive establishes may have to be directed primarily toward one goal and only secondarily toward others. One of the purposes of business policies is to resolve any conflict there may be between the several objectives. The policies guide the action of the company along a path toward the objectives; they represent the best thinking of the company management as to how the objectives may be achieved in the prevailing economic and social conditions.

Hierarchy of goals. Objectives may be broad or narrow in scope; they may be immediate or long-range in time for achievement. We are concerned in this chapter with long-range, company-wide objectives. In actual operations, however, these general objectives will be translated into departmental goals, section goals, and on down to aims of a specific individual for next week.

Thus, a proprietary drug firm selling antihistamine tablets for cold symptoms will set a sales objective of X dollars for the coming year. This, in time, will lead to a sales promotion goal of physical distribution to Y drugstores and advertising in media reaching Z customers. Each sales district will have its assigned quota, and the district sales manager will agree with individual salesmen on the number of calls to be made each week.

The setting of sub-objectives, and sub-sub-objectives is an important management technique. We shall refer to the process often and discuss it in the chapter on programming. Here, however, we focus on a limited number of basic objectives that shape the "character" of a company. The aim is to develop, first, a view of a company as an organic unit.

The "character" of a company. A business firm may have "no body to be kicked" but it does have *character*. In addition to a separate legal existence, every company develops its own traditions, habits, and reputation which give it individuality. This group of habits and attitudes endows a company with character or personality quite beyond the people who work for it at any given time.

There is nothing strange in the idea of a social institution which has an individuality separate from its members. When we speak of the Kiwanis Club, the Episcopal Church, or the City Government, the words have fairly definite meanings. The people who happen to be officers, or the buildings these institutions occupy, are only parts of the picture; these could be changed and yet the organizations would continue very much as they had been before. More enduring are the purposes, the activities sponsored, the services rendered, and the relationships engenderd.

Similarly, business firms become social institutions. For example, Macy's in New York, Marshall Field's in Chicago, and Bullock's in Los Angeles, each have clear-cut identity in the minds of their respective employees and customers. Consulting firms, banks, manufacturers, and other enterprises each have their own objectives and customs which make them separate entities.

A very useful way to discover the key features of the character of a company is to concentrate on its basic objectives. These basic objectives will indicate, to a large degree, what the firm wants to be. They tend to override and to permeate the rest of its administration, and in this way they shape the company character.

Basic objectives that shape the character of a company. For purposes of studying company character and developing a sense of the company as a whole dynamic unit, its basic objectives may be classified under the following headings:

    A. What place or niche does the company seek in its industry?
    B. Does the firm want to emphasize stability or dynamics, i.e., what is its disposition toward change?
    C. What kind of a business citizen does the firm want to be, i.e., what is its social philosophy?
    D. What type of administration is desired, i.e., what is its management philosophy?

All too often company objectives in these four areas are not well defined. This leads to confusion in planning and makes it difficult for company executives to work in a consistent manner. The basic objectives need not be written up in a company manual, although this practice has been found to be valuable in some companies. What is important is that all key executives of the company develop, by some means, an appreciation of the basic objectives of the enterprise they serve.

PLACE COMPANY SEEKS IN ITS INDUSTRY

The first decision to be made for any company is the industry in which it will operate. Indeed, it is hard to conceive of a company except as a member of some industry. The original choice of industry, made by the founders of the company, may be modified if a company adds an entirely new line of products or if it devotes a significant part of its resources to produce its own raw materials. Such changes as these will be explored in the chapters on product policies and purchasing policies.

The choice of industry, however, still leaves considerable need for refinement of objectives. The place a company seeks in its industry may be defined in terms of:

    1. Major functions to be performed.
    2. Specialization *vs.* diversification of activities.
    3. Quality or price level sought.
    4. Size of operation.

Major function to be performed. Within any industry there will be found a variety of types of companies. Some serve a particular set of customers; others perform either a basic or a service process; some concentrate on one type of material. In the women's hat industry, for instance, some firms make felt hat bodies while others specialize in feathers. In the insulation field some firms concentrate their attention on a particular type of material such as asbestos and often stick to only the mining and the preliminary refining of the material. A great many industries have wholesalers or jobbers who do no manufacturing but give their entire attention to marketing. An early step in defining the objectives, then, is to decide upon the major function or functions which the company will seek to perform.

Specialization vs. diversification. A related issue in defining the particular niche the firm seeks in its industry is the basic question of specialization *vs.* diversification. Many firms achieved distinctiveness by concentrating on some one type of product such as printing machinery, whereas others will make a widely diversified line of equipment. A book publishing house may handle a wide variety of books, as does Harper & Brothers or Macmillan Company; or, it may concentrate on children's books, business texts for colleges, or some other relatively narrow field. In this industry specialization is much more common than diversification.

The largest companies in the country typically carry on a diversified group of activities. This fact, by itself, suggests that a variety of functions and products is a desirable objective. It should be borne in mind, however, that many of the companies which specialize earn a higher rate of return on invested capital than do the industrial giants. Also, we should not overlook the many firms that tried diversification and failed in the process. This variety of experience clearly indicates that diversification *vs.* specialization is another one of the basic objectives which should be given careful attention.

Quality level. Most firms seek to become leaders in a particular range of quality in their industry. For example, the manufacturer of occasional tables has a choice of making what are known in the trade as "museum pieces." These include original artistic designs and authentic copies of period furniture. They are typically hand-carved and often are individual pieces.

A second quality range is good reproductions. Here, production runs are 40 to 400 tables, and a larger company will often make as many as 200 to 300 different kinds. This range of patterns in relatively small production runs permits the company to give each outlet in a given city distinctive patterns. The tables are produced primarily on machinery but considerable care is exercised in tracing the master copy and the tables are usually hand cut.

Still a third possibility for the occasional table manufacturer is to select a few patterns which have been selling successfully and manufacture them in runs of 5,000 to 10,000. These are almost entirely machine manufactured, and quality is sacrificed so that the tables may be sold at a low price.

The production, selling, purchasing, and finance problems of a table manufacturer will be drastically affected by this choice of quality range, and rarely is it practical for a single company to operate at more than one level.

In a great many industries this question of quality range arises; a choice of objectives must be made between the Tiffany and the time-payment store, between the Marshall Field's and the Woolworth's.

Size of operation desired. Growth has been such a dominant characteristic of the American economy that many people assume that the objective of every company should be to get bigger and bigger. Increase in size may be desirable but this is not always the case. For example, some of the most successful management consultants and other professional men have found that the need for their personal contact has placed definite limits on the volume of activity they should undertake. Similarly, high transportation costs or other difficulties in reaching distant markets may place sharp restrictions on how large it is profitable for firms to grow in other industries. This matter of size objective will have a profound influence on sales promotion activities, financial structure, organization and executive personnel, investment in facilities, operating procedures, and other phases of management.

The aim of a company regarding size, quality level, specialization *vs.* diversification, and major economic functions will go a long way in defining one set of basic objectives for a company. In a specific industry, there may be still other ways to mark off the role or the niche a firm seeks to occupy. However it is defined, a clear understanding of the place a company seeks in its industry is essential to effective central management and will have a marked effect on company character.

EMPHASIS ON STABILITY vs. DYNAMICS

The place a company seeks in its industry can be defined in fairly specific terms, whereas its disposition toward change is a much more intangible type of objective. Nevertheless, the emphasis a firm puts on seeking stability as compared with dynamics has a profound influence on its character and administration. This facet of character can be considered in terms of a company's objectives as to:

1. *Progressiveness*—the seeking of better ways.
2. *Aggressiveness*—drive in making changes.
3. Willingness to take *risks*.
4. Willingness to share *ownership control*.

Progressiveness. Some companies undertake a continual search for new and, presumably, better ways of performing their activities. The objective of the management of these companies really is to use the most modern facilities, policies, and techniques. One soap manufacturer, for instance, prides itself on being in the forefront, if not the leader, of new personnel practices in regard to selection, training, salary administration, employee services, and the like. This company also is a leader in the adoption of materials handling equipment and continuous methods of manufacture; its accounting system is entirely mechanized; and it employs the latest techniques of market research and analysis. Other companies are progressive leaders in only some of their departments, but usually the desire to be progressive is fairly contagious and will be found to a greater or lesser extent throughout the enterprise.

Progressive management sounds appealing; it is definitely "fashionable" to be progressive. Some practical managers feel that this idea can be carried too far; they place greater emphasis on stability of operations. New policies and techniques naturally require changes, and there is considerable human energy and financial cost in introducing changes into a going enterprise. If these changes are introduced frequently, a feeling of insecurity and instability is likely to develop among the executives and operating employees.

Moreover, as the executive of a large steel company pointed out, the development of new methods is almost always accompanied by unanticipated difficulties and mistakes. "Our experience indicates that the man who initiates the change often doesn't make the most money out of it. He incurs high costs learning what not to do and may have to discard some projects entirely. As a general rule, we prefer to wait until a new product or new method has been demonstrated to be sound. We may have to pay royalties on patents and may be at a slight disadvantage because of a late start; but, on the whole, we believe we are better off to wait and profit by the other man's mistakes."

There are, of course, other companies, such as some financial firms, that, because of the nature of business and/or the disposition of their executives, place great stress on stability and prefer to make changes in their operations only when it is essential to do so.

Aggressiveness. Closely associated with progressiveness is the aggressiveness of a company. This refers to the energy, the self-assertiveness, and the disposition to attack with which a company seeks its objectives. One business executive whose aggressiveness has been widely publicized is Henry J. Kaiser. He became a public figure in World War II because of his bold and insistent approach to shipbuilding. He not only employed novel methods but went to great lengths to overcome obstacles in his path. If necessary, he did not hesitate to go directly to the President or to Congress, asking for modifications in existing laws.

Following the war, Mr. Kaiser entered both the aluminum and the automobile industries, in spite of the firmly entrenched positions of the existing producers. Here again, his attack was bold and determined; for example, when his production of automobiles threatened to be delayed because of a lack of steel, he purchased a small steel company of his own. Not all of the Kaiser ventures have been successful, but each has been pursued aggressively. Mr. Kaiser's disposition toward change permeates his entire organization and has become a characteristic way in which his associates do business.

There are fields of business where too much aggressiveness will cause serious trouble. A commercial bank or an exclusive women's dress shop, for example, may well find itself in trouble if it becomes too aggressive in developing its business. An aggressive firm is likely to annoy other members of the industry and its suppliers, and, consequently, may find it difficult to secure the cooperation of other firms in troubled times. There are also limits to the aggressiveness which customers will accept. Consequently, in setting the basic objectives of a company it is well to consider how aggressive a company should be.

Willingness to take risks. Change in business operations almost always involves a move from the known to the unknown. Even when the change is based on a thorough investigation, there will be some unknown factors that tend to make the new policy or method more risky than the existing one. Therefore, an important element in a company's disposition toward change is its willingness to take risks.

One moderately successful company, for instance, had operated under a conservative management for over a decade. This management was inclined to play safe and make changes only when it knew that policies or methods had proved to be successful in another company, or when the possible gains were so great that there was little room to question the wisdom of the move. The stockholders then installed a new management which took quite a different view toward changes. This new management quickly abandoned lines of business which had a poor outlook, reorganized the internal administration, and took other steps to make the company a leader in its field. The new program clearly involved more risk, and when some of the steps taken proved to be unwise, numbers of the "old guard" were quick to point out the losses resulting from the progressive actions of the new management.

The heated discussion that arose at this time was fundamentally a debate on the extent to which the company should take steps that involved a considerable degree of risk. In this particular case, the decisions of the new management, when viewed as a whole, appear to have been wise; but there is still doubt in the minds of some whether the objectives of the company should have been centered more around stability than around the more risky, dynamic approach to company problems.

Willingness to share ownership control. Major changes in company operations always require considerable investment of new capital. Some companies are profitable enough, or have sufficient borrowing capacity, to raise the capital needed for any changes they desire to make. Not infrequently, however, a progressive and aggressive company can obtain the necessary capital only by selling more common stock. Whenever the stock is sold to outsiders, it means that the original owners of the business give up a share of the profits and also a share of the ownership control. There are many stockholders, particularly of small companies, who do not want to dilute their ownership control in this way. In situations like this, a willingness or unwillingness to share ownership control has a marked influence on the basic objectives of the company with regard to changes in operation.

A desire to keep ownership control was illustrated recently when a successful manufacturer of plastic toys had an unusual opportunity to enter the manufacture of plastic garden hose. The new line offered the advantages of use of excess plant capacity, better balance of seasonal fluctuation, and easy entry into a rapidly expanding field. However, the plastic toy manufacturer turned down the deal; it required that he merge with another smaller company and in the end he would have had only 40 per cent of the outstanding stock instead of his present holding of 60 per cent.

Objectives of a company with regard to stability *vs.* dynamics usually are not stated in writing. There can be no doubt of their importance, however, as the various illustrations already cited clearly show. When an executive is sitting back thinking about just what kind of a company or department he wants, one aspect he should consider is just how progressive and aggressive the company should be and just how willing he is to take risks and to share ownership control should this be necessary.

SOCIAL PHILOSOPHY OF THE COMPANY

A third set of basic objectives which shape the character of a company deal with its social philosophy—what kind of a business citizen does a company want to be? In this connection, the company should consider:

1. *Community* relations
2. *Government* and economic responsibilities
3. *Customer* service
4. *Supplier* contact
5. *Competitor* contact
6. Regard for *employees*

Community relations. Companies take widely different attitudes towards the community in which they operate. Some firms believe that they have no responsibility other than paying local taxes and obeying local laws. This has been a fairly widespread point of view in the city of Philadelphia, for example, and is aggravated by the fact that the political limits of the city do not include the suburbs where most of the executives live.

In contrast, some firms set a definite goal of being "good neighbors." In communities where they have plants or offices, they try to promote good schools, sound local government, city planning, adequate provision for receation, and other things which make the community a good place for people to live. Such community activities probably cost more money than can be justified, at least in the short run, in terms of direct returns. Nevertheless, the firms feel that it is part of their responsibility as citizens in a democracy.

For many years, large corporations with absentee management were criticized because of their failure to feel a responsibility for local communities. A marked change in this regard has occurred; many large companies now definitely state—and show by their actions—that building good communities is one of their objectives.

Government and economic responsibility. In government relations, as in community relations, there is a wide variation in company objectives. One view is a "what can I get out of it?" attitude. Companies with such an attitude seek contracts for government business only if it is to their financial advantage to do so. They often take an active part in lobbying for legislation that will give them tariff subsidy or other protections, and against legislation that will interfere in any way with their activities. They seek to influence government officials and regulatory bodies so as to secure favorable treatment.

With the increasing influence of government on business, it behooves any intelligent management to give some attention to the matters just listed. The real question is whether the company objective is solely in terms of reaping short-run benefits regardless of the effects such actions may have on the nation as a whole.

Another common attitude toward participation in government and economic affairs is indifference. Besides grumbling about taxes and making the conventional remarks about the "damn bureaucrats in Washington," executives with this view take no direct part in shaping governmental policy.

An increasing number of companies are becoming concerned about the total economic climate in which they must operate.

Consequently, when dealing with the government, these companies think in terms of the general economy as well as of their immediate interests. These companies are likely to cooperate with governmental activities by loaning necessary technical personnel and by accepting contracts that show small prospect of immediate profit. These companies are no more in favor of large-scale governmental operations than are the others, but they accept the governmental work as inevitable and make it their objective to help improve the efficiency of such government action as is taken.

Both community and government relations impinge upon company activities in many ways—materials supply, markets for goods, prices, employee relations, financing, taxes, competition, and plant expansion, to mention only the more obvious ones. Consequently, the basic objectives that control these relationships will affect the actions of almost every department of a company.

Customer service. Service to customers may be regarded only as a sales appeal; it is treated in this light in Chapter 8. In the present discussion of basic objectives, we are concerned with the long-run relationship a company seeks with its customers.

There is considerable difference, for example, in the service rendered by the Parker Pen Company, which sells a "lifetime" pen, and the services of one of the early manufacturers of ballpoint pens who sold as many as he could for over $10 each and then, as competition increased rapidly, reduced his price to below $1 and finally withdrew from the market altogether. Parker Pen is playing for a long pull, whereas the other firm is interested in a quick sale with an unannounced motto of "caveat emptor." If a company deals with other business concerns rather than with final consumers, the contrast is between an objective of helping the customer to prosper versus charging what the traffic will bear.

This facet of company character is important not only to customers but also to everyone in the production, sales, and credit departments who make the product or perform activities directly or indirectly related to customers.

Supplier contacts. A similar problem arises in deciding the type of relationship to seek with suppliers of raw material, supplies, and equipment. Some firms play one supplier against another in an effort to get the greatest possible concessions in price and services. In fact, a few large companies have been accused of first making their business so important to a small supplier that the supplier gave up his other outlets, and then driving such a hard bargain with the supplier that he finally went bankrupt.

In contrast, other companies try to develop relations with suppliers that can continue over a long period of time. They believe that the sound relationship is one that develops wholesome, vigorous suppliers as well as providing them with a continuing and dependable source of materials. This question is explored in more detail in Chapter 10, but underlying the more specific policy decisions will be the general social philosophy as to the kind of a business citizen the company wants to be.

Contact with competitors. Under a "lone wolf" objective, a company will have as little as possible to do with competitors and will reject various suggestions for cooperative effort. This point of view has been decreasing in popularity in the United States for several decades; in fact, European visitors remark on the freedom with which all sorts of problems are discussed in industry association meetings.

Many companies actively cooperate with their competitors within certain limited areas. There is often a substantial exchange of operating data. These data may be summarized by some central agency so as not to reveal individual company results, but on a surprisingly large number of matters there will be a frank and direct exchange of "know-how." Companies which engage in this practice believe that they stand to gain substantially more than they will lose.

In some industries, the companies join together for united trade promotions or public relations activities. Thus the Wallpaper Institute promotes the use of wallpaper for the benefit of the entire industry. Another cooperative activity is representing the entire industry to the federal and state legislatures. The combined force of an entire industry is often much more effective than the separate individual efforts of the companies. In fact, the pressure of some industry lobbies is so great that Congress has taken steps to control their activities.

Industry cooperation may, of course, slip over into areas prohibited by our antitrust laws. Price agreements, allocation of customers or territories, production quotas, and other restrictions on trade must be avoided. Unfortunately, there are many activities, the legality of which is not clear. In the petroleum and other industries, there have been certain activities sponsored by government units at one time that are later declared to be illegal. Consequently, in deciding how far to go with industry cooperation, each company must consider the possibility of legal complications.

Regard for employees. By no means the least important part of the social philosophy of a firm is its regard for its employees. Tangible evidence of this regard will be found in its personnel policies, discussed in Chapters 11, 12, and 13. However, a genuine desire to make a company a "good place to work" affects all activities. It leads to traditions regarding the way personal relationships are handled which become part of warp-and-woof of company operations. Many an executive has incurred extra expense simply because "that is the way we treat people here."

In other instances, the employment of people may be regarded simply as a necessary step toward some other objective. This is clearly the point of view of a New York manufacturer of air-conditioning equipment. The founders of this company are engineers whose primary interest has always been in the technical side of the business. The personnel policies of this firm are "enlightened" and "reasonably modern." These policies have been adopted, however, because they are regarded as necessary to attract and maintain the skilled work force the company needs. The management of the business would be quite willing to abandon any or all of these policies if their machines could be produced more economically under some other system. This mechanistic view of personnel relations is sensed by the employees, and the company has had to provide employees services and protection that probably would not have been required of a more friendly management.

Summarizing: a whole range of possible objectives relating to community, government, customers, suppliers, competitors, and employees have been suggested in this section on social philosophy of a firm. There are, of course, many other variations that have not been mentioned.

One of the disturbing things about such a review of possible social objectives is that a company's aspirations may far exceed its capacity to fulfill them. Is it possible, one may ask, to take an active part in community, industry, and government affairs and maintain good relationships with suppliers, customers, and employees all at the same time? There are two general answers to this question: (a) At this point we are discussing long-run objectives rather than specific plans of action, and for this purpose it may be all right to set some goals which will be difficult to achieve. To be most useful, however, the objectives should be ranked, or given relative weight. These weights will, of course, shift from time to time as circumstances change, but recognition of basic objectives leads to a consistent direction of effort rather than a series of opportunistic actions. (b) The objectives do not necessarily conflict with one another; in fact, they may be selected so that one supports the other. For example, the desire to provide good employment conditions is quite compatible with the objective of giving customers dependable merchandise over a long run. An important part of policy making and programming is planning activities so that the various objectives may be achieved to an optimum degree.

MANAGEMENT PHILOSOPHY OF THE COMPANY

Three broad types of basic objectives have been discussed—the place a company seeks in its industry; its emphasis on stability or dynamics; and the kind of a business citizen it wants to be. A fourth type of objective also has a profound influence on the entire administration of a company. This is the management philosophy desired by the company. It is clearly reflected in:

1. *Centralization vs. decentralization* of decision making.
2. *Quality* of key personnel.
3. Extent of *advance planning* and research going into plans.
4. Manner of *supervision*—strictness of control.

Here again, we are not concerned with specific management techniques for dealing with each of these topics; this more detailed treatment has been given in other parts of the book. The interest here centers on the general character of the enterprise that the managers wish to create.

Centralization vs. decentralization of decision-making. Some companies are ruled closely from the top. This is likely to be true of a small company that is still managed by the founder. He knows the customers and watches over sales made to them. He personally approves the selection of and pay increases for each of the employees. He negotiates credit with the bank and actively participates in the selection of new equipment or other changes in production methods. In fact, there are few, if any, major decisions that he does not personally make or approve.

Even in some medium-sized and large companies this type of centralization may be found. For instance, while Henry Ford, Senior, was still active, there was a highly centralized management in the Ford Motor Co. With the growth of size of such a company, there is an increase in the number of special assistants who investigate and recommend; production managers, sales supervisors, and accountants are, of course, authorized to take action but they must operate within closely prescribed limits. This method of operation tends to secure uniformity of action; it takes advantage of the special skill and knowledge of the central executives. On the other hand, it tends to make the supervisors and managers "doers" rather than "thinkers." It is less adaptable to local conditions, since exception to the standard rule must be made at central headquarters.

Decentralized administration gives the local managers and supervisors considerable leeway in the direction of their units. Each local manager is expected to figure out for himself the programs and methods best suited to his particular situation. In American Brakeshoe Company and J. C. Penney & Company, two well-known examples of decentralized management, the managers of local branches or stores have considerable choice in the operation of their particular units. A variety of service divisions at the headquarters office may be called upon for advice and assistance, but the local manager decides whether such advice fits his local needs.

This matter of centralization *vs.* decentralization affects the whole way of doing business. The type and nature of plans needed, the selection of personnel, the building of company morale, the organization structure, the types of controls necessary, are all affected. It is a major aspect of company character for anyone working within the organization.

Quality of key personnel. A second vital aspect of the management of any firm is the quality of its key personnel. Over a period of years a company can, if it sets about it, build a corps of executives who, as a group, have a number of distinctive characteristcs. A well-known commercial bank, for example, has developed a group of officers who are highly competent and dependable in the performance of their particular tasks. Typically they are conservative and stable men who place a great store in the traditions of the bank and are cautious about making any changes. Consequently, the bank is a stable, respected, conservative institution. The president of another bank in the same city decided that he wanted to surround himself with executives who were farsighted, energetic and interested in developing new ways of being of service to the community. It has taken a decade of promotions, transfers, and retirements to develop a corps of key men having these qualities. Now, the whole atmosphere of the second bank is quite different from that in the first.

Many different qualities might be set up as objectives for the key personnel of a company. Technical competence, daring, rugged individualism, social attitude, persuasiveness, and many other qualities should be considered in establishing the personnel goals. This is one area, of course, where the objectives will probably never be fully achieved because of great differences between individuals and the changes within a single person over a period of years. Nevertheless the expression, "He is our kind of a man," has real meaning.

The personnel objective should be related to several of the other basic objectives. For instance, if a company decides it wishes to emphasize stability rather than dynamics, it would not normally seek highly aggressive men as executives. Likewise, if it is going to emphasize decentralized administration, it will have to get key executives who are resourceful and able to carry responsibility.

Extent of advance planning. Some companies make a general practice of "crossing their bridges when they come to them." They rely upon experience and intuition in meeting new problems. This way of managing has the advantages of being flexible and simple.

Such an opportunistic approach to management is in sharp contrast with the modern development of "scientific management." Under the latter, business operations are forecast as far ahead as is practicable, and then considerable analysis is done in order to find the best way of dealing with the anticipated problems. On the basis of the research, a plan or blueprint is prepared showing just what is to be done, as well as a schedule of when it is to be done. Actual performance, then, consists of carrying out this plan.

It should be smooth and efficient (assuming the forecasting and planning was well done).

For each company there is a real question—how far ahead and in how much detail such planning should be attempted? In a public utility with fairly predictable demand, it may be possible to plan in considerable detail. On the other hand, many deptrtment store executives believe that in their type of business detailed, advance planning must be confined to accounting and materials handling, because of the unpredictability of style changes, competition, and consumer behavior. There is no simple answer as to how much advance planning should be done; it depends partly upon the nature of the activity, but it is also influenced to a marked degree by the management philosophy of the company.

Strictness of control. "When my boss says 'jump,' he means jump." "We give very few orders around here, and rely on guidance and leadership to get things done." These two quotations suggest a difference in the manner of supervision and the strictness of control that may be found in modern business. At one extreme, there is prompt, unquestioned obedience to orders which we associate with military management; at the other extreme, there is the highly informal relationship between a group of skilled workers who understand their jobs and work through their own volition, with only general guidance and stimulation coming from their supervisors. Most boss-subordinate relationships (including the relations between the president and the vice-president all the way down to those between the first-line supervisor and the unskilled laborer) fall somewhere between these two extremes.

Within any single company, of course, the manner of supervision may differ from department to department. Some supervisors will be "strict," while others will be "easy." Nevertheless, taking the company as a whole, a general pattern, or underlying tradition, is likely to prevail; the way employees are directed and controlled is part of the management philosophy.

SUMMARY

No business firm is completely static, like a building or machine with stationary framework and standard parts that may be replaced from warehouse stocks. Instead, shifts in demand, in competition, and in other external forces call for continuous adaptation; and, the ambitions and drives of executives within the company keep it evolving, And, as changes are made in one part of the company, compensating adjustments are necessary in other parts. Consequently, we should think of each company as a dynamic, integrated entity.

Each of these business entities develops character, an individuality of its own. This character is shaped, not only by physical resources and technology, but also by basic objectives set by top management. A useful way to clarify our thinking about the kind of company we want is to ask ourselves the following questions:

1. What particular role or niche do we seek in our industry? This may be defined in terms of the major function or functions the company will perform, the extent to which the company will specialize or diversify its activities, the quality range it will try to cover, and the size and scale at which it hopes to operate.

2. Do we want to emphasize stability or dynamics? This is a more intangible phase of business character in which the desire to be progressive and aggressive must balance against willingness to assume risks and perhaps to share ownership control with others. This disposition toward change will have a marked effect on how quickly and in what manner the company moves from its present position in the industry to the desired position as outlined under the first set of basic objectives.

3. What kind of a business citizen do we want to be? In working toward our desired position in the industry, the company will have many continuing relationships with other groups. There is need for goals as to desired relationships with community, government, competitors, customers, suppliers, and employees.

4. What type of management do we desire? Our long-range concept of the company is not complete without some sense of the basic management philosophy that will be employed. Important considerations are the extent to which decision making will be decentralized, the quality of key personnel, the extent of advance planning, the manner of supervision, and the strictness of control. This set of objectives deals with the internal mechanism of the company, whereas the preceding set is concerned with external relationships.

These basic objectives cut across and permeate other phases of management. They influence, directly or indirectly, the policies, the organization, the resources, and the execution. Few, if any, companies can achieve all their objectives within a limited period, and consequently we have a continuing task of adjusting our more specific plans so as to approach our basic objectives to an optimum extent.

QUESTIONS FOR CLASS DISCUSSION

1. Several economists have suggested that business firms would better serve the general welfare if they subordinated all other objectives to maximizing return on investment. This includes breaking up large firms into smaller units that will not have to consider social issues since they will be too small to affect the general community. Do you agree with this view? Does it provide clearer guidelines to central management than other views?

2. Is it necessary, or important, that executives and other key men in a company *personally* believe in the objectives of the company, or is it satisfactory if key men follow the objectives because they have been established by top management? Explain.

3. (a) Distinguish between: an objective and a policy; an objective and a control standard; an objective and a program. (b) How are objectives related to policies, to control standards, and to programs?

4. A major machine tool manufacturer, through its reputation for quality, finds itself shut out of over 60% of its potential market. Buyers looking for lower-priced and less accurate machines turn elsewhere. Since the executives wish to insure growth for the firm, they face the special problem of defining the company's desired place in its industry. What points should they consider and how can they reach a decision?

5. One company's statement of objectives calls for "a decent return to stockholders, an example to the community of corporate citizenship, payment of better than a living wage and stability of employment for all employees, honorable treatment of suppliers, and the willingness to undertake business risks to provide an example of dynamic management." How do these goals conflict? In what way can a balance among them be achieved?

6. Two patterns of relationships with suppliers have been explained in this chapter: (a) the "most important buyer" strategy and (b) the "mutual benefit" or "continuing relationship" strategy. How can a company go about choosing between these two? What significance does a decision either way have for the question of relations with other groups?

7. Do you believe that the management philosophy should or will vary from one bank to another? Consider such institutions as (a) the major bank in a medium-sized city, (b) the largest bank in the country, (c) a savings and loan association in a rapidly growing segment of a western state.

8. A company typically develops a character of its own, distinct from the individuals who work for it. This character often continues through several generations of executives. (a) How does a new employee of a company learn its character? (b) Why does this character persist even after a complete turnover of directors, executives, and other employees?

CASE IV
The Textron Mills at Nashua

On the morning of Monday, September 13, 1948, the mills at Nashua were busy as they had been for a century and a quarter turning out blankets, sheets, and Indian Head cloth. One-third of the working population of the town was employed in the two weaving and spinning mills, and the new resident manager, Robert Cushman, was smoothing out difficulties with the union over work loads and was making changes in production. In the midst of this activity the teleprinter clacked out a bulletin from the head office which a secretary immediately rushed to the mill manager:

"During the summer of 1947 the 'New Nashua Plan' was adopted in an attempt to save one of New England's oldest and largest textile operations. Success of the plan required the reduction of labor, overhead, power, and tax costs by more than $2,000,000 during the first year.

"We regret to announce, however, that results to date do not justify the continued operation of the Nashua Mills. On September 8, the board of directors of Textron Incorporated voted to run out all work in progress prior to December 31, 1948, and to dispose of all physical properties in Nashua, New Hampshire."

Copies of the notice were soon posted on bulletin boards around the mill and small groups of employees gathered around each one, speculating on this sudden change in the plans for the mills. Mr. Cushman said later: "They pulled the rug from under me without any warning."

When the Nashua shutdown was announced, Harold Daoust, of the Textile Workers' Union, wrote a letter to all New England senators and representatives accusing Textron of having destroyed ten thousand jobs in a few months (for tax reasons Textron had taken on the loss of liquidating the Esmond Mills which went out of the blanket business in May, 1948). Within two days a subcommittee of the Senate Committee on Interstate and Foreign Commerce was appointed to make an investigation of the closing of textile mills in New England and the operations of Textron Incorporated, and Senator Tobey was on his way to Nashua.

Textron—something new in the textile business. During the early years of World War II, Royal Little, president of Atlantic Rayon Corporation, saw a rare opportunity for profits and growth in the textile industry in the coming years, and, in 1943, when Atlantic Rayon received the first cancellation of its parachute contracts, he began to move. Little's plan called for an integrated system to manufacture a well-styled, well-made line of branded garments for men and women, sold at a good markup with the aid of wide national advertising, and priced just above the broadest mass market. The new concern would be put together in time to share in the booming market for clothing which Little foresaw coming at the end of the war and would be based on New England plants which could be bought cheaply because of the owners' long memories of depression in the textile industry during the 1920's and 1930's. The system, if built in war time, would have to be integrated, since a newcomer could get cloth only by buying the mills that made it. Integration, in the case of Textron, combined under one management operations ordinarily performed by independent companies, such as spinning, weaving, finishing, designing, cutting and sewing, and merchandising.

Textron's policy, adopted in 1943, was to turn out five lines of branded articles—women's "intimate apparel," blouses, negligees, home fashions, and men's wear—to be sold direct to about 3,000 department and specialty stores throughout the United States. In carrying out this policy, Little went looking for mills.

His first acquisition was the 1,400 loom Suncook (N. H.) weaving mill, a producer of cotton, rayon, and other synthetic grey goods. Little borrowed most of the money for this purchase from the First National Bank of Boston and then set about converting the Suncook looms from coarse rayons and cottons to fine, light rayon crepes and satins suitable for women's slips, gowns, etc. In 1945 the Manville Jenckes Corporation, a producer of cotton, and rayon and wool blend fabrics, and the Lonsdale Company, a producer of fine count cotton cloth, were added to the system. Textron, after the purchase of Manville Jenckes, had no money with which to acquire Lonsdale, so Royal Little, as sole trustee of a charitable trust for the benefit of the Providence Community Fund, borrowed $4.5 million from the First National Bank of Boston. With this loan, together with notes to the stockholders of Lonsdale of $2,500,000, the trust acquired all of the Lonsdale stock in November of that year.

Then trustee Little caused Lonsdale to sell the mills to two other charitable trusts, the Lansing Foundation and the Rayon Foundation Trust, the latter of which had been formed by Mr. Bayard Ewing at Mr. Little's instigation on June 30, 1944. As controlling stockholder of Lonsdale, Mr. Little declared to himself as trustee a dividend of $4,600,000, which enabled him immediately to pay off the Rhode Island Charities Trust Loan from the First National Bank of Boston. (The mill properties were leased back to Textron.)

During the period when the mills were being acquired, Textron was also building up its merchandising organization, mainly by hiring able merchandise managers from other companies. The merchandise managers were put in charge of styling, pricing, and distributing the various Textron lines and proved so successful that in 1947, according to *Fortune* magazine, Textron was probably the largest-selling U. S. brand name in the business.

By late 1945 the Textron system was in a crisis for lack of cloth to meet the demands of its cutting and sewing plants. Only the Suncook cloth had proved really suitable for the Textron medium-priced garments. The beautiful Lonsdale cottons were of high quality but too expensive, and the Manville Jenckes coarser cloths had not proved adaptable to the Textron needs. Output of these two mills was thus sold outside the system. Mr. Little, hat in hand, went looking for cloth from big competitors such as J. P. Stevens, Deering-Milliken, and Burlington Mills and they had the pleasure of turning him down. While the search for grey goods sources was on, a golden opportunity came Little's way.

The Nashua purchase. A principal stockholder of the famous old Nashua Manufacturing Company was anxious to get rid of his holdings and, in December 1945, Royal Little, acting for Textron Incorporated, acquired about 45% of the Nashua common at $100 per share (the market price then ranged from $68 to $72). The following month all but 3% of the balance of the stock was bought from other stockholders at the same price and Textron owned a business with total assets of about $17 million and a net worth of about $13.5 million for an outlay of about $10.5 million. Of the funds necessary to acquire the stock, $7.8 million were obtained through a five year term loan from the First National Bank of Boston.

Nashua Manufacturing Company had been founded in 1823 and for a hundred and twenty-three years had produced cotton blankets, cotton and wool and rayon and wool blankets, cotton sheets and pillow cases, and the well-known Indian Head cloth, all of which were sold direct to retailers. Through depression and boom, in peace and in war, the mills had been operated and Nashua Manufacturing Company had become the town's principal source of industrial employment until in 1944 it employed almost 50% of the working population.

Three generations of Amorys from Boston ran the mills after 1840, and, while there had been cutbacks in production, the mill had always remained open. In 1937, in the midst of a textile depression, Robert Amory promised to keep the mills open "so that their thousands of employees might not face hardship."

Following World War I, there had been few advances in ideas and techniques at Nashua, and although the plant and equipment were in good repair, some changes were needed to make Nashua fully competitive.

"At the time of acquisition, Little told Nashua's businessmen, at an off-the-record, country-club luncheon, that he had come to the city to stay. He was a gambler, he said, and this was a good gamble; the big mills fitted perfectly into his program for an integrated textile industry. He proposed to retain the former management and recommend only such changes inside the mills as were necessary to improve their efficiency." [1]

NASHUA MANUFACTURING COMPANY

Balance Sheet—October 31, 1945

ASSETS

Cash on hand and in banks		$ 782,600
U. S. Treasury Tax Notes (In excess of current requirements)		795,000
Accounts Receivable	$ 2,034,000	
Less Reserve for Allowances and Doubtful Accounts	$ 30,300	2,003,700
Inventories		
Merchandise	$ 5,227,800	
Supplies	282,200	5,510,000
Excess Profits Tax Refund Bonds		72,700
Cash Surrender Value—Life Insurance		22,300
Premium Deposits with Mutual Insurance Cos.		155,400
Total Current Assets		$ 9,341,700
Claims for Refund Federal Taxes		186,400
Plant—at cost	$16,787,000	
Less Reserves for Depreciation and Amortization	9,688,700	7,098,300
Prepaid and Deferred and other Items		204,600
		$16,831,000

LIABILITIES

Accounts Payable and Accrued Items		$ 1,964,300
Provision for Federal Taxes on Income	$ 1,525,000	
Less U. S. Treasury Tax Notes	1,525,000	
Reserve for Commitments and Contingencies		650,000
Total Current Liabilities		$ 2,614,300
Reserve for Deferred Maintenance Charges ..		600,000
Total Liabilities		$ 3,214,300
Capital Stock		
Second Preferred—no par value, 32,097 shares at stated value of $1.00 per share (Redeemable at $42 per share)		$ 32,100
Common—no par value, 108,805 shares at stated value of $50 per share		5,440,200
Capital Surplus		5,647,700
Earned Surplus		2,496,700
Total Liabilities, Stock, and Surplus		$16,831,000

---

[1] Arthur W. Hepner, "The Nashua Story," *Harper's Magazine* (February, 1949), p. 74.

NASHUA MANUFACTURING COMPANY

Statement of Profit and Loss and Surplus

Year Ended October 31, 1945

SALES, less Returns and Allowances		$32,361,500
COST OF SALES, including Selling and Administrative Expenses		29,612,900
GROSS OPERATING INCOME		$ 2,748,600
DEDUCT:		
Depreciation and Amortization	$424,000	
Miscellaneous Taxes	26,300	450,300
NET PROFIT before provision for Federal Taxes on Income and Contingencies		$ 2,298,300
PROVISION FOR Federal Taxes on Income		1,525,000
		$ 773,300
PROVISION for Sundry Contingencies		100,000
NET PROFIT for Year		$ 673,300

NASHUA MANUFACTURING COMPANY

Summary of Sales and Earnings

Fiscal Year Ended	Gross Sales (less returns and allowances and discounts)	Profit before Provision for Federal Income and Excess Profits Taxes, Reserve for Contingencies
Oct. 31, 1937	$14,453,600	$ 795,700
Oct. 29, 1938	8,376,800	(227,100)
Nov. 4, 1939	11,319,800	14,100
Nov. 2, 1940	12,440,400	(246,100)
Nov. 1, 1941	22,017,300	1,910,400
Oct. 31, 1942	32,265,300	3,782,600
Oct. 30, 1943	35,666,900	3,338,200
Oct. 28, 1944	33,493,600	2,608,900
Oct. 31, 1945	32,361,600	2,298,300

Nashua had two principal plants, the Nashua Mill and the Jackson Mill, with 2,714,000 square feet of floor space. There were about 2,590 looms and 131,700 spindles, all in good repair, although the average age of the machinery was about 30 years.

Gossett Mills—a source of cloth is found. Within a few weeks after the Nashua purchase, Little learned that Gossett Mills, a producer of low-priced cottons and rayons in North and South Carolina, was for sale for $12 million (its current book value was less than $10 million). This was the answer to Textron's need for cloth, which was by then desperate, but Textron had no money for the purchase and the Boston First National Bank had just loaned Textron $7.8 million against a legal limit of $8 million. Attempts to sell Nashua failed, but finally New York banks and the charitable trusts put up the money. Textron Southern, Inc. (a subsidiary of Textron Incorporated) got the twelve million dollars together, as shown below.

Loan from N. Y. Chemical and Central Hanover	$6 million
Sale of Textron Southern preferred to Rhode Island Charities Trust, MIT Trust, Rayon Foundation Trust	$4 million
Sale of Textron Southern common to Textron Incorporated	$2 million

The loan from the New York banks provided that Textron was to add $6 million to Textron Southern capital before May 1, 1947, by public sale of stock or by putting up the money itself.

The search for cash. The Textron system was now heavily in debt to the Boston First National for the purchase of Nashua Manufacturing and to the New York banks for the purchase of Gossett Mills. During the summer of 1946, registration statements were prepared for public sale of Textron stock and, in the meantime, Royal Little went to work on Nashua.

The cotton inventory required by the slow-moving cotton-blanket business amounted to 40,000 bales and was worth $3 million more at market than at book value. Nashua stopped hedging cotton in early 1946 (when it became apparent that OPA controls would soon be removed) and rehedged in October of that year shortly before a break in the price of cotton. In the meantime, cotton had risen 14 cents per pound and Nashua had doubled its $3 million. To take advantage of this situation, cotton blanket production was cut by two thirds and the excess inventory sold off until Nashua Manufacturing was loaded with cash. A sale of the North Monmouth, Maine, division of Nashua for $325,000 plus an unreported amount for its inventories helped swell the coffers. Production changes and changes in machinery released spindles which were sold in the export market at high prices.

The stock market break in the fall of 1946 washed out any hopes of public issuance of stock to pay back the Boston and New York banks, but Nashua's cash was available to meet the squeeze on capital. A dividend on Nashua common could not be declared because preferred holders would share dollar for dollar so two non-operating subsidiaries (Textron Mills and Manville Fabrics) were sold to Nashua for $7.5 million and Textron Southern Class B stock went to Nashua for $2 million. Thus, Nashua provided $9.5 million cash in one year to pay the banks and still its plant was going strong.

The New Nashua Plan. In spite of a net profit of $3 million for the year, 1946, operations at Nashua Manufacturing were not satisfactory to Textron officials. In July, 1947, Mr. Little said: "The present mills are inefficient operations. Direct and indirect labor costs are at least $1 million a year higher than they would be on similar products and similar equipment in the South. In addition, the physical layout of the plant is bad." The new plan, which was meant to produce more efficient and lower cost operations, called for:

(a) The sale of about 30% of the spindles, looms and related machinery.

(b) The transfer of 20% to 30% of the spindles and looms to southern plants.

(c) The consolidation of the most modern and efficient remaining machinery at Nashua, expected to consist of about 50,000 spindles, looms and related machinery, in the modern Jackson mill and the blanket mill and the operation of this revamped plant on a full three-shift basis.

(d) Spending $1,200,000 over the next five years in modernizing and improving the remaining plant at Nashua.

(e) Adjusting work loads to more nearly approximate those in the South (an agreement was reached with the union).

(f) Reducing the work force from 4,000 to 2,500. (Severance pay was given to elderly, long-term employees who were laid off.)

The annual report for 1947 gave the following "Progress Report":

"By the end of 1947, the Company's operations were consolidated into three major subsidiaries. All New England manufacturing plants other than Lonsdale, and all consumer product sales were consolidated into the former Nashua Manufacturing Company, now named Textron Inc. All southern manufacturing operations are conducted by Textron Southern, Inc. The Lonsdale Company continues to operate the Berkeley and Blackstone Mills and Lincoln Bleachery, all located in Rhode Island.

"The New Nashua Plan announced on July 29, 1947 is currently being put into effect and all operations have been discontinued in certain of the Nashua mill buildings. The best equipment, supervisors, and operating personnel are being concentrated in the Jackson Mill, the bleachery, and the blanket mill. All surplus machinery and equipment has been sold. As a result of an agreement with the Textile Workers' Union of America, the mill will be operated on a three shift basis with work loads comparable to any modern plant. When this plan has been completed, there will be a reduction in working force from 4,000 to 2,500 persons with approximately the same dollar volume as in the past.

"The blanket mill will continue to manufacture blend and cotton blankets and automotive and shoe fabrics. Nashua combed percale and carded muslin sheets and pillow cases, wide Indian Head cloth, and drapery fabrics will be made in the Jackson Mill.

"The production of narrow Indian Head cloth has been transferred to Cordova Mill Division of Textron Southern but is shipped to the Nashua finishing plant for dyeing, inspection, and distribution.

"Since December 28, 1946, the Company has sold the high-cost Nemasket spinning mill at Taunton, Massachusetts, three surplus New England warehouses, and has cancelled its lease on the high-cost spinning and weaving plant at Manville, R. I., as of July 1, 1948.

"Textron Southern, Inc. has made an equity investment of $500,000 for 100% of the capital stock of Textron Puerto Rico, Inc. The latter company has entered into a contract with the Puerto Rico Industrial Development Company to purchase the land, new building, and new machinery and equipment necessary to equip a modern, windowless, air-conditioned, 25,000 spindle print cloth plant for approximately $3,500,000 on a long-term mortgage. This mortgage is not guaranteed by Textron Incorporated or any of its continental subsidiaries. Textron Puerto Rico will operate the first cotton textile mill ever built in Puerto Rico. A resident manager is already living in Puerto Rico supervising the construction of the mill and the selection of key personnel for training in various of our existing plants. Ground has already been broken for the foundations, and all major contracts for building and machinery have been placed. The mill should commence operation late this year.

"As part of the plan to industrialize the island, Textron Puerto Rico has been granted complete tax exemption through June, 1959. Federal income taxes are not applicable to this Puerto Rico subsidiary."

During 1947, Mr. Little said, in connection with the New Nashua Plan: "We have full confidence that one year from now, the mills in Nashua will be among the most efficient textile operations in the country. A fine old textile name and industry has been saved for New England."

Shutdown. The New Nashua Plan did not work. Squabbles over work loads arose with the union and production reforms did not come fast enough to enable efficient operation. The accounting system, in the view of the directors, failed to provide adequate information on which operations were low cost and which were not. In an attempt to remedy this, a new resident manager was appointed in July, 1948. He settled some of the work load cases and had restored peace with the union, but the work force remained at about 4,000, and the directors believed costs were too high to enable the mills to compete with Southern operations.

When the directors became convinced in the fall of 1948 that the outlook for sales of Nashua products was not profitable, the board voted for the shutdown.

As soon as the bulletin from New York was made public, Mayor Oscar Maynard asked a group of three businessmen and three aldermen to form a committee, hoping to find new firms to occupy the plant space that Textron intended to vacate.

On September 22, Senator Tobey opened public hearings at which Royal Little; Emil Rieve, general president of the Textile Workers' Union of America; and representatives of the Department of the Interior and the Department of Commerce testified. The hearings became wild and charged with emotion and, on the evening of September 23, Little was hanged in effigy outside the blanket mill.

The comment of Mr. A. Schmidt, executive secretary of the Nashua Chamber of Commerce, was: "The sooner we get rid of Textron the better off we'll be. . . . They've given us nothing but trouble since they've come here." And Emil Rieve stated: "Mr. Little hasn't used Nashua as a mill; he has used it as a mine. He has mined it and stripped it."

Mr. Little's views were:

"In accordance with this program" (the New Nashua Plan) "the Company carried out in substantial measure its plan for modernization. However, the arrangement for increasing work assignments to reduce costs to competitive levels did not develop as rapidly as expected and in the summer of 1948, when the market for the principal products of the Nashua Mills, namely sheets, pillow cases, and blankets, gave every indication of a return to traditional narrow profit margins, it became apparent that serious losses could no longer be postponed if production were continued on the same high cost operating basis. Accordingly, the closing of the mills was authorized by the directors early in September.

*   *   *   *   *   *

"It has been charged that the Company avoided taxes through the use of charitable trusts and thus shifted some burden of taxation to the small taxpayers. The facts are that none of the trusts referred to by the Subcommittee Chairman has been created by the Company and none was controlled or dominated in any way by the Company. No tax advantage accrued to the Company itself through transactions with Trusts. Further, any corporation wholly or partially owned by any of the trusts paid all income, property, social security, and other taxes imposed on any of its competitors. These points are here mentioned for the reason that they were largely ignored by the Subcommittee and were not featured by the press.

"It is important to note that at no point was there made any charge of illegal activity on the part of the Company or its officers.

"The Subcommittee also touched upon the matter of the industrial development of Puerto Rico, where a subsidiary of the Company is presently constructing a print cloth mill as you were advised in the last annual report. The inquiry into this subject developed nothing new. It was brought out that the Puerto Rican government has offered inducements in the form of tax advantages and otherwise to attract industries to Puerto Rico and that some thirty New England firms have considered locating plants there."

After two days of testimony, and with the Mayor's Committee enjoying no success, an alternative to complete shutdown was proposed to the board. One mill was to be kept open for ten years as a sheeting operation to employ 750 people and the bleachery and dye house would remain open as a source of work for 250 more.

TEXTRON INCORPORATED AND SUBSIDIARY COMPANIES
Summary of Consolidated Earnings

	Gross Sales (less Returns and Allowances and Discounts Subsequent to 1941)	Profit (Loss) before Provision for Federal Income and Excess Profits Taxes
1938	$ 5,821,200	$ (72,000)
1939	7,468,900	159,600
1940	7,479,600	(18,900)
1941	8,142,600	220,000
1942	13,606,200	908,600
1943	23,742,600	1,747,700
1944	26,254,600	2,347,800
1945	46,853,300	2,016,900
1946	112,951,900	16,193,900
1947	124,776,000	14,904,000
1948	93,037,700	8,777,900

All other departments were to run out their inventory and close down. Provisions of the 1947 New Nashua Plan regarding increased work loads and severance pay were to be continued.

Although the mill to be kept open contained the most modern facilities, members of the board were reasonably certain that it would be only a marginal operation at best and probably not earn a profit except in unusually good years such as 1946.

REQUIRED: If you were the Textron board of directors at the time of these hearings and public protest, would you stick with your announced decision to shut down the Nashua Mills? For purposes of this discussion, accept as your own the board's forecast of operating costs and profits at Nashua.

PART

2

DEFINING MAJOR POLICIES

Ch. 5 · Sales Policies—Products

Ch. 6 · Sales Policies—Customers

Ch. 7 · Sales Policies—Pricing

Ch. 8 · Sales Policies—Sales Promotion

Integrating Cases—Sales Policies

Ch. 9 · Production and Purchasing Policies

Ch. 10 · Production and Purchasing Policies
(Concluded)

Ch. 11 · Personnel Policies—Selection and Training

Ch. 12 · Personnel Policies—Compensation and Arrangements for Work

Ch. 13 · Personnel Policies—Employee Services and
Industrial Relations

Integrating Cases—Production and Personnel
Policies

Ch. 14 · Financial Policies—Uses of Capital

Ch. 15 · Financial Policies—Sources of Capital

Ch. 16 · Financial Policies—Protection of Capital and
Distribution of Earnings

Integrating Cases—Financial Policies

5 SALES POLICIES—PRODUCTS

Nature of policies. Certain major issues confront the central management of every company. Time and time again questions about product line, pricing, purchasing, wages, and similar basic matters arise. *Policies* give central management's standing answers to these questions. Policies indicate how these recurring problems are to be resolved so as to attain basic objectives.

Policies aid the process of managing an enterprise in a number of ways: (a) With policies clearly understood, a busy executive can delegate duties to subordinates with confidence that these duties will be carried out along the general lines he wishes. (b) Each executive knows how others will act, and this makes coordination easier to achieve. (c) There will be a consistency of action taken by different members of the firm, and a consistency from time to time.

Policies should, of course, be modified when necessary to fit new conditions in the industry and within the company. Usually this should be done only after careful study and the change should be made known to all executives and operating employees affected. In many companies, clear policies exist even though they are not written; through oral training and supervision an employee learns the guide posts which channel his efforts toward desired ends. Policies, then, are not a set of inflexible rules; instead they are the living precepts which guide the company in a continuing and consistent pattern of behavior.

Since our present study is focusing on central management, we shall deal with those policy issues that involve the entire company —directly or indirectly. In every company there are major questions regarding:

    I. *Sales policies.*
    II. *Production and purchasing policies.*
    III. *Personnel policies.*
    IV. *Financial policies.*

These groups overlap to some degree, and it is impossible to make final decisions with reference to one group of policies without considering other groups. Some companies may have still other policies for specialized activities. Nevertheless, the sequence does provide a logical approach to overall company activities.

Classification of sales policies. Central management needs sales policies relating to:

A. *Products* to be offered for sale.
B. Types of *customers* to whom products will be sold.
C. *Prices* at which the products will be sold.
D. *Sales promotion* used to induce the customers to buy the products at the established prices.

Here, again, the groups are interrelated. For instance, a manufacturer of women's gloves was considering the addition of a line of men's gloves as a means of increasing his sales volume. He decided against the plan, however, because the retailers who might buy the men's gloves would be a different group of *customers* than were currently buying his present *products* in the women's line. When this same company reviewed its policies regarding *sales promotion,* it recognized that the *products* which it sold were subject to such frequent changes in style that appealing to customers on the basis of long-wearing quality was unwise. Thus, decisions regarding one type of sales policy affect the success of other policies.

The interdependence of sales policies—and of all phases of central management—makes a logical sequence of analysis especially valuable. Then, as we examine each part or issue, we know what the other parts will be and how they all fit in the total framework.

Product policies. Continuing the analytical framework one stage further, the major questions of policies arising in connection with products usually involve diversification versus specialization of the products to be handled, product differentiation, and frequency of design change.

DIVERSIFICATION VERSUS SPECIALIZATION

Each company must decide how many products it will offer for sale and the variety in which these products will be offered. This is a recurring problem as markets change, competition grows, and new technology becomes available.

Expansion of a product line. The number of products offered for sale may vary greatly among companies even in one industry. For example, one of the large meat-packing companies in the United States engages in the production and sale of numerous lines of products having both direct and indirect connection with its primary activity, that of butchering. In fact, the company has a large pharmaceutical department selling all sorts of products, such as liver extract made from hogs, cattle, or sheep. Other by-products that the company processes and sells include wool, soap, glue, and leather.

Some of these supplementary lines extend to businesses even farther removed from the original meat-packing operations. For example, the company manufactures and sells a line of sandpaper to insure a steady volume of glue consumption.

Fertilizer is another natural by-product of slaughtering operations. To market effectively its own brand of fertilizer, the company added other types of fertilizer made from materials that had to be secured from outside sources. These other lines have been expanded to such an extent that less than one tenth of the fertilizer now sold by the company is made of by-products of the packing operations. Actually the fertilizer plant has been moved to another city where it can more economically handle the products that are not derived from slaughtering.

In the production area, the company entered the ammonia business to provide the large quantities that were needed for refrigeration throughout its plant. Having entered the ammonia business to provide its own requirements, the company undertook the sale of ammonia to outside concerns and thereby assured itself of economies of large-scale production.

For quite another reason it added a produce line. Its refrigerator cars, trucks, branch houses, and other marketing facilities were well adapted for handling poultry, butter, and eggs. Moreover, such produce could be sold primarily to the same customers who were buying fresh meat. This company is now the largest produce dealer in the country.

Here diversification has carried the company into by-products, raw materials, and products using similar manufacturing and marketing facilities. Then to assure success of these subsidiary ventures, the added lines have been expanded.

In contrast, other leading packing companies have followed a policy of selling most of their by-products to independent manufacturers rather than finishing the products themselves. The managements of these companies believe that more profits can be earned by concentrating their attention upon meat-packing operations.

Dangers of unwise expansion. Diversification may lead to trouble. For example, several years ago a leading watch manufacturer decided to expand into the electronics and scientific instruments businesses. The company had many of the production skills needed to make electric microscopes and similar instruments. Ever-changing technical and scientific developments were opening up new uses for precision instruments and opportunities for manufacturers who had the technical skills to keep abreast of these changes. A new plant was acquired and three new divisions— Research and Development, Precision Products, and Electronic Products—were formed.

The results were unsatisfactory. Two of the three divisions reported steady losses. Although sales increased, the constant demand for funds to fulfill engineering requirements and to maintain inventories for government work drained cash resources. The company had to borrow heavily from an investment bank, and control of the company went over to the bank. Then, a new chief executive decided to abandon the new lines and to concentrate on the watch business, which, though shaky, was profitable.

Variety of products. The problem of variety of items within a line is often as pressing as the question of additional lines. Customers are continually requesting additional products, and salesmen will contend that the sales volume could be increased materially if they had a larger variety of products to sell.

One manufacturer of soaps yielded to this pressure. Whenever the sales manager became convinced that competitors were offering a new soap or that a number of customers had requested a new soap that differed in color, size, shape, fragrance, or composition, a new product meeting these specifications would be introduced. Examination of sales records showed that sales of most of these new products were satisfactory for several months but would gradually dwindle.

Apparently the initial sales were due to the enthusiasm of the salesmen for a new product and a willingness on the part of the retailers to try an original stock to see how the product would sell. After this original distribution, however, most new products were discovered to have no unique appeal. This particular company, therefore, was found to have a large number of products for which the sales volume was inadequate to justify the cost of manufacturing, warehousing, and selling. By careful study the company was able to reduce the number of items carried to comparatively few products that really had significant differences. It then concentrated its attention on selling these products rather than dissipating its efforts on new and unnecessary additions to its line.

Occasionally there may be specific reasons for a wide variety of products. A leading department store, for example, undertakes to show 300 colors of fine broadloom carpet ranging over the entire color spectrum. By so doing, the store can match any color of wall paper, drapery, or upholstery material. Such wide variety is, perhaps, more important as a sales-promotion device than as a useful service to customers. Most stores and manufacturers believe that consumers can be adequately served with about a tenth as many colors.

A common policy is to fix a limit on the number of items. Then any proposal for a new item must be accompanied by a recommendation for dropping an existing one. While exceptions may be necessary, this plan has the advantage of forcing attention to pruning along with justifying the new item.

Factors favoring diversification. What, then, are possible benefits a manager should look for when deciding how far to extend diversification?

In some lines the customer desires to buy a variety of products from the same source. For example, a dealer in plumbing supplies must offer several types and sizes of valves to meet the needs of his customers, and he may prefer to purchase all of these from one source. If a manufacturer of valves offers him only one type, he may refuse to buy this valve because he would prefer to secure it from the same manufacturer from whom he purchases other types and sizes. Again, the retailer may desire to purchase a *complete line* of hosiery from one manufacturer and may refuse to buy from a manufacturer who offers only one style of product. This attitude is most likely to be taken by the retailer who desires to use the brand name in his advertising and does not wish to incur the expense of advertising more than one brand.

If the customer buys only a small quantity of any one product at a time, it may be necessary to offer several products to the customer so that the salesman may secure sufficient sales on each call to justify the expense of making the call. For example, some bakeries operate trucks that sell bread directly to housewives. To secure an *economical sales unit* that will warrant the cost of the call, the salesman must offer a variety of bakery products—not just bread—to the housewife.

Products may be included in a line in order to prevent a competitor from establishing a *relationship with the customer.* Thus, a manufacturer of electric dishwashers may find it desirable to sell refrigerators also. Otherwise, competitors who sell both dishwashers and refrigerators may develop a close business relationship with dealers through refrigerator sales, thereby inducing the dealer to buy both products from the same source and under the same brand name.

It may also be desirable to sell more than one product in order to decrease the severity of *seasonal or cyclical fluctuations.* A manufacturer of electric storage batteries, for instance, is experimenting with the production and sale of paint because it has a complementing seasonal fluctuation.

Product lines contributing to cyclical stabilization are more difficult to find. A manufacturer of automobiles may produce low-priced cars as well as high-priced cars since in the periods of depression he can secure a better sales volume on the low-priced cars.

Sometimes a company may offer additional products in order to *utilize more fully* the type of organization, facilities, or other assets that it thinks desirable for operating its business efficiently. For example, a manufacturer of textiles may desire to maintain a research department to study markets, and to maintain a bureau of style and design to concentrate on product development. To justify the expense of these units, the company must secure a high volume of sales, and to obtain this volume, the company may have to add additional products. Such a procedure has led a number of concerns into serious difficulty because it is often less painful to add new products than to cut overhead expense.

Other firms diversify to *spread their risks.* A company highly successful with a component for missiles, for instance, sought civilian products to guard against cancellation of its military contracts. The du Pont company can risk failure on a new product because profits on other lines will provide financial support. In practice, this argument has been overworked. Companies have gone into lines they were unqualified to manage, thereby increasing their risks far more than spreading them.

The effect upon a company of increasing the number of its products. Before deciding diversification is preferable to specialization for one or more of the reasons just described, a company must consider the impact of an increase in product lines.

The typical salesman is able *to sell only a few products efficiently.* If he is given a large number to sell, he will usually concentrate on the sale of a few and neglect the others. For instance, a leading breakfast food company added a special brand of coffee to its product line. Analysis of sales results indicated that the main line of cereals was neglected when pressure was put on the salesmen to secure coffee sales. In this particular case the coffee line was discontinued.

Usually a production organization *cannot produce efficiently products of widely different quality.* Manufacturers of high-grade watches have found it difficult to adjust the thinking and acting of their organization to the production of cheaper products. An organization manufacturing products in which a large degree of tolerance is permissible will find it difficult to manufacture products of high quality where variations from standards must be very slight. A carpenter shop cannot easily be transformed into a high-grade furniture factory.

Another of the dangers in increasing the product line is that the *ability of the management to supervise activities required in selling a large number of products* will be exceeded. In many cases the management of a company may be capable of supervising the sales of a few products, but if new lines of products are added with which the executives are not familiar, they may spend an amount of time administering the venture that is quite out of proportion to the importance of the new products.

A factor of major importance in determining whether to diversify is the *suitability of a company's present facilities to the production and service of new products.* If new products are to be manufactured in the company's plant, the additional investment required must be carefully considered. The company may lose considerable flexibility and add materially to its costs if the required investment is large. Even if the new products are to be purchased from an outside concern, management must give attention to the suitability and adequacy of storage, display, and delivery equipment for the contemplated new product.

The production of a wide number of products has a marked *effect upon production costs,* if they are produced at the same plant. Frequent adjustments of machinery may be required. Special dies and other tools are needed for some products; unless the article can be sold in a substantial volume, these expenses for "tooling-up" materially increase the total cost per unit. The modern trend for low-cost mass production has been possible only by producing large quantities without the necessity of making frequent adjustments in equipment.

If a company sells a wide range of products, especially products of different qualities, it is *likely to lose its distinctiveness.* For example, a large store in an Eastern city had achieved prominence by selling high-quality, distinctive women's apparel. A new management attempted to capitalize on the firm's reputation by adding a line of medium-priced clothing, with the result that the exclusiveness of the store rapidly diminished.

We should note that many of the drawbacks of diversification just discussed can be overcome and the benefits of specialization can be obtained by creating a new separate division for the added product line. This new division might manufacture the product, *or* market the product, *or* perform all activities related to the product as a self-sufficient operation. However, the more the new line is divorced from existing operations, (a) the fewer will be the benefits of diversification and (b) the larger will be the potential volume necessary to support the new venture.

Clearly, many factors should be weighed in deciding whether to diversify or specialize. The outlook for proposed new lines and the situation existing within a company at a given time vary so much that no single answer is best for all companies. Experience does indicate that many companies have suffered from seeking to sell too many products rather than from restricting their activities to too few products.

PRODUCT DIFFERENTIATION

In a competitive economy every company must develop some reasons for customers to prefer its products over those of its competitors. Service, price, and other appeals may be used. And small firms may follow a policy of making their products as much like leading brands, or widely accepted industry standards, as possible. More often companies seek product differentiation.

This raises a question—in what respects will a company try to make its products distinctive? Usually the company will have a standing answer, because it wants a continuing and consistent reputation in the market and because its engineers and production people need guidance on what to emphasize.

What is quality? Quality is not is not capable of an exact definition. It depends on the type of customers to whom a product is sold and the nature of the appeal used in its sale. The basement customer of a department store may define quality in terms of *durability,* while a purchaser of a high-priced hat who expects to use it only one season may define quality in terms of richness in *appearance.* In the case of medical products, quality usually refers to *purity;* customers will pay a high premium for a product they feel confident is pure.

Within the industrial field, quality frequently refers to *uniformity.* For instance, some foundrymen prefer to get their pig iron from the same source in order to assure the uniform character of the iron.

Consumer attitude toward style. Increased interest in style and design has made some types of customers somewhat less sensitive to certain elements of quality. For example, the purchaser of an evening dress is so much interested in style and appearance that she may be willing to sacrifice quality from the point of view of the length of service.

Style is also important in automobiles and television sets. Their intrinsic performance may be no better than last year's model, yet having the latest gadget or different shaped chrome increases their salability significantly. The policy of a company in regard to style must conform to the desires of the group of consumers to whom it seeks to sell its products. A furniture producer, for example, must decide whether it will concentrate on modern furniture of the extreme type or follow more conservative lines. Firms manufacturing "period" furniture must decide whether they will copy original pieces in minute detail as an appeal to potential customers who are fastidious about interior decoration or merely use some of the characteristic features of the period. Within the furniture industry there is a well-recognized demand for what is know as "borax furniture" that tends to be gaudy, ornate, and cheap in construction.

Consumer recognition of product differences. In deciding on the kind of specifications to emphasize, the manager must consider not only the desires of his customers but also their ability to appreciate variations in quality. The purchaser of a low-priced or medium-priced radio may not be able to detect differences in tone qaulity; thus, he will not be willing to pay the extra cost necessary to provide a fine quality tone. The manager must therefore determine (a) what characteristics of his product his customers feel are important; (b) the extent to which his customers can appreciate the differences in such features and how much they are willing to pay for this extra quality; and (c) whether the cost of producing extra features is more or less than customers are willing to pay for them.

FREQUENCY OF DESIGN CHANGE

Related to the question of how product distinction is to be achieved is the troublesome issue of how frequently changes in design should be made.

Costs of change. Design changes are costly. First comes the technical and marketing research, engineering, testing, and tooling-up for the redesigned product. For simple products, such preparation expenses often amount to thousands of dollars; for complex products, like automobiles or airplanes, to millions of dollars. Then, manufacturing costs tend to increase if frequent changes are made. New skills have to be learned, production runs are shorter, and overhead builds up.

Next, inventory problems are complicated. Enough but not too much of the old product is needed as it is being phased out, and stocks of the new product must be built for an uncertain demand. The same problem arises at each stage in distribution—wholesaler, retailer, and perhaps consumer. In fact, anticipation of new models often leads to wide fluctuations in distributors' inventory and irregular orders for the manufacturer. If the manufacturer wants to keep distributive channels well stocked, he may have to accept return of old merchandise or make price concessions.

Finally, service problems are complicated by frequent design changes. The user of the product will expect repair parts to be readily available and servicemen to understand the idiosyncrasies of each model. As users of foreign products know from bitter experience, adequate service on a product has a significant effect on its usefulness and its resale value.

But these costs—development, manufacture, distribution, and service—are only one side of the picture. In setting a policy for frequency of design changes, the manager must also consider the benefits of changing.

Pressures to change. The most recent style, as already noted, may be so important to consumers that frequent design changes are inevitable. Today even staple products are styled according to the current mode. Kitchenware and bath tubs, which still render the same service they did thirty years ago, are streamlined and styled to the modern taste. Bath towels and sheets have blossomed out in all colors of the rainbow; even steam hammers are now streamlined.

Change may be necessary for more technical reasons. Technology is advancing in many fields—in the home and in the office, as well as in the plant. New developments are occurring every year in color television, microfilming, and transistorized controls of machines, to mention only a sample. If customers are to be well served, a company must from time to time adapt its products to such technological developments.

The pressures of style or technology are strong by themselves. Competitors' actions, however, may make the need to change irresistible. When a clearly preferred product is offered by a competitor, a company must respond in some manner, usually by redesigning its own products.

Frequency of change. Several alternative ways of reconciling the pressures and the costs of redesign of products are available to managers. Annual models are often used for consumer goods. This practice tends to accentuate the changes, because strong promotional stress is laid on "new" features—whether they are significant advances or not. And the annual model may hasten obsolescence, thereby raising replacement demand. The annual change does consolidate revisions into a single package and this package is retained for at least a year, so the timing of production adjustments is predictable. The best known example of annual models is in the automobile industry. In recent years only Volkswagen has had significant success with "continuous improvements" instead of annual models. All large-volume cars in the United States have annual models.

Another tack, more common in industrial goods, is a policy of "product leadership." Here the firm wants to be first on the market with improvements, and new designs are introduced as rapidly as new technology is developed. An illustration of this practice was IBM's switch to unitized computers, even though at the time the new design was presented the company enjoyed a dominant position in the electronic computer field.

A few firms try the leapfrog approach. Once they have a good design, they stick with it, letting competitors try various modifications. Then when significant improvements are evident, they make a major adjustment—incorporating not only competitors' advances but hopefully many more. The presumption here is that production and marketing economies of few changes will more than offset a temporary lag in improvements. In those fields where technological change has been slow, this policy works well.

A mixed strategy is to use standard parts year after year, but to combine them in different ways or to change the outside shell to give an up-to-date appearance. The Swiss watch industry, for example, follows substantially this practice with excellent results. The standardized parts simplify manufacturing and service problems, while the watchcases can be adapted to the latest styles.

Because design changes are so important to company success, top management often at least approves specific changes—using the best available data on customer preferences, estimated costs, competitors' actions, and the like. In addition, a more basic and longer-run decision is the company policy of how frequently detailed plans for changes are to be prepared. The alternatives just discussed suggest the form such a policy can take.

SUMMARY

A basic and recurring question for every business firm is, "What product or services are to be sold?" Nonprofit concerns and departments within a company face similar problems regarding the services they should render. Therefore, policies are needed to resolve (1) the recurring questions about diversification versus specialization—of lines and of items within a line, (2) how differentiation of products is to be achieved, and (3) the frequency of design changes.

Deciding upon the scope of product line is one of the most crucial issues that top management faces. In dealing with it, the wise manager should consider: need for a complete line, economical sales units, building close relationships with customers, smoothing seasonal and cyclical fluctuations in volume, full utilization of resources, ability of salesmen, production organization and management to handle diversified line, and effect of different products on production efficiency and company reputation.

The basis for product distinction should be derived from what customers feel is important, their ability to discriminate, and the cost of providing the desired features.

Frequent design changes appeal to customers but also generate a variety of added costs. These conflicting pressures may be met by such policies as annual models, product leadership, leapfrog changes, or many arrangements of standard parts.

Closely related to product policies is the choice of customers to whom the products will be sold. The next chapter will consider this second basic policy issue.

QUESTIONS FOR CLASS DISCUSSION

1. The ordinary large food store carries many nonfood items—power mowers, toys, lawn fertilizer, cosmetics, and drugs, for example. On the average across the country, 10% of supermarket sales comes from such items. A large, fast-growing chain views this with disapproval. The president says: "Space is at a premium, and nonfood items cut down on the number of brand lines we can carry. The selection of nonfood items is much too narrow to give the buyer an effective choice. We want to be a good grocery store, not a poor general store. We prefer shopping centers where a hard-selling department or specialty store doubles customer traffic for both parties." Do you agree? Why are nonfood items added by some food stores?

2. Classify the sales problems of the manager of an office building and of a producer of packaged shows for television. Are the problems similar?

3. A well-known breakfast food company is thinking of adding canned dog food to its line of products. Sales of canned dog food have been growing and most manufacturers are making good profits; it is sold through the same channels and by the same merchandising methods as breakfast food; some of the company executives believe the company's reputation for high-quality health food will help the sale of the new product. Do you recommend that the dog food be added to the company's present line?

4. A large percentage of phonographs and components sold today are called "hi-fi" in the advertisements when their performance is nowhere near that promised. Turntables have some flutter and significant amounts of "rumble," or amplifiers add objectionable "noise." Why is the designation "hi-fi" used, then? Is this ethical?

5. A company that manufactures small electric appliances (irons and toasters) once thought of adding room air-conditioners to its product line by buying out another firm. The air-conditioners would be made in a separate plant in a different city and sold by a different sales force under a different brand name to the same ultimate consumers and to the same direct customers—retail chains, large department stores, and hardware and appliance wholesalers. Does this seem a wise addition to the product line to you? What effect would such an addition have on the work of the central managers?

6. Volkswagen had a considerable success in the United States from 1957 through 1964 selling a car with very few styling changes while United States automobile manufacturers were going through the usual gyrations of annual model changes. How can Volkswagen's success over that period be explained?

7. A hardware wholesaler added charcoal briquettes at the urging of salesmen to complement a line of outdoor barbecuing equipment. Two years' experience has shown that prices and demand hold up well in the spring, then demand drops as grocery stores begin to "feature" charcoal as a traffic-builder. Average gross profit has worked out to be 5% as against 15% for all other items. Net profit per item for the 3,000 different items carried is not computed. Advantageous purchase prices can only be obtained by buying carload lots in the early spring. Charcoal is reasonably easy to handle, but torn or burst bags (2% of the total) scatter carbon around the warehouse. Do you recommend continuing the product?

8. Indian Head Mills, an offshoot of Textron Incorporated, had considerable success until 1964 in the textile business by buying other companies and discontinuing the unprofitable parts of the firms acquired. In late 1964 it purchased Detroit Gasket—a supplier of automotive parts. Why would Indian Head undertake such a venture? What questions of product policy are raised?

9. Following a deliberate policy of diversification, a manufacturer of heavy industrial presses and of pipeline handling equipment bought out some small companies and formed additional divisions to produce and sell self-generated items. It developed a line of teaching machines, self-tutoring books, and scientific equipment for sale to primary and secondary schools. Other products added were an assembly robot for small parts, automatic post office equipment, automatic pilots for airplanes—especially drones —and for trains and automobiles, and automated book recovery equipment for libraries. The companies purchased did development work for defense and atomic energy industries, made automatic dairy farm equipment, made high-energy-rate metal forming equipment, and worked on plasma generators. Some ventures were immediately profitable; others were not. What product policy do you see at work here? What aims does it serve?

CASE V
Metzger Chemical Company

Directors of the Metzger Chemical Company must decide whether the Company should submit a bid on a synthetic rubber plant that has been put up for sale. Top management of the Company has desired for some time to diversify the product line; it has had the Commercial Development section looking for opportunities suitable for the Company.

Present Operations. The Metzger Chemical Company has three divisions, the Ethical Products Division, the Industrial Division, and the International Divison. The headquarters of the Company are in Philadelphia, where the headquarters and the main plant of the Industrial Division are also located. In addition, the Industrial Division operates plants in Virginia, Pennsylvania, and South Carolina. The headquarters and one of the plants of the Ethical Products Division are in Baltimore. That division also operates plants in two small towns within 30 miles of Baltimore. The International Division operates plants and distribution centers in about a dozen foreign countries.

Products. The Industrial Division manufactures between 1,000 and 1,500 products, chiefly fine and medicinal chemicals which require further compounding or minor processing, such as tableting, before they can be sold for use by ultimate consumers. About 65 percent of the total sales volume is in vitamin and hormone preparations and antibiotics. It supplies the Ethical Division with many of the materials used in compounding its products and the International Division with many of the articles it sells abroad.

The Ethical Division produces about 450 pharmaceutical and biological items which are ready for application to human beings or animals by a doctor or veterinarian or on his prescription. The products include blood plasma, antibiotic compounds, vaccines, serums, insulin, narcotics and sedatives, and anesthetic agents.

The International Division distributes abroad all the products of both the other Divisions except those which it has been found advantageous to produce in or near the countries in which they are to be sold.

Customers. The customers of the Industrial Division are pharmaceutical and veterinary manufacturing houses, food processors, feed manufacturers, government agencies, and wholesalers and industrial distributors. These wholesalers and distributors resell to any of the above groups, and they also distribute prescription chemicals to retail drug stores and hospitals, laboratory chemicals to industrial and educational users, and other chemicals to general users.

The Ethical Division sells to retail druggists, wholesale druggists, hospitals, and governmental agencies. Since the products of the Division must be prescribed by physicians, the Division does considerable missionary sales work in calling on them, supplying them with samples, explaining the uses of Metzger products to them, and trying to induce them to prescribe those products for their patients. In one sense, the doctors may be regarded as customers of the Division. Sales to dispensing physicians are made directly or through distributors who service them.

The customers of the International Division belong in the same categories as those of the domestic divisions although the channels used in reaching them tend to vary from country to country according to local commercial practice.

System of distribution. The Industrial Division has about 100 salesmen. Practically all of these men have technical backgrounds and have received considerable additional technical training from the Division. The leadership of the sales department emphasizes good will and service work. The selling pitch is built largely on the basis of the uses to which Division products can be put. Each salesman sells all the products of the Division to all types of customers. The largest customers, however, are sold directly by one of the five regional Managers or their Assistants.

The Division also operates three branch distribution warehouses, located in Chicago, Philadelphia, and San Francisco, out of which it services the needs of its customers. Complete stocks are carried in each warehouse.

The Ethical Division operates a force of between 600 and 700 salesmen out of 20 combination selling and distribution branch houses. All the men have received extensive training by the Division. They call on wholesalers and on a selected list of retail druggists, comprising about one-third to one-half of the total number, for the purpose of making direct sales. They likewise call on the larger hospitals to make direct sales and to promote the prescription of the Division's products. They visit a selected list of the more important physicians to dispense samples, pass on information about Division products, and induce the doctors to prescribe their use. Except in calls on doctors and hospitals, their emphasis is on the resale possibilities of the products they sell.

The International Division sells a varying percentage of the total sales volume of the Company, usually somewhat smaller than the portion sold by either of the other two Divisions. The Industrial Division and the Ethical Division usually divide the remaining sales volume about equally.

Research and engineering activities. The Company is committed to a heavy program of research. The Industrial Division usually spends about 2 percent of its sales in this activity; the Ethical Division's expenditure for this purpose is generally much more, amounting to about 10 percent of its sales. The result is that the composition of the lines of both divisions is constantly changing. A surprisingly large percentage of the sales volume of both divisions is of products that were entirely or relatively unknown ten years ago.

These discoveries would be of little value were it not for the Company's engineering talents. Conversion of a test-tube process into an operation which can be repeated over and over on a large scale, economically, and with high quality standards poses many obstacles and pitfalls. The engineering staff at Metzger Chemical has an excellent record in overcoming these problems.

Production. The production of finished products of the Company is typically on a small scale. The value of most products per physical unit is high. A carload shipment of a single product is not unknown but it is certainly an unusual event. However, products such as the biologicals often require great tanks for fermentation or other large processing equipment inasmuch as the end-product may be very small in relation to the raw material required. This range in scale of operation poses special production problems, and the production departments are continually struggling to achieve as many as possible of the advantages of mass production even though the finished goods are likely to be measured in pounds or grams.

Along with this goes the necessity for unusually high quality standards. Many of the chemicals the Company produces have lethal as well as curative properties. Exactness in the properties of materials sold for further processing or compounding and in the quantities and purity of the materials used in the compounding activities of the Ethical Division is vital to the very existence of the firm. There is, therefore, a strong tradition of unimpeachable purity and rigid quality control which extends throughout the organization. This tradition sometimes becomes a matter of pride instead of merely a matter of recognition of commercial benefits or survival value.

The devotion of top management to a program of research and engineering, together with the rapid changes which have taken place in the chemical and pharmaceutical industry, have endowed the Company with considerable knowhow in the techniques of introducing and capitalizing on new products. They have also engendered in the Company personnel an attitude of reliance on new products to help resolve problems.

Financial condition. Company net sales and total assets have both fluctuated around $150 million in recent years. Working capital is very high, and there are no long-term debts.

The diversification opportunity. The high ratio of current assets to current liabilities ranging in recent years from 3.6:1 to 8:1, and of current assets to total outside obligations, ranging from 4:1 to 6:1, together with a general feeling that it would be good policy to seek to escape the heavy dependence of the Company on the fluctuations of the medicinal business, has led the corporate executives to think in terms of diversification into an industry not so closely associated with the general field of health. Fluctuations result from the risk aspect of new products and from heavy demands for one product in the case of epidemics.

A significant opportunity for diversification has arisen through this chance to purchase an operating synthetic rubber plant. The corporate executives appointed a task committee to explore the prospects of this as a possible area of expansion for the Company. The following is a summary of the committee report. The nature of the committee's discussion of raw materials available, plant facilities, and probable costs of operation indicates a thorough and sound report.

The Industry—Supply and Demand

An ever increasing portion of the world's rubber supply must come from synthetic sources because of steady long-term growth in demand

and a ceiling on natural rubber capacity. In fact, demand is already over 90 percent of existing world capacity and additional synthetic plants should be required in three years.

Synthetic rubber can hold its own against natural on both price and performance. Butadiene-based GR-S has no serious challenger among other synthetics for the majority of uses for two reasons. The technical problems of producing it have been reasonably well solved. Half a billion dollars more have been invested in facilities for making it than have been invested in plant for other synthetics.

The committee forecasts an increasing market and a minimum market opportunity for synthetic rubber of three times current output in twenty years.

Estimated Butadiene Requirement

	Per Cent of Existing Capacity
Last year	113
Current year	75
Next year	82
Succeeding year	93
Succeeding year	102

Research and developmental possibilities

Butadiene and its raw material, butylene, are starting points for new products in the branch of chemistry with which the Metzger Chemical Company is most familiar—organic synthesis. While their development has been neglected, a whole family tree of chemical descendents from there versatile materials is thought to be potentially available; with proper development their derivatives may rival those of ethylene and acetylene in number and scope of application, though probably not in tonnage. Preliminary investigation indicated that derivatives of butadiene should be of existing or potential value as intermediates in the production of a wide range of polymers, solvents, plasticizers, drugs, and other organic chemicals. It might yield low cost coating and flooring resins and a drying oil with excellent properties. Butadiene is now widely used in making "cold rubber" for tire treads.

Sources of materials and markets

The plant under consideration uses as a raw material natural gas which is available in abundant quantities nearby. It produces many thousands of long tons of butadiene annually and is a major factor in the synthetic rubber field.

Butadiene rubber must at present be sold to a few large buyers. As a result, the initial work of marketing would be conducted at a very high level and no great increase of personnel or organization would be needed. As research and development effort is applied and new products are created or new uses are discovered resulting in wider distribution, a specialty sales force would probably become necessary. This could be developed as needed. The committee foresees no significant difficulty during the next three to five yars in disposing of the output of the plant under consideration. Competitors include all of the large rubber companies and several of the major chemical companies which produce "basic" chemicals sold in large quantities to further processors.

Financial considerations

The seller and a larger financial intermediary offer liberal purchase terms which would not strain the company's cash resources.

Committee estimates of future butadiene demand and prices indicate that a successful bid could be made which would allow a long-run return on investment equal to the average for the chemical industry. Expected demand and prices after three years would make up for lower operating rates and prices in the near future, in the opinion of the committee.

There is considerable difference among the operating top management group as to what action the Metzger Chemical Company should take.

Several executives feel that the Company could much more appropriately devote its personnel skills and available funds to developing a line of products that would enable it to expand into the animal health and nutrition or the plant health and nutrition fields and become a major factor there. Others are of the opinion that the proprietary drug business with its wide margins of gross profit offers opportunities worth exploration. It has also been pointed out that profitable investment might be made in developing facilities to produce some of the chemicals that the Company buys in quantity, thus becoming "basic" in such materials.

A meeting of the Board of Directors is scheduled for tomorrow to decide whether the Company should submit a bid on the butadiene rubber plant.

REQUIRED: As Company president, what would you recommend to the board? Give the reasons for your choice and why other alternatives were rejected.

6 SALES POLICIES—CUSTOMERS

Customer policies of every company should be reviewed periodically to make sure that they are attuned to shifting markets. The long-term changes we examined in Chapter 2 have a major impact on customer selection. The revolution in distribution of incomes alone has had a profound effect on markets for luxury goods and for mass production items such as television sets.

The five-day week, with the resulting long weekend, has expanded interest in hobbies, sports apparel, and related items. To cite still another example, the sharp drop in the number of household servants, coupled with a higher average income, has promoted women's emancipation from household drudgery—prepared foods, automatic washing machines, electric mixers, electric dishwashers, and simplified household designs are only some of the more apparent results of this shift. The mechanization of the farm, rising industrial activity in the South, new synthetic materials, and drastic changes in our foreign trade give further evidence of the dynamic nature of markets.

In the face of such changes as these, it behooves every business administrator to keep a vigilant eye on his customer policies.

Distinction between customers and consumers. Confusion sometime arises due to failure to distinguish between "customers" and "consumers." The term *consumer* means the one who *uses* a product (or service) for his personal satisfaction or benefit; or in the case of industrial raw materials, the one who so *changes* the form of the product as to alter its identity. A *customer,* on the other hand, is anyone who *buys* goods. A customer may be a consumer, or he may be a dealer who will resell the product to someone else.

The habits and wishes of the ultimate consumer of a product are of vital interest to all businessmen having anything to do with the product, for the major purpose of economic activity is to create consumer satisfaction. In the original design of a product, during its production, and throughout its distribution, consumer satisfaction is ever a controlling consideration. While the businessman should always keep the consumer in mind, nevertheless a vast number of sales are made to customers who are not final consumers.

Problem arising in the selection of customers. In laying plans for effective relationships with consumers and customers, central management should establish policies regarding:

1. The types of consumers that offer the best market for company products.
2. The locations that it will seek to cover.
3. The channels of distribution to be used to reach desired consumers in the selected areas.
4. The size of customer that will be most efficient and strategic for the company to serve.

SELECTION OF CONSUMERS

Various types of consumers demand services of a widely different nature. In fact, the activities necessary to sell to different consumers vary so widely that most companies find it pays to select certain types and to concentrate their attention on selling goods to these groups.

Selecting consumers for a retail store. The difficulties in selling to more than one type of consumer may be illustrated by a retail store in Boston that had grown and prospered by appealing primarily to well-to-do women of mature age. When a new manager was installed, the store had a sales volume of over a million dollars. The new manager had assured the owners that he would be able to increase the profits within a short period of time. Contrary to his expectations, he found himself faced with declining sales and operating losses. A business depression occurred soon after he took charge, and many of the store's well-to-do customers were affected very adversely.

Under these conditions there was a strong temptation for the store to seek to serve a wider group of customers. Some of the department managers were permitted to operate their departments on a definitely popular-priced basis. This middle-of-the-road policy brought a number of serious problems.

The former customers were accustomed to receive a great deal of personal service and were disgruntled when they were treated in a summary and routine fashion by clerks in the departments attempting to do a volume business. The managers of the popular-priced departments justly contended that they could not afford the expense of serving all customers in the manner desired by the well-to-do women and that it was necessary to treat alike all customers coming into their departments.

On the other hand, the customers seeking popular-priced merchandise were unable to shop throughout the store because some of the departments carried only high-priced merchandise. These departments also limited their selection primarily to conservative styles that did not suit the taste of newer customers, many of whom were young in age. A few of the departments tried to carry merchandise that would appeal to both classes of customers, but they found that the popular-priced merchandise was usually sold in small amounts, not warranting the selling effort and personal service that should be rendered by these departments. The general economic conditions and the confusion of sales policies finally resulted in a completely new administration for the store.

Department stores that desire to sell products of widely different price ranges usually find it necessary to organize a basement or "shops" where the low-priced merchandise is sold. These units are often operated as separate organizations and are able to adjust their services to the group of customers to whom they cater.

A similar sort of problem is found in many industries. The restaurant catering to business executives offers a different service from the campus kitchen seeking the trade of students. A hotel primarily serving commercial travelers must maintain a different atmosphere and render a different type of service than a hotel seeking resident guests. A patent medicine company found as a result of studying its market that a major group of its consumers were people who spoke only foreign languages. These groups were located primarily in large industrial centers and could be reached by foreign language newspapers and circulars printed in foreign languages.

Types of consumers for consulting services. Even the clients of management consulting firms may be grouped into major types in much the same way as the customers of an industrial firm.

Bankers sometimes desire a general survey of a business as a means of appraising its management and determining its financial possibilities. If it is the board of directors or the general manager who calls in the consultant, the problems are likely to deal with policies or organization. Departmental managers often call in consultants to help them with more detailed problems, such as factory layouts, sales incentives, accounting procedures, or systems of expense control. Each type of client requires studies made from its particular point of view. Some consulting firms seek to adapt their activities to satisfy any of these consumer groups, whereas other firms follow a policy of rendering a special and limited type of service.

Market analysis. The need for a clear definition of the consumer groups a company hopes to serve is evident in the preceding examples. Fundamental steps in arriving at such a definition are:

1. Estimate the size and the nature of the future market. The number of potential consumers, shifts in their needs and desires, and their probable economic ability to buy will point to growth or contraction in the total volume. Then a detailed study of particular preferences or technical requirements will refine the estimates of demand for specific products.

2. Appraise the present and potential competition. Some markets are served well; competitors are strong, progressive, and firmly entrenched. Other markets may be served by companies predominantly interested in a different field or companies that may lack the financial resources, the technical know-how, and perhaps the leadership to provide the services desired.

3. Compare the ability and the products of your own company with (a) market needs and (b) competitors' strengths. Then, select market segments in which growth prospects combined with your relative strength show the most profitable market possibilities.

If a company has carefully studied its outlook, much of the data needed to identify the most attractive consumer groups will already be available. However, more specific information on various consumer groups, and especially estimates of future changes in groups not currently served, will probably be necessary. Also note that decisions on customers are entwined with product policies. The two sets of decisions are as inseparable as Siamese twins; a company must either make what a selected group of consumers want or find consumers for the products it makes. Often adjustments are necessary in both product and consumer policies so that the two are fully compatible.

The relation of a company to consumers of its products is normally continuous over a period of years. Reputations are established, and expectations—so vital to careful planning—are built up. Consequently, a company cannot move in and out of a market from week to week. Instead, well-established and relatively stable policies regarding consumers to be served are very useful.

LOCATION OF CONSUMERS

Another dimension of customer policies is the geographical location to be covered. The following examples show that knowing where to place sales efforts may become a complicated question.

Location of consumers of an electric range manufacturer. A manufacturer of moderately priced electric ranges for household use had a peculiar distribution of customers. The company was organized on the idea that there was a place for a Henry Ford in the electric range business. It was believed that a company could afford to sell a simply designed range at a moderate price provided a sufficient volume of business was obtained. The company's location in a southern city placed it in an excellent position to cultivate the southern market, which was expanding at the time because of rising per capita income and increasing availability of electric power in rural areas.

The company was actually securing a significant volume of its business, however, in the Minneapolis, Des Moines, and Seattle territories, because the president of the concern had formerly worked in these areas and was able to secure orders from distributors with whom he was personally acquainted. At the same time sales in many of the southern states were being neglected.

It was true, of course, that the company might have had to serve households in these western areas to secure the volume of business that it desired. Also, if the company had been producing ranges in large volume, the average production cost might have been low enough to permit it to pay the heavy shipping cost into distant territories and still make some profit on the operation. At the time, however, the company did not have a sufficient volume in production to make business with these more distant buyers desir-

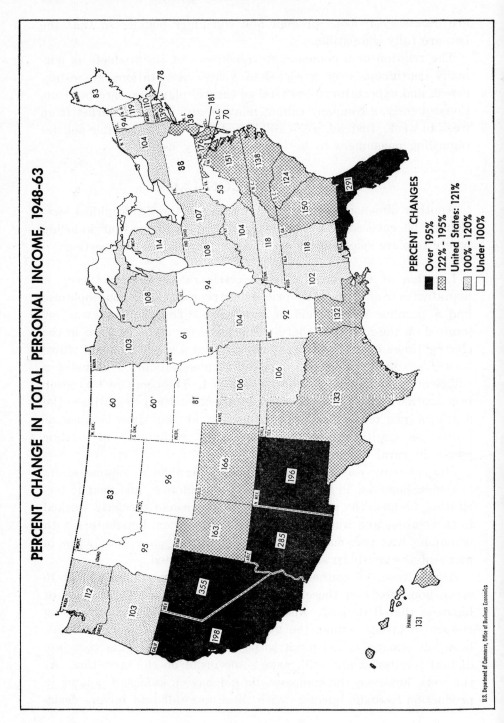

PERCENT CHANGE IN TOTAL PERSONAL INCOME, 1948-63

PERCENT CHANGES

Over 195%
122% - 195%
United States: 121%
100% - 120%
Under 100%

U.S. Department of Commerce, Office of Business Economics

able. Moreover, it was neglecting the local market that was growing in importance and could be more economically served. Clearly the company should have adopted a policy of first cultivating the southern market where lower selling and shipping costs made current operating profits a reasonable possibility. When this was accomplished, the company would have been in a better position to seek users in other areas.

From rural to urban consumers. The large mail-order houses such as Sears, Roebuck and Montgomery Ward built their business with rural consumers—people who had difficulty getting to cities to shop. But conditions have changed. Now there are fewer farmers, and they drive automobiles. One adjustment to this shift has been an impressive expansion of retail stores operated by these companies.

Nevertheless, the mail-order business also continues to prosper. How? Through a shift in definition of potential consumers. The largest mail-order market now is the suburban housewife, whose children and other duties make shopping a chore, and her do-it-yourself husband. They find the semiannual catalogs a storehouse of merchandise information and a convenient way to select many items. To be sure, the merchandise offered has been adapted to appeal to the nonfarm consumer, and telephone ordering is replacing the mailed order. But, vital to the planning of what will be offered is a clear concept of where the potential buyers live.

Foreign markets. With the United States increasingly involved in world affairs, more and more companies are considering exports as a way of expanding sales. Selling in foreign markets, however, presents several special factors that should be weighed. Many countries have tariffs or import quotas that interfere with free trade. Local competition may be strong and in some countries local firms received favored treatment. The United States exporter must, of course, be prepared to do business in accordance with local customs and not attempt to impose United States business codes where they do not fit. Currency regulations may make withdrawal of money difficult after the goods are sold.

In spite of these difficulties, export business often is attractive. In analyzing foreign markets, as any other new markets, the added or *incremental* costs should be balanced against the added income. Once a company has completed its product engineering and is "tooled-up" for production, the cost per unit of turning out an added 5% or 10% is less than the total average cost of the basic output. If the company has idle capacity in its plant, this incremental cost may be very much lower. So, even though there are difficulties in selling abroad, the net revenue received may still be above the incremental cost.

Foreign markets may be tapped by means other than exporting. One arrangement is to license a local firm to make products with United States patents and know-how. Another is to build a foreign plant. Neither of these plans calls for export of United States products (except perhaps, special parts that cannot be made economically in the foreign country), but they have enabled a number of companies to secure profits from foreign operations.

Delimiting the market area. Involved in every decision regarding the location of consumers to be sought are costs of selling and of delivery.

Usually the costs of selling to customers increase as the distance of the customer from the location of the manufacturer or retailer increases. Even though a manufacturer may have salesmen located in the territory where the customer lives, it is more expensive to supervise salesmen working a considerable distance from the central office. It is also difficult to maintain intimate contact with the customer who is situated far from the central office, and as a consequence the cost of selling to such customers is higher because of greater sales resistance. Delivery costs, particularly on heavy or bulky articles, may place definite limits on the territory that can be served economically.

In addition, full utilization of an existing strength may be a factor. Most common is adoption of national distribution because national advertising of the company—already necessary for part of the market—is reaching consumers in all areas. In these cases, sales promotion considered to be necessary dictates the market scope, rather than customer policy determining what promotion is feasible. A somewhat similar situation arises when a company invests heavily to acquire technical know-how for a specific problem and then feels impelled to serve all people with this problem regardless of where they are located.

Competitive strategy may also influence the choice of markets. For instance, Company A may immediately follow Company B into a new area—say the West Coast—because A does not want B to acquire a possible source of strength that might be extended to other markets. On the other hand, if a pattern of normal territories has evolved, Company X may not move into Company Y's home market for fear that Y will reciprocate. Such intangible considerations may result in a firm not pushing its territorial limits just to the point where incremental selling and delivery costs match incremental revenue.

CHANNELS OF DISTRIBUTION

Nature of the problem. By *channel of distribution* is meant the *steps* by which products are *distributed* from the one who first converts them into usable form to the consumer. Many enterprises, of course, render services rather than manufacture products; for example, banks, public accountants, and all sorts of retail stores. Because of their nature, such services are almost always sold directly to consumers. But for manufacturers the selection of the proper channels of distribution is a very real problem.

Changes in buying habits, transportation, communications, and market locations have modified methods of distribution greatly during recent years. This whole field is in a state of flux, and few companies are justified in assuming that their traditional channels are necessarily the most effective ways of reaching the consumer they prefer.

The most important channels of distribution are through jobbers, direct to retailers, direct to consumers, or through brokers or agents.

Through jobbers. For many years the jobber (or wholesaler) was regarded as the orthodox method of distribution. The jobber assembles products from many manufacturers, stores them, and sells them to retailers. In so doing, he also assumes risks of price change, damage, or obsolescence; he extends credit to retailers; and he sorts and ships products according to retailer needs.

All of these functions are essential in the distribution of merchandise; regardless of the channel of distribution used, someone must perform them. When a large part of consumer purchases was secured through small retailers scattered over a wide territory,

it was more economical for the manufacturer to have the wholesaler perform these services than to undertake them himself.

During the past half century, an increased interest in style and
price, coupled with improved transportation, have resulted in a
decline in the importance of the small retail store and a growth in
the department store and the chain store. The latter types of retail
outlets buy sufficient quantities of merchandise to make it economical for the manufacturer to sell directly to them. Nevertheless, a
local jobber is still needed to serve small retailers located both in
small towns and in trading centers. These still cannot be sold
economically by the typical manufacturer.

Moreover, in some lines of merchandise, such as millinery, it is
difficult for a single manufacturer to produce a sufficient variety
to meet the needs of retailers. A *specialty jobber* who concentrates
on a limited type of merchandise fills this gap. Also, there are auto
supply jobbers who serve repair shops, plumbing supply houses
that serve plumbers, and similar concerns that assemble a wide
variety of supplies needed by some particular trade or industry.
Thus, while the trend may be away from the use of jobbers, there
are situations in which the local jobber or the specialty jobber
performs a very useful service.

Direct to retailers. Distribution by the manufacturer direct to
retailers has some distinct advantages. By using specialty salesmen to concentrate on the sale of his products, the manufacturer
may secure more aggressive selling efforts, for a jobber's general-
line salesmen sell a wide variety of products and cannot concentrate their efforts upon the sale of one particular product. This
plan may also enable the manufacturers to ascertain better the consumers' desires, since he has firsthand contact with the final "point-
of-sale," namely the retailer.

The manufacturer exercises more control over the final sale of
his goods if he has direct contact with the retailer. He builds his
own personal relationships and goodwill and consequently is not so
dependent upon the jobber for sales volume. He also has a better
opportunity to influence retail prices, display, and other factors
that affect the popularity of his product with the consumer.

The plan of selling direct to retailers, however, may lead to excessive costs if it is used unwisely. If the manufacturer eliminates
the jobber entirely, he may incur unbearable costs because many

retailers buy in such small quantities that the expense of selling and servicing them may exceed the gross profits on the goods they purchase.

Some companies that manufacture a variety of products set up their own *sales branches*. These branches perform in many respects like a jobber, except that they sell only products of the parent company. One firm, for example, has eleven separate manufacturing divisions—each operated like an independent company. The sales division is another fairly independent unit with several branches that perform the functions of a jobber. A sales branch with its own salesmen enables a company to secure improved selling effort and at the same time have a local distributing point. Coordination of sales and production is easier with a branch, and the branch is more willing to make market surveys.

Direct to consumers. This plan is usually employed when the product is of such a nature that the salesman needs a high degree of technical training to sell it and when technical services must be rendered in connection with the product after it is sold. For example, this plan is used by manufacturers of office equipment such as adding machines, addressographs, and computers. Salesmen must be able to operate such equipment to sell it, and the manufacturer must assure himself that the equipment is kept in proper repair or the customer may become dissatisfied with it. For similar reasons most industrial equipment is sold directly to users.

Manufacturers of many types of consumer goods have used the direct-to-consumer method to some degree. For example, it has been used by manufacturers of such articles as brushes, hosiery, and medicines. Although the concerns using this channel of distribution often advertise the fact that the expenses of jobbers and retailers are eliminated, most costs arising from the activities of these middlemen must still be met by the selling company. For consumer goods there is not sufficient evidence to warrant the belief that distribution direct to the consumer can be widely applied.

Use of exclusive dealers, as is done by automobile manufacturers and many oil companies, combines many advantages of direct sales to consumers while retaining the initiative of local businessmen. The dealer "runs his own business," but to retain his franchise he must join in company sales programs and conform to service standards set by the company. Obviously, the producing company must have a good enough line of products for the typical dealer to make a profit or competent men will not apply for dealerships and the whole system will collapse.

Through brokers or agents. The broker usually performs only one major function of distribution—selling. As contrasted with the jobber, he usually sells only one type of product, or at most only a few closely related products. Although the broker is used most frequently in the distribution of producer goods, he may also be used in the distribution of consumer goods. For example, he is used extensively in the distribution of farm products, notably livestock and fresh fruits and vegetables. The farmer does not have an economical means of reaching the wholesaler of these products, so it is customary for him to consign them to a local broker or agent who, in turn, sells them to the jobber who distributes them to the retailer. Brokers are often used in the same way by small canneries that do not have sufficient output to justify a full-time sales force and therefore need the services of someone who is familiar with the potential market for their product. Anyone who has publicly announced his intention of buying a house or a suburban lot knows that brokers are also used in the real-estate field. Here, again, it is difficult for buyers and sellers to get together without the aid of someone who is in close contact with the market.

Selecting a channel of distribution. Professor Thomas L. Berg [1] suggests that selecting a channel of distribution be viewed as an organization problem and that the activities analyzed include the total distribution system. More specifically, his approach involves:

1. Listing all actions necessary between producer and consumer—promotion, actual selling, transportation, financing, warehousing, repackaging, risk-taking, installation and repair service, and the like.

2. Grouping these activities into jobs that can be effectively and efficiently performed by separate firms. These firms may be banks or warehousemen who also do other things, or they may be firms exclusively involved in this particular channel. The crucial matter here is to conceive of jobs (packages of activities) that are the most effective combinations.

1 See T. L. Berg, "Designing the Distribution System" in W. D. Stevens, ed., *The Social Responsibilities of Marketing*, American Marketing Association, 1962.

3. Defining relationships between the jobs that will assure cooperation and necessary flow of information. Also define how each firm involved is to be compensated for its efforts. And work out necessary, minimum controls to be exercised by various members over other members.

4. On the basis of this organization design (the *policy* adopted by the designer), developing specifications for the firms that are to fill each job.

5. Then moving on to execution of the plan by recruiting people to take the specified jobs (some negotiation may arise here since independent firms will be participants), educating people on how the plan is to work, supervising the day-to-day operations, and exercising necessary controls.

One of the significant aspects of this approach is that the channel of distribution problem is not viewed as a choice between a few predetermined alternatives. Instead, each company should work out a design that is the best way to get its products to the consumers it has selected. Also implied is the idea that tasks assigned to participants are apt to need modification as economic and competitive conditions change.

Since a channel of distribution typically creates a complex set of relationships, a policy is needed to provide consistency and stability of action. And top management is vitally concerned because—as experience in the automobile, watch, liquor, and many other industries testifies—a strong, well-designed distribution system may spell the difference between success and failure of the entire enterprise.

SIZE OF CUSTOMERS

Small customers. Often a company needs a policy guide on the size of customers it seeks. Customers, that is the people it deals with directly, can be either too small or too large. A company should know how much it costs to serve each type of customer and the amount the customer must buy if his business is to yield a profit to the company. One manufacturing concern, for example, was selling to 8,000 retail accounts. An analysis of these accounts revealed that 55% of the total number purchased only 5% of its entire sales volume and that none of these 55% purchased more than $200 worth of merchandise a year. The company decided to eliminate all such accounts, which, it was thought, would not develop into better accounts, and as a consequence the number of customers was reduced to 4,000. This enabled the company to reduce its salesmen from 82 to 43 and to make a number of other substantial reductions in selling costs.

This is not an unusual case. In his eagerness to secure sales volume, the manufacturer may seek to sell to all customers who desire his products. And the typical salesman is inclined to sell to whoever will buy. Consumers wanting only a small quantity of a particular product should be served, of course, and some firms will find a way of selling them merchandise profitably. Unless, however, the company designs its product line, services, and other policies to serve customers of this type, it will probably find that sales to them do not yield a profit.

In deciding whether to eliminate customers who purchase in small quantities, consideration should be given to the potential purchases of these customers as well as the actual purchases now made from the company. If a small customer has the capacity to increase his purchases substantially, it may be desirable not to eliminate him but to concentrate on securing a larger percentage of his trade.

Large customers. On the other hand, a customer may purchase too much merchandise! If a concern is dependent on one or two customers for most of its business, its position is vulnerable because loss of patronage of such an important buyer will disrupt the entire organization.

A comparatively small tire company had been selling tires to a large mail-order house for years at the time of an investigation. The relative importance of sales to this one customer increased from year to year, constituting approximately 36% at the end of the first 5 years, 50% at the end of 10 years, and increasing to over 65% in the year the investigation was made. The tire company had earned a satisfactory profit on its business from this customer; in fact, the company had substantially expanded its production facilities so that it would be able to meet the requirements of its large customer during the coming years. The sales contract with the customer had been renewed for another 5-year period, and the additions to the plant were made primarily at the request of the customer who wished the company to be equipped to handle a greater volume of tires. There was, however, a provision in the contract that made it cancellable by either party upon 6 months' notice prior to the end of any calendar year.

Although sales to other customers of the company had been increasing, they had not risen as fast as sales to the one mail-order customer. The business with the other customers was not sufficiently large and profitable to enable the company to operate without the volume secured from the mail-order house. The company recognized that it was in an unsound position and decided to promote the independent business. Before this was accomplished, however, changes in economic conditions and in the buying practices of the mail-order house resulted in the cancellation of the contract, and the small tire company was thereby forced into bankruptcy.

The fact that the preceding illustration happened to end disastrously does not necessarily mean that a company should refuse business from one large customer. It should, however, be prepared to withstand insofar as possible the loss of this one customer. This can be accomplished by building up sales with a large number of customers, by securing a contract from the single customer that protects the company against a precipitous drop in the volume of business, and by avoiding a large investment in facilities and other commitments that cannot be curtailed if the sales to the large customer are lost.

SUMMARY

Customer policies, along with product policies, define broadly the function or economic service of an enterprise. They lay out what is to be done and for whom. No manager can plan wisely unless he has a clear concept of these "end products" of the operations of his company.

More specifically, top management should set up policies regarding the types and the location of final consumers the company hopes to reach, the distribution system to be used in getting products to such consumers, and the upper and lower limits on the size of direct customers. These adjustments to the market are vital to success; they have to be nurtured over time; and they need wise policy guidance for consistency and dependability.

There has been frequent occasion in this chapter to note how customer policies are closely related to many other aspects of a company's activities. For example, the customers sought will affect the kind of sales promotion needed, the size of plant, the type of sales and perhaps production personnel, the need for large accounts receivable, and other phases of operations. These interrelations will become more apparent in subsequent discussion of the other aspects of business administration and in the analysis of the cases found throughout the book.

QUESTIONS FOR CLASS DISCUSSION

1. Stretch Wire Company, of Houston, Texas, sells wire rope to oil and natural gas producers. It desires to expand sales to the Pacific Coast lumber industry and to the steel industry in the Middle West and the Middle Atlantic states. Personal selling ability —including personal acquaintance with purchasing agents and engineers plus the technical knowledge necessary to specify the right kind of rope for the buyer's purposes—is the key to getting orders. Should the company expand its own sales force to cover the new territories and customers or should it use manufacturer's agents?

2. The S. and K. Corporation, manufacturer of plumbing supplies, has for years sold its products through plumbing wholesalers to plumbers. It is well known in the trade but has never advertised to consumers. One of its best lines is high-quality, well-styled towel racks, soap dishes, and similar fixtures. To share in the growing "do-it-yourself" market, S. and K. now wants also to sell this fixture line to homeowners who install the fixtures themselves without the help of a plumber. What channel of distribution should S. and K. use to reach this new market? What major hurdles will have to be overcome in marketing fixtures to these new consumers?

3. A retail furniture store that had been catering to families with annual incomes from $15,000 to $20,000 experienced a decline in sales that resulted in operating losses. It considered (a) going into the interior decorating business so as to secure business from a higher income group, and/or (b) adding a line of cheaper furniture that might be sold to people with lower incomes. List the points you would consider before making a recommendation regarding such a change in policy.

4. The Lincoln Box Corporation, a producer of set-up paper boxes, sells about 60% of its output to one large candy manufacturer. There has been a close relation between the two firms for over 15 years and the two presidents are good friends. What steps, if any, might the Lincoln executives take to protect their company against the possible loss of this one customer?

5. Should the manager of a summer resort be interested in changes in the income distribution in the United States? How might income distribution affect his customer and product policies?

6. The leading manufacturers of rugs sell their products directly to retailers. Some companies perform all the distribution functions in their home office; others maintain showrooms in two or three buying centers but perform all other activities at their plant; and still others establish branch offices and warehouses at which the branch manager has full responsibility over selling operations within the territory. What reasons may account for this difference in organization? How might product and customer policies influence the extent to which branches or jobbers are used in this industry?

7. "Many companies sell to a large number of customers even when the gross profit on sales to these customers does not equal the cost of selling." Is this ever justified from the point of view of the seller? Is it desirable from the point of view of the buyer? May this be desirable from a social point of view?

8. Commercial banks that once specialized in lending only to business firms are now often seeking out the individual borrower who wants an auto loan, a home-mortgage loan, or even an unsecured time loan. They are also seeking to merge and expand geographically as far as the law allows—and to have the law changed. Do you see any limits to these drives toward smaller customers and larger territories? Why have they occurred?

9. A major machinery manufacturer has been asked to license a foreign manufacturer to use its name, patents, and know-how in a country in which the United States-based firm has little hope of making sales because of import restrictions. The machines, though of a standard kind, are always modified to some extent to each ultimate purchaser's production needs. Under the license, the United States firm would have no effective control over future modifications made to the machinery. Would you recommend that it grant foreign licenses?

CASE VI

Phoenix Company

The Phoenix Company is a manufacturer of tools with its general offices and one plant at Pittsburgh, Pennsylvania, and a second plant at Coraopolis, Pennsylvania, about fifteen miles distant. The Coraopolis plant was formerly owned by the Perfection Tool Company. Eight years ago, these two companies were merged and the firm name of Phoenix was retained. During the past five years, the Phoenix Company has refused to sell to many chain store companies that desire to handle the regular branded Phoenix lines. The management has considered that its policy of confining the distribution of its regular brands almost entirely to the jobber-retail channel is the wisest one to pursue. At the present time, the management is reviewing this policy.

Product lines. The Phoenix Company manufactures the following fifteen lines of products:

Planes	Scrapers
Mitre boxes	Grinders
Drills	Auger bits
Glass cutters	Screwdrivers
Electric tools	Forged tools
Precision tools	Hacksaw blades
Braces	Hacksaw frames
Levels	

Repair parts really constitute a sixteenth line. Certain inexpensive tools are manufactured and identified separately from the above lines and might be said to constitute a seventeenth line. There are many different types and sizes of tools within these various lines. All lines together contain close to 2,000 items.

Within the company it is customary to group the above lines into three major classifications:

a. Hand tools
b. Hacksaws
c. Electric tools

About 18% of the business is done in hacksaws (frames and blades) and about 18% in electric tools. None of the lines within the hand tool classification approaches the hacksaw and electric tool classifications in volume.

The company makes high-quality tools primarily. It is known as a "quality" house. It does make some hand tools in a cheap grade, and at little or no profit, to meet the competition of the chain stores and mail-order houses in their cheap lines. This low-quality line has its own brand and is in no way identified as a Phoenix product. The salesmen are instructed not to push this line.

Branding. Most of the company's products carry the Phoenix brand. For years, the company has promoted this name as a symbol of quality, and executives believe that the reputation of "Phoenix" is one of the company's major assets. There are two types of exceptions to the use of the Phoenix name on company products.

1. The Perfection Brand is retained on a few items. At the time the Perfection Tool Company was purchased, a major decision

was made not to continue the promotion of both the Perfection and the Phoenix brand, even though "Perfection" enjoyed a very good trade name on certain lines. It was felt that promotion of a single name would, in the long run, give the company greater strength than would attempts to spread its resources over a second brand. Nevertheless, the company was anxious not to lose sales volume, and the Perfection name has continued to be used on some products. Perfection products were especially important for the export business where limited contact with customers makes it difficult to transfer their allegiance to the Phoenix brand.

Curtailing the use of the Perfection brand name has enabled the company to reduce the number of items in its lines. At the time of the merger there was much duplication, whereas now a given type of product will be made at only one of the two factories.

2. None of the lower quality products carry the Phoenix brand. Various names are used on these items, depending upon market strategy, and occasionally the private brands of important jobbers or the mail-order customers are used for large orders from these sources.

Distribution. The principal users of Phoenix products are factories and artisans, such as plumbers, contractors, and carpenters. These consumers are generally interested in Phoenix quality, dependability, and availability of repair parts. The household market is not as important as the others.

The company faces considerable competition on each of its lines. While some of these competitors make as broad a line as Phoenix, in each of the lines there are from two to twelve competitors who concentrate on that line alone.

Hand tools. Hand tool lines are sold through a variety of middlemen: hardware jobbers, mill supply jobbers, electric goods jobbers, plumbing supply jobbers, marine jobbers, and automotive goods jobbers. As the names imply, these various jobbers cater to particular segments of the market. The company follows the typical industry practice of selling its products to as many different jobbers as are willing to handle the line.

According to Dun & Bradstreet, the median ratios for hardware jobbers over the past five years have been: net profit on sales— 2.12%; net sales to inventory—4.2; and net sales to tangible net worth—3.19.

In addition to the use of jobbers, the company sells to one of the largest mail-order houses and to a few small chains. One chain of 200 stores in Chicago and vicinity was sold because the jobbing representative there did not seem to be getting the sales volume it should. Although the jobber threatened to throw out the line if the chain store was allowed to handle the line, he did not do so, and in fact he increased his sales of Phoenix products. However, a competitor of the Phoenix company that took the same step was induced, through the threats of dropping his line, to confine his sales to the jobbing house.

This question of whether to sell to chains is one of the most difficult ones faced by the company. Chain or syndicate buyers are becoming stronger all the time. On the Pacific Coast, for example, there are five syndicates with hundreds of stores. These organizations are anxious to handle the Phoenix line. Ten or twelve jobbers on the West Coast who work very closely together do not want the company to sell to these syndicates. The jobbers claim that chain stores resort to price-cutting to increase their share of the market, use some items as "loss leaders" thus making them unprofitable and disrupting the market, and exert great pressure on the manufacturer to lower his prices to the chains once they have become his major customers. Undoubtedly, hundreds of thousands of dollars of volume could be obtained in a fairly short time by selling to these chains and syndicates.

Prior to the merger, the Perfection Company sold directly to retailers. Naturally this policy was looked upon with disfavor by jobbers. When the Phoenix Company bought the Perfection Company, it decided to discontinue this type of distribution and dropped the 4,500 Perfection retail accounts, along with most of the Perfection salesmen. The retailers expressed dislike for this change, but for the most part they now carry the Phoenix lines.

Hacksaws. The hacksaw line is sold through distributors who have exclusive territories. They sell this particular group of Phoenix products, along with other non-competing products, to industrial users. The Phoenix Company supplements their efforts with specialty salesmen who work with potential users of the products and try to get them to place orders through the distributor. These men are technically trained and are able to offer expert advice to the industrial concerns.

Electric tools. The electric tool line is sold in the same manner as hacksaws. Here again the company feels that it can secure the greatest volume by a distinct kind of sales effort and use of specialized knowledge.

Export sales. About 20% of the company's business is secured from foreign countries. The company has its own agent in England. In all other countries it sells through representatives who sell on a commission basis.

Advertising and pricing. The Phoenix Company issues a catalog describing its entire line, in a large trade edition and in a small trade and consumer edition, every three years. It also publishes a special Electric Tool Catalog. In addition, it advertises in trade papers (such as *Hardware Age, Hardware World, Mill and Factory, Mill Supplies,* and *American Exporter*), by direct mail, and with window and counter displays. It prints some pages to be inserted in jobbers' catalogs.

Prices are quoted in the catalogs. Distributors are given a discount sheet that shows the various discounts allowed on the various types of tools. The discounts range from 30% to 40%, with one exception where it is 50%. A few distributors, who sell but do not stock the line, receive only a 15% discount. Typically Phoenix products are sold to consumers at the list prices, but the company does not attempt to police the resale prices of its products.

Prices are in line with those of competitors, quality being equal. Frequently, when "price" competition arises, a new, cheaper item is introduced and the price on the established item is not lowered.

The mail-order business is obtained at regular jobbing prices except for some items especially designed for these outlets in which case the price quoted is somewhat lower. In general, the company believes that its selling costs to mail-order houses represent a 12½% saving as compared with selling costs of the line in general. The mail-order house does not feature cut prices on "Phoenix" products. When shipping costs are included, the mail-order price is only slightly below the suggested list price.

Credit management. Since customers are of two main types, credit problems are not identical. Mill-supply jobbers are prime risks so that investigation and losses are at a minimum. The main problems concern hardware wholesalers, and here losses run from ¼ to ½%. Credit terms are net 30 days with 2% for payment in 10 days. Receivables as a whole average 45 days' sales. Credit investigation involves a preliminary analysis based on Dun & Bradstreet's information; but since this is a year to a year and a half old, more recent data are needed. Although the company belongs to a hardware trade credit exchange, main dependence is placed on the salesmen. They receive credit training and are required to make out reports regarding the credit standing of their customers.

The treasurer would like to decrease receivables, even though these represent only 25% of current assets, since a large part of company assets must necessarily be tied up in inventories to supply adequately the many kinds of tools sold and since cash has always been in short supply. Reduction of the large inventory carried by Perfection before its acquisition helped somewhat with the cash problem, but most of the funds released from the decline in inventories were used to pay off a bank loan that financed the purchase.

An index of sales, from which price changes have been removed, is:

Current year 135
Past year 159
Previous year 156
Previous year 121
Eight years ago 100

REQUIRED: (a) Following its purchase of the Perfection Tool Company, the Phoenix Company had a choice of at least three methods of distribution that might be employed:

(1) Continuing to sell the output of the two companies through the same channels as before, that is, Phoenix products through jobbers and Perfection products direct to retailers.

(2) Selling all products direct to retailers.

(3) Selling all products through jobbers.

As stated in the case, the third method, with minor exceptions, was selected. In your opinion, did the Phoenix Company make the best choice? Give reasons.

(b) After reviewing policy on jobber-retailer channels, the executives have determined not to expand the manufacture and the sale of private-brand merchandise to additional chain outlets under any circumstances. Do you agree with this policy? Explain.

(c) The policy of confining distribution of the regular Phoenix brands to the jobber-retail channel is still under review. Would you advise the Phoenix Company to alter its traditional policy of refusing to sell its regular line to chain store organizations? Explain.

7 SALES POLICIES—PRICING

Need for pricing policies. The particular price at which a product is sold reflects numerous influences on the production and the distribution of the merchandise and on the desires of consumers for such products. Moreover, there are some legal restrictions on pricing policies. The final market price is the net result of these different forces.

This complexity of the pricing problem has led many managers to regard pricing as a subject that could be properly handled only on the basis of experience, and in some firms it is surrounded by an air of mystery not to be penetrated by analytical thinking. Actually, the very complexity of the problem makes necessary some general policies to guide executives in their daily actions.

The pricing policies of a company should be coordinated with its policies regarding products, customers, sales appeals, and sales promotion. If a company has decided to sell a product of high quality to a selective group of customers, obviously its pricing policy will differ from that of a company that has planned to sell products of lower quality to a wide range of customers. Thus, the pricing policies followed by the editors of a distinctive magazine like *Fortune* must differ considerably from those of the publisher of a "western thriller."

But even after the place of the product in the market has been decided, a whole set of questions regarding prices still calls for answers. The most important of these are:

1. What will be the general relationship to *prices of competing products?*
2. What will be the relation to *costs* of production and distribution?
3. How will *prices of specific items* in the company's line compare?
4. Will all customers be charged the same price; if not, on what basis will *differences* be established?
5. How often and under what conditions will prices be *changed?*

155

RELATION TO PRICES OF COMPETING PRODUCTS

Prices at which competitors offer similar goods or services always have a bearing on pricing policies. In comparing sales prices, a company should consider among other things the quality of its products and services in comparison with that of its competitors and the reaction of competitors to a price that is more or less than the prevailing market price.

Comparative quality and price. *Pricing of highly standardized products.* The quality of some products can be accurately and readily measured, and in such instances recognized grades may be established. For example, cotton, wheat, coffee, and certain minerals and chemicals are described with such accuracy that permanent variations from going prices in a market are impossible. Insofar as the quality varies, such products fall into different standard classifications for which there is a standard differential in price. Thus it is possible to fulfill a contract for future delivery of wheat or cotton by delivery of any standard quality, the price being adjusted a given number of "points" or fractions of a cent for any variation of this quality from the standard grade used in the future contract.

In somewhat the same way, pig iron is quoted at so much a ton; then, as the sulphur content increases, there is a corresponding reduction in price because this is considered an undesirable quality. If the content of manganese or other desired elements increases, the price is raised accordingly. Companies dealing in such products must anticipate prompt reaction of competitors if they deviate for long from the established price.

Differences in quality and services. For the vast majority of products, however, there are no commonly accepted standards of quality. In fact, the characteristics that constitute quality in many products depend upon the personal taste of individual customers and are not susceptible to accurate measurement. We all recognize that meals served by different restaurants may vary greatly in quality and that the quality of men's suits may vary because of differences in materials used and in workmanship. When formulating pricing policies for such products, a manager must consider any acknowledged differences in quality between his products and those of competitors.

Differences in services rendered also affect pricing policies. An independent grocer may deliver orders free of charge and permit his customers to run charge accounts until the end of the month. This service is different from that which the customer receives in a supermarket where the transaction is completed at the counter when the clerk exchanges a paper bag filled with groceries for a full cash payment. The service that a manufacturing concern renders its customers in such things as credits, deliveries, sales aids, and returned goods often varies as much as if not more than the service provided by retail stores to ultimate consumers.

When significant product or service differentiation is achieved, the company must decide whether (a) a higher price than that of competitive products will be charged, or (b) a comparable price will be set and the superior quality or service will be used as a means of building sales volume, or (c) a high price will be used initially to "skim the cream off the market" and then the price will be cut to competitive levels. The choice of one of these alternatives depends, in part, upon how long the distinctiveness can be maintained, how much premium consumers are willing to pay for the superior quality, and how much unit costs would drop if volume rather than a higher price is sought.

Reaction of competitors. In establishing a pricing policy, a company must take into consideration not only the immediate effect of a price above or below the prevailing market, but also the reaction of competitors to such a price. For example, a company by establishing a price below the market may secure a temporary increase in sales volume; but it may lead competitors to lower their prices, which in turn will result in a general lowering of the prevailing market prices. As a consequence, the original company will gain a little in additional sales volume but will have to be satisfied with a lower profit.

Sensitivity of markets. At the peak of a recent business cycle, for example, a number of textile companies had excessive inventories of sheets that they were having difficulty in selling because their retailers were facing a declining consumer demand and wished to reduce inventories already on their shelves. There was not an immediate and drastic reduction in price because each manufacturer recognized that his competitors would probably match any reduction he might make and thereby eliminate his competitive advantage. Actually, the pressure for sales was so acute in this case that the wholesale price eventually did fall approximately 20% in the course of a six-month period.

An example of a similar situation in the retail field is the price of gasoline. If any one of the large oil companies cuts its retail price, it can be reasonably sure that there will be a corresponding and immediate reduction in the prices of competitors' products and a "price war" may result.

If the quality of the goods is quite indeterminate and customers cannot easily compare price schedules, the reaction of competitors may be much slower. They may decide to permit a differential in prices to exist on the assumption that the demand for their products will not be materially affected by the lower price of the competitor. In the same way, they may not follow a competitor in an increase in price.

Influence of size of company quoting low prices. The effect of a price change on competitors will depend partly on the size of the company. Price changes by a large and dominant firm in an industry are very likely to affect the prices of the entire industry. For example, in the farm-machinery industry all small companies follow the leadership of one or two large companies in pricing. On the other hand, it is sometimes possible for a small company to quote prices lower than those of its large competitors because its total sales volume is not important enough to the large company to warrant an adjustment of its entire price schedule. In the steel industry, for example, several small concerns have been able to increase their business by shading the prices quoted by the leading companies.

Price agreements among competitors. In some industries a company's freedom to adjust its prices upward or downward, and particularly downward, is restricted. This restriction may be imposed by a voluntary agreement among all vendors that prices will not be changed or by the control that a single company or group of men exercise over all important vendors in the industry. Any such price control that prevents free competition is a violation of our federal antiturst laws and is subject to criminal prosecution. It is also contrary to the theory of free competition on which our business structure is based. Surprisingly enough, there are businessmen who willingly become a party to a price-control agreement and who at the same time object to government interference with a competitive system of business. The pricing policy of any company in an industry in which there is even partial monopoly control over prices must be adjusted in recognition of these facts.

RELATION TO COSTS

Companies that have some discretion in pricing their product above or below the market frequently establish a general policy regarding the relation of price to cost. In this connection they consider selling products at a price that permits a normal profit above cost, selling below cost, and the effect of volume on cost and profit.

Selling at a normal profit above cost. *Effect of high profit margins.* Many managers state that they establish prices covering all costs of production and distribution plus a normal profit. Even assuming that the total cost attributable to a particular product can be determined, there still remains the question as to what constitutes a normal profit. One is tempted to believe that the profit margin will be made as large as possible without inviting competition within the field. The steel industry, for example, has followed a policy of maintaining prices at comparatively stable levels during depressions as well as periods of prosperity. When operating at a reasonable volume, these prices permit the large steel companies to realize a "normal" profit. Actually, the price has been so high that new producers have been able to enter the field and capture part of the business. In this instance maintenance of prices by large companies is said to have provided an "umbrella" under which the small companies have developed until they were strong enough to offer serious competition.

A somewhat similar situation arose in one of the food industries during a period of falling prices. The cost of raw materials declined substantially, but the selling prices of the finished products were not reduced significantly. This resulted in a larger profit margin for the producers. In fact, the profits were so handsome that several new competitors entered the field and secured a significant share of the market by offering goods at prices below those of the established concerns. The older companies finally recognized what was happening and reduced their prices to a point where additional companies would have difficulty in breaking into the market.

Therefore, if a company is in a position to establish prices on the basis of total cost plus normal profit, it should consider the effect of such prices on future competition.

Selling below cost. *Pricing on the basis of out-of-pocket expenses.* There are a number of conditions that may lead a company to establish prices below the total cost of a product. Every firm has certain expenses such as interest, rent, and executive salaries that must be paid regardless of the volume of sales. Other costs, such as materials and direct labor, vary with the volume of products manufactured. These latter costs are sometimes called *out-of-pocket expenses,* and it is rarely desirable for a company to produce and sell merchandise below the total of such costs. There is, however, a general zone between the out-of-pocket expenses and the total cost including overhead items. Under some conditions companies may establish prices within this range.

There is a strong feeling in many industries against selling goods at a price below the total cost. The manager of a printing establishment, for instance, recognized that he might secure additional business if he reduced his price to slightly more than his out-of-pocket expenses, but he refused to do so because he did not want to "spoil the market." He pointed out that if he reduced his price, competitors might follow suit and soon all business would have to be taken at the low price. Moreover, after the price had once been generally used throughout the market, it would be difficult to return it to the present level. In other words, pricing followed at one time may materially affect the price structure for subsequent sales.

Liquidation of inventory. When goods are already produced and on hand in the form of finished inventory, it is occasionally desirable to sell them below cost. In fact, it may be desirable in special circumstances to sell such merchandise at a substantial sacrifice. A lamp manufacturer, for example, had exhausted his cash resources and needed funds for taxes and notes at the bank. Unless he secured capital from some source, bankruptcy appeared inevitable. Under these circumstances the inventory was sold at a very low price in order to raise cash.

Even firms in a strong financial condition sometimes follow a policy of selling inventory for any price it will bring. Thus, if a general decline in prices is anticipated, a firm may be better off to dispose of its stock immediately rather than carry it over a period when prices are even lower. A similar situation sometimes arises for firms handling perishable merchandise or goods that will soon pass out of style or become obsolete. A manufacturer of men's suits, for example, followed a policy of selling all regular numbers at prices that were at least equal to the total production cost, but any inventory of suits dropped from the regular line was sold (with the brand label removed) at whatever price was necessary in order to secure an immediate sale.

Some firms have a policy that their first-quality, branded goods will be sold only at a fixed price. Hence, when they want to liquidate inventory, they have to remove all brand identification and often they use entirely different outlets. Second-quality merchandise, soiled goods, and odd lots may also be sold at below-average unit costs; here again some unknown brand label is often used to avoid "spoiling the market" for the regular line.

Loss leaders. Still another reason retail stores sometimes sell below cost is to attract customers to the store. In such cases one or more standard products are sold at a loss, which loss it is hoped will be more than offset by the profit on the sale of other merchandise to the customer while he is in the store or on subsequent visits resulting from the contact established by the special sale. In many states there is agitation to prohibit the use of loss leaders, but from a strictly business point of view it is difficult to see any valid distinction between incurring a loss on certain types of merchandise and spending money for other forms of advertising. (Misrepresenting the reasons for selling below cost or selling below cost for the purpose of eliminating competition are already contrary to federal law.)

Occasionally companies will sell some minor item at a price below the total cost just to render a service to their regular customers. This may be done on a certain part of the product, or it may be done on a particular item necessary to complete the line. Such a practice is distinct from loss leaders in that it is done as an accommodation and is not featured.

Effect of volume on costs and profits. *Variations in average unit costs.* Thus far we have assumed that costs were fixed and could be easily measured. In many companies, however, the total cost of products varies with the volume sold. A partially filled motion picture theater, for example, may handle a substantial increase in patrons with little change in total operating cost. In the production of many metal products, the cost of making dies and setting up machinery for production is often half of the total expense of producing a normal volume. This fixed expense will remain the same whether the volume is cut in half or doubled. Thus, there will be a substantial variation in the *average cost per unit.*

The producer of a high-class automobile estimated that it would just be able to cover the costs of production with the income from the sale of 1,800 cars. If the sales volume was 2,000 cars with no change in price, a profit of at least $100,000 would be earned. The actual sales volume of approximately 1,400 cars resulted in a loss substantially larger than this amount because the total cost could not be reduced in proportion to the decline in volume, and consequently the average cost per unit increased. Most companies have at least some overhead expenses that will not vary with changes in volume, and they also have other expenses that will vary only to a small degree. Such costs tend to make the average total cost per unit increase or decrease with opposite changes in volume.

It should be noted that the foregoing tendency holds true only when the production capacity of facilities is not fully used. If a motion picture theater, for instance, had to build an addition and increase its staff of attendants in order to handle additional customers, its profit on each customer might not increase at all. In the same way, so long as the tire company described in Chapter 6 could produce tires for the mail-order house with its existing facilities, an increase in business from this source permitted it to spread a fixed overhead over a larger volume of buiness. When the augmented volume made necessary an enlargement of the plant, the overhead was substantially increased and consequently the added business did not result in a reduction in the total unit costs.

There are, of course, many companies in which the fixed expenses are comparatively small and consequently the unit costs do not change greatly with the changes in volume. For example, the expenses of a commission merchant dealing in fruits and vegetables consist largely of material costs.

Costs will also vary because of many other factors, such as changes in prices paid for raw materials, variations in the efficiency of the employees, and increased or decreased selling and promotion expense. All of these factors should be considered by an executive in estimating the cost for various volumes of business.

Estimating profits for different price levels. When the cost varies with the volume, the manager should estimate the quantity of merchandise that can be sold at different prices; the effect of change in volume on the cost of goods produced as well as upon the cost of selling; and the combined effect of changes in the price, the volume, and the cost on the total net profits.

A hypothetical illustration will serve to indicate the possible variations resulting from changes in price. A company may be able to sell 800 dresses at $10 a dress. By reducing the price to $9, 1,200 dresses may be sold; and at a price of $8, 2,000 dresses may be sold. Additional reductions in price may increase the demand for the product further. The possible effects of variations in price on the sales volume, the cost, and the net results are shown in the following table.

The Effect of Price on Volume, Cost, and Profit

(1) Price	(2) Number of Units Sold	(3) Cost per Unit	(4) Profit per Unit	(5) Total Profit (2) x (4)
$10	800	$7.00	$3.00	$2,400
9	1,200	5.75	3.25	3,900
8	2,000	5.50	2.50	5,000
7	2,500	5.40	1.60	4,000
6	3,000	5.30	.70	2,100

It will be noted that the cost per unit decreased as the volume increased. As already pointed out, many companies find that the average cost of producing and distributing products falls when the total volume of business is expanded. In most instances, however, unit costs do not decline as rapidly as the prices must be reduced in order to secure the additional volume. Consequently, the *profit per unit* diminishes as is indicated in Column 4.

Profit per unit, however, is not the final answer regarding the desirability of a particular price because recognition must be given to the number of units on which this profit is earned. Thus, if an increase in price results in a significantly higher profit per unit and a comparatively small reduction in volume (from $7 to $8 in the illustration), the total profit will be increased. But if the drop in volume is sharp, it may more than offset the higher profit per unit (from $8 to $9 in the illustration).

Factors affecting response of volume to changes in price. The total profit secured at each price, as can be seen by the preceding table, depends upon the volume of sales as well as the average cost per unit. Clearly, the manager must estimate as best he can not only the effect of volume on the total cost but also the volume of sales that will be secured at different prices. In actual practice the response of volume to price changes depends upon many factors, some of which are considered in the following discussion.

The *reaction of competitors to price changes* by one company is an important factor to be considered. If an entire industry acts almost simultaneously in the adjustment of any price, then there is little reason to assume that one company will gain volume at the expense of its competitors because of the price change. Only if the entire volume of the industry expands or contracts because of the price change is it reasonable to assume that there will be a significant change in the volume of a specific company. If, on the other hand, price advances or reductions are not copied by competitors, then a company can consider the demand for its own products.

Another factor in the response of volume to price changes is the *elasticity of the demand.* We have observed that if a retail store has a big sale with prices on standard articles significantly reduced, the volume of sales will be greatly expanded. In fact, the sale of certain articles will be doubled and trebled. The use of synthetic fibers has expanded greatly as its real price has declined. On the other hand, a doctor would not greatly increase the volume of his business if he were to make a 25% reduction in his charges, nor would an electric power company sell much more current for household use if it were to make a similar reduction in its rates.

The behavior of the price of one product may affect the response of volume to price changes in another product. Packing companies have observed that if the price of pork falls while the price of beef remains constant, there will be a significant increase in the consumption of pork. Should beef prices decline at the same time pork prices are reduced, there will be a much smaller expansion in the volume of pork consumed.

Professional buyers for industrial concerns, as well as retail stores, *adjust the volume of their purchases to anticipated prices* as well as to changes that have actually occurred. Thus, if a company reduces its price and the buyer anticipates that this is just the beginning of a series of price reductions, he may actually diminish his volume rather than increase it. Contrariwise, if an increase in price is interpreted as a sign of future scarcity of goods, the buyer may place large orders so as to be assured of an adequate supply at the current market price. This is one of the reasons for temporary spurts in business activities during periods of business prosperity and a sharp contraction in activity when a decline in prices is anticipated.

There are other influences that may affect the response of volume to price changes in a particular industry. The complexity of the problem is due not only to the numerous influences that may affect the response of volume to price, but also to the fact that it is difficult to obtain adequate information. Often the short-run adjustments to a price change are quite different from those that will occur in the long run after costs and volumes are well known.

Composite policies. Often companies use both competitors' prices and their own costs in formulating their general pricing policy. A local manufacturer of electrical fixtures who uses price as a sales appeal, for example, follows a policy of (a) 10% below prices of a well-known competitor, except (b) this differential is narrowed to avoid selling below "cost" (total manufacturing costs at estimated sales volume), and (c) sales below "cost" are made only temporarily to close out an item or to combat a "price leader" of a competitor. In contrast, a company producing high-quality, shortwave intercommunication systems relies on technical service and quality to attract customers. This firm normally quotes prices on the basis of total engineering, manufacturing, and selling costs (with a liberal allowance for overhead) plus 10%. However, downward adjustments are made when it is known that the normal price is more than 20% above either of two reputable competitors.

POLICIES REGULATING PRICES OF INDIVIDUAL ITEMS

Price lining. If a company sells several different grades of same product, the price of one grade must be established in relation to the prices of the other grades. This problem often becomes important in department stores where a rather wide selection of each type of merchandise is handled. Some stores have established a definite policy of carrying only one or two styles of a certain product at each price level. Furthermore, they attempt to have prices spread throughout the range from the highest to the lowest rather than concentrated at some points and having wide gaps at others.

Manufacturers that sell their products under several brand names, only one of which is advertised, must decide on the differential between the advertised brand and the unadvertised brands. If there is a significant difference between the products, then each may be priced on the basis of its particular market and its costs. When the products are similar and are available to the same customers, the problem becomes more delicate. Some obvious characteristic of the product must be different if the higher-priced line is to continue to sell. Surprisingly enough, this variation may consist of a relatively unimportant change such as the kind of finish or the addition of a special gadget—for example, more chrome trim on an automobile.

Several manufacturers have a regular line of products and a deluxe line; and if price competition is keen they may add a "fighting brand," which is the basic product stripped of almost all the surface features that give extra convenience or attractiveness to the regular line. Thus, product design and pricing policy are coordinated so that the company can tap several different segments of the total market.

Using accepted market prices. For some types of merchandise there are well-established prices in the market. For instance, women are accustomed to buy hosiery at standard prices, such as $1.15, $1.35, or $1.50 a pair. These prices are so generally accepted that the volume of sales secured at $1.29 a pair is often less than the volume for identical hosiery at $1.35 a pair.

A company confronted with a standard price structure must decide whether it accepts the customary price ranges. The Hershey Chocolate Corporation dealt with this problem by *varying the size* of its chocolate bars retailed at the standard prices of 5 and 10 cents. Small companies, in particular, usually find that they secure better results by improving the quality of their product or the services rendered rather than by cutting prices below the accepted amount.

DIFFERENT PRICES FOR DIFFERENT CUSTOMERS

The "one-price policy." Every enterprise must decide whether its products will be sold at the same price to all customers. In the United States the so-called one-price policy has wide acceptance, particularly in retail transactions. Retail stores typically have a set price marked on the merchandise, and every customer coming into the store must pay this set price. In fact, an American is frequently at a loss when buying goods in foreign countries where dealers name a high price and expect to haggle before the sale is finally made.

The horse-trading days in the United States, however, are by no means over. New automobile prices are not rigidly fixed, and the secondhand market and trade-in values retain many opportunities for deception and bargaining. A wholesale fruit company considered a one-price policy but rejected the plan because the prices in the market changed so frequently and the products were so prishable that standardization of prices would have prevented the flexibility for success in this type of business.

Discounts from established prices. Many manufacturers and other concerns wish to have the benefits of a one-price policy, but they find it desirable to have different prices for different types of customers. This is often accomplished by maintaining a list price and then granting discounts to certain classes of customers.

Discounts are necessary when a company wishes to sell to wholesalers as well as retailers. The wholesaler performs services for which he must be paid, and unless he can buy products for a lower price than the retailer, his resale price will be so high he cannot get business. This need for *trade discounts* is generally recognized, but there is much debate as to how large such discounts should be and who are entitled to them. For example, one firm with three retail stores set up a "wholesale department" in an attempt to get an extra 20% discount. Most manufacturers would refuse to grant a wholesaler's discount to such a firm because it is not really performing wholesaling functions. In some industries, such as tires, it is a common policy to have a whole series of discounts that presumably reflect the differences in actual services performed by the various distributors. Clearly, a company's discount policy will have a marked effect on its success in winning patronage from different types of customers and hence should be coordinated with customer policies.

Quantity discounts are commonly offered to anyone who purchases in large volume. Here, again, the difficult questions are under what conditions the discounts will be granted and how large they should be. Large customers may be so important to a company that there is a temptation to give them very high discounts. Under existing legislation, however, quantity discounts are limited to actual savings in producing and selling the larger orders.

There are, of course, other forms of discounts such as cash discounts and advertising allowances that are not intended to be price reductions. In actual practice, however, they are sometimes so large and are granted in such a way that their effect is a price reduction in a somewhat disguised form.

In addition, a company may offer price concessions in an effort to build up volume in slack periods. A 10% discount for early orders of Christmas cards is not uncommon; moving picture theaters have lower prices in the afternoons; electric utility companies offer special "off peak" rates. When a well-recognized policy has been set up, such discounts can be granted without upsetting the basic price structure.

Regional differences in prices. Still another pricing problem deals with regional differences in prices. If the cost of shipping the finished goods from the plant to the customer is a significant part of the cost, as is true for most heavy or bulky articles, this problem can hardly be avoided. If the manufacturer receives a uniform price, then customers in more distant locations will have to pay more for delivered merchandise than will customers located closer to the source of supply. On the other hand, if the manufacturer pays the freight, he will receive a lower *net price* from the most distant customer.

The policy of many companies is to absorb most or all of the shipping costs to distant customers whenever a competitor is located in that territory. In some cases the courts have ruled, however, that this is an unfair price discrimination and there are legal questions as to how far a company may go in regional pricing. Clearly, if a producer with excess capacity wants to sell products in a highly competitive, distant market at a *lower* price than he charges in his local area, he will be on sounder ground if he differentiates the products sold in the two areas.

PRICE CHANGES

Markdowns in retail stores. There is wide variation in the frequency with which companies change their prices. Prestige stores that feature the quality of their merchandise and service rather than price may not take markdowns as rapidly as the stores that feature popular-priced merchandise because their sales will not respond as quickly to price reductions. Such stores are more likely to reduce their prices only for semiannual clearance sales.

In popular-priced department stores and specialty shops, prices on style merchandise are reduced as soon as it appears that the stock on hand will not be sold by the end of the current season. Sometimes more than one reduction is necessary. For this purpose Mr. Filene, of the Wm. Filene's Sons Co., one of the leading department stores of Boston, Massachusetts, developed a novel plan under which merchandise was placed in the basement and reduced 25% after the second week. If it was not sold during the third week, another 25% reduction was made, and again after the fourth week, at which time the price was 25% of the original figure. All merchandise left after the fifth week was given to charity.

Difficulty of changing widely announced prices. Not all companies are in a position to make such frequent adjustments in their prices. Many companies selling industrial goods distribute a printed price list to potential customers and it is not expedient to change such prices frequently. An increase in price is likely to cause dissatisfaction on the part of customers who have been relying upon the printed list, and even a decrease may cause some confusion in ordering and billing. In somewhat the same way, the large mail-order houses cannot readily adjust prices for at least a season once their catalogs are distributed. Automobile companies, likewise, hesitate to change prices for a particular model once the price has been publicly announced.

Price protection. Changes in prices on industrial raw materials create a special problem because these products are often an important item of cost to the customers. To get orders on the books and thus facilitate production planning and also to assure the customer of a supply of material at a known price, it is customary to place orders for such material a long period in advance. The order specifies the price and protects the customer against an increase in the price of his raw materials. In practice, the customer is often permitted to cancel his contract if the price falls. Thus, he is in a position to take advantage of a falling price or to protect himself against an increase in price as circumstances may warrant. The raw material producer follows such a pricing policy because it is the only way he can secure advance orders that greatly assist his production scheduling, and also because it is necessary if the goodwill of the customer is to be maintained.

Price protection is also granted by some manufacturers to wholesalers and retail dealers. In such instances if prices are reduced, the manufacturer agrees to reimburse the dealer for the nominal loss in inventory value he suffers as a result of the price reduction. Tire companies, for example, have found it necessary to protect their dealers against price reductions in order to encourage the dealers to carry a complete stock. Such a practice obviously is important in maintaining a dealer's goodwill, for otherwise he might feel that the manufacturer had loaded him up with stock and then caused him to take a loss in order to compete with other dealers who held off buying until the new prices were in effect.

In almost every instance the handling of a price change may create complications, and recognized policies are often essential if the transition to the new price level is to be accomplished smoothly.

SUMMARY

Every company needs policies covering the prices to be charged for its products and services. Often the setting of these price policies is one of the most complex problems central management faces.

An orderly approach to pricing has been suggested in this chapter. First, policies regarding the basic level of company prices should be considered. The policies are usually expressed in terms of relationships with prices of competing products and relationships with company costs. Then policies dealing with pricing of specific items and "price lining" should be set. Closely related are policies regarding price differentials for various types of customers;

there will be need for standing answers to questions regarding trade discounts, quantity discounts, freight and advertising allowances, and similar adjustments to list prices.

Once a price structure is established, there is the further issue of how often and under what conditions prices will be changed. Warning of price increases and protection from price cuts are often important in relations with customers.

Throughout this discussion of pricing policies frequent reference has been made to the quality and variety of all products in the company lines, the types and sizes of customers sought, and the nature of company services and other sales appeals, as well as to many factors affecting company costs. Clearly, pricing policies are intimately connected with other policies; final pricing decisions should not be made until their repercussions on all company operations have been considered.

QUESTIONS FOR CLASS DISCUSSION

1. A large department store in Cincinnati with a reputation for quality found its appliance business hit hard by discount houses. The merchandise manager received three main policy proposals from other executives: (a) "Sell at discount prices and let the manufacturers clean up the price-cutting." (b) "Sell only big-ticket items that require product knowledge and some special sales effort to help the customer. Do away with items she can buy on price only." (c) "Continue to sell these products but do not advertise, promote, or display them. Have them available if customer want them and will not buy our private brands." How should the merchandise manager proceed?

2. At one time when its output was 85% of capacity (equal to the industry average), a major aluminum producer found its profits shrinking because costs had risen steadily while its prices of ingots had remained stable for two years. Mindful of events prior to 1962 when a 3¢ per pound higher price had clearly prevented industry expansion, executives hesitated. The last price decrease had increased sales 5% and cut profits 23%. Was this now the time to increase prices by 2½%?

3. Following the last war, Marine Trampship, Limited, of England owned and operated five freighters specially designed to carry certain types of war cargo. The boats were slow and not very efficient in carrying peacetime goods, and within a few years they were operating at a substantial loss. Estimates showed that a cut in freight rates might increase the volume of business but that, even with the increased volume, depreciation and interest on the capital investment would not be earned; consequently, the vessels were sold at substantially below their book value to a Greek concern.

The Greek concern proceeded to cut the freight rates to a point where the vessels were kept reasonably busy. Marine Trampship, Limited, protested strongly against the low rates. The Greek concern replied that, because of the low purchase price and the resulting low depreciation and interest, it was able to operate at these low rates and show a profit.

Assuming equal efficiency of operation, should Marine Trampship, Limited, have sold the vessels or should it have cut rates to the same level as the Greek concern did?

4. A southern shipyard, faced with keen foreign competition and declining shipbuilding in the United States, was invited to bid on three new freighters. With jigs and tooling remaining from a similar job, it had an estimated 2% (of bid price) cost advantage over two competing yards. These yards had bid in at 9.2% and 9.3% profit margins on several recent bids. But a third competing yard decided to bid and little was known or could be found out of its past actions. Should the southern shipyard bid in at 5% profit at which it would be almost certain to win the contract or should it bid at a higher margain and how much higher?

5. In the automobile tire business, wages constitute approximately 15%, materials 43%, and overhead 42% of the total costs. The typical costs of sugar refining are labor 4%, materials 85%, and overhead 11% of the total costs. Suppose that the X Tire Company and the Y Sugar Company each suffered a $33\frac{1}{2}$% decline in volume of business. Which company would have the largest increase in average total unit costs? Should each company raise its prices to cover the increased costs? Why?

6. One basic assumption typically made in economic theory is that a company meets competition by raising or lowering its prices. (a) How may a company meet competition aside from adjusting its prices? (b) Why might a company prefer not to alter its prices each time there is some change in its local supply or demand situation?

7. (a) The Novins Wallpaper Company grants the following discounts from its list prices: paper hangers, 34%; retail dealers, 50%; local jobbers, 66%; and distributors, 80%. Do you think the company is guilty of unfair price discrimination?

(b) For a given type of customer, for example a jobber, prices are uniform across the country. Is this unfair discrimination against customers close to the plant?

8. What connection may there be between a company's policy to sell above, at, or below the market and its policy regarding national advertising?

9. Block Ice Cream Company sold soft ice cream from highway stands. It proposed to multipack assorted parfaits in polyethylene bags for take-out and home consumption. Single units sell at the stands for $.20. The proposed pack is six for $1. The advertising manager objected: "$1 is too high a price and six is too many. It should be two for $.39 or maybe four for $.69." The decision hinged on what was the "right" price. Would it be more comfortable and easier to pay $.39 or $.69 or $1.00? "Consider the psychology of the husband and father providing for the family or taking the kids out for a big treat," said the advertising manager.

CASE VII

Andersen Starch Company

The Andersen Starch Co. is one of several manufacturers, importers, and sales agents of starch products and dextrines. The company has carried on profitable operations for many years and currently is a leading supplier to the paper industry, textile manufacturers, foundries, bakers, confectioners, corrugated box manufacturers, carpet mills, manufacturers of pharmaceuticals, soap manufacturers, and furniture manufacturers.

Among the products merchandised are corn starch, tapioca flour, potato starch, wheat starch, dextrines (converted from all of the above starches), sago flour, and natural gums. For many years, some of these products have been sold to wholesale and large retail grocers. Included among the Andersen Co. customers are Alpha Supermarkets, First Union Stores, and Grand National Groceries, Inc. These three concerns are among the most profitable and aggressive food distributors in the country and have large capital investments in the most modern plants and equipment that can be purchased. All of them have extensive laboratory facilities and are well staffed with research and development personnel.

Recently a competitor of these firms introduced a pudding using a starch base that gained immediate consumer acceptance throughout the country. The techniques of manufacturing this starch base are different from any used by the three firms in making products sold under their private brand labels, and special equipment is required to produce it. As a result, the three firms individually approached the Andersen Co. and requested assistance in the development of a competitive product that could be sold under their private brands.

Since the research department of Andersen Co. had been working on problems closely related to the pudding, it was soon able to develop a base product that, when submitted to slight additional processing and packaging by the grocery firms, produced a superior competitive product. The long experience of the Andersen Co. in the field of starches and dextrines contributed significantly to the problem. Three important raw materials—potato starch, wheat starch, and tapioca starch—could be used alternately in the manufacture of the base depending upon their price and availability. Successful production of the starch pudding base required an exact knowledge of the markets for these three raw materials and skill in purchasing them. Such knowledge and skills were ordinarily only available in firms, such as Andersen, that dealt to a major extent with starches and dextrines.

The quantities required by Alpha, First Union, and Grand National were far in excess of the available production capacity in the Andersen factory. To meet the demand, a large capital investment in new processing equipment was necessary. The Andersen management committee decided to proceed with an investment in equipment to the limit of the company's current ability to finance the investment. Enough equipment was acquired to process 3½ million pounds per year of the starch base, 80% of the total pounds that the three concerns desired to purchase during the coming year.

Once the decision to buy the equipment was made, it immediately became necessary for the management committee to make a policy decision on pricing the product.

Should the starch pudding base be classified as a specialty and be priced accordingly, or should it be considered a bulk commodity? As a specialty, a profit margin of 4½ cents per pound would be established on top of a cost of manufacturing and selling of $9.75 per 100 pounds. A decision to price as a bulk commodity would mean that an average margin of 60 cents per 100 pounds would be established on a current cost of $9.75 per 100 pounds. Margins of these sizes were consistent with those of other Andersen products. Such prices would be f.o.b. the plant. These prices would enable the company to recapture its capital investment in 8 months in the case of a specialty price and in 5 years in the case of a bulk commodity price.

The new pudding introduced by the competitor of Alpha Supermarkets, First Union Stores, and Grand National Groceries, Inc. has put these firms at a considerable competitive disadvantage and they are now pressing the Andersen Co. for as much output as possible. In an attempt to secure large quantities of the starch pudding base, Alpha has offered Andersen a contract to cover output for the next 18 months. The contract, which is typical of those this grocery firm is willing to offer and sign, calls for delivery of a minimum of 1 million pounds and a maximum of $2\frac{1}{2}$ million pounds at a firm price. Alpha is to be protected against a decline in the market price through a provision that Andersen meet any lower price offered by competitive suppliers of the starch product base. Should the estimates of consumer market acceptability prove too high, Alpha can reduce the quantity specified. The other firms are also anxious to sign contracts to obtain a supply of the base and are willing to contract for delivery of 1 to $1\frac{1}{2}$ million pounds per year each.

Since demand for the base is currently so large, the Andersen management committee has considered the possibility that the grocery firms will install their own facilities for producing the starch product. It is definitely known that these firms could not get into production for another eighteen months. The management committee is almost certain that Grand National Groceries will continue to purchase from Andersen and will not install its own equipment. The behavior of the other two firms cannot be forecast with any degree of certainty. It is known that, in the past, Alpha has purchased new items introduced by others, has watched the sales of such items and, if the sales proved sufficiently interesting has built its own facilities. This is the limit of the management committee's knowledge.

Other products besides this pudding base are sold to the three grocery firms and the management committee is anxious to do all it can to maintain good relations with these customers. Good will is important to the Andersen Co., and the company wants to protect its reputation for dealing fairly with its customers. However, since the grocery business is highly competitive, maintaining good relations is a very tricky and delicate matter at best. The pudding base is more important in volume than all of the other products sold to the three customers, for the dollar sales of all other items are probably less than 10% of the dollar sales of the starch base. If the base should continue to be produced by Andersen over a period of years, it would be a very important member of the total product line and possibly one of the big money-makers.

The Andersen management committee has a practice of considering projects such as the production and sale of the base entirely as individual matters. Installing the equipment and operating it to produce the pudding base is to be justified by the profits from this project only. Other uses for the machinery might be developed with a great deal of effort in an emergency situation, but it is felt that the possibility of such other uses should not enter into the original decision. Similarly, the committee believes this project should bear all the costs that can be charged to it under any reasonable accounting convention; the project should not be consid-

ered on an out-of-pocket basis. The management committee feels
that the costs cited earlier were established fairly and completely
on the basis of this policy.

In considering whether or not any one of the customers might
install its own facilities and then no longer purchase from Andersen, the management committee concluded that the customer might
well decide that its costs were less than the bulk commodity price
that Andersen might establish. This might occur because of the
method of allocation of overhead expenses used by the customer.
The management committee was certain that its costs were complete and that its bulk commodity price would be less than the production costs of any customer provided that customer's costs were
also complete.

The management committee felt that no matter which price of
the two Andersen established, the price charged by the grocery
firms to their customers would remain the same, since the final
starch product had to meet competitive prices of other brands and
also the competition of other types of foods.

REQUIRED: (a) What pricing policy do you recommend?

(b) What kind of price agreement should the Andersen Starch
Co. reach with the three customers?

CHAPTER 8

SALES POLICIES—
SALES PROMOTION

Product and customer policies define the economic service a company is to perform and the people who are to receive this service, Along with these vital decisions must be pricing policies, which set the monetary conditions of sales. These central issues, which every enterprise faces, have been discussed in the preceding chapters. There remains a fourth basic type of sales problem to be considered in this chapter—sales promotion.

The object of sales promotion is to induce the selected customers to buy the company products at its established prices. To achieve this end, the manager should assume the point of view of his customer and consider what actions the company should take to lead the customer actually to complete the purchase of the product. Key decisions in this area are:

1. Selecting *sales appeals* that are important to the customer.
2. Determining the use that will be made of *advertising*.
3. Deciding the role of *personal solicitation*.

SALES APPEALS

Most customers have an opportunity to purchase products from several companies. Consequently, a company must present some definite appeals to persuade the customer to purchase its products rather than those of a competitor. The most customary appeals are the following:

a. Price.
b. Service.
c. Quality.
d. Style or design.
e. Personality and ability of salesmen.
f. Reputation of the company.

Typical use of the price appeal. Price has some influence on the sale of all products. However, the emphasis that is placed on

177

price to secure the sale of an article varies greatly. Large mail-order houses stress the price appeal, and throughout their catalogs the price of each article is given a prominent place. The price appeal is also used by other types of business. In all large cities, for example, dry-cleaning establishments may be found that feature lower charges than those generally prevailing.

It is not necessary that a company offer products at the lowest price available in the market if its product is of higher quality than that of competitors. The consumer does not consider price alone; he thinks of price in relation to quality. For example, a really high-grade pair of shoes for $18 may have more price appeal than a low-quality pair marked at $11.50. In using the price appeal, most companies try not to give the impression that quality is sacrificed for price.

For some products the price appeal is not important, as a standard price may be used by all vendors. For example, there is no difference in the price of fresh milk delivered to your doorstep by any of the recognized dairies. For many years the prices asked for steel products at a given location have been the same for most producers. Consequently, in selling these products, appeal to the customer must be made on some basis other than price. Furthermore, high-quality products such as grand pianos sold to wealthy consumers cannot be sold on the basis of price. Thus, each company must have a policy as to the extent to which price will be used as a sales appeal for its products.

Services offered by retail stores. Service is used as a major appeal by many firms. We all recognize that the better-class department store provides free delivery throughout the local area as well as monthly charge account privileges to its regular customers. These two services, however, are only a beginning of things done for the convenience of the department store customer. One large store, for example, provides a parking service for customers who wish to drive to the shopping center. Hats, coats, and other articles may be checked inside the door in order that the customers may shop in comfort. If a mother's enthusiasm for "just looking around" is greater than her child's there is a supervised playroom where the child finds toys and slides and hobbyhorses to suit his fancy. Should the mother become weary or wish to meet a friend, convenient waiting rooms are available. Here may be found a general information booth, a telegraph office, a counter selling theater tickets, a travel bureau, a separate room with special desks for letter writing, and a small postal station close at hand. If the customer is unfamiliar with the store and wishes to purchase merchandise from several locations, a personal shopper is available to guide and assist her in her selections.

There are further shopping services created for the convenience of the shopper. Articles to be used as gifts are wrapped in fancy packages. If the gift is to be sent out of town, the store will ship it by parcel post, express, or freight. Should the customer need her purchase before the next day, a special-delivery service is available. Customers buying articles at several locations in the store may have them assembled and wrapped in a single package. Merchandise may be held with only a partial payment, and large durable articles may be purchased on deferred payments.

For the absent-minded, an anniversary desk keeps a record of Aunt Jenny's birthday, Clare's wedding anniversary, and similar occasions; telephones you in time to select a gift; and, on request, selects the gift for you. At the wedding bureau a bride learns the correct thing to do and, if she wishes, may leave the name of her silver and glass patterns for the benefit of her generous friends.

Regular customers are provided with a charga-plate that not only serves as identification but also may be used to stamp the customer's name and address quickly and accurately on the sales check without tedious spelling of a peculiar name. Any article of a type sold in the store may be brought in to be cleaned and repaired. If the customer has mislaid some personal article, the man at the lost and found desk lends willing assistance.

This list of services, which is by no means complete, illustrates the type of conveniences that this particular store is offering to its customers.

A discount house, by contrast, provides almost none of the services listed. And the suburban branches of department stores have cut back on the variety of accommodations provided. The policy issue is which service (and to what degree) are sufficiently attractive to the type of customers the store hopes to reach to justify their expense. The dramatic rise of discount houses and supermarkets indicates that the modern customer can do without many conveniences formerly provided. On the other hand, bankruptcies and trading-up within the discount-house group suggests that these institutions may have gone too far in stripping off service.

Other service policies. Industrial firms also stress service rendered to their customers. This frequently takes the form of prompt delivery or technical assistance in the use of their products. Air-conditioning companies, for example, use trained engineers as salesmen so that they may be able to advise the customer on air-conditioning problems. Some machinery manufacturers maintain a stock of repair parts for all equipment sold during the past thirty years.

Most companies are continuously seeking new types of service that will appeal to their customers and that may be rendered at comparatively low expense. Oil companies have stressed the point of rendering special services to customers and actually call their retail outlets "service stations." Manufacturers of electric driers and other mechanical articles provide free service for six months or a year. The extent to which a company can afford to give special services depends upon the amount of profit made on each sale and the importance of the service to the customer.

Quality as a sales appeal. The importance of quality in certain types of products has already been indicated in the discussion of product policies. Minimum quality standards are absolutely essential for many products. Certainly airplanes cannot be sold unless the quality of the workmanship and the dependability of the materials are beyond question. Most of us insist on high quality in any medicine that we buy; we like to have good quality in our clothing; and the quality of paper and ink in our shool work may be of some interest to us. In the purchase of medicines, quality is a very important appeal; whereas in the purchase of notebook paper, quality is likely to be subordinated to service and price.

Use of style and design in selling. Effective styling or designing is the crucial factor in the sale of some commodities. For example, a small brass company making hinges, handles, drawer pulls, and other metal trimmings for furniture found that there was almost no sale for poorly styled articles. A tool company making tools for farm use was successful in selling its products to amateur gardeners because it redesigned hand cultivators, lawn sprinklers, and other tools for this particular purpose. The style of wearing apparel obviously plays an important part in its salability.

It should be remembered that some classes of customers like extreme styles and insist on the latest thing, while others are attracted by more conservative styles. As was pointed out in an earlier chapter, style is playing an increasingly important part in the sale of even those products where convenience and economy in operation are usually considered to be the controlling factors.

Conditions in which salesmen are a controlling appeal. When price, quality, style, and service appeals of several vendors are approximately equal, the personality and the ability of the salesmen presenting the merchandise are likely to be a determining factor in the sale. We have noted that pig iron is sold at a uniform price by all vendors. It is one of the few products that completely lacks style (although a few companies feature the shape of a pig because of the effect on the rapidity with which it melts), and differences in service and quality are small if not entirely imaginary. Consequently the personality of salesmen representing the pig iron producers is likely to play an important part in the sale of the product.

A wholesale hardware company found it was in a somewhat similar position. Its line of products did not differ much from that of competing wholesalers. The salesman who got the order was likely to be the one most skilled in selling technique and best liked by the local retailers. Consequently, this company laid great stress on selection and training of its men.

A survey among housewives sponsored by a large dairy showed conclusively that the personality of the milkman, his care in filling orders accurately, and such little things as setting the milk inside the screen door or on the shady side of the porch were among the determining factors in the selection of a dairy.

Effect of a company's reputation upon sales. Banks, insurance companies, and other financial institutions must guard their reputations jealously because this is a major factor affecting the business they secure. Some manufacturers have developed a reputation for well-designed and reliable products and use this reputation as one of their important sales appeals. For example, there are several well-known manufacturers of electric refrigerators whose brand name adds a definite attractiveness to the product. In the same way the name of the manufacturer is likely to receive consideration in the purchase of a wrist watch. Canned fruit is sometimes purchased on the basis of the reputation of the canner, although much of it is selected on the recommendation of the retailer irrespective of its source. Retailers also may use their reputation as a sales appeal, some retailers being held in such high regard that gifts are purchased from them in order that the package may bear the retailer's name.

Other sales appeals. There are other sales appeals that may be used. Reciprocity, for instance, is frequently employed by industrial concerns that purchase supplies from companies which are also their customers. Professional purchasing agents strongly oppose use of reciprocity because substantially higher prices may have to be paid for items bought; consequently top management should weigh carefully the extent to which its use will be permitted.

Assistance in reselling, financial reliability, accessibility, and conspicuous consumption (prestige) are additional possible appeals.

No company can stress all the sales appeals we have discussed. Some are incompatible (for example, low price versus high quality and service); others are inappropriate; all involve some expense. In setting a policy on which appeals are to be emphasized, central management should consider, first, the product or the service—(its uses and distinctive characteristics), then the needs and the attitudes of the groups sought as customers, and finally how this company can differentiate itself from competitors.

ADVERTISING

Today we are bombarded on all sides by many types of advertising. No matter whether we walk on the streets, drive an automobile on the highways, ride a bus, watch television, read a newspaper or magazine, or open our mail, we are brought face to face with advertising. This creates a difficult situation for the manager, for he must determine what advertising on his part will justify its cost amid the bewildering array of advertisements by other companies. The major questions of policy with reference to advertising that the manager must answer are (a) the purposes for which it is to be used and (b) the media employed to accomplish these purposes.

Analysis shows that advertising is used for numerous purposes. It also shows that many companies have not given adequate thought to the question of exactly what they are trying to accomplish with their advertising. Let us, then, take a closer look at the major purposes of advertising.

Bringing customers to the place where goods are sold. Retail stores frequently use advertising for this purpose. In such cases the display of merchandise and the efforts of salesmen are depended upon to close the transaction. We are all familiar with advertisements of special drugstore sales that feature twenty-five or fifty different items. The store usually hopes to sell substantial quantities of the merchandise advertised; but more important, it hopes to get customers into the store so that they will buy other types of merchandise and will develop a habit of coming to that establishment for their subsequent requirements.

Department stores use advertising in a similar manner. Those stores that feature price appeal undertake extensive advertising of "economy day," "president's birthday," and pre-season or post-season sales. Stores desiring to use a prestige appeal may have the author of a popular book give a lecture or secure designers of furniture, dinnerware, or clothing to talk about these particular products. A number of stores provide space for local art exhibits or a showing of crown jewels; a pair of unusual and very expensive fur pelts or the elaborate doll houses of a well-known T.V. actress may be featured for the purpose of attracting customers to the store.

The point is well illustrated by a story told of two keen partners operating a store located in a very low-income neighborhood. Upon observing that a large number of customers were patronizing their near-by competitors, they set up a table filled with small articles, such as pickle forks, salt shakers, and cigarette holders. This table was placed near the front door where it would be passed by everyone entering or going out of the store. The sales of the articles proved to be very unprofitable, however, since they could easily be slipped into a pocket and the near-by door allowed easy escape for would-be purchasers. According to the story, however, there was a substantial increase in customer traffic. When asked to explain the situation one of the partners said, "We call that our steal table. We place ten dollars' worth of merchandise on the table each morning and know that most of it will have disappeared by evening, but when people come in to steal from this table, they have to act like customers and look at other merchandise, and sometimes they buy. They like to come to the store because they can go home with an extra ten-cent article that probably cost us three cents. All for ten dollars a day—it's cheap advertising."

Persuading the customer to ask for a specific product. Retailers use advertising for this purpose to some degree, but it is probably used to the greatest extent by a manufacturer who wishes to create consumer demand, or at least consumer acceptance, for his brand of products. For example, a number of children's television programs are sponsored by manufacturers of food products. The program may consist of adventures in space, a detective serial, or anything that arouses the intense interest of a child. Somewhere in the program the youngsters are instructed to insist that their mothers buy the product of the sponsoring manufacturer.

This kind of advertising has proved very effective under certain conditions. In fact, almost the entire advertising programs of the large cereal companies are directed towards the ultimate consumer for the purpose of getting her to ask for that specific product. Although the goods are usually sold through a jobber, who in turn sells them to a retailer and thence to the consumer, it is the policy of these companies to advertise only to the consumer and thereby create such an active consumer demand that the retailer and the jobber will be glad to carry the products and benefit from the quick turnover resulting from the strong demand.

Any of a number of advertising techniques are used to induce the customer to purchase specific products. Some have a rational basis while others are largely psychological or emotional. Thus, when you buy aspirin, you are to insist on a given brand because it is pure, it dissolves, and it acts more quickly. At other times reliance is placed primarily upon repetition of the brand name so that the consumer will automatically select that particular product. The Coca Cola Company follows this technique extensively. Whatever the technique, the purpose it to get the consumer to ask for, or at least willingly accept, a particular brand of product.

Assisting the salesman in making sales when he calls on the customer. The manufacturer uses advertising extensively for this purpose. He seeks to familiarize the customer with his products and create a favorable attitude toward his company before the salesman approaches the customer. For example, concerns producing basic metals frequently advertise in trade papers that are read by their customers. The advertisement itself will not induce the potential customer to take any action, but it is hoped that the salesman will receive a more cordial welcome as a result.

A firm manufacturing a line of luggage had for several years advertised extensively in national magazines. This was discontinued when a special study convinced the management that style, design, quality, and price were so much more important to the ultimate consumer than a particular brand name that directing its advertising toward the ultimate consumer was not economical. Nevertheless this company does a limited amount of national advertising because retailers are more inclined to stock a product that can be said to be nationally advertised. Thus the primary purpose of the national advertising campaign of this company is to assist the salesman in his negotiations with the retailer.

Other companies provide the retailer with attractive window displays and store decorations that serve the dual purpose of creating consumer interest and providing the salesman with a favorable reception by the retailer.

Producing direct sales. In some circumstances advertising is used for the purpose of persuading the customer to submit an order as a direct result. The catalogs of mail-order houses, for instance, present merchandise in such a way that the customer can write out or telephone an order without going to a shopping center and without further promotional effort on the part of the vendor.

One company has been successful in selling men's shirts as a result of direct-mail advertising to the consumer. This company stresses a price appeal that, it claims, is justified by its distribution "direct from the factory to you." How-to-do-it and reference books that appeal to a particular type of reader are often sold by direct mail or magazine advertising.

Building institutional goodwill. Practically all advertising is expected to build institutional goodwill to some degree, but in some cases this may be the primary objective. The advertising by telephone companies is largely for this purpose.

One of the leading small-loan companies has made extensive research on the problems of consumer buying and distributes a large number of pamphlets guiding housewives in the selection of merchandise. Intelligent expenditure of a limited income is, of course, related to the collection of small loans made to individuals for personal use. Nevertheless, the primary purpose of the distribution of these pamphlets is the development of goodwill toward the company.

Enough illustrations have been given to indicate that advertising may be undertaken for widely different purposes. Central management normally does not become involved in detailed aspects of advertising, but it can and should exercise a significant influence on company advertising by setting policies regarding the purposes of the expenditure.

Choice of advertising media. After a company has decided on the purposes of its advertising, the media must be determined. The principal media include:

    (a) Magazines
    (b) Newspapers
    (c) Trade papers
    (d) Television and radio
    (e) Billboards
    (f) Direct mail

This list is not intended to be complete. Other types of sales promotion that might be included under the general heading of advertising are displays, dealer's helps, and sampling.

Rarely does a single company use all of these media. It must select those that will accomplish its objectives most economically. For example, one large hosiery company that used advertising primarily to influence retailers formerly spent approximately $800,-000 annually advertising in magazines having a national circulation. A survey among retailers showed that dealers liked nationally advertised products, but that they were influenced to a greater degree by dealer helps such as counter displays and leaflets, and by cooperative advertising in local newspapers in which the name of the local dealer was mentioned along with the company's products. The expenditure of the company on magazine advertising is now less than $50,000 a year.

An airline company faced a serious problem in the selection of media to build familiarity and goodwill among a large number of people. Advertising that would produce traffic on its planes immediately was also wanted. For this latter purpose expenditures are confined primarily to direct-mail letters, circulars, and announcements to business executives and other people believed to be potential passengers in the near future. Considrable effort is directed toward passengers on its planes because these passengers as a general rule do not travel by air as much as they might, and the fact that they do use planes occasionally indicates they are interested in this method of transportation. The institutional program consists largely of magazine advertisements and general newspaper publicity.

We see in both of these cases the need to match media and purpose carefully. Too often the virtues of a particular medium are advanced without reference to the mission of the advertising.

Other advertising problems. Problems of advertising are by no means limited to a determination of the major purposes and selection of media. In addition, decisions must be made as to the general type of advertising to be used. Some companies feature testimonials; others employ cartoons to a large extent. Some use flashy advertisements and large print; others make their advertising more dignified. The use of premiums and of contests can open up many additional possibilities for the imaginative copywriter. Then there are numerous questions regarding such things as layouts. Primarily these are questions of advertising techniques rather than general sales promotion policies.

PERSONAL SOLICITATION

Differences in the use of salesmen. Although in nearly all types of selling salesmen must be used to some degree, the extent and purpose of personal solicitation varies greatly. The nature of the product to be sold, the type of customer to be solicited, the channels of distribution to be used, the types of sales appeals to be employed, all affect a company's policy regarding personal solicitation. An accounting firm, for example, operates on a professional basis and consequently is prevented from using advertising beyond a few dignified announcements. Such a firm secures its business primarily through personal solicitation. As a general rule, specialized salesmen are not employed. The partners and supervisors are expected to seek new business among their acquaintances, but in so doing they must maintain the professional dignity of the firm.

The selling activities of a clerk in a five-and-ten-cent store consist of little more than making change and wrapping packages; therefore, the amount of constructive selling such a clerk can perform is very limited. In contrast, a good insurance salesman is usually well-versed in problems of personal finance in addition to knowing facts regarding insurance premiums, cash reserves, cash surrender values, mortality rates, and contingent beneficiaries. He must also have considerable skill in approaching people and developing their interest in insurance to a point where a policy is purchased.

Some companies use what are known as missionary salesmen. Most of the leading soap manufacturers, for instance, distribute their products through grocery wholesalers. Experience has shown that the salesmen of these jobbers handle such a wide variety of products that they do not effectively promote the sales of any particular brand of soap. As a result, the soap manufacturers employ salesmen to travel among retailers, sometimes with the jobber salesmen, to advise the retailer regarding his problems in connection with selling soaps and to secure his cooperation in promoting the company's products to the retail consumers. The jobber fills orders, keeps the accounts with the retailer and makes collections; he also contacts the retailer at more frequent intervals than is possible for the specialty salesman. The missionary salesman, however, is an essential part of the sales promotion program of the manufacturer.

Sales personnel, organization, and techniques. From these examples it is evident that every company must adopt definite and clear-cut policies regarding its use of salesmen. It is essential that the company not only decide the extent to which salesmen are to be used but also must clearly define the purpose of their activity. Unless such a program is adopted, a considerable amount of misdirected sales effort and expense will result. The administration of a sales force involves, of course, many problems in addition to the establishment of general policies. There will be personnel policies relating to the selection, training, and compensation of these salesmen. A sales organization must be provided and detailed techniques must be worked out for specific activities to be performed. These problems are discussed in later chapters of this book.

An approach to sales promotion problems. The particular needs of a company should dictate its sales promotion policies. The array of possible methods complicates the choice. Moreover, the results of sales promotion activities are usually difficult to measure accurately. There are numerous factors, many intangible, that affect the final consummation of a sale. Consequently an increase or decrease in sales volume may not be a satisfactory measure of the effectiveness of the sales promotion policies.

Furthermore, as in all questions of policy, the costs of securing the desired results by alternative methods should be weighed. The complex and somewhat intangible nature of sales promotion makes such a comparison of costs and results extremely difficult. It is not surprising that, as a result, many concerns lack a sales promotion program based on a thorough analysis of their promotional problems. This means that expenditures of time and money are misdirected and sometimes entirely wasted.

One method of analyzing complex sales promotion problems is to answer these four questions:

1. *Who consumes the product to be sold or alters it so that its identity is lost?* The answers to this question should be found by a study of the customer policies of a company.

2. *Who makes the final decision as to the products that the ultimate consumer buys?* A study of this question will often lead to interesting results; for some products it is the housewife; for other products it is the breadwinner or the head of the family, and for still other products the ultimate consumer actually has little influence in the choice of the product. For instance, in purchasing fresh meats, the housewife usually is not interested in the packing company from whom the retailer secures his products. The retail butcher, therefore, determines whether he will purchase beef from packing company A or from packing company B. In the same way the student buys the textbook specified by his instructor, and consequently sales promotion efforts of a textbook publishing company are directed toward the teacher rather than the student.

On the other hand, the ultimate consumer usually makes the decision in the selection of the brand of cosmetics she buys. The purchase of producer goods is often influenced by several individuals. For example, the engineering department, production department, and purchasing department may all exercise an influence in selecting the company from which steel or coal is bought.

The answer to this question is often the key to a proper sales promotion policy. It certainly was for a company manufacturing piston rings for automobiles, since the entire advertising program depended upon whether the car owner or the garage manager actually selected the brand of piston rings that was to be used in the repair job.

3. *What factors influence those who make final decisions?* Note that this question focuses attention upon the factors that influence the person making the decision. The more common factors have been discussed in detail under sales appeals, and added illustrations are not necessary at this point. For example, a small difference in the price of piston rings is of little importance to the ultimate consumer, nor is he concerned with the delivery service of the manufacturer since he depends upon the local garageman to carry a supply of such parts. If, however, the garageman makes the decision regarding the rings to be used, then some of these things become of vital importance.

4. *How is it possible to influence these factors by means of sales promotion?* To what extent is it possible by national advertising, by sampling, or by personal solicitation to influence the thinking of those who make the final decision regarding the purchase of the product? There are some factors, such as the price or delivery service, that no form of sales promotion can change. On the other hand, an explanation by a salesman may be effective in pointing out the distinctiveness of quality and design of a particular product, and an advertising program may greatly affect the reputation of the company.

The method of approach to sales promotion problems indicated by the discussion of the foregoing questions does not provide a ready answer, but it will often lead to very significant conclusions. As the advertising manager of a company securing annual sales of approximately $60 million said, "I have asked a large number of advertising men those four simple little questions and frequently found a lack of adequate understanding of the problems they were pretending to solve. The questions are keen because they go right to the heart of the problem."

SUMMARY

To operate at maximum effectiveness every enterprise needs sound sales promotion policies. These policies should define (1) sales appeals the company will stress, (2) the nature and use to be made of advertising, and (3) the functions to be performed by salesmen. Important issues and alternatives in each of these areas have been discussed in this chapter, as well as a successful method of approaching sales promotion problems.

Sales promotion policies along with policies for products, customers, and pricing provide the basic framework of plans for a company's sales activities. There are, of course, many detailed decisions which remain to be made. For instance, a sales organization must be provided and programs worked out for specific sales activities. These and other operating problems will be considered in later parts of the book.

Before following through from broad policy to final execution of selling activities, however, we will explore other basic policies. This is important if we are to see sales in relation to over-all company operations. Also, in practice sales policies cannot be finally set until central management is sure they are compatible with other policies. Therefore, the chapters immediately following turn to questions of production, purchasing, personnel, and financial policies.

QUESTIONS FOR CLASS DISCUSSION

1. An old-line machine tool manufacturer faces massive resistance to a new, tape-controlled drilling machine because its United States customers are generally running at 60% to 70% of capacity and the new equipment is priced at two to three times the price of drills it is designed to replace. The new machine was priced at what everyone recognized as a "volume price" for its type even before it was introduced. The company decided to follow the auto industry pattern of volume pricing and accepting trade-ins. It has also shifted from direct factory sales to a distributor network. All major machine tool builders have agreed to exhibit at no general trade show except the National Machine Tool Show, held every five years. Private exhibits are occasionally held on a small scale. Now the sales vice-president proposes a nationwide series of private exhibits in at least twenty-five major cities. "No matter how many thousands of dollars this may cost, we must get across to each and every possible buyer not only our new product but also our whole new marketing concept!" Do you agree with sales vice-president? Why?

2. Assume that you are the sales manager of a coffee company using missionary salesmen. A member of the board of directors asks you why the company continues to use jobbers, who naturally charge retailers a higher price than the company receives from the jobbers, when the company already has salesmen in the field contacting retailers. Prepare a statement in reply. Include any assumptions you make regarding products, salesmen's activities, and other features of the method of distribution in use.

3. What advertising, if any, should be undertaken by the manufacturer of products like basic chemicals that cannot be effectively branded? Would the same reasoning apply to cut flowers, which are also rarely branded?

4. What justification can you see for the business ethics of the legal and medical professions forbidding advertising and personal solicitation as practiced by a commercial enterprise such as a washing machine company? How can a doctor or a lawyer promote his business? Do you think it might be desirable to require all businesses to restrict their sales promotion to such means?

5. A method of approach to sales promotion problems has been outlined at the close of this chapter. Apply this outline to the development of a sales promotion program for (a) soap flakes, (b) women's shoes, (c) office supplies, (d) television sets, and (e) the Empire State Building in New York City.

6. To what extent do the sales appeals discussed in the text rely upon the rational behavior of customers and to what extent on emotional reactions? Do you believe rational appeals are more effective? Should one type be preferred from a social viewpoint?

7. A manufacturer of power tools found a need among automobile repair garages for ruggedly designed hand power tools (sanders, air hammers, drills, wrenches) to offset the rougher treatment given these tools in garages than they usually get in industry or home repair shops. It also found that automotive jobbers do not extend credit to garages, while hardware stores selling the ordinary line of power tools do. A recheck of the market research indicated that 55% of the garages and service stations regarded the purchase of a power tool or tools as "important and not routine." Executives

were then undecided as to how significant the extension of credit was in selling to garages and how this question might be handled in promoting the new line. What do you suggest?

8. Explain to what extent you believe a life insurance company should use each of the advertising media discussed in this chapter.

CASE VIII

Prometheus Steel Corporation

The Finance Committee of Prometheus Steel Corporation had before it a proposal to increase the company's contribution to its industry trade association by $300,000 for the coming year. The additional money was to be spent to further the trade association's institutional advertising program.

Prometheus Steel, with annual sales of about $300,000,000, net worth of $130,000,000, and net profit last year of $7,000,000, had integrated plants near Pittsburgh and Youngstown. It sold a wide range of sheet, strip, bars, and tubular products to other manufacturers, but it was known best as a producer of specialty steels— stainless, electrical sheet and strip, alloy bar for use in machine manufacturing where special strength was needed, cooperage steel, and steel clad (coated) with aluminum, vinyl, zinc, and other finishes.

The case for the additional contribution was essentially that an institutional advertising program was needed to increase general public awareness of the value of steel in its many uses and to influence, to some extent, the buyers and the managers of the hundreds of thousands of firms using steel. Average production in recent years by the American steel industry had been below the 1955 to 1957 average of 115 million tons per year. Also there had been no substantial increase over the period. Meanwhile, sales, production, and use of aluminum, plastics, reinforced concrete, and other substitute products had climbed 40% to 70%. Although the inroads into steel's markets were not large in tonnage, they were highly visible—as in the cases of aluminum cans, glass and aluminum curtain walls and siding, and reinforced concrete buildings. Advertising campaigns to increase general public awareness of steel's value, relative low cost, and its many applications were instituted to help offset these events.

During the meeting two other proposals were offered. One was to expand the "sales team" program. The second was to reduce the contribution to the trade association by $100,000 from previous levels and to expend the entire $400,000 on special catalog advertisements in several selected trade journals.

An initial trial in one test market had demonstrated that sales calls by a two-man group, a metallurgist and the territory salesman, had brought increased sales. With the support of the data indicated below, the corporate marketing director proposed to expand the "sales team" program.

RESULT OF SALES TEAM TEST

Products   — Alloy Bar, Electrical Sheet, Stainless
Market   — Area M
Test Period — 6 Months

	Previous Year (comparable 6-month period)	Plan	Actual
Number of men	1	2	2
Sales	$600,000	$660,000	$645,000
Variable manufacturing expenses (standard)	$450,000	$495,000	$485,000
Fixed manufacturing expenses (standard)	60,000	60,000	60,000
Gross profit	$ 90,000	$105,000	$100,000
Variable selling expenses	15,000	30,000	30,000
Contribution to other expenses and profit	$ 75,000	$ 75,000	$ 70,000

The major points of his argument were that any increase in sales (especially one of 7.5%) was to be cherished in light of the lack of industry growth, that the contribution to profit would increase substantially if the program were extended, and that the most effective means of influencing buyers of specialty steel was through personal contact with engineers and purchasing agents. Adding metallurgists to the sales team increased the team's technical knowledge.

Following an extensive study of media, the corporate advertising director proposed a special test of catalog advertising. Advertisements in existing media were to be maintained, but two major trade journals and one buyer's directory were to be selected for special 12-page inserts. These inserts were, essentially, condensed product catalogs. Test objectives were: to inform top management (not often seen by salesmen); to provide manufacturing management with product information; and to reduce casual inquiries (by providing detailed product data) and thus restrict sales time to the most profitable calls. Two studies were offered in support:

READERSHIP PROFILE
Journals A and B and Directory Y

Level	Readers	Readers[1] per dollar
Top Management	26,000	6.5
General Purchasing Agents	18,000	4.6
Buyers	72,000	18.2
Engineers	102,000	26.0

[1] Based on one-page rates.

SALES INFLUENCES, STEEL BUYERS
(National sample, 485 buyers)

Results in: Effort	Awareness	Understanding	Ordering
Personal Selling	10%	40%	80%
Trade Advertising	60%	60%	35%
General Publicity	40% [1]	10% [1]	5% [1]

[1] Results necessarily add to more than 100%.

In a final comment to the Finance Committee, the public relations director said: "To be a good industry member we have to support our trade association. Ultimately, it's the general buying public that determines whether it wants articles made of steel. General advertising and publicity reach the top management of our customers just as effectively as does trade advertising. We can't let the association down."

APPENDIX
Selected Financial Data, Prometheus Steel Corporation

	Current Year	Previous Fiscal Year
Sales	$290,000,000	$305,000,000
Sales Force Expense	$ 6,000,000	$ 6,000,000
Advertising Expense	$ 600,000	$ 600,000
Trade Show Promotions	$ 90,000	$ 90,000

REQUIRED: Which of the three proposals should the Finance Committee accept? Explain how your answer furthers the objectives of Prometheus Steel Corporation.

THE HOOPES RIBBON COMPANY

The Hoopes Ribbon Company has for many years manufactured a limited line of ribbons and other classes of narrow fabrics for sale to manufacturers of lingerie, millinery, typewriters, fancy packages, blankets, and other products. At times the company has made parachute bindings and other webbings in large volume for the Air Force. Currently, the sales manager of the company is urging that the company expand into the home market for ribbons. He feels that the industrial market is so competitive that it offers small opportunity to enlarge sales and profits. On the other hand, there are fewer firms serving the home market and the gross profit margin is much larger.

Production. Ribbon manufacturing is a typical textile fabrication process. Yarn, purchased from cotton or synthetic yarn producers, is woven into ribbons. The ribbons may be dyed or finished in various ways or sold as grey goods, depending upon the desires of the purchaser. All ribbon going to the home market is dyed or finished. Weaving may be done on special ribbon looms which have narrow beams and can be changed rather readily to make different kinds of ribbons. Mills also have looms with wide beams which are loaded with enough yarn for four to eight months production of one type of weave. Down time for these looms, for changeovers, is two weeks.

The Hoopes Ribbon Company is now completing a new mill in the South in which all looms will be of the large-capacity, wide-beam type. One of the company's two older mills in Pennsylvania is gradually being shut down as looms are installed in the new mill.

All the looms of The Hoopes Ribbon Company are capable of making the different weaves such as plain, rib, or satin, which are required for ribbons and narrow fabrics used either by manufacturers or by the home trade. Although the new Southern mill is not equipped for dyeing and finishing, the other two mills of the company, both located in the Middle Atlantic states, can produce any type of finish normally required.

Competition. The ribbon industry is highly competitive in its sales to manufacturers. Low profit margins are the rule and firms enter and leave the industry yearly. Of the 238 firms currently in the industry, only 6 have more than 500 employees and only one of these more than 1,000. The Hoopes Ribbon Company has almost 400, which is much larger than the average mill of 25 employees. Ninety percent of all the firms are located in New England and the Middle Atlantic states.

Cost of materials, supplies, fuel, and electricity average 49% of sales price for the entire industry and salaries and wages to all employees average 30% of sales price, leaving 21% for additional overhead and profit. The Hoopes Ribbon Company calculates its total overhead costs to be 20% of the sales price.

Despite general price competition, Hoopes emphasizes quality. A consistent effort is made to maintain uniform yarn tension on the looms in order to have uniform edges and widths—the two most important factors in ribbon quality. The new Southern mill is air conditioned for employee comfort and because weather changes affect quality. Loom speeds are kept low, in some cases 50% below competitors', in order to achieve the best quality. The Hoopes Ribbon Company can do this, and still compete price-wise, by having its Southern operators tend more looms than is customary in Northern mills.

Gross profit margins on sales to the home trade are typically double the margins on sales to industry. Only five or six companies are in this part of the business, but they include all the large companies. Burlington Mills Ribbon Division is by far the largest of any of the companies and maintains nation-wide sales to wholesalers and retail outlets, as well as to manufacturers. This company is a division of one of the country's largest integrated textile manufacturers.

Finance. The company is family owned with outstanding stock closely held. Earnings have been quite consistent, with deficits in 6 of 72 years of operations. (See table on following page.)

Company policy in recent years has been to pay out ⅔ of net income in dividends. When low earnings are incurred, dividends are still paid. The amount is determined by average dividends of a few previous years. Then, in profitable years, dividends are kept below the normal ratio until enough profits are made so that the

(All figures in thousands)

	Net Sales	Net Income		Dividends
Current year	$4,099		$138	92
Preceding year	2,724		147	98
" "	2,481		87	80
" "	3,025		179	119
" "	2,741		151	101
" "	2,331		189	126
" "	1,925		97	65
" "	1,727		84	56
" "	2,199		73	44
" "	1,848		64	20
" "	1,242		19	20
" "	1,056	deficit	(93)	20
" "	1,105		70	27
" "	982	deficit	(119)	20
" "	1,121		34	23

⅔ ratio can be restored. The balance of net income is retained in the business to provide for expansion.

Expansion of assets has taken place at a greater rate than was provided for from retained profits. For the past fifteen years, increases in current liabilities have provided the major share of funds for expansion.

Additional looms for the Southern mill will require a cash outlay of $50,000 in the coming year. Retirement of the long-term debt calls for a yearly outlay of $62,000. Any attempt to make sales to chain stores and other retail outlets would require increased working capital. The capital requirement would probably rise more than proportionately to sales, at first, as lines were broadened. It is expected that earnings would remain at about 3% of sales because the higher margins available in the home trade would be offset, at first, by costs of breaking into the market.

Balance sheets as of December 31, for the past two years, are given at the top of the following page.

Six to seven weeks raw yarn is carried in inventory, and in-process inventories are even larger since the looms can be loaded for four to eight months production. Finished-stock inventories are carried at a planned level of eight weeks sales, but may actually be higher so that long runs can be obtained and so that sea-

(All figures in thousands)

Assets	Last Year	Current Year
Cash	$ 422	$ 457
Receivables (net)	1,002	1,106
Inventories	1,437	1,549
Land, buildings, and equipment (net) .	617	727
Other assets	161	155
Total assets	$3,639	$3,994

Liabilities and Capital		
Notes payable	$ 111	$ 287
Accounts payable	1,634	1,829
Long-term debt	437	375
Common stock	1,000	1,000
Retained earnings	457	503
Total liabilities and capital	$3,639	$3,994

sonal demands for Christmas ribbons can be met. The company's finished inventory turnover was six times in the past year. For the industry as a whole, inventories of materials, supplies, and work in process are about two and one-half times the size of finished goods inventories. The company calculates that 50 cents must be added to current assets to support each $1.00 of increased sales, if sales are to be made to the home market.

Channels of distribution. The Hoopes Ribbon Company has 15 salesmen who sell direct to manufacturers for a 6% commission and it employs one jobber for West Coast sales. In the industry, sales of ribbons to chain stores and retail outlets for use by the merchants in wrapping and decorating gifts, or for further sales to the general consuming public (known as the home trade) are made either direct or through jobbers; jobbers are most active in selling to small retailers. A typical commission on sales to chain stores is 3%. On sales to other retail outlets a commission of 8% is paid.

Customers. The company has so far sold only to manufacturers of lingerie, hats, millinery, blankets, or typewriters, who in general buy a limited range of products in large volume. These customers often order well in advance of their requirements so that production can be scheduled readily and the looms set for long runs. Currently the company has 800 regular customers and 600 customers who purchase occasionally.

Sales to the home market would be made through chain stores, department stores, and other retail outlets.

Type of Store	Number (Total U. S.)
Millinery	12,433
Women's ready-to-wear	18,253
Department stores	4,221
Variety stores	12,110
Dry goods, general merchandise	38,305
Gift, novelty, souvenir	5,186
Retail chains with 4 or more retail stores	6,159
(107,409 total stores in the chains)	

Source: Statistical Abstract of the U. S., U. S. Bureau of the Census.

Chain and department stores ordinarily buy only from manufacturers who provide a reasonably complete stock of widths, colors, and textures. Buyers for large stores, like purchasing agents of manufacturers, are familiar with the industry code of ribbon widths and with various company brand names which identify different ribbon qualities. Ribbon widths are not easily identified without special knowledge of code numbers. For example, a #9 ribbon is $1\frac{7}{16}$ inches wide. It has been found that ribbon-counter clerks very frequently do not know the width code nor are they acquainted with the brand names which identify quality. The Hoopes Ribbon Company has always wound its ribbon in bolts on wooden cores or on wooden spools with the code number stamped on the end.

Ribbons purchased in retail stores are used mainly to make and remodel clothing. At Christmas there is a heavy seasonal demand for red and green ribbons for tying packages. Overall, the home trade demand is stable, and may even increase in depressions. Fancy ribbons make up 10% of the home trade market. A change in dress fashions may increase or decrease total demand 15% to 20% in any one year. However, the retailer can readily carry over unsold inventory.

Women buy practically 100% of the ribbons and tapes sold in retail outlets. Their choice has often been found to depend on colorful point-of-sale display. Many women also insist upon a direct examination to test quality. The quality of each firm's products tends to be more important to the customer than minor price differentials. One manufacturer has met the point-of-sale requirements by packaging ribbons in cellophane and leaving one end sticking out through a slot in the package. Some retailers have expressed preference for this type of display since it cuts down depreciation losses which run high when the ribbons are wound on bolts and kept under the counter.

Burlington Mills Ribbon Division advertises ribbons for the home trade through pamphlets which illustrate various uses for ribbons or carry patterns for children's and doll's clothing. These pamphlets are given to the retail stores for free distribution to customers. Pamphlets showing how to gift-wrap packages and tie with ribbon are also given to the stores for their own use or for distribution to customers.

The Hoopes Ribbon Company has not estimated the number of retail and chain stores and jobbers to which it might be able to sell. One of its competitors, which has about double the sales volume of Hoopes and is well established in the home market, has 4,000 regular customers and 3,000 occasional purchasers. This competitor has 10 retail salesmen. Its total sales are divided:

Type of Customer	*% of Total Sales*
Retail	33
Chain	23
Jobbers	4
Total home trade	60
Manufacturers	40
Total	100

A buyer for a large variety chain stated that a new supplier would have to offer him either a better ribbon at the same price he now pays, or the same quality ribbon at a lower price, to receive a major share of his business. He felt that a 3% to 5% reduction in price would attract his serious consideration. Another buyer was looking for an additional supplier to take 5% of his total purchases so that he could increase the number of his sources of supply. This buyer required comparable quality of the ribbons and an attractive package, but no reduction below the prices he was currently paying. Both buyers indicated that they expect any manufacturer serving them to carry a "full line" of ribbons.

REQUIRED: (a) If The Hoopes Ribbon Company enters the home market, what phases of its operations, in addition to customer policy, would have to be changed?

(b) Should the company try to sell to the home market in addition to the industrial market?

HARGROVE, O'DONNELL AND COMPANY [1]

After some years of experience working for different Wall Street banking firms, Stephen Hargrove and Albert O'Donnell, friends since college, founded their own investment banking firm.

Stephen Hargrove had worked for a moderately large investment banking house in the buying department. Eventually he managed the department that purchased blocks of securities. Albert O'Donnell had been employed as a research analyst for a large brokerage firm that sold securities to individuals and performed other investment banking work.

Their experience had led them to question many aspects of the investment philosophy and management practices of the "traditional" securities industry. Their primary concerns were:

(1) Investors seemed to have been oversold on the growth potential of the "blue chips." The tripling of price-earnings ratios since 1950 plus the doubling of corporate earnings during the same period had produced large capital gains. As a result, investing in "blue chips" seemed to offer a relatively riskless route to large gains, but the projection of further increases overlooked the historically high price-earnings ratios already attained as well as "disguised" relatively slow earnings growth.

(2) Emphasis on "blue chips" had limited the research done on small and medium-sized companies with good records of increasing sales and earnings. These were felt to be too risky or to offer too limited a brokerage volume relative to the cost of research and relative to customer demand for recommended issues. Indeed, Mr. Hargrove was himself skeptical, especially since most work in this area had the added problem of original spadework into the industry.

(3) The securities industry was not meeting all the needs of institutional fund investors. The funds—insurance companies, pension funds, and especially mutual funds—were growing at a very rapid rate. Hargrove and O'Donnell believed that the demand by funds for stocks such as General Motors and Du Pont would eventually be satisfied and that these funds would seek new investment outlets—either in foreign securities or in smaller

---

1 An investment banking firm (a) assists companies to obtain long-term capital by underwriting the sale of stocks and bonds and by arranging other long-term financing, (b) counsels and sells stocks, bonds, etc. to investors in long-term securities, and (c) performs other services related to (a) and (b). Primarily it is a middleman in the long-term capital markets.

United States companies likely to grow much faster than the general economy. Very few investment banking houses, however, were studying and analyzing such firms in any depth.

(4) The securities industry was also failing to meet the needs of institutional funds, it was believed, in the way that it serviced these funds. Typically, fund buyers were called upon by salesmen. Occasionally, these salesmen were accompanied by reasearch analysts. Hargrove and O'Donnell had observed that institutional buyers were interested in fairly sophisticated presentations by analysts who had studied the companies and who could give new ideas. Buyers were less interested in talking with the "usual" salesmen who could only transmit information and who could rarely develop and explore his own ideas. It therefore seemed inefficient and expensive to have these salesmen call on institutional buyers even though some sales could certainly be made based on service and personal relationships.

(5) Too frequently the securities industry passed off as investment research what was only financial reporting—trends and comparisons of earnings per share, price-earnings ratios, yields, sales per dollar of plant, depreciation, and other statistical data. Hargrove and O'Donnell believed that this type of "traditional financial analysis" merely projected the past and failed to appraise adequately the marketing, production, product development, and management policies and structures of a firm as they affected the future. Furthermore, most securities firms attempted to give answers to customer queries on any of hundreds of companies, thus tending to limit thorough analysis on any one or a few investment opportunities.

(6) Investment counselors spent too much time writing letters to clients. The letters were frequently filled with cliches, such as "Company X has cut costs" or "Company Y anticipates a 10% increase in earnings," without satisfactory independent analysis. The letters did not contribute to better investment results and were often written largely to impress customers with the attention being given to their accounts.

Hargrove, O'Donnell and Co. was established to meet the needs represented by the founders' questions. Accordingly, they planned:

(1) Research focused upon firms whose annual sales ranged generally from $5 to $50 million, but up to $100 million if ap-

propriate. Chances of finding growth situations among firms this size were better than among larger firms, since in many cases they believed companies began to reach maturity and to grow at a slower rate after they approached a certain size or age. Furthermore, these small and medium-sized companies lent themselves to evaluation by a small team of individuals. Each company and industry could be appraised in 4 or 5 man-months in terms of its products, product development, market, market potential, managerial abilities, financial strengths and weaknesses, and so on.

(2) Growth companies were defined carefully as (a) a steadily improving record of sales, per-share earnings, and to a lesser extent profit margins; (b) a good record of new product or process development and/or old product or process improvement resulting in sales volume generated in new markets or through a steadily growing share of existing old markets; (c) management abilities to implement policies for future growth, and (d) an area of operations characterized by rapid development of new applications and new products within an expanding overall market. Recommendations would be made only on "proven" situations with a history of earnings increases, and then only after a thorough analysis of other factors that would influence future performance. The firm eliminated speculative situations and turn-around situations.[2]

(3) Recommendations would be limited to no more than ten or twelve stocks each year. This would permit detailed analyses of each stock. No attempt would be made to have informed opinions on other stocks.

(4) An effort would be made to develop a close and continuing relationship with each of the companies recommended. As growth companies, they would probably need additional financing, that is, sale of additional stock or long-term loans of some sort. It seemed natural for Hargrove, O'Donnell and Co. to apply its knowledge and become their long-term bankers. Also, owners of the firms would probably be willing to diversify their holdings, that is, to sell part of their large holdings. This would provide Hargrove, O'Donnell and Co. with blocks of stock for their institutional clients. The selling stockholders would also be potential clients

---

2 They defined a turn-around situation as one in which an historically mediocre company shows promise of renewed growth because of something new—new management, a product breakthrough, a new market, etc.

for the firm's Investment Management Service. All these were reasons why a close working relationship with recommended companies was essential.

(5) Sales of securities would be made primarily to large institutional funds. Researchers, not salesmen, would call upon these accounts. In each instance the researcher who developed an idea would present it to the potential buyer. No salesmen as such would be employed. Accordingly, several persons would call upon each account.

(6) Although the firm would not attempt to sell securities to individuals generally, it would handle personal accounts for a fee on a discretionary management basis (that is, the firm can buy or sell securities for the account without securing approval of the investor). These accounts would be administered by the firm's Investment Management Service and invested in the firm's recommended issues. No accounts would be taken on a non-discretionary basis, thus preventing time-consuming and nonproductive letter and personal contacts with accounts.

This was the framework within which the three founders decided to operate. They hoped to build a firm that would eventually offer a complete investment banking, counseling, and brokerage service, including specialized individual and institutional fund management, principal markets in selected securities, block placement facilities, assistance in raising new capital, underwriting, and private placement services.

One of the firm's first steps was to buy a seat on the New York Stock Exchange. This cost $135,000. Several months later, Mr. Hargrove said:

> "The purchase of the seat was a major decision and very definitely the right one. We felt that we wanted it, in part, as a Good Housekeeping Seal of Approval! We are young and unknown. Just having a seat makes it easier for us to get credit, to do over-the-counter business, and to gain acceptance with the few companies with which we work. In the short run, the seat was purchased more for prestige than for trading. We do considerable NYSE business also, even though many of the stocks we recommend are traded over-the-counter. Some institutions place orders with us on listed securities which we have never mentioned to them, but we had no way of anticipating how much business there would be when we started."

The founders were pleased with the first year's results. Institutional and discretionary managed accounts had built up more rapidly than was originally anticipated. A substantial profit was in sight for the year. Nine companies had been recommended and the prices of all except one had risen substantially. That one had declined 10% since its recommendation. Overall, the managed portfolios had appreciated 30%. This record compared with a general market decline of 15% during the same period. In fact, Hargrove and O'Donnell were frankly afraid that their initial successes with rapid price rises, more rapid than they had anticipated, might create the wrong impression, since they could not hope to maintain that pace of increase.

Success was also achieved in relationships with firms whose shares were recommended for purchase. Two used Hargrove and O'Donnell to sell newly issued stock. The two founders were able to obtain a great deal more stock in smaller companies than they had expected. Management's confidence was usually gained as a result of the detailed study and understanding developed by Hargrove, O'Donnell and Co. In addition, the offer to place stock with some of the prestige institutional funds appealed to the managements to an extent. Finally, it made sense for many of them to diversify their own investments for estate reasons if for nothing else. The net result was that while the acquisition of sufficient stock in each of the selected companies was frequently a problem to Hargrove, O'Donnell and Co., it could be reasonably well overcome with patience and effort.

The early success was accompanied by gradual growth in personnel. There were 18 employees by the end of October. Two new senior executives, both to become partners, were to be added within the next three months.

Many activities having only future benefits had been undertaken. A 15-page booklet describing the firm's investment philosophy had been published. Another one was planned. Lunches were given for executives of institutions and of corporations so that they could meet each other. The two founders felt that a part of their profits might as well be invested in these ways.

Despite their initial successes, the two founders saw problems ahead, only some of which they were beginning to meet. All professional employees had been responsible for suggesting companies to research and for doing some research. The two founders took care of all client contacts.

(1) "How can we maintain the quality of the initial reports in the face of pressures for more work? As we get busier following up companies already reported and catering to the visits and calls of institutions, the days are busy and research gets shoved to weekends and evenings. We believe that the answer is to try to budget our time better, hire more people, and move to offices with more privacy. Our main limitation is to find people who can do our type of work."

(2) "What should be the role of our research people as salesmen? We have avoided the 'salesman' in the traditional sense of communicating the efforts of wise research men in New York. As a matter of fact, we have had the opportunity to add two salesmen who were anxious to join us although they are partners in other firms.

"The question that arises is how our researchers can service the institutional accounts and still avoid weakening our research effort. They have spent much time in selling. There has been a real correlation between the time they spent in selling and the volume of sales. But can we operate without salesmen and still maintain a satisfactory research effort? Also, by having several persons call on each account and attempting to avoid personal identity with accounts, do we lose personal rapport? Should we have only one man call on an institution?

"We are coming around to the conviction that some form of salesman might fit into the organization after all. We have hired one man as an experiment, a classmate who has been given a major metropolitan market to develop. We have done little business in that city, and this is an extraordinary young man whose business training seems to go beyond the usual sales type of parroting information. We feel that he has a pretty good understanding of what makes a company tick and that he can interpret the information our research comes up with. But the question is: Should we have more people of this type, which means giving certain key institutions to them as a sort of franchise?"

(3) "Should we participate in the sale of large issues underwritten by other investment bankers—as is customary in the industry? We have had several opportunities for syndicate

participations thrown our way by a leading banking firm, but we have refused almost all of them. These have presented grand opportunities to make money. We have screened them very carefully. In the early days of our business we spent too much time screening underwritings. Most of them have been rejected as poor investment opportunities—we did not want to put our accounts into them. In other instances, few in number, not enough stock was available to make it worthwhile to do the necessary research. We feel a responsibility for our customers that many other houses don't seem to feel, at least to the same extent. A third reason for rejecting several participations was their possible reflection upon our company image, either because of the product or because we did not want to be linked with other firms that were participating for one reason or another. Is it now time to bring in a man who is more expert than we in the mechanics of group investment banking in order to accelerate this function?"

(4) "Should we have our own mutual fund?[3] As an investment vehicle, this would relieve the burden of managing some small accounts, we could accommodate others that we presently turn down as too small, and we could establish a public record—for better or for worse. Would this kill off our very important brokerage with other mutual funds, which might then regard us as a competitor? Could a small internal mutual fund be set up for friends without antagonizing these funds?"

Hargrove and O'Donnell did not believe that these problems demanded immediate solution, but they viewed them as sufficiently basic to affect the direction of growth of the firm and therefore hoped to resolve them within the next few months.

REQUIRED: Do you recommend any changes in the product, customer, or sales promotion policies of the firm? If so, what?

---

[3] The typical mutual fund is an extension of discretionary managed investment accounts. Individuals buy shares in the fund; the managers of the fund treat this money as a pool and invest it in securities according to their best judgment.

PRODUCTION AND
PURCHASING POLICIES

In preceding chapters we have discussed the sales of company products. These products must be obtained someplace, somehow. So we now turn attention to major procurement policies.

Although many firms have separated departments for purchasing and production, the basic problems that demand attention of central management are so entwined it is simpler to consider production policies and purchasing policies together.

Historical changes in procurement problems. For many years procurement of merchandise was the primary problem of businessmen. The rounding of the Cape of Good Hope and the discovery of America were actually attempts to find new trade routes. The enterprising merchants of those days were seeking products of the Far East because these products had a ready market in European nations. For centuries thereafter merchants searched the four corners of the earth for goods that they might bring back to sell in their home markets. These early merchants had some sales problems, but their major task was that of finding goods to bring to the markets.

Following the Industrial Revolution in the latter half of the Eighteenth Century, with its application of power and large-scale production methods to the processing of goods, more attention was given to the production than to the buying of goods. In the United States particularly, businessmen gave their energy to exploiting natural resources, developing more efficient methods of production, and harnessing steam and electric power. Nevertheless, the problem still remained one of securing goods that could be offered for sale.

During the last fifty years problems confronting central management have shown a still further change in emphasis. The great increase in variety of goods produced and the improvements in transportation have compelled the businessman to give added attention to selling his wares. This increasing attention required by the sales end of business has changed procurement problems in some respects but cannot be said to have diminished them. Because of the increased competition for markets, more attention must be given to timely production, keeping costs low, and maintaining quality standards.

Issues requiring central-management attention. Production and purchasing, like other phases of a business enterprise, involve a myriad of detailed problems. The proper handling of such problems is essential, and we shall discuss several of them in later parts of this book. At this point, however, we will focus on broad policy issues that need central management attention. Many, if not all, of these issues have a profound effect on the destiny of virtually every firm. Also, the way they are resolved should be carefully integrated with other key policy decisions. Consequently, they should be included in any overall analysis of a company.

These major production and purchasing policy issues will be discussed under the following headings:

1. Deciding the extent to which vertical integration is strategic.
2. Selecting the general processes to be used in production.
3. Setting total capacity and facility balance.
4. Providing basic guides for maintenance and replacement.
5. Resolving make-or-buy questions regarding services and supplies.
6. Selecting vendors from whom purchases should be made.
7. Correlating purchasing, production, and sales.

The first four sets of problems will be considered in this chapter; the last three in the next chapter.

EXTENT OF VERTICAL INTEGRATION

"Should we manufacture what we sell or should we buy it? If we manufacture, should we just assemble purchased parts or should we make the parts? Should we make or buy raw materials for the parts? Should we produce the supplies needed to make the raw materials?" These are questions of vertical integration. Every firm faces them, and for many firms a sound answer is the key to long-run success.

Vertical integration in the automobile industry. The problem of deciding whether to make or buy products is well illustrated in the automobile industry. Forty years ago the typical automobile manufacturer bought most of his parts from other manufacturers. The entire body of the car might be purchased from one manufacturer, the motor from another, and the differential from a third manufacturer. In fact, a substantial number of the so-called automobile manufacturers did little more than assemble these various parts into a complete automobile. They frequently exercised considerable influence over the design of parts, but the actual production operations within their own plant were quite limited.

Since that time large automobile manufacturers have decided to manufacture many of the 15,000 parts that go into a typical car. They may stamp and weld the metal that goes into the automobile body, and they often cast the original parts that go into making the engine. It is interesting to note, however, that even the large manufacturers do not make certain automobile parts. The production of a speedometer is a specialized operation, and most automobile manufacturers have considered it more economical to purchase their supply from a company that specializes in the production of speedometers for several different makes of automobiles. This specialized company can make speedometers more economically for several manufacturers than one automobile company can make a limited number for its own automobiles.

Piston rings and tires are other examples of purchased parts. Expertise is the main reason piston ring manufacturers have withstood the swing to vertical integration. For tires, an added factor is that most successful tire companies make a wide array of other rubber products and the automobile firms do not want to become involved in activities so far removed from their main business.

Combining publishing, printing, and paper making. The sharp differences in integration in the publishing field throw more light on the nature of the problem. Most book publishers do not print or bind their products. Their printing needs fluctuate in volume; one week they may have six typesetters and printers working for them and the next week none at all. Also, being free to get printing done anywhere gives them greater flexibility in the design of their books. On the other hand, contract printing is expensive. The former president of the company publishing this book, for example, often said as he passed the plant that did most of his printing, "My business made that man wealthy. But, I have enough worries already."

In contrast to book publishing, larger newspapers always do their own typesetting and printing. Probably this saves them money. The dominant consideration, however, is the need for very close coordination—literally down to a few minutes—between writing copy, setting it in type, proofreading, headlining, layout, and printing. And when a hot story breaks, much of the work may be redone in an hour or two. Such fast coordination can be best supervised by a single management.

Fewer newspapers have their own paper mills and timberlands. The big papers and the chains have a large, fairly steady need for a single product. Production economies are a natural result. To be sure, these same economies might be obtained by an independent supplier under a long-term contract, but some risk would remain for both newsprint producer and newspaper. So, at least those papers that predict a long-term rise in newsprint prices and that have capital for investment try to reduce supply risks by integrating clear back to the forest.

To farm or not to farm. Still unsettled is the extent to which frozen food companies should raise their own vegetables and fruits. Seabrook Farms, to cite one case, is heavily engaged in farming. Most firms, however, rely on local independent farmers. A farmer tilling his own land conforms to the centuries old cultural pattern; and reliance on independent growers presumes that the resourceful, close supervision of a farmer over *his* crops will be more effective than hired management. But the frozen food packer must be assured of a supply of quality produce suitable for freezing. So he signs annual contracts with farmers well in advance of planting, provides selected seed, and offers advice. We see here, not vertical integration in the usual sense, but an arrangement with supply sources that accomplishes several of its benefits.

Key factors in vertical integration. The examples just discussed show that a variety of factors may influence a decision on when to integrate. Among the many possible considerations, the following are likely to be key ones.

Possible savings resulting from coordination. If a company manufactures the products or the materials it needs, the promptness of delivery and adjustment to emergencies may be easier. When the parts have to fit together into a complex balance, the engineering may be more easily coordinated. Unusual quality requirements may be easier to meet. A firm knowing its own needs and being assured of continued use of equipment may develop more specialized machinery than is feasible for an outside supplier.

Elimination of marketing expenses. If a firm produces its own materials, the selling expenses incurred by the outside vendor are automatically avoided.

Effect of patents and restricted supply. The control of patents by other companies may make economical manufacture impossible; but if the company itself should obtain control of patents, then a policy of manufacturing may be particularly desirable. If there is reason to doubt that raw materials will be readily available, then a company may acquire its own sources as a means of protection. For example, virtually all the basic metal processors mine their own ore, and the leading oil companies want a controlled supply of at least part of their crude oil requirements.

Flexibility. Vertical integration tends to limit flexibility in product design. Heavy instruments in plant or raw material sources hamper the shift to completely new designs or materials, whereas the firm that buys its requirements is not concerned with making a large investment obsolete.

In the short run, too, the nonintegrated firm may cut down its purchases or shift to another supplier, whereas the integrated firm must recognize the effect of such action on unabsorbed overhead. To guard against such a stultifying effect, General Motors has a longstanding policy that none of its divisions is required to buy from another division if the profit or the long-run development of the first division would suffer from doing so.

Volume required for economic production. Many small companies simply cannot consider backward integration because the volume of their requirements for any one part or material is too small to keep an efficient plant busy. Also, the requirements may be so irregular that a plant would be kept busy only part of a year. Occasionally a company builds a plant larger than needed for its own use and then sells the balance of the output to other users. Such an arrangement, however, does divert both financial resources and managerial attention from the major activity of the firm.

Financial status of the company. Many firms have only enough capital to operate their principal line of business and may not be in a position to acquire new capital under favorable conditions. This precludes substantial investments in manufacturing facilities for the production of parts or raw materials. On the other hand, financially strong companies may undertake vertical expansion because their suppliers are financially weak. In such circumstances, the added financial strength may permit substantial improvements in the manufacturing operation.

Capacity of management to supervise additional activities. In a great many instances, a decision to produce products that formerly were purchased means that the executives of the company are undertaking activities of a distinctly different nature from those with which they are familiar. While they can employ an executive from that industry, central management cannot escape giving some attention to the new undertaking and bearing responsibility for making final decisions regarding it. Sometimes central management becomes so absorbed in directing the new activity that it fails to give adequate guidance to the older part of the business where it has demonstrated competence.

On the other hand, if inadequate managerial attention is given to the new venture, expected savings may not be realized. Perhaps low cost will exist when production is first started because the new plant will have new equipment and the latest methods; but with only secondary attention by central management and the opiate of an assured market, there is real danger that the plant will fail to keep up with other concerns.

General conclusion. Vertical integration decisions of the type that we have been considering in this section are of substantial magnitude. Each proposal should, therefore, be thoroughly examined in terms of the key factors listed, estimated ratio of savings to investment, and unique considerations such as idle plant or lack of technical knowledge. But underlying such a detailed analysis—and guiding a decision to devote time and energy to the study in the first place—should be a consciously determined disposition (policy) to move toward vertical integration or to stay away from it. Such a general policy should be based on an appraisal of what is required for success in the industry, the distinctive competence and resources of the company, desire for diversifying economic risks, and similar factors reviewed in Part I. Few policies are more crucial to the long-run development of a company.

PRODUCTION PROCESSES

Closely related to decisions on what production activities the company itself will perform are choices of processes to be used. Broad issues in this area are:

1. Choice of technology.
2. Extent of division of labor.
3. Extent of mechanization and automation.
4. Size and decentralization of plants.
5. Involvement in process research.

Choice of technology. In the production of many products the manager has no choice regarding the process to be used. Thus, a manufacturer of wallboard, using fiber of sugar cane as his primary raw material, need be in no quandary about the process to be employed in removing the small quantity of sugar remaining in the cane after it passes through a sugar mill. The only commercially practical method is fermentation. By allowing the sugar to ferment, it can be almost completely removed and the remaining fibers are then in a light and workable state. Since there is only one feasible process, the manufacturer really faces no problems in this regard and turns his attention to the detailed methods and facilities for carrying out the process.

Not all manufacturers can solve their production process problems as readily as a wallboard company. Even in a comparatively simple operation, such as the ice business in northern Wisconsin, a company must decide whether it will manufacture its ice artificially or cut it from some neighboring pond or lake. In the same way a company manufacturing steel must decide upon the extent to which it will use electric furnaces, open-hearth furnaces, or oxygen inverters. Stemming from such basic decisions will come a whole array of plans for equipment, personnel, methods, and organization.

Technology is not confined to physical processes. Universities, engineering firms, mental hospitals—to mention only a sample—

face similar choices. A management consulting firm, for instance, can either design standard solutions (production control systems, sales compensation plans, budget procedures, and the like) and adapt them to each client, or it can make a fresh analysis of each situation with no preconceived ideas about the solution. The choice here does not involve large investment in facilities, but it does affect personnel, organization, sales appeals, and other facets of the business.

Extent of division-of-labor. Practice differs among manufacturers of inexpensive dresses and aprons as to the use of the "section system." Sewing constitutes a major part of production activity, and under the older system each sewing machine operator did a whole series of operations on either the blouse, the skirt, or the other parts of the dress. The newer system has each operator do a much smaller piece of the work and then pass the garment on to the next operator for another small seam. Thus, when work can be standardized and secured in sufficient volume, the idea of line production is applied. While not so called by men in industry, students of economics will recognize this as an example of the *extent of division-of-labor.*

Fine division-of-labor has been a common, and usually productive, policy in business operations since the establishment of pin factories in the early days of the Industrial Revolution. Recently it has faced two challenges—mechanization and automation of routine work, and "job enlargement" in which the duties of a worker are deliberately diversified to give him more nearly a "whole" operation. In deciding how much emphasis to give division-of-labor, then, the manager should weigh his policies regarding standardization of products, mechanization, and type of labor to be employed.

Extent of mechanization and automation. Some companies adopt definite policies regarding the extent to which they will automate their operations. One manufacturer of automobile frames, for example, established a policy that operations would be mechanized from start to finish. As a result, the final product might carry the same label as appears on some food products, "Not touched by human hands." Likewise, the telephone companies adopted long-run plans for the introduction of dialing equipment in place of manual switchboards. Incidentally, in this case the rate of change is slow enough so that few operators have to be discharged. Normal turnover plus need for service operators of the new equipment avoid most layoffs, but the net reduction in personnel is substantial.

The rising cost of labor and the inflexibilities in the use of labor that are being introduced as a result of unionization and government regulations are leading more and more companies to mechanize wherever practical. They recognize that machines also are often inflexible, but machines are tractable and their costs do not rise after they are placed in operation.

A similar decision regarding mechanization has been followed on the large collective farms in Russia and the large farms in the United States. In the South, crop dusting from the air, flame throwers for killing weeds, mechanical harvesting equipment and other power driven machines are creating a change that alters the plantation more than did the Thirteenth Amendment.

Size and decentralization of operating units. Large manufacturing companies have considerable choice in the size and location of their plants. For many years, most of them assumed that the larger the plant the more economies would be possible; transportation costs of raw materials or finished products were usually considered the limiting factors on the size of a plant. Present thinking challenges these assumptions. At least the advantages of large plants are not taken for granted.

One concern that produces nine related products, for instance, has a clear-cut policy that each product is to be manufactured in a separate plant even though three of the plants employ fewer than two hundred people. Plants are to be located in relatively small communities, rather than big cities, preferably within seventy miles of the home office so as to make face-to-face contacts easy. Several of the plants have already been relocated in accordance with this policy.

A firm in the clothing industry has adopted a similar view toward separation of production into several operating units. Production technology does not require large-scale operations, and the company believes the optimum size plant is one just large enough to support specialized service divisions such as accounting, personnel, and maintenance. In this case, plant location is determined primarily by nearness of consuming market and availability of women workers—but again, not in a big city.

In some industries, such as the chemical industry, technology requires a large-scale plant. Once a plant is large enough to use economical processes and to support specialized service divisions, there is question whether expansion should be at the same plant or a new location. Smaller plants, especially those in smaller communities, have advantages of closer and friendlier relations among all employees—operators and executives, easier identification of the worker with the product he is producing, less bureaucracy, more face-to-face contacts in place of expensive and impersonal communication systems, executives who have first-hand knowledge of what is going on, less commuting time and expense for employees, etc. Moreover, modern means of transportation and communication have reduced the disadvantages of having several plants separated from the home office.

A similiar challenge to size of operating unit is occurring in the retail field. Here, traffic and transportation congestion in large cities has led department stores to open branches in suburban locations. These branches cannot, of course, offer customers the same selection of merchandise as the larger downtown stores. Several different policies are used to overcome this limitation. Some firms have their branches carry only certain lines, such as women's ready-to-wear and domestics, and do not attempt to stock all kinds of merchandise. Other companies place at least samples of a wide variety of goods at their branches and rely upon the main store to supply a full range of sizes and colors. Still other firms have only large branches and stock each with almost as wide a selection as the main store. The decision as to which of these policies to follow makes a fundamental difference in the branch operation.

The smaller company with a single place of business does not face this issue, but for larger companies a wise policy regarding the optimum size of operating units is of crucial importance.

Involvement in process research. How much initiative and money should a firm invest in improving its production processes? Again, there is no single answer. In industries with rapid technological change—such as electronics, pharmaceuticals, and chemicals—some technical research is necessary for survival. In contrast, firms in the furniture, printing, and textile industries rarely engage in technical research; they rely primarily upon equipment manufacturers and materials suppliers for new processes.

To formulate a broad research policy, managers should distinguish first between basic and applied research. Basic research (at least from a manager's viewpoint) is search for knowledge in a field related to the company's business but without any specific application of that knowledge in mind. Only the largest companies can afford to engage in an activity where a commercially valuable result is so uncertain and remote. Basic research may lead to new processes, new products, or activities unrelated to present operations. Consequently, if a firm does basic research, it should be financially able and willing to diversify in directions that will exploit discoveries.

Applied research has a stipulated objective, such as a substitute raw material, a cheaper process, or a new product to serve an identified need. Even so, it is risky. Except for the simplest applications of well-developed techniques, no one knows whether the end will be achieved, how long it will take, or what the accumulated expense will be. Most firms that do their own applied research have a variety of projects and hope that enough will be successful to carry the expense of the failures.

Often research is a defensive activity. Competitors have laboratories, and our company fears that sooner or later someone will find the improved process—leaving us with obsolete operations. By doing some research, at least we will have men conversant with current developments and prepared to advise how to move if the lightning does strike. If defense is our main motive, then the nature and the scope of our research can be somewhat restricted; policy is determined largely by what our competitors are doing.

Since technical research is both expensive and risky, firms may pursue a policy of sharing the risk. They may support industry research institutes, help finance projects at universities, or pay suppliers for part of the cost of an experimental model. Such a policy is especially suited to a smaller company that cannot afford the expense of its own laboratory.

Research is a long-range matter; it cannot be easily expanded or contracted; and as we have seen, technical research may vary in nature and scope. Consequently central management should provide policy guidance regarding appropriate involvement, if any.

HOW MUCH CAPACITY

Data from a variety of sources must be brought together to estimate the productive capacity a company needs. Sales forecasts of physical volume, policy decisions on what will be purchased instead of made, engineering estimates of machine productivity, production plans on how equipment will be used all contribute to projections on size of plant needed. In addition and overriding such data are several central management policies regarding capacity desired. These policies deal with provisions for peak versus normal requirements, backward taper of capacity, allowance for growth, and balance of facilities.

Peak versus normal load. A completely stable level of operations is virtually impossible. All types of business activity are affected by cyclical fluctuations, and most industries experience seasonal, daily, or even hourly variations in volume of business. In addition, the demand for a company's product may increase or decrease because of wars, governmental regulations, inventions, floods, changing fancies of the consumer, and many other influences. Moreover, mere random distribution will lead to peaks and valleys. The manager must decide whether he will provide capacity large enough to satisfy all demands during peak periods, knowing that some of this capacity must remain idle during slack periods, or whether he will maintain a smaller capacity and hope that failure to render service during peak requirements will not have unbearable consequences.

A leading example of companies that try to meet peak requirements is found in the electric utility industry. On dark winter evenings or hot summer days, we expect to have current available on the flip of a switch. Utilities have a policy of building capacity to meet such peak demands (occasionally there are some restrictions on industrial customers). Fortunately, the demand is predictable; nevertheless, the investment made for peak needs is tremendous.

Most companies follow a policy of letting the customer bear part of the peak load burden. This is obvious to the subway or bus commuter during rush hours and to the Christmas shopper on December 24th. Neither the bus company nor the retail store are indifferent to crowds of customers. They provide capacity several times their volume during slack periods. The problem is one of balancing the amount of delay and inconvenience to X% of the customers versus the cost of providing the increment of capacity to meet the peak. Perhaps the policy will be to meet 90% of the requirements without delay.

Other means of meeting peak capacity will, of course, be incorporated in the policy regarding maximum capacity. (a) Manufacturers of standard, durable products may manufacture stock during slack periods. This arrangement is explored in the next chapter. (b) Overtime work may be feasible for operations not already run 24 hours a day. (c) Obsolete or high-cost equipment may be maintained on a standby basis and placed in service just during the peak. (d) Some of the work may be subcontracted, although this is often difficult because potential subcontractors are likely to be busy during the same peak period. (e) Off-peak discounts, "mail early" campaigns, and other measures may be used to induce customers to avoid peak periods. These devices also involve extra expense and may be more or less satisfactory to customers. Clearly, policy guidance is needed to indicate the reliance on these various ways of responding to peak needs.

Backward taper of capacity. Vertically integrated companies may deliberately follow a policy of backward taper of capacity. Such firms normally perform final operations on all their finished products, but they manufacture only parts of their material requirements. A tire manufacturer may have its own textile mill in the south to weave tire fabric. This mill will probably have the capacity to supply only the minimum needs of the tire manufacturer. Additional fabric for peak requirements will be purchased from an outside concern. Such an arrangement has the obvious advantage of keeping the units in the earlier stages of production operating comparatively near their productive capacity. The feasibility of this policy depends on the presence of potential suppliers who are willing to supply fluctuating amounts of material.

Provision for growth. Experience indicates that a business enterprise does not stand still. During the last century, many executives were warranted in anticipating an increase in the volume of their business. Whether the executive who built facilities 50% larger than he needed for current operations had a clear vision into the future or was simply lucky, his decision was justified in a great many instances.

It is both expensive and inconvenient to customers and employees to have additions to facilities made at frequent intervals in piecemeal fashion. On the other hand, the financial downfall of many firms can be traced to the construction of excessive facilities, which construction absorbed a large part of the company's liquid capital and entailed annual charges that further depleted the company's resources.

Again, some middle ground is desirable if it can be arranged. Often provision for expansion may be included in the amount of land purchased and the shell of the building, while only part of the equipment is purchased initially and a work force is hired as needed. Perhaps the original plant can be used for both manufacturing and warehousing, and then a warehouse may be added later. Offices may be treated in a similar fashion. Whatever the specific scheme, the basic decision to be made by central management is how much growth to anticipate and the extent to which investment will be made now in anticipation of that growth.

Balancing capacity. Each phase of an operation—materials handling, processing, warehousing, selling, and the like, along with their subdivisions—has its own capacity. A recurring task is trying to keep the volume of business that each subdivision can perform about equal.

A lack of balance was illustrated in a striking way at a plant making electric cooking ranges. The operations included stamping, welding, painting of some parts, pickling and enameling of other parts, assembling, and testing. The plant had ample capacity for all operations except enameling. A small furnace originally installed for experimental work was used for this purpose. Not only did it limit the number of products that could be enameled at any one time, but it was of such a size and shape that the operation was quite inefficient when large pieces were being enameled. The capacity of this one unit placed a definite limit on the total usability of the entire plant.

Even if balance is achieved through careful planning, it is hard to maintain. Over time, the character of work may change, small modifications will be made in the techniques employed, and people will move about. With such shifts, some one operation becomes the bottleneck. Consequently, there seems to be a never-ending task of overcoming one bottleneck after another. On the other hand, there is the task of trying to reduce the expenses in those phases of operations where the workload has dropped off.

Most of the examples of problems with capacity have been in terms of physical facilities. Nevertheless, similar issues arise in stores, offices, and firms dealing with intangibles. Capacity to meet requirements, provision for growth, and problems of balance are likely to arise in any kind of enterprise.

MAINTENANCE AND REPLACEMENT

Closely associated with issues of how much capacity should be provided are questions of maintaining and replacing existing capacity.

Levels of maintenance. The statement "Captain Svenson runs a tight ship" conveys meaning to any sailor. It refers to much more than caulking the hull; everything throughout the vessel—engines, galleys, winches, and whistle—are kept in excellent running condition. Sloppiness and procrastination are not tolerated.

Similarly, a tourist driving through Kansas can easily tell when he is in a Mennonite section. The fences are mended, the barns are painted, the fence rows are weeded, and the crops look good.

Plants and offices, likewise, may be run like a "tight ship" or in a more casual and relaxed fashion. The level of maintenance results partly from the personal preferences of key executives, perhaps a cultural value inherited from their forebears. It may also reflect a calculated decision on the kind of maintenance that will most effectively support the other objectives and policies of the particular company. Maintenance involves expense (the Mennonite farmer in Kansas works hard and long). And the "tight ship" approach may be unwarranted in, say, a sawmill located on a tract that has just been cut over. Railroads appropriately vary the level of track and right-of-way maintenance on their main lines compared with a branch line soon to be abandoned. Incidentally, railroads also accelerate or hold back on deferrable maintenance depending upon their financial condition from year to year.

Preventive maintenance. Prevention of breakdowns, rather than repair after a stoppage has occurred, is now widespread practice. This is achieved by proper use and care of productive facilities, coupled with regular inspections to identify potential trouble. Repair of worn or defective parts is then scheduled when it will cause the least disruption to regular operations. We are all familiar with this approach in the care of an automobile— regular greasing and oil changes, driving within prescribed limits, 5,000-mile checkups, prompt inspection of unusual noises or performance, and replacing tires when they are worn. Observing such practices enables us to depend on the automobile instead of wondering when we will have a flat tire or whether the motor will start. The same general concept can be applied to a sales organization or an accounting office, except that here we deal with people, social relationships, paper forms, and procedures.

Again, there are questions of degree. The attention given a fire engine should differ from that given to a wheelbarrow; an integrated chemical plant, from that given to a roller rink. If a breakdown can be repaired quickly and the interruption is not very serious, the intensity of preventive maintenance can be relaxed.

Scheduled replacement. In this day of mass production, regular replacement may be simpler than careful maintenance. The typical trouble-free life of electric bulbs, salesmens' autos, water meters, and airplane engines can be measured and replacements can be made regardless of the apparent condition of a specific piece of equipment. Compulsory retirement of air pilots at age sixty—or professors at age seventy—is based on the same logic. Perhaps the replaced item will be salvaged for other use, or it may be rebuilt, but the aim is to make the change before performance falters.

Central management rarely becomes involved with the maintenance or the replacement of specific units. To maintain effectiveness and efficiency, however, senior executives need to provide guidance on how tight to run the ship, when and where maintenance is to be slowed down or pushed ahead, the level of preventive maintenance desired, and the extent of the use of scheduled replacements.

QUESTIONS FOR CLASS DISCUSSION

1. By adding an alkylation unit to its hydrogen and platinum reforming capacity, an oil refining and marketing company could supply benzene to a large, nearby chemical company. The added investment would be about 2% of company assets. The alternative would be to operate the reformer for high octane gasoline sold to a large number of independent jobbers and through company stations. The price of benzene had dropped steadily for some years while its sales volume was growing rapidly. Gasoline sales depended on the number of company stations and on the price to jobbers. Retail price wars affected profits intermittently. Is integration forward into petrochemicals likely to be a sound move for the refining company?

2. A relatively small manufacturer of grinding wheels, which has done well in selling vitrified wheels, now hopes to expand by selling resinoid bonded wheels. Past success has come from imitating Norton Company's and the Carborundum Company's products, from careful cost control, and from closely tying production in relatively small lots to sales requirements. Success in the resinoid bonded field will require continued close attention to these factors and probably some "research" to allow the firm to do better what it is already doing. The amount of research effort will have to be limited and its direction is undetermined. Three possibilities are (a) product development, or (b) engineering development work on production processes, or (c) systems work on costs and budgeting. Which of the three do you think would be most suitable?

3. A policy to make rather than to buy raw materials leads to "vertical integration of industry." (a) Which business risks are increased, and which decreased, by vertical integration? (b) Some economists criticize vertical integration as tending to limit competition. Do you believe it is socially undesirable for this reason?

4. Salesmen of companies that manufacture all or part of the items necessary to place their finished product in marketable form often argue that they can offer the customer a better product at a lower price. They contend that competitors who purchase the major portion of their materials from outside concerns must pay the vendors a profit, whereas their company can eliminate this profit due to its vertical integration. Do you think this argument is sound?

5. Motorola and Delco both make automobile radios in large quantities—Motorola for Ford and Delco for other divisions of General Motors. Delco uses an automatic assembly machine to perform 46 successive assembly tasks without the aid of a human hand. Motorola uses women for hand assembly of parts and subassemblies. Both companies make sets based on printed circuit boards. Delco makes its own parts; Motorola buys outside, especially the preassembled components. These preassemblies have up to 10 connecting pins and are therefore suitable for hand assembly but not for the machine, which can take only 2 or 4 connections at a time. Explain how such different processes could be found suitable for essentially the same task.

6. (a) What effect, if any, do you think the policy of some companies to set up smaller decentralized operating units will have on opportunities for "small business" in those industries? (b) Do you believe operating units will become larger or smaller in the following fields: banking, grocery retailing, the leading industry of your state, universities?

7. Redstone Sweaters, Inc. anticipates a 20% increase in sales from a new territory. Shipments in past years have averaged:

January	3,100 doz.	July	1,600 doz.
February	3,000 doz.	August	2,200 doz.
March	3,900 doz.	September	4,100 doz.
April	3,600 doz.	October	4,800 doz.
May	2,500 doz.	November	4,300 doz.
June	1,600 doz.	December	3,300 doz.

The company tries to fill orders promptly from stock on hand, but style and other changes have led to a policy that no production will be started more than three months prior to anticipated shipment. Two basic operations are required for production: (a) knitting fabric and (b) cutting, sewing, and finishing. Present knitting capacity can provide material for 160 dozen sweaters per day; cutting, sewing, and finishing capacity is 130 dozen per day. The mill can run a maximum of 26 days per month. The storeroom has capacity for 3,500 dozen sweaters. How much additional capacity, if any, does Redstone Sweaters, Inc. need?

8. Compare the ratio of actual operation to theoretical maximum capacity of a typical electric utility plant, a dress factory, a restaurant, and a brick factory. Among the possible ways of improving that ratio of use to capacity are (a) not accepting peak business, (b) manufacturing to stock, and (c) buying goods or otherwise using idle capacity of another company in the same industry. To what extent can these ways of reducing necessary capacity be used by each of the four enterprises mentioned in the first part of this question?

9. An Eastern railroad, in financial troubles, had postponed and slowed down expenditures on maintenance-of-way until it was now necessary to reduce freight train top speeds from 60 to 50 mph over the system if a sustained maintenance improvement program was not introduced immediately. Train schedules and interchanges with other roads would be considerably affected by the reduced speed. How much could not be completely determined. A maintenance program could be carried out by the old system of section

gangs using temporarily hired labor or callbacks from the layoff board, or, in half the time, by investing heavily in mechanized equipment that would have to be financed by borrowing at high interest rates. Detailed quantitative studies had led to the qualitative conclusions just stated. What would you recommend?

CASE IX

Middle States Steel Corporation

Executives of Middle States Steel Corporation were justly proud of the company's new 120-inch blooming and plate mill. After two years of planning and two further years of building, the mill had just come into production. With this facility, Middle States was fully equipped to serve all the foreseeable needs of its prime plate customers as well as the input of slabs needed by its hot strip mill.

Middle States sold steel plate to manufacturers of heavy industrial and transportation equipment whose products were boilers, oil refinery towers, railroad cars, ships, and the like. In addition, Middle States turned out hot-rolled sheet and strip up to 48 inches in width for sale to manufacturers of lockers, steel shelving, kitchen cabinets, home appliances, and the like. Overall demand for steel products is notoriously cyclical, and sales of Middle States were no exception to the pattern. Its participation in the heavy capital goods market is reflected in the following output data:

EXHIBIT 1

Year	Federal Reserve Board Index of Industrial Production (1957-59=100)	Production of Steel Ingots, United States, millions of net tons	Percent of Capacity, United States	Middle States Steel Corp., Ingot Production, Millions of net tons
1947	66	84.9	93.0	1.0
1950	75	96.8	97.4	1.1
1955	97	117.0	93.0	1.5
1957	101	112.7	84.4	1.4
1958	94	85.3	60.6	1.0
1960	109	99.3	66.8	1.2
1961	110	98.0	n.a.	1.1
1962	118	98.3	n.a.	1.2
1963	124	109.3	68.0 est.	1.3
1964	132	126.9	77.0 est.	1.4

Middle States was an integrated, although not a balanced, steel producer. Capacity of its facilities at the various stages of production after the installation of the new blooming and plate mill is shown in Exhibit 2 on the following page.

EXHIBIT 2

Capacity of Equipment (annual)

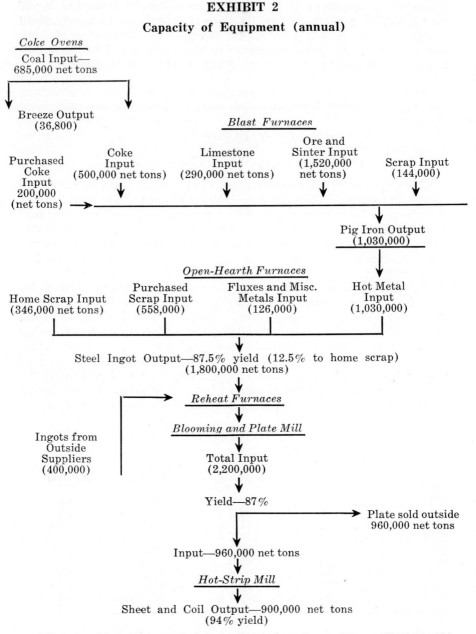

The new blooming and plate mill replaced an older mill that did not roll the wider plate (over 50 inches) being demanded by Middle State's customers and that did not readily hold the flatness tolerances expected.

Since the capacity of the new mill was well above Middle State's steelmaking capacity, consideration was being given to installing oxygen converters to add to ingot-producing capacity or to replace some of the present open hearths. Although ingots could be purchased from other steel companies, there was usually a cost advantage and some product quality advantage to using home ingots. Because of the high temperatures necessary to produce steel (from 1500°F. to 3600°F. at various stages) and the great tonnages involved, steel producers attempted to conserve heat and to minimize transportation whenever possible. Cold ingots bought outside added 12% on the average (including a 2% reheating charge) to input costs at the semifinished (blooming mill) stage in periods of high output. At other times, however, outside ingots had been offered at delivered prices up to 5% less than Middle State's total standard cost of ingots from its open hearths. Investment costs for new oxygen converter plants were:

Annual Capacity	500,000 tons	1,000,000 tons
Buildings	$0.9 million	$1.2 million
Equipment	1.9	2.4
Utilities	2.6	3.4
Air Pollution Control	1.5	2.0
Storage	2.2	2.4
Total	$9.1 million	$11.4 million

Investment costs for added open-hearth capacity were $20 million for 500,000 tons of annual output, of which $5.5 million would be for buildings.

OPERATING COSTS

	Oxygen Converters [1]		Open Hearths [2]	
	Lbs./net ton	$/net ton	Lbs./net ton	$/net ton
Steel scrap at $43/gross ton (2240) pounds) ..	475	$ 9.12	660	$12.65
Hot metal at $33/net ton	1,650	27.23	1,340	20.10
Other materials		1.17		4.00
Materials cost		$37.52		$36.75
	at 500,000 tons	1,000,000 tons	500,000 tons	1,000,000 tons
Other manufacturing costs [3] ...	$ 6.95	$ 6.86	$ 9.88	$ 9.73
Total mfg. cost	$44.47	$44.38	$46.63	$46.48

1 Oxygen converters in other plants currently operated with a 77% to 90% hot metal charge. Technical experiments underway indicated that this could probably be reduced to a 50% hot metal charge within the next 7 to 10 years.

2 Open hearths operated most efficiently at a 60-68% hot metal charge. Their effective range was 30-70% hot metal. Other manufacturing costs were $1.50/ton higher at the 30% end of the range. Above a 70% hot metal charge, quality was very difficult to control .

3 Including fuel, repairs, direct and indirect labor, supplies, and benefits but excluding all fixed charges for plant and equipment such as depreciation, local taxes, and interest. These capital charges for the open hearths were calculated to be $7,200,000 per year at present.

Oxygen converters produced steel with low carbon (below .09%) and with fewer impurities (primarily sulphur and phosphorus) than open-hearth steel. It was, therefore, superior to open-hearth steel for cold rolling and for customer applications that required severe bending of a flat sheet, such as the deep-drawing process used to make automobile fenders. The two steels were about equally suitable for hot-rolling. Oxygen steel was not as suitable as open-hearth steel for alloying.

The blast furnaces of the company had been either recently installed or recently rebuilt and were highly efficient. Additional pig iron output could be obtained from a new blast furnace of 45,000 tons per month capacity, which, with an ore screening and sintering plant, would cost about $35 million. After construction (two to three years), it would produce iron at a full cost of $38.50 per ton. (The past year's average market price for pig iron had been $56.20/net ton.)

Steel scrap prices changed even more rapidly than steel output:

AVERAGE PRICE IN DOLLARS PER NET TON

1947	$32.41	1958	$35.20	1963	$24.00
1951	40.34	1960	29.44	1964, Jan.	25.90
1956	48.35	1961	31.15	1964, July	32.10
1957	42.44	1962	25.10	1964, Nov.	34.90

Middle States had a sound market position in plate sales. Last year its sales of 610,000 tons of plate at an average price of $106 per ton had given it a 30% share of the relevant market. Company executives confidently expected that the new mill would allow an increase to a 38% share of the same market. Of the plates sold, 80% were of plain carbon steel and 20% were alloy (small percentage of columbium or vanadium or molybdenum added). The outlook was for an increasing demand for alloy steel—perhaps up to 40% within 10 years.

REQUIRED: (a) Explain why external sources of inputs were needed *at capacity* for the various stages of production.

(b) Was enough pig iron available for the open hearths *at the present level* of steel ingot production?

(c) Should Middle States Steel increase ingot-producing capacity by adding oxygen converters to balance steel output with the blooming mill's input capacity?

(d) Should Middle States Steel replace existing open-hearth capacity with oxygen converters?

(e) Should Middle States Steel plan to build an additional blast furnace? (Assume that financing is available at a capital cost of 6% per year.)

PRODUCTION AND
PURCHASING POLICIES
(CONCLUDED)

MAKE-OR-BUY SUPPLIES AND SERVICES

Every company uses a variety of supplies and services—paper, soap, transportation in and out, telephone, packaging, heat, power, and a thousand-and-one other items. Time and again the question arises of whether to make or buy these supplies and services. The following examples suggest the nature of the problem.

Production of containers and printed forms. All firms must decide whether to purchase or manufacture printing and packing supplies such as cans, cartons, seals, and twine. Some companies have a small printing shop in which they print their own forms, circulars, and notices, and do other job printing. While this practice has its definite advantages, a thorough analysis shows that in the majority of cases a single firm rarely has enough printing of a similar type to justify the most economical machine methods. Consequently, the wiser policy usually is to have such printing done by an outside firm that has a large number of customers.

A similar situation exists in connection with packing boxes. For example, the Taft Medicine Company, which had its own box shop, needed boxes in a considerable range of shapes and sizes for the packing of its various products. Because of the variety, several different machines were needed; however, most of these machines were used only part of the time. While the boxes made in the local shop were satisfactory, analysis showed that it would have been less expensive for the company to have purchased boxes from a manufacturer that specialized in this type of work.

On the other hand, a leading manufacturer of prepared breakfast foods concluded, after an exhaustive study of the relative costs of manufacturing and of buying packages and cartons, that a considerable savings would result from his own manufacture of these products. In this instance large quantities of identical boxes and cartons were required, and the cereal company was able to install specialized machinery and efficient methods equal to the independent box companies. Furthermore, the advantages of installing this specialized machinery more than offset the added complexity of managing the additional operation. Under this arrangement the company was able to exercise direct control over all phases of production and to coordinate under the same roof the manufacture of the packing boxes with the packing of the final product. This same company, however, decided that its job printing could be done more efficiently and more economically by an outside concern.

Company power plants. Larger companies must decide whether they will produce their own power and light or buy all their electric current from a public utility. The policy sometimes followed in this case is to manufacture the minimum load and purchase from the public utility only for the purpose of meeting peak requirements. Thus, the company plant can be operated continuously and the burden of fluctuating demand can be shifted to the public utility. The feasibility of such a plan depends, of course, upon the rates charged by the public utility. If the peak demand for a particular company occurs at the same time that other utility customers have peak demands, the rates charged by the utility companies are likely to be high.

Guides to make-or-buy policy. The following line of analysis provides an answer to most make-or-buy questions relating to supplies and services.

1. Does a dependable outside source exist? If the answer is "no," then we presume that our own production is best unless unforeseen obstacles arise. For instance, a cement plant in Chile has its own foundry and machine shop because no reliable source of repair parts is within reach. Similarly, most large industrial plants in Argentina have their own power plants because public power is unreliable.

2. When a dependable outside source does exist, we will use it unless a strong case can be made for not doing so. The reasons for this preference include simplifying the total managerial burden, focusing executive attention where major opportunities lie, reducing capital investment, retaining flexibility regarding sources, and—in competitive markets—gaining some of the economies that suppliers serving several customers will obtain.

3. Possible reasons for making exceptions to the preference for buying, just stated in (2), are: (a) Coordination with outside sources would be very cumbersome; for example, although office buildings frequently contract for janitor service and window washing, industrial plants rarely do so because cleaning up is intimately related to plant operations. (b) A large volume of a uniform item would result in unusually low costs. (c) The supply source is unwilling to provide special services (for example, speedy delivery or unusual sizes) we desire.

This approach at least puts the burden of proof on the executive who suggests deviating from the main activities in which his firm is staking its success.

SELECTION OF VENDORS

Regardless of how a company resolves its problems of vertical integration and of make-or-buy supplies, some sorts of goods must be purchased. The manufacturer must buy raw materials and factory supplies, the retailer must buy finished goods, even the professional firm must buy office supplies. In most business it is possible to purchase satisfactory products from several vendors. This raises the question of (1) whether purchasing from several vendors is wiser than concentrating the business on only one or two. Even after this policy is settled, (2) the type of vendor that will be the most satisfactory source for materials has to be settled.

Number of vendors. The number of suppliers of at least the essential products purchased by a firm should receive careful attention. Entire operations of the firm can be jeopardized if this issue is not wisely handled.

Allocating buying to secure vendor's services. A school supply jobber for instance, followed the practice for a number of years of buying from as many different manufacturers as possible so that the firm name might be widely known. The company later became involved in financial difficulties and regretted its policy of using a large number of vendors. The purchases it made from any one manufacturer were not important enough to that manufacturer to justify granting special credit terms, and each vendor sought to collect bills promptly. Had this firm concentrated its purchases to a greater extent, it might have induced its vendors to be more lenient in making collections during the period of financial stress.

Advantages and dangers of concentration. A few companies that buy large quantities of merchandise concentrate their purchases to such an extent that they buy the entire output of the supplier. By so doing, they are able to secure favorable prices because the manufacturer is relieved of all selling cost and he is able to concentrate his production operations on just those commodities desired by his one customer. The danger in this practice is that the manufacturer may fail to make delivery because of labor troubles, lack of capital, fire or some other catastrophe, thus leaving the company deprived of its supply of products at a time when they are sorely needed.

A large mail-order house that was buying the entire output of a refrigerator plant guarded against this to some degree by having at the plant its own representative who reviewed the books of account and was familiar with plant operations. Such a representative could warn the mail-order house of any impending difficulties. Another large firm followed the policy of buying no more than 25% of its requirements of any one product from the same manufacturer. If for any reason something happened to one of these sources of supply, the company would be able to continue to get at least 75% of its requirements from its other vendors.

Many firms follow a policy that seeks to gain the advantages of both concentration of purchases and multiple vendors. They find that buying most of their needs of a particular material from one source is desirable; the quality, price, delivery service, or some other factor makes concentration clearly the best arrangement. So, they give 70% to 80% of their business to this one vendor. The remaining part of the business is divided among several other suppliers. In this manner, business relations are established, specification problems are met and resolved, and the way is prepared for much larger purchases at a later date. Placing these small orders with several vendors is probably more expensive than buying all requirements from the chief source, but it serves two important purposes: (a) if a strike, fire, or other catastrophe hits the main supplier, the firm can shift to other services much more quickly than it could if no relationship had been established; and (b) the main supplier is "kept on his toes" because the buyer is in close touch with the market and in a position to shift to other suppliers if the price, quality, or service from the main source does not continue to be the best.

Buying distress merchandise. Some retail stores appeal to their customers primarily on the basis of price, and in order to make a profit continually seek to buy merchandise at "distress" prices. These stores usually offer to pay cash for merchandise, and they are not particularly concerned about being able to secure additional products from the same company. Such stores will deal with any vendor who has merchandise to offer for sale at a reasonable price, and they are continually "shopping around" for more favorable terms. Although such a policy appears to be good for companies operating on a purely price or cut-rate basis, most concerns have learned by experience that it is preferable to cooperate with vendors. A cooperative relationship will not be disrupted by either party because of apparent temporary advantages that may be obtained from time to time under special conditions.

Factors determining number of vendors. These illustrations show that there are both advantages and disadvantages to limiting the number of vendors from whom purchases are made. It is often necessary to balance the advantages of better service and quantity discounts that can be secured by concentrating business with a few vendors against the disadvantages of possible failure of supply and the passing up of occasional bargain merchandise. The problem often resolves itself into the following questions:

1. Can a limited number of vendors supply the variety of products required?
2. How much special service and price concession will result from concentration?
3. How important is such service to the purchaser?
4. Is the company too dependent upon any one company for materials?

Type of vendor. *Importance attached to quality.* The type of vendors selected by a company will depend, in part, upon the quality of the product that it wishes. Thus, a publishing house, desiring all its books to be made of a high-quality material, bought only from mills that made paper of dependable quality. Although the paper was purchased according to detailed specifications, the company was aware of the difficulty every paper mill has of controlling the quality of its product. The publishing house therefore preferred to pay somewhat higher prices to those mills that had a reputation for exercising care in maintaining the quality of their product.

If the quality of the product to be purchased can be easily determined by test, the reputation of the vendor will not be as important as in a case where quality is difficult to determine. For example, a company may be willing to rely upon its testing laboratories to determine the quality of steel or coal that it buys, but a doctor will not take the same attitude toward drugs purchased for his patients.

Even a product that is highly standardized and has a recognized market price may be purchased from one vendor rather than another in order to secure certain intangible qualities. Operators of textile mills, for instance, point out that there is considerable variation in the way raw cotton of identical staple and grade will work up in cloth. Consequently, when a textile mill discovers that cotton coming from one region through a given broker is more easily handled on their equipment than cotton from any other region, that mill will try to concentrate its future purchases on cotton coming from that particular section.

Service of vendors. Vendors may be selected because of the service they render their customers. For example, companies manufacturing typewriters, adding machines, billing machines, duplicators, and other types of office equipment often give their customers a great deal of aid in designing office forms and in establishing new systems. Most of these companies also maintain an extensive repair service. If a machine should break down, it may be quickly repaired without serious interruption in the work of the office using the equipment.

The importance of such service became striking in Brazil when that market was flooded with relatively inexpensive office equipment of German manufacture. The machines had entered Brazil under a barter agreement in which Brazil exchanged coffee and other raw materials for a specified quantity of machinery from Germany. As a result, the German machinery could be purchased in Brazil at substantially lower prices than equipment made by American companies. Inadequate provision had been made for servicing the German machines, however. Consequently, when one of these machines broke down, it was both expensive and time consuming to get it back into working order. As a result, many of the office managers were turning to more expensive American machines because of the repair service maintained by the American manufacturers.

Under some conditions promptness of delivery is a controlling factor in the selection of vendors. This has been one of the primary reasons why small steel companies have been able to secure in their local territories business that otherwise might have gone to the big steel companies. With standardized products and uniform prices prevailing in the industry, such special services as delivery often become controlling influences. The large companies have recently given more recognition to this factor and have spent substantial funds in an effort to expedite the handling of customers' orders.

Reciprocity. Under special circumstances vendors are selected on the basis of reciprocity. Thus, railroads are careful to place orders with concerns that are in a position to route a large quantity of freight over their lines. Sometimes the reciprocity may be a three-cornered deal. For instance, a Great Lakes steamship company decided to place a large order for motors with a particular manufacturer as a favor to a pig-iron producer. The pig-iron producer shipped large quantities of ore and could therefore demand favors from the steamship company in exchange for a contract to transport ore. To complete the circle, the pig-iron producer used its control over the order for motors in selling pig-iron to the motor manufacturer. Hence, each of the three concerns selected vendors with an eye to the indirect effect such election would have on sales.

Role of price. Thus far, no mention has been made of price in connection with the type of vendors. Prices for many products are uniform, and for other products the differences are not of sufficient importance to offset such factors as quality and special service. It should be clear, however, that price is an ever-present consideration, and if for some reason one type of vendor charges higher prices than another, the former is automatically eliminated unless there is some special reason for dealing with him. As already noted, the significance of differences in prices depends partly upon the emphasis that the company buying the material gives to price in reselling the material, and also upon the importance of that particular product to the total cost of the company.

Summary regarding selection of vendors. In selecting vendors a company is responding to the *sales appeal* of the numerous companies desiring to sell merchandise of the type used by the company. The point of view, however, is essentially different because the purchasing company is concerned only with its own specific problems and has no interest in the sales activities of the vendor unless these activities are of some value to it. There are also a number of questions, such as the number of vendors, that do not have an exact counterpart for the seller. The more important foctors that should be considered in making vendor selections are indicated in the following table:

Factors Influencing Vendor Selection

Capacity and Willingness of Vendor to Meet Company Needs	General Characteristics of Desirable Vendors	Factors Limiting the Choice

Quality of product:
   Specifications
   Dependability
 	
 Services offered:
   Delivery
   Technical aid
   Repair
   Credit terms
   Guarantees
   Adjustments
 	
 Price:
   Competitive level
   Inclination to squeeze
   Protection on changes
	Size of vendor:
	   Interest in our
	     business
	   Financial stability
	
	 Geographic location:
	   Support of "local"
	     industry
	   Dispersion of risks
	
	 Manufacturer *vs.* jobber
	
	 Maintenance of alternative sources:
	   Divide equally
	   One main source,
	     others minor
		Reciprocity
		
		 Time and expense of locating and dealing with new vendors
		
		 Habit and conservatism:
		   Potential "headaches"
		   in new relationship
		
		 Friendship and loyalty
		
		 Willingness of using departments to try new vendors.

Company policies are needed to show which of these factors should be given primary consideration and which should be disregarded.

COORDINATION OF PRODUCTION, PURCHASING, AND SALES

Even after policies regarding integration, capacity, processes, procurement of supplies, and selection of vendors are clear, a cluster of problems on *timing* of purchasing and production remain. We are concerned here not with specific programs—a topic explored in Chapter 23—but with several underlying guides that must be established before programs can be built. As a basis for coordination of purchasing and production with sales, central management should set policies regarding:

1. Procurement for stock or "to order."
2. Minimum inventories.
3. Size of production run or purchase order.
4. Stabilization of production operations.
5. Adjustments to anticipated price changes.

Procurement for stock or "to order." *The made-to-order policy.*
Coordination of procurement with sales is accomplished in some
industries by buying or making goods only if the sales order is
already received. The purchase of raw materials and supplies is not
undertaken and production is not started until the order is actually
at hand. Manufacturers of heavy machinery—or space ships—
almost always follow such a make-to-order policy.

Other companies, such as producers of radio and television
broadcasting equipment, make finished products only "on order";
but, in fact, they produce many parts and even subassemblies for
stock. Then when an order is received, only the final assemply
operation has to be done according to customer specification.

Concerns manufacturing high-class, upholstered furniture may
follow the same policy to even a lesser extent. In this industry, it
is customary to manufacture the furniture up to the point where
the upholstery is to be put on. This final covering is not applied
until a specific order is received from a customer designating the
kind of cover desired.

While a policy of making-to-order does reduce inventory risks
and gives the customer just what he wants, it also has serious
drawbacks. Delivery is inevitably slow and costs tend to be high
because mass production techniques cannot be fully utilized.

Carrying stock. A majority of products are purchased or produced long before the customer's order is received. Orders are
filled from inventory already on hand. This is true of most of the
products that we, as ultimate consumers, purchase, and it is also
true of a great many products purchased by industrial concerns.

A compromise policy is followed by some firms that carry only
standard products in stock. If their customers want an article that
is not standard, the merchandise will be purchased or produced
according to their choice. For example, a shop dealing in dinnerware and glassware may carry an open stock of certain popular
patterns. Should a customer wish other patterns, the manager of
the shop will be glad to order them from the factory.

Since there are various degrees of making-to-order and of carrying stock—as the preceding examples show—and the degree affects purchasing, production, and selling activities, management should provide policy guidance. This is not a decision to be made from the viewpoint of any one department alone.

Minimum inventory. If stock is to be carried, a company must establish some general guide to assist the purchasing and production departments in determining how much inventory to have on hand at any one time. Let us look first at the more mechanistic aspects of the problem—ordering points, size of production runs, and purchase quantities—and then note two main reasons for further adjustments, namely, stabilization and speculation on price changes.

How low should inventories be permitted to go before they are reordered? Each retail store in a modern grocery chain, for instance, is expected to maintain a minimum of all items regularly sold. Since the store gets frequent deliveries of additional merchandise, the minimum may be only a week's supply. In contrast, because of slow turnover the minimum inventory carried by many independent furniture stores is equal to a full year's sales.

Manufacturing firms must establish some general policy for minimum inventory for both finished goods and raw materials. Thus, a manufacturer of rugs had a policy of carrying finished merchandise only at the beginning of each selling season and gave no assurance to his customers that he would carry an inventory throughout the year. On the other hand, he did wish to carry a minimum stock of raw materials so as to avoid possible delay in production operations. Here the policy was to carry approximately three months' supply of yarn and other raw materials.

It has been suggested, as a general rule for finished merchandise, that the stock level at which replacements will be ordered should be approximately equal to the sales of that merchandise during the period required for replenishment. Thus, for stock that can be replenished within two weeks, the reordering point would be equal to approximately two weeks' sales. If it takes three months or six months to procure new inventory, then the minimum at which orders should be placed would be correspondingly higher. The same general idea can be carried back into the inventory of raw materials, in which case the rule might be that the reordering point should not be less than the probable production requirements during the period required to replenish the stock.

Since the sale or use of stock on hand will continue during the period of replenishment, it is customary to add a reasonable margin of safety to any such reordering point as a protection against possible contingencies. The size of the safety margin will depend upon the likelihood of delays in getting replacements and the seriousness of the delay to production operations or customer service. These considerations lead many firms to follow a policy of carrying a minimum inventory much higher than strict interpretation of the replenishment rule requires.

Size of production run or purchase order. When reordering is necessary, how much should be ordered? Primary considerations are economical production runs in a company's own plant or quantity discounts offered by vendors due to economic production runs in the vendor's plant or warehouse.

A company producing waxpaper wrappers for bakeries and candy companies, for example, found that the cost of preparing plates, setting up plates in the printing presses, threading the proper weight paper through the presses, and making other preparations necessary for actual printing was often a substantial part of the total expense incurred on small orders. It was found that the labor and idle machine charges were often $40 per order, and when this cost had to be charged to a few hundred wrappers, the cost per unit was quite high. If the order was for several thousand sheets, the expense could be spread over the entire order, and thus the cost per unit could be lowered.

To meet this situation, the company often printed more wrappers than were actually on order by the customer, thereby securing a low production cost per unit. The extra stock was then held until the customer placed a reorder. This substantially increased the company's inventory but was the only way that the company could secure satisfactory production costs.

Several years ago companies manufacturing circle saws and other saw blades for lumber mills and wood shops faced a similar situation. At that time each mill preferred a blade with the particular shape of teeth that it believed to be most efficient in cutting wood. The mills insisted on having blades cut to their specifications, and the blade manufacturers were consequently forced to make a special run for each customer. In this case, however, the industry was successful in standardizing blades carried in stock and in educating a majority of customers to buy these standard blades.

This same factor may lead a company to purchase larger quantities of goods than are necessary to maintain minimum stocks. To get the customer to purchase in larger quantities, the vendor will often offer quantity discounts. The possibility of obtaining these discounts may induce the customer to purchase more goods than are required for current sales or production. It should be noted that this applies to the production of a special and distinctive product for each customer. Once the product becomes standardized, the manufacturer can sell a small quantity of the product to one customer because the balance of what constitutes an economical production run will probably be sold to other customers.

Policies regarding size of purchase orders, like size of production runs, may be stated in total quantities or so many weeks or months supply. Then order standards for specific items may be computed, giving effect to economy of large lots, cost of storage, perishability and obsolescence, and related factors.

When the time at which sales orders will be received (or supplies needed) can be predicted with reliability, at least for a frequency distribution, and dollar values can be attached to carrying inventories, to savings on large quantities, and to loss resulting from failure to accept or deliver a sales order—then minimum inventories, ordering points, and size of production runs or purchase orders can be calculated statistically. Even in such situations, however, the judgment of central management is needed to establish safety margins on receipt of goods and to evaluate the seriousness of disappointing a customer. These judgments are often stated as policies. Moreover, management may choose to modify a statistically optimum schedule (a) to stabilize production or (b) to adjust to price changes.

Stabilization of production. The business of every company fluctuates by seasons and by cycles. For example, a manufacturer of blankets may find that he sells two thirds of his products in the last half of each calendar year, and a manufacturer of gloves may find that he sells 45% of his products in the last three months of the year. Even articles in daily use, such as soap and cosmetics, have a seasonal fluctuation.

Production for stock. Faced with such a seasonal fluctuation in the volume, a company may decide to manufacture and purchase merchandise in harmony with its sales volume so that it will not carry inventory in excess of its sales needs at any time. Most glove manufacturers, for instance, do not attempt to produce very far ahead of the season in which they will sell their gloves. Frequent changes in style may make gloves produced in advance of the season unsalable, or salable only at a reduced price.

Other firms produce at approximately a level rate throughout the year. This means that they accumulate during the seasons of slack sales an inventory that may be used to satisfy the demand during the peak periods. One of the leading manufacturers of bathing suits follows this policy in order to avoid having an idle

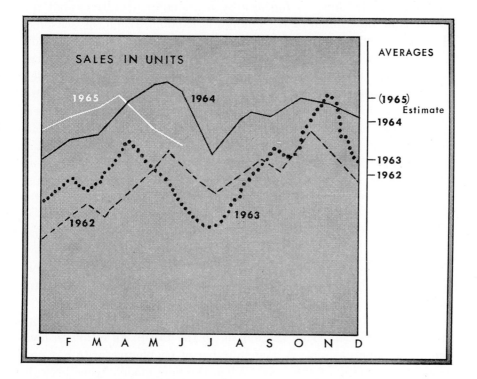

The Household Appliance Company decided in January, 1965, to stabilize production at the estimated 1965 average. In June, central management had to decide whether to cut back because inventories were at an all-time high.

plant during part of the year and to keep a group of efficient workmen employed the entire year.

Theoretically, a similar policy of production stablization could be applied to cyclical fluctuations. In fact, International Business Machines did continue manufacture of tabulating equipment during the depression of the early 1930's because Thomas Watson wished to avoid layoffs. Fortunately, demand picked up before the company was financially exhausted and the high inventory was gradually liquidated. (Technological change was not so rapid then as now.) But other companies went bankrupt with more modest stabilization efforts.

Any company that considers producing during slack periods for sales in later boom times must reckon with obsolescence, deterioration, storage costs, and financing. Fully as important is the ability to forecast the duration and the amplitudes of downswings and upswings. Even seasonal drops are difficult to interpret during the downswing because a manager usually cannot tell *at the time* how much of the change is random, trend, or seasonal. So, an important aspect of a policy to stabilize production is how long production will be maintained above sales—or how large an inventory will be built up— in the face of below normal sales.

Other ways of dealing with fluctuations. It should be noted in passing that production in excess of demand during slack seasons is not the only way companies have sought to adjust to fluctuations in sales volume. We have already seen in Chapter 5 that some companies have been successful in adding to their line products that have complementary seasonal fluctuations. The combination of the radio and electric refrigerator business was among the illustrations cited.

Subcontracting at times of peak demand has been used by some companies in place of a temporary expansion in their own work force. This is not always practical, however, since subcontractors are likely to be busy just at the times when the prime contractor has his peak load.

The automobile industry has changed the date for bringing out new annual models from the spring to the fall in an effort to level out season fluctuations. A large number of people prefer to buy new cars in the spring of the year. When the new models were brought out at this time, there was a double incentive to buy during the months of March through June. By changing the time of introducing the new models to the fall, the companies were able to attract customers in the fall of the year who otherwise might have purchased in the spring.

These methods, like almost all stabilization devices available to private enterprise, apply best to seasonal fluctuations and have only limited application to cylical changes.

Adjustment to anticipated price changes. Many companies adjust their purchasing and production schedules in anticipation of changes in prices of raw materials and finished products. When price increases are anticipated, goods will be procured in excess of immediate requirements; and when declines are forecast, inventories will be reduced. In this way the companies hope to secure additional profits by buying at lower prices goods that can be sold at higher prices.

Setting up a sound policy regarding anticipation of price changes is complicated by the fact that availability of goods often fluctuates with price. At times of rising prices demand is brisk, and it may take twice as long to get delivery as is necessary when business is dull. Consequently, a purchasing agent who is responsible for having an adequate supply of inventory on hand, may buy ahead in boom times just to make sure that he gets goods on time. On the downswing, prompt deliveries are easier to get and the purchasing agent may safely cut back his inventory. Assuming that some adjustment for variations in delivery time is prudent, the question of trying to outguess price changes still remains.

"Shrewd buying." The difficulty of establishing a wise policy regarding size of inventories was illustrated during the Korean crisis. Immediately after the invasion of South Korea, department store sales jumped 20%. This increase in business plus the possibility of a war scarcity of goods, led store executives to increase their orders for goods at least 25%. Within three months, however, the initial scare-buying had passed and department store sales dropped back to their former levels. About this same time the large orders which had been placed earlier were being shipped. Business was down, receipts of goods were up; inventories on hand jumped as a result.

At this moment the United Nations forces received a severe setback in Korea, and the possibility of an all-out war seemed imminent. Retail sales bounded back to even higher levels. This meant inventories no longer looked large; instead, the earlier decision to build up stock was vindicated. Under these circumstances, store executives placed new orders for goods in greater volume than before. Demand was high, prices rising, shortages likely.

Had a major war developed at that time, the inventory policy these executives followed might now be considered great wisdom. As events turned out, the second bulge in sales was no stronger than the first and sales again dropped almost to the earlier level. And again deliveries poured in when goods on hand were already too high. Soon inventories were almost 40% too high, and orders had to be cut back drastically. The dislocations created by these two buying sprees precipitated a minor depression in the soft good industries that took them over a year to work out of, and department store profits fell because high-priced inventory had to be sold at sale prices.

This illustration happens to be keyed into war scares, but the buying and inventory problems are typical of business fluctuations which have beset business for years. The inventory problems described for retailers are duplicated in greater magnitude for manufacturers. In this connection, note that firm commitments to buy goods are equivalent to goods on hand, as far as price risks are concerned.

Conservative buying. A conservative approach to the problem of adjusting purchases to anticipated price changes is illustrated by the policies of a relatively small tire company. It normally carries on hand from three to six months supply of rubber; and variation within these limits is determined by the management on the basis of anticipated ease or difficulty of getting deliveries.

Fabric, a second raw material needed for tires, is usually purchased in the early fall in sufficient quantities to meet a year's requirements. The management believes that this is the most satisfactory way of purchasing this product. Lower prices can be secured if fabric is purchased in large quantities, and the fluctuations in price during the year are not sufficient to cause large inventory losses. Reclaimed rubber and other materials are purchased in amounts sufficient for sixty days' supply. Thus, this company varies its procurement in anticipation of prices only within comparatively narrow limits. Some manufacturers go even further and purchase all materials a fixed period in advance, making practically no adjustment for anticipated price changes.

The case against inventory speculation. Although companies are sometimes able to secure substantial benefits from procuring products in excess of current requirements and in anticipation of price increases, it is questionable whether from a long-run point of view this is a wise policy for merchandising or manufacturing institutions. There are so many factors affecting price trends that accurate forecasting is very difficult. The typical merchandiser or manufacturer is not well equipped to make such forecasts, and even those who specialize in the study of price trends do not have a very satisfactory record of accomplishment.

There are many other risks that a business concern cannot avoid, and it would appear wiser for executives to concentrate their attention on these rather than incur risks that may be avoided, at least in part. Few companies would be willing to give their manager or their purchasing agent a large sum of money to be used for speculation in the stock market, and ket they do permit these men in behalf of the company to risk similar sums of money on price changes in order to buy necessary commodities. If these men were able to predict price changes accurately, it would be better that they retire from manufacturing or retailing responsibilities and devote their attention to speculating in commodities.

There are, of course, a few times when it is evident that there is to be an increase in prices. On some occasions vendors announce price increases a substantial period before they become effective, and under such conditions it may be wiser to purchase in excess of current requirements. But if a company follows the policy consistently of speculating in commodities, it is likely to secure unsatisfactory results over a period of time.

Conclusion regarding timing of procurement. In producing and in buying, wide differences exist in anticipating customers' actions or waiting until orders are in hand. Many companies carry larger stocks than are required for customer service to secure economic production runs or to obtain discounts from vendors. Sometimes the procurement of merchandise is adjusted in an effort to stabilize production operations, but more frequently it is adjusted in an effort to profit from anticipating price changes or to assure adequate supply.

The more important factors that an executive should consider in dealing with such timing issues include:

1. Customer requirements for specially designed merchandise or for prompt deliveries of standard merchandise.
2. Economies possible from larger production runs.
3. Economies that may be secured from level production, including more complete utilization of facilities, maintenance of a well-trained labor force, and possible reductions in tax burdens.
4. Expenses of carrying goods in inventory, including the storage charges, the financial cost, the insurance expense, and the deterioration or obsolescence of merchandise.
5. Accuracy with which price changes may be predicted.
6. Accuracy of prediction of the volume and nature of products demanded at a subsequent period of time.

This list, though incomplete, does indicate that the timing of procurement is a complex problem. Central management should provide policy guidance in this area because actions will affect the company's ability to render good customer service, influence its operating costs, change its circulating capital requirements, and may bring about special losses due to adjustment in valuation of inventories.

SUMMARY

Every business enterprise will face many of the production and purchasing issues discussed in the last two chapters. There is the inevitable question of "make-or-buy," and this applies to the whole range of finished products, parts, supplies, and raw materials used.

Production processes must be selected, and here policies regarding division of labor, automation, size of plant, and process research are needed.

Then comes the issue of how much capacity. Plans for meeting peak loads should be set up. Provision for growth, balance between departments, and backward taper of capacity also have to be fitted into the general scheme. Guidance on the level of maintenance and on replacement should be correlated with product line, customer service, and financial policies.

For goods to be purchased, policies dealing with the number and the types of vendors are necessary. And there are basic issues of when and how much to buy and to produce.

In this array of issues we are concerned with the company's basic strategy for generating the goods and the services that its marketing strategy requires. Each set of policies should support the other and also should be consistent with personnel and financial policies—to which we now turn our attention.

QUESTIONS FOR CLASS DISCUSSION

1. A common-carrier pipeline company, which gathered natural gas from various locations and pumped it several hundreds of miles to distributing companies in several cities, had used the telephone wires and microwave communications of American Telephone and Telegraph and several independent telephone companies for remote control of its gathering and pumping stations. Now a manufacturer of microwave equipment proposes to the pipeline company that it set up its own communication system. Based on present technology and experience with other installations, the private microwave system would pay for itself in ten years, would have total operating costs no higher than the telephone companies' toll charges, would decrease downtime from $1\frac{1}{2}\%$ to 1%, and would open up the possibility of carrying administrative traffic as well as scheduling and control traffic on the company's own microwave network. A new communications department would be necessary. Should the pipeline company install its own communications system?

2. What factors should be considered in establishing a minimum inventory policy for raw materials? How do these factors differ from those affecting minimum inventories of finished goods? Of finished parts?

3. The managing director of the Volkswagen Company once made a special trip to attempt to persuade companies located in the United States to become regular suppliers of parts to the Volkswagen Company and to make bids on a list of parts he brought with him. The mission was generally a failure. Why do you think he made the effort and why was the objective not adequately realized?

4. An electronics company assembles its 30 models to order only —usually in lots of 10 to 30 units. In these products it uses 5,000 purchased or fabricated parts, many of which are used on all models. A bank of parts and subassemblies is kept in the stock room. Perpetual control of parts and materials inventory is by the Production Control Department. Reordering is based on minimum quantities from historical usage. Difficulties with not-infrequent shortages of parts for final assembly are overcome by personal expediting by the assembly foreman. Management, to prevent borrowing, has ordered inventory reduced 20%. To comply, Production Control has cut reorder points and quantities. What difficulties, if any, do you visualize?

5. How, if at all, should a company adjust its policy on timing of procurement and selection of vendors to governmental attempts to influence prices? Consider such actions as support of farm prices, Federal Reserve and Treasury fiscal policies, antimonopoly suits, minimum wages, reciprocal tariff agreements, and the like.

6. Contrast the factors, and the emphasis on each, in deciding the number of vendors to be used by (a) a small manufacturer of paper boxes with (b) a large oil refinery and with (c) an electric public utility company.

7. A large hotel chain that specialized in conventions and business travel and that had several hotels in one major city once operated its own laundry but discontinued this in favor of using commercial laundries. Would you recommend this for a luxury hotel catering to families and travelers? For a YMCA hotel?

8. Use the table of *Factors Influencing Vendor Selection* in contrasting (a) the purchase of groceries by a family and (b) the purchase of coal or iron by a factory.

9. "The production department should be consulted in the preparation of the sales program." If so, why? In what situations would it be more accurate to say that the sales department should be consulted in the preparation of the production program?

CASE X

Automatic Lathe Company

Automation of its customers' production lines made obsolete the design of one basic machine type produced by the Automatic Lathe Company. Redesigning the machine has resulted, in turn, in a question of supply and vendor policy.

The Automatic Lathe Company makes screw machines and tracer lathes, which it sells to automobile manufacturers, munitions makers, and office machinery firms. The main use of these machines is to cut metal from the surface of an object by rotating it against a cutting tool which is held at the side of the object. The machine type being redesigned is the "multiple spindle chucker," which performs up to twelve simultaneous machining operations on three to seven work pieces. The parts worked on are held in a device known as a chuck which rotates rapidly at the end of a spindle. Although work is removed automatically, the parts must be loaded by hand and an operator must be present to check on the satisfactory working of this high-speed machine.

The new automatic handling equipment on customer production lines brings parts from other machines to the chucker built by Automatic and carries parts away at high speed. Recently devised testing devices which check the dimensions of finished parts, and new controls which set the sequence of operations and start and stop machining automatically, cut down the amount of work for an operator so that now a single attendant should keep several machines in operation rather than one as before.

To further cut down operator time and to allow his manual operations to keep up with the machine operations, it was necessary to redesign the base of the chucking machine as well as the housing space for air valves and related equipment. The redesign resulted in (1) a rectangular cut-out in the splash pan and the lower base to allow the operator to move 8 inches closer to the loading area, (2) a housing compartment (box-like covering) for the air valves, and (3) a cut-out area at the bottom near the floor with a platform adjustable to operator height in order to reduce his fatigue. These requirements present a difficult problem for the foundry which has been making the base. The sharp angles and intricate moulding work result in a machine base hard to keep cleaned out and subject to unusual stresses. Indeed, the first base broke in two while being removed from the sand.

As they looked at the broken pieces, the design engineer turned with delight to the works manager and said: "Good! Now we can go to weldments!"

The machine base looks like a huge rectangular dish with one or more high sides. Its purpose is to provide rigidity for the entire lathe, to support the working parts, to provide reservoirs and piping for the lubricating oils and coolant, and to collect machining scrap. The base which broke is 10 feet long and weighs 9,500 pounds.

If the new base is a casting, it will be handled in the Automatic Lathe Company shop in the same manner as the present cast base. Gray iron castings for the base are presently purchased from a foundry next door to the Automatic Lathe Company plant and from two other nearby foundries. The base is made in two sections which are brought in at one end of the plant and then cleaned to rid them of sand and small projections of metal. After cleaning, the base is machined and moved further into the plant for assembly. Machining takes 40% of the total preparation time before assembly begins. After assembly of each major operating section such as the gear box or the cross slide frame assembly, the base must be releveled and possibly scraped in order to correct alignment. Following assembly the entire machine is prepared for painting, then painted, crated, and shipped from the other end of the plant. The preliminary machining of the base includes drilling holes for piping. Final filling and painting requires 30 hours.

The neighboring foundry that supplies bases and other parts makes 75% of its sales to the Automatic Lathe Company at an average price of 18 cents per pound of castings. The other foundries are used less extensively.

Weldments are made from sections of heavy steel plate which have been cut into a particular shape by a gas torch. The sections are welded into a unit. If the base for the new Automatic Lathe Company chucker were a weldment it would be made of $\frac{5}{8}$-inch thick steel plate cut to shape and then welded to make the complete base. The production of weldments for heavy use is a new industry and requires a much higher degree of skill and technical knowledge than is found in the typical welding shop. Only one firm in the area, Avery and Saul, could supply the Automatic

Lathe Company needs. This means that the weldment bases would have to be shipped 120 miles as a complete unit. Upon arrival at the Automatic Lathe plant, they would be ready for machining prior to assembly, that is, no cleaning would be necessary. During assembly the single unit welded construction would reduce deflection to a great extent and in some cases no adjustment of the initial level would be necessary. (Piling heavy sections on top of the base would not twist it out of alignment.) The weldment, which would weigh 6,000 pounds, would arrive with the oil and coolant piping completely provided; it costs $65 to install this piping in a present machine. Finished painting of the chucking machine would require 25 hours if weldments were used.

The design advantages of using weldments are felt by the engineers to be considerable. The addition of a compartment for air valves to the weldment is very simple whereas it is a complex casting problem. Continual minor additions and changes in the basic machines must be made for convenience in fitting them into the variety of customer automation lines. These changes can be readily accomplished in the case of weldments by making minor additions of cut shapes. However, if castings are used, the pattern must be altered. This takes considerable time. Delivery of special or adapted machines may be greatly speeded up by the use of weldments. In the design of the cast base, continuation of the splash pan for the full length of the upper base adds strength and rigidity and also eases the molding problem. This, however, obviously detracts from the appearance of the machine and does not add to it functionally. The designer felt that weldment use would affect a considerable improvement in general appearance.

The works manager remarked about the design engineer's enthusiasm for weldments, "Well, you know the engineers are always looking for something new and are really happy if they can make a big change which will make the design simpler. Without any question we could continue to use castings for the chucking machine base although the foundry work is hard and they would get some breakage. These weldments cost 34 cents a pound delivered and the standard purchasing procedure in getting steel means that deliveries run from two to six months. When no pattern change is necessary, we can get a cast machine base in a hurry. If we stop buying cast bases for this chucking machine, we will cut down our use of the foundry next door to about 50% of its capacity. We pay an average of $2.25 an hour for labor and it takes about 60 hours to clean up one of the cast bases before assembly. Avery and Saul makes lots of other items besides our base; I think it would complicate scheduling to work with them."

REQUIRED: Should the Automatic Lathe Company use weldments for the base of its chucking machine?

PERSONNEL POLICIES—
SELECTION AND TRAINING

Personnel policies—a 20th century concept. Sixty years ago personnel policies and personnel departments were unknown. The hiring and firing of employees were left to the foreman or executive who had immediate supervision over the worker; problems of training, compensation, and discipline were handled by numerous supervisors throughout the company largely as the saw fit. Proper treatment of employees, or the lack of it, depended primarily upon the humanitarian interests of the bosses.

The personnel movement, as we know it today, received its greatest impetus during World War I. During this period there was a demand for increased industrial production. Manpower was scarce and expensive. It was only natural, therefore, that business executives should turn to the pioneers in personnel work for assistance in handling their labor problems. Actually there were several currents contributing to the personnel work of that day which gradually became integrated into a body of ideas regarding personnel relations.

Among these currents was the safety movement in the steel industry and other fields, which received added impetus from the more drastic provisions of workmen's compensation laws. The scientific management movement under the leadership of Frederick W. Taylor, with its emphasis on detailed job analysis and scientific selection of workmen, was influential particularly in the handling of factory personnel. The study of psychology had emerged from the domination of philosophers in university classrooms, and men interested in applied psychology injected their slant on human problems in business operations. Still another contributing movement was the development of corporation schools that gave vocational training to their younger employees. In addition, many companies were beginning to give greater attention to lunch rooms for employees, company picnics, athletic meets, and similar welfare activities designed to build a friendly *esprit de corps* among the workers. All of these movements affected personnel practice as we know it today and many have become an integral part of the broader modern concept of personnel management.

We should note in passing that the personnel movement in its early days experienced a period of growth and popularity that led many business concerns to undertake activities that were expensive and yet contributed little to the mutual trust and understanding between employees and employer. Often some of the more obvious surface activities were undertaken while more fundamental underlying policies were neglected. The last twenty years have done much to debunk these glittering but shallow programs. At the same time management has become more keenly aware of the need for sound personnel policies.

New attitude toward personnel problems. The haphazard way in which personnel problems have been handled in the past is now recognized as unsatisfactory by many business leaders. This change in attitude has been due in part to: (1) recognition by employers that the enthusiastic support of a group of properly qualified employees is of vital importance to the success of every business enterprise; (2) demonstrated benefits that can be secured through well-conceived personnel policies and methods; (3) the need for consistency in dealing with employees especially in *large* enterprises with many supervisors; (4) federal and state legislation that has taken a significant part of the control of labor activities out of the hands of the employer and at the same time has increased the variety and extent of legal regulations regarding employment; and (5) increased power of labor unions.

Classification of personnel policies. Personnel policies deal with the procurement and maintenance of an efficient work force. The major policies that set the pattern of personal relations throughout a firm can be grouped under the following headings:

1. Selection.
2. Training.
3. Compensation.
4. Arrangements for work.
5. Employee services.
6. Industrial relations.

SELECTION

Selection embraces all policies a company may have regulating the choice of employees. In this broad sense it includes not only the *hiring* of new employees but also the selection of employees to be *promoted* and the further problem of *discharging* employees. The process of selection goes on almost continuously.

Hiring college students. There was a time when the man with a college degree who applied for a job was regarded as having some distinctive quality. Today a greater proportion of young people are going through college, and many firms have revised their policy of hiring college graduates. For example, one medium-sized public utility company was enthusiastic about hiring college graduates because it was believed that they would develop into capable executives. Over a period of years thirty or more college men were employed and sent from one department of the company to another so that they might learn all parts of the business. Promotion to supervisory positions was difficult, however, because the company did not want to discharge the experienced men already in those jobs. Even when normal vacancies did occur, capable men who had worked for the company for a longer time than the college graduates had to be considered in order to convince the rank-and-file employees that there was an opportunity for advancement if they put forth their best efforts. Consequently, advancement of the college graduates was slow, and many of them became impatient with the progress they were making. The company therefore modified its policy and restricted the college men employed to a number that could normally be absorbed without upsetting the morale of other employees.

A retail store operating in a better suburb of a large city had a different experience. A number of the young women in that area attended a neighboring university and had many acquaintances among the potential customers of the store. Following graduation, these girls often became ladies-in-waiting. The store adopted a policy of hiring as many of these girls as possible for salesclerks on the assumption that their friends would be likely to come into the store and buy from them. In terms of ability, appearance, and bearing, most of these girls were very well qualified. They took the positions partly for the income they received, and partly because they wanted something to do.

The result in this case was definitely unsatisfactory. The girls sold merchandise to their friends, but they did not care enough about their positions to observe the store rules. They were frequently late or absent, and they sometimes assumed a superior attitude toward the customers whom they did not know. This had a disrupting effect upon all the salespeople, and it gave many of the customers the impression that the store was not interested in their patronage. The store had to change its policy of seeking these girls for salesclerks. While it continues to hire college graduates, it tries to select only those who will be interested in their jobs. The store makes it clear to them that they will be expected to observe the store rules and to carry out the selling policies of the company.

Racial discrimination. Discrimination in most employment on the basis of color, race, or religion is, of course, illegal. Nevertheless, companies vary widely in their vigor in observing this law. Some firms now are systematically trying to increase the proportion of Negroes in their work force and in higher ranking jobs. Reasons for doing so range from fear of racial trouble, to belief that high potential ability can be tapped (as occurred in major league baseball when the color ban was first lifted), to a moral conviction that in our society all men should have equal opportunity.

Such a policy does, of course, discriminate against white applicants and is probably a technical violation of the law. For instance, a consumer credit company has a policy of employing 32% Negroes —the same percentage that Negroes are of the total population in the area. At present, over 80% of the employees are white. Consequently, a white applicant must have most unusual qualifications to get a job—because he is white.

The task is to redress three centuries of wrong and to modify social mores so that classes of jobs—including supervisory positions —do not "belong" to a racial or religious group. This can be done, as experience in Hawaii and elsewhere indicates. However, the process calls for more perceptive policies than a mere head count such as the policy noted in the preceding paragraph.

Companies with operations abroad face different problems, especially pressure to employ local people. IBM World Trade in recognition of such nationalistic feeling—and to have employees who are familiar with local customs—has a policy of employing in its fifty or more local offices only nationals of the respective local countries. To make this possible, the company spends a great deal

Occupational Distribution of Employed Males in the United States, 1960

	White	Negro
Managers, officials and proprietors	12.0%	1.9%
Professional and technical workers	11.5	3.4
Sales and clerical workers	15.2	6.7
Craftsmen and foremen	21.4	10.8
Operatives and kindred workers	20.4	26.6
Service workers	5.5	16.0
Non-farm laborers	5.9	22.3
Farmers and farm laborers	8.1	12.3
	100.0%	100.0%

Future selection policies will have a significant influence on occupations of Negro workers.

of effort in recruiting and training; without the extensive recruiting and training (and the high prestige and pay IBM can offer), its selection policy might well result in unsatisfactory operations. In any event, racial discrimination in this form pays off.

Selection of salesmen. Salesmen represent their company to customers whose patronage is necessary to the very existence of the concern. They spend a large portion of the company's gross income and are responsible for the effectiveness of much of the sales promotion. Clearly, the type of men to be selected as sales representatives deserves careful thought and attention.

The sales manager of a company having 38 salesmen developed his sales force from men who had had previous selling experience, preferably with a similar line of products. This meant that the men were usually already matured when hired and had often worked for some competing firm. In fact, out of 38 salesmen, 4 were over 50 years of age and 12 were over 40 years of age at the time they were first employed. Furthermore, the company was very loath to discharge men after they had built up personal contacts with customers throughout a given territory. In several instances the company reduced the area to be covered to a size that an elderly man could effectively handle. As a result of these practices, the sales force included—at the time of an investigation—7 salesmen over 60 years of age, 16 salesmen over 50 years of age, and 25 salesmen over 45 years of age. They were indeed veterans in the business; and not infrequently they were opinionated and did not welcome suggestions from the sales manager.

Another company having a much larger sales force made a scientific study of its experiences with salesmen in an effort to develop definite policies that might be used in selecting new employees. This analysis showed that failures were heaviest among men who were outside the ages of 23 to 40 years when they started on the sales job, and that an age of approximately thirty years seemed to be preferable. High school graduates were desirable, for, surprisingly enough, college graduates as a rule did not make the best salesmen. (The product of this company did not require technical knowledge for its sale.) The best prospects were high school graduates who had worked in the office of the company or in the retail establishment of a customer.

This analysis clearly showed that the least successful salesman was the man who had worked for a competitor and had resigned or was dissatisfied with that position. If a salesman had had four or more previous employments, or if he had left this particular company once before, he usually did not prove successful. Application of the policies developed through that study enabled the company to reduce the annual turnover in its sales force from 44% to 15%. Had the company been selling a different product or catering to a different group of customers, the standards developed would have been different. The study clearly showed that the selection policies previously followed by the company were either wrong or certainly inadequate.

Nepotism and cliques. Companies also vary in the extent to which they guard against the development of cliques or political factions resulting from the selection of employees on the basis of friendship or family relations. A friendliness among employees is certainly to be desired and cultivated, but occasionally the selection of new employees and the promotion of men within the company is based almost entirely upon personal friendships or family relationships. If the person receiving the new appointment has the proper qualifications, there is nothing wrong with such a procedure, although a feeling is likely to develop among other employees that the appointment was not made on merit. Those instances in which individuals lacking in ability are given preference over those more capable or otherwise deserving of the new position are to be strongly condemned.

Selection policies classified. We have illustrated only a few of the specific problems arising in connection with the selection of employees. From a general point of view, selection involves the following types of problems:

1. Selection from within or outside the company.
2. Hiring new employees from outside the company.
3. Promotion within the company.
4. Discharge of old employees.

Selection from within or outside the company. A company of any size will often have vacancies created by withdrawals or by expansion of operations. When these vacancies are in the lowest rank, they must, of course, be filled from the outside. If the vacancy arises in the upper levels of the organization, there is always a question as to whether the position should be filled by promoting an employee within the company or by hiring someone from outside the company. Policies in this regard are by no means uniform. Most companies prefer to promote men from within the organization, if a satisfactory candidate is available, for the following reasons:

1. A man already in the company knows its policies, organization, personnel, and techniques. The employee selected from within the company should, therefore, be able to function effectively more quickly than could someone secured from outside.

2. The suitability of a particular employee for a specific position can be judged more accurately if he has previously worked for the company. Information secured from a relatively brief interview with a stranger and from other individuals who are familiar with his past experience is rarely as complete and satisfactory as the knowledge about an individual the company has gained from actually working with him for a period of time.

3. Promotion of employees from with the company is likely to have a beneficial effect upon the morale of other employees. When employees see that they have a chance for advancement, they are more likely to render efficient service. This does not mean that all vacancies must be filled by promotion, but the practice must be common enough so that employees within the company believe they have an opportunity to secure promotion.

It may be advantageous, however, to secure employees from outside the company under the following conditions:

1. An employee with the proper ability and training may not be available within the company. Just because a company has an efficient sales force does not mean that there is a suitable person to fill the position of sales manager within the sales ranks. The qualities of an efficient salesman are not necessarily the quali-

ties of a capable sales executive. Experience has shown that one who has been an office boy *may* become an efficient president, but no one has yet proved that the efficient office boy necessarily has the ability to become president of the company. If the company has an adequate training program, the lack of suitable candidates within the company is less likely to arise.

2. Unexpected vacancies may occur due to withdrawals or disability. The president of a bank, for example, may leave suddenly because he has obtained another position or because of death. It may be that the management was training an assistant to take his position but had not anticipated so sudden a change. Consequently, the assistant may lack the maturity or experience required by the position.

3. A new point of view in a company is sometimes desirable. The present executives may have a narrow and unprogressive attitude toward current problems. They may have been trained to use methods that were effective in the past, but failed to adjust their thinking to changing conditions. Under such conditions, "new blood" will probably have a stimulating effect upon the entire organization.

Hiring new employees from outside the company. The selection of new employees is important not only to fill existing vacancies adequately but also to develop the core of workers who will be competent to conduct the affairs of the company for many years to come. Increasing emphasis on security, seniority, and promotion from within means that the new employee is likely to be a potential asset or handicap to the company over a long period. Even if the worker stays only a limited time, the cost of employing and breaking him into a new job is substantial, and considerable economy can be secured by selecting the right man on the first try.

A great deal of study is being given to the improvement of the techniques of selection. Many leading companies now insist that a thorough job analysis be made and from this a list of qualifications needed by a person to fill the job be prepared. In addition, for some general occupations such as selling, clerical work, and the like, a wide variety of psychological analyses are being made in an attempt to identify traits and attitudes which lead to successful performance. In addition to these efforts to define just what kind of a man is needed to fill a given position, methods of appraisal are being improved. Effective interviewing is now recognized as a highly developed skill and many companies use aptitude and performance tests to supplement the information gained from the work history and outside references.

Detailed consideration of these techniques is outside of the scope of this discussion of broad personnel policy. The qualifications for specific jobs will vary, of course, even from company to company in the same industry, so that the most that can be done here is to urge that careful analysis be made of qualifications needed for each job before people are hired to fill them. Nevertheless, companies often do establish general policies regarding the qualifications of new employees that apply, at least, to a large number of positions. Examples of such general policies are:

1. Most companies have some general standards of physical fitness. Often the policy is that new employees must have no major defects. Unfortunately, such a policy rules out people partially disabled or otherwise handicapped. An increasing number of companies are making provisions for employing such people on jobs where the handicap does not interfere with effective performance. This is not only a humanitarian act but when done with the proper precaution usually provides a source of efficient and loyal employees.

2. Companies may follow a general policy of hiring only people, who at least have a high school education. Within certain departments there may be further requirements regarding technical or specialized training. These general policies should not be followed too rigidly because knowledge and mental habits can be acquired in a variety of ways, and a person should not be judged in terms of the methods by which this ability has been developed.

3. Sometimes it is not desirable to employ people from one geographical location to work in certain other geographical locations. For example, salesmen from the North may not be the most effective in selling to some types of customers in the South.

4. There is considerable evidence that people who have recently held a large number of jobs are likely to quit the new one within a brief period. Consequently, some companies have a policy of not employing, as a regular employee, anyone who has held as many as say four jobs in the last two years. Another policy occasionally followed is not to employ men whose previous salary was more than 50% higher than the new beginning salary will be. The assumption here is that personal adjustment to such a drastic cut in income is so likely to lead to discouragement and trouble that the man is a poor risk.

5. Occasionally, companies will not normally employ men currently working in competing firms. It is argued that if a man cannot make a success at his present job there is little reason to suppose that he will be successful in the new plant where the work is substantially the same. The policy may also be aimed at "labor pirating." A standing exception to this policy is almost always made if the new job provides a clearly better opportunity than the man has in his present position.

Promotion within the company. In promoting employees, consideration should be given to the desirability of horizontal versus vertical promotion and the desirability of securing assistants who complement rather than supplement their superiors.

Vertical promotion. It is customary in many companies to establish vertical lines of promotion; that is, the employee is promoted from one rank to the next highest rank in the same department. This plan is based on the belief that it is the most effective way to give the employee the experience that he needs for each position to which he is promoted. If a company is organized into a few major departments, as most companies were a few decades ago, this plan of promotion has fewer disadvantages than when it is used rigidly .in a company that is subdivided into numerous specialized units. In the latter case, it limits both the experience and the opportunity of an employee because he has only a limited contact with the business as a whole. Furthermore, an employee may be deprived of an opportunity to secure promotion because vacancies do not occur in his department at the right time.

Horizontal promotion. In order to overcome this difficulty, some companies have a policy of horizontal promotion. Under this plan an employee may be transferred from a position in one department to a position of higher rank in another department, or he may be transferred to the same rank in another department if the transfer gives him an opportunity to acquire broader experience or provides a larger opportunity for promotion.

This plan of horizontal promotion is most easily followed in a company that has a number of units performing similar activities of varying sizes. For example, the assistant manager of a large store in a dry-goods chain may be appointed general manager of a smaller store instead of being retained as assistant manager of the larger store until there is a vacancy in the general managership of that store. After he has served as general manager of the smaller store, the employee may be promoted to general manager of the larger store when a vacancy occurs. By appointing him as general manager of the smaller store, the company secures an efficient employee for this position. Such a promotion also gives the employee valuable training because it provides him with an opportunity to assume more important responsibilities.

In a company that does not have several units of the same type, horizontal promotion is somewhat more difficult but may nevertheless be quite useful. The man will need more time to learn his new job and may need counsel on specific technical details. Even in this case the employee will obtain a much broader experience and will have more opportunity for promotion than if he remained in his original department.

Type of man to be promoted. There is a natural tendency for an executive to select as his assistant one who has abilities similar to his own. This may not result in the most efficient combination. Most executives have both abilities and weaknesses, and it is often desirable that the assistant be able to aid the executive with problems that his boss copes with less efficiently. For example, in a mercantile concern the manager of a department may have a thorough knowledge of the products but he may not think soundly on organization policies or be effective in the development of personnel. In such a case it may be wise to appoint as his assistant a man who is adept at organization and personnel issues even though he lacks a feel for merchandising problems. If this assistant later becomes head of the department, he should probably have an assistant who, in a like manner, will complement his abilities.

Promotion is a part of the general problem of selection. It will be evident from what has been said, however, that promotion is also related to training and to incentives.

Discharge of present employees. *Transfer rather than discharge.* Some firms handle discharges on the assumption that if a man is unsatisfactory in his present position in the company, he will be of no use in other places in the concern. A different policy, which has had increasing acceptance in many firms, is that the company should try to place an employee released from one department in some other department before he is discharged from the company entirely. His release from his first department may be due to an unusual personality clash with his superior, lack of a particular quality required for work in that department, or some similar reason.

The employee is already familiar with many of the internal procedures of the company, and consequently he should be able to learn his new position more quickly than an entirely new employee secured from the outside. Moreover, it is highly desirable from the point of view of employee morale to make the worker feel that the company is doing its best to find suitable work for him.

Reasons for discharge. No matter how careful a company may be in hiring, promoting, and transferring its employees, it sometimes is necessary to discontinue their services for one of the following reasons:

1. Changes in policies that may result in discontinuing the activities in which the employee has been engaged.
2. Seasonal and cyclical trends that make necessary a reduction in the number of employees.
3. Unadaptability or inefficiency of the employee.
4. Disability of the employee through age, illness, or other causes.

When it is necessary to discharge the employee, he should be told in a frank but friendly manner that his services are no longer needed. An employee should never be discharged as a result of any sudden feeling of anger on the part of his superior. It is desirable that the employee be discharged with as little humiliation and ill feeling as possible, both because this is humane and because it is advantageous from the point of view of the company. The employee is a member of the general public, and it is desirable that he not speak unkindly of the company for which he has worked.

Seniority and discharge. Policies covering discharge may have to be adjusted to union requirements if the union is powerful. A typical provision in a union agreement is that regular employees be discharged (and re-employed) on the basis of seniority; that is, when operations are curtailed, the newest employee is the first one to be discharged and the employee with the longest service is the last one.

While there is considerable fairness to such a rule and many companies follow it voluntarily, its application is not always economically sound. Some managements prefer to discharge the least efficient worker first and keep the more efficient men on the payroll. Efficiency and length of service are not always closely correlated. Even less related are mere length of service and ability to assume greater responsibilities, and consequently seniority is not an adequate guide in selecting men for promotion.

The pros and cons on this particular rule are too involved to discuss here. Suffice it to say that a rule can be worked satisfactorily to all concerned if the management recognizes its responsibility for giving reasonably secure employment, and if the employees appreciate the necessity of high efficiency in the work force.

The adoption of a seniority policy in connection with discharges places greater importance upon having only competent persons in the work force. The obligation to an employee, under this policy, becomes a long-term commitment instead of a short-term arrangement that the employer is free to terminate at his convenience. Thus, original selection of employees must be done more carefully, prompt corrective action must be taken if any employee is found to be unfitted for his job, and training often must become a continuing process.

TRAINING

Need for training. Whenever a man takes a new job, he will need at least some training. He must be familiar with his surroundings and with the names of people and things connected with his new employment. He must also develop skill in performing the operations assigned to him. In many cases he must thoroughly understand the reasons for his employment and the reactions he secures from the machines and people with whom he is working. In all cases he must learn what his employer expects of him. This may require careful, patient, and often long training even though the man has been transferred from another position in the same company.

There are, of course, some simple tasks in which the operator does not have to understand the "why" of his job any more than a person has to be a mechanic in order to drive an automobile. All that is asked by the employer is dexterity in performing the task. On the other hand, a large number of employees in any business must be more than skillful operators, and consequently their training becomes more complicated. Most of us do not care to ride in an airplane with a pilot who knows how to fly only when everything is running well.

Basic training issues. In discussions of training, as in several phases of management, there is a tendency to jump into technical details before setting up the general purposes and limits of the activity. The manager should first decide:

1. The *place* training is to occupy in management activities of the company.
2. The *purposes* which are to be covered in company training.
3. The *types* of training which will best meet these purposes.

Place of training in company management. Training may be regarded as a necessary evil, as an extra burden imposed on executives because their subordinates are not as competent as they should be. Where this view prevails, and it is by no means uncommon, training activities are held down to those which are obviously necessary. Some learning inevitably takes place, of course, as younger men watch older associates and as some plans succeed while others fail. But most of the training any man gets is what he is able to garner as a by-product of his day by day assignments. In such companies men literally "come up the hard way."

Another policy is to treat training as a device to overcome certain specific problems. New employees must be instructed in their duties; a course in safety or salesmanship may be needed; perhaps formal apprenticeship is established in the plant. Here training is accepted as desirable when a clear-cut need is identified. Typically the training will be a course with a definite, limited objective; once given, the effort probably will be discontinued. In many respects this viewpoint is like that of a student who thinks he can learn all he needs to know about, say accounting or business policy, by taking a course with that title.

Still a third view is to regard training as one of the important aspects of the process of management. From this viewpoint, an executive gets things done by training his subordinates rather than giving them many detailed orders; he trains his men and then sets goals which he helps them meet. It is a continuing relationship, and it applies to all members of the enterprise. In fact, under this view, continual learning is fully as important for executives as for operators. The recognized training activities are intended to stimulate, aid, and supplement a pervasive process that is vital to a healthy enterprise.

Clearly, it will be difficult to build any kind of a training program until some one of these viewpoints, or variant of them, is adopted. The choice will affect the nature and extent of training and also the provision for training in the company organization. Most growing concerns take at least the second view—training to meet specific, limited needs—and many companies are shifting to the third view —that training is an integral part of the management process. Assuming the top executives will support recognized training, what then are the more definite purposes that may be sought?

Purposes of training. *Induction.* Important among the various purposes training may serve in a company is the induction of new employees. A new relationship between the company and the employee has to be established, and there is question as to how much planning and specialized attention should be given this early orientation. Many companies believe this is a critical point in developing good personnel relations and as a matter of policy insist that the induction be carefully done.

In one company, for example, the new employee is told in a simple, clear manner, highlights of the major developments and organization of the enterprise. In particular, he is informed about the firm's personnel policies, terms of employment, disciplinary rules, and employee services and benefit plans. The employee is then carefully shown his physical environment—plant facilities, lunch rooms, rest rooms, bulletin boards, locations of offices and departments he may have occasion to visit, etc.; if he is a new resident, he is given information about community facilities.

Attention is likewise given to social relationships. The new man is introduced not only to his immediate supervisor, but to union stewards, safety supervisor, inspectors, and other people with whom he will have direct contact. He is also introduced to his fellow workers and an attempt is made to establish a relationship with one or more of these associates to whom the new man may talk freely and get the lay of the land. And finally, the induction includes an introduction to his job, his duties, standards, safety rules, work place, compensation, and related matters. The importance of the job and its relation to the total work of the firm is also made clear.

Companies that stress such orientation feel that it is important, not only in providing new employees with needed information, but also in creating a favorable and lasting impression of the company as a place to work. It is hoped that the employee will quickly develop a sense of "belonging" and that this will contribute to job satisfaction and subsequent training.

Development of skills. The whole host of skills are, of course, needed for the operation of any company. Mechanical operations, clerical work, and selling all have numerous subdivisions which vary from industry to industry. Every company faces the question of the measures it will take to assist its employees in developing the needed skills.

The need for company effort in building special skills depends in part upon its selection and promotion policies. Companies that attempt to employ only people who already have the needed skills, such as skilled machinists, experienced salesmen, and trained book-keepers, place less emphasis on training. On the other hand, firms that stress promotion from within may have to take special steps to assure that employees develop the skills which will be needed. In this connection, note that much of the training in skills is directed toward improving performance in present jobs, and this may be undertaken even in a highly static situation.

Two trends have contributed, in recent years, to more attention to the development of skills. Fewer and fewer skills are now regarded as "an art" that defies analysis and cannot be taught in any systematic manner. Many, though not all, aspects of jobs ranging from department store buyers to brewmaster are now written out in instruction manuals. Second, the accelerated rate of technological change—in the plant, office, and marketplace—is making many skills obsolete. Workers have to be retrained to do new tasks.

Human relations and supervisory training. The ability to get along with people, to understand them and their problems, and to utilize this knowledge in obtaining maximum effectiveness, is being given increasing emphasis in training activities. Human relations are being stressed particularly in supervisory training. While the more technical aspects of supervision, such as scheduling of work, control of materials and equipment, quality control, and safety are still essential parts of the well-balanced supervisory training program, more and more people feel that the greatest opportunities for improvement lie in the human side. The difficulty here is the development of training techniques which are effective in dealing with the complex and somewhat non-rational aspects of human behavior.

Adequate information regarding company operation. The task of keeping operators and supervisory personnel accurately informed of the company rules, policies, and programs is a major one. Most top administrators agree that their employees are entitled to much more company information than formerly was given them. At the same time, the increasing size of business enterprises adds to the difficulty of communicating with employees. Consequently, a number of companies are looking to their training divisions to make sure that employees fully understand company policies and facts about company operations, as well as reasons for such changes as may be made. Mere publication of the data is not enough; executives, supervisors, and other key people must clearly understand it so that they can explain it to their fellow workers in ordinary language at such times as questions arise.

Economic education. Half a century ago several large corporations had schools to help educate their foreign-born employees to become United States citizens. Sharp restrictions on immigration have led to the discontinuance of almost all corporation schools of this nature. Today, however, there is renewed interest in education for citizenship of quite a different nature. The challenge of the free enterprise system by communists and the underlying current toward attempting to solve social and economic problems with governmental action throws a heavy task on the United States citizen.

Some companies feel that they should help their employees meet this task by giving them at least basic training in both economic and business problems. They believe that an understanding of business economics will help their employees be more intelligent and farsighted union members. There is, however, no clear-cut agreement as to how far the company should go in this respect, and many activities are far more indoctrination than education.

There are, of course, other purposes toward which company training may be directed. The preceding paragraphs do indicate the range of the topics that might be considered. They also suggest the need for clear-cut policies on just what is to be covered.

Types of training. Once policies regarding the place of training and its more specific purposes have been defined, the manager is in a position to consider the types of training that will be most effective. No simple formula defines the form of training to be used for a given purpose. The size and the traditions of the company, the maturity and the background of the employees, the abilities of supervisors and other executives and the work load they are already carrying, and training activities that have been carried on by the company in the past, all will affect the type of training that will be most successful in a given situation. Nevertheless it will be helpful to indicate briefly the principal alternatives from which the manager may choose.

The most important type of training always has been and always will be *training-on-the-job.* The experience of actually doing some-

HOW TO INSTRUCT

Step 1. PREPARE THE WORKER.

Put him at ease.

State the job and find out what he already knows about it.

Get him interested in learning the job.

Place in correct position.

Step 2. PRESENT THE OPERATION.

Tell, show, and illustrate one **Important Step** at a time.

Stress each **Key Point.**

Instruct clearly, iompletely, and patiently, but no more than he can master.

Step 3. TRY OUT PERFORMANCE.

Have him do the job—correct errors.

Have him explain each **Key Point** to you as he does the job again.

Make sure he understands.

Continue until **You** know **He** knows.

Step 4. FOLLOW UP.

Put him on his own. Designate to whom he goes for help.

Check frequently. Encourage questions.

Taper off extra coaching and close follow-up.

If the worker hasn't learned, the instructor hasn't taught.

thing makes a lasting impression and has a reality that other types of training cannot provide. The chief difficulty of training-on-the-job is to make sure that it actually does take place in a reasonably effective manner. Merely doing a task does not assure that it will be done in the best way, nor does it develop an understanding of the reasons and consequences of the action. For training-on-the-job to be effective the supervisor, or some other designated trainer, must take time to see that learning really occurs.

For this reason, if a policy of training-on-the-job is wisely followed, it is usually necessary to make sure that supervisors are trained and motivated to be good trainers. The outline on the preceding page was developed by the War Manpower Commission as a guide for supervisors instructing new workers. Many companies have given their supervisors a "Training Within Industry" course built around this outline, and it illustrates one of the outstanding attempts to make training-on-the-job more effective.

Apprenticeship training has been developed by a number of the craft unions and typically combines several years of work experience with at least some formal schooling in the trade. A definite progression in type of work is outlined, and the apprentice is expected to get considerable training-on-the-job from the skilled journeyman with whom he works. Apprenticeship training has worked out quite well in the development of skills in a number of trades, such as machinists or typesetters; however, it is only available to companies employing men in certain crafts and, generally speaking, it is a rather slow and inflexible process.

Conference training provides an important supplement to on-the-job training. Here, relatively small groups of men get together to raise questions and exchange ideas. There is much stimulation in this give-and-take as well as exchange of actual information. Conferences may be used to discuss company operations or case problems may be introduced. An outside case may be used to encourage objectivity during the early part of a conference, and then similar company situations discussed later. Conferences have been found to be particularly useful in human relations training, provided they are under skilled leadership.

There are a whole variety of more *formal programs* that a company may use. A series of lectures and discussions, dinner meetings, and moving pictures or slide films are among the devices available in this area. Another type of formal training is vestibule schools. Here new workers are taught how to operate machines in a separate room before they are assigned to a regular production job. In such a school the learners can be under the guidance of an experienced instructor and they do not interfere with regular production. The plan is suitable, however, only when there is a fairly large number of trainees and they can be trained to work in a manner satisfactory to the regular supervisors. There is by no means full agreement as to the advisability of using vestibule schools.

Still another form of training available to a company is that provided by *outside institutions*. A whole variety of vocational refresher courses are available at the high schools in industrial areas. Universities offer evening courses, and the wide offerings of correspondence schools are available for those who cannot attend regular classes. Companies vary greatly in the extent to which they encourage their employees to use outside educational facilities. Some companies consider that training is an individual matter which an employee takes entirely on his own initiative. Other companies encourage such training and often pay part or all of the tuition costs for successfully completed courses. In some instances the company actively cooperates with school authorities in designing courses which will meet the needs of their employees.

There are, of course, many variations of these basic types of training. Each company will probably use some combination of types which fit its situation best. In developing such a detailed training program, it will be very helpful to establish general policies as to the types of training that are to be emphasized.

SUMMARY

Securing and maintaining an efficient work force are crucial to the success of every enterprise. The first broad part of this task is selection of the right workers. As used here, selection includes hiring of new employees, deciding who is to be promoted, and facing the unpleasant duty of discharging those who cannot be used effectively. Many delicate, individual problems are naturally involved. In addition, a variety of important issues, such as the use of seniority, promotion from within, the use of physically handicapped workers, and horizontal promotions, can be treated best when a clear-cut policy has been established.

A second part of the overall personnel job is training. A dominant question here is how training is to be related to the process of management. Assuming the answer is that training will be an integral part of the process, the specific purposes need to be defined.

Policies are needed indicating the emphasis to be placed on induction, job skills, human relationships, company operations, and economic education. Then the types of training, for example, on-the-job, conferences, lectures, or correspondence courses, that are most likely to achieve these purposes should be selected.

Workers carefully selected and properly trained must be paid. The next chapter takes up this matter of compensation.

QUESTIONS FOR CLASS DISCUSSION

1. Four personnel policies of a large producer of drugs (both ethical and proprietary), cosmetics, veterinary medicines, and food products were a constant subject of discussion. (a) The "up-or-out" policy of automatic promotion after one year from trainee or probationary employee and then dismissal if the employee was not promoted again after two more years. The "up-or-out" policy continued until an employee was 40 years old, with increasing time spans allowed for promotion periods. (b) Employees were very rarely hired or fired if they were over age 40. Circumstances had to be highly unusual. (c) "First-bouncers" were welcomed—those who quit first jobs elsewhere or were released by their first employers. (d) Employees over 40 who failed at further promotions were removed from line positions into staff jobs or listed as "consultants." The comment was that these practices lost the firm the services of skilled people who could do a job well at a particular level—regional sales manager or research department head, for example. Would you recommend any changes?

2. A recent study of the effects of a two-week training program in human relations given to foremen has shown that the foremen demanded more work from their men after the training and were not so much a part of the working group. The study concludes that this is unfortunate and that it results from increased identification with management by the foremen because they were singled out for training. Do you agree that this is unfortunate? How can such training be evaluated?

3. Seniority with respect to lay-offs may be defined in terms of work experience (a) on a type of job, (b) in a department, (c) in a plant, or (d) company-wide. Which definition will cause the most confusion at times of a curtailment in company operations? Which definition will facilitate transfer of men from job to job? If you were an administrator of a company, which definition would you prefer to use?

4. What complications is a company likely to face if it adopts a policy of employing handicapped workers? What can it do to minimize the likelihood and effects of such complications? Do you think this is a sound policy for most companies to adopt?

5. The Matthews Department Store adds 500 temporary sales people to its force each fall to handle the seasonal peak in business that ends at Christmas. Most of them are new to the store and need training in (1) store rules, (2) general information about the store, (3) merchandise carried in the department where they will work, (4) selling techniques, and (5) writing sales checks for various kinds of transactions. Outline a training program for these employees.

6. Make a table showing which of the various types of training (on-the-job, conferences, evening courses, etc.) is best suited, and which is least adequate, to use for *each* of the major "purposes of training" discussed on pages 266 to 269.

7. What type of training would you recommend for the following: (a) a crew of men responsible for cleaning the buildings and the grounds of a university, (b) an interviewer in a market survey, and (c) a football team?

8. Discuss the desirability, from the point of view of a business administrator, of the use of *seniority* for rehiring, promotion, and discharge. What kind of rules would you want adopted if you were an employee in a company where the adoption of seniority rules was being considered?

9. Explain how selection policies affect, and are affected by, training policies. Also, what are the interrelations between selection and compensation policies?

CASE XI

Blue Island Plating Co.

Within eight years after leaving his job as a plant foreman at Equipco Steel Company, a steel fabricating concern near Chicago, Bob Reynolds had built his own small but successful electroplating company in Blue Island, Illinois. He financed this venture through his personal savings accumulated over fifteen years, with the further aid of a loan from his brother. Slowly, the company, Blue Island Plating Co., Inc., achieved a fine reputation in the area. Now it is doing almost $2 million worth of business a year.

The following situation was explained by Hi Phillips, Production Manager:

Maybe I should say first that Bob Reynolds is well known to have a temper. When he left Equipco Steel, he unsuccessfully attempted to entice two other foremen from their jobs by offering them more money to work for him. Ed Riley gave as his reason for refusing Reynolds' offer, "Bob is a good guy, but I wouldn't want him for my boss; he's got a wicked temper." Fred Aley replied, "You've just got to let Bob blow off steam and not pay any attention to him. He gets mad as hell one minute, and then two mintes later he acts like your best buddy." Bob Reynolds has done well, even though he occasionally does blow his top.

Blue Island Plating now employs 40 workers—25 on a day shift, and 15 on a night shift. The background of almost all of the workers is similar. They migrated North from the hills of Kentucky and Tennessee in order to earn better wages. Many of them live in neighboring apartment buildings in Harvey, Illinois, a town about 2 miles from Blue Island. All the others live around the same area. They spend both work and leisure hours together. Because of their common background and interests, the workers form a close-knit group. I have been careful to organize the work to take advantage of this.

Jed White has worked with the company since its founding and is a popular member of this group. He is 35 years old, married, and the father of two children.

About eight months ago, I selected Jed for a special job. His duties were to come to work an hour before the regular shift to light and adjust the gas burner in each electroplating line so that the acid used in plating the metal parts would be at the correct temperature by 8 a.m., to add occasionally to the acid for the proper concentration, and to line up some of the orders for proper sequencing through the plating lines. The job meant that he had to talk with me several times a week at the end of his regular shift to get instructions.

I chose Jed because I knew about his popularity in the group and because he was one of the most capable linemen. I had also observed that he was one of the three men who were the centers of lunch hour activities. It was my hope that he would work out well enough so that he could be a foreman in the not-too-distant future. We are growing fast enough so that one, or perhaps two, first-shift foremen will be needed. As Production Manager, I have worked without any other first-shift supervisors up until this time. I have been able to do so because of low turnover, the men's background, and their off-hours residences. Although I could easily have brought in experienced foremen from among my acquaintances in other shops, I thought I would try Jed.

Plating work can readily be learned on the job. New men start as helpers on those lines that require someone to load and unload the buckets or racks and then progress to being linemen. Some linemen have one or two helpers, some run lines by themselves. The skills are considerable after awhile—in loading properly, in running the parts through the solution at the correct rate to achieve the plating desired, in making minor adjustments to the equipment—but this can be learned by experience with my guidance or guidance from the other men.

Some linemen eventually move into the two highest-skilled jobs. The first is preparing parts by barrel tumbling and acid dipping for later high-quality plating. The men on this job also do some specialized, high-quality, acid-etching work. The second job is running an automatic tank for high-quality, special-design parts.

In addition to the helpers and linemen, we also have a man running a steam degreaser on the day shift and a rack repair man. These jobs are semiskilled, can be learned by experience, and serve all the plating lines.

Now, if he were to be a foreman, Jed needed to learn more than a regular lineman—proper job sequencing for cost control among other things.

The other men all consider Jed's extra work to be a good job. It is easy work physically and assures Jed of at least 5 hours of overtime each week. The other workers felt Jed was in a responsible position.

During the past year, I heard some rumors that interested me. If any worker had difficulty obtaining the correct plating thickness on the job he was doing, Jed was always happy to give his advice— whether asked for or not. Whenever his work was questioned by Bob Reynolds or me, Jed would stand with his hands in pockets and nod his head. (I have seen him do this.) Then later, so the rumor ran, Jed would proceed to "cuss them out" in front of the other workers and boast that he knew more about the electroplating business than either Reynolds or Phillips.

About every four months the acid in the electroplating lines is filtered from the tanks and cleaned. After the acid is removed, all dirt and waste materials are shoveled out of the tanks. It is common to find about 10 pounds of small metal parts on the bottom of the tank. These parts have fallen out of the plating buckets as they were being submerged in the acid. The parts, considered waste, are thrown away. Three days ago, when the acid in Jed's electroplating line was being filtered and cleaned, about 250 pounds of small nuts, bolts, screws, springs, and other parts were found on the bottom of the tanks. When Reynolds, who happened to be going through the plant with me that day, saw this excessive amount of waste, he turned to Jed and shouted, "Goddamit, how'd all that get in there? Whatta you doing, dumping it in by the handful?"

"It's not my fault," replied Jed, "the plating bucket has a leak."

"Leak, hell, you know it doesn't have a leak. You're just being careless when you run the bucket through the line."

"If you don't like the way I do my work, I'll quit."

"Then quit, Goddamit." Reynolds stormed from the line back to his office.

Jed went to the locker room and gathered his personal belongings together. As he walked out of the locker room to his car, he shouted to the other workers, "He ain't gonna push me around! Let's see how he does without me."

The lunch hour discussion centered around that morning's incident between Reynolds and Jed. All the workers supported Jed's walkout. They knew Reynolds had a quick temper, but agreed that they would probably have walked out too. They thought Reynolds had been unfair by jumping on Jed so quickly.

I moved Al Benson into Jed's old job on Line 5 where he had two helpers. Production proceeded. Unrest was obvious among most of the workers who thought Jed had gotten a "raw deal."

This morning, Fred Harris, a line worker, talked to Whitey Miles, the plant maintenance man. Fred said, "I saw Jed when I was coming to work this morning. He still hasn't found a job and doesn't think things will get any better. What makes it worse, his old lady is biting his tail for him to get some work. He's got them two kids to worry about and feed. Reynolds was a real bum to let him go."

Whitey later talked to me and wondered whether someone should ask Reynolds to give Jed his job back. I was interested in what he had to say because, although we are a little slack at the moment and not having any trouble meeting schedules, I know that we will soon tighten up again. In addition to replacing Jed, we will need one or perhaps two more men.

One factor I have to consider is a call from the United States Employment Service. They have both unskilled men and a few skilled platers looking for jobs. The call mentioned only the number of men and their skills. It said nothing about race, but we are near South Chicago and, naturally, I know about the high rate of unemployment among Negroes. I know also, of course, about the Illinois Fair Employment Practices Law.

In the past, the pool of Tennessee mountaineers provided all the men we needed. The men in the plant frequently have asked me about jobs for their friends. Since we have not done any hiring for six months, their requests have dropped off.

This afternoon Jed walked into the Blue Island Plating Company office and asked to see me. I called him into my office.

Jed started talking immediately. "Mr. Phillips, Fred Harris told me you still haven't hired a new man. I guess it's pretty tough to get a guy to do that job, and I was thinking if you need a man, I'd maybe come back to work for you."

REQUIRED: (a) What do you think of the policies of this firm as to hiring, training, and promotion? How have they worked out?

(b) Should Mr. Phillips turn to the United States Employment Service as a source of plant workers? For what jobs?

(c) What would *you* say to Jed White if you were in Mr. Phillips' position? State the exact words you would use in response to what Jed has said.

PERSONNEL POLICIES— COMPENSATION AND ARRANGEMENTS FOR WORK

COMPENSATION

Compensation deals with wages, salaries, bonuses, and other forms of direct financial remuneration. Of course, additional kinds of remuneration, such as power and similar intangible values, often provide important incentives for human effort. But financial remuneration is the most basic form of compensation. The major compensation issues are:

1. Amount of compensation.
2. Method of payment.

Amount of compensation. A significant portion of the expense of almost every business enterprise consists of wages it pays to its employees. Therefore, the manager must be sure that the amount of compensation paid to employees is commensurate with the services they render. He must seek to pay a fair wage—fair to the employee, the customer, and the investor. This is no simple matter, and policies governing the amount of compensation of each employee deserve the careful thought of the business executive.

There are three basic components in deciding how much an employee should be paid:

1. The relation of his wages to those being paid by other employers in the area for the same kind of work.
2. The difficulty and importance of this job compared with other jobs in the company.
3. The quality of performance by the individual in this job.

Experience indicates that wages and salaries can be administered more satisfactorily and efficiently if each of these components receives separate consideration.

Relation of wages to "the market." Most companies seek to follow a policy of paying competitive wage rates, that is, wages in line with those paid by other employers in the area. Unfortunately, this usually provides a rather crude and inaccurate basis for determining the exact amount to be paid to a specific employee. Often neither employer nor worker has reliable information regarding pay rates in other enterprises. Even if they do, the duties of the particular worker are likely to differ from those of men in other plants. Consequently, there is need to refine the idea of paying competitive rates.

In almost every company there will be 15 to 25 jobs that are quite similar to jobs in other companies in the area. These will probably be positions such as typist, elevator operator, auditor, and the like. Assuming these jobs are a fair sample, they may be used to compare company wage rates with those in the market. A company wage level may then be said to be higher or lower, depending upon how the pay for these comparable jobs lines up with the average for all firms having similar jobs. Note that these sample wage rates are not necessarily what a worker could earn if he quit and went elsewhere, for if business were slack other employers probably would not be interested in hiring him at any price. Nor is it the rate that would induce an employee to leave his present job, because he may be loathe to break the personal acquaintanceships and social ties connected with his present job and mode of living. The so-called wage level of a company is simply a comparison with the average wages being paid by other companies, for a representative sample of jobs.

High wages. Some companies deliberately pay their employees a higher wage level than that prevailing in the community in an effort to secure the "cream of the crop." For many years this was the policy of the Ford Motor Company. There is considerable difference in the ability of workers doing a given job. By offering to pay more than the average compensation, companies hope to secure the best workers. In other instances the higher rate must be offered to offset an unfavorable location or poor working conditions. Other companies interested in low labor turnover pay their employees above the general competitive rate.

Low wages. There are circumstances in which the amount of compensation paid is less than the level generally prevailing in the labor market. A few well-known concerns that pay less than the competitive rate have taken advantage of the employees' desire for training, for prestige, and for possible promotion connected with a white-collar job. As a general rule, this policy has not proved to be satisfactory because the employees sooner or later become dissatisfied with the low wage scale and seek employment elsewhere. Also, the company's reputation for low pay may prevent it from attracting capable employees. A few of the large commercial banks experimented with this policy. They found that the unfavorable effect on the morale of the employees and the high turnover that resulted more than offset the saving secured by the lower wage scale.

Some companies pay comparatively low wages because satisfactory results can be secured from mediocre employees. A retail store, for example, that expects the salesclerks to do little more than make change and wrap packages may quite legitimately have a lower wage scale than a store that expects its salespeople to give intelligent counsel and advice to customers. As a matter of fact, in this illustration the two stores desire a different quality of worker, and actually each store may be paying the competitive rate for the type of employee it is seeking. As already pointed out, a comparative wage rate should refer to workers having similar abilities and rendering similar services. When a specific company requires a significant difference in ability, either more or less, there may very appropriately be a differential in the wage rate.

Industry rates. In some industries, primarily as a result of union pressure, the industry-wide wage level is more important than the wage level in the local labor market. A national union, after being recognized in key plants throughout the country, may choose to negotiate wages with most or all of the employers as a group instead of dealing with each firm separately. In these circumstances, comparison with local rates is usually less significant than ability to pay, changes in cost of living, and general bargaining strength of the two parties. In fact, there is no agreement as to what should be the basis for establishing industry-wide wage levels once the union secures and operates as a national monopoly of the labor supply for that industry.

The policy questions facing a company in these circumstances are largely concerned with the extent of joint action with other managements in the industry. This subject will be considered in the next chapter.

Relation of pay for different jobs within company. Policies regarding the general level of wages by no means cover all the compensation problems of a company. As already explained, a great many jobs in any firm have no good counterpart in the market. They must be related in some manner to the sample jobs that can be keyed into the market.

Increasing recognition is being given to the importance of the relation of wages paid to different employees within a company. Several psychological studies of the attitude of workers revealed that they are as interested, if not more so, in how their pay compares with that received by their fellow workers as they are in the actual amount they receive. For example, a steel company that paid average wages among the highest in the industry also had the highest number of wildcat strikes during the last war. The explanation lay in differentials in earnings within the company; the group bonus plan then in effect gave groups with lots of green help low bonuses and groups with few green hands high bonuses, with the result that the skilled men in the former groups were paid less than the green men in the latter groups. When the relatively low-paid skilled men discovered such an inequity, they got mad and struck in protest.

While in most companies the amount of pay a particular worker receives is regarded as confidential between the employer and the employee, the information sooner or later leaks out and becomes generally known by the grapevine. Workers have a deep sense of justice and fairness, and they may become very disgruntled if some of their fellow workers are overpaid, in much the same way as if they themselves are underpaid.

To meet this situation, a company may adopt a policy of using a consistent wage scale for all employees. The application of this general policy is illustrated by the compensation plan of a utility company that was formed through the consolidation of nine separate corporations operating in more than one hundred cities. As might be expected, these different companies had followed different wage policies, so that when they were consolidated, there was considerable variation in the amount paid to people doing identical work in different cities.

When the company attempted to iron out this difficulty, it found no basis on which to compare different jobs. People doing almost identical work in different cities often held different titles, and even after standard job classifications had been established, there was the more difficult task of deciding how much difference in wages there should be between each class of workers. For example, what should be the relationship between the wage paid the head janitor, the bookkeeper, the chief clerk, the lineman, or the receiving teller? Some of the jobs required considerable experience and judgment, whereas others could be filled by young persons having comparatively little business experience.

In order to develop a fair basis for wage differentials, it was necessary to evaluate each of the numerous jobs. Each job was rated in terms of the education and experience required, the degree of supervision received, the degree of supervision exercised, the nature of duties performed, and the working conditions surrounding the job. This *job evaluation* provided a basis for classifying all jobs up to the "executive" level into fifteen different grades. Jobs in any one grade are about equal in difficulty and importance, and hence are entitled to the same pay, If, say, the experience required was greater for one job than another, it would be classified in a higher grade. In other words, the company adopted a policy in which the pay differentials between *jobs* would be based on systematic job evaluation.

Recognition of differences in individual performance. Sound policy regarding external alignment of the wage level and the internal alignment of individual jobs will go a long way towards a satisfactory wage plan for a company. A third factor should also be recognized. The quality and the quantity of work turned out by individuals on the same job are not equal. Rarely is a man recently assigned to a job as valuable to the company as his fellow-worker who has been doing that kind of work for several years. Most companies believe it is desirable to adjust pay in recognition of these differences in individual performance.

If a company uses piece rates, commissions, or other forms of incentive compensation, individual differences in performance will be reflected directly in the pay envelope. Such incentive schemes will be discussed later in this chapter. For a great many jobs, however, output bonuses are not practical. Consequently, companies often have a range of pay for each job or job grade. Beginners will be paid at the minimum of the range and then, as they improve their skill and usefulness, their pay is increased up to, but not above, the maximum of the range.

The public utility already discussed decided it wanted a range of pay for each of its job grades. It made provision for five in-grade increases above the minimum, each of approximately 5% giving an overall pay range from the minimum and the maximum of any grade of about 28%. The resulting salary schedule (including several adjustments made since the plan was first installed) is shown below. Under this plan it is relatively easy for an employee to move up one or even two steps within his grade, but only the exceptional employees have pushed on to the maximum.

Salary Scale Used by Public Utility Company
(in communities of 15,000 to 100,000 population)
Weekly Pay for Steps Within Each Grade

	A	B	C	D	E	F
Job Grades	Learning	Mastery	Skill	Versatility or Skill and Long Service	Exceptional or Versatility and Long Service	Exceptional and Long Service
15	$236.25	$248.25	$261.00	$274.20	$288.00	$300.00
14	214.50	225.00	236.25	248.25	261.00	274.20
13	194.40	204.00	214.50	225.00	236.25	248.25
12	176.40	185.10	194.40	204.00	214.50	225.00
11	159.70	167.70	176.40	185.10	194.40	204.00
10	144.90	152.10	159.70	167.70	176.40	185.10
9	131.40	138.00	144.90	152.10	159.70	167.70
8	119.10	125.10	131.40	138.00	144.90	152.10
7	108.00	113.40	119.10	125.10	131.40	138.00
6	97.80	102.90	108.00	113.40	119.10	125.10
5	88.80	93.30	97.80	102.90	108.00	113.40
4	80.40	84.30	88.80	93.30	97.80	102.90
3	72.90	76.50	80.40	84.30	88.80	93.30
2	66.00	69.30	72.90	76.50	80.40	84.30
1	60.00	63.00	66.00	69.30	72.90	76.50

A company following this plan must decide how wide its salary range is to be. If the nature of the work and the management of the company is such that employees can exercise considerable initiative, or if there are other reasons for a wide variation in individual performance, then the salary range should be wide. Most companies, if they have a salary range at all, allow for a spread of 20% to 35%. There are several drawbacks to a wide spread, however. Control of salary costs is more difficult. People in low salary grades may be earning as much or more than people holding considerably more difficult jobs, and this can create a bad morale. Also, for certain kinds of labor, notably in the skilled crafts, it is a tradition in some markets to have a single rate, or at most only a 5% or 10% differential, for all workers in that craft. The implicit assumption here is that anyone who qualifies as a regular carpenter or plumber is as good a workman as anyone else in the same trade.

Administration of wage plan. No wage plan, even one as well worked out as that described for the utility company, can be administered in a mechanical fashion. There are many personnel problems involved in wage and salary administration. Some of these, however, are of such importance and arise so frequently it is desirable that top executives establish policies governing them.

One of the most widely recognized problems is when to make changes in the general wage level of a company. This is often a subject of collective bargaining but even so policies may be useful. Some companies will make an across-the-board adjustment any time there is a 5, 8, or 10% change in the cost of living. Other companies make adjustments when the general level of wage rates in the local labor market, or for the industry, has shifted a given percent. A few companies, notably in the automobile industry, make an annual "productivity" increase. When for any such reason a company decides to increase its wage level, it may either increase its entire scale a given percentage or it may add a constant amount to the pay of every worker. The latter action, of course, narrows the percentage spread between grades, but in either case the general pay structure is maintained.

Another type of policy has to do with the frequency of salary increases in a grade. Some companies have a limit such as two steps within a year. A more ticklish question is when, if ever, employees will be permitted to earn more than the maximum established for their jobs. Generally speaking, unless these maximums are respected, the usefulness of the plan will degenerate over the years. Nevertheless, some companies allow a 10% increase above the maximum for employees who have been in the same job, at the same rate of pay, for a considerable number of years. One company following this practice has a large proportion of employees who will probably stay in their present position for the rest of their working lives and it feels that some possibility of salary increases should be held out for those who give long, loyal service.

Provision must, of course, be made for reclassifying jobs whenever there has been a significant change in the duties. Without this, a pay schedule that provided a fair differential when it was adopted would be outmoded. In other words, basic policies of paying wages that are in proper relationship with general levels prevailing in the community, that provide fair differentials between jobs, and that recognize individual merit cannot be successfully executed without continuing detailed attention to their administration.

Method of payment. *Basis upon which compensation is paid.* Basically, there are two ways of paying an employee. He may be paid so much per hour or per week, in which case the compensation is based on the *time spent;* or he may be paid on the basis of his accomplishments, that is, the compensation depends upon the *results.* In either case the total compensation will approximate the amount fixed by policies already considered.

The use of these two different bases of compensation are an everyday experience. When children, we may have been paid so much a quart for picking berries; whereas we were probably paid by the hour or the day for hoeing corn, inasmuch as a piece rate for the latter work might have resulted in a kindly attitude toward little weeds and/or a failure to discriminate between weeds and corn. We know that a streetcar conductor is paid so much a week rather than a percentage of the fares he collects, whereas the salesman who stops at the door in all probability receives a commission on the sales he secures.

Use of time rates. A great many employees are paid a fixed amount for which they are expected to work a certain number of hours. This simple basis of compensation has many advantages. It is easily understood by the employee, and he is assured of a known income for working a given period of time. From the employer's point of view, such a policy is easy to administer. It has the serious disadvantage, however, of not providing an immediate incentive for the worker to increase his productivity. Under a time rate the only financial incentives are keeping one's job (stability of income), securing an arbitrary raise in pay for the same job, or getting a promotion to a better job. The worker has no assurance that if he works hard today and tomorrow, he will be rewarded in one of these ways.

An extreme example of the separation of output and remuneration occurred in a printing plant in which all workers were on a standard daily rate. In this instance, the union went so far as to insist that the company not even suggest or state the amount of work it expected the employees to accomplish within a given period of time. Accomplishment and compensation were completely divorced from each other. All the management could do, unless the worker was grossly negligent, was to hope that the employee would put forth reasonable effort and do what he considered to be a fair day's work.

Problem of installing incentive rates. It is only natural that the management should prefer a policy of paying by piece rates or some other incentive plan, provided an equitable and satisfactory plan can be devised. This, however, is not always possible. For example, a company dealing in air conditioning equipment wished to put its salesmen on an incentive wage, but it found this difficult because many sales were made on a contract basis for which there was no standard price. The salesman, in his desire to increase sales volume, was likely to offer the product at such a low price that the company could make no profit on the transaction.

As an alternative it was proposed that before a contract order was accepted, the company engineers make an estimate of the total cost of installation. Salesmen would then be paid a percentage of the margin between the installation cost and the price received from the customer. Under this arrangement salesmen would be interested in profitable business rather than mere sales volume. The difficulty with this suggestion was that the company often wanted to accept business at a very narrow profit margin in order to keep its plant active. In such a case the salesmen would receive very little pay for selling an order. The management recognized that some form of compromise between these two bases might have been developed. The company felt, however, that such a system would be so complicated that it would be difficult to administer and that the salesmen would not respond because they would not understand just how the system worked. Consequently, the idea of an incentive plan was at least temporarily set aside.

Plans for incentive do not always work just as anticipated. When quality work is desired, an incentive on volume of output may lead to difficulties. A company manufacturing electrical appliances experienced a sharp increase in complaints from customers shortly after the incentive plan was installed, and only after a new quality control procedure was established did the incentive plan work satisfactorily.

Combined piece rates and time rates. Many companies, wishing to place their employees under some financial incentive, have found that the most successful arrangement is a combination of time rates and piece rates. A dairy, for example, pays its route men delivering milk to retail customers a standard amount per week, plus 12% of the amount collected from customers. Thus, the amount of compensation varies with the quantity of dairy products sold. As an added incentive to build up new business, a special bonus is paid each time the weekly sales increase above a certain fixed amount. Similar plans developed for factory employees provide for a fixed amount a day or week, plus a bonus for all work exceeding a standard output for a given job. In fact, considerable attention has been given to the best way of combining the different bases of compensation for factory workers.

Workers' attitude toward incentive pay. Workers often feel that the piece-rate system places standards so high that these can be achieved only by the most skillful men. Workers also hesitate to work hard to secure large bonuses, because they feel that the management may cut the rate of compensation and thus force them to put forth extra effort in order to earn their original pay.

Unfortunately, these fears of the worker have been well founded in too many instances. Incentive forms of compensation have been used to drive workers beyond their endurance, and managements have cut piece rates as soon as it was discovered that employees were earning compensation beyond the amount considered fair for that type of worker. Because of this attitude, a company should not adopt a policy of paying workers on an incentive basis unless it is willing to take the time to establish fair standards of performance and unless it can secure the cooperation of at least a majority of its employees toward the achievement of these standards.

In many companies and some industries, piece rates or other forms of incentive pay have become the standard method of compensation and the workers would undoubtedly resist a change to straight-time rates. The unions in such industries as hosiery, dresses, and steel often have expert time-study men on their own staffs and may participate in setting or check the output standards set by the management. In fact, a few unions such as the International Ladies Garment Workers Union have taken the initiative in developing standard time data and establishing fair production standards.

Conditions affecting success of incentive wage policy. There are many conditions upon which the success of a policy of paying incentive wages depends. Among the most important are:

1. The final result must truly reflect the effort of the worker. In many types of work the nature of the job, the raw materials, the conditions surrounding the work, and other factors outside the control of the worker are primarily responsible for the accomplishments achieved. If the worker sees that his efforts do not affect the final outcome very much, the incentive will not be effective.

2. All important elements that are subject to the control of the worker should either be included in the compensation plan or be carefully controlled by other means. Output or sales are frequently not the only factors that must be controlled. The quality of output, the waste of materials, the care of machines, the selling expenses, the prices received for products, the cooperation with other employees, and the service rendered to the customer are some of the details that may suffer under an incentive form of compensation. Frequently, however, such details are included in the basis on which the compensation is computed or are controlled by other means.

3. The method of computing compensation must be simple enough so that the employees can readily understand it. Unless the employee recognizes the connection between his actions and his wages, the incentive form of compensation will likely be ineffective.

4. The effect of good performance on the amount of compensation received should become apparent quickly so that the worker will realize the importance of good performance. If the typical employee is not rewarded until a month or perhaps a year after exerting the extra effort, the reward will lose much of its potency.

5. The confidence and the cooperation of the employee should be secured. If workers believe incentive wages are merely a device to cut wages or to increase the amount of work without added benefit to them, the plan is likely to run into snags. On the other hand, if they believe the management is fair and is offering them an opportunity to secure extra pay by added effort, the whole system is much more likely to succeed.

Unless these conditions can be reasonably met, the better policy would probably be to pay employees on a time basis.

Profit-sharing plans. In connection with compensation, brief mention should be made of the policy of sharing profits with employees. In recent years there has been much talk about the possibility of improving employee relations by permitting them a share in the profits of their company. Without attempting to analyze such plans in detail, it can be said that profit sharing is not a very effective device for the rank-and-file employees. Low-salaried workers do not like to have their compensation dependent upon the profits earned by their employer. They expect to be paid whether a profit is earned or not. Profit sharing must therefore be over and above the regular pay of workers.

When considered in this light, profit sharing becomes a special bonus or incentive so far as management is concerned. If we look back at the requirements of a good financial incentive, we soon recognize that profit sharing lacks some of the important elements. In the first place, the profits of an employer are not a good measure of an employee's performance. In the second place, the various factors that enter into the profit or loss of a company are difficult for a rank-and-file employee to understand. And finally, the distribution of profits will probably occur a long while after the employee has either put forth extra effort or loafed on the job.

Profit-sharing bonuses to top executives have much more to recommend them. Since the profits are more closely related to the efforts of these particular men, they can understand how their activities affect the amount they receive.

ARRANGEMENTS FOR WORK

While problems of selection, training, and compensation of employees are perhaps more widespread and basic throughout all types of business enterprise, there still remain other problems that frequently loom large in the development of an efficient work force. Management must also consider arrangements for work, because compensation alone is not going to develop an enthusiastic group of employees. In this connection we shall briefly discuss:

1. Hours of work.
2. Vacations.
3. Working conditions.

Hours of work. *Trend in hours of work in American industry.* One of the striking facts of the industrial development in the United States and other industrial countries during the last century has been the marked reduction in hours of work. In 1851, for example, a printers' union in New York recommended to the newspaper industry a work week of six 12-hours days or 72 hours per week, whereas now their work week is 37½ hours. As late as 1900, employees in the steel industry were expected to work 12 hours a day for 7 days a week or a total of 84 hours per week; their standard week is now 40 hours. These figures are even more

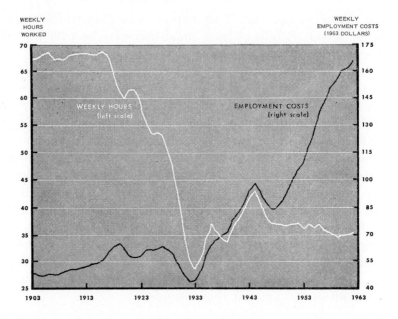

Trends in hours and earnings of United States Steel Company employees. Employment costs include wages and benefits. (Data are three-year moving averages.)

impressive when we realize that at the same time that the number of hours has decreased, real wages paid to employees have more than doubled.

The 40-hour week—five 8-hour days—is now regarded as standard in a great majority of industries. This does not mean, of course, that employees may not work more than 40 hours; but when they do, they expect to be paid time and a half for all the hours in excess of the standard.

When Saturday morning work was eliminated, it frequently was done on the assumption that the employees would accomplish as much in 5 full days as they had in 5½. At first, while employees felt grateful for a completely free day on Saturday, this proved to be correct. As Saturday has come to be regarded as a regular day off, however, the lull that used to occur on Saturday morning has often shifted to Friday afternoon. This experience suggests that we have long since passed the time when the long hours of work caused sheer exhaustion, when a reduction in the number of hours would be made up in a large measure by the increased tempo of work in the shorter period. Now the tempo of work depends upon attitude and work habits. A reduction in hours, or a free Saturday, may temporarily improve worker attitudes, but the effect wears off within a few years.

Adjusting hours to operations. Many companies operate more than 40 hours a week. If so, they need policies indicating how the 40-hour week will be adapted to the company operating schedule. For instance, retail stores are often open evenings for a total of 60 hours a week, so they must arrange for employees to take time off in the morning when there are the fewest customers.

Most plants that maintain continuous operations will have three separate shifts, but occasionally they follow a rotation plan. All sorts of schedules are possible and it is important that they be worked out with the employees so that there is a full understanding. Obviously unexpected changes in the hours of work can cause considerable personal inconvenience. Some employees are regularly assigned the undesirable hours and paid a "shift differential" or are given some other special consideration.

Thirty-five hour week. A few industries, such as coal mining, already have a 35 hour week. Also, offices often work from 9 to 5 with an hour off for lunch, or a total of 35 hours a week. With these instances as an example, managers should be prepared to face the question whether they too should adopt a 35-hour standard, or perhaps a 37½-hour standard.

Should the standard work day be cut from 8 to 7½ or 7 hours, employees will, of course, expect to receive the same pay. Possibly, in times of slack employment, a short work week with a corresponding reduction in pay might be acceptable as a means of "spreading the work." Aside from such an unusual circumstance, a short work week will probably result either in higher prices of products sold to the customer or a reduction in net profits.

Vacations. *Typical practice.* A question of personnel policy related to hours of work is that of vacations. When employment is irregular as is true in many industries, vacations are no problem because there are already too many forced vacations and employees want all the work they can get.

A great many companies now permit their regular employees to take vacations with pay. One company grants a vacation of 1 week to any employee who on June 1 has been working continuously since the preceding October 1, and any employee who has been continuously employed from May 1 of the preceding year receives 2 weeks' vacation. Another company has a plan whereby employees who have worked for the company for 3 months are considered regular employees and for each 2 months' service following that time are allowed one day's vacation, Sunday excluded, up to a maximum of 3 weeks.

The length of the vacation period and the requirements for eligibility naturally vary greatly from company to company. Two weeks' vacation with pay for regular employees who have worked with a company for several years is the most common practice.

Reasons underlying vacation policies. Opinion differs among executives regarding the purpose of granting vacations. Some executives contend that a vacation is an opportunity for the employee to get a change from his regular daily routine so that he may come back to work refreshed, rested, and prepared to render more efficient service to the company during the balance of the year. According to this philosophy, a vacation is not something to which the employee is entitled. Consequently, the employee does not have a claim to vacation pay if he voluntarily leaves the company, nor can vacations be carried over from one year to the next.

Other executives look upon vacations more or less as a bonus or a special compensation. One large company, in which approximately 70% of its 23,000 employees are eligible for vacations with pay, permits its employees to work during the vacation period and take extra compensation in lieu of time off if they so desire. Incidentally, the cost to this company of granting vacations is approximately $1,350,000 per year.

Just as in the case of shorter hours, the business administrator must ask himself, "What is the actual cost of granting vacations?" If vacations can be scheduled in slack periods, the actual expense may not be great. If temporary help has to be employed or the efficiency of the organization is reduced during the employee's absence, then the administrator must compare this cost with the improvement in general employee morale, the possibility of attracting a more efficient work force because of the liberal vacation policy, and any increased efficiency of the worker after the rest period.

With 2 weeks paid vacation, a 40-hour week, and the customary 8 paid holidays, "full-time" work accounts for only about 22% of a man's total time. Yet many people regard this as a tough schedule. To a considerable degree, vacations are like a standard of living—one feels either rich or poor depending upon what he is accustomed to.

Working conditions. Attitudes and practice with respect to working conditions have changed as sharply as hours of work during the 20th century. For example, the importance of safety—once the center of a crusade—is no longer a concept that calls for debate. And the record in modern companies is impressive; accidents per man hour in the steel industry are less than 10% of the 1907 hazard. Likewise, the need for adequate washrooms and lockers is accepted by all progressive companies. Performance is not ideal in all companies, of course, and executives must persistently keep alert to careless practices. But rarely do problems of this sort require policy decisions by central management.

Indicative of the shift that has occurred are the kind of issues we do hear about now: length of coffee breaks, parking space for employees' cars, air-conditioning. As the more elementary human needs become more nearly satisfied, new wants come to the surface. There is a rise in an acceptable standard of living on-the-job just as there is off-the-job.

The real problem for management is not whether working conditions affect efficiency, but just which improvements are important enough to warrant the outlay of money required to accomplish them. Improved lighting by the installation of special fixtures that will be used at least part of the time every day in the year is one thing, whereas the installation of expensive air-cooling equipment that may be operated for only 20 hot days during the summer is quite another matter.

Moreover, management's attitude is significant. Mayo found in his famous Hawthorne studies that the worker's belief that the company was concerned about him as an individual and was interested in his work and welfare was more important than details of his physical surroundings. Experience generally shows that expenditure of money on plant is not enough; the way and the spirit in which changes are made are fully as important.

SUMMARY

Policies providing for fair compensation are among the most important that a business administrator makes. Fairness of pay involves (a) a reasonable alignment with what other companies are paying, (b) differentials between jobs within the company based on differences in job difficulty and importance, and (c) recognition of variations in individual performance. Job evaluation and formal salary scales often aid in achieving fair compensation, but they are merely tools to help bring into reality a basic concept of equitable pay.

In the right situations, financial incentives serve as an effective method of compensation. They stimulate effort and provide an automatic reward for superior results. They are likely to be successful, however, only if results and effort are closely related, noncompensated factors are controlled, the plan is simple and prompt, and mutual confidence prevails.

The traditional trinity in labor relations, "wages, hours, and working conditions," has undergone considerable shift in emphasis with respect to hours and working conditions. The 40-hour, 5-day week has become standard. Current issues are: when to drop below a 40-hour week, how to schedule the short work week over the total time the company must operate, and how long and for what purpose to grant paid vacations.

Similarly, *debatable* problems regarding working conditions are no longer preservation of life and limb; rather they deal with how far to go with comforts and conveniences.

Policy formulation in these areas requires care, as employee response is difficult to predict because of shifting expectations. Fairness and equity are highly prized, and the manner and the spirit of making changes is as important as spending a lot of money.

QUESTIONS FOR CLASS DISCUSSION

1. A wholesale company wants to pay piece rates to all its warehouse employees. A study of packing has shown that the number of cartons packed in a day by one worker depends on the worker's efforts, on his position on the packing conveyor, on the season of the year, and on the number of items in each order. Can an individual piece-work standard be established? Can any sort of group standard be established? Would you be interested in administering an incentive pay scheme for the packers?

2. Suppose 500 men were running in a half-mile race for which prizes totaling $1,000 were being offered. How would you distribute the prize money to get the maximum effort from the group as a whole?

3. "Long service normally helps a man do better work and increases his chances of promotion. He is entitled to more pay if, in fact, the quality of his work improves or if he gets a promotion; but length of service, as such, should not be a factor in deciding whether an employee gets a pay increase." Do you agree? How, if at all, should long service be recognized in setting pay rates? Explain.

4. When should a man's pay be cut under the following circumstances: (a) if he slows down because of ill health but retains his same position; (b) if, as a result of reorganization or introduction of machinery, his job is discontinued and he is transferred to another job in a lower grade; (c) if he slows down because of age and the company transfers him to another job in a lower grade; (d) if, for purposes of giving him broad training, he is transferred for a year or two to a job that normally pays less than he has been earning.

5. A company making jet engines now shuts the whole plant down for two weeks in July for vacation, rather than scheduling these through the year as before. Some dissatisfaction is expressed with this policy, but the turnover rate has not increased and no difficulty is found in hiring. What are the advantages of such a policy? Would your answer be the same for a pig-iron producer, a large bakery, a restaurant, or a commercial truck gardener?

6. (a) "We pay our employees a fair wage, which entitles us to their best efforts; therefore I do not believe in financial incentives." Do you agree? (b) How do you account for the fact that companies with incentive plans typically set "normal" output below what an average worker should produce so that workers frequently get a 20% bonus if they do a "fair day's" work?

7. A company near E. M. Barnet, Inc. recently constructed a new air-conditioned office building. Last summer several Barnet employees asked, "Why can't we have air-conditioning, too?" Barnet's normally closes its office when the temperature goes above 90°; plant workers may go home on very hot days, but they are not paid for the time they take off. The personnel manager has estimated that the annual cost, including depreciation and interest, of air-conditioning the offices would be $12,000. If the office were closed when temperatures rose above 85°, the salaries paid-but-not-earned would be $6,200. What changes, if any, should E. M. Barnet, Inc. make?

8. If a man were promoted in the company having the salary plan shown in the table on page 283, how many salary groups would he have to be advanced so that his pay as a beginner on the new job would equal his compensation in the top bracket of the old job? Do you think workers would accept promotions to positions classified just one group higher than their existing position?

9. Shortly after shipping facilities were moved to a different building, the number of grievances of all kinds from the shipping department tripled. Since the new facilities were designed to be more efficient and to reduce physical labor, the management was surprised. Investigation showed that the shipping personnel (25 of them) now worked near an assembly line using women workers. For various reasons, including time on the job and job ratings, some of the women were taking home more pay than any of the nonsupervisory shipping workers. The men said this was unfair and that, furthermore, their jobs were harder and demanded much exposure to the weather. Industrial engineers claimed the jobs were rated and evaluated fairly. Can anything be done?

CASE XII

Major Spectacle Corporation

Robert Baer, president, controller, and proprietor of Major Spectacle Corporation, producers of plastic and plastic and metal eyeglass frames, was concerned about a bottleneck operation in the piecework room. Since he had only owned the company for a relatively short time and had had limited personal production experience, he decided to call in a local consulting firm, Katzenbach, Coffin and Lear. Athol Grim, a principal of the firm, was a friend of Mr. Baer's. The instructions to Mr. Grim were to find out how to get some output out of that room and to find out why more overtime was being paid than was called for in the production plan. Furthermore, Mr. Grim was supposed to find out why the workers in the piecework room seemed to resent having to work overtime.

Mr. Grim talked first to Thaddeus Griffon, head of industrial engineering and quality control. Griffon said, "I don't think those people in the 'playroom' respond as they should to a piece rate system. We designed the pay so that they would take home $1.80 an hour, which is a good rate in this area. Since the cotton textile mills shut down or reduced their operations in this area, there hasn't been much employment available and pay is fairly low. We are, however, interested in a pretty healthy rate of output from the piecework room and therefore I set the standard so that the workers' take-home pay would be decent if they put out some real effort. The room has the unfortunate name of the 'playroom'— I'm not exactly sure why, but you might find out in your investigation. There's one thing that might help us. We do have one other small operation that is on piecework and the people there are taking home about $2.20 an hour. This means that the standards must be loose. If you have any recommendations on the failure of piece rate in the playroom, this would give us an opportunity either to tighten standards in the other shop that I am talking about or to go back to an hourly rate as we have in most of the rest of the operation."

Mr. Grim found that the eyeglasses came out of the plastic molding machines, then went to a gluing operation in which laminations were glued to the top half of the frames. After sitting in a curing or drying room for three days, the frames were then moved to the piecework room for a series of machining operations. After preliminary machining, the frames were tumbled to remove sharp edges, sent back to the piecework room for a few final machining operations, and then shipped out. To have a more complete perspective on the problem of compensation and its possible contribution to what was going on in the piecework room, Mr. Grim asked Mr. Griffon about pay in the other parts of the plant. Griffon explained, "Most of the jobs around here are machine paced so that we pay people by the hour. There's no point in an incentive rate when they can't influence the output. Our average hourly rate for machine operators is about $1.50. This is a little bit low, but people are easy to get here for jobs that don't require much training. We do pay the tool and die men a range from $2.90 an hour to $3.50 an hour and the machine setup men a range at about 25 cents less. These fellows are crucial to both the plastic molding and the metal stamping operation. It's their skill that allows us to have high output and low costs in the molding and stamping rooms. We stamp out some metal temples and metal hinges in one of the shops, as you will see. We even have a special pay arrangement for the tool and die men and the setup men in that they get six paid holidays. None of the other production people here get any paid holidays. Our work is uneven so that the production people get three or four days off at a time at different seasons of the year, depending upon how many orders are in the shop. Sometimes this may run as much as ten days at a time. You'll probably find that the six paid holidays are a constant subject of conversation. This hasn't hurt production any. If the days off have any result, it's given more status to the tool and die men and helps us keep them here so that we don't lose them to the bright lights of some big city."

Mr. Grim then spent some time in the piecework room. He found that all the machining work was done at a series of benches at which people were engaged in special machining operations. The first step done in the piecework room was grooving. The operation was to cut a groove around the inside of the eyeglass frame. Lenses were later fitted into this groove. The grooving operator worked with a milling machine with a vertical shaft that pointed up. A small milling cutter on the shaft projected 1/8 of an inch beyond some protective washers so that a groove of equal depth could be cut all the way around the frame. The frame was placed with the shaft inside the eyelet, then a fixture was clamped over the frame to hold it steady, and the operator moved both the fixture and the frame, holding the fixture so that his fingers would not get caught. Mr. Grim noticed that the operator had several bandages on his fingers. He later learned that no protective device seemed to be able to prevent operators from cutting their fingers. The operator also oiled the inside of the frame to prevent burning the plastic. A second operation was called outer frazing. The outer edges of the frame eyelets on the lower half of the frame were rounded off on the milling machine by running the eyelet between two blades. Some care was needed so as not to cut into the wing tips (where the front of the frame and the temple, or earpiece, were joined). Additional steps in the machining process included inner frazing and bridge frazing to cut out the space on the frame between the eyelets where the nose tabs were later placed. In bridge frazing, the frame was placed backside down on a fixture and the fixture was pushed against the milling cutter. After another cut, known as top frazing, that removed excess plastic from the top of the frame, the eyeglasses moved on to the tubbing room. In the tubbing room they were tumbled in barrels for further smoothing. They then returned to the piecework room for hinge notching and hinge drilling. A notch and a hole were cut in the wing tip so that the metal hinge could later be fitted into it.

Mr. Grim found that very little experience was needed to do each one of the jobs except for a few hours of beginning training. Mrs. Benoit, notch-cutter, said to a new girl, "This job ain't hard. Oh, you might flub the first 20 or 30 until you get the feel of the tool, but then it's nothing. I learnt it in 10 minutes." Bob Cole, a frazing operator, said "Grooving is the hardest 'cause they can't fix that afterwards and the damn tool never fits, which cuts hell out of even making a day's pay as well as your fingers." A local boy, known as "B.J.", who had gone away to college but who still worked summers in the plant, told Mr. Grim that Cole had said to him on his first day in the playroom, "You can learn grooving fast —you're a bright college kid."

There were 16 workers in the piecework room, 6 of them women who specialized on hinge notching and drilling. The remaining jobs appeared to belong to the men. Although each man tended to specialize on one job, they frequently interchanged. "I usually do the top frazing, but I like to get away from it, so Bob and I switch." This was a comment by one of the two younger workers to Mr. Grim. He noticed that each man spent about 50% of his time at his special job. There were two exceptions: B.J., who stayed with one job about 80% of the time, and grooving, which was split equally among all the men. The reason for dividing grooving equally appeared to be so that each one would suffer the same hazard of cut fingers. After a while, Mr. Grim noticed that B.J. was often kidded about working so hard to beat the standard. Mrs. Benoit occasionally commented to someone else or to him, "Look at the professor go," or "Grease 'em and groove 'em, kid," or "Did you make $16 today, B.J.?" This was all said in a joking tone.

Mr. Grim's judgment was that the attitudes of the workers toward each other were always congenial. The men were quite free with their language, but the women didn't seem to mind; quite often a worker would stop to help another set up for his piecework; occasionally the people in the room made a game of seeing who could make the least scrap in one day. This was a little surprising because most of the scrap was due, not to them, but to the tools and the amount of excess material on the frames they received. The workers did not seem to care much about what order the work was done in so long as they had some work to get done even if it was just to pass the time of day. In a conversation with B.J., Mr. Grim learned that B.J. thought that there was a pattern to the process that should be developed but never was. He thought the grooving should be done last since the pieces didn't seem to fit well into the tools used for grooving. Mr. Grim and B.J. together took a look at the process and concluded that a sequencing of top frazing, outer frazing, inner frazing, bridge frazing, and then grooving would allow the tools to fit most adequately. They conjectured that this would also smooth out the flow of work.

When Mr. Grim talked to Mr. Griffon about the sequencing, Griffon said, "Yes, that's the sequence. The men are all trained in it and the fixtures are designed for it. If they deviate, it's for some particular reason of their own. Each job has its own rate— from $.25 per hundred for bridge frazing to $.85 per hundred for templet hinge notching. Top frazing pays $.75 per hundred. The rest are close to $.50 per hundred. Presumably the foreman starts the jobs off right, but he has to spend most of his time in the stamping room. Downtime on the machines is a lot more expensive than labor time."

In talking with the workers in the piecework room, Mr. Grim learned something of their goals and attitudes.

The four women in the room were working to earn extra money and "for something to do after the kids are out of the house." They liked the people with whom they worked and weren't bothered much by the boss, whom they all called "Chick."

Of the three older men, two were married and had no children. Their wives worked also, elsewhere. They owned their own homes and cars. They "earned what they wanted and saved." "What the hell do I have to work for unless the work becomes interesting," was a comment by Pete Barrett, 38 years old. The third man, a widower with no children, wanted money for his two hobbies, photography and fishing. The three younger men, B.J., Fishman, and Mudd, were working for school spending money.

"I like the work, but it can be boring. I do know that our job is important, because if we slow down, the whole plant does—after all, we do all of the basic work here. We could bottleneck the whole operation." This was a comment by Mr. Chair. Mrs. Benoit agreed with him.

One of the younger fellows, Fishman, said to Mr. Grim, "If I can earn $60 a week, what the hell!"

Mr. Grim happened to mention Mr. Griffon, and two of the women said, "Whatever you do, keep him out of here! Excuse the language, but he's a b———."

"Why is that?"

"He's never satisfied. Even Chick, our foreman, appreciates our work although he says it could be improved on, but Griffon. . . .!"

B.J. also said to Mr. Grim, "Griffon seems to be the hatchetman to a number of people although he always struck me as being okay. I just thought he was a hard-hitting, ambitious fellow."

REQUIRED: (a) What has Mr. Grim learned that would help him answer the three questions of (1) how to get more output from the room, (2) why the workers appear to resent overtime work, and (3) why there is excessive overtime?

(b) Evaluate the company's compensation policy in its totality.

(c) Explain how the frame shop got the name "playroom."

(d) Explain why the men rotated jobs and the usefulness of this from their point of view and from the company's point of view.

(e) Would you recommend a change to an hourly rate system of pay from the piece rate system?

PERSONNEL POLICIES—
EMPLOYEE SERVICES AND
INDUSTRIAL RELATIONS

EMPLOYEE SERVICES

Sharp challenge has been raised to company policies that intrude into the private lives of employees. Paternalism is frowned upon; modern attitudes require that employees be regarded as mature, self-respecting individuals. Why, then, should any company go beyond proper selection, training, compensation, and provision of good working conditions?

The answer lies in the fact that each employee is a whole person. His working self is the same man as the person who is head of a family, goes to a ball game and argues about politics. If the man gets in trouble away from the job, his production on the job is seriously affected. Without interfering with his personal independence, there may be things his company can do which will help him enjoy himself and overcome his problems. If these can be done in a friendly manner, and not as "handouts," then the employee will be better off and the company will have a more competent worker.

Part of the company relationship with the "whole man" concerns the manner of supervision. This will be discussed in a later chapter. Efforts may also be directed along the following lines:

1. Sponsoring social and recreational activities.
2. Providing protection against some of the financial risks of the employee.

Social and recreational activities. *Typical activities undertaken.* The following list of company-sponsored activities will indicate the way some companies have attempted to build a friendly feeling among employees and help them find outlets for their interests:

Athletic teams. One of the simplest and perhaps most effective forms of recreational activity is the organization of athletic teams among employees. A bowling league may be organized within the company, or an indoor baseball team may compete with teams from other companies. The men who participate have fun, and the other employees are interested in the outcome of the contests.

Picnics. Some companies have very successful annual picnics. The offices and the plant are closed down (the workers' pay continues), transportation is furnished for the entire family of each employee, and the company furnishes refreshments. A committee of the employees provides varied activities for people of all ages and interests.

Musical organizations. Choral societies and other musical organizations among employees are encouraged in some firms. These are made up of employees that enjoy music, and often include enough talent so that they can give public concerts and sing on other public occasions. Most of us are familiar with the television broadcasts of several such groups.

Company libraries. The primary function of many company libraries is to assist in training employees and to provide technical books that may not be readily available elsewhere. Some libraries are extended to include a wide range of popular books and magazines that are circulated among the employees who enjoy reading.

Company magazines. Company magazines, or "house organs" as they are often called, may be used for general announcements or general training. A large part of such magazines, however, is usually given over to items and stories of particular interest to company employees. There are usually one or two pages of personals, and often stories about prominent men in the company are included. One such magazines carries information about possible vacation spots and notices about rooms to rent and articles available for sale or trade by employees. The activities of any athletic teams and other organizations within the company are given publicity.

In general, the two objectives of social and recreational activities such as those just described are: first, to create a friendliness among the employees; and second, to have the employees remember pleasant associations when they think of the company. Much of the coldness of business activities and the bickering that frequently arises within an enterprise can be eliminated if the employees know each other on a friendly, personal basis. Furthermore, the employee who develops pleasant contacts and activities through his employment hesitates to change jobs, and it is probable that he will tell his friends about the desirable place in which he works.

Limitations of entertainment activities. Recognizing what social and recreational activities should *not* be is fully as important as deciding on their scope. First, this type of personnel activity cannot be substituted for proper policies regarding selection, training, compensation, and work arrangements, or for adequate supervision. Some companies have made a bad mistake in assuming that a flourishing program of outside activities would eliminate the necessity for proper treatment on the job itself. At best, these outside activities can only supplement the general personnel program.

Moreover, the activities are a service for employees. There is no virtue, at least no profit, in making employees play together. Company sponsorship of a program should not be carried to the point where employees are more or less forced to do things they do not really enjoy. A more successful policy is for the company to cooperate with employees in providing facilities, equipment, and perhaps assisting in the organization of various projects that the employees really want to undertake. It is much better to have the foreman report "Some of the boys want to get up a horseshoe tournament," than it is for some social-minded personnel manager to put on a dance, especially when the interests and background of the various employees are so different that a dance could not be successful. In recent years the trend is toward administration of recreational activities by the employees themselves through clubs or through their unions.

Employee risks. *Types of risk.* Anyone who depends upon working for a livelihood is subject to a number of serious financial hazards. The most important of these are the following:

1. Loss of work due to accident or sickness.
2. Unemployment; that is, loss of present job plus inability to find other suitable employment.
3. Premature death, leaving family or other dependents without adequate means of support.
4. Old age without adequate means of support.
5. Emergencies requiring large sums of cash, such as serious illnesses of other members of the family, fire, theft, or similar catastrophes.

Ways of handling risks. A vast number of workers either do not earn enough money or lack the self-discipline necessary to accumulate personal savings or to buy insurance that will give them a minimum protection against these risks. For many years this problem was considered to be of no concern to the employer. The employer paid wages for work performed, and what the worker did with the money and how he met emergencies was his own personal problem. Actually the problems were met in numerous ways: the old folks moved in with their children; the widow's older children worked to support the younger children; relatives were called upon for assistance in emergencies; and if worst came to worst, appeal was made to private or public charity.

Within the last thirty years recognition that some more adequate provision should be made to care for such situations has been increasing. Many business executives feel that their company has some responsibility for the economic risks of its employees, and they have undertaken programs to help alleviate the troubles. And the federal government has stepped into the picture with a far-reaching program of social security.

When the federal program was first started, many people expected it to replace company programs. No wholesale transfer of employee protection from companies to government has occurred. Modifications have been made, to be sure; but, in general, company-sponsored protection has increased in variety and amount along with enlarged federal programs. As a consequence, this whole field is constantly changing. Generally speaking, management must adopt policies governing:

1. Activities to be undertaken.
2. Methods of financing protection.
3. Management of protection plans.

Kinds of employee protection. Almost all states have workmen's compensation laws that provide, in addition to the payment of doctors' bills, a minimum compensation for all serious accidents arising in connection with employment. In addition to these legal requirements, many business concerns undertake voluntarily a program designed to prevent accidents and to improve the physical well-being of their employees. Such a *health program* usually includes health examinations, treatment of minor ailments, and diagnosis of major difficulties. As a general rule, the employee is expected to call upon his family physician for care in a serious illness.

Every company must establish some policy regarding payment of salary to an employee who is absent because of sickness. Some companies establish a maximum number of days of *sick leave* and then permit no further allowance. Other companies may continue the employee at half pay for an additional two or three weeks. Beyond this period there is the question of whether a job will be kept open for the employee when he recovers.

In some companies, mutual benefit associations have been established that provide *medical care* for employees and that occasionally pay a weekly allowance to an indisposed employee who no longer draws a salary. The extent of company and union participation in such mutual benefit associations varies a good deal. Provision for Blue Cross hospital insurance is, however, quite common. More recently, insurance against *major medical expenses* has been added.

Most companies pay a tax to finance the various state *unemployment insurance* plans. These are added to in some cases, notably the automobile companies, by private supplementary unemployment benefit plans negotiated with the unions as part of the employment contract. Also business concerns are giving increasing attention to stabilization of operations through a varied product line or the handling of inventories to provide regular employment as discussed in previous chapters. A few companies have enough confidence in their ability to stabilize operations that they are willing to guarantee their regular employees work for 48 or 50 weeks a year. Such *annual wage plans* or the *supplementary unemployment benefit plans* are heralded by some people as the next major step forward in employee security.

If, despite these efforts at stabilization, the volume of operations must be curtailed, the question then arises whether the available employment should be spread among all the former employees so that each has at least part-time work, or whether some of the employees should be laid off. Many firms follow a share-the-work policy if they believe that the slump in operations is only temporary and that full employment will be restored to all of their regular employees in the near future. This plan has the serious disadvantage that none of the employees, not even the most efficient or those with long service records, earns a full wage. Moreover, keeping a larger number of workers on the payroll than is necessary complicates the administrative problems and increases the overhead expenses to some extent. For these reasons, few companies carry a share-the-work policy beyond the point where the remaining workers get less than half-time employment. Of course, if the reduction in operations is considered more or less permanent, it is usually better policy for the company to face the situation at once and make the necessary reductions immediately.

An increasing number of firms sponsor group *life insurance* plans that give all participating employees some protection against *premature death*. While the amount is limited to a few thousand dollars, it does provide funds for funeral expenses and something for dependents during the period of readjustment. Federal social security benefits also provide limited protection against premature death.

Thousands of companies now have some sort of *old-age pension* plan that supplements social security payment. The federal plan provides only modest protection, and with the rising interest in security, many firms have expanded their retirement plans to cover all long-service employees. Unions have pushed hard for company pensions, especially when increases in cash pay cannot be justified by a rise in the cost of living.

Several difficult problems are connected with pensions. A liberal pension plan is very costly, and there is considerable doubt whether the average employee, and certainly the younger ones, care enough about it to warrant the expense. Then, for the long-service employees a ticklish question arises as to when company financed plans "vest," that is, when an employee may quit the company and still take his pension rights with him. Even more troublesome is the age of compulsory retirement. Spending one's years after sixty securely in a rocking chair is not as attractive as it sounds. Many people are still able and vigorous at that age, and both they and their company would like to have them continue working. Men vary in the age when they ought to retire, and no clear, objective measure of this time has been devised. Increasingly, companies are adopting a policy that permits voluntary retirement at about sixty and compulsory retirement at sixty-five.

The typical way a company helps its employees meet *emergency needs for cash* is an advance in salary. Unfortunately, if a company becomes too lenient in giving employees an advance, the privilege is likely to be abused and payroll records decidedly complicated. Consequently, most companies have established a definite policy as to the amount and the conditions under which advances may be made, and they see to it that employees understand this policy. Another successful device for meeting temporary cash needs is the credit union. A credit union is a cooperative venture among employees for the accumulation of small savings from which members may borrow.

Methods of financing protection. A second underlying problem faced by management in connection with employee risks is financing the protection offered. The simplest and most obvious plan for support of these activities is to have the employer pay expenses of any activities that he is interested in promoting. Some employers have followed this policy, paying the cost of group life insurance, health service, employment stabilization, pensions, or other protection plans.

Few companies can afford the cost of an adequate security program for their employees because it results in a substantial increase in labor cost. Another important objection to the employer's paying all of the expense of a security program is the attitude of the worker toward something for nothing. It is human nature to prize a thing that requires sacrifice to attain and to deprecate the free gifts of nature and society. Even if union leaders stress the fringe benefits they have won for their members, the workers are likely to regard employer-financed benefits as ordinary as fire and police protection.

The opposite policy of having the employee pay all the bills is occasionally used. Group life insurance is often entirely financed by employees' contributions. Cooperative organizations, such as mutual benefit associations or credit unions, are ordinarily supported entirely by employees. The management may encourage such activity, but it may also hold tight to the purse strings. Here we encounter the obvious difficulty that many workers cannot afford to pay the cost of adequate protection. Furthermore, many employees prefer to spend their money otherwise and to meet trouble when it comes. Obviously, if the employee pays all or part of the bill, his participation should be voluntary.

A compromise policy between these two extremes is now popular. Under such a plan both the employer and the employee contribute to the support of the various activities. Sometimes the employer merely contributes the administrative and overhead expenses. At other times there is an equal sharing between employee and employer. In many cases the employee pays enough so that he becomes personally interested in the protection plan while at the same time the employer lightens the financial burden by contributing a larger share toward the expense of the plan, thus making it attractive to the employee.

Management of security plans. The management of various plans for employee security, like their financing, may be entirely in the hands of the management or of the employees, or it may be under some form of joint control. When the company pays all or part of the bill, naturally the executives want to see that the money is properly expended. Even if the company has nothing at stake, it may be interested in the success of the venture. It will certainly want to avoid any ill feeling that might be created by the failure of any plan upon which it has put its stamp of approval and to which the employees have contributed their money.

The executives will undoubtedly make the assumption that they are more competent than the employees or the unions to administer the plan. This is probably true where technical financial questions are involved, but it does not necessarily follow that the executives would prove more competent so far as dealing with individual employees is concerned. For example, one of the reasons for the outstanding success of credit unions is the knowledge employees have of their fellow workers at the time loans are being granted. Ordinarily, they can effect collection of the loans by bringing a certain type of social pressure to bear on those employees who have borrowed money. The same advantage applies to the operation of a mutual sickness benefit plan.

Moreover, a plan operated entirely by company executives is likely to be administered on a paternalistic basis, thus failing to build an employee sense of self-respect and joint participation. After all, problems of financial risks of employees are traditionally individual and personal, and the employer should follow policies that will create and maintain a feeling of individual responsibility. The business executive should therefore assume the role of helper in situations that call for cooperative assistance rather than the role of a dominating administrator.

INDUSTRIAL RELATIONS

For managers and employees to work together to accomplish the objectives of an enterprise, there must necessarily be an agreement between them as to wages, hours, working conditions and other factors having immediate bearing upon the conditions of employment. For many years, these agreements have been made primarily between managers and individual employees. Even today, over two thirds of the employees in the United States bargain individually with their employers. However, there has been a dramatic rise in the power of labor unions, and the agreements reached with the unions set the pattern for most of the individual agreements. Consequently, policies guiding the relationship between unions and management are a vital aspect of personnel administration.

Some people contend that the existence of a union makes the objective consideration of personnel policies futile. The assumption is that if management is not entirely free to make final decisions on such matters, the alternative is an irrational patchwork of agreements based on the bargaining surrounding each issue. Such a view is both unrealistic and unproductive. The manager designs products in terms of what customers will buy, he sets prices on the basis of competition and within the limits permitted by law, he buys materials and borrows money under terms he can negotiate with the supplier. The views and strength of the union will, of course, influence the personnel policies finally established, just as the operating situations influence other policies. But the fact that the decisions are not made by the manager alone does not remove the desirability of a workable, integrated plan of action. The need for unemotional, careful analysis remains unchanged.

Policies regarding the selection and development of a work force, compensation, and conditions surrounding employment have already been discussed. Consequently, attention here will concentrate on the way relations with unions are conducted. In this connection, a company should establish policies regarding:

1. Character of union relations.
2. Support of union organizations.
3. Scope of bargaining.
4. Recourse to outside agencies.

Character of union relations. A key aspect of all union relations is the underlying attitude or approach of a company to its relations with the union. The following examples will illustrate the wide choice and the importance of these policies.

Belligerent policy towards unions. Companies engaged in interstate commerce are required by federal law to bargain with unions which represent a majority of their employees. Similar state laws require collective bargaining of most local businesses. Nevertheless, some employers balk at union activities whenever possible, make no concessions unless unavoidable, and do anything in their power to weaken the strength of the union.

Such a policy usually stems from a conviction that unions are anti-social. It may be supported by experiences with corrupt union officials or Communist-led unions, or with unions failing to live up to their contracts. Whatever the causes, there is strong dislike and mistrust of the union by the company executives. They try to conduct themselves so as to discredit the union in the eyes of the employees. There is the hope that sooner or later the employees will repudiate the union and it will no longer have to be recognized as the bargaining agent.

Obviously such a militant policy keeps the union stirred up and it will probably continue to use scurrilous tactics which typify organization efforts. At best there will be only an armed truce between the two factions.

The horse-trading approach. Another view accepts the union as being inevitable but conducts relations along horse-trading lines. The union is assumed to be unreliable and conniving. Consequently negotiations are conducted in an air of suspicion and sharp bargains are quite in order. In keeping with this approach would be deals which resolved immediate difficulties but are acknowledged to violate sound principles of human relations. As one advocate of this policy said, "It is just a question if you can outsmart the other guy."

Follow the leader. Often smaller companies try to establish a general understanding with the union that the company will grant any wage increase or fringe benefits that have been agreed to by the leading companies of the industry, or sometimes in the local labor market. These firms feel that they are too small and weak to stand out against the union. The most they hope for is to be no worse off than their large competitors.

This is undoubtedly a practical policy to follow in some circumstances. It does, of course, have the weaknesses of any policy of appeasement. Naturally, the union is going to ask for, and probably get, the most favorable clauses that are granted by any of the leading companies. Having won these points, the union leader may ask for even more, particularly if there are political problems within the union and the leaders feel they must win further concessions to strengthen their own position. Moreover, one of the important ways a small company competes with a large one is by making special adaptations to the local situation. The follow-the-leader policy sacrifices this potential source of strength insofar as industrial relations are concerned.

Straight business relationship. When both company executives and union leaders take a mature view of their relations, it is often desirable for a company to approach union negotiations as a straight business proposition. This can occur only after questions of union organization and recognition have been resolved and the bitterness that so often is associated with such activities has passed into the background. There is mutual confidence, respect, and trust, just as there should be between the company and its major suppliers of raw materials.

This sort of business relationship does not mean that there may not be disagreements. The company may take a firm, even tough, position on certain matters but the positions it takes are based on long run business considerations and there is a strong undercurrent of sound principles of personnel relations.

Company executives must recognize that the union leader holds an elected office and that at times he must press grievances or present a request simply in response to pressure from some of his constituents. Under the straight business policy these do not create a strong emotional reaction but are regarded simply as a normal part of the relationship. This type of relationship is often found in industries that have been organized for a period of several years by a union that itself is stable and follows a bread-and-butter philosophy.

Union-management cooperation. Still another policy in dealing with unions is to regard the union as an ally in improving the efficiency of the plant. One of the best examples of union-management cooperation is the working agreement developed over a generation ago between Hart, Schaffner & Marx and the union representing a large number of its factory employees. The union recognized that the company was in a highly competitive industry; consequently, it worked with the employer in making improvements in labor productivity. On the other hand, the company acceded to demands for higher wages and better hours.

Both recognized that long, bitter strikes worked a hardship on the employees and caused business losses to the employer which he could ill afford. From the start there was emphasis on the settlement of disputes by means of arbitration. The arbitrators were highly respected individuals, and always insisted that questions regarding interpretation and application of an agreement be examined objectively. More important than wise administration of the fixed agreements have been the methods developed to deal with technological and economic changes in new agreements. The actual operation of the plan has required a great deal of patience. Nevertheless, there is substantial evidence that the employer and the employees alike have benefited by the spirit of cooperation and tolerance created by working together under such circumstances.

Union-management cooperation has taken different forms on the railroads, in the steel industry, and in other places where it has been tried. In some cases there has been a sharp distinction between the cooperative activities at the plant and the bargaining over a new contract. In other instances, as in some of the agreements in the hosiery industry and the ladies garment industry, plans for improving productivity have become part and parcel of the basic contracts. Whatever the form, the important point here is that the company followed a basic policy of union-management cooperation.

The foregoing illustrations, ranging from a belligerent policy to union-management cooperation, are among the more common policies followed in union relations. There are, of course, many other combinations and variations. Until a company formulates some kind of a policy on this basic issue of the character of its union relations, and gets this policy thoroughly accepted throughout its executive ranks, there is little hope for consistent and really effective industrial relations.

Support of union organizations. In addition to policies regarding the general character of union relationship, guides are needed for several more specific issues. While in some respects these are extensions of the general policies, they usually are of sufficient importance to warrant top-management attention. One such troublesome area is the support which the company will give to the union organization.

Having fought for existence, unions are much concerned about maintaining their position. This can be assured if the employer will grant a closed shop in which he agrees to employ only union members in good standing. Almost as satisfactory, from the union point of view, is a union shop in which the employer hires whomever he wants but the men must join the union in order to keep their jobs.

Many employers are strongly opposed to either of these arrangements or variations thereof, and the closed shop was made illegal by the Labor-Management Relations Act. The employer objections center primarily on two points. First, if the unions have an assured monopoly position, there is danger of racketeering, as has existed in some of the longshoremen's and building crafts' unions. Or, there is the possibility that the union leaders will become irresponsible because of their assured control. On this point the union shop, which does not give the union leaders control over admission to membership, is much to be preferred.

The second objection is one of principle. Employers may feel that a man should not be forced, against his wishes, to become a member of a union in order to hold a job. The unions, on the other hand, argue that it is unfair for a few employees to get all the benefits of the union activities without paying dues. Fifteen or twenty years from now, these arguments over the union shop will probably look like a tempest in a teapot because there are examples of very strong unions that do not have the protection of a union shop and there are also many union shops in which, apparently, the workers do not feel that their liberties have been seriously curtailed.

A related issue is whether the employer will deduct union dues and assessments from the worker's pay and turn the funds thus collected over to the union treasury. Such a check off gives the union financial strength and avoids a cumbersome collection problem. Most companies that accept unions as a legitimate part of the business scene are willing to grant the check off, provided the individual employee authorizes the action.

A much more intangible question is the support a company will give a union that is having a jurisdictional fight with a rival union. Theoretically, the employer is supposed to exercise no influence over the employees' choice of a bargaining agent. Nevertheless, an employer is vitally concerned about interruptions in work that may result from jurisdictional squabbles. From time to time there are things that a company can do to make a particular union appear in a favorable light. The question of policy then is whether the company will throw this intangible support to one or more of the unions. The answer to this question will be determined in a large measure by the character of the relationship that the company seeks with the union.

Scope of bargaining. Recognition of a union does not, of course, indicate what activities are to be covered in the union-management relationship. By tradition and law questions of wages, hours, and physical working conditions are normal subjects of collective bargaining. More recently, employee pensions and similar services have been added to this standard list. Most companies would also agree that job assignments, the use of seniority and other factors in selecting men for lay-offs or promotions, and other supervisory activities were legitimate subjects for discussion although they might be firmly opposed to any written agreement as to how these matters were to be handled. We have already noted, in connection with the union shop issue, that employers are much concerned about union interference with their selection of new workers, and as soon as discussions extend beyond the traditional subjects there are likely to be objections that the union is interfering with "management prerogatives."

There can be no doubt that employees have a real stake in the stability of operation in their company. Their income and their economic future is strongly influenced by the prosperity of the firm for which they work. If the function of the union is to protect the interests of the worker, is it not reasonable then that they should participate in decisions regarding pricing, new customers, product line, and similar matters?

This line of reasoning led unions in post-war Germany to insist on membership on boards of directors and other means of co-determination. With a few exceptions, American unions have shied away from such arrangements. Union leaders have recognized that if they participated in such decisions, they would share responsibility for them. By staying away from such matters, they avoid such managerial responsibility and continue to be in a position to criticize (a significant weapon in union politics).

While neither union nor management leadership wants unions to become involved in the entire managerial process, it is likely that an increasing number of topics will fall within the orbit of union-management relations. Unions can be helpful on such matters as absenteeism, productivity, and installation of new processes. They are concerned about changes in plant locations and mechanization.

Some firms follow a policy of keeping unions as far away from such matters as possible. In other cases, such as the union-management agreements regarding the mechanization of hosiery mills, and the contracting arrangements in the garment industry, union contracts deal with what typically are regarded as management matters. A more common and much more flexible policy is to restrict the formal collective bargaining process to conditions of employment and to work out other matters of mutual interest in a much more informal manner.

Recourse to outside agencies. Union-management relations are not wholly a matter between an individual company and the union or unions representing its employees. Other parties may be brought into the picture and a company will do well to consider carefully its policy regarding recourse to outside agencies.

Impartial arbitration. Most union contracts provide for arbitration of disputes over the interpretation and application of the contract. Typically, the dispute follows a grievance procedure moving up from the worker and his first-line supervisor through several administrative levels. If the matter cannot be settled by top-management and union representatives, an impartial arbitrator is called in to make a decision that becomes binding on all parties concerned.

Some such provision as this is necessary if strikes are to be avoided during the period of the contract. Where a single impartial arbitrator has been used over a period of years, a sort of "common law" develops. Once this common law becomes accepted, many potential disputes are settled without ever reaching the arbitrator. On the other hand, many companies take the position that minor disagreements can be worked out best by the parties directly concerned. They follow a policy of making minimum use of outside arbitrators.

Group bargaining. The negotiation of a new labor contract is quite a different matter than its interpretation, which has just been discussed. The distinction is like that between the legislative and judicial branches of the government. Usually the company itself works out the new agreement with its employees. To an increasing extent, however, employers are joining together in groups in order to negotiate new contracts with labor unions. Roughly a tenth of all the contracts in effect are negotiated through employer groups and these cover approximately a fourth of all workers under union agreements.

Industry-wide bargaining is found in a few industries, such as coal mining and glass. More often group bargaining covers employers in a city or a region. There are several reasons why a company might want to join such a group. The executives in small firms are busy with many things and lack the time typically consumed in negotiations. In many instances they are not as skilled in the process as the professional union representatives with whom they must deal. Even the larger companies that have full-time industrial relations men may join an employer group in an effort to increase their bargaining strength. Moreover, the union has less opportunity to play one company against the other, pushing for different concessions with the several companies and then requesting everyone to agree to the most favorable concessions any competitor made.

On the other hand, such group bargaining makes it much more difficult to adapt the agreements to the particular situation of a given company. Also, at times the company may find itself being pushed into agreements that it would not make had it bargained alone. Consequently, companies whose industrial relations policies differ significantly from others in the industry, or whose economic position is distinctive, are often reluctant to participate in group bargaining. Wise choice of a policy regarding bargaining through groups is then clearly a matter that each company must make.

Government mediation and arbitration. When a company and a union cannot agree upon the terms of a new contract and a strike threatens or actually begins, it is possible to call for the assistance of a government mediator. This man explores the nature of the dispute and tries to find some basis upon which the two sides may agree. The attitude of the company will determine in part when a mediator should be called in and how effective he is likely to be. Some companies believe that this type of mediation is very helpful while others resent the intrusion of an outsider.

If the impending strike is of sufficient importance to the public interest, the company may be faced not only with the offer of federal mediation but with other forms of outside assistance. Public utilities and basic industries are subject to fact-finding boards and impartial commissions of various kinds, depending upon the state or federal laws under which they fall. In this country we have not yet adopted compulsory arbitration in which parties to such a disagreement have to submit the dispute to an arbitrator whose decision would be binding. But government seizure and other forms of pressure bring us pretty close to that point.

Each dispute has its own unique problems, and general policies governing the way a company will conduct itself in this type of negotiation are difficult to establish. Nevertheless, it is evident that some companies very carefully steer away from government intervention, whereas other firms either are willing to submit to governmental decision or they permit themselves to be jockeyed into that kind of a position. The reason why the general policy of resorting to governmental intervention has detrimental value is that the whole preliminary bargaining process tends to break down if it is assumed that the dispute will be carried to mediators, political bodies, and public opinion. There is no strong pressure for the negotiators to try to arrive at agreement if they feel that a final settlement will not be reached at their level. On the other hand, if the feeling is that some type of an agreement must be hammered out without recourse to outsiders, then local negotiations can be carried on in an atmosphere where results are likely to be achieved.

SUMMARY

Preceding chapters have dealt with selection, training, and compensation of employees and with hours, safety, and other arrangements for their work. Personnel policies cannot stop at this point, however.

This chapter opened with emphasis on the fact that employee morale depends on more than the job itself. The attitudes, worries, and enthusiasms developed by employees off the job have a marked effect on their productivity. Consequently, a company should set up policies indicating how far it is prepared to go in assisting employees with social and recreational activities and in meeting their economic risks such as sickness, old age, and unemployment. Any activities that are undertaken in this area should be financed and administered so as to develop the genuine interest and the individual integrity of each employee. Supervision that also has a marked effect on morale will be considered later in this book.

Finally, policies guiding a company's relations with unions were discussed. The underlying approach of the company, which may be anywhere from a militant policy to union-management cooperation, will permeate all union contacts and consequently should be selected as objectively as possible. More specific issues on which policies are needed are the way the company will support existing union organizations, the scope of activities that will be considered with the unions, and the extent to which the company will participate in group bargaining and will use outside arbitrators and mediators. Just as in the relationship with customers or creditors, industrial relations policies should be adapted to realities of the situation, for example, maturity of the union and size of company. But this need for reality does not lessen the value of sound, consistent policies for dealing with the unions that the employees designate as their representatives.

We have now discussed major policies in three areas vital to every business enterprise—sales, production and purchasing, and personnel. Finance, a fourth phase of every business concern, is the subject of the next three chapters.

QUESTIONS FOR CLASS DISCUSSION

1. For many decades the United Mine Workers stressed wage increases and tonnage royalty payments to its benefits fund while encouraging coal companies to substitute machines for men and thus automate the mines. This led to a 75% reduction in the work force in the mines, industry-wide bargaining, severe unemployment in several states, and the recent reopening of small, inefficient, low-pay, nonunion mines that are probably not very safe. Can or should the coal operators bargain for any other pattern of wages, employment, and manpower policy?

2. Legislation is now being introduced in some states to outlaw union and closed shops—the so-called "right-to-work laws." What philosophy lies behind such laws? Why do unions think union shops are so necessary?

3. For almost two months when the country needed steel badly, the steel industry was shut down by a strike primarily over the union shop issue. Both sides recognized that a very small percentage of the workers were not already union members. The final settlement provided that all new employees had to join the union, but that they had the privilege of resigning at certain very limited times. Do you believe the steel companies were justified in holding out against the union shop for so long? How do you explain the union's adamant stand? Should the issue have been resolved quickly by compulsory arbitration?

4. The directors of O.R. MacKenzie & Co. have just decided that 3% of its payroll should be spent on insurance and pensions for its 1,200 employees. How would you allocate this sum among various kinds of insurance such as hospitalization, surgical benefits, medical expense, group life, pensions, widows' allowances, etc.? The appropriation is in addition to social security and unemployment insurance taxes, workmen's compensation insurance, and sick leave (company maximum is one month per year).

5. Review the discussion of the role of the employer in the management and the financing of various plans for protecting employees against financial risks. How much of this reasoning can be applied to governmental financing and management of security schemes? What are the advantages and the disadvantages of having the government assume the responsibility for protection against such risks rather than the administrators of individual companies?

6. The union business agent representing the workers of the Superior Hosiery Company has objected to the company's subcontracting some of its knitting and has asked that the company come to an understanding with the union on this issue. Do you think the company should bargain with the union on this issue? Do the reasons for the subcontracting have any bearing on whether the union should have some say in the matter?

7. The J.B. Lyon Company, of Albany, New York, employs about 1,000 workers at its printing plant. It is operated on a strictly union basis, and it is engaged in the production of magazines, business papers, books, and a large variety of general commercial printing. The unions in this plant are strongly opposed to any form of individual incentive system. In fact, the management is not permitted to set tasks directly, nor may it make time studies. Hart, Schaffner, and Marx manufactures a wide line of men's suits and overcoats and is also highly unionized. In this company the union not only permits individual incentives, but it cooperates with the management in improving operating efficiency and establishing output standards. What reasons can you suggest for the differences in the positions taken by the unions in the two situations?

8. Do you think that industry-wide bargaining would be desirable for: (a) a company with 40% of its employees members of the union; (b) a company in a highly competitive industry almost completely organized (for example, men's suits) ; or (c) a company that had contracts with several unions in addition to those participating in the industry-wide bargaining?

9. The Apex Furniture Company produces moderately priced household furniture that is sold directly to retailers. The entire output of the company, which employs 800 workers in its plant, is sold by its 15 salesmen. The company has been maintaining its position in the industry, but operations last year were unprofitable and the company is still paying off a bank loan incurred during that period. To what extent would you recommend the same personnel policies for both the plant employees and the sales force, and in what respects should the policies differ? Explain.

CASE XIII

Blends Woven Label Company

One week after the National Labor Relations Board certified that Blends Woven Label Company was an unorganized shop with no union at all to represent its workers, the weavers struck. About 80% of them, plus men brought in from the outside, picketed the plant in an attempt to force recognition of the United Textile Workers (A. F. of L.). After some pushing on the picket line and a few threats, the warper tenders, doffers, slash hands, and card cutters gave up trying to enter the plant. Only the settling dust stirred in the silent rooms as looms, warpers, slashers, and dyeing machines lay quiet—eating overhead at a galloping rate.

Enraged as he was at a strike that he believed both immoral and illegal, Mr. Powell, president and part owner, also sweated with the anxiety of keeping accounts, getting out orders, and beating competitors.

Blends was one of the 15 largest companies in a specialized segment of the textile industry. It counted 52 direct competitors—all making narrow tapes and woven labels. Since its founding, Blends had been unorganized, but it had always kept abreast of the national unions' wage demands in order to keep the workers satisfied. The managers saw many advantages in staying out of the A. F. of L. The most important was that if the A. F. of L. went on strike, Blends workers did not have to follow. The workers lost no pay and the firm lost no production. Organized firms did. In addition, at a strike's end, Blends employees received the wage benefits that the organized workers had struck for. For years the company had experienced no trouble from the workers or the national labor unions; that is, until this latest effort by the local A. F. of L. labor organizer and the NLRB decision.

Manufacturing woven labels is no exception to general conditions in the textile industry. A large number of firms with identical products, constant excess capacity, and continual drives for improved productivity mean severe price and service competition and a premium on cost-cutting. Return on investment in textile manufacturing was half that of the average of all manufacturing. In the woven label field particularly, production was now "slow." Although no workers had been laid off at Blends, weavers at some of the nearby plants had been.

The plant was located in Paterson, New Jersey, a city of about 150,000 people in a heavily unionized area. Nearby there were about 17 other plants manufacturing woven labels. In all, 32 firms in the industry were not organized. The remaining 20 were. Of the top 15 firms in the industry, 5 were not organized—a competititive advantage for the 5, as no time was taken up with bargaining difficulties and contract demands. Unorganized firms could run 5 to 10% more looms per weaver at a lower average pay rate, although the minimum union rate was observed by most of them. But they had no pension system, a cost saving of 8¢ per hour. For lower labor costs, some firms had moved south or had established branch plants in the south. The need to be close to the New York garment market limited such moves.

The 20 firms mentioned were organized by the United Textile Workers (A. F. of L.). A few of the other 32 had company (sometimes called "shop") unions. These shop unions had been established in the late 1930's to head off organizing efforts by the Textile Workers Union. In general, the shop unions were not militant, seldom called strikes, and followed the pay pattern of the national union while lagging on bargaining for benefits.

As far as Mr. Powell knew, his workers were getting wages equal to those demanded by the A. F. of L. However, he knew that some of the employees still held union cards because of their previous association with the national union. Also, he believed that if any of the other workers desired association with the union, it would be the older ones who naturally felt job insecurity the most.

The plant employed about 50 people, 20 of whom were weavers. Mr. Powell felt that a kind of family relationship existed between the management and the workers. He had worked in the plant since he was 18. People called each other by first names throughout the organization. Managers had always treated the workers with respect. In recessions when Blends, like other firms, had rough times financially, it had tried to take care of the workers, keeping many of them employed when it would have been easier on finances to lay them off. Also, recently one of the workers had been ill and had not worked in over a year; yet during this entire period the company continued to give him his weekly pay, since Mr. Powell knew he needed the money to pay his doctor bills and support his family. For these reasons and others, Mr. Powell had always felt that the workers had confidence in the management and would resist the A. F. of L.'s attempt to organize.

Nevertheless, he worried because some of the workers already had A. F. of L. union cards. With the natural turnover of help in a heavily unionized area, workers who had union cards continued with their dues just in case they left their present jobs and took work with another plant that was unionized. They felt protected through greater assurance of some work. They also would not have to pay initiation dues again. Although Mr. Powell felt that these workers were satisfied and had no particular desire to have a union shop, he knew that they were affected by their previous union association. Also, he realized that, since the average age of the weavers was 60, many of them might feel that the national labor union would provide more security.

To have an election to decide if the workers wanted to join a union, 30% of them had to sign a petition. They did. To that point, Mr. Powell said nothing to the workers because he felt that it would only cause more trouble and friction between the workers and management and among the workers themselves. Then Mr. Politz, the A. F. of L. organizer, made several visits to the shop and to the workers' homes. He and some of the older workers pressed the A. F. of L.'s case vigorously.

Mr. Powell, from years of acquaintanceship, thought he knew why they wanted the A. F. of L. The national union said that it would provide more benefits than the workers were now getting. Mr. Powell knew this was not true because the only thing the workers were not getting was the pension. Several of the workers were campaigning around the shop about the pension. These were mostly the older workers who would not be able to build up a sizeable pension anyway. If they did join the A. F. of L., they could be fired when they became 68 years old. The firm did not do this now. So, in Mr. Powell's eyes, they would not be getting job security since many of them were already at that age or fast approaching it. He discussed this with several of the workers.

Bill Marvis and Tony Belletti, older workers who were not in the national union, said they had friends working in the other plants who didn't have to run the loom loads that they did and were still making as much money. Some others said that Bill and Tony and others like them wanted the union because they thought they would be fired if other weavers could be found to take their places. Mr. Powell reflected that they might be right, for he had often thought about bringing in some younger weavers so as not to be strapped when the older ones had to leave. He had recently hired 3 young men who were being taught by the other weavers in the plant. It usually took about 3 to 6 months before the weaver could operate a Jacquard loom efficiently by himself. Also, Mr. Powell had brought in some women for other jobs than weaving because he felt that on the whole they caused much less trouble than some of the older men. He had found that they would work better for him without causing as much dissension among the workers.

Woven label manufacturers are not integrated textile companies; that is, they do no spinning or any prior steps in the yarn manufacturing process but buy yarn from a few specialized spinners. Some labels are woven from cotton yarn, but most are all rayon. The highest quality labels may, in some cases, be made with a silk blend in the lettering shuttle.

An artist working for the label manufacturer develops a sketch of the label. Once this satisfies the garment or cloth manufacturer, it is turned over to a card cutter who punches out the directions for the Jacquard loom on the cards that govern the loom's operation.

Yarn, after receiving, is warped on to the loom beams in a separate warping room and then moved to the weave room. After weaving, the labels move on to the makeup room. There they are rolled on counting machines and inspected. Finally, they are cut and taped for ease in handling by the user. Recent developments in this final process mean that some labels may have their ends folded after cutting to simplify the later sewing processes, or a glue finish may be applied to certain grades to help bind down the labels, or a polyethylene backing may be applied by machine to the folddown part of the label to allow the label to hold up better under dry cleaning.

Mr. Powell was legally able to talk to the workers up until 24 hours before the election. Other than the conversations mentioned, he did not talk with them to attempt to persuade them not to join the union. He felt that this was not the proper thing to do and he thought that he would lose respect rather than gain anything by such action. He knew from some of the workers who had spoken to him how many of the individuals were voting. He was sure that many of them did not want the union and would not vote for it. He decided the best course of action would be not to instigate any more trouble than was already present at the plant.

The National Labor Relations Board conducted the election. The result was a tie. With this, the NLRB said that the union was not certified. At this ruling, Mr. Politz of the A. F. of L. concentrated his efforts on the essential workers, that is, the weavers. He succeeded in getting 80% of them to strike. Powell talked with Politz the second day after the picketing had started.

"How come all this, Joe? We played it fair and square right along and the workers don't want it. At least they didn't vote for the national union. Is this the right thing to do now that you lost?"

Politz answered: "I know how the vote came out, Mr. Powell, and I know what we have done. This is our way."

Powell was angry. He felt that he had acted morally correctly throughout the whole affair and that he hadn't campaigned among the workers. Now he knew that the other workers would be afraid to come into the plant. To get the weavers back to work, Mr. Politz said that Mr. Powell would have to bargain with the A. F. of L.

With the competitive nature of the industry as it was and with no rosy outlook for the near future, Mr. Powell knew that he could not afford to have the plant closed for very long. He had orders to get out, and if he didn't get them out, competitors would grab the accounts. He believed that he could not afford to lose several large accounts that he was producing for at the moment. By dealing with the A. F. of L. his costs would go up—something he felt he could not afford. Profits last year had been $20,000 after taxes. He felt that he had won the issue and that these were underhanded methods that the union was employing.

Mr. Powell called in his lawyer and checked through the situation with him. The lawyer, Mr. Cromwell, had been kept up to date with the proceedings as they went along so that the management would be sure to abide with the legal procedures. Now the union was using illegal methods and Mr. Powell wanted to know what he could do about it.

Mr. Cromwell stated that he could obtain an injunction against the picketing. However, he added that by the time he could gather the necessary documents and information, show some damage, and find a judge who would issue an injunction, it would be three or possibly even four weeks before even a temporary injunction could be obtained.

Mr. Powell wondered whether he could outlast the workers who were leading the strike. He knew that they were the type who lived from weekly pay to weekly pay and that they didn't have savings to live on. They couldn't stay out of work long.

Powell felt very dejected. He had received no help at all from the NLRB. He believed that he could not afford to have the plant shut down for longer than two or three weeks at the outside. He knew that the union was acting illegally, but he felt himself trapped. He also knew that the vote had been a tie and thus many of the workers did not want A. F. of L. representation. Mr. Powell concluded that the majority of the workers wanted a shop union if they had any union at all.

Mr. Powell believed he was faced with several conflicting objectives. He wanted to do what was best for the workers, and that was not having an A. F. of L. shop. He knew that he had to get out several large orders and that if he didn't he was liable to lose the accounts. He did not particularly want to get mixed up with a national union because he would then be at a disadvantage competitively with the other firms in the industry. He knew that he had won the issue but the union had resorted to illegal methods to organize the workers. Moving to the south or to another non-unionized area would cost $200,000 or more—three fourths of the firm's total free capital. By dealing with the union now, he also realized that he would be subjected to bigger demands in the future. The situation could only get worse.

REQUIRED: (a) Explain why the company's past personnel policies have not been effective in preventing the strike.

(b) Appraise Mr. Powell's actions during the time after he first learned of the organizer's activity (just before the petition for an election was signed). Have they been useful in achieving his purposes?

(c) What policies as to employee services and industrial relations do you recommend for Mr. Powell in the future?

INTEGRATING CASES
Production and Personnel Policies

ORIENT MAGNETICS COMPANY

John Sullivan, president and chief stockholder of Orient Magnetics, was considering several decisions that he believed to be among the most important the company had faced. The chief engineer had proposed that Orient invest almost $100,000 in a foundry to make its own castings, the head of the heat-treating department was about ready to leave in search of what he termed "a more challenging opportunity," and Mr. Sullivan had just about decided to move a subsidiary from Columbus, Indiana, to Cincinnati, Ohio—site of the headquarters and the main plant.

Orient Magnetics primarily produced permanent magnets and transformer laminations—products in which the residual magnetism (either high or low) was of major significance. It sold permanent magnets made of various aluminum, nickel, and cobalt alloys to manufacturers of radios, television sets, and electrical control equipment and instruments. It sold pieces of steel stamped out of a special grade of steel with a high silicon content to transformer manufacturers. The flat pieces were called "laminations." When assembled properly, they made up the cores of various small sizes of transformers used in radios and other communications equipment.

The silicon steel was purchased in large quantities from one of the very few steel producers that made this special grade. It was delivered once a quarter in coils of about 3,000 pounds each. The infrequent delivery caused Orient to have a large average investment in raw materials inventory—about twice the normal for other metal-working firms of the same size. Mr. Sullivan disliked the risk associated with such an investment, but he had found no way to alleviate it. The steel mill was on a quarterly rolling schedule and shipped each order as it was completed.

Once taken from inventory, the silicon steel went to the stamping room where it was punched out to the desired sizes and shapes on dieing machines and presses ranging from 15 tons to 250 tons capacity. From the stamping room the laminations moved to the heat-treating room where they were heated in either electric or oil-fired furnaces and then quenched in oil or water baths. Time and temperature were controlled to help impart the desired magnetic characteristics. After heat treating, the laminations were shipped out.

Columbus Coil Company. This firm had, for some years, been a major purchaser of transformer laminations from Orient Magnetics. It specialized in small transformers used in radios and amplifiers. About fifteen months ago Orient had purchased almost all of the stock from the former owner. Since then Columbus Coil had continued about as before except that Mr. Sullivan spent one day a week there attempting to give it overall supervision. During other times three men—the production manager, the accountant, and the sales manager—ran the firm. They had all been at Columbus Coil for some time and were thoroughly familiar with its operations.

Orient had purchased what it believed to be a profitable firm, but events had not borne out this belief. Costs seemed to have risen steadily through the past year and the subsidiary was at best breaking even. Among the costs that could be avoided by relocating in Cincinnati were shipping costs of the laminations and of the copper wire used to wind the transformers, which was also produced in Cincinnati. Mr. Sullivan estimated that these costs were about $10,000 a year. In addition, Orient would then be able to furnish Columbus Coil with its requirements of transformer covers, which were drawn or stamped from ordinary mild steel $\frac{1}{16}$th to $\frac{1}{8}$th of an inch thick. Orient had the technical capability to do the work in its stamping room. It did not do so now because a Columbus supplier consistently underbid Orient's prices by about 10%—Orient's desired profit margin on the bid. The total sales amount involved was about $30,000 to $40,000 annually.

Mr. Sullivan estimated that operating costs in Cincinnati would be about the same as in Columbus. A leased plant was available a half mile away. Assembling transformers was a simple hand operation done by women using bench tools and jigs. The total cost of moving the inventory and the equipment and setting up in Cincinnati would be no more than $3,000 to $4,000. Whether or not the executives of Columbus Coil would be willing to move was problematical. Should they not, Mr. Sullivan believed that the accountant need not be replaced and that the accounting system could readily be merged with Orient's.

Labor supply was also estimated to be not much of a problem. About 50 women were needed to do the assembly work and 10 men were used for various jobs such as maintenance, shipping, and materials moving. The workers in Columbus did not belong to a union, but their pay rates were the equivalent of those Mr. Sullivan expected to pay in Cincinnati.

Workers at Orient's plant belonged to the United Steel Workers of America. Whether that union or the Electrical Workers' Union would attempt to organize the new coil shop was uncertain. An analysis of the current contract with the Steel Workers to compare it with the pay and benefits of Columbus Coil indicated that pension and insurance costs in Cincinnati added 14¢ an hour to the total pay package. There were also seniority provisions on layoffs and job transfers.

A foundry. Orient currently purchased its magnet castings from a plant in another city. Once received, the castings were either cut from bars into small cylindrical shapes or rough-ground to remove gates and spurs. They were then finish-ground in surface or cylindrical grinders, packed, and shipped.

The chief engineer had been with Orient for a little less than a year after five years' work with a major electrical manufacturer. He had become curious about the quality of Orient's finished product and had found some unevenness in the magnetic characteristics of the castings. This, he claimed, could only be due to obsolescent casting techniques. No customers had yet complained about these characteristics, but the chief engineer showed some fairly convincing test results. He went further ahead to investigate the possibilities and the costs of a specialized foundry for Orient. The purchasing agent, the only man at Orient with any operating foundry experience, assisted in gathering the estimates.

The results of their investigation were:

Land: ½ acre needed; available next to present building
         as part of employees' parking lot.

Building: 75' by 100'. Monitor roof with 16' sidewalls.
Fireproof construction .... $ 30,000
Equipment and fixtures (melting furnace, lining, blower, hoist,
    scale, core oven, molding machines, jolt roll-overs,
    ladles, tram rail, crane system, flash equipment,
    grinder, tumbler, air compressor) .... $ 49,000
Training Costs .... $ 17,500
       Total Capital Investment .... $ 96,500
Annual Operating Costs:
    Direct Materials $152,500
    Direct Labor (19 men) 105,000
    Indirect Labor (manager, foreman, 2 clerks) 36,000
    Indirect Manufacturing Expenses (power, supplies, taxes) 6,000
                                              $299,500

Mr. Sullivan estimated that the capital needs listed could be financed by the company but that additional working capital would be required amounting to 60 days of raw materials and 30 days of work in process. The current annual cost of magnet castings, as received at the Orient plant, was $311,000.

For the firm as a whole, excluding data for Columbus Coil, last year's results were: sales, $2,100,000; stockholders' net investment, $900,000; net profit after taxes, $120,000.

Heat-treating. This department, like the grinding shops, had once had excess capacity (entire second shift and 15% of first shift) beyond the ordinary needs of Orient. The foreman, who was also a graduate metallurgist, had tired of seeing his equipment stand idle and had built up sales of heat-treating services to other metalworking shops in the area. The department now ran on a two-shift schedule 6 days a week. Beyond regular heat-treating it did some experimental work on a development project basis. The centerless grinding room also did development work of this kind occasionally at customer's requests, but neither it nor the surface grinders had much in the way of outside work. Mr. Sullivan had speculated at times about selling grinding services, but he did not have the time to do it himself (nor did the sales manager) and the shop foreman had no interest in sales activities. There was a much greater demand in the area for ordinary steel stampings, but Orient's stamping room had been working at capacity for some time. The demand for grinding services or for stampings was cyclical and only high when other shops were overloaded.

In talking with Mr. Sullivan, Robert Barlow, the heat-treat foreman, had indicated that he was looking for "a large organization, with better furnaces and more complex metallurgical problems, where more interesting development work was needed."

REQUIRED: (a) In what ways are the three problems facing Mr. Sullivan interrelated?

(b) What action do you recommend with respect to each problem?

J. FINDLAGER & SONS, INC.

John Findlager, Jr., executive vice-president and general manager of the family's wholesale and retail lumber and building materials company, was bothered by success. "Our rapid growth in sales, which has come along as we opened new retail stores, has posed some problems for us in the central warehouse that are pretty sticky and are not easy to solve." More particularly, he was concerned about turnover of order pickers in the warehouse and about the profitability of the door and window manufacturing shop.

J. Findlager & Sons, Inc. now operates 20 branch outlets. Two years ago, the company centralized its warehousing activities in Fulton. Earlier the majority of warehousing had been done at the Door & Window Warehouse in Hudson and at the Building, Plumbing & Supply Warehouse in Van Wyck. Both of these warehouses had filled orders and made deliveries to branch outlets and customers, but they had carried almost completely different inventories. After the opening of the Fulton Central Warehouse, these two warehouses had been closed. The workers of the two divisions were given the opportunity to transfer to the new warehouse, and they all accepted. These men, along with 6 others from the company's branch yard at Yonkers and 2 newly hired men, constituted the initial work force at the new warehouse.

The Fulton Central Warehouse was a two-story concrete and brick structure with 100,000 square feet of storage space. The main floor of this warehouse was divided into three main sections (Door, Window & Plumbing; Door & Window Shop; and Home Accounts & Building Materials). Also, the company's general and executive offices were attached to the structure (see Exhibit 1).

Exhibit 1

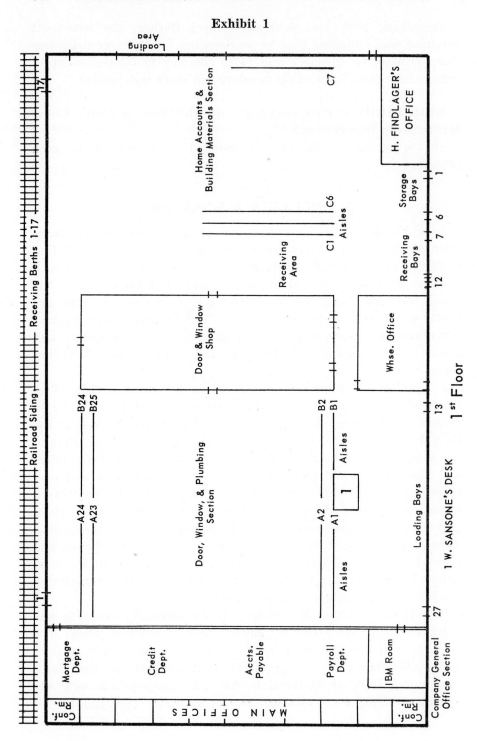

EXHIBIT 1

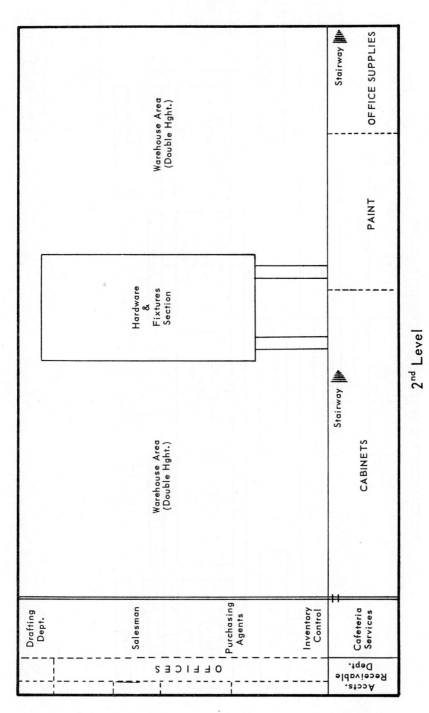

2nd Level

Exhibit 2

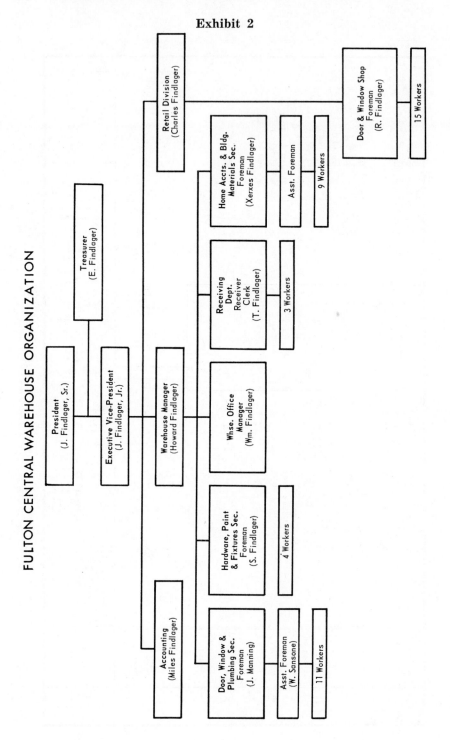

FULTON CENTRAL WAREHOUSE ORGANIZATION

Sixty-nine people worked in the warehouse performing various tasks. The various departments' work occurred in response to orders from the branches or direct sales orders that continually changed. The organization of operations at the Fulton Central Warehouse is shown in Exhibit 2.

Door, Window & Plumbing Section. The Door, Window & Plumbing Section was located directly adjacent to the general offices of the company (see Exhibit 1). There were 11 workers in this section, 5 of whom were "order pickers" who had responsibility for filling sales orders for immediate delivery. All of these men operated electric forklift trucks. One other worker in this section operated an electric forklift, but his main responsibility was to see to it that all "picking locations" were fully stocked; 3 men loaded trucks for delivery on a full-time basis; and the other 2 workers in this section handled only orders for kitchen cabinets and parcel post deliveries. These men were under the direct supervision of a foreman, John Manning, and his assistant, Bill Sansone, both of whom had been transferred from the Yonkers branch yard.

The turnover in this section was very high; 6 men from this section had left the company in the last two years. Four of these men were order pickers, all of whom had long seniority with the company. Howard Findlager was concerned with this turnover because it took at least three months for a new order picker to learn the stock and the picking locations well enough to be able to fill a complete branch order sheet without assistance. Even then he did not gain full efficiency for at least a year. The men had to learn the location and the description of over 3,000 items of stock in this section.

All except one of the original order pickers of this section had formerly worked in the Door & Window Warehouse. Before and immediately after the move to the new warehouse, these men had been responsible for filling only orders of a specific product line. These men had considered themselves to be specialists in wood stock, plumbing items, door and window items, etc., and they handled only orders for these goods. All but one of these men filled their orders on foot rather than from forklift trucks. They had worked through several small buildings and across two yards with open sheds.

In planning the move to Fulton, the Findlagers decided that it would cut costs if the order pickers were to fill a complete set of branch orders rather than only those orders that fell under their specialty. This would allow stocking all "heavy-movers" near the exit doors and minimize the pickers' travel. For efficiency the order pickers were all taught how to operate forklift trucks and were required to fill their orders using the machines.

Finally, the assistant foreman, Bill Sansone, was assigned the task of passing out the orders to the order pickers and recording the time necessary to fill a lot of orders and the number of items picked in each lot. Shortly after these changes, turnover among the order pickers increased.

Door & Window Shop. This shop was located exactly in the center of the warehouse and was closed in on all sides by four brick partitions. There were 15 workers in this section; they were split about evenly into two groups, both of which were arranged along two lines of work benches. One group built prefabricated door units and the other built prefabricated window units. All the men had worked in the old Door & Window Warehouse at Hudson and they were performing essentially the same tasks as before the change.

This shop was the only section where the men were paid by piece rates for their production. Finally, these men did not mingle with the other employees of the warehouse and took their coffee breaks and lunches together in the Door & Window Shop. There was very little turnover in this section.

Home Accounts & Building Materials Section. This section was at the farthest end of the warehouse from the company's general offices. There were 9 workers, of whom 5 were order pickers for home accounts and worked on foot at all times. All of the materials they needed were in stand-up racks in their picking area. The 4 other workers were heavy forklift truck operators and were responsible for filling orders for bulk building materials and loading these on "open-tail" trailer trucks. All except one were former employees at Van Wyck and had transferred to Fulton when the former warehouse had been shut down. All of the men who had transferred from Van Wyck to this section of the new warehouse were still working for the company.

Management personnel at Fulton. Howard Findlager, a nephew of the president of the company and a former branch manager, had held his present position since the opening of Fulton. It was common to see him at least once a day in the new warehouse. He would walk around the warehouse with John Manning or by himself, and he was continually asking the workers what they were supposed to be doing. During one of these tours he became engaged in an argument with a forklift operator over some damaged materials and dismissed the worker on the spot. The workers commonly called him "Digger O'Dell" or "Sea Gull."

John Manning had formerly been an assistant foreman at the Yonkers branch yard. He was transferred to Fulton as a foreman when it opened. He was known by the men as "Howie's Boy," since he almost always accompanied Findlager on his tours of the warehouse. Bill Sansone had also come from the Yonkers branch yard. He had the responsibility of giving the order pickers their orders to fill and of recording the time used. He also had to see that the trucks were loaded in time for delivery.

Conversations with workers. John Findlager remembered an exit interview with Fred Wilkins, a former order picker in the Door, Window & Plumbing section.

Fred had said, "It's the way things are done around here. I'm through taking any more from Sea Gull and the rest of them no good b - - - - - - s. They want me to operate a forklift and pick plumbing orders which I never picked before. They're crazy. It will take me all day to fill one branch order because of this. I wouldn't care if it took me all week, except for Sansone and his little time chart. That's something else—you'd think we were loafing all the time by the way they watch over us and write down everything we do. It was never like this before our move to this cement prison! I can remember when I worked at Hudson we were lucky if we saw any of you big shots twice a year."

John: "Did Howard ask you to stay on here?"

Fred: "Yeah, he said that if I left I would never be able to come back again! And then he asked me what I would rather do. I told him the only job I would want here was in the Door & Window Shop. He said he didn't mean that, but rather what jobs in the warehouse. I told him I didn't want to work any place here and that I felt it would be better if I left the company."

John: "Did you know we need the information that Sansone keeps for costs and for pricing?"

Fred: "I wouldn't trust Sansone as far as I could throw him."

Sometime later the personnel manager told John Findlager, Jr. that Bill Collins wanted to see him under the open-door policy.

John: "Bill, I hear you are leaving us after today."

Bill: "Yeah, I finally smartened up! I've been with the company 15 years and thought I might be able to get somewhere, but this is a dead-end street. I'm 33, and if I don't leave now I never will."

John: "But I thought you liked your job; you never complained before."

Bill: "I did like it before. I used to work only plumbing orders for special accounts and would even go out and give estimates on the cost of a new plumbing system to customers and sometimes install the equipment. But since they changed this place all around, all I do is fill orders all day long. They put you on a forklift and hand you some orders and say go to work! What happens when you get too old to work fast? I'll tell you what: they'll kiss you off as worn-out."

John: "Did you ever ask for something else?"

Bill: "Sure, I went and asked Howie if I could continue working only on special plumbing jobs right after they made the big switch to full-line picking. He said my vacation was all over and I had to handle all orders now. Then, about three months ago, I went up to Personnel and asked if they had anything else open."

John: "What did they tell you?"

Bill: "Well, I had been 'moonlighting' over at the Fulton Retail Store as a plumbing salesman nights and Saturdays. I told them I had been doing this and was selling as much as some of the full-time salesmen. Then I asked them if I could do this full time. They told me that they didn't think I would enjoy that kind of work, but that if I insisted upon it, they might find an opening within the next year, but I would have to go on salary starting at $85 a week take-home until I became used to the job. I've got two kids and a wife to support and couldn't get by on that."

John: "Well, did they ever call you back after that to discuss what they had open for you?"

Bill: "I never heard from them again, so I went out on my own and found a job with the Edison. It doesn't pay as much as this job, but I will be making the same in two years and have a union to watch out for me and see that I'm not just treated like another piece of machinery."

John: "Didn't you just see Howie and Sansone this morning?"

Bill: "Sure, I saw them. They said they hated to see me leave and what could they do to keep me with the company. I told them I wanted a change of jobs, the same as I told Manning one hundred times before. You know what he said? 'Well, Bill, we'll try to find something else for you, just give us a little time.' They gave me the whole story about my seniority and how if I left I wouldn't be able to come back.

"I have 15 years with the company! It doesn't seem to mean anything. They give other pickers who have less than a year's seniority more overtime than they give me."

Door & Window Shop. Materials, labor, and manufacturing supplies costs had varied little for this shop; but with the move to Fulton, the overhead allocated to it had doubled. This reduced its profitability to less than that of a typical retail shop and John Findlager was considering reallocating the capital tied up in it.

The finished doors and windows were sold half to the Findlager warehouse and half to large-scale building contractors. Other door and window manufacturers could easily fill in the supply. Using outside sources might have some advantage for the warehouse since the warehouse had, at times, stocked heavily on inventory to keep the Door & Window Shop running when building operations slowed down. If the Door & Window Shop were closed, the brick walls could be knocked out and other sections of the warehouse expanded.

John Findlager saw continued growth for his firm. Even now there were good opportunities to open two more retail stores. Within 5 to 7 years it might be necessary to use the entire building for warehousing only. This, of course, presumed that no particular technological or efficiency improvements could be made in the warehouse or the door and window operations.

REQUIRED: (a) Explain the differences in employee turnover in the two warehouse sections and the Door & Window Shop.

(b) What policies should the company adopt as to transfers, promotion, and overtime?

(c) Should the Door & Window Shop be discontinued and the funds be reallocated to the Retail Division?

FINANCIAL POLICIES—
USES OF CAPITAL

Need for capital. The very nature of business operations requires outlays of cash before customers pay for goods or services. Plant and equipment must be obtained, raw materials purchased, production employees paid, sales and administrative expenses met— all before goods are available for sale. Then a month or more may elapse before customers pay for purchases. Even a law firm selling only services will incur payroll expenses and have accounts receivable. Capital fills the gap between the time outlays are made and revenues flow back in.

The required capital has to be secured somewhere—from the owners of business or from long-term or short-term creditors. These suppliers of capital, and others vitally concerned with the company as a going business, want to be sure that the capital is protected against extreme risks. Eventually, if the flow of income has exceeded expenses, someone must decide whether to reinvest these profits or to distribute them as dividends.

Central management should make sure that the company has the proper amount of capital because an inadequate supply will hamper operations, prevent the adoption of efficient methods of operation, and perhaps lead to more fiscal difficulties or bankruptcy. Too much capital, on the other hand, means that the earnings will have to be spread over an unnecessarily large amount of capital. Moreover, the ready availability of funds may lead management to make unwise investments in inventory, fixed assets, or other assets that have no direct connection with the operation of the firm. In every business, no matter its size, watching over the flow of capital in and out of the firm is essential.

Effect of profits and losses on capital requirements. In any consideration of financial policies we should recognize that an accounting profit or loss and the need for additional capital in the form of cash are two different things.

For example, it is quite possible for a company to incur large operating losses and still be in less need of new capital than it was when business was profitable. The losses may occur during periods of declining sales volume when there is a corresponding reduction in both inventories and accounts receivable, or there may be a reduction in the net investment in fixed assets due to a decision not to reinvest the amount set aside for depreciation.

Such a situation arose in one large company having assets of approximately $65,000,000. Although in one year this company lost $1,850,000, the president was able to report that "bank loans which stood at $18,500,000 on July 23 were reduced rapidly from that date and at the end of the year the company was free of debts to the bank. The reduction reflects liquidation of inventories as well as decreases in accounts receivable due to inactive business." It is when operating losses are not offset by liquidation of assets or depreciation charges that a company may find itself in need of additional capital.

Profitable business operations often lead to a need for additional capital, especially if the total volume of sales expands rapidly. Under such circumstances there is likely to be substantial expansion of inventory and accounts receivable. Thus, capital may be required either when a company is profitable or operating at a loss. In securing additional capital, financial embarrassment is less likely to arise when a concern is enjoying satisfactory earnings than when losses are being incurred.

Classification of financial policies. A useful way for central management of a company to view its capital problems is in terms of:

1. Use of capital.
2. Sources of capital.
3. Protection of capital.
4. Distribution of earnings.

Primarily these problems are concerned with *cash flow*—what the cash will be used for and where it will come from. Some direct trades are made, to be sure; for example, stock in Company A may be traded for stock in Company B, or stock in Company A for assets of Company B, as in a merger; or inventory may be sold on credit, thus creating an asset and postponing the cash flow until the account is paid off. But we can avoid trouble from abstractions by focusing on cash flows and treating the other exchanges as convenient shortcuts.

USES OF CAPITAL

Circulating and fixed capital. Cash, inventory, and accounts receivable constitute the *circulating capital* of an enterprise. The expression "circulating capital" is used for the total of these amounts because the form in which the capital is invested changes frequently. The original capital is typically in the form of cash. This is first invested in inventory, and additional sums are spent on sales promotion and general administrative expenses. The inventory should be sold at a price that will cover all these outlays of cash. The capital then takes the form of accounts receivable. When the customers pay their bills, the capital is again back in cash ready to start on another circuit.

The amount of circulating capital needed varies. Fluctuations in sales will result in varying quantities of capital invested in accounts receivable. These fluctuations in sales may be anticipated in purchasing and production programs, and large inventories may be built so as to insure prompt delivery during peak sales periods. A desire to adjust inventory in anticipation of price changes may cause the investment in inventories to rise or fall. Adverse business conditions may slow up the rate at which customers pay their bills, thus increasing the capital tied up in accounts receivable. Since both external conditions and management decisions regarding internal operations affect circulating capital, policies and internal controls are necessary to be sure that the total amount does not get out of hand.

Especially in manufacturing, the amount of capital required for facilities is often large. A retail store has to make some investment in counters, fixtures, and perhaps delivery equipment or a building. Even a professional firm must have desks, typewriters, and other office equipment. Capital invested in such forms is called *fixed capital* because these assets typically render their services over a period of years. Fixed capital is turned back into cash much more slowly than circulating capital.

We should not assume that fixed capital represents the only long-term investment needed in a company. Actually, a growing business always needs a minimum amount of capital invested in inventory, accounts receivable, and other circulating items. The inflow of cash from receivables must be again invested in inventory. Circulating capital is, therefore, just as much a regular requirement as fixed capital. Only the extra circulating capital needed for seasonal and irregular requirements can be treated as temporary. Consequently, the financial program should provide long-term capital to cover both fixed capital and normal circulating capital requirements.

Relation of other policies to the use of capital. Policies regarding the use of capital are related to almost every activity of a business. In a sense, plans for sales—such as products to be sold, sales appeals to be stressed, plans for production and purchasing, decisions to "make" rather than "buy," and heavy use of automation—and plans for personnel—such as vestibule training, company pensions, and other comparable plans—dictate the uses of capital. Capital has a supporting, facilitating role; it is essential and not directing. Financial policies concerning the use of capital do not stipulate the specific uses of capital; these are determined by other management decisions.

Nevertheless, every company should have some underlying financial policies that will act as limits for the use of capital for specific purposes. Any decision that calls for the use of additional capital must fall within the limits established by this general financial plan. In other words, there may be several policies bearing on a particular proposal, such as building a new plant on the West Coast, and unless the proposal is compatible with these several policies, it must be modified (or an exception to one or more of the policies authorized). In this sense, financial policies are not subservient to other policies. Rather, they deal with another dimension of a complex operation. They guard the financial health of the enterprise.

Major issues regarding the use of capital will be discussed in terms of:

1. Regulating investment in fixed assets.
2. Use of circulating capital.
3. Mergers and acquisitions.

REGULATING INVESTMENT IN FIXED ASSETS

General restrictions. In every active company, all sorts of proposals are made for additions to facilities. Executives concerned with a particular operation naturally think of new equipment that would enable them to do their job better or at lower operating expense. One way to regulate such proposals is to set forth general areas where investment will or will not be made. Here are some examples of this approach.

Financing of special equipment used by distributors. The Universal Company promotes a product known as vermiculite or zonolite, an unusual mineral that expands many times its original size when heated and that possesses important insulating properties. This company owns the largest known deposit of the mineral, and after some years of research has developed processes that make the use of vermiculite for insulation of homes feasible.

Because the original ore can be shipped more cheaply than the expanded vermiculite, the company decided that all kilns required for expanding the material should be erected near the point at which the material was used. The company also decided that the potential volume of sales to home owners did not justify the establishment of numerous sales offices throughout the country. Building supply companies, which already had contacts with many of the potential customers, offered a channel for the distribution of this particular product. The plan was to grant exclusive local territories to building supply houses, and to ship the ore to these companies where it could be expanded by heat treatment and then sold by them to the ultimate consumer.

This naturally raised the question as to who would supply the capital needed for kilns and other equipment at each of the distribution points. If the dealers made the investment in fixed assets, the company recognized that the price of the ore would have to be kept low enough so that the dealers could make a satisfactory return on this investment in addition to a reasonable commission for their selling activities. Moreover, if each dealer owned and operated his own facilities, there was a greater possibility that the quality of the final product might not be uniformly satisfactory, and consequently there was some danger of losing customer goodwill for the product.

On the other hand, the primary purpose of the company was to develop different uses for this new mineral. There were several other possibilities in addition to the home insulation field that needed further research. If the company invested its capital in processing equipment in each local territory, the available capital of the company would be absorbed and the development of additional fields would be retarded. For these reasons, the company adopted a policy of making no investment in fixed assets used in connection with distribution through building supply dealers. It was recognized that this would probably reduce the profit secured from this type of business, but the company wished to keep itself in a flexible position and to retain its capital for use in other fields.

Long-term outlook. A paper company with a mill in northern United States became concerned about the increasing costs of its pulpwood. Careful study showed that on many of the types of paper it was making, Southern mills using Southern pine enjoyed a cost advantage. While there was the possibility of shifting to specialty papers, the company concluded that a satisfactory return on an additional investment made in its present plant located in the North was quite uncertain.

Consequently, a policy of making no major investment in fixed assets in its northern mill was adopted. Only the purchase of miscellaneous equipment necessary to operate existing machines would be permitted, and the purchase and installation of new machines or susbtantial expenditures on the existing building would be postponed at least until the outlook for a northern mill improved.

Another firm adopted a similar policy because the probable shift in demand for its product would make its present plant somewhat obsolete. If new processes had to be adopted, then the firm wanted to move into a new building in a suburban location. In the meantime it chose to keep itself in a flexible position and made only essential investments in fixed assets.

A policy that places definite limits on the use of capital for fixed assets must be administered with discretion. A change in technology may necessitate installing new equipment if a company is to continue to compete in a particular industry. If the concern wishes to render distinctive service to its customers, investments in fixed assets may be essential. Nevertheless, investment policies should be disregarded only in unusual circumstances.

Minimum rate of return. The policies just illustrated stipulate a type of fixed asset to be avoided or encouraged. A different kind of investment guide is a minimum rate of return that must be anticipated if capital is to be assigned to a proposal. For example, the policy might be that any new investment in fixed assets must earn at least 10% annually on the initial investment after provision for depreciation and taxes. Then, a proposal to buy a machine costing $10,000 that was expected to result in an average net saving of $700 per year during its life would be rejected because the 7% return falls below the acceptable minimum.

For such a policy to be useful, the method of calculating the rate of return should be defined. Depreciation, taxes, interest, net investment, and several other items can be treated in different ways. So, to avoid ambiguity, the policy should indicate the formula that was assumed when the minimum was set.

Theoretically, the minimum permissible rate of return should be the average cost of capital to the company (a weighted average of the company's long-term borrowing rate and the earnings/price ratio on the company's common stock). In practice, desire for expansion, willingness to sell more stock, funds already available, judgment about future risks, and similar considerations affect management's choice of the minimum rate. Since most executives who propose new investment in fixed assets tend to be optimistic in predicting the benefit of the action, central management of many companies counter by setting the minimum acceptable rate higher than the theoretical minimum.

Capital budgeting. Frequently, a company has many more possible investments in fixed assets than it can prudently finance. The issue then becomes which projects to endorse and which to reject. *Capital budgeting* is a method for making this selection.

First, all major proposals for additions to fixed assets are described and analyzed and predictions are made of the amount of the investment and the resulting benefits of each proposal. Obviously, this analysis and prediction must be carefully done because the soundness of all subsequent steps can be no better than the data fed into the process. The whole task will be simplified by promptly screening out all proposals not consistent with sales, production, purchasing, and personnel policies and with general investment policies such as those discussed in the preceding pages.

Next, the predicted investment and results should be expressed in dollars insofar as possible. The figures that are pertinent are *additional outlays* the company will make if the project is undertaken and *additional receipts* (or reduced expenditures) that will result from the project. Intangibles should also be recognized, both intangible costs and intangible benefits—for example, flexibility or strategic advantage of a controlled supply of raw material. These intangibles must be listed because the budgeting process deals only with dollar figures and time and tends to deemphasize intangibles.

Then, proposals should be ranked, with those showing the highest rate of return to outlay at the top and those with the lowest return at the bottom.

Finally, management can proceed down the ranked projects until (a) the capital available is exhausted, assuming overriding reasons exist for keeping the total within a fixed amount, or (b) the rate of return falls below the minimum acceptable rate. Before projects below the cutoff point are completely rejected, intangible benefits should be appraised to decide whether the added advantages are important enough to move a project up into the acceptable list. Similarly, intangible cost of projects above the cutoff point should be assessed with an eye for projects that might be dropped.[1]

Discounted cash flow. Among the problems arising in the application of the capital budgeting procedure is how to compute the rate of return for each investment. The aim here is to follow a method that compares each project fairly.

A clearly specified way of computing the average rate of return [1] can be used for capital budgeting also. For a great many projects, this method is as precise as the basic data (predictions) warrant. However, major investments often require outlays at different times and yield their benefits over varying periods. The use of annual *averages* blurs such differences in time of outlays and receipts. The best way to handle these time differences is the *discounted cash flow* method.

We all know that a dollar a year from now is not as valuable as a dollar in our pocket, and that a dollar ten years hence is worth even less. Compound interest tables deal with this aspect of time and enable us to compare the value of dollars at various periods in the future by discounting each to its present value. The discounted cash flow method uses the compound interest concept by reducing all receipts and disbursements to their present values. Thus, if one project will create income promptly, these dollars have more *present value* than the same dollar income from another project that won't start paying off for, say, five years. Of course, the difference

---

1 For brief examples of computation of average rate of return on investment in equipment, see pages 585 to 587.

Rate of Return Computed by Discounted Cash Flow Method

Investment (cash outflow)	Actual net amount	Present value discounted at: 16%	18%	20%
		Investment in Canadian Assembly Plant (in $1,000)		
Building & Equipment—1st year	100	100.0	100.0	100.0
Building & Equipment—2nd year	20	17.2	16.9	16.7
Start-up cost —2nd year	30	25.9	25.4	25.0
Totals	150	143.1	142.3	141.7
Savings (cash inflow)				
3rd year	10	6.4	6.1	5.8
4th ″	20	11.0	10.3	9.6
5th ″	40	19.0	17.5	16.1
6th ″	60	24.6	22.2	20.1
7th ″	80	28.3	25.1	22.3
8th ″	80	24.4	21.3	18.6
9th ″	80	21.0	18.0	15.5
10th ″	80	18.2	15.3	13.0
Salvage value	40	9.1	7.6	6.5
Totals	490	162.0	143.4	127.5

Notes: All actual amounts are *net* cash flows, including changes in taxes and interest due to the investment. Investments are made at beginning of year, savings at end of year (a simplifying assumption). Only cost savings are estimated; the effect, if any, of local assembly on sales volume is considered an intangible.

Conclusion: Rate of return is higher than 16% since at this yield the present value of benefits exceeds investment; by same test, the rate is less than 20%. Correct rate for this proposal is 18%; at this yield the present value of benefits is virtually the same as the present value of the investment.

in present values will reflect both the time of the income and the interest rate used in discounting.

Now, in capital budgeting we know (predict) when and how much will flow out and in for each project. The unknown is the rate of return, or interest rate, that each project will yield. So we try different interest rates until we find the rate at which the present value of future income will just equal the present value of outlays; this will be the rate of return for that project. The table above illustrates the procedure.

By using the above method for each project, we can determine the rate of return for each, reflecting the time when cash flows. Projects are then ranked and selected as already outlined.

Central management will not, of course, become involved in the detailed computations necessary in the application of the discounted cash flow method to capital budgeting. However, it should decide whether the reliability of projections and the relative significance of the factors that can be expressed in dollars warrant the use of this refined method.

Leasing versus purchase of fixed assets. Analysis of investment proposals may reveal more attractive opportunities than can be absorbed by a company's normal financial structure. When this occurs, the long-term leasing instead of the buying of the fixed assets should be considered.

Of course, reasons other than financing may make leasing attractive. The outlook may be so uncertain that owning your own building is imprudent, or prospects of rapid expansion and relocation may suggest flexibility in asset commitments. However, in the present discussion we are concerned with leasing as a way of reducing the need for tying up capital in fixed assets. Here's the way it works. An investor, perhaps an estate or an insurance company, with funds for long-term investment buys a building we want to use and at the same time leases it to us for a long period. The rental payments are high enough to cover real estate taxes, depreciation, and repairs, as well as interest on the capital tied up. Note that these are all expenses we would have to pay if we owned the building. The main difference between owning and leasing is that with a lease we show neither the building as an asset nor the source of funds as a liability on our balance sheet.

If the asset to be leased has to be constructed for our own peculiar requirements, we may actually build and equip the structure and then *sell and lease back*. Also, we may have an option to buy the asset when the lease expires, 10 or 20 years hence, at a depreciated value. Both these provisions make leasing even more like owning. The investor, in turn, is in much the same position as a mortgage holder; he relies on our contract for his interest and the return of his investment.

A few companies have a *policy* to lease rather than to buy certain types of assets. For example, oil companies and retail chain stores may regularly use such an arrangement for their many retail outlets. Most firms resort to leasing only occasionally for some large asset. Whatever the frequency, the operating cost and the tax implication should be carefully studied because a long-term lease obligation is just as binding as mortgage or debenture bond obligations even though it does not so appear on typical financial statements.

Since a long-term lease creates a continuing financial burden in many respects comparable to owning fixed assets it must not be used promiscuously. The general policies of a company regarding its investment in fixed assets and capital budgeting comparisons of alternative uses of company resources should normally apply to property leased for a long term as well as property that is purchased.

USES OF CIRCULATING CAPITAL

Financial restrictions on inventory. Policies governing circulating capital must include some general restrictions on the amount of capital invested in inventories. The size of inventories should be consistent with other possible uses of this capital. Thus, if a company is having difficulty financing accounts receivable, it should see whether its inventories might be reduced. On the other hand, if the firm is using service as one of its sales appeals, its capital allocation for inventory should not be so niggardly that prompt deliveries are difficult.

Moreover, financial restrictions on inventories should be tied in with the maintenance of a good *current ratio,* (the ratio between current assets and current liabilities). The credit standing of a company is judged in part by its current ratio. If the purchase of inventories has to be financed by an increase in accounts or notes payable, growth in inventories can lower the current ratio. This is another reason why inventory policies must be considered as an integral part of the whole financial picture.

The task of determining the proper size of particular types of inventories will not be considered here since it has already been discussed in Chapter 10. The treatment of inventories as primarily a procurement problem instead of a financial problem is consistent with the practice followed by many companies in which the attention of the treasurer to inventories is limited, first, to checking on the speculative and obsolescence risks involved and, second, to seeing that inventories do not become so large that the financial program is thrown out of balance.

This task is significant, however, since any extensive and unnecessary speculation of inventory would certainly be frowned upon in most financial circles in which the company might wish to borrow capital. Even when conservative inventory policies have been adopted, eternal vigilance is necessary to see that inventories for one reason or another do not become much larger than anticipated.

Extension of credit. *Typical practice.* Credit policies vary widely in different industries and in different localities. One large department store takes pride in the fact that its credit policies are so conservative that bad debt losses are less than ½ of 1% of total credit sales. In contrast, the credit managers of some low-priced clothing stores, which feature easy-payment terms, would be criticized if their bad debt losses were less than 5 or 6% of total sales, as this would be interpreted to mean that credit is being granted so cautiously that many potential customers have been refused.

Many hardware and grocery merchants in rural western towns make a practice of extending liberal credit to farmers. Such merchants do not expect to be reimbursed until the farmer receives his large cash income from the sale of this year's crop. In the more arid grain belts, where crop failures are all too common, the merchants may be forced to carry accounts for a second year until a new crop has been raised and marketed by the farmer. The liberality of the credit policy will, of course, have a significant effect upon the capital used for accounts receivable.

The administration of credit should be consistent with other policies of the company. The difference in credit policies was one of the reasons why a textbook company preferred to deal directly with private schools that purchased substantial quantities of books in place of having a book jobber handle the account. If the company felt that there was a good prospect that the school might continue to buy a large number of books each year for a period of years, it wished to be more liberal in its extension of credit than many of its jobbers would be.

Factors influencing credit policy. As suggested by the preceding illustrations, the credit policy must be based on a balance between two factors: first, the cost of extending credit, which includes interest on money, probable losses on uncollectible accounts, and the expense of handling the account—that is, granting credit, making collections, and maintaining necessary bookkeeping records; and second, the net profit that may be earned on sales resulting from the extension of credit. In this connection it must be remembered that no one likes to be refused credit. Therefore, turning a customer down may lose not only the net profit on the current sale, but it may also lose future sales to the same customer and his friends.

Installment credit. Installment credit is, of course, merely a variation of general customer credit. The old idea that the article should always have a resale value at least equal to the unpaid balance on the account is now commonly disregarded. Today companies making installment loans depend primarily upon the earning capacity of the purchaser rather than upon the resale value of the merchandise purchased. This is particularly evident in the case of some mail-order houses that will sell anything they carry in stock on the installment plan.

The granting of installment credit raises the same general question of a balance between costs and potential profit on additional sales. A service fee, which substantially reduces and often eliminates the cost of granting credit to customers, is customary in most lines of installment credit.

Transferring installment accounts to banks and loan companies. The growth of installment finance companies and the entry of commercial banks into the small loan field have enabled many companies to transfer installment accounts to these specialized houses. Usually the credit is extended by the bank or loan company directly to the consumer who has made a large purchase. The selling company is not involved, except in assisting its customer to get credit. This, of course, greatly reduces the capital a company has tied-up in accounts receivable. On the other hand, the finance company is glad to get the business and cooperates with the retailer in giving service to the customer. Installment sales of automobiles, electrical appliances, furnaces, and many other consumer durable goods are financed in this manner. And, installment financing of industrial equipment is growing.

Use of finance companies becomes more complicated when the retailer wants to give his customers more liberal credit terms or better service than the finance company feels is justified. Sales of clothing on installment credit, credit to doubtful risks, and leniency on collections are examples. One arrangement is for the retailer to guarantee the finance company against losses on bad debts. A more drastic modification is for the retailer to extend the credit and make collections, but to use his installment accounts as collateral for a bank loan. This is, of course, a source of capital rather than a means of lowering accounts receivable, but from the viewpoint of financing, the dividing line is fuzzy.

Any company that wants installment credit extended to its customers should carefully consider a policy of having this done entirely or in part by an outside financial agency. The effect of this decision on capital requirements may be substantial.

Collection policies. Extension of credit involves not only policies as to the amount and type of customer to whom credit will be extended; general rules of action regarding collection are also necessary.

When there is little doubt as to the customer's ability to pay, various types of courteous reminders of amounts due are usually all that are required. A point will be reached with some customers, however, when it is necessary to "get tough"; legal suits, garnishment of wages, and repossession of property are among the actions that may be threatened if the bill is not paid. Actual practice in the use of these collection devices varies widely, some companies resorting to them only when there is clear evidence of intent to evade the obligation; whereas other companies at least threaten such action as soon as a bill is, say, three months overdue.

A different problem arises when a customer is unable to meet his obligations, or when payment would require that the customer liquidate his business to secure the needed cash. In this type of situation the customer needs help, and many companies follow a policy of postponing the payment date, especially if the customer can make a partial payment. Other firms and banks often take more positive steps and work out with the customer a financial plan embracing all his needs, and if the amount involved is large they may make suggestions regarding management of the enterprise as well. This is done to increase the possibilities of full collection and, even more, to build goodwill among customers who may provide a substantial volume of business in years to come.

Here again, the policy adopted should be based on a balance between the cost of collection and the net return; the net return includes both a reduction in loss on the amount currently due and any increase or decrease in future net profits resulting from the collection action.

Miscellaneous investments. *Large bank balances.* It is not uncommon for a company to find that it has more capital than is required for current operations. This naturally raises the question of how such capital shall be invested. If the sum is not large, this extra capital often is kept on deposit at the bank. Here it serves little purpose other than reassuring the executives that their cash account will not be unexpectedly depleted and impressing those stockholders who read the annual report with the great financial strength of the company.

Securities. If the amount of cash on hand is large, the executives responsible for the finances of the company will naturally seek to put some of the excess capital to a use that will yield a return. A conservative policy is to invest the funds in government bonds or other high-grade securities. Furthermore, if the employment of excess cash is to be of a temporary nature, the financial executive will probably purchase government bonds or high-grade securities having a near maturity. Such securities can easily be sold at any time the funds are needed for operating purposes, and fluctuation in their value is comparatively small. Treasury notes that mature at the time income tax payments fall due are regularly purchased by some companies.

Many companies invest surplus cash in their own securities. This is particularly true if the company has an outstanding bond issue. The company many times is able to purchase its own bonds at less than par or redemption value, and it is therefore able to effect a saving not only in interest but also in principal. Companies may also purchase their own stocks. In the case of preferred stock, purchases may be made for retirement or for treasury stock. In the case of common stock, purchases may be made to be held in the treasury for retirement or for resale to employees or executives under stock-purchase plans.

Some companies buy stocks or low-grade bonds in order to secure a larger current return on their investment, and often in the hope that such stock or bonds will appreciate in value. This is, of course, out-and-out speculation, and it is not ordinarily considered legitimate business except for investment firms.

Conservative policy. If excess capital is in the form of cash, then the conservative policy would seem to be:

   (a) Investment in high-grade securities, if it is anticipated that the company will require the capital for its normal operations sometime in the near future; or,

(b) Distribution of the capital by paying off debts, provided these could be retired under favorable conditions, or by payment of dividends to stockholders.

MERGERS AND ACQUISITIONS

Development of a company typically occurs by channeling its capital into various assets in a step-by-step process. The growth may be slow or rapid; but, as implied throughout this chapter, it tends to be an unfolding of events by each change of policy being built on preceding accomplishments and difficulties. By contrast, a *merger* moves in a grand leap. Entire companies are absorbed— including their physical assets, their personnel, and much of their reputation—without opportunity for managerial scrutiny of the usefulness of each part.

Clearly, a merger will have a profound effect on how capital is used as well as on sources of capital. For any single company, mergers are an infrequent occurrence; but they have such a marked effect when they do occur that we should note at least briefly the major management issues involved. We shall discuss:

1. Reasons for entering a merger.
2. Alternate ways to finance acquisitions.
3. Problems of compatibility.

Reasons for entering a merger. *Financial expediency.* Some mergers are arranged solely for financial reasons. These are examples:

(a) Large stockholders in a closely held company want to convert their assets into marketable securities or cash, frequently in anticipation of high inheritance taxes. Poor health or old age makes them willing to merge at an attractive price.
(b) A rapidly growing company may absorb a declining firm because the latter has a large amount of cash (or marketable securities) that is much needed by the growing company. For tax reasons, the owners of the declining company prefer to hold stock rather than to receive a high cash dividend.
(c) A company may have suffered severe losses for several years and may have accumulated a large tax credit. If this company absorbs another firm with high profits, the past losses can (within limits) be used to offset profits of the second firm and thereby to avoid paying about half of these profits to the government as income tax.
(d) Company X is too small to have its securities listed on the Stock Exchange. By merging with one or more other firms, the new combination can be listed and additional capital can be obtained

at lower cost. If mergers happen to be in fashion at the time, the glamour of a new merger and of diversification may also assist in the sale of stock to the public.

Financial benefits such as those just listed are significant. However, if a merger has no other advantage, it is essentially a "marriage of convenience" with all the dangers of incompatibility and future trouble. Obviously, when sound economic reasons exist as well as potential financial benefits, the situation is ripe for a merger.

Economic benefits. The combined operations resulting from a merger should have clear economic advantages that were not available when the companies operated independently. Typically, one company has some asset needed by the second company that the second company cannot obtain at all or could obtain only slowly and at great expense. Less often, unnecessary duplication exists and the merger leads to savings by elimination of the excess effort or capacity.

A typical example is the merger of an oil company already strong in refining and marketing with a producer of crude oil. Such an acquisition provides a quick way to gain control over a *supply of raw materials*. Often backward integration is achieved via the merger route rather than by developing a completely new source of materials.

Getting into a *new line of business* may be a sound basis of merger. For example, a heating equipment company, facing a static demand for its established products, merged with an air-conditioning equipment firm, a related business where demand was growing rapidly.

Over recent years the tin can companies have been involved in mergers for two reasons. They have sought national *market coverage* because several of their large customers wanted service in all regions of the country. Acquiring a local can company with facilities and a flow of local business was much more economical than starting in a new territory from scratch. Also, the can companies have moved into paper, plastics, and glass containers to offer customers a more *complete line* of packaging. Here again, merging provided an established volume of business necessary for economical production, personnel with technical know-how, and operating facilities more quickly than a new unit could be built up.

A company may merge to obtain *fuller utilization* of one or more of its resources. Thus, a firm with a full-fledged marketing organization for its refrigerators, washers, and driers acquired a kitchen range producer. The ranges could be sold through the existing organization with relatively little added expense.

In all these companies, the merged operations picked up some economic advantages. Each merger was sound because it reflected the sales or procurement policies and objectives of one of the combined firms.

Alternative ways to finance acquisition. Once a merger possibility with clear benefits has been identified, a financial arrangement has to be negotiated. Naturally, this will be based on the desires of the owners of the two companies—their need for cash, tax position, desire to withdraw or remain active, and the like— and on the strengths and the policies of the respective companies. Broadly speaking, the final agreement will probably be some variation of the elements indicated in the following diagram:

Company X gives:	*Company Y gives some combination of:*
Assets, including name and going-concern	Cash
	Bonds, notes, or long-term lease
or	Assumption of Company X liabilities
Stockholders of Company X give controlling stock interest	Stock—common or preferred
	Stock options, employment contracts, etc.

in exchange for

The financial and legal details of most mergers become quite complicated, and the final negotiation of specific payments or stock exchange ratios often is tense. Consequently, the major economic and financial benefits being sought should be kept clearly in mind so that they do not become lost in the shuffling of papers.

Problems of compatibility. Mergers involve more than identifying a major economic advantage and negotiating a deal. The two enterprises have to be fitted together into a new composite institution. Unless this true amalgamation is done effectively, many of the anticipated benefits may not materialize. Let us note some of the possible sources of friction.

The character and the operating policies of the merged firms may differ so sharply that living together is impossible. Drastic change must then be made by at least one of the groups, and when this occurs, its morale and going-concern value may disintegrate. For example, a volume producer of electric switches took over an electronics research firm as a means of developing new products subject to less competition. Unfortunately, the driving attitude and policies of the manufacturing executives in getting products out on schedule at budgeted costs was so foreign to the research group that most of the key men resigned and the dominant firm was left with little more than physical laboratory facilities.

Individual personalities of key executives must be recognized. Rugged individualists may object to being "Number two" men in their departments, or a revered senior executive may have difficulty in adapting to the new regime. The task here is to build a new team, using the able men where they can be effective and by-passing the weak ones.

The task of combining facilities is more objective and is often considered before a merger is consummated. Nevertheless, experience indicates that companies may have difficulty actually closing down plants and/or reassigning work. Because of technological and union complications, for instance, one merged firm took five years getting production economies it had assumed could be achieved within a year.

Significantly, a large manufacturing firm that uses the merger route for expansion now includes compatibility as a major consideration in deciding to go through with a merger. This firm explores carefully—before an agreement is concluded—how the merged activities will be run. Other firms, usually with less merger experience, deliberately avoid talking about "those messy operating problems because the other party may withdraw from the deal when he sees that his pet project will be scuttled or his friends upset." Occasions may arise when this latter evasion approach is strategic; but if it is followed, central management should be well aware of the added risks it entails.

Mergers, then, occasionally provide a fast and economical way to move toward company objectives, but they also take a lot of central management time to negotiate and to place on an operating basis. Therefore, the anticipated benefits should be clearly appraised before such a major step is undertaken.

SUMMARY

Policies regulating the use of capital cut across and intertwine with almost all other policies of the enterprise. (a) Restrictions on inventory are directly involved in the coordination of procurement and sales. (b) Credit limitations tie in with customer service policies. (c) Fixed asset controls will affect, to some extent, almost all divisions of a business. (d) The soundness of a merger is largely determined by the way the acquired firm can fit in with and contribute to the whole array of company policies.

Financial policies should not attempt to stipulate the *specific* uses of capital, because this would extend the financial arm too far into the responsibilities of other departments. Instead, policies on the use of capital are primarily concerned with general soundness, total size, and balance between the various types of assets. Only in such activities as credit administration and security investment do capital-use policies give positive direction.

In addition to identifying issues that central management should consider in establishing capital-use policies, we have briefly outlined methods for approaching major problems in this area. Capital budgeting, and in some situations the aiding technique of discounted cash flow, is a useful mechanism for allocating funds to fixed assets.

With respect to mergers, three important steps have been suggested: (1) identify clearly the anticipated economic and financial benefits, (2) work out an exchange of securities, other assets, and obligations that permits both companies to gain from the merger, and (3) check the compatibility of the two companies to be sure that the anticipated benefits will be realized.

QUESTIONS FOR CLASS DISCUSSION

1. The example on page 346 of calculating a rate of return by the discounted cash flow method indicates an expected useful life of a particular number of years and the correct rate for the proposal. Certain studies have indicated that major automobile companies have a target rate of return of 20%. Would you accept the proposal if you were a member of the finance committee of an automobile producer? Would your answer change if you worked for a steel producing and fabricating company? a toy manufacturer?

2. Prepare a detailed list of possible reasons why a profitable company may be short of cash. When may a company operating at a loss find itself with an increasing amount of cash? with a decreasing amount of cash?

3. The Nelson Construction Company, which specializes in building highways, has a clear policy of selling its bulldozers, cranes, heavy trucks, cement mixers, and other equipment as soon as a major job is completed. What reasons do you think account for this policy regarding fixed assets? What effect does it have on capital requirements and on operating costs?

4. Suppose, as a member of the finance committee concerned with the example on page 346, you were convinced that the engineering estimates were excessively conservative as to building time and that the plant and equipment would be in place within one year. Start-up would still occupy the second year and savings would begin as indicated. How would your conviction affect your judgment as to the proper rate of return? How would your judgment be modified by the effect of local assembly on sales volume?

5. An integrated lumber and paper manufacturing company has a choice between two investments—one in laboratories to do development work on dimethyl sulfoxide (a drug produced from wood), the other in high-grade Southern pine timber lands in Arkansas. The two appear to promise about the same rate of return. How could the company's capital budgeting procedure work to give an answer to the choice between the two possibilities (doing both is not possible)?

6. A company needing additional warehouse space had the choice between (a) buying a warehouse that has an estimated life of 20 years or (b) signing a renewable 10-year lease for the same property. How would you decide which of the two plans to follow? Suppose your calculations showed that the average annual expense of both propositions was about equal. What other financial considerations would be involved? What nonfinancial considerations?

7. Over a period of 15 years, the Walter C. Wycomb Company, manufacturers of fire brick, built up its cash and government securities accounts to a total of about 20% of its total assets. The treasurer argued that these funds "were not costing the company anything" and could well be kept as a safety reserve. The sales manager argued that, since the company had the money, a new sales territory should be opened up with a large sales promotion campaign and that a warehouse should be established in the area. One director thought a large dividend should be declared; another director suggested investment in common stock of customers. What approach would you use to get a sound policy regarding the use of this capital?

8. For many years Schussnig Brothers was strictly a textile converting firm. Grey cloth was purchased and shipped directly to dyers and finishers who sent the finished cloth to Schussnig's customers. Schussnig's fixed assets consisted of office furniture and a few drawing boards. Recently Schussnig Brothers decided to integrate backwards and purchased two textile mills. How will this recent action affect the financial policies needed by the firm?

9. (a) Make an outline of the sales, procurement, and personnel policies discussed in Chapters 5 through 13. Indicate how, if at all, choice of policies in each of these areas will affect the need for capital. (b) How can policies covering the use of capital be set so that they will not usurp the significance of these other policies?

10. To expand and to take advantage of a tax loss provision, a Pittsburgh firm, which specialized in heavy machinery, acquired through an exchange of stock a manufacturer of light industrial machinery and home power tools. The company acquired had significant overseas sales and producing operations. Within two years the combined firm was losing money since profits of the acquired division, which was still set up independently, had declined further. Executives of the division acquired complained bitterly "that their hands were tied by Pittsburgh" and that they could not seize profitable opportunities for leasing sales facilities in foreign countries. What problems of merger do you see here? What might be done about such problems?

CASE XIV

Quality Watch Company

The situation of the international watch industry kept on changing, as it always had, in the 1960's. Directors of the Quality Watch Company were concerned about the most appropriate use of the firm's financial strength in light of the new circumstances.

Quality Watch Company, a United States-based company, produced very high-grade, 19- and 21-jewel, men's and women's jeweled-lever and battery-powered electric wrist and pocket watches in its United States plant and a line of medium-grade, 15- to 17-jewel, watches in company-owned plants in Switzerland and in the Virgin Islands. Using its own sales force, it sold these in the United States to a select group of jewelers.

Some directors believed that the firm had more than adequate financial strength to support current operations (see Exhibits 1 and 2). Therefore, they asked for a consideration of additional uses of the company's funds. Among the proposals offered were advance payment of a long-term loan, adding further to the product line by moving to the production of inexpensive watches, or buying some of the stock of other watch manufacturers who specialized in different segments of the watch industry than did Quality.

Exhibit 1

Quality Watch Company

Current Balance Sheet

Assets		*Liabilities and Shareholders' Equity*	
Cash	$ 2,800,000	Short-term bank notes payable	$ 3,750,000
Short-term government securities	4,000,000	Current portion of long-term debt	400,000
Notes and accounts receivable	6,000,000	Accounts payable	1,950,000
Inventories:		Accrued wages and expenses	700,000
Raw materials	3,300,000	Accrued taxes	600,000
Work in process	4,400,000	Total current liabilities	$7,400,000
Finished stock	3,800,000		
Investment in subsidiaries	2,300,000	Subordinated, convertible notes, 6%	4,000,000
Plant and equipment:		Preferred stock—5% cumulative	4,300,000
Cost .. $18,000,000		Common stock	4,000,000
Depreciation . 10,000,000		Retained earnings	14,900,000
Net	8,000,000		
Total assets	$34,600,000	Total liabilities and shareholders' equity	$34,600,000

NOTE A—The long-term notes due to various insurance companies had a remaining term due of 10 years. The notes were convertible at any time to common stock at a price of $27 per share. (Authorized common stock amounted to 1,000,000 shares; shares outstanding were 342,000.) The notes could be retired in advance of the date due according to the following schedule:

Date due—par.
One year in advance—110% of par.
Two or more years in advance—115% of par.

NOTE B—The preferred stock was cumulative as to dividends. Should dividends be in arrears more than two quarters, the preferred stockholders had the right to elect one-fourth of the directors. Should dividends be in arrears more than six quarters, preferred stockholders could elect a majority of the board. Par is $100 and 43,000 shares were issued and outstanding. Preferred stock could be called by the corporation at 140% of par.

Exhibit 2

Quality Watch Company
Selected Financial Data

Year	Sales	Net Earnings	Dividends
1964	$34,100,000	$ 652,000	$215,000
1963	30,200,000	100,000	215,000
1962	31,000,000	620,000	415,000
1961	30,900,000	750,000	415,000
1960	31,100,000	932,000	415,000
1959	28,300,000	1,100,000	345,000
1957	26,000,000	1,450,000	517,000
1954	30,000,000	2,570,000	690,000

Price range of stock of Quality Watch Company over the past year:

	High	Low	Current
Preferred	105	97	104
Common	15	12	14⅛

Industry conditions. Worldwide output of both pin-lever (non-jeweled) and jeweled-lever watches has been increasing steadily over the past decade. Substantial industries have been built in Japan, West Germany, Great Britain, and Russia. These are now providing active competition for watches made in Switzerland—the world leader. As an example, Japanese firms sold to the United States market in 1962, 800,000 watch movements and in 1963, 1,500,000 watch movements. The Swiss share of the total of 12 million jeweled-lever movements imported into the United States in 1963 declined 1½% from 1962 to 1963 and another 3½% from 1963 to 1964, while the number of Japanese watch movements imported increased another 30% above the 1963 quantity. A second development that has affected imports into the United States is the practice of sending watch movements and partly assembled watches to the United States' Virgin Islands. Under a law designed to spur the economy of the Islands, the movements come in nearly duty-free. The complete watch can then be assembled in the Virgin Islands by adding dials, cases, and straps and then be sent duty-free to the mainland. Current Swiss laws ban such re-exporting of Swiss-made movements and parts.

The watch and clock industry of Switzerland is integrated partly along vertical and partly along horizontal lines. It includes about 70 manufacturers who produce most of their own parts and assemble them into finished movements or completed watches that are tested, adjusted, and made ready for shipment anywhere in the world. A second group of manufacturers buy most of the component parts and assemble movements. Supplying these manufacturers are a large number of small to medium-sized firms specializing in particular parts such as mainsprings, hairsprings, hands, and dials.

Another group of firms specializes in the production of subassemblies such as the escapement train or an incomplete movement known as an ébauche (sometimes called the "chassis" of a watch). These subassemblies are sold to the second group of manufacturers, who make complete movements that are marketed throughout the world under many different brand names. Regardless of the name, movements built on ébauches are identical within any given category of quality, size, and style. Interchangeable parts are available from the factories on short notice and are also stocked in main distribution centers all over the world.

Unlike the Swiss industry, the Japanese jeweled-lever watch industry has only 4 producers. Its output of 21 million units in 1963 represented a 10% increase over 1962 and a 100% increase over 1958. With labor costs 20% below those in Switzerland, Japanese producers are now seeking to market abroad.

Like other United States producers, Quality Watch Company has taken advantage of foreign production skills and cost structures. It now has a Swiss subsidiary making both its medium and high-grade watches and a plant in St. Croix in the Virgin Islands that assembles its medium-grade watches.

Tariff changes. In 1954 the tariff on jeweled watches imported into the United States was raised substantially, up to 50% in some instances. At the same time, the tariff on pin-lever watches was increased very slightly. After this tariff increase, Swiss imports declined from an average of about 10 million watches a year to about 7 million watches. This, however, did not help United States producers, for their sales of jeweled-lever watches made domestically declined from about 2.3 million down to 1.6 million units and has remained at about that level since. However, pin-lever watches have risen substantially in the number sold. Less than 2 million were imported in 1954, but the quantity has gone up very substantially since that time.

Shipments from the Virgin Islands amounted in 1960 to 44,000 watches, in 1962 to 420,000, and in 1963 to 1 million watches. Movements and other parts for these watches were made in France, West Germany, and Japan. Although current Swiss laws forbids re-exporting through the Virgin Islands, there have been some statements to the effect that if the United States tariff on jeweled watches is not lowered, then the Swiss law will be changed. The United States tariff commission holds hearings several times each year, but recent hearings have been on only the $10.50 tariff on movements containing more than 17 jewels. Presently, there is a bill in Congress to close "the Virgin Islands tariff loophole," but only one United States-based manufacturer is backing this bill. Other United States manufacturers have claimed that they will fight any lowering of tariffs, since they state that without the duty no jeweled-lever watches will be made in the United States and skills necessary for national defense will thereby be lost. On the other hand, the American Watch Association (a group of import firms) has claimed that there is no need for the high tariff on jeweled watches. Their claim is that the electronics industry with its micro-miniaturization practices has rendered watchmaking skills obsolete for defense purposes. They claim further that no major United States company will suffer substantially if tariffs are lowered since each firm will merely step up the imports in its product mix.

The United States market and consumption. In 1962, watch sales in the United States increased 16% over the year before to 26.1 million units (a new record). Sales in dollar volume went up 21% to $151 million, which is close to the 1953 peak of $157.4 million. Comparable gains occurred in 1963 with sales close to 30 million units. Low-priced pin-lever watches were taking an increasing share of this market. Sales of pin-lever watches jumped from 7.5 million units in 1954 to 15 million units in 1963. Of these, 7 million were imported from Puerto Rico, Germany, and Great Britain while the balance were made in the United States.

At one time, the United States market for watches appeared to be segmented according to a combination of price and the number of jewels in a watch. High-priced watches of 19 to 21 jewels were sold at retail for $70 and more on the basis of luxury and prestige. An upper middle segment of 17-jewel watches priced from $50 to $70 at retail were sold on the basis of styling and features such as an extra thin or a self-winding watch. These watches were also expected to keep very good time. A lower middle segment of the market consisted of 15- to 17-jewel watches sold at retail for $30 to $50 on the basis of special features such as an alarm watch, a calendar watch, an antimagnetic watch, or a self-winding watch. Watches in this price range tended to be discounted or sold in department store basements. Below this lower middle price range were pin-lever watches. Such a watch may have some jewels, but the teeth of its escapement wheel touch upright cylindrical metal pins in contrast to a jeweled-lever watch whose escapement wheel teeth touch flat pallet jewels. The original pin-lever watches were the good old $1 pocket watch and the Mickey Mouse wristwatch that was sold to children by the millions.

However, in recent years pin-lever watches have become a new factor in the United States market. As was mentioned above, their sales have risen substantially. This has been attributed to various factors: (1) their comparative low price, $5 to $15; (2) the great variety of sizes, shapes, and styles offered, including self-winding and waterproof features; (3) improvements in quality, so that a pin-lever watch now keeps reasonably accurate time over a substantial period; and (4) the increasingly higher repair cost of jeweled-lever watches. It has been noted that recessions clearly affect jeweled-lever watch sales.

What has been the effect on the state of the United States market? It appears that the situation is now mainly uncertain. It seems to be clear that the market is undersaturated. United States production and sales of watches has certainly not kept pace with increases in disposable personal income. One estimate by a market research firm is that only 70% of Americans over 14 years old own a wristwatch and only ⅓ of those over 10 years old own a watch. The average retail price fell substantially from $75 in 1948 to $55 in 1958. As far as attitudes are concerned, over half of the United States consumers seem to believe that a good watch now costs much less than it did in years past and about half of them could not see much difference between an expensive and an inexpensive watch. A large proportion also believed that inexpensive watches would last almost as long as expensive watches. There has been a tendency for consumers to buy cheap watches and throw them away rather than attempt to have them repaired. Perhaps the increasing number of unknown brands, as well as vigorous discounting, has contributed to this practice. Up until 1960 the $15 to $30 price range was "the emptiest." It demonstrated the smallest amount of sales increase and was the segment of the market occupied by unknown brands that suffered the most discounting and the most consumer distrust as to what they were really getting.

It was into this segment of the market that U. S. Time moved with vigorous promotion of its Timex brand. The firm was able to persuade consumers that it could sell "a fine watch at a fraction of a fine watch price." It sold pin-lever wristwatches for $6.95 and up. These watches were sturdy, dependable, and well-styled. One market analyst contends that sales of pin-lever watches have been so successful because they tapped a segment of the market not recognized before, that is, both low and high income buyers who looked for a watch that worked reasonably well but was sold at such a low price that it could be thrown out and replaced if it failed after a year. The pin-lever watches also appeared to tap another market segment that was looking for products with good styling, the latest features, and what appeared to be good workmanship. U. S. Time also emphasized sales all year round, while others concentrated on the November-December season, the traditional high point for watch sales. From this point of view, it appeared that most manufacturers of high-grade jeweled watches were selling a product that symbolized a big occasion and that was purchased on the basis of a brand name, a jeweler recommendation, or a gold or diamond case.

Opportunities. In the context of the watch industry there appear to be several possibilities for Quality Watch Company. It could continue as it has with emphasis on selected distribution of the very high-grade line that had had a distinguished name among consumers for years and with the same kind of distribution for the upper medium-grade line sold under a different brand name.

The company could also maintain its diversification into miniaturized electromechanical products sold to the defense industry and certain customers in the electronics industry. These latter products increased sales volume and kept plant and employees busy, but generally they were sold with a small profit at best because of competition and the pricing practices necessary on government bids. The return on investment in this part of the company's effort fluctuated from 0% to 4%. Domestic watch production averaged a 3% to 4% return on investment, and sales of imported watches averaged an 8% to 10% return.

If Quality Watch Company continued with the same watch lines, then it could use any extra funds available for appropriate changes in its financial structure.

There were other possibilities in the watch industry. Quality Watch Company could use another Virgin Islands plant and Japanese sources to expand sales of jeweled-lever watches in the $20 (at retail) to $40 price range. Costs in the Virgin Islands were less than those of the Swiss subsidiary for watches landed in the United States. These watches would be sold as private brands or to very large accounts in order to minimize the sales effort required and so as not to affect the image of the company's other brands. Price pressures would probably wipe out any extra cost advantage, but probably the company would realize a return close to that of its other imported watches once it had gained real experience in this market. Total investment for fixed and working capital would be about $1,200,000.

Another possibility was to use such a proposed Virgin Islands plant to back up a wider distribution of jeweled-lever watches by direct sales of the medium-grade line to retailers. The attempt would be to increase the number of jewelers carrying the medium-grade line. It would be expected that such an action would be reasonably profitable since the watches would not be sold at discount prices. However, the action would require considerable marketing effort, major additions to the field sales force, and substantial promotional costs. Presumably these tasks could be carried out since they would be an extension of skills the sales division already had. But the larger risk was that consumer acceptance was uncertain.

A further possibility was to enter the rapidly expanding pin-lever watch market. One advantage of such an action would be that the company could produce the watches entirely within the United

States at no major cost disadvantage as compared to foreign producers. Selling these watches, however, would require substantially different marketing efforts than were currently used. New kinds of promotion would be required and entirely different channels would have to be utilized, such as drug wholesalers, rack jobbers, and stationery wholesalers. Other firms have made a major success at this, but results could not be predicted with any certainty for Quality Watch Company.

A final proposal had been put forth by the treasurer of the company. He suggested buying shares of common stock of a manufacturer of pin-lever watches. These shares were not generally available but could occasionally be bought over the counter. The treasurer had a limited amount of financial information on one such firm. He reported that its capital structure was 60% long-term debt and 40% common stock and retained earnings. The book value per share of common stock was $38.82. In the most recent year, interest had been earned 3.12 times. The company had never paid a dividend on its common stock. The latest prices quoted over the counter were; bid, $30; offered, $35. The treasurer stated that the earnings rate on the common stock appeared to be high to him, since pre-tax earnings per share were $6.36.

REQUIRED: What uses of capital do you recommend for Quality Watch Company? Consider both the extent of its investment in fixed assets and investment in the various alternatives proposed.

CHAPTER

15

FINANCIAL POLICIES—
SOURCES OF CAPITAL

The cultivation of adequate sources of capital is of prime concern to central management. Other aspects of company operations may be just as crucial to success, but none is more relentless in insisting on proper attention. For small and medium-sized firms, especially, the supply of capital is frequently a restraint on the successful execution of many policies and programs.

The principal sources of capital available to most companies may be classified under:

1. Owners.
2. Long-term creditors.
3. Short-term creditors.

We shall first review the typical ways capital is obtained from each of these sources and shall then consider how a management can combine the use of various sources to form a financial structure suited to the strengths and needs of its specific enterprise.

Owners. *Typical policies.* The owners of a company must supply at least part of the capital at the time of its organization, and they frequently make additional contributions to meet subsequent requirements. These additional contributions may consist of an increase in their original investment or may arise by leaving profits in the business. The use of profits for financing business expansion in place of paying these out to the owners has long been regarded as a conservative policy, and a large number of our present companies have secured a major portion of their capital in this way.

Effect of legal form of organization. The amount of capital that may be secured from owners will depend upon the legal form of organization and the particular rights granted to each class of owners. In a sole proprietorship the amount of capital is limited by the personal resources of the individual who has complete control of the business. For example, capital required for the operation of a ferry across the Hudson River about one hundred years ago

367

was supplied entirely by the owner of the boat that plied between the shores. As the business grew and improvements had to be made in both the dock and the boat itself, the owner provided the capital either by failing to withdraw the profits of the enterprise or by making additional contributions from his personal savings.

In time a much larger ferry was required and the operation of freight boats up and down the river appeared to be a profitable expansion. To finance this development, a partnership was formed with the owner of a small freight boat and a third party who supplied additional funds. The three partners had to agree upon a distribution of profits based on the amount of capital and the value of services each contributed to the partnership. The business prospered, and the third financial partner was called upon to make further contributions of capital. This required a readjustment in the basis of distributing profits.

Common stock. The business of operating boats up and down the river grew rapidly. Soon a number of additional boats were needed to carry on the business adequately, and since the three partners were unable to finance the purchase of additional equipment from their own resources, they decided to form a corporation instead of taking another partner. The partners were given shares of stock for their interest in the business, and new capital was raised by selling additional shares to a number of people who became convinced of the profit possibilities of the enlarged business. All these stockholders had a share in the ownership of the company.

To finance further expansion, the company followed a policy of plowing back a large part of its earnings, and as further additions of capital were required over and above the earnings that could be retained, more shares of stock were sold.

Preferred stock. The enterprise eventually became a large steamship company operating far beyond the Hudson River, and now it has a total capital greatly in excess of the wildest dreams of the original ferryman. After the company was well on its way to success, one of the original partners, who owned a large block of the stock, wished to retire from active participation in the management. He was willing to take a limited return on his money if the company could give some assurance that special effort would be made to pay dividends on his stock. For this purpose preferred stock was issued on which the possible dividends were limited to 7% per annum.

As a protection, no dividends could be paid on the remaining stock, now called common stock, until the preferred dividends had been paid. Furthermore, dividends on the preferred stock were made cumulative so that if no dividends were paid by the corporation during any year, the 7% dividend preference of the preferred stock would carry over from year to year. Thus, if no dividends were paid on a $100 share of preferred stock for two years, $14 for back dividends and $7 for current dividends would have to be paid to the preferred stockholder in the third year before any dividends could be declared on the common stock.

The steamship company now has hundreds of stockholders. The common stock has been *split* (several new shares issued to holders of each old share) and new 5% preferred stock has replaced the original 7% preferred stock. Each share entitles its holder to one vote, and since there are many more shares of common stock outstanding than preferred stock, the common stockholders control the company. The owners of preferred stock enjoy cumulative preference on dividends of 5% per annum, but all dividends in excess of this sum are distributed among common stockholders.

Frequent use of stock to raise capital. Almost all large enterprises today are incorporated, having many owners or stockholders. Stockholders may be divided into various classes with varying rights, the most usual classes being preferred and common. Preferred stockholders invariably have preference as to earnings, which preference may be cumulative (as in the example already given) or noncumulative. Usually the preferred stockholders have a preference as to assets in case of dissolution; that is, they may be entitled to receive a stipulated amount of the proceeds from liquidation before the common stockholders receive any share. Occasionally, the return on preferred stock is not limited to the preferred amount, in which case the preferred stockholder participates with the common stockholder in any dividends in excess of a specified return on each class of stock.

The common stock, on the other hand, has all the rights that have not been granted to the preferred stock. As a matter of fact, both common stock and preferred stock may be further subdivided into classes of stock with varying rights. The rights granted to any particular type of stock depend largely on (1) the securities that the company has outstanding at the time new securities are issued,

(2) the condition of the securities market at the time of issue, and (3) the position and financial standing of the issuing company.

The policy of a corporation in regard to procuring additional capital by the sale of stock should be established in relation to the availability and the cost of securing capital from other sources. The effect of issuing new stock on the rights and equity of present stockholders must also be considered. Each time additional common stock is sold to new investors, the present owners give up a share in the profits, and naturally no common stockholder wants capital raised in this way if some other satisfactory source is available.

Preferred stock, with its limited participation in earnings, might be a more desirable source of capital if investors would buy it without insisting on so many special priviliges that the position of the common stockholder is seriously weakened.

Long-term creditors. *Borrowing as a source of capital.* Capital may also be secured by borrowing it from long- or short-term creditors. Some of the problems and possible policies in connection with borrowing can be illustrated by two companies, each of which sought to raise capital by this means. One was a comparatively small printing plant that had grown up as an adjunct to a larger manufacturing concern and was just being established as an independent enterprise. The manufacturing concern sold some machinery and miscellaneous assets to the new company, The Long-Shot Printing Company, and accepted promissory notes and a part of the common stock of the company as payment. The president of the new company invested all of his available capital, but this was inadequate to provide necessary working capital and to pay for additional machinery. It was not possible to sell stock to outside investors because they were not interested in purchasing securities of a new, unknown company. Additional capital had to be borrowed from some source if the enterprise was to operate.

The other enterprise whose borrowing problems we shall consider is a local electric company with assets of approximately $26,-000,000. This company, the Red River Power Company, wished to finance an expansion program that required approximately $6,000,-000. The new expansion might have been financed by the sale of additional stock. The present common stockholders, however, did not wish to use this source of capital because (a) high income taxes make earning of net profits more difficult than earning bond interest, and (b) all profits would have to be shared with the new stockholders.

Interest on borrowed capital is an expense deducted from income *before* income tax is computed. Profits available for stockholders are net income *after* income tax has been paid. Consequently, a corporation in the 50% income tax bracket has to earn $2 for each dollar available to stockholders. If capital is borrowed, less earnings are needed to pay for the use of the capital because the tax collector has not yet taken his toll.

The effect of these factors on the Red River Power Company can be seen by comparing the disposition of operating profits (before paying bond interest) under bond and stock financing. The company already had outstanding $9,000,000 of 4¾% bonds, $6,000,000 of 5% preferred stock, and $6,000,000 of common stock. It was estimated that an average annual operating profit of $2,000,000 would be earned when the expansion was completed. The effect of borrowing the necessary $6,000,000 at 4¾% or selling common stock at par would have been:

	Borrowing $6,000,000 at 4¾%	Selling $6,000,000 of Common Stock
Estimated annual operating profit	$2,000,000	$2,000,000
Less bond interest	712,500	427,500
Net profit before income tax	$1,287,500	$1,572,500
Income tax @ 50%	643,750	786,250
Net profit	$ 643,750	$ 786,250
Less preferred stock dividends	300,000	300,000
Available for common stockholders	$ 343,750	$ 486,250
Rate of return on par value of common stock outstanding	5.72%	4.05%

The present stockholders would profit by borrowing because a larger rate of return is being earned on capital than would be required for interest. If for some unforeseen reason, however, the operating profit of the company fell to $1,600,000 or $1,300,000, the earnings on common stock would have been as follows:

	Rate of Return on Common Stock Outstanding	
Annual Operating Profit	Borrowing $6,000,000 at 4¾%	Selling $6,000,000 of Common Stock
$2,000,000	5.72%	4.05%
1,600,000	2.40	2.39
1,300,000	— .10	1.14

Thus, by borrowing, the common stockholders increased their possibilities for profits but also incurred a greater risk of loss. Such use of bonds for raising capital is referred to as *trading on the equity*.

Trading on the equity may be accomplished through the use of any of the following instruments for long-term borrowing:

1. Mortgages.
2. Secured bonds.
3. Debenture bonds.
4. Long-term notes.

Mortgages. The Long-Shot Printing Company, for example, needed additional machinery. A machinery manufacturer was willing to sell the particular equipment for only part payment in cash provided the company would give a mortgage on the equipment as security for payment of the unpaid balance of $80,500. Under the mortgage if the company failed to make interest payments or to pay the principal at the time of maturity, the manufacturer had the privilege of foreclosing on the mortgage and forcing a sale of the property pledged. If the proceeds from the sale were not adequate to retire the entire debt, the borrower would still be liable for the remaining balance. To secure an order, the manufacturer was willing to take the risk of not being able to collect from the company or to liquidate the machinery for the amount due.

The agreement provided for the payment of $8,000 per year on the principal, in addition to the interest due, thus reducing the amount of the debt as the value of the machinery depreciated. The company was able to secure the equipment it required by this means, but it still needed funds for working capital. Since the equipment had been mortgaged for a large part of its value, the company had to endeavor to secure circulating capital from some other source.

Mortgages on equipment or buildings are frequently used by individuals or partnerships that wish to borrow money for a period of several years. Occasionally, as explained in the preceding chapter, long-term leases are used to finance buildings or plants.

Secured bonds. The Red River Power Company had ample fixed assets that might have been pledged as security for its $6,000,000 loan. The corporation, however, wished to borrow more than a single lender would probably care to risk in one enterprise. A simple mortgage loan was not adequate, and the company therefore found it necessary to issue mortgage bonds. This means that the loan was divided into a series of identical parts, or *bonds* as they are called, each having the same face value. These bonds could then be sold to as many lenders as was necessary to secure the total sum required.

The company was reasonably sure it could sell such bonds. Its assets were substantially in excess of the amount of bonds to be issued, and the estimated annual operating profit would be almost three times the interest charges on its entire debt. Since any shrinkage in asset value or earnings must first be borne by the stockholders, a good cushion of protection was provided for the bondholders.

The rate of interest on the bonds had to be adjusted in terms of the risk of loss that was associated with such bonds and the interest rates prevailing in the money market at the time the bonds were issued. Since this was a public utility company with reasonably stable earnings, bonds bearing a 4¾% interest rate could be sold. Had the earnings of the borrowing company been uncertain and subject to wider fluctuations in amount, and if the assets pledged under the mortgage were likely to have a substantial shrinkage in value, the ratio of bonded indebtedness to the investment previously made by the stockholders would necessarily have been correspondingly smaller and the interest rate higher.

Since the bonds of the Red River Power Company were to be owned by a large number of bondholders, it would not have been convenient to have each bondholder deal directly with the corporation. As is true of most bond issues, a trustee was therefore appointed who was responsible for performing the routine matters of looking after the interests of the bondholders as a group. A contract, called the *bond indenture,* specified in considerable detail the agreement and obligations of the borrower and the procedure to be followed in event of default. Such indentures often restrict the right of the borrower to incur further debts having prior claim to the bondholders, and the payment of dividends may be prohibited if such payment reduces the current assets below a stated amount.

Capital may also be raised by selling other types of secured bonds. Under some circumstances a borrowing company may pledge as security stocks or bonds of other companies that it happens to own, instead of giving a mortgage on property as security. Such bonds are typically called *collateral trust bonds.*

Debenture bonds. Another form of long-term securities that is used by some corporations is known as the *debenture bond*. Such bonds may be issued by corporations that have a sufficiently strong financial position that money can be borrowed without the pledge of any specific security. Sometimes the issuing company has no suitable assets that can be mortgaged or pledged. This type of bond, however, proves useful since it may be issued by any financially strong concern.

Before capital can be raised by the sale of such bonds, the investors must be convinced that the earnings of the company will be much more than adequate to meet all outstanding obligations, and that there is little likelihood that the company will fail to meet interest payments and to repay the principal at maturity.

Long-term notes. The tremendous growth of life insurance companies, trust companies, and other financial institutions has greatly increased the use of long-term notes in recent years. These institutions have such large assets that they are in a position to make loans up to several millions of dollars by themselves. Consequently, a company in good financial condition can go directly to such a large lender and get all the additional capital needed from this single source. Private placements of this sort account for about half of the long-term borrowing by corporations.

Sometimes bonds, like those already described, are sold to the financial institution. More often the loan is made simply on the basis of 10-, 15-, or 20-year promissory notes. There is, however, an accompanying agreement similar to a bond indenture that spells out the conditions under which the loan is to be repaid and the various protective measures requested by the lender. While negotiations for such long-term loans may become involved, they usually are much simpler and less expensive than the public sale of bonds. Moreover, a firm commitment from a single lender avoids much of the uncertainty connected with the public sale of securities. Only when the capital needed is so large that an insurance company cannot provide it, or when a company's reputation is so well-known in the financial markets that it can borrow at low rates, will most companies resort to *public* issue of bonds.

Special bond provisions. As a special protection for the lender and also as a convenience for the borrower, provision is often made for reduction in the amount of the principal of the loan each year. This is frequently done by issuing *serial bonds*, a part of which must be paid off each year until the entire loan is finally retired. In other cases a *sinking fund* is created by setting aside a stated amount each year. This fund will provide cash with which to pay off the entire bond issue at the time of maturity.

Sometimes, in order to increase its attractiveness to an investor, the bond is made convertible into stock; that is, the bondholder may exchange his bond for a given number of shares of stock of the same company if he wishes to do so. Of course, a bondholder will only do this if the company is unusually prosperous and the stock becomes particularly desirable.

Another feature found in many bond agreements is that the company, by giving proper notice and by paying a premium that often ranges from 5% to 10%, may call the bonds for retirement prior to their specified maturity date. This enables the company to eliminate or refund its outstanding debt if and when its financial requirements change. On the other hand, the investor knows he will receive an extra premium if the company decides to take advantage of this privilege. Similar provisions for "calling" are usually made for preferred stock; conversion privileges are likewise often attached to preferred stock as well as to bonds.

There are many other detailed features of bonds and mortgages too technical for this discussion. In most cases, however, these technical features are not of sufficient importance to affect a general policy decision as to what sources of capital shall be used.

Short-term creditors. The sources of capital discussed thus far provide capital for a long period of time. Short-term creditors, however, are better adapted to provide funds to meet seasonal requirements or other temporary needs. The most common short-term creditors are (a) commercial banks and (b) merchandise vendors. We shall consider each of these briefly as possible sources for borrowing additional capital for The Long-Shot Printing Company and the Red River Power Company.

Commercial banks. Borrowing from commercial banks is a general practice followed by most firms and is one that the president of The Long-Shot Printing Company sought to use. The company had already opened a regular bank account to use for depositing daily receipts, making up the payroll, paying merchandise vendors, and carrying on other ordinary financial transactions, and therefore its president was acquainted with the banker. During the interview the banker was courteous but inquisitive, asking questions about the character of the men operating the company, the nature of its existing assets, the use to be made of the money borrowed, the obligations that had already been incurred, and the earning record of the company. He was also interested in seeing a budget of the cash receipts and disbursements anticipated month by month during the coming year.

Since the company had no current assets and was seeking a loan to be used as permanent circulating capital, and because of the fact that an ability to earn profits while operating on an independent basis had not been demonstrated, the banker refused to extend credit to the company. He explained that commercial banks normally grant credit for only a few months to meet seasonal or unusual cash requirements and that the borrower is expected to have enough capital to finance his regular needs.

The banker went on to say that if, after the company had become established, it needed credit for a short period of time, the most desirable arrangement was to establish a *credit line* with the bank. Under such an arrangement the company would anticipate its needs for temporary cash and would reach an understanding with the bank, prior to the time the cash was required, that credit up to a certain maximum would be granted. This would give the bank ample time to make its customary credit investigation, and it would also enable the company to plan on the bank as a temporary source of capital. In other words, the banker made it clear that the bank was not in the business of extending credit without knowing the likelihood of getting its money back.

The Red River Power Company had used bank credit to the extent of $1,800,000 for the purpose of commencing its expansion program just prior to the time its new bond issue was floated. Inasmuch as the capital was invested in fixed assets that would not turn into cash except through operations over a long period of years, a question may be raised as to whether this was a legitimate use of a bank loan. Actually, both the company and the bank recognized that the loan was a temporary measure and that the company had to seek permanent capital through the sale of either additional bonds or stock. Until a single, long-time issue could be sold to provide capital for the entire expansion program, the company wished to secure capital temporarily from the bank so that its program could continue without interruption due to lack of finances. The bank felt it safe to make the loan because the company had a sales volume of almost $8,000,000 a year and was earning a net profit after a deduction for bond interest of approximately $1,000,000. Thus, the loan could be paid off out of earnings if future events should prevent the completion of a bond issue to finance permanently the proposed expansion program.

In some types of business a commercial bank makes loans that are secured by collateral. For example, the investment banker pledges stocks and bonds as security for his bank loans, and the dealer in commodities backs up his loans by means of warehouse receipts or bills of lading. Occasionally, a manufacturing concern will pledge marketable securities that it does not care to sell as collateral for a bank loan. When such security is provided, the preliminary investigation by the bank will be less extensive.

With secured loans, as with unsecured loans, the commercial bank will normally extend credit for only a few months at a time; furthermore, the bank will hesitate to renew the loan if there is doubt about its liquidity. Perhaps it should be added that if for some unforeseen reason a borrower is unable to pay a loan at maturity, a commercial bank will very often take a friendly attitude toward the borrower and endeavor to help him work out his situation. More often than not, however, the other sources for short-term capital that have no personal relationship with the borrower will probably press him for immediate payments as soon as his loan matures.

In passing it may be noted that while commercial banks are traditionally regarded as a source of short-term capital, they do lend substantial sums to be used for fixed capital. Marketable bonds and real-estate mortgages have long appeared in the asset column of financial statements of banks. In recent years many banks have engaged in loaning money direct to business enterprises for terms ranging from 2 years up to 10 years. The practice of occasionally making these long-term loans, however, in no way detracts from the primary role of commercial banks in providing short-term capital.

Merchandise creditors. Most companies purchase products and services "on account"; that is, they agree to make payment in a stipulated period of time after the products are shipped. Although each particular bill is paid at the close of this period, additional obligations are being contracted continuously. In other words, companies usually have a certain quantity of merchandise on hand for which they must still make payment. In effect, then, the vendors are supplying part of the capital being used to carry on operations.

The Long-Shot Printing Company made substantial use of this source of capital. Suppliers of paper and ink were anxious to establish trade relations with the new company and shipped goods without a careful credit investigation. Some of the vendors assumed that the company was still closely associated with the manufacturing concern and shipped goods on the basis of the credit standing of the latter. The company took advantage of this availability of trade credit. Goods were purchased from several sources so that bills with any one vendor were not large, and payments on all bills were stalled for a month or more past the due date.

Question may be raised whether such extensive use of trade credit is a wise policy as a general rule. Vendors often offer substantial discounts for prompt payment of bills, which means that this is an expensive source of capital. It was estimated, for example, that The Long-Shot Printing Company was losing discounts of $9,000 a year, or 14½% of the total capital secured from vendors, that might have been taken had bills been paid promptly. Furthermore, a company with a reputation for slow pay will not receive favorable treatment from vendors when there is a shortage of merchandise or when close-outs are being offered at low prices. Then too, there is always the danger that the supply of materials will be shut off altogether until bills are paid. So if possible, capital from vendors should normally be limited to trade credit customarily provided in the industry.

It will be recognized, of course, that buying on credit is but a counterpart of the use of capital to finance accounts receivable from customers.

Other short-term credit. Several other methods of raising short-term capital may be used under special conditions. As noted in the preceding chapter, the popularity of installment payments for consumer goods has given rise to finance companies that assist the retailer in carrying the installment accounts that might otherwise absorb a considerable part of his working capital. These companies may make loans to the retailer on the basis of the installment paper, although in the automobile field, and also in a number of other fields, the finance company deals directly with the purchaser and the retailer is out of the transaction as soon as the purchaser has made the necessary arrangements with the finance company.

Some large, well-known companies with a very high credit rating secure short-term capital by selling commercial paper that takes the form of short-term promissory notes. The credit of these companies is so well known that these notes can be easily sold to financial institutions seeking a temporary investment for idle funds. There has been, however, a marked decrease in the use of commercial paper.

When a company cannot secure the required funds from other sources, it may turn to a commercial credit house, or factor, that advances funds on the basis of customer accounts receivable. The accounts receivable are either pledged as security for the loan or actually turned over to the credit house for collection. As a general rule, this source of capital has been expensive and has often led to ill will on the part of customers, because customers dislike buying from a company that has to resort to such a source of capital. In a few limited fields, this method has a much more favorable reputation. As is sometimes done by factors in the textile industry, the financing house undertakes supervision of the payment of bills as well as the selection of accounts.

Postponing payment of taxes, installment payments on machinery, loans against inventory placed in a bonded warehouse, and even advance payments by customers can be resorted to during periods of stringency. Few companies, however, care to have a continuing policy of obtaining short-term capital from such sources.

FINANCIAL STRUCTURE

Meaning of financial structure. The various sources of capital employed and their relative importance make up the financial structure of a company. In establishing policies regarding sources of capital, this general structure must be considered because the use of one source will affect the desirability of others.

The size of the company, the nature of its assets, the amount and stability of its earnings, and the condition existing in the financial market at the time the capital is raised, all have an influence on the sources of capital used by the company. From time to time changes will be made in the sources employed, either because capital can be secured more advantageously from some other source or because some lender decides to withdraw his capital from the enterprise. Expansion or contraction of the total amount of capital used will, of course, affect the relative importance of the various sources. The financial structure for a company is therefore based on the proper correlation and adaption of its financial policies to existing conditions.

At any given time the right-hand side of the balance sheet of a company will reflect its financial structure. In order, therefore, to review the policies followed by a few different companies, we will examine briefly their condensed balance sheets.

Financial structure of Schultz Electronic Controls, Inc. The balance sheet of Schultz Electronic Controls, Inc. is typical of many comparatively small manufacturing companies.

Schultz Electronic Controls, Inc.
Balance Sheet
December 31, 19—

Assets		Liabilities and stockholders' equity	
Cash	$ 140,000	Accounts payable	$ 117,000
Accounts receivable (net)	410,000	Accrued liabilities	84,000
Finished inventory	196,000	Long-term serial notes	550,000
Materials and in-process		Preferred stock, 5½%	600,000
inventory	439,000	Common stock	1,000,000
Fixed assets (net)	1,500,000	Earnings retained in	
		business	334,000
		Total liabilities and	
Total assets	$2,685,000	stockholders' equity	$2,685,000

Almost three fourths of the total capital of $2,685,000 was supplied by owners of this company. Par value of preferred and common stock is $1,600,000, and earnings retained in the business have increased the stockholders' investment by another third of a million dollars. Limited use of long-term notes is shown. These notes are only about one third of the depreciated value of fixed assets. Thus the notes appear to be protected by an ample margin of assets, and the serial feature provides for a regular reduction in the amount of the long-term debt.

The short-term debt of the company at the time of this balance sheet was comparatively small, the accounts payable to trade creditors being only a fraction of the total assets and actually less than the cash on hand. The company did, however, have a bank line and normally used bank credit to finance a seasonal peak in inventories and receivables from March through August.

Financial structure of the Red River Power Company. The sources of capital used by the Red River Power Company reflect the difference in the nature of operations of an electric utility company as compared with a manufacturing company such as Schultz Electronic Controls, Inc. The balance sheet below shows the financial condition of Red River Power Company after its expansion program was completed.

Red River Power Company
Balance Sheet
December 31, 19—

Assets			Liabilities and stockholders' equity	
Cash	$	400,000	Accounts payable .....$	400,000
Other current assets .		300,000	Accrued taxes, etc.	100,000
Fixed			Mortgage bonds, 4¾%.	15,000,000
assets . $36,700,000			5% preferred stock ...	6,000,000
Less al-			Common stock	6,000,000
lowance			Retained earnings	4,800,000
for de-				
precia-				
tion ... 5,100,000				
		31,600,000	Total liabilities and	
Total assets		$32,300,000	stockholders' equity .$32,300,000	

Perhaps the most striking feature of the financial structure of this company is the large bond issue that represents almost 50% of the total assets. This company could obtain such a large bond issue at favorable rates because of the stable earning records of operating utility companies and also because of the large amount of fixed assets that the company could pledge under a mortgage issue. This company has also issued both common and preferred stock. Earnings retained in the business instead of being paid out as dividends amount to about 28% of its total proprietorship.

Inasmuch as there is no such thing as inventories of finished goods in a utility company and accounts receivable can be collected from customers promptly, the assets of this company are virtually all in the form of fixed assets. As already noted, the company has used bank loans to finance temporarily the expansion of its facilities.

Financial structure of The Long-Shot Printing Company. The balance sheet of a company financed on the proverbial shoestring offers an interesting contrast to those already considered. At the end of its first year of operation, the balance sheet of The Long-Shot Printing Company was as follows:

The Long-Shot Printing Company
Balance Sheet
December 31, 19—

Assets		*Liabilities and stockholders' equity*	
Cash	$ 5,200	Trade accounts payable ..	$ 61,600
Accounts receivable—net .	28,400	Notes payable	18,000
Inventories	52,500	Accrued liabilities	7,600
Total current assets	$ 86,100	Total current liabilities ..	$ 87,200
Deferred charges	3,000	Mortgage on equipment ..	72,500
Machinery and other fixed		Common stock	40,000
assets—net	115,300	Retained earnings	4,700
		Total liabilities and	
Total assets	$204,400	stockholders' equity ...	$204,400

The owners of this company have actually contributed less than 25% of the total capital and are relying heavily on both long-time and short-time creditors. Machinery, which is the principal fixed asset of the company, was purchased on time payments; and the vendor, in order to protect his claim, still holds a first mortgage on the machinery amounting to almost two thirds of its book value. It is doubtful, however, whether even the book value could be realized if it became necessary to sell the machinery at a forced sale. Credit from material suppliers has been used to a point where it exceeds the value of the inventory actually on hand. This means that the vendors are not only financing the entire inventory of the company but other assets as well.

Fortunately, the notes payable are due to an affiliate company that will probably not force their collection at maturity but will accept new short-term promissory notes in exchange for the old ones. Nevertheless, the current ratio is approximately one to one, and any shrinkage in the value of current assets would probably cause immediate financial complications. The company has no bank loan and has been unsuccessful in securing a line of bank credit that it may use in an emergency. It is doubtful if new capital can be attracted to correct the existing weak cash position, with the possible exception that the company might offer a new investor the speculative possibility of sharing in future profits if they are earned. Under such a plan, however, the present management would probably be required to give up part of its control over affairs of the company.

SELECTING CAPITAL SOURCES

Typical financial structures of companies in his industry will give a manager a lead on what the financial community will accept as satisfactory. Oftener than not, however, the great variations in assets, in earnings, and in existing capital structures, in addition to the differences in management, make reliance upon typical industry patterns both unsatisfactory and even dangerous. The policies adopted should be suited to the particular company and to the conditions existing at the time plans for the financial structure are made. The more important factors to consider relate to:

1. Use to be made of the capital.
2. Cost of this capital.
3. Rights granted to persons or concerns from whom capital is secured.

Use of capital. Funds to finance seasonal peaks or other temporary needs can probably best be obtained from short-term creditors, such as commercial banks. This is a comparatively inexpensive way of raising capital and permits an immediate reduction in the total amount owed after the peak requirements are over. On the other hand, capital for fixed assets or for circulating capital that will be permanently retained in the business calls for a different solution. Because the company cannot expect to have cash to return to the lender for several years, owners or long-term creditors present a more logical source for such funds.

The use of capital will also affect the ability of the company to offer the lender some special security for his loan. As an effective guarantee that a loan will be repaid, a company may pledge as security one or more of the following assets: inventories that can be readily sold on the market, machinery that is standard in design and can be easily moved from one plant to another, buildings located and designed so that they are suitable for use by other companies, or marketable securities. If valuable collateral can be given to the lender, borrowing will be much easier. If the funds are to be used for purposes that cannot be made to yield cash readily, the raising of capital from owners is indicated.

Cost of capital. To ascertain the cost of capital, consideration should be given to the original cost of obtaining it, and secondly to the compensation to be paid for its use. In sole proprietorships and partnerships, capital is usually secured by negotiations between the owners and those with whom they are intimately acquainted. Other persons or concerns not intimately acquainted with the owners would not be likely to provide capital to such organizations. The cost of procuring such capital will therefore usually be nominal.

Underwriting and registration. In the case of a corporation, securing capital by issuing bonds or selling stock to the public often involves a considerable expenditure. Frequently these securities are sold through an investment banker who is equipped to reach prospective purchasers of securities, and in most instances substantial commissions must be paid to the investment bankers for these services. Also, complicated legal requirements must be complied with before such securities can be sold. Federal legislation requires the registration of all widely distributed securities with the Securities and Exchange Commission, and the expense involved in preparing the detailed statements required for registration is quite large. In fact, the minimum cost of registration is so large that it makes the public offering of less than $1,000,000 of securities uneconomical.

Private placement of bonds and long-term notes also entails legal and accounting fees and perhaps a fee to a consultant who helps arrange the loan, but the total expense of procuring capital in this manner is normally less than half the expense of a public sale.

Use of rights. Some companies are able to sell securities directly to present stockholders. This applies particularly to the sale of additional stock similar to that already outstanding. The charters of many corporations require that when additional stock is to be sold, it must first be offered to the present stockholders; and if the new stock is offered for sale at a price somewhat lower than the current market price, the present stockholders will probably exercise their right to buy the new issue. When this procedure is possible, the cost of securing additional capital may be reduced substantially. If, however, there is any doubt about stockholders exercising all of their rights, it may be necessary to employ an investment banker to underwrite the issue, in which case many of the expenses incident to an initial public sale of securities must be incurred.

Adjusting sources to prevailing interest rates. The compensation, or interest, that must be paid for the use of capital varies not only according to the use to be made of the capital, but it is often affected materially by the stage of the business cycle. To note an extreme case, speculators in the stock market were willing to pay as high as 20% for call loans during a period in 1929 because of the large profits anticipated from the purchase of securities. During the 1940's, however, the rate of return on call loans fell as low as a fraction of 1%. Although the interest rate on other types of loans will not fluctuate over such a wide range, it does vary; and if a long-term loan is being negotiated, the fluctuation in the interest rate will affect the cost of capital for a period of many years.

Many companies seek to sell bonds and other long-term obligations during periods of low interest rates in order to protect themselves against the higher costs that they anticipate later. In fact, many well-known companies in the United States during recent years have called outstanding securities and refunded these with new obligations bearing a substantially lower rate of interest. Usually these companies had to pay a premium for the privilege of calling their outstanding debt, but they found it profitable to pay this premium so as to secure the lower interest rate over a long period of time.

When interest rates are high, a company may choose short-term obligations, with the expectation that these can be paid off from the proceeds of long-term bonds which will be sold at a later date when interest rates are lower. The success of such a plan depends, of course, upon the accuracy with which movement in interest rates is forecast. There is always the danger that the interest rate on the long-term obligation will be even higher when the short-term notes mature, or other changes may occur that will make it difficult for the company to sell its long-term obligations as planned. Income taxes play such an important part in corporate profits that the timing of changes in capital structure may be based on an attempt to get the most favorable tax status.

Return paid on new stock. When common stock is sold to obtain additional capital, the company does not agree to pay a specific amount of interest for the use of the new capital. Nevertheless,

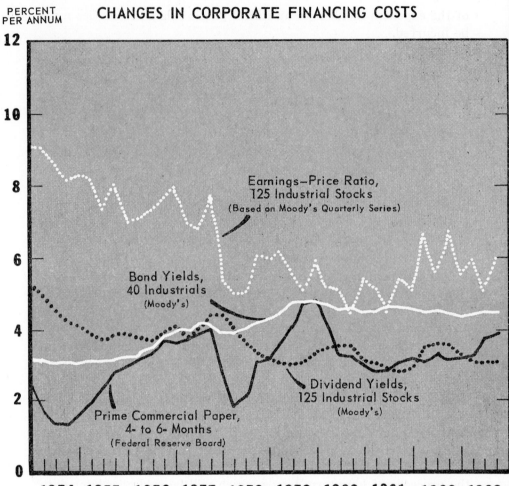

PERCENT PER ANNUM

CHANGES IN CORPORATE FINANCING COSTS

Earnings–Price Ratio, 125 Industrial Stocks (Based on Moody's Quarterly Series)

Bond Yields, 40 Industrials (Moody's)

Dividend Yields, 125 Industrial Stocks (Moody's)

Prime Commercial Paper, 4- to 6- Months (Federal Reserve Board)

1954 1955 1956 1957 1958 1959 1960 1961 1962 1963

the new stockholders will share in any dividends paid, which will reduce the amount of dividends available to the former stock-holders. This sharing of dividends is a cost of capital so far as the former stockholders are concerned.

Many companies prefer to secure capital from the sale of stock, even though it is anticipated that the dividends paid on this stock will exceed the interest that would have to be paid on bonds. Their willingness to pay this larger cost lies in the fact that divi-dends do not have to be paid when there is not a sufficient amount of earnings or cash to justify their declaration. Conversely, inter-est on bonds must be paid regardless of the amount of earnings and the cash on hand. If this interest is not paid on time, the stockholders run the risk of losing control of their company and perhaps their investment in it.

We have assumed that capital can be secured from any source at any time provided the compensation offered for its use is high enough. As a practical matter the sale of bonds or stock becomes so difficult in some phases of the business cycle that new capital is virtually unobtainable from these sources.

Rights granted with new securities. *Rights granted to creditors.* A final factor to be considered in selecting the source from which capital should be secured is the authority exercised by the different contributors of capital. If capital is obtained from short-term creditors, they usually have no control over the affairs of the company. Of course, if the obligations of these creditors are not paid at maturity, they have the right to bring legal action against the company to enforce their claims.

Likewise, long-term creditors ordinarily have no voice in the current operations of the company, although a bond indenture may impose certain restrictions upon the management. For example, the indenture may restrict the amount that the company can invest in fixed assets, it may restrict the future debts that the company can incur, or it may require that the ratio of current assets to current liabilities be not less than 2 to 1.

The loan agreement may also restrict the freedom of the company in the payment of dividends. Some agreements provide that dividends cannot be paid if the ratio between various types of assets is below the standards established or if there is any default in the payment of interest or principal on the long-term obligations. If any of these requirements are not met or if any interest or principal payments on the bonds are not made, the company may be declared in default. In case of default the trustee under the mortgage may be given the right to take legal action against the company in order to enforce the payment of the *total* amount of the bonds. These restrictions may become so burdensome that the management prefers to seek capital from other sources.

Rights granted to stockholders. If capital is secured by the sale of stock, the new stockholders have certain rights with reference to the company. The new stockholders frequently have full voting rights, and they thus become participants in the future management and control of the corporation. Sometimes present stockholders wish to retain a balance of control of the company and do not care to grant the right of participation to others outside of their group. The possibility that the sale of stock will change the balance of power in the board of directors depends, of course, upon the relative size of the new issue as compared with the stock already outstanding, the amount of stock held by those already in power, and the extent to which the present stockholders exercise their right to purchase the new issue.

Preferred stockholders normally do not exercise control over company operations. They usually, though not always, have the right to vote for directors just as do the common stockholders. The par value of a share of preferred stock, however, is typically higher than common stock (often $100 and $10 respectively), so a given investment in preferred stock gives considerably fewer votes than an equal investment in common stock. The common stockholder usually runs a risk of losing control to preferred stockholders only if preferred dividends are unpaid for several years and if the charter provides that voting powers of the preferred stockholders are increased under such circumstances.

SUMMARY

An important task of central management is to see that necessary capital is provided at a reasonable cost and with a minimum of risk. Short-term creditors, such as commercial banks and suppliers of materials, can be used to cover seasonal needs or other temporary requirements. It is risky, however, to place too much reliance on short-term loans because the capital might be withdrawn when business conditions become unsettled, and if used to the maximum for continuing needs, short-term credit will be unavailable for temporary rises in capital requirements.

Long-term loans in the form of bonds or long-term notes are a natural source of capital for companies with relatively stable income. Since the credit is extended for a period of years, various types of protection may have to be granted to the lender, such as mortgage liens, regular reduction of the debt, and limits on additional debts. The greater the stability of a company's earnings and the greater the protections offered, the easier long-term loans will be to obtain and the lower the interest rate. Conversely, unless a company can meet these conditions few, if any, lenders will extend long-term credit. And, from the viewpoint of the company, heavy fixed interest and debt retirement charges may cause financial disaster for concerns with volatile earnings.

Owners' contributions of capital may take the form of either preferred or common stock. The special provisions of preferred stock, like those of bonds, should be tailored in terms of conditions prevailing at the time of issue. Moreover, the total owners' contribution should be a large enough part of the whole financial structure to be able to absorb shocks and losses of bad times. Typically, the owners' capital is increased as a company grows, by retention of earnings, as will be discussed in the next chapter.

The ever changing requirements for capital and the shifting conditions in financial markets make necessary frequent review of a company's sources of capital. In adjusting to these pressures, financial policies adapted to the specific enterprise are a vital management tool.

QUESTIONS FOR CLASS DISCUSSION

1. What effect, if any, should a prediction of "gradual inflation averaging 2% per year" have on the sources of capital used by a company? What inference about the firms' forecasts of inflation do you draw from the lack of trading on equity by many leading companies?

2. (a) Most of the bonds of Matthews Department Store are 4½%, debenture, serial, callable at 106, convertible, junior, publicly issued, registered bonds. Explain what each of these terms means and its significance in financing a company. (b) The store also has authorized and outstanding an issue of $3, cumulative, voting, nonconvertible, callable at $53, privately held, $50 par stock, preferred as to assets and dividends. Explain what each of these terms means and its significance in financing a company.

3. Several major hotel chains have, over the past ten years, changed their policy from owning the hotel properties to leasing them from real estate corporations that were established to buy the hotel and, perhaps, the land on which it sits. How can this be explained? What did inflation through the late 1940's and 1950's and more recent general price movements contribute to such a change? What effect would the age of a building have on such a change in policy? The location of a building in the downtown section of a major city?

4. With corporation income tax rates about 50%, it would be logical to expect corporations to raise capital through short-term or long-term debt instead of stock issues that earn a return only *after* income tax is paid. In fact, there has been no great shift from equity securities to debt securities since the tax rate has been at such high levels. Give several reasons why companies have not made greater use of interest-bearing securities.

5. How can you explain the fact that many companies offer cash discounts to their customers that are substantially higher (terms of 2/10, n/30 are equivalent to about 36% per year) than the interest rate at which these same companies might borrow from commercial banks?

6. The treasurer of a well-established industrial firm is very reluctant to give his short-term or long-term creditors any mortgage liens or other preferred rights. One of his associates criticizes this policy, saying, "You know we are going to pay the money back. Why be so concerned about giving creditors specific protection if they want it?" Do you think the treasurer is taking a sound stand?

7. Suppose the average operating profit of the Red River Power Company had been estimated at $2,300,000. Would you advise present stockholders to sell stock or bonds? What would you advise if the anticipated profits had been $1,500,000? (Assume all securities are sold at their par value.)

8. A steel company was seeking to sell 5% mortgage bonds to finance a major expansion. The company had been earning a small return on invested capital, and the president hoped the new mill would increase profits substantially. The earning record of the company left some doubt whether interest would be earned in slack years. Compare the likely attitudes toward this proposed issue of (a) an investment banker asked to sell the bonds, (b) a preferred stockholder, and (c) a common stockholder.

9. The balance sheet of a strong regional trucking company, whose ton-miles of freight carried had grown more rapidly than the national average but which had still seen some cyclical variations, showed long-term debt amounting to 40% of total liabilities and stockholders' equity. Since this was well above the industry average of about 20%, it had been suggested to the treasurer that he "clean up" the balance sheet by a sale and lease-back of company-owned terminals to reduce the debt ratio to 25%. He, too, was worried since current liabilities amounted to 38% of total liabilities and the equity base thus seemed very thin. Should he pursue the suggestion?

CASE XV

Industrial Scale Company

The Industrial Scale Company is a relatively small manufacturing firm that concentrates on the production of automatic weighing, bagging, and proportioning equipment. Its scales are used in almost every grain elevator in the country and a wide variety of manufacturing plants in which the flow of material is controlled by weighing. Typical uses include the weighing of coal going into steam plants, the automatic proportioning of chemicals being mixed together in chemical plants, and the weighing of batches of material for brick making. Most of the scales are operated by automatic electric controls and weigh with an average accuracy within one-quarter to one-tenth percent. Most of the scales are designed for a particular use in a given factory, and they often include bins and materials handling equipment. Prices per unit range from $1,500 to $25,000.

This company differs from Fairbanks Morse and Toledo in its concentration on specialty products. None of its scales are manufactured by mass production methods. Its plant is set up for job lot production and is equipped for all types of machining operations, sheet metal forming and welding, electric control assembly, and related operations. The company also operates a foundry. Out of a total of almost 400 employees, about 50 are engineers and skilled draftsmen devoted to the design of products for the particular needs of customers.

The company experienced substantial increases in both sales and profits following World War II, as is shown on the accompanying comparative profit and loss statement (page 392).

Top executives are now giving thought to the future size of the company and any additional financing that may be necessary to provide for growth. They recognize that future volume will depend, in part, upon the level of industrial activity and, more specifically, on the general demand for capital goods. In addition, there is a question whether the company will occupy a more, or less, important part in the re-equipping and expansion of factories. In this connection, the company has a new research building, fully equipped to experiment with a variety of problems in weighing and handling materials. The research program also includes a study of automatic electric controls.

The chief financial officer of the company states in this connection, "The usual management problems of a small manufacturing firm are present with us, and are not to be minimized, but it is apparent to us that even though we succeed in solving them, our big problem is to come up constantly with new variations of our machines. Future progress of the company depends on its in-

Industrial Scale Company

Comparative Profit and Loss Statements for Years 1940, 1945, 1950, 1955, 1960 through 1964
(in $1,000's)

	1940	1945	1950	1955	1960	1961	1962	1963	1964
Sales	634	1048	2505	3427	4207	3343	4383	4084	4160
Cost of sales:									
Material	153	254	587	1082	1297	1084	1574	1393	1347
Direct labor	132	195	478	492	722	554	565	482	468
Factory overhead	150	294	599	747	958	777	877	938	944
Gross profit	199	305	841	1105	1230	928	1367	1271	1401
Selling expenses	97	137	288	342	370	362	418	460	472
General and administrative expenses	64	92	210	246	290	320	339	380	407
Other expenses and income, net ..	10	12	52	6	32	15	22	38	66
Retirement plan	...	12	88	110	125	125	140	145	154
Operating profit	27	52	206	400	413	106	458	248	302
Income taxes	4	20	79	193	206	45	221	121	146
Net profit	23	32	127	207	207	61	237	127	156
Cash dividends	18	19	68	48	48	38	68	48	48
Percent of sales:									
Gross profit	31.4	29.2	33.6	32.3	29.2	27.8	31.2	31.1	33.6
Operating profit	4.3	5.0	8.2	11.7	9.8	3.2	10.4	6.1	7.3
Net profit	3.6	3.1	5.1	6.0	4.9	1.8	5.4	3.1	3.7
Ratio—net profit/net worth	5.9	6.3	9.7	14.0	12.7	3.7	12.9	6.7	7.8

Industrial Scale Company

Comparative Balance Sheets for Years 1940, 1945, 1950, 1955, 1960 through 1964
(in $1,000's)

	1940	1945	1950	1955	1960	1961	1962	1963	1964
Cash and government securities	13	60	182	106	347	213	229	117	143
Accounts receivable	65	118	334	382	457	342	391	597	637
Deferred charges	4	6	11	9	20	25	25	26	32
Inventories	138	176	573	1282	906	837	783	905	1197
Total	220	360	1100	1779	1730	1417	1428	1645	2009
Investments	15	15	15	15	15	15	15	62	59
Fixed assets:									
Real estate	79	91	101	101	101	101	71	71	71
Buildings	241	295	421	603	651	656	759	1003	1010
Machinery and equipment	292	379	630	662	510	503	537	575	602
Less: Depreciation	−322	−397	−511	−546	−402	−423	−456	−493	−549
Net total	290	368	641	819	860	837	911	1156	1134
Total assets	525	743	1756	2613	2605	2269	2354	2863	3202
Bank notes payable	50	84	100	500	500	300	0	400	600
Accounts payable	81	116	147	153	122	131	146	178	180
Accrued items	6	11	102	208	74	116	124	251	262
Customers' advances	··	8	19	85	67	19	28	6	···
Federal income tax	5	20	79	193	207	45	226	123	147
Total liabilities	142	239	447	1139	970	611	524	958	1189
Preferred stock	177	172	167	167	167	167	167	161	159
Common stock	100	99	497	497	497	497	497	497	497
Retained earnings	106	233	645	810	971	994	1166	1247	1357
Total stockholders' equity	383	504	1309	1474	1635	1658	1830	1905	2013
Total liabilities and stockholders' equity	525	743	1756	2613	2605	2269	2354	2863	3202
Ratio—current assets/current liabilities	1.55	1.51	2.46	1.56	1.73	2.32	2.72	1.72	1.69

genuity to meet the ever-increasing demand for automatic materials handling machinery."

Machinery in the plant has been kept modern. Until recently, however, many of the buildings dated back to the founding of the company over fifty years ago. To correct this situation, a new office building was built in 1962 and a new building for the machine, tool, and assembly shops was constructed in 1963. An additional investment of about $200,000 for buildings would put the company in first-class physical shape. Idle capacity and overtime could absorb some increase in sales, but additional machinery will be needed if sales expand more than 30%. Added volume would also require a normal increase in circulating capital.

In addition to the $200,000, which, as noted above, might well be invested in facilities, the research engineers recommend an increase of $100,000 per year for additional research. They think such expenditures would return the company a profit in less than ten years. A considerable part of these expenditures might be capitalized, that is, shown as an asset on the balance sheet of the company.

During the last two years the company set up subsidiaries in England and Switzerland to manufacture (largely through subcontracting or licensing) and sell company scales in the British Empire and Europe. Sales volume of the English subsidiary has increased rapidly. While it was hoped that this operation could be expanded through retention of its own earnings and through local borrowing, the rise in sales has been so rapid the parent company will have to make additional investments or slow down the growth. A minimum of $50,000 is needed immediately, and an additional $200,000 will be required in a year or two if business continues to expand at its present rate. Profit prospects are good, though not exceptional, and the usual difficulties of foreign exchange are present.

There is no clear seasonal fluctuation in company sales. The peak requirements for cash usually arise in March when approximately half of the preceding year's accruals for income tax and retirement plan must be paid.

Past expansion of the company has been financed almost entirely through the retention of earnings. For many years, the company has had no mortgages or long-term debts of any kind. When retained earnings were inadequate to meet capital requirements, the company has taken short-term loans from its commercial bank. Policies of the company regarding the use and the sources of funds during the past decade are indicated on the accompanying comparative balance sheet (page 393). The sources of funds and the applications of funds from 1950 to 1964 are summarized in the following figures:

Sources		Applications	
Decrease in cash	$ 39,000	Increases in assets:	
Increases in obligations:		Accounts receivable..	$ 303,000
Bank notes payable..	500,000	Deferred charges ...	21,000
Accounts payable ...	33,000	Inventories	624,000
Accrued items	160,000	Investments	44,000
Federal tax payable..	68,000	Fixed assets	493,000
Increase in retained		Decreases in obligations:	
earnings	712,000	Customer advances ..	19,000
		Preferred stock	8,000
	$1,512,000		$1,512,000

The following ways of meeting future capital requirements are under consideration by company executives:

1. Continue present policies. This is based on the belief that retention of a large portion of the company earnings will be adequate to finance future requirements, except for relatively short-term needs which can be financed through loans from commercial banks. The company has total credit lines of $700,000 from its two banks, $400,000 from Bank A and $300,000 from Bank B. Last year, notes due each bank were paid off for at least 45 days, but this seasonal "clean-up" was done at different times.

2. Obtain a long-term loan from an insurance company or other institutional lender. Such a loan would bear interest of about $5\frac{1}{2}\%$ and would be paid off in equal quarterly installments during a term of 10 to 12 years. Probably $800,000 would be borrowed from this source; but if this were done, the bank loan would have to be paid off and further borrowing from the bank confined to strictly short-term needs. The lender would probably insist on certain types of financial protection, such as a restriction on dividends, current ratio, executive salaries, etc.

3. Issue debenture bonds or bonds secured by a real estate mortgage on the company property. The use of a real estate mortgage might enable the company to get the loan for a longer period of time and make the issue attractive to several different lenders. The interest rate would be about the same as that charged by an insurance company for a term loan; however, underwriters would insist on a 5% to 8% discount for such a small issue.

4. Issue additional preferred stock. The present preferred stock is 5% cumulative, voting, and nonparticipating. Since the present issue is small and closely held, any additional preferred would probably be sold privately. There is no market demand for the present issue.

5. Sell additional common stock. Most of the present 57 stockholders are employees of the company and a majority of the common stock is controlled by the members of the family who are currently senior executives in the company. These executives have no large sums to invest and they have no desire to dilute the value of their shares unless this would result in a clear advantage to the company.

REQUIRED: What action should the Industrial Scale Company take during the next year to provide capital for future operations?

FINANCIAL POLICIES—
PROTECTION OF CAPITAL AND
DISTRIBUTION OF EARNINGS

PROTECTION OF CAPITAL

Business risks. Every concern is subject to numerous risks that may result in a loss of capital. The risks of fire, tornado, or flood are present at all times. Burglary or embezzlement of funds by employees occur occasionally. Accidents or explosions may not only damage property but may injure employees or other nearby persons to whom the company must pay substantial damages.

Changes in style or general business conditions may cause a substantial reduction in goods demanded and force a company to liquidate large quantities of inventory at very low prices. Prices fluctuate, and an investment in goods and machinery at one price level may be worth only 75% of that value at a new price level. Strikes may cause large operating losses. New processes may make fixed assets obsolete. The possibility of war or unexpected taxes and legal restrictions are additional risks faced by almost every enterprise. A formerly profitable company may find itself confronted with so many competitors that none of them can earn a profit.

To pilot a business enterprise through these various hazards is one of the tasks of the manager. In dealing with this problem he must establish policies regarding:

1. Reduction of hazards.
2. Insurance.
3. Hedging.
4. Calculation of profits.

Reduction of hazards. In a variety of ways the risks faced by an enterprise can be reduced. A safety program may reduce the accident hazard, and a deliberate policy to diversify the product line may reduce the wide fluctuations in sales volumes caused by changes in demand for particular products. Likewise, policies regarding number of suppliers, size of inventories, dependence on one large customer, specialization of equipment, and many other factors all have degrees of risk as an important criterion of choice. Reduction of business risks is part of the art of wise management.

There is considerable truth, however, in the saying, "Nothing ventured, nothing won." The very nature of business includes risks that cannot be avoided.

Insurance. One way of dealing with the risks that cannot be eliminated is through insurance. While insurance is not available for all risks, it does offer a protection against loss of capital from some of the major hazards faced by a business concern.

Nature of insurance. Insurance is simply a device for the sharing of risks. Each person faced by a common hazard pays a small known amount called a *premium* in order to avoid a large loss in case the lurking danger should happen to fall upon him. For instance, out of a thousand factories there will be a serious fire in at least one or two each year. The managers of these factories do not know where the fire will break out, yet they can be reasonably sure that some one of them will incur a substantial loss. If each contributes a one-thousandth part of the probable loss during the year, a fund can be built up with which to reimburse the owner of the plant in which the fire does occur.

The main function of an insurance company is to discover a large enough group of people interested in protection against a certain type of hazard so that the premiums received from those who do not suffer any loss will offset the damages that must be paid to those suffering the loss. Many technical problems relating to reserves, settlement of claims, and the like must also be cared for, and the premium will include a charge for administration as well as a share of average settlements.

A wide variety of insurance is available to every business enterprise. The following partial list suggests possible types of protection.

Fire	Plate-glass breakage
Burglary and theft	Steam boiler
Fidelity bonds	Flood
Public liability	Automatic sprinkler
Employee compensation	Tornado
Automobile	Weather
Marine	Life insurance on officers

Although carrying some insurance is now almost universal practice, considerable difference exists in policies regarding:

1. The type and amount of insurance carried.
2. The selection of insurance companies used.

Type and amount of insurance. Some companies carry a minimum amount of insurance. They cover themselves only against large losses, such as losses from fire and explosion, for which the probability of occurrence is quite small. The firms contend that other smaller risks will not break the company and that since there are so many different types of losses to be covered by insurance, only a few of which will probably occur in any one year, it is better to concentrate on eliminating risks and paying such losses as do occur rather than attempt to cover all possible contingencies with insurance.

At the other extreme are the companies that carry insurance against almost every possible type of insurable risk. The executives of these companies argue that business is subject to so many risks that cannot be covered by insurance, such as changes in prices and in volume of demand, that the wise policy is to avoid all risks possible and then concentrate attention upon the remaining uncertainties that are uninsurable.

In between these extremes is a company with assets of several million dollars that followed a policy of insuring only those risks that might result in the loss of more than $10,000. Several of the insurance contracts of the company provide that the first $10,000 of a loss will be borne by the company. This provision is justified on the grounds that the company can stand a loss of $10,000 without seriously impairing its capital, and that over a period of years the premiums paid on insurance for smaller amounts will more than equal the losses.

Railroads and some other business enterprises use a self-insurance plan. They are able to insure themselves because the individual risks involved are scattered and relatively small. For instance, it may be known with reasonable accuracy by a railroad company that a fire will occur in a few of its stations each year; just as it is known by the fire insurance company that each year, in all probability, a fire will occur in several out of a large number of houses that it has insured. It is unlikely that the number of fires occurring in railroad stations during any given year will vary much from the average. A certain amount may therefore be allocated each year by the railroad companies and other similar companies to meet any damages arising from fires or similar contingencies.

Perhaps the greatest difference in actual practice is in regard to insuring the lives of officers. A hosiery company with assets of approximately $7,000,000, for example, carries insurance of $1,250,000 on its president. At one time the president was active in the business, and the success of the business undoubtedly depended upon the continuance of his management. In recent years, however, an executive vice president has been appointed, and it is doubtful that the operations of the company would be seriously handicapped by the death of the president. Nevertheless, the company continues to pay premiums on this large amount of insurance.

Other firms only rarely insure their executives. There appears to be considerable justification in the contention that if the money paid for insurance premiums was spent in training a man to take the place of the executive, the company would eliminate its risk of financial loss and at the same time lend stability to its operations by providing for a successor.

The extensiveness of the insurance program of a company reflects in part the temperament of its administrators. In making a rational appraisal of any insurance program, certainly the following factors should be considered:

1. The nature and extent of insurable risks of the company. If important risks are overlooked, the company may be subjecting itself to unwarranted hazards. On the other hand, if the possible loss from an unfavorable event is overestimated, the company may be spending entirely too much for insurance protection.

2. The adequacy and cost of insurance coverage available, considered in relation to the nature and extent of the hazards faced by a particular company. Care must be exercised to see that the form of policy purchased actually protects the company against important risks. Also, the company may be a preferred risk, and the probability of the unfavorable event may be much lower than that assumed in computing the cost of the insurance. Under such circumstances, the company would be paying more for its insurance than is theoretically justified.

3. The ability of the company to withstand loss. A large company in a strong financial position will not be crippled by a loss of a few thousand dollars, whereas a small enterprise with total assets of only $10,000 to $15,000 might be bankrupt by such an event.

Selection of an insurance company. In all fields of insurance there are several strong, well-established companies that have large investments in marketable securities. Such investments serve as guarantees to the purchaser of insurance that the company will be able to pay even a large loss. Most of these large companies are privately owned corporations, the profits of which accrue to the stockholders.[1] These corporations are commonly referred to as stock companies.

In competition with the large stock companies are smaller stock companies and mutual companies. The smaller stock companies often operate in a limited area and frequently quote lower rates than the large standard companies. The mutual companies, as the name implies, are basically cooperative associations owned by the various policyholders. In calculating the cost of insurance from mutual companies, any dividends should be deducted from the original premium paid, inasmuch as any profits remaining after proper reserves have been provided are distributed back to the policyholders. Another characteristic of a typical mutual company is that the policyholders are subject to further assessment should the regular premiums paid prove inadequate to meet the claims against the company. While such additional assessments are unlikely in the great majority of mutual companies, cases have occurred where these additional assessments have substantially increased the cost of insurance.

The very existence of these different types of insurance companies suggests considerable variation in business practice regarding types of companies selected. A great many firms take the position that they are buying insurance to eliminate risk. Consequently, they wish to place their insurance with those companies whose ability to pay claims is unquestionable.

The other side of the argument emphasizes possible savings in insurance costs. Executives point out that a small company or a mutual company can be just as sound financially as any of the large companies. The additional premium paid to large companies is regarded as unnecessary cost. To be sure, the purchaser of insurance must examine the company with which he places his insurance, but when this company shows a satisfactory financial condition, there is no need to pay higher premiums.

---

[1] This is not true in the life insurance field where mutual companies predominate.

Other factors such as the particular form of the policy offered and the attitude of the company toward adjustment of losses may enter into the selection of insurance companies. As a rule there is not a great difference between companies in these respects.

In practice, insurance is often purchased through an agent or broker who is authorized to represent almost any of the large companies. Often the final selection of companies is left to this agent. While a reliable, well-informed agent may be better equipped to pick specific companies than is an administrative officer who gives only a small part of his time to insurance problems, the financial executive should take at least enough time to decide upon the type of insurance company that is to be used.

Hedging. *Future contracts.* Another protective device that has much the same effect as insurance, but that is fundamentally different in operation, is *hedging*. There are a few basic products, such as wheat, coffee, cotton, and other textile products, that are bought and sold for future delivery by means of future contracts. Anyone interested in a particular commodity can buy a contract by which he agrees to accept delivery of a given quantity of the product several months hence at approximately today's price. The other side of the contract is, of course, the agreement by someone else to deliver the product in the future at approximately today's price.

Hedging process. Firms dealing in products in which there is future trading can protect themselves to some extent against price fluctuation by engaging in hedging. For example, cotton textile mills manufacturing sheets will have to buy raw cotton from which to manufacture the sheets. Before the sheets are sold, the price both of cotton and of sheets may fall, thus causing an inventory loss for the mill. To avoid this loss the mill at the time it purchased the actual cotton for processing might have entered into a future contract to sell cotton. If by the time the sheets were ready for sale the price of cotton had declined, the mill would be able to profit on this future contract. At that time the mill, in order to fulfill its agreement, could go into the market and purchase raw cotton at a price lower than that agreed upon in the future contract. Thus, in event of a fall in the price of cotton, the mill would make a profit on its future contract but would suffer a loss on the cotton actually on hand.

Similarly, if the price of cotton went up during this period, the value of the actual cotton that the mill had in inventory would increase. The mill, however, would have to buy cotton in the open market in order to be able to fulfill its future contract; therefore a loss would obviously be sustained on the contract because the market price of cotton would be higher than the original contract price. The mill, then, that follows the process of hedging is usually in a position to offset losses from one part of a transaction with profits from another part regardless of whether the price goes up or down. Thus, by hedging, a mill may seek to protect itself from adverse changes in raw material prices and concentrate its efforts on securing a normal manufacturing profit.

Limitations on the use of hedging. Hedging can be employed by only a limited number of companies because only a few commodities have organized future trading. Moreover, a perfect hedge requires that the finished goods market, the raw materials market, and the future market all move in harmony with each other. For example, if the price of sheets should fall temporarily because of an overstocked condition of the market while the price of raw cotton remained constant, a sheet mill would suffer an inventory loss even though it hedged its cotton position. In practice, fluctuations in prices of futures, spot raw materials, and finished goods are rarely proportionate with each other. Thus, even in those industries where hedging is possible, there is no complete protection against declines in the value of inventory.

Calculation of profits. Capital should be protected against unwarranted distribution of profits. If the profits are overstated, dividends to stockholders may actually be paid out of capital.

Management has significant discretion in how profit is calculated. And, more than protection against unwarranted dividends is at stake. Income taxes, reputation in the financial community and hence ability to raise new capital, perhaps executive bonuses—all are affected by this calculation. The three main areas where policy guidance is needed on this matter in a going concern are:

1. Accounting reserves.
2. Capitalization of disbursements.
3. Inventory valuation.

Accounting reserves. The extent to which accounting reserves are set up may affect company profits significantly. The issue is what expenses to anticipate in accounting reserves and what decline in asset value to show in such reserves.

Expenses that involve an immediate outlay of cash or those for which there is written evidence, such as a bill from a vendor of raw materials, are easily recognized. On the other hand, expenses that require no immediate outlay of cash but that must be met eventually are subject to greater error or manipulation. Depreciation of equipment and buildings, provision for uncollectible accounts, and anticipated expenses such as unassessed taxes or contingent losses are examples of this latter type. Often the amount of the expense is not known accurately, and opinion as to how much should be charged against the operations of a particular year may differ.

The customary way of handling such items is to make a reasonable estimate of the amount to be charged against operations each year, and then include this figure along with other expenses as a deduction from the gross income in the calculation of the net profit. At the same time a so-called "reserve" is set up on the accounting books in anticipation of the time when the cash payment or discarding of assets will take place. It should be remembered that this reserve is not a special cash fund put aside to meet an anticipated cash payment. Such an account does, however, perform an important function in preventing the overstatement of profits.

Some companies follow a conservative policy and create large reserves, whereas other companies are interested in showing immediate profits and consequently build up reserves slowly. For example, a steel company may depreciate equipment that will not wear out with 20 years of continuous use at the rate of 10% a year because improved methods of operation will probably make this equipment obsolete in 10 years' time. In contrast, a large resort hotel depreciated its equipment at an average rate that would have taken 50 years to cover the original cost, even though this hotel catered to high-class customers who expected up-to-date service and modern equipment.

Capitalization of disbursements. A similar issue arises in the treatment of product development expenses and improvements of fixed assets. Here the cash has been paid out, but the question is whether to treat the disbursement as an expense in the current year, and thereby reduce profits, or to *capitalize* it.

The treatment of patents illustrates the problem. If a company buys a patent, it clearly has an asset the cost of which should be charged as an expense, not all at once, but year-by-year during the life of the patent. But when a patent comes out of the company's research laboratory the situation is not so clear. How much research cost should be attached to that patent, treated as an asset, and written off year-by-year? The more cost that is capitalized as an asset, the higher the profits in the current year.

Likewise, when a wooden floor in the plant is replaced with a concrete one, should the cost be treated as a repair expense or should at least part of the outlay be shown as an asset? Disbursements for intangibles like training or advertising a new product are regularly treated as expenses, but what of the cost of an elaborate demonstration model built for a Worlds Fair though to be used for several additional years?

Inventory valuation. Still another fuzzy area in the computation of profits is valuing inventory. Judgment has to be exercised in deciding what is obsolete, damaged beyond its point of usefulness, or missing an essential bearing. Value depends upon future demand as well as physical condition of the inventory; but future need in the company for repair parts, or demand by customers, often is uncertain. Someone has to say that a specific item is still a good asset or that it should be written off (or down). Here, again, the higher the value attached to inventory carried as an asset, the higher the profit.

Policy issues in profit determination. Limitations surround the size of reserves, the capitalization of costs, and the valuation of inventories. The public accounting profession has devoted much effort to establishing "acceptable practice" in these and related areas. Federal tax regulations of what may be treated as an expense on income tax returns (and hence not taxed) are comprehensive and complex. Securities and Exchange Commission stipulations stress full disclosure in annual financial reports. Nevertheless, a substantial latitude for management action remains.

Central management does not, of course, deal with the numerous specific entries involved in profit computation. Instead, it should set general policies indicating the degree of conservatism to be followed throughout the company. When room for judgment is present, should it be resolved in favor of low value of assets, large reserves, and, to the extent that these entries are acceptable to the

Internal Revenue Service, low taxes? Or will the policy be to show as high a profit as is legitimate within the area of judgment?

A related policy issue is *when* guides for profit computation should be changed. If a given method for computing profits is followed consistently year after year, the effect of the method chosen tends to balance out—profits postponed from last year show up this year and largely offset this year's potential profits that have been deferred until next year. However, if a conservative policy is followed one year and then a liberal policy the next, the effect on results reported for any one year can be much greater. Consequently, many prudently run companies stress *consistency* fully as much as the particular valuation methods employed. Other companies have a policy to postpone and *minimize income taxes* in any legitimate way, including a shift in treatment of matters of judgment if such should be propitious.

Like so many other policy problems we have examined, calculation of profits is interrelated with several aspects of central management. Protection of capital calls for conservative estimation of profits; but income taxes, executive incentives, and ease in raising new capital also should be considered. The policies adopted should reflect a careful weighing of the importance of each aspect to the particular company in its current situation.

DISTRIBUTION OF EARNINGS

Net profits of a company after income taxes belong to the stockholders. This does not mean that stockholders will receive a cash dividend equal to their share of the profits, because the board of directors may decide that part or all of the profits should be kept in the company. Policies regarding the disposition of profits vary widely.

Plowing back profits. A very common practice in American business is to use profits as a source of additional capital. Profitable enterprises typically are growing concerns, and additional capital is required to finance this expansion. Rather than distribute profits in the form of dividends and then seek new capital from other sources, many managements believe that it is wiser to use earnings to meet this need.

One prominent company manufacturing office equipment has relied exclusively on profits to finance its expansion. The founder of this company had an idea but no capital. A loan from a bank was therefore sought to launch this enterprise. The unsympathetic treatment that the founder received at the hands of the bankers made him resolve never to seek their aid again. Finally a partnership was formed with a man who had some capital. The partnership soon became successful enough to finance further expansion from its earnings. This meant, however, that the original partners could not withdraw any profits from the business and that the use of this single source for additional capital would not permit a rapid expansion or exploitation of the market. On the other hand, it did permit a healthy growth of the company, which now enjoys freedom from any long-term financial obligations.

The process of plowing earnings back into the business rather than distributing them in the form of dividends has proved to be such a desirable practice in the past that some authorities advocate a standard policy of distributing no more than half of the profits to the owners in the form of dividends. Such a policy certainly contributes to the financial strength of a company, but it may lead to the accumulation of unnecessary capital if the company is not expanding the scope of its operations. One small company, for example, kept about 20% more capital than it needed for over 10 years simply because the directors thought it was "sound" to plow back half of the earnings.

Except in special circumstances, traditional attitude frowns upon the payment of dividends in excess of earnings. For instance, one company seeking the aid of investment bankers in the public sale of a large block of its stock was required to make a detailed explanation of its dividend policy because it had paid out more money in dividends during the preceding year than it had earned. Without a good explanation, this was regarded as a blot on the record of the company and a handicap to the sale of its securities.

Stable dividends. Another dividend policy, and one that is sometimes contradictory to the idea of plowing back at least part of the profits, is the payment to stockholders of a regular amount of dividends each year. Of course, the payment of regular dividends on cumulative preferred stock is not uncommon, because companies wish to avoid large accumulations of back dividends that must be paid before any dividends can be paid to common stockholders. Common stock and preferred stock on which dividends are paid regularly tend to have a better market and are more likely to be regarded by purchasers as an investment rather than a speculation.

To maintain a stable dividend rate, it is often necessary to retain part of the profits earned in prosperous years, irrespective of the present need of the company for additional capital, so that dividends in less prosperous years can be assured. Thus, a company might pay dividends of $2 a year over a 10-year period rather than pay dividends of $4 a year for the first 5 years and no dividends for the next 5 years. This policy, however, is likely to lead to the payment of dividends in excess of earnings during depression years. If it is clear that a company has refrained from paying large dividends in prosperous years in order to be in a position to continue the stable dividend rate in lean years, then payment of dividends in excess of earnings need not be condemned. On the other hand, if profits are retained in order to provide needed capital, then the payment of dividends in excess of earnings may lead to an inadequacy of circulating capital.

Even within the same business there may be a considerable variation in dividend policy. This may be seen in the charts on page 408, which show profits and dividends of a large beet sugar company from 1929 to 1964.

The Great Western Sugar Company paid regular dividends of $1,050,000 on its 7% preferred stock each year regardless of the size of the profit or the loss. In addition, in all except two years it paid dividends of varying amounts on its common stock. For over ten years the company followed a policy of paying out more than was earned! A sharp change in the common stock dividend policy of the Great Western Sugar Company is evident in 1947. Prior to that date, dividends were very high in relation to profits and tended to vary. After 1947, dividends were relatively stable and permitted some retention of profits.

Need for adequate retained earnings. Net profits left within a company are generally shown in a surplus account, which is more aptly called "earnings retained in the business." [2] It is illegal to pay dividends that wipe out the retained earnings account and create a capital deficit; in fact, most companies prefer to show a surplus that is much larger than current dividend payments. A relatively large retained earnings account is desired because any

---

[2] Surplus may, of course, be created in other ways, such as by purchasing bonds at less than par value and retiring them or by reducing the par or stated value of stock.

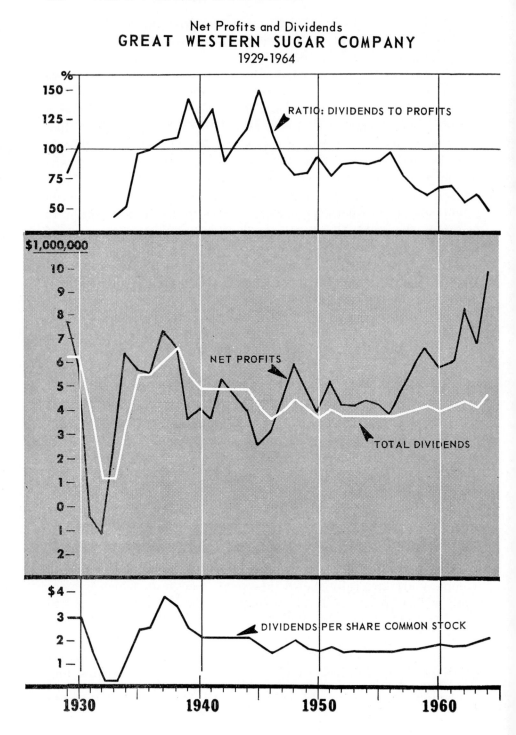

Net Profits and Dividends
GREAT WESTERN SUGAR COMPANY
1929-1964

operating losses or dividends in excess of profits may be charged against this account without impairing the original capital invested.

Before leaving this topic, one distinction should be made clear. The condition of the retained earnings account may be a restraining factor on the payment of dividends if the account is not as large as the management believes it should be. On the other hand, a large retained earnings account does not mean that the company is in a position to pay dividends. The capital represented by this account may be tied up in buildings or inventories, and dividends are paid in cash—not bricks or commodities. In addition to adequate retained earnings, there must be adequate cash in order to pay dividends. This goes back to the need for additional capital that has already been discussed in connection with plowing back earnings.

Conclusion regarding dividend policies. Major factors to be considered in the distribution of profits may be summarized as follows:

1. Present cash position and need for additional capital.
2. Desire to maintain a stable rate of return to stockholders.
3. Adequacy of the retained earnings account to meet present and future reductions due to dividends and losses.

In establishing a dividend policy, the attitudes of people outside the company should be considered as well as of those inside. A stable dividend payment, for instance, will affect not only the income of present stockholders but also the marketability of stock to new holders. Likewise, care to maintain a strong cash and retained earnings position will influence the credit rating of a company and its ability to borrow long-term capital. In addition, the effect of high income taxes on large individual stockholders should be kept in mind when the dividend policy is set.

SUMMARY

The distribution of earnings is a fitting subject with which to close this review of business policies, inasmuch as profits are the indicator of the overall success or failure of a company in a competitive, free-enterprise economy. Major policy issues of sales, purchasing, production, personnel, and finance have been considered. For convenience in grasping the range of policies as a whole, a summary of the main topics discussed is given in the following outline.

Summary Outline

MAJOR POLICY ISSUES IN BUSINESS ENTERPRISES

SALES

A. *Products and services*
  1. Diversification vs. specialization
  2. Product differentiation
  3. Frequency of design change

B. *Customers*
  1. Types of consumers
  2. Location of consumers
  3. Channels of distribution
  4. Size of customers

C. *Prices*
  1. Relation to competing products
  2. Relation to costs
  3. Prices of individual items
  4. Quantity and trade discounts
  5. Price changes

D. *Sales promotion*
  1. Sales appeal
  2. Advertising
  3. Personal solicitation

PRODUCTION AND PURCHASING

A. *Extent of vertical integration*

B. *Production processes*
  1. Choice of technology
  2. Division of labor and automation
  3. Size and dispersion of plants
  4. Involvement in process research

C. *Capacity and facility balance*
  1. Peak vs. normal load
  2. Backward taper of capacity
  3. Provision for growth

D. *Maintenance and replacement*

E. *Make-or-buy supplies and services Pur.*

F. *Selection of vendors Pur.*
  1. Number of vendors
  2. Type of vendors

G. *Timing production and purchasing*
  1. Stock vs. to-order
  2. Size of inventory and orders
  3. Stabilizing production
  4. Anticipating price changes

FINANCE

A. *Uses of capital*
  1. Fixed asset investment
  2. Uses of circulating capital
  3. Mergers and acquisitions

B. *Sources of capital*
  1. Owners
  2. Long-term creditors
  3. Short-term creditors
  4. Financial structure

C. *Protection of capital*
  1. Reduction of hazards
  2. Insurance
  3. Hedging
  4. Calculation of profits

D. *Distribution of earnings*
  1. Plowing back earnings
  2. Stable dividend rate
  3. Adequacy of surplus

PERSONNEL

A. *Selection*
  1. New employees
  2. Promotion
  3. Discharge

B. *Training*
  1. Place in management
  2. Specific purposes
  3. Types of training

C. *Compensation*
  1. Amount of pay
  2. Methods of payment

D. *Arrangements for work*
  1. Hours of work
  2. Vacations
  3. Working conditions

E. *Employee services*
  1. Social and recreational
  2. Protection from risks

F. *Industrial relations*
  1. Character of relations
  2. Support of union
  3. Scope of bargaining
  4. Use of outside agencies

No single outline can include all policy questions. Any specific company will have problems peculiar to itself or its industry. Also, there are many minor policies, consideration of which would have cluttered up the broad picture we have been seeking. The approach to central management planning suggested by the outline of policies is useful because (1) almost every enterprise will face probably 90% of the issues in some form, and (2) the sequence provides a logical flow of thought about a company as a whole. We need some structure for our thinking about general management problems, and this one has proven to be highly practical in many companies.

A danger in any pattern for analysis into parts and subparts is that in identifying each part we lose sight of their interrelationships. Throughout the preceding chapters attention has frequently been called to the interdependence of problems of administration, and cases have been used to emphasize that real problems do not stay in compartments that are helpful to orderly thinking. Seeing these mutual relationships, and developing a sense of relative importance, are vital to integrated understanding of the job of central management.

The execution of business policies requires organization, resources, and operative management. It is to these subjects we shall give attention in the following parts of this book.

QUESTIONS FOR CLASS DISCUSSION

1. Some companies seek to reduce their risks by diversification of product lines. Examples are a steamship company going into the chemical business; a rubber concern, into television broadcasting; a whiskey firm, into pharmaceuticals. What are the advantages and the disadvantages of this way of protecting capital?

2. Stewart Warner Corporation each year spends for replacements of machinery a sum equal to its annual depreciation charge on machinery. Does this policy assure that capital invested in machinery is kept intact? Do you think this is a wise policy for all companies to follow?

3. Explain exactly how the creation of an accounting reserve protects the capital of a company. Would the creation of cash funds accomplish the same purpose?

4. A number of manufacturing concerns have formed a mutual insurance association. The association (a) devotes considerable effort to reducing fire hazards in its member plants, (b) reinsures with a large stock company against very large losses, and (c) gives its members who cooperate with the prevention program somewhat lower rates than those charged by stock companies. Would a company be wise in placing its insurance with such an association? Do you think the general approach has other applications?

5. Suppose a textile mill received an order from the government for 40,000 blankets to be delivered in equal monthly shipments during the ensuing year. Each blanket requires 1 pound of cotton and 2 pounds of wool. Trace step by step the hedging operation this company might follow to protect itself against a rise in raw material costs before the order was completely filled. If the mill had received no advance order, but instead had manufactured blankets for stock so as to be in a position to fill customer orders as they were received, what kind of hedging program should have been followed?

6. From 1958 through 1963 the percent of passenger miles flown by jet aircraft in United States scheduled airlines increased from 8% to 83%. During this same period the airlines reported very low profits. Their policy was to depreciate the planes rapidly in order to maximize cash flow to pay for the jets and to get out from under the very heavy debt burden and high interest charges incurred to purchase the planes. Now the heaviest burden of payment is in the past and the prospect of higher operating profits is ahead—as is the possibility of supersonic transports, which will be far more expensive than any equipment yet purchased. What financial policies relating to calculation of profits and earnings distribution can you recommend for such a future?

7. Would you, as a stockholder, prefer the distribution of a large or a small percentage of net profits in the form of dividends? Suppose you were a member of the board of directors and had shared responsibility for deciding what dividends to pay, would your answer be the same? Finally, suppose you were an executive of the company, interested in building up the financial strength of the company so as to insure continuation of your job, would your answer still be the same?

8. At some stage in a corporation's growth, its common stock, formerly held by a few individuals, is likely to be sold publicly to many people. Explain how such a sale of stock, and even its anticipation, is likely to affect dividend policies.

9. Several noted economists have, at times, recommended "sabbatical leaves" for businessmen to refurbish their intellectual capital. These recommendations have been an offshoot of serious studies of education as a capital-acquisition process and of investment in human capital. Might a company capitalize the cost of such sabbatical leaves? Or the cost of sending high-salaried executives to 6-week or 13-week executive training programs? Or the cost of indoctrination programs for new employees who will not be earning their keep for some time?

CASE XVI

Premier Paper Company

Following his review of the year-end financial statements (see Exhibit 1), the treasurer of Premier Paper Company was considering recommendations to the president and the board of directors for changes in financial policy. He felt that certain changes in policy in recent years had strengthened the capital position of the company, and he was considering what else might be done.

Premier Paper Company is a manufacturer of fine writing and printing paper. Its plants are located in the paper-making district of central Wisconsin. The company was incorporated over 40 years ago as the consolidation of two small paper companies near Appleton and has grown through increased sales and acquisition of other small firms to an important position in the high quality and specialty paper industry. Since the original merger, three competitors have been purchased and equities in four other subsidiaries have been acquired. The company owns the majority of the stock of each of these subsidiaries.

The principal directors of Premier are all active officers of the company and include Albert Warren, president; A. M. Strawn, vice-president of sales; and L. F. Pearce, treasurer, as well as several other officers. Mr. Warren, now 83 years of age, has been general manager of the company since its founding and is still active, although recently he has given much of the responsibility to Mr. Strawn, who is assistant general manager in addition to his sales duties. All of the major executives have been with the company for twenty years or more.

Capital stock. There are three classes of Premier capital stock—employees' stock, preferred stock, and common stock. Employees' stock is preferred as to assets and is entitled to 7% cumulative dividend. Any employee continuously employed for one year or longer may subscribe for not more than $5,000 of this stock. Purchases may be made in installments. The certificates are issued when payment has been made in full. Stock may be resold only to the company. This stock has no voting rights. The company also has the option to call this stock for redemption on any dividend date in whole or in part and to select the shares called for redemption at a slight premium plus accumulated dividend.

Preferred stock is entitled after the employees' stock to 6% cumulative dividends and, in the event of liquidation, to payment of par and accumulated dividends. It may be called for redemption at $105 and accumulated dividends on any dividend date. If two dividends are passed, or if the value of net working capital (current assets minus current liabilities) is less than the aggregate par value of employees' and preferred stock outstanding, the pre-

EXHIBIT 1

Financial Statements

(000's omitted)

Account	Current Year	Past Year	Previous Year	Previous Year	Previous Year	10 Years Ago	15 Years Ago	20 Years Ago
Net Sales	$12,136	$10,462	$ 9,572	$ 9,942	$ 9,232	$ 5,035	$ 4,661	$ 2,819
Profit after Tax	593	489	378	346	311	223	288	144
Cash	$ 263	$ 336	$ 166	$ 316	$ 238	$ 478	$ 194	$ 107
Accounts Receivable	1,698	1,353	1,264	1,053	1,064	522	675	802
Inventories	3,704	2,861	2,874	2,191	2,198	1,241	1,169	1,015
Prepaid Insurance	277	206	250	269	247	230	205	179
Net Property	3,913	3,100	3,192	2,581	2,606	2,685	3,103	3,775
Goodwill	5,492	5,492	5,492	5,492	5,492	5,492	5,492	5,998
Investments in Subsidiaries	889	1,460	1,460	938	888	592	1,762	1,456
Total	$16,231	$14,808	$14,698	$12,840	$12,733	$11,240	$12,600	$13,332
Notes Payable	$ 300	$ 225	$ 51	......	$ 50	$ 200	$ 500	$ 600
Accounts Payable	590	208	534	$ 297	347	221	103	74
Tax Reserve and Accruals	748	497	463	215	310	96	355	53
Mortgage Payable	944	1,000	1,000	......	......	......	......	......
Employees' Preferred	350	350	365	346	332	316	353	336
6% Preferred ($100 par)	939	939	939	953	953 [1]	1,623	1,833	1,833
Common Stock	2,016	2,016	1,940	1,940	1,940	1,940	1,940	2,024
Surplus	9,303	8,355	8,188	7,871	7,718	6,844	7,438	8,412
Replacement Reserve	688	865	865	865	730	......	......	......
Inventory Reserve	353	353	353	353	353	......	78	......
Total	$16,231	$14,808	$14,698	$12,840	$12,733	$11,240	$12,600	$13,332

[1] Mandatory sinking fund of 20% of annual net income after taxes was made permissive by stockholder vote. Fund used to redeem at call price.

ferred stockholders may elect a majority of the board of directors so long as a default exists.

Ownership of the common and preferred stock is almost identical. The bulk of both issues is owned by executives of the company, relatives, and foundations or trusts. All of the preferred and a large part of the common shares outstanding were issued as stock dividends and were not, therefore, paid for in cash. There is an uncertain, unlisted market for the stocks.

The president of the company, his wife, and a foundation he established own over 50% of both the preferred and common stock. There are two other very large holdings within his family.

Employees can, and some do, own some of the regular preferred and common stock of the company as well as the employees' preferred stock. Employees are represented by an A. F. of L. union with which the company has excellent relations. For example, the men have refused in the past to 'join in sympathy strikes that have crippled other manufacturers in the area. Among other factors, the employee stock ownership plan contributes to these cordial relations, in the opinion of the executives.

Dividends on employees' stock have been paid in full every quarter. Dividends on preferred stock have been paid with the exception of a period in the 1930's when dividends were passed for four years and paid only in part for another three years. All accumulated dividends were made up in the early 1940's. Since then, current dividends have been paid. Cash dividends were paid on the common stock during the early years of the company's operation at rates of 10 to 12%. Since the early 1930's, no dividends have been paid on this stock. A requirement of the mortgage loans used to finance the most recent acquisition of a competitor is that dividends on common stock can be paid only if net working capital is 150% of the first mortgage debt. The only other restrictive covenant is that any proceeds from any sale of the assets mortgaged must be applied to pay off the mortgage.

A competitor (Alpha Paper Co.) was acquired two years ago. A $1,000,000 mortgage loan at 4½%, due in twenty years, was made to finance the acquisition and to provide funds to erect a new plant for one of the subsidiaries. Investments in other subsidiaries also required large borrowings, mainly from banks. These amounted at the maximum to $950,000 in 1930. The loans were paid off slowly over the next two decades.

Comments on financial statements. Inventories—it is typical of a mill in the fine paper industry to have a large inventory. Prepaid insurance—this is the cash surrender value of an insurance policy on the life of the president and of a new policy on Mr. Strawn. Investments in subsidiaries—this represents the cost of controlling equities in the subsidiary companies mentioned before.

The Alpha Paper Co. has just been liquidated. Notes payable—the company has established credit lines with eight banks and uses these at various times. Currently, the money is owed to four banks at 4% interest.

Several years ago the management provided a replacement reserve and an inventory reserve in the surplus account (see Exhibit 1). This was done because the executives contemplated extensive replacement of fixed assets for efficient operation and rising paper prices as well as increasing raw material prices for an extended period. In reviewing this policy, the treasurer noted that fine paper production had increased threefold in the past 35 years. This increase was by no means steady since output was almost the same in 1940 as it was in 1930. However, the general trend was definitely upward. Over the past five years, the index of wholesale paper prices had indicated an increase of about one quarter in the average of all paper prices.

Views differing somewhat from those of Premier executives have recently been expressed by the head of the American Paper and Pulp Association. He noted that expansion plans of the major producers were "flattening out." Plants scheduled for completion in the 1960's were being delayed a year or two. His own company was postponing several projects. He concluded, however, "I haven't run across anyone who is bleary-eyed from lack of sleep over our situation."

Five years ago the company switched to the LIFO method of inventory valuation. The effect of this in the year the switch was made was to state inventories at about $600,000 less than if the prior year's method had been applied in determining cost. The net result was to lower the reported gross profit.

Mr. Pearce, the treasurer, has for some time been considering making recommendations on common stock dividends. All executives are currently paid on a straight salary basis. Salaries are of course changed from time to time, but there is no bonus or profit-sharing plan. Executives and directors who own stock, as well as minority stockholders, have expressed considerable interest in receiving cash dividends from common stock.

Mr. Pearce will meet at the end of the month with Mr. Warren, who now limits his duties to monthly meetings with the other executives and quarterly meetings of the board. Mr. Strawn carries on operations at other times.

REQUIRED: (a) Evaluate the financial policies of this company. Have they been useful in promoting the welfare of the company? Do they provide for protection of capital and sound distribution of earnings?

(b) State your recommendations for changes in financial policy.

INTEGRATING CASES
Financial Policies

WESTERN PLYWOOD MILLS, INC.

Western Plywood Mills, Inc., a company engaged principally in the manufacture and sale of Douglas fir plywood, is subject to financial pressures from many sources. The proposed acquisition of new timberlands for an assured source of supply of logs, the expansion of plant to maintain its position in the industry, the addition of warehouses to meet competitors' selling methods, and pressure from stockholders for increased dividends are currently straining the company's financial resources. These pressures are likely to increase in the future, and it is necessary for the officers of the company to review thoroughly its capital structure in order to maintain a sound financial position.

This company was organized about fifteen years ago by a group of employees who saw the possibility of a major expansion of the plywood industry. This method of organization and ownership is fairly common in the industry, and currently about 15% of total production is carried on by worker-owned companies. Since its founding, the company has been successful, and its sales now amount to about 4% of the industry total. However, its portion of industry sales is not as large as before. Five years ago Western's sales were 6% of the industry total and its share has dropped steadily since then.

Plywood is made from many different kinds of softwood and hardwood. The major species used, however, is Douglas fir, which is also known as Oregon pine. Douglas fir plywood is widely used for many exterior and interior construction purposes. Fabrication begins with the debarking of choice "peeler" logs. These logs, sawed into sections, are first skinned with a debarking knife. They are then centered on a lathe that rotates the section against a long, hollow-ground blade, and a sheet of smooth veneer is cut from the entire length of the section. This wide ribbon of veneer is cut or "peeled" from the section much as a large roll of paper is unwound. The veneer is then carried on a conveyor to the clippers where it is cut to the desired width. After sorting for quality, the sheets are conveyed to an oven dryer. Following the drying, waterproof glue is applied by rollers to the surfaces of the veneer layers, and the plies are cemented together with the grain of each sheet at right angles to that of its neighbor. Heat and pressure in a hot press weld the panels together to form a permanent bond.

A tremendous expansion has taken place in the industry, which in the past thirty years has increased plywood production from about 235 million square feet to about 10 billion square feet.

In making plywood, only the bottom 55% of a Douglas fir tree can be used. The top 10% is used for making sawmill or dimension lumber and the balance for shop lumber that goes into doors, pipe, tanks, etc. To meet the growing demand for plywood, the industry has moved south from Washington through Oregon into California in its search for good supplies of top-grade peeler logs. Less than one third of all fir logs are of peeler grade, and clear-growth, virgin timber with knot-free trunks is fast disappearing.

Shortages of high-quality logs and continued expansion have forced some of the larger companies to purchase their own timberlands so as to assure themselves of logs at a constant price. On the average, the cost of logs amounts to 55% of total manufacturing costs. Once timberlands are purchased, it is necessary for a company to enter other parts of the lumber industry so as to utilize the balance of the fir tree that cannot be used for plywood. Roads and sawmills have to be built, and investment in machinery must be made in order to develop the timberlands.

A revolution in industry marketing practices has gone along with the expansion in production. At one time the plywood mills sold through agents who handled the entire distribution program. Now marketing emphasis has shifted, and a large proportion of output is sold through controlled channels. The major companies have their own warehouses and their own salesmen. Some of them engage in extensive brand promotion. For example, United States Plywood's consumer advertising program featuring its brand name "Weldwood" is very extensive. Western Plywood currently markets 13% of its output through its own warehouses. It would like to extend its chain of warehouses and its dealer promotion program so that 50% of its sales are made through these channels within the near future. This will give it a good start towards a strongly competitive marketing organization.

The original group of 49 worker-owners who started the company have, by now, changed their attitude toward the use of profits. From the beginning, the company has financed its expansion by plowing back profits, as is shown by the increase in earned surplus to about $5.5 million. Many of the older owners have retired or died and only half are still active in the company. More of these will retire in the near future. Their interest is now in having a higher percentage of profits paid as dividends. They also want a ready market for their stock so that it can be sold quickly, thus providing an emergency source of cash. Some of them would like to sell their stock now, so that they can diversify their investments. In the past, the company has purchased common stock from estates of deceased partners, and several retired partners are urging that the company adopt a policy of buying back any stock that former partners wish to sell. Retained earnings have provided the major source of funds in the past, as is indicated in the table below. The treasurer is, however, by no means sure that profits will be sufficient for the capital needs that he sees arising in the near future.

SOURCES OF FUNDS
(000's omitted)

	Current Year	Last Year	Preceding Year
Net profits	$ 644	$1,600	$1,390
Depreciation and depletion	247	121	179
Long-term bank loans	(94) minus	(111) minus	384
Liquidation of other assets	....	62	302
Total	$ 797	$1,672	$2,255

USES OF FUNDS

Increases in working capital	(252) minus	449	218
Plant & equipment additions	593	699	208
Timber additions	162	30	1,350
Dividends	258	398	398
Investments	....	75	13
Deferred assets	36	21	68
Total	$ 797	$1,672	$2,255

The company estimates that an expenditure of $3,600,000 during the next year will enable it to acquire timberlands that will be adequate to provide the supply of logs necessary within the foreseeable future. Executives believe these timberlands could be purchased at an average cost that would yield 7% per annum before income taxes, based on current log prices, when all the timber is cut. It might be anywhere from fifteen to thirty years before all the timber is cut, however, and the realized profit would depend upon the trend in prices during that interval. The profit earned in any one year would depend upon how many logs were cut, and the margin between the current value of the logs and depletion, property taxes, logging, and other costs.

Additions to plant and equipment, necessary to exploit this supply of logs, will call for expenditures of $1,000,000 within the next two years. Finally, an additional $1,200,000 will provide the working capital necessary for extended production operations and for expanding the company's marketing program. Executives are confident that these additional investments in production and marketing facilities will yield about the same profit as the company is earning on its present assets, assuming industry conditions continue as they have prevailed in the last few years. Detailed estimates have been postponed until the basic policy regarding expansion is settled.

The past profit history of the company has been good, as is shown by the income data below.

SELECTED INCOME DATA
(000's omitted)

	Net Sales	Net Profit	Dividends
Current year	$7,475	$ 644	$258
Preceding year	8,590	1,600	398
" "	7,500	1,390	398
" "	5,450	789	89
" "	5,170	233	...
" "	5,430	304	...
" "	6,025	338	...
" "	5,650	352	42
" "	5,520	596	168
" "	3,860	339	310

Continuous future profits are not assured, however. Plywood has shown considerable price instability in the past. This affects sales and also causes inventory losses, as was true in the last year. Price drops are caused largely by the activity of small manufacturers who buy veneer and make plywood from it. These companies are typically weak financially and will often cut prices rapidly and drastically in an attempt to maintain sales volume. Although sales prices of the finished plywood may fluctuate widely, costs typically do not. Both log costs and labor costs (which together make up 85% of total costs) have risen rather steadily since the founding of Western Plywood. Log prices on the open market occasionally drop 10% from one year to the next, but more commonly increase because of the shortage of peeler logs. Labor rates have risen 110% on the average, in the past ten years.

Beside the problem of how much capital the company needs and how it should be obtained, the treasurer is concerned with the allocation of any funds obtained among the various claims on capital. The officers feel that it would be highly desirable for the company to own additional timberlands and would prefer to buy them if the capital is available. Purchase of timberlands is not absolutely necessary, however. The government owns two thirds of the timber in the Northwest and each year cuts and sells at auction enough peeler logs to meet about one quarter of the industry's needs. In addition, there are private timber operators who supply logs to the open market. Before World War II, most plywood companies bought their logs on the open market and some of them have continued to do so since. Open market prices of logs naturally fluctuate and may rise quite steeply when demand is high. Three years ago, for example, they increased 33% over the year before. A decision not to buy timberlands would also mean a reduction by about one half of the contemplated expenditures for additional plant and equipment.

The company sees no other way of meeting competition than to continue the planned marketing program, which calls for additional warehouses, more finished inventory, and expanded sales promotion efforts.

The desires of the stockholders pose a difficult problem. The treasurer is not sure just how far the company should go toward increasing annual dividends, nor is he certain what should be done about the stock held by retired employees.

The company's balance sheets for the current year and past year are as follows:

BALANCE SHEETS
(000's omitted)

Current Assets	Current Year	Past Year
Cash	$ 675	$ 569
U. S. Government Bonds	262	262
Accounts Receivable	609	405
Inventories	869	1,508
Total	$2,415	$2,744
Investments	544	544
Plant and Equipment, net	2,315	1,917
Timber	1,930	1,820
Deferred Charges	266	230
Total Assets	$7,470	$7,255
Current Liabilities		
Loans Payable	$ 180	$ 94
Accounts Payable and Accruals	837	1,000
Total	$1,017	$1,094
Long-Term Loans [1]	179	273
Capital Stock	414	414
Capital Surplus	367	367
Retained Earnings	5,493	5,107
Total Liabilities and Capital	$7,470	$7,255

[1] Repayable at a future rate of $74,000 per year.

REQUIRED: What financial policies with respect to uses of capital, sources of capital, and dividends do you recommend Western Plywood Mills, Inc., follow during the next few years?

CENTRAL WIRE COMPANY

Betty McCormick, trim, charming, and gracious, smiled at me as I walked across the soft green of the lawn from the drive. "Jack called a few moments ago," she said, "to say that he would be delayed. Shall we sit in the garden for awhile until he returns?"

As always, I admired her walk as she led me around the side of their country home. We stopped beneath the red oaks at the edge of the gardens. "Here are the martinis, dry as you like yours." She poured with the graceful motions of experience.

We chatted for awhile, then Jack came up the drive. I caught the black flash of his Mercedes 300 SL; by the time the dying roar of the engine had faded from the ice-blue air of the late afternoon, he was with us. After several minutes, Betty left to confer with the children's nurse and the cook.

Jack began. "Let's postpone your forecast of economic conditions until after dinner. Right now I'd like to talk about some general company matters, if you don't mind.

"You remember that last year I worked out a deal with my father whereby I would take over the presidency since I wasn't learning enough as assistant to the executive vice-president. I'd like to just sit here and free-associate as I reflect a bit on what I've seen. Then perhaps you could give me your reactions to my appraisal." (Central Wire was family owned; Jack and his father held the controlling interest.)

"You remember that I was doubtful about that order of magnet wire from Sylvania for their telephone sets. We had always specialized in very high-quality copper wire, plain or coated with silver, nickel, or gold or insulated with Formvar, polyurethane, teflon, or nylon. Usually our wire is sold for pretty fancy electrical or electronics stuff, but in this one case we took on some price business to fill up the Indiana plant. I pushed it through for three reasons. First, so that we could get experience in marginal cost pricing. None of our men had ever thought this way before and I wanted to educate them to it. Second, so that we could run the Indiana plant full blast to see if we could get the bugs out under capacity operating conditions. My third reason was to see what a different product grade and quality really meant to the whole operation. The trouble is that I did the selling and so the order was outside our salespeople's experience. They haven't really learned anything yet about this grade of product. The costs were above those that we predicted, but that's all right; I view it as a training cost. The order still represented a big contribution to overhead that we would not otherwise have had. Now Sylvania is back. The wire was a bit better than they had expected. It handled and performed well for them. They want to give us more big contracts. What would be the influence on our organization? We would have to bid in below full cost. It would overload the plant even on a two-shift basis and it would take out some of our capacity for specialized business. Of course, we don't have the specialized business on the books now. We would have to grub for it as always. While we are getting it, the plant will operate just as it used to, up and down at less than full capacity. I suspect that under current conditions profits would be about the same either way, with or without the Sylvania orders; but what profits might be in the future I am uncertain about.

"If we take on the telephone wire grade, then we will also have to rethink our purchasing. In the past we have bought only special brands from two suppliers. I think we could buy copper rod (which we draw down to wire) to specifications rather than by brand name or number. If we can do this—that is, buy to specification—then we can get the copper companies to sell us lower-priced rod according to published specifications.

"However, there is something about buying these two brands. We have learned from sixty years' experience that these are the best for our high-grade wire. Our research section agrees with my father on this. They are working to isolate the reasons why, but they don't have any answers as yet and they probably won't for a long time to come, if ever. But, buying by brands means that we stick with two sources. If we bought lower-priced wire, we could get it from several other sources. If we bought by specifications, then we could presumably get their highest grade wire from these other sources as well.

"You can make an awful lot of money speculating in copper inventories. We are in touch with copper producers and are a large user of copper rod, so we should have the knowledge to be able to buy throughout the market rather than just rely on two suppliers and purchase automatically from them.

"There are many firms around who claim that their brands are just as good as those we use; but to really find out, we would have to buy a large amount of inventory, probably as much as $130,000 worth. To find out how good the other companies' high-grade copper rod is, we would have to test it under innumerable operating conditions. We would not know whether or not it worked well until it broke down in our own processes and caused us trouble and until customers complained. Just off the top of my head, I think it would take us two years to find out anything. But, if we did learn something, I estimate that we could reduce our raw materials cost about $30,000 a year just by buying the highest grade of copper rod to specification or by using additional suppliers for the very highest quality. Perhaps there is some other way to reduce purchasing cost that I haven't thought of.

"The Indiana plant, in its three years, has not really produced as it should. Roy Harson, the executive vice-president, told me over a year ago that he knew why. The Sylvania order was an attempt to give them volume experience. Perhaps the people there just don't have the total fund of experience necessary. Wire drawing and stranding is a high-speed operation. It requires very delicate control of tension and of lubricants. So far, here at the Camden plant, we haven't found any substitute for the sight, the ear, and especially the touch of skilled foremen or head machine tenders. In the home plant we have several machines with the fanciest of electrical sensing devices and electronic controls, but they are not as effective in achieving output and preventing breaks as are our good machine hands. Pulling the wire through the dies at rapid speeds, laying it properly, and winding it without breaks are the real keys to cost controls and profits in this business. Product innovations count—new coatings, larger spools, annealing to customer specifications—but any smart merchandiser can think of those things by keeping close tabs on customer needs. It's getting the wire through the machinery that pays off.

"Camden worries me." Jack stopped and swirled the remains of one martini. "Something is wrong in our labor force. The older men, the experienced men, are topnotch. They have been with us for a long time—15, 20, 25 years—and make up a sizeable group who know each other well. They work together effectively. I am talking about the foremen, the chief machine tenders, and the lead hands. It is the work attitude of the younger fellows that disturbs me. High school graduates or not, they don't seem to want to help and to learn on a wire drawing machine. The work is easy, it's not hard, it just takes patience and application and careful attention. From what I have been able to gather by talking with a couple of them, the work is just not glamourous enough. The pay is low here, less than they can earn at RCA or Owens-Corning, but more than at Campbell Soup. But the work is steady, it's long-term work. I guess it's just not flashy enough for them, it's not a big enough deal. I don't really know. We have a high turnover, higher than I like. Our benefits are okay; they are not those of an auto plant, but they're decent for this area. On the whole, I think the pay is fair for the area and the working conditions are good for an industrial plant. It's clean, not excessively heavy physically, the plant is noisy. We have few grievances, just a lot of turnover. This hurts training and it's no good for the future. The plant manager is not at all concerned. Production will get out okay this year and next year and the year after that. We all agree to this, but I'm still concerned. I'm not sure that raising the general level of our wages or the rates for the less skilled grades would help. This is certainly one of the points on which your advice would be helpful.

"You know about the research effort I instituted two years ago. It really should be called development work. The major project we are on is annealing the wire, and I think there are some definite long-range possibilities here. My father and Harson don't agree. They don't like the expenditure of $120,000 a year and the time of three men on this work. 'Leave it to universities or consultants,' they say. 'If the outsiders can develop something, then we'll pay royalties later.' But my point is, Let's get the royalties if anything develops. It's true that research expenditures reduce our before-tax profits by 8 to 9%, but what better way to do so? We don't need the money for dividends. There are no interest charges that might suddenly loom large in a bad year, the Indiana plant is all paid for, and working capital is in sound shape. If anything, a current ratio of 3.2 to 1 and an acid test of over 1.2 indicate that we have excess cash. I think we should be looking for ways to spend the money, not conserve it. On the average, we need about half of our present profits after tax for plowing back into new or rebuilt plant and equipment. (Last year's sales were $13,000,000; total assets, $5,000,000; stockholders' equity, $3,300,000; number of employees, 250.)

"One thing we might do is invest in our own sales force on the West Coast. We use manufacturing agents there, and I'm not sure they get all the business they should. A rough analysis of territorial potential shows us well behind in Los Angeles, which is just the place we should be strong. Furthermore, we don't have the knowledge of and control over that market that we should have. Aerospace and defense electronics can shift rapidly, it is true. Using agents may then be wise. Our own sales force would cost us more initially and might be a little more dangerous in tough times. Let's say it would take an extra $200,000 a year invested for three years to build up an effective West Coast sales force. Who knows what the payoff would be? Is there any way of estimating this? Can we resolve it just on a policy basis?

"Our combined product mix out of both plants is now:

Defense electronics	28.4
Commercial electronics	20.6
Home appliances	20.2
Communications and utilities	16.3
Industrial machinery	11.1
Automotive	3.4
	100.0

"The agents tend to specialize in one or a couple of closely related industries. Our own salesmen could be allocated by territory and we could control more closely the customer groups on whom they called.

"Speaking of allocation, I've just allocated the last of these martinis. Dinner should be about ready. Let's wander in and put a little pressure on Cook if it isn't. Then after dinner we can take a look at your forecasts."

REQUIRED: (a) As an advisor on general economic affairs and on problems of central management, what would you say to Jack McCormick?

(b) What is your appraisal of the issues you have learned from his running commentary?

PART

3 ⠂ **ORGANIZING FOR ACTION**

Ch. 17 · Grouping Activities for Effective Operations

Ch. 18 · Organizational Relationships

Ch. 19 · Balancing the Organization Structure

Ch. 20 · Board of Directors and Central-Management Organization

Integrating Cases—Organization

GROUPING ACTIVITIES FOR
EFFECTIVE OPERATIONS

ALL COOPERATIVE EFFORT REQUIRES ORGANIZATION

Modern life makes cooperative action necessary. Individuals work together in the home, the school, the church, the state, and business. If a group of people are to work together effectively in such enterprises, their activities must be planned, directed, and controlled. Whatever may be the group goals, an organization with various roles and authority for the members must be understood and accepted.

College organization. Administrative organization is essential in a college or university, to cite an example close at hand. Someone must be responsible for the supervision of buildings and grounds; and provision must be made for heat, light, janitor service, and similar activities. There must be a business office that handles the college income and pays the bills. In many colleges annual receipts and disbursements amount to hundreds of thousands of dollars. Moreover, many colleges and universities have endowments that must be invested and supervised so as to secure the greatest income that is commensurate with safety of principal.

Still another unit of the college organization will be required for the supervision of the dormitories, the dining halls, and the other living facilities necessary to accommodate the college students. Another group of people will be concerned with managing the library, and there is likely to be a further unit of the college organization responsible for the athletic activities. All of these departments are in addition to the teaching staff, which in itself is divided into schools and departments. The objectives of the university are far different from those of a business, and yet both a university and a business require some form of administrative organization.

Need for organization in a growing business. The need for administrative organization in a commercial enterprise can be illustrated by a growing retail establishment. As long as the shop is small, the storekeeper has no organization problem aside from that of organizing the use of his own time. He performs all the activities of his small enterprise and has only himself to blame or praise for the results.

Organization problems, however, appear as soon as assistants are hired, and these problems continue to increase in complexity with the addition of new employees. A single assistant to a storekeeper may help with most of the activities in the store, including estimating stock requirements, arranging displays, contacting customers, and keeping books. When three or four more employees are added, this loose form of administrative organization is no longer possible. If all the employees make entries on the books, errors will arise from duplication or from the assumption that another employee made the entry. One assistant may refuse credit to a customer, while a second assistant may readily grant it.

To avoid confusion and to use the services of the employees to best advantage, the authority of each employee must be limited. For example, the general manager may assign to one individual authority for granting credit and to another individual responsibility for keeping a record of all business transactions. By limiting the duties in some such manner, each employee can apply himself to the activities for which he is best qualified rather than attempt to participate in all activities of the company. Moreover, by limiting the authority of each employee, the general manager will be able to hold an employee responsible for performance.

As the number of employees grows, the general manager will have increasing difficulty giving detailed supervision to each of them. If a store has over 50 employees, it will employ several sales persons, 6 or 7 men to deliver goods, and 2 or 3 persons as bookkeepers. Under such circumstances the natural thing to do is to group all sales persons under a single sales manager and then to make the sales manager responsible for supervising all selling activities. In the same way, bookkeeping may be placed under a head bookkeeper, delivery under a delivery superintendent, and so on. The general manager can then deal with 6 or 7 group managers, and each group manager in turn can supervise 8 or 9 people.

Organization hierarchy in large concerns. The administrative organization of large companies with thousands of employees is very complex. There must be several levels of authority, for if the employees were merely placed in groups of tens, the general manager would still have an impossible task of supervising hundreds of group supervisors. Also, the relationships between the various units have to be defined, since the work of any one unit must be synchronized with several others and some specialized units will exist merely to aid the rest of the organization. Systems and procedures will guide the flow of routine work through the various departments, and specified contacts will aid in coordinating nonroutine problems.

Research to identify problems facing top executives of our leading companies always shows organization to be a major issue.

Factors to be considered in establishing an organization. The objectives of a business enterprise are reflected in its policies, and we have seen that they vary considerably from one company to another. Consequently, no one form of organization can be applied generally to all types of business units, and even within any one concern the form of organization should be changed from time to time to meet varying conditions. This means that central management will frequently face problems of organization and reorganization.

Certain factors should be considered in establishing any organization. Most significant of these are the following:

1. What activities must be performed to carry out the policies?
2. How should these activities be classified or grouped to facilitate their administration?
3. What authority should be granted to insure effective performance of activities by each group?
4. What use should be made of committees, and how may all departments and committees be welded into an integrated organization structure?
5. How may the process of organizing be done so as to recognize the individual people concerned and at the same time provide for efficient achievement of objectives?

All of these factors are interrelated, and a final decision with reference to any one of them should not be made without considering the others to some degree. For convenience in presentation, however, we shall discuss them separately.

ACTIVITY ANALYSIS

Bearing of policies on organization. The objectives and the policies of a company may affect materially its form of organization. For example, when the J. C. Penney Company gave up its long-standing "cash sales only" policy and started to grant credit, an array of new activities arose in the bookkeeping, customer credit, and financial control sections of each store as well as in the home office. Likewise, Dole Pineapple Company's decision to make rather than buy its tin cans in Hawaii added activities ranging from purchase of tinplate to running a conveyor from the can shop to the warehouse.

Because policies of a company affect its form of organization so greatly, the first step in building an organization should be an identification of its policies, and the second step should be an analysis of the activities necessary for achieving these policies.

Suggested approach. A useful approach is to prepare an outline of the policies of the company. The chart at the end of Chapter 16 gives headings that may well be used in such an outline. Then all the activities necessary to execute each of these policies can be listed.

The degree of detail to which this analysis should be carried depends upon the scope of organization being considered. When an executive is studying broad, overall organization structure, a listing of major activities is usually adequate. However, when the organization of individual jobs is the aim, listing of minute details may be useful. In either case a lot more detail is analyzed in the design process than appears in the final conclusions because (a) the organizer must be sure he has a complete and realistic grasp of the work involved, and (b) novel and strategic combinations of duties are apt to be missed if the organizer thinks only in terms of large customary groups of work. Also, greater detail should be considered in those areas that are new, that are especially crucial to success, or that have been sources of trouble.

As we noted in Parts 1 and 2, the dynamic business environment calls for frequent revision of policies. This, in turn, makes changes in organization necessary. The analysis that is used as a basis of establishing organization is, therefore, a continuing process.

With the activities in mind, our next step is to decide how they can best be grouped together into manageable divisions, departments, sections, or other units. In management circles, this grouping is called *departmentation* even though the final units are not necessarily called departments. A related issue is *span of supervision*—the number of people reporting directly to one supervisor. The span of supervision is a factor in deciding how many groups and subgroups should be created.

In the following pages we discuss bases for departmentation and span of supervision, and then we conclude with an application of these concepts to a composite organization.

BASES OF DEPARTMENTATION

The more common ways of grouping activities are by:

1. Products.
2. Processes.
3. Territories.
4. Types of customers.
5. Functions.

A brief examination of situations where each of these patterns is used will suggest basic criteria for departmentation.

Product departments. *Use in packing companies.* Any company that handles two or more products may wish to group activities pertaining to each product in separate organization units. Meat packing companies, which perform all operations from the purchase of livestock on the hoof to the sale of a wide variety of meat products to the retailer, use product grouping in varying degrees. A few companies have a beef department, a pork department, and perhaps a mutton department. The manager of the pork department, for example, directs the purchase of hogs, the processing operations, the storing of the finished product, and the selling of pork products. The primary advantages of this arrangement are that a single executive can follow closely conditions both in the supply market and in the selling market, and he can take whatever steps are necessary to make a profit on the handling of his particular product; coordination is eased, control is clarified, and each product receives the full attention of a set of executives.

Note, however, that even in these instances several activities are performed for the company as a whole. Accounting, credit, finance, personnel, and other service activities can be performed more economically and consistently by a single department that serves all of the product groups. Also note that the product division is not carried to the point where, for example, a sausage section performs all of its purchasing, production, and selling work. Two main reasons for not doing so are:

1. The volume of business in sausages is not large enough to support a separate purchasing, production, and selling organization—or at least it would be uneconomical to do so.
2. The sausage activities are very closely related to similar work for fresh pork and other cured meats; consequently, having a separate sausage section would create many problems of coordination.

In some packing companies, the activities assigned to a product department are even more restricted than in the example just cited. These companies find economies in having a single selling force for all products and a single processing division that is in charge of all physical handling from the time animals are purchased until products are delivered to retailers. Nevertheless, the product departments continue to have important responsibilities. They buy, schedule production, establish price, watch inventory, and assist in the promotion of sale of their products. Thus they watch closely over the rate of flow of their product and its profitability.

Under such an arrangement, responsibility for final results is hard to place, but operating economies are achieved.

Department store organization. For many years in the typical department store the buyer was king. There would be separate buyers for hosiery, jewelry, gloves, shoes, millinery, and dozens of other products. Normally, each buyer was responsible for the purchase of his merchandise, its pricing and display, and its sale. Of course, there were storewide departments for such activities as building operations, delivery, finance, accounting, advertising, and personnel. Nevertheless, the very crucial trading function remained the domain of the respective buyers. This provided close coordination of buying and selling each product, and it aided control by localizing responsibility.

With the recent substantial expansion of suburban branches, the role of the department store buyer has been changing. Because of the distance factor, he cannot directly supervise the people selling his product in the several outlets and he has difficulty maintaining his former close observation of display and proper maintenance of stocks. Many companies are still wrestling with the question of how far to cut back the domain of the product buyers. There are advantages in having the manager of each suburban branch responsible for sales volume and merchandise turnover. When this is done, however, the product buyer exercises little direct supervision; he buys, prices, and advises on sales promotion. He is a provider of merchandise that he hopes someone else will sell. With luck, sales volume goes up, but responsibility is diffused.

Process departments. Manufacturing and other types of business often perform several distinct processes that may serve as the basis for departmentation. For example, in steel production separate departments ferquently are established for mining, transportation, reduction of ore to iron and steel, and fabricating. Each process involves a distinct technology and is frequently performed in a separate location; consequently, these divisions can operate on a semiautonomous basis.

In contrast, the use of process grouping in a company manufacturing small cutting tools such as drills, taps, and reamers is more debatable. The production operations of this business are turning original stock down into desired size, milling the cutting edges and the grooves that provide for the escape of waste material, giving the metal a hardness by tempering it in a high-temperature oven, and finally polishing the otherwise finished product. Each of these operations might be placed under the supervision of a single superintendent. An alternative is to organize the shop by product groups and to assign machinery necessary for the various processes to a product manager.

The grouping of activities by process tends to promote efficiency through specialization. All the key people in each department become expert in dealing with their particular phase of the business. On the other hand, process classification increases problems of coordination. In the tool company example, scheduling the movement of work from department to department on each order becomes somewhat complex. Also, since no department has full responsibility for the order, a department may not be as diligent in meeting time requirements and other specifications as a group of people who think in terms of the total finished product and their customers.

The organization issue just posed—product versus process grouping in manufacturing activities—has additional ramifications.

It ties in with plant layout, extent of mechanization and type of equipment selected, the desirability of subcontracting, and of course the characteristics of executives needed.

The conflict between a desire to increase skill in performance through specialization and mechanization, and the need for coordination to secure balanced efforts recurs time and again in organization studies.

Territorial departments. Companies with salesmen who travel over a large area almost always use territorial organization. Large companies will have several regions, each subdivided into districts, with a further breakdown of territories for individual salesmen. Chain stores, finance companies with local offices, and gasoline companies all by their very nature have widely dispersed activities and consequently use territorial organization to some degree.

The large dairy companies provide an interesting example whereby not only sales but also production are localized. The proper handling of fresh milk requires rapid movement from the farm to processing plants, to bottling plants, and on to the customer. To assure local coordination and control, each geographical unit is self-contained and semiautonomous. This arrangement does not apply to the manufacture of cheese, canned milk, and other dairy products that are shipped long distances and sold through grocery stores.

The primary issues with territorial organization are three:

1. What related activity should be physically dispersed along with those which by their nature are local? For example, should a company with a national sales force also have local warehousing, local assembling, local advertising, local credit and accounting, and local personnel? And how far should the dispersion occur— to the regional level or to the district level? Typically, whenever such related activities are dispersed, they are all combined into a territorial organization unit.
2. How much authority to make decisions should be decentralized to these various territorial units? In other words, how much of the planning and control work should go along with the actual performance?
3. What will be the relations between the home office service and staff units and these various territorial divisions?

We will discuss these last two issues in the next chapter, but it is important to recognize that they must be satisfactorily resolved if territorial units are established.

The major advantage of territorial organization is that it provides supervision near the point of performance. Local conditions vary and emergencies do arise. Persons located a long distance away will have difficulty grasping the true nature of the situation, and valuable time is often lost before an adjustment can be made. Consequently, when adjustment to local conditions and quick decisions are important, territorial organization is desirable. On the other hand, if a lot of local units are established, some of the benefits of large-scale operation may be lost. The local unit will probably be comparatively small, and consequently the degree of specialization and mechanization will be correspondingly limited.

Customer departments. A company that sells to customers of distinctly different types may establish a separate unit of organization for selling and servicing each. A manufacturer of men's shoes, for instance, sold to both independent retail stores and chain stores. The chain-store buyers are very sophisticated and may prepare their own specifications; consequently, any salesman calling on them must have an intimate knowledge of shoe construction and of the capacity of his company's plant. In contrast, a salesman who calls on retailers must be able to think in terms of retailing problems and be able to show how his product will fit into the customer's business. Few salesmen can work effectively with both large chain-store and independent retail customers; consequently, the shoe manufacturer has a separate division in his sales organization for each group.

Commercial banks, to cite another example, often have different vice-presidents for types of customers—railroads, manufacturing concerns, stockbrokers, consumer loans, and the like. These men recognize the needs of their particular group of customers and they also are in a good position to appraise the credit worthiness.

Ordinarily, customer groups include only selling and direct service activities. Anyone who has been shunted around to five or six offices trying to get an adjustment on a bill or a promise on a delivery will appreciate the satisfaction of dealing with a single individual who understands his problem and knows how to get action within the company. On the other hand, this form of organization may be expensive and a customer-oriented man may commit his company to actions that other departments find hard to carry out.

Functional departments. In each of the types of grouping already discussed we have observed that at least a few activities are reserved in divisions serving the entire company. These departments that are responsible for performing one group of similar activities for all other departments—such as credits, record keeping, and maintenance—are called *functional departments*. The functional grouping of activities can be extended until all of the activities of a firm are classified on this basis.

Most colleges are organized on a functional basis. There will be executives in charge of buildings and grounds, the living accomodations, the business office, the student records, and perhaps other groups of activities. Instruction, however, is usually organized on a product basis. Typical functional departments in a manufacturing business include sales, purchasing, production, finance, controllership, and personnel. In more technical industries, research and engineering will be fully as important as any of those just listed. And within many major departments the subdivisions are made on a functional basis.

Deciding the scope of a functional department is by no means simple. The nature of a particular company's business will influence where a given activity can best be placed. Two general guides are helpful in this respect:

1. Place in the same department those activities that have the same immediate objectives. For example, activities as diverse as running a cafeteria, performing medical service, and administering a pension plan may be placed in the personnel department because all of these contribute to the objective of building an efficient work force. In the same manner, the management of salesmen and of advertising may be placed under the sales manager, because the objectives of both these activities is the same—to procure sales orders.

2. Place in the same department activities that require a similar type of ability and experience for their efficient management. For example, in pharmaceutical companies quality control is often placed in the research department. Control of the quality of pharmaceuticals requires someone who is objective, analytical, and expert in laboratory techniques. These similarities with research seem to warrant combined supervision even though the mission of the two activities differs significantly. Budgeting and finance might be placed in the same department for similar reasons.

Advantages of functional departments depend partly upon the integrating theme for the particular unit. Expertness with a similar type of problem, adequate attention to an activity that otherwise might be given hurried treatment, consistent action in such matters as labor relations, and easy coordination of activities having a common purpose are among the benefits often secured.

Basic factors in departmentation. The types of groupings we have discussed suggest possibilities for dealing with specific problems. Nevertheless, we have noted that each type has some advantages and some disadvantages and that no one type is applicable to all the activities of a business at each of several levels. Therefore, we must conclude that wise departmentation depends upon finding a particular grouping that in a specific situation provides an optimum combination of:

1. Specialization or expertness (with respect to function, product, customer, or other factor that is important in a specific situation).
2. Aid to control.
3. Aid in coordination.
4. Adequate attention.
5. Adaptation to local conditions.
6. Low expense.

Finding an optimum departmentation obviously, then, requires considerable ingenuity and judgment.

LIMITS ON SPAN OF SUPERVISION

Once the basis for grouping activities has been decided upon, the question of *how many* subdivisions of work there will be is sometimes settled automatically. Thus, if departments are set up by products and a company handles four types of products, there will be four major units.

In other situations, the issue of how many units to establish is not so easily resolved. For instance, when territorial or functional grouping of activities is used, many subdivisions of work are possible. Likewise, a department store carries literally thousands of products, each of which might conceivably be used to form a separate unit of organization. Obviously, these small units or cells of work must be grouped together into divisions or departments, but each time this is done, the question arises of how many or how few divisions there should be.

Factors restricting effective span of supervision. It is desirable in any plan of organization to limit the number of departments. If too many departments are established, senior executives cannot supervise them effectively. The time and energy any executive can devote to his job is limited; even if he is willing to work very long hours, his judgment and leadership ability will decline. Moreover, as the number of immediate subordinates increases, the task of coordinating their efforts is likely to rise.

The number of people an executive can supervise effectively depends, in part, upon what they are doing. If each subordinate is doing the same kind of work, for example, bookkeeping or routine assembly, more can be supervised than if their work is varied. The time and energy needed to keep track of varied work is greater and the job of coordinating it is more difficult. For this reason, it is generally thought that an executive should not supervise more than 5 to 8 people doing varied work, whereas he might handle 15 to 20 doing similar routine work. These limits are only rough guides, as we shall see.

Too narrow a span of supervision. Too few subordinates is also bad. The most evident drawback is the payroll expense. If each executive supervises only a few divisions, the total number of executives needed by a company will be relatively large and the executive payroll correspondingly high.

A further difficulty is that narrow spans of supervision inevitably mean more *layers* of executives between the operators and the general manager. In a company with 81 operators (salesmen, production workers, bookkeepers, and the like), only one layer of executives between the general manager and the operators will be needed if the average span is 9 people. However, if the span is only 3 people, there will be three layers between top and bottom.

Additional layers of executives between the general manager and actual operations are objectionable on several counts. Human beings are poor conductors of ideas. This is notorious with respect to witnesses of an accident; even the eyewitnesses do not agree on what happened, and by the time each has told a friend and each friend told some of his acquaintances, the account of what took place is garbled indeed. The same inaccuracy of communication may occur in a company, with the result that the general manager and operators fail to understand each other.

Moreover, additional executive layers contribute to inflexibility. It takes time to communicate, especially if men are busy or out of town, and this slows down the speed of adjustments to changing conditions. When a company is divided into many segments, vested interests are likely to arise, and those who see the company only from the viewpoint of their own little section are likely to resist changes.

Morale tends to be lower in companies with many layers of supervision. Operators often do not know the "big boss" personally; they may lack a sense of participation and feel like just a cog in the wheel. This remoteness can be overcome to some degree by deliberate efforts of top executives to keep in touch with the men "down the line." Nevertheless, additional levels of supervision are likely to have an adverse effect on morale.

Other factors affecting optimum span. Reasons have been suggested for having as many people report to an executive as the limits on his time and energy will permit. Several additional factors are involved. Most executives are expected to give time to duties other than supervision. The sales manager will have to contact some customers personally, the production manager may spend time designing new equipment, and so with other executives. The more of these other duties an executive has, the fewer subordinates he can supervise effectively.

If an executive has competent, well-trained people working under him, they will require less supervision than inexperienced workers. This will be especially true if a high degree of decentralization is practiced. Also, it is easier to direct stable activities than new and changing ones. Still another factor is the staff assistance an executive may have.

The variations in such factors as those just mentioned, as well as differences in individual capacities, make it impossible to set arbitrary rules as to the number of subordinates an executive should have. Part of the art of organizing is to assign work so that the total duties of each executive keep him busy but do not overload him.

When it appears that an executive will be overloaded, combining some of the units under him is often possible. For example, credits, collections, receipt and custody of funds, and related activities may be combined and placed under an assistant treasurer. In a department store, all women's wear may be assigned to a divisional merchandise manager if the general merchandise manager cannot supervise the buyers of coats, dresses, and other related lines.

Consequently, in grouping activities to form an administrative organization, the optimum span of supervision for each executive must be considered along with the basis on which the activities are classified and combined into units.

THE COMPOSITE ORGANIZATION

Several bases of classification used in every company. No one of the bases of classifying activities that have been discussed is used to group all activities of a particular business. Ordinarily, two or more bases are used. For example, the major departments of a company may be set up on a functional basis with a sales department, a production department, a finance department, a personnel department, and a controller's department. The method of classifying activities within each of these major departments does not necessarily have to be functional, nor need it be the same for each department. Thus, the production department may be organized on a process basis; while the sales department may first be grouped according to customers, making a division between bulk customers and smaller customers, and then subdivided into territories.

An organization needing improvement. The way these different bases of grouping are used in a concrete case is illustrated by a manufacturing concern located in central United States. The organization of this company at the time of an investigation, as indicated in the chart on page 446, was the result of a gradual development over a period of years. Although this organization worked reasonably well and was not nearly as unsatisfactory as many organizations now in actual use, the management recognized that it could be improved. An analysis showed that it was subject to the following weaknesses:

1. There were too many men reporting directly to the president of the concern for him to give adequate attention to each. When he did try to consult with each of them regarding their daily activities, he had no time left to consider the broader, underlying problems affecting the company.
2. The president had to coordinate several activities that could just as well be coordinated by someone subordinate to the chief

executive if the proper organization were adopted. For example, there were two sales managers and a branch manager, besides a sales promotion director, all reporting to the president. To secure coordinated sales activities, the president had to take time to consult with each of these men.

3. The company was not securing all the benefits that could be derived from a specialization of activities. For example, personnel problems were handled by a number of different executives. The manager of the production department was the only department head who had provided for a full-time employment director. All employment and training problems of the other departments were considered to be under the jurisdiction of the respective department managers. The company had one man in charge of industrial relations, and a medical director had been employed.

Revised plan of organization. To correct these difficulties, a new grouping of activities was adopted, as is indicated in the chart on page 447. The activities classified under each of the major executives shown on the chart may be briefly described as follows:

The president, who is also general manager, is the chief executive officer of the company. He is responsible for carrying out the broad policies laid down by the board of directors. The activities under his direction are grouped into seven major departments, with the following executives in charge:

1. Sales manager.
2. Production manager.
3. Treasurer.
4. Personnel manager.
5. Controller.
6. Branch manager.
7. Research director.

It will be noted that activities have been classified on a functional basis, with the exception of the branch manager. The distance from the home office to the West Coast made it necessary for this company to establish a branch office in San Francisco, California, that would be responsible for all activities performed west of the Rocky Mountains.

1. Sales manager. The sales manager is responsible for all selling activities of the company. He has the following assistants.

a. Sales promotion and advertising director, who is responsible for advertising, displays, and sales promotion methods.
b. Bulk sales supervisor, who is responsible for sales to large customers, such as mail-order houses, chain stores, and other customers who buy in very large quantities.

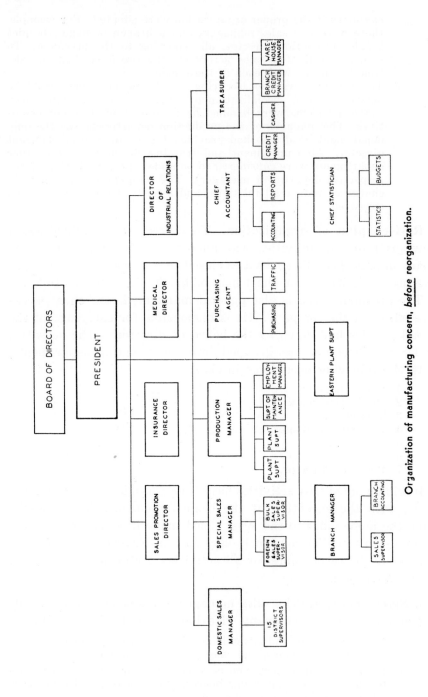

Organization of manufacturing concern, before reorganization.

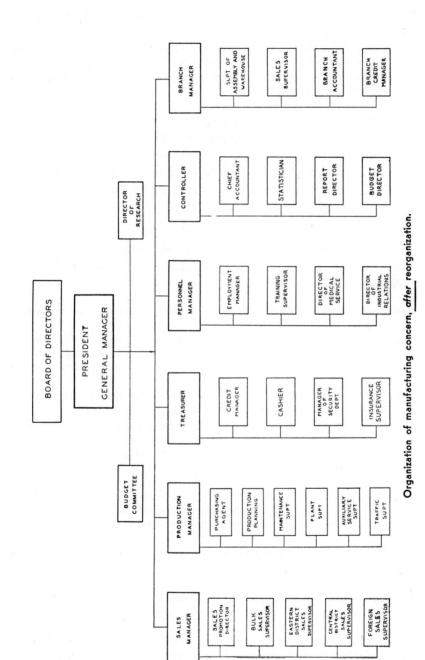

Organization of manufacturing concern, *after* reorganization.

c. Eastern district sales supervisor, who is responsible for selling activities in the eastern part of the United States.

d. Central district sales supervisor, who is responsible for selling activities in the central part of the United States.

e. Foreign sales supervisor, who is responsible for sales made outside of the United States.

Several bases are used in grouping the activities performed under the supervision of the sales manager. The functional basis is used to separate sales promotion from the actual solicitation of customers; customer classification is used in setting up bulk customers as distinct from other customers; and finally, a territorial basis is used in dividing eastern, central, and foreign sales.

2. Production manager. The production manager is responsible for all procurement activities extending from the purchase of raw materials to the shipment of merchandise to customers. He has the following assistants:

a. Purchasing agent, who is responsible for buying raw materials and factory supplies.

b. Production planning superintendent, who is responsible for the scheduling of production in accordance with sales requirements and the issuing of production orders to the various units in the factory.

c. Plant superintendent, who is responsible for the operation of all factory units engaged in direct production activity.

d. Maintenance superintendent, who is responsible for maintaining buildings and keeping equipment in good condition.

e. Auxiliary service superintendent, who is responsible for the providing of steam, electricity, water, and similar services throughout the factory.

f. Traffic superintendent, who is responsible for the movement of raw materials from the vendor to the plant and the shipment of finished goods from the plant to customers.

Activities under the production manager have been classified on a functional basis.

3. Treasurer. The treasurer is responsible for all financial activities of the company. He has the following assistants:

a. Credit manager, who is responsible for the extension of credit to customers and the collection of accounts receivable.

b. Cashier, who is responsible for handling cash within the company, issuing the checks of the company, and maintaining connections with banks.

c. Manager of security department, who is responsible for maintaining a record of stockholders, for sending out notices of stockholders' meetings, and for similar activities involving stockholders.

d. Insurance supervisor, who is responsible for handling all insurance matters.

4. Personnel manager. The personnel manager is responsible for the personnel activities of the company. He has the following assistants:

a. Employment manager, who is responsible for recommending new employees to other executives and also for recommending promotions and discharges.

b. Training supervisor, who is responsible for training activities of the company.

c. Director of medical service, who is responsible for the health program of the company.

d. Director of industrial relations, who is responsible for safety work, employee recreation, union contacts, and other miscellaneous personnel activities.

In the personnel department, the functional basis of classifying activities is used. The personnel department determines how personnel problems should be handled and then depends upon its influence over executives of other departments for the execution of these plans.

5. Controller. The controller is responsible for all accounting activities and for checking the performance of other departments. He has the following assistants:

a. Chief accountant, who is responsible for maintaining accurate accounting records throughout the company.

b. Statistician, who is responsible for collecting and analyzing statistical records other than the financial accounts.

c. Report director, who is responsible for preparing periodic accounting and statistical reports for the use of officers and other executives of the company.

d. Budget director, who acts as secretary to the budget committee and assists in the preparation of budgets for the company.

6. Branch manager. The branch manager is responsible for all activities of the company performed west of the Rocky Mountains. He has the following assistants:

a. Superintendent of assembly and warehouse, who is responsible for assembling the parts sent from the main factory, the storage of finished products, and the shipments to customers.

 b. Sales supervisor, who is responsible for all selling activities in the West Coast area.

 c. Branch accountant, who is responsible for all accounting activities at the branch office.

 d. Branch credit manager, who is responsible for handling credits and collections and other financial matters for the branch office.

It will be noted that the classification of activities under the branch manager roughly parallels that of the entire company.

7. Research director. The research director is responsible for making studies of important problems within the company. Except for a few personal assistants, he has no authority over other employees. He makes studies of problems and recommends to the president and other executives the action that should be taken.

8. Budget committee. Provision is also made for a budget committee. This committee is important in securing coordination between the various departments. Future plans are discussed by the committee and budgets are agreed upon. It is an important device for informing each major executive of the general plans.

A study of this company reveals that the organization problem is a very complex one even for a medium-sized firm. Moreover, such a problem cannot be solved by the use of rules. Thus, the type of organization that should be used by any specific company depends upon the objectives of the company, the nature and volume of its activities, the conditions under which it must operate at any specific time, the ability of its executives, the nature of its personnel, and the stage of its development in organization thinking and practice.

SUMMARY

The execution of policies of a company involves a variety of activities. These activities can be performed efficiently only if they are properly organized. A basic feature of this organization—the grouping of activities into departments, divisions, sections and other administrative units—has been discussed in this chapter. Grouping of activities for purposes of administration takes place at all levels, from the division of work under the chief executive to the assignment of duties to individual operators.

The most common bases for grouping business activities are according to processes, territories, customers or functions. From a consideration of the advantages and disadvantages of these typical forms, the following basic factors emerge. When grouping activities seek an optimum combination of (1) the advantages of specialization, (2) aid in coordination, (3) aid in control, (4) adequate attention, and (5) adaptation to local needs and expense. Attention to these basic factors is more important than sticking to a standard type of organization.

Along with the question of how best to group activities is the issue of how many groups should be set up under each executive. The choice of a proper span of supervision again requires weighing several factors. Important factors include (1) the time and ability that the executive has to devote to supervision, (2) the variety and importance of the work supervised, (3) the effect on morale, communication, and flexibility of additional layers of executives, and (4) the competence of subordinates and the authority delegated to them.

Because of possible changes in activities of a company from year to year, the grouping that works best at one time may need to be modified at a later date. Just as policies need to be adjusted to changing conditions, so too is organizing a continuing job.

QUESTIONS FOR CLASS DISCUSSION

1. Compare a railroad with a large milk company in regard to assigning the following activities to major departments, that is, where do you think these activities belong in each organization: (a) sales promotion, (b) setting prices, (c) selection and training of employees, and (d) quality control.

2. What factors should be used to determine whether it is desirable to have one sales force sell several products or to have a separate sales force for each product?

3. "As an enterprise grows, its organization becomes more complex." Explain why this is so. What can be done to reduce or overcome this complexity?

4. In assigning authority and responsibility to individuals working for a business enterprise, what advantages can be secured from (a) limiting the authority of each employee, (b) having each employee specialize on one or only a few activities, and (c) restricting the number of subordinates reporting to each executive? Explain the effect on the growth and development of the persons in the company of your answers to (a), (b), and (c). Explain also the effect of your answers on the objectives of a firm.

5. (a) In a department store organized on a product basis, who should be responsible for the amount products are marked down from the price at which they were originally offered to the public? (b) If a department store is organized on a functional basis, with all sales activities under one executive and all buying activities under another executive, who should be responsible for controlling markdowns? (c) Which is the better form of organization insofar as handling markdowns is concerned? Would your answer be the same for all kinds of businesses?

6. The Juvenile Dress Company has just decided to open a plant in Puerto Rico to supplement, at low costs, the output of its main St. Louis plant. The St. Louis production superintendent, who heretofore has directed all of the company's production, has assumed that he would also direct the new plant. The treasurer, who has been responsible for negotiations for the new plant, recommends a Puerto Rico plant manager reporting directly to the president. Currently, the sales manager, production superintendent, treasurer (also purchasing agent), chief accountant, and personnel director report to the president. Prepare arguments supporting each proposal. Which factors do you think will be most important in making the final decision?

7. The sales manager of the Hoopes Ribbon Company, which sells its products to clothing manufacturers and industrial users, contends that the credit department should be under his jurisdiction. The treasurer contends that it should be a subdivision of the financial department. What is your opinion? Why?

8. The American Refrigerator Corporation, manufacturer of domestic refrigerators, has a repair service that trains repairmen of local dealers and also does difficult repair jobs that local men cannot handle. The nature of the work is, of course, akin to production, and the head of the repair service thinks he should report to the production vice-president. The production vice-president says he can make refrigerators run but does not want to get involved in dealer and consumer problems. Where do you think the repair service division should be placed in the organization?

9. Many companies are vitally concerned about their public relations or public image. Should such companies have a public relations division, and if so, what activities should be assigned to this division?

10. In analyzing the administrative problems of a business, is there any advantage in considering policies, organization, and executive personnel in that sequence? Under what conditions might it be desirable to deal with these three topics in some other order?

CASE XVII

St. Louis Blues, Inc.

The St. Louis Blues, Inc., a major league baseball club, has been consistently unprofitable and just as consistently finished at the bottom of its league standings. A new group of stockholders, including a leading businessman, has just bought the club. All the new owners are interested in getting the club on a profitable basis and the businessman especially is convinced that sound organization can do much to bring this about.

The sources of gross income, in the order of their importance, are: ticket sales, television and radio rights, concessions (programs, refreshments, souvenirs, parking, etc.), and rental of the ballpark for football games and other events. Except for rentals, the amount of the income is greatly influenced by the popularity of the team and its success. Consequently, in addition to a certain amount of advertising and sales promotion, careful attention is given throughout the year to the publicity, news stories, and public reaction to the team and its various players.

During the season attention is naturally focused on the playing activities on the field. The selection of pitchers, use of pinch-hitters, the batting order, decisions to walk a man or to bunt, and many other tactical maneuvers have to be made. In the background of these specific plays are, of course, matters of training, coaching, and team morale.

The main expenses are payroll; maintenance of the stadium, playing field, loudspeakers, clubhouse, etc.; uniforms and supplies for the team; carfare, hotel, meals, and other traveling expenses; and spring training. The concessions are operated on a decentralized basis with the manager of each buying his own food, programs, or other required supplies and reporting only his net revenue.

The club owns its own ballpark, although this has been rather heavily mortgaged to raise capital for other purposes. Substantial sums have been invested in contracts for players, and there is a continual question of whether particular players should be bought, sold, or traded. A related activity is the setting of players' salaries and the dropping or "farming out" of unsatisfactory players.

A substantial investment has been made in minor league clubs in order to form an effective "farm" organization. Some of these clubs are owned outright, others have been helped financially through loans or purchase of minority stock, while with still others there is a working agreement but no ownership. This farm organization is considered important in testing and developing players. Related to the farm organization are a group of scouts (often part time) who locate promising players at high schools, colleges, sandlots, and other minor league teams. These scouts advise both major and minor league team managers about acquiring or transferring of players.

In addition to the activities already indicated directly or indirectly, provision must be made for collection and payment of taxes, purchase of insurance, legal work, scheduling and other relations with members of the league, exhibition games, team physician, and trainers.

At the time the new owners bought the St. Louis Blues, Inc., the following persons were on the payroll: 25 players on the regular team, 55 regular park operations men (the number of ushers and gatemen is substantially increased by part-time help for big events) ; 3 coaches, the doctor, and the trainer; 40 men on concessions; and 30 office and executive personnel (including ticket sellers). These figures do not include the farm organization; each of the minor league clubs has an organization of its own, although substantially smaller than the major league club.

REQUIRED: The new owners of St. Louis Blues, Inc., would like to have your recommendations for organizing the club. Prepare an outline or a chart showing the groups and sub-groups you propose, and give reasons supporting your plan.

18 ORGANIZATIONAL RELATIONSHIPS

The grouping together of activities for purposes of management discussed in the preceding chapter does not complete the organization structure. Assignment of activities to departments and to jobs within these departments provides for the performance of activities; but if these activities are to be integrated to obtain common objectives, clear understanding of the flow of authority between and within groups also is essential.

These organizational relationships help shape the character of an enterprise. A "one-man company" dominated by its president is a distinctly different kind of institution than the General Electric Company with its many semi-independent divisions. The ability of a firm to act swiftly, the kind of employees it attracts, its competence to handle complex technology, the uniform quality of its services, for instance, are all strongly influenced by internal relationships. And just as departmentation should be adapted to objectives and policies, so too should relationships be designed to fit each company.

The chief elements that make up the design of relationships in an administrative organization are:

1. Line authority.
2. Decentralization of authority.
3. Staff relationships.
4. Functional authority.

Central management is, of course, primarily concerned with the appropriateness of overall design, but it cannot avoid pesky jurisdictional squabbles. To deal with these problems, we must understand each of the elements.

LINE AUTHORITY

Horizontal strata in an organization structure. The grouping of activities into major departments and units within these departments may be regarded as a vertical division of activities. From another point of view, the organization process may be considered to create horizontal strata within each of these vertical divisions. In a plant, machine operators will be on one level, foremen on another, then shop superintendents, and on to plant manager. A strata of vice-presidents will probably be placed between the plant manager (and his peers) and the chief executive of the company.

In some companies these strata become numerous. For example, in a large grocery chain, the strata between the stockholders and the clerks who deal with the customers are:

    a. Board of directors.
    b. Executive committee of the board.
    c. President.
    d. General merchandise manager.
    e. General superintendent of stores.
    f. District supervisors.
    g. Branch managers.
    h. Store superintendents.
    i. Store managers.
    j. Clerks.

Nature of line authority. The term *line authority* refers to the common relationship between a member of any one of these strata and his immediate subordinates. In the grocery chain mentioned above, the general superintendent of stores has line authority over the district supervisors, and a store manager has line authority over the clerks working in his store. Anyone with complete line authority plans the activities, issues the orders, stimulates greater effort, and checks up and evaluates the performance of his subordinates.

Authority should always carry with it a corresponding responsibility. There are basically three almost inseparable aspects of every relationship between an executive and his subordinates. First is the *assignment of duties*, that is, what the man is expected to accomplish. Second, this assignment must be accompanied by *authority* (permission) to use materials, make commitments, give orders to other employees, and take such other action, within the framework of company plans, as are necessary to fulfill these duties. Third, there is then a *responsibility* (obligation) on the part of the subordinate to the executive for satisfactory performance of his duties.

Experience shows that trouble is likely to arise if authority and responsibility are not coextensive. When a man is permitted to do things, such as adding people to the payroll or refusing to repair defective merchandise, and he is not at the same time held responsible for the expense or the results of his actions, administrative control will soon break down. Contrariwise, if a man is blamed for something, say big payroll expense, and he has no authority regarding the number of people employed, then a feeling of injustice and low morale will almost surely develop. In many situations an executive may be quite wise in restricting the authority of a subordinate; but when he does so, he should be careful to hold the subordinate accountable only for results that could reasonably be expected of a man working within such limits.

Delegation to a subordinate does not relieve an executive of his responsibility. This is not always recognized, and some executives give as an excuse for poor performance the fact that they had assigned the work to someone else. As in borrowing money, if Mr. Rockefeller borrows some money from the bank and reloans it to a South American firm, the second transaction does not reduce Mr. Rockefeller's obligation to the bank. In this sense, responsibility cannot be delegated. Of course, additional obligations can be created between an executive and his subordinates, but this does not permit the executive to duck out of the relationship.

Dual subordination. Only one manager should have line authority over an employee. For instance, the packing company, referred to in a preceding chapter, that used salesmen to handle both beef and pork products found that giving the managers of both departments line authority over the salesmen was not practical. Such dual subordination often results in conflict and inefficiency because it has long been recognized that an individual cannot serve two masters well.

A simple illustration of this difficulty was found in a department store where a salesclerk was subject to the authority of the personnel manager, the floor manager, and the buyer of the department in which she worked. The personnel manager had given her instructions regarding the time of her lunch hour in accordance with the general plan adopted for all employees. The buyer wished to have his entire sales force available during the noon rush, and he had therefore instructed the salesclerk to take her lunch half an hour earlier. When the salesclerk started to follow the latter instructions, the floor manager asked her to wait on some customers who had been standing for several minutes at the next counter.

Each of these men considered that he had line authority over the salesclerk, with the result that the clerk was forced to decide whether she should disobey one of her bosses or go without lunch. The result in this instance was a disgruntled, uncooperative, and perhaps hungry salesclerk. Again, if conflicting orders come to a buyer from both the merchandise manager and the store superintendent, the same principle is violated with perhaps more serious results from a net profit point of view.

DECENTRALIZATION OF AUTHORITY

Delegation of authority to make decisions. For an organization to function most effectively, ideas should flow freely from one strata to another. This is difficult to obtain because most people are poor conductors of ideas. Any idea that must be passed through a series of individuals is likely to become modified, warped, and misinterpreted; and even if the basic idea is retained, a considerable period of time may elapse before there is a meeting of minds between two individuals who must work through several intermediates. The resulting difficulty of transmitting ideas from the board of directors to the rank-and-file employee, and vice versa, will be readily recognized.

One solution for this problem is to decentralize authority. Thus, the top executives issue only general instructions and give to their subordinates authority to interpret these general instructions in a way that meets the specific situations that arise. For example, the general manager of a company may give the production manager general instructions and may then depend upon the production manager to see that the instructions are appropriately applied. If there are several plants, the production manager may delegate much of this authority to the plant managers. These plant managers, in turn, may leave a large part of the interpretation to the shop superintendents, or they may retain the authority themselves and give specific instructions to the superintendents. By delegating authority to make decisions regarding specific situations, the need for passing ideas up and down the lines of command can be reduced materially.

In considering the delegation of authority, there should be a clear distinction between the granting of authority for making decisions and the granting of authority for executing them. In any large company it is always necessary to delegate authority for "doing." This discussion, however, is devoted to the extent to which authority for making decisions may be delegated.

Decentralization of authority in chain stores. The problem may be further illustrated by the grocery chain store company that operated branches in several states. Each branch manager might be given complete authority to operate the individual stores in his branch area as he sees fit. If this practice was followed, each branch would be operated as an independent unit, subject only to the general supervision of the vice-president in charge of stores at the home office. Rarely is this degree of local independence desirable. The grocery company prefers to maintain centralized authority over certain features of store operations.

One of the advantages that may be gained from operating a large number of retail units under a chain management is that merchandise can be purchased in large quantities at lower prices. Moreover, the expenses of shipping and storing the merchandise can be reduced by centralized control. The grocery company also feels that major financial problems can be handled more economically in the central office.

On the other hand, flexible administration requires supervision of some activities by the branch managers rather than by the home office. After studying the question of what authority should be decentralized, the company has concluded that:

1. Some of the functions obviously have to be placed under the jurisdiction of local store managers. This includes authority over the following activities:

   (a) Arrangement of displays and maintenance of the store so that it will be attractive to customers.

   (b) Selling merchandise to customers. Most stores have one or more clerks in addition to the store manager, and thus the responsibility of selling includes the selection, training, and general supervision of these clerks.

   (c) Under certain conditions the store managers are permitted to buy a few products, such as butter and eggs, from their customers. Also, the store managers are permitted to pay incidental expenses.

    (d) Keeping some simplified records of sales, stock, cash receipts, and cash disbursements.

2. The responsibilities of the branch office are considerably greater than those granted to the individual stores. In addition to supervising the operation of stores, the branch office has authority to:

    (a) Select merchandise from that supplied by the central purchasing department which the local stores will carry in stock.

    (b) Determine the price at which each article of merchandise should be sold, and make such adjustments to the price as current competitive conditions and the size of inventory necessitate.

    (c) Direct the advertising for all stores of the branch, and work out plans of sales promotion to be followed by the store manager.

    (d) Compile and analyze accounting and statistical information regarding the operations in the branch area, which will aid the branch manager in appraising the results of past activities and in making decisions regarding future activities.

3. Decisions regarding other types of problems are made only by the executives in the home office. Some of these activities are classified under separate functional departments. The home office exercises complete authority over the following activities:

    (a) Selection of new locations, and designing and constructing the appropriate facilities.

    (b) Buying merchandise to be sold by the stores if the branch managers determine it can be done profitably. The company also manufactures a few products, such as bread and candy, and these operations are supervised from the home office.

    (c) Warehousing merchandise and supervising the transportation of merchandise from the warehouses to the stores. These warehouses are located in various parts of the country, but one warehouse often serves more than a single branch. Moreover, having warehouses supervised by a single department rather than placed under the direction of the branch managers assures adequate attention.

    (d) Supervising the financial activities of the company.

    (e) Conducting special studies of the merchandising and advertising problems of the company. The results of such studies are made available to the branch managers so that they may conduct their advertising campaigns more intelligently.

This case illustrates two issues. One is really departmentation; buying, warehousing, and finance are assigned to functional departments and not to the stores. Second, some authority is delegated to the branches but not to the stores (for example, pricing), while authority over other matters is passed clear down to the store manager (for example, display and sales training).

Authority to make exceptions. A large number of firms follow the general practice of making decisions as to policies, procedures, and methods in the central office. Authority is then granted to subordinates to conduct activities in accordance with these instructions, and frequently the men "down the line" are permitted to make modifications or exceptions within certain limits. The men close to the actual operation may have knowledge of more of the factors that should be considered in making this exception than the general manager. For example, a company may adopt a general policy concerning the price at which it will sell its product to different types of customers. However, in order to meet competing conditions, 5% variation in price may be permitted. The district sales manager may be able to decide more intelligently what conditions justify such variations than can the sales manager located a hundred miles from where the need for the variation arises.

A further advantage of such delegation is that it frees the top executives from the burden of making many decisions of a routine nature. On the other hand, when problems arise that do not fit within the established procedures and cannot be disposed of by the limited discretion granted to subordinates, the case is referred to the top executive. Thus the executive avoids the repetitive cases and concentrates on major exceptions, an arrangement often referred to as "the exception principle."

When to delegate. We cannot state exactly what problems are sufficiently important to require a decision by the top management rather than by a divisional or junior executive in some unit of the company. Those responsible for general management must depend largely upon their experience and judgment in deciding when it is desirable to increase or decrease the authority of men down the line. The extent to which authority for making decisions should be delegated depends primarily upon:

1. What factors must be considered in making the decisions, and at what point in the organization it is possible to be aware of all or most of these factors.

2. The ability of the members of the organization to whom the authority is to be delegated.
3. The need for speedy "on the spot" decisions.
4. The importance of the decision to successful operations.
5. The need for consistent and coordinated action by several divisions of the company.

Profit decentralization. A special form of delegation occurs when a company sets up self-contained, semiautonomous divisions. Johnson & Johnson, for instance, has a pharmaceutical division with its own research, production, sales, and finance operations; this division has almost complete authority to decide how to run its own affairs. In most respects the division is like an independent company (legally it is), and its officers are held responsible for resulting profits.

Du Pont, General Motors, General Electric, and other large firms use this form of decentralization because each division becomes more manageable, easier to coordinate and control, and more challenging to the executives who run it. Such profit decentralization is probably the best way to overcome the managerial difficulties of very large size.

Note that the concept of profit decentralization involves a combination of both (a) departmentation—placing all key activities necessary for making a profit into a self-contained unit—and (b) delegation—granting a high degree of independence over most activities so that the unit is semiautonomous.

Of course, use of profit decentralization is feasible only when production and marketing technology permit the clear separation of a sizable, stable chunk of business. Boeing Aircraft Company, for instance, has not been able to divide up its production activities into independent, self-contained units and consequently can use profit decentralization only in a modified form.

Delegation of authority and the task of control. The separation of planning and making of decisions on specific problems from the place where performance occurs inevitably creates control difficulties. Thus, when a sales manager sitting in the home office decides to solicit sales in a new territory, he also needs a control mechanism to insure proper execution of the plan. Or, if authority as well as performance is decentralized (for example, the salesman is given authority to decide which customers to solicit), a different control mechanism is required. In the first situation, a means of making sure the salesman did an effective job of calling on the specified customers is needed; in the second case a measure of how wisely the salesman selects his customers would be helpful.

We shall discuss the design of controls in a later chapter. The significant point here is that when central management approves decentralization plans, it should at the same time check on the controls to be used for appraising results of the delegation.

STAFF RELATIONSHIPS

Line authority is by no means the only relationship included in an administrative organization. Numerous criss-crossing of influence and communication is an essential part of every organization design. Procedures establish normal, routine paths for passing information, and many other lateral contacts are incorporated into systems for planning and control. In addition, advisory or "staff" relationships play an increasingly important role as a company grows and engages in more complex activities.

In practice, the scope of a staff assignment may vary widely— from office flunky to a key member of central management. Consequently, care is needed in figuring out just what staff relationships will be effective in a given setting.

General staff assistants. In its simple form, the idea of staff is used when a busy executive appoints an assistant to help him do his work. At first, an assistant may be primarily a fact finder, gathering and analyzing information for use by the executive in resolving troublesome problems. As the assistant gains experience, the executive may ask for recommendations; in fact, the assistant may prepare written instructions so that the executive receives recommendations and papers needing only his signature to put the proposals into effect. This kind of help enables an executive to deal with problems in a relatively short period of time; in fact, a more careful study may have been made than if the busy executive tried to do it himself.

A good staff assistant also works with other subordinates of the senior executive and with people outside the department and the company. He must, of course, contact such people in the process of gathering information. In addition, he normally discusses possible solutions to a problem with all people concerned. It some-

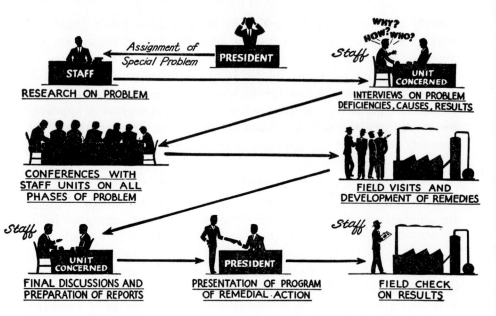

RESEARCH ON PROBLEM

INTERVIEWS ON PROBLEM DEFICIENCIES, CAUSES, RESULTS

CONFERENCES WITH STAFF UNITS ON ALL PHASES OF PROBLEM

FIELD VISITS AND DEVELOPMENT OF REMEDIES

FINAL DISCUSSIONS AND PREPARATION OF REPORTS

PRESENTATION OF PROGRAM OF REMEDIAL ACTION

FIELD CHECK ON RESULTS

Chart used in company training manual to explain role of staff.

times happens that in this examination and exchange of ideas, the problem resolves itself. The staff man has served as a catalyst or mediator and need only report to his senior that the problem is solved.

On other problems that require centralized decision, the staff man may play an important role in explaining and interpreting the plan of action. His detailed knowledge about the problem and intimate association with the senior executive put him in a good position to explain what is wanted. This interpretative function of a staff assistant again saves time of a busy executive and improves mutual understanding throughout the enterprise.

In still other situations, the busy executive may ask his staff assistant to keep an eye on some particular aspect of operations such as expense ratios, governmental regulations, or inventory turnover. Then, if there is need for executive action, the assistant takes the initiative in preparing a recommendation and calling the whole matter to his superior's attention. In this way the staff assistant serves as eyes and ears for his boss.

Specialized staff. The general staff assistant, such as has just been described, typically carries the title of *Assistant to* the sales manager, the president, or whoever his senior may be. These assistants may be asked to help with any or all of the activities of the executive.

The staff concept also may be applied to assistants who concentrate on some one function, or aspect, of operations. For instance, one staff man may concentrate on legal problems, while another works on public relations. Perhaps enough engineering problems arise so the executive needs personal help in this area. The chief executive of a large company may have a specialist on organization planning, another for expense control, and still a third working on executive personnel.

Although such men may be specialists in some one area, the nature of their relationship with the senior executive and with other employees is like that of the general staff assistant. They investigate, recommend, interpret, and follow up on problems in their particular sphere. Being specialists, it is quite likely that they possess technical knowledge that may be superior to anyone else's in the organization. Through the staff arrangement, this technical knowledge is put at the disposal of the senior executive and all of his subordinates who come in contact with the staff man.

The work assigned to a staff specialist may become so heavy that he needs people working with him. Consequently, there may develop a small organization unit on public relations, expense control, or other fields. This group may be called an "office" or a "service division." Size and title, however, do not change the nature of the relationship.

Essential factors in good staff relationships. The preceding illustrations of staff have assumed that it always is a full-time job. While this is often true in larger companies, it is not a necessary feature of the staff concept. The important thing is the relationship, and it is entirely possible for an executive to devote part of his time to staff work.

The staff relationship implies that the man is working on behalf of an executive; he is doing things the executive himself would do, if the time permitted; he has no authority to issue orders, and if he does pass along instructions or interpretations, this is done in the name of the senior executive.

Staff relationships may be used in any department of a business enterprise. Most of the examples already cited have been of staff work directly under a chief executive, but the idea has many other applications. The sales promotion director in the sales department, an industrial engineer in the production department, the cost analyst in the accounting department, an economist in the purchasing department, and a safety director in the personnel department are all positions where a considerable amount of staff relationship typically is found.

In some of these positions a man may be given functional authority (described in the next section) with respect to certain types of problems and work in a staff capacity over a much wider area. If such a dual arrangement appears necessary, care must be taken that all people affected understand the limits of the man's functional authority. In fact, many students of organization believe that a competent staff man can accomplish as much through recommendation and persuasion as he can by issuing orders. Actual practice in most companies suggests, however, that both staff relationships and functional authority are needed to deal with the complex business problems of the modern day.

FUNCTIONAL AUTHORITY

Functional authority is permission to issue directions to people not under your line supervision; such directions deal only with specified activities or certain aspects of those activities. Except for their source of issuance, these directions are to be treated as though they came from the senior executive himself.

Situations warranting use of functional authority. *Controller's relations with a branch.* The use of functional authority is illustrated in a manufacturing firm that has a general office in Chicago and plants in Kansas City, St. Louis, and Cleveland. Each plant manager "runs" his plant. He has line authority over all employees at the plant, including local accountants. On the other hand, the chief accountant at the central office is responsible for maintaining accounting records for the entire company; he has functional authority over *how* the records are kept at each branch.

The reason for granting functional authority in this instance is fairly clear. The weekly sales report of the company might be misleading if one branch accountant reported orders received as sales, whereas another unit of the company did not report goods as sold until they had actually been shipped. Likewise, one branch accountant might charge depreciation on machinery at his plant at a much lower rate than was used by another branch, with the result that the combined figures for the company as a whole would lack the consistency needed for comparisons and for income tax returns.

The branch manager continues to be the line supervisor of the branch accountant, but he is not free to keep the branch books any way he chooses any more than he is free to make different products or to double the size of his plant. He acts within the plans of the company, including the accounting procedures specified by the chief accountant.

Other departments exercising functional authority. A large part of the authority of several important departments is functional. For example, an industrial engineering unit in a factory often selects equipment and prescribes the tools and the methods to be used in production operations. The sales promotion departments of some companies stipulate the methods for presenting new products and the time the products will be introduced. In the meat packing house discussed in the last chapter, the product departments decide the total quantity of each end-product to be produced and also stipulate price ranges to be observed by the sales department.

In all these examples, the executive with functional authority does part of the planning of the activity. He may prescribe policies, set up methods, or determine the time when activities are to be undertaken. In doing this, he is saying how the activity is to be performed. The line executive, on the other hand, is responsible for seeing that the instructions issued by those with functional authority, as well as instructions "coming down the line," are carried out.

Through the use of functional authority, similarity of action by employees who are under several different line executives may be secured. Such similarity often is desirable in accounting, union relations, and some aspects of dealing with customers. Also, the following of expert judgment in technical matters such as engineering and law can be assured by using functional authority.

Reasons for cautious use of functional authority. Functional authority is a useful concept in the proper situations, but like many good things, if used in excess or at the wrong time, it can cause trouble. Among the dangers and disadvantages of functional authority are the following:

1. If several different people exercise functional authority over a given operating executive, he may be swamped with specialized instructions. A branch manager, for instance, may find it almost impossible to carry out all the directions received from the chief accountant, maintenance manager, warehouse manager, sales promotion manager, credit manager, personnel manager, and public relations manager—if each of these home office experts has a wide degree of functional authority. Moreover, under such circumstances, it is quite possible that some of the instructions will be inconsistent with others in actual operations.

2. The effectiveness of line supervisors may be weakened by heavy use of functional authority. As more and more instructions come from the functional specialists, the status of the line boss may be undermined. In the eyes of his subordinates, the boss has become merely a go-between, and they will often turn directly to the specialists for guidance. Some companies today are having serious difficulty keeping the loyalty of their foremen because of such dilution of their authority.

3. Functional authority sometimes leads to autocratic and inflexible administration. The functional specialist may become narrow in his viewpoint and insist that his plans be followed even though they are not well suited to a specific local situation. In a large concern he is likely to be distant from the scene of operations and reluctant to make modifications in his generalized plans.

For these reasons functional authority should be granted only when it is clearly desirable, and provision should be made to see that it is not used arbitrarily. Functional authority works best when (a) only a minor aspect of the total operating job is covered, (b) technical knowledge of a type not possessed by the operating executives is needed, and (c) consistency of action in several departments is important.

Composite relations. A single executive often has a variety of relationships, depending upon the subject and who the other person is. A controller, for instance, normally will (a) have line authority over employees within his department who keep company books and prepare reports, (b) have functional authority throughout the company over accounting systems, and (c) act in a purely staff capacity when suggesting how expenses may be cut. Similarly, a personnel director is likely to (a) have line authority over the employment office, cafeteria, and other employee service operations; (b) exercise functional authority with respect to compensation ranges, length of vacations, dismissal procedures, and the like; and (c) provide much constructive advice regarding training, promotion, motivation, etc., in a staff capacity.

These illustrations show that designating a man as "line" or "staff" is at best vague. For a real grasp of relationships, the authority or the influence of each executive should be defined for each subject he deals with and for various groups he contacts. *Customary* roles help clarify such definitions, but we should guard against oversimplification.

SUMMARY

The formal relationships established in administrative organization play a vital role in tying the work of all employees together. There are, of course, many informal relationships that affect people's attitudes and responses, but the formally designated relations are needed to hold the structure together.

Line authority is used in the normal worker-supervisor relationship. It involves assigning duties, granting permissions, and establishing obligations. Care should be taken to keep all three phases in balance and also to avoid dual subordination.

A further consideration in line relationships is the decentralization of authority. Delegation of authority and responsibility to perform work is essential. The significant question is how much authority to *decide* is delegated, that is, to what extent is the subordinate free to do what he thinks best and in what respects must he act only in accordance with instructions from his boss? There are no standard answers to this question, but the factors listed on pages 461 and 462 will usually suggest a sound solution for a specific situation.

In most modern businesses there will be some added relationships that supplement the line authority. In specialized and technical areas, an executive may give instructions to people under someone else's supervision. Such functional authority invites abuse, however, and should be used with great care.

A more flexible supplement to line authority is the staff relationship. Here the person outside the "line" only advises and explains. He can be of real value in providing expert counsel and in serving as eyes and ears for his senior, but he does not issue orders (except when he serves as a spokesman).

QUESTIONS FOR CLASS DISCUSSION

1. Multiproduct companies, such as General Motors and Johnson & Johnson, often establish product divisions each with its own engineering, production, sales, and related departments; each division is like a self-contained firm and is responsible for showing a profit from its own operations. A great deal of authority is delegated to each division manager. (a) What advantages does the company get from such a decentralized organization? (b) What benefits does a division of such company have compared with a completely separate firm of comparable size in the same industry? (c) What are the limitations of this kind of decentralization?

2. Is it good practice to permit the rank-and-file employees the privilege of communicating their ideas direct to the general management since it is difficult to transmit ideas through various intervening strata? Why? What are the dangers?

3. "Decentralization" has become such a popular word that its meaning is vague. Distinguish between (a) decentralization of performance, (b) decentralization of authority, and (c) decentralization of an activity such as research or stenographic work.

4. "Responsibility cannot be delegated." Authority to take action and authority to decide frequently are delegated. How, then, is it possible to abide by the principle that authority and responsibility for each executive should be equal (coextensive)?

5. Several executives of divisions of large electrical manufacturing companies served criminal sentences as the result of price collusion among these companies. One of the reasons cited to explain their behavior was pressure from central management for sales and profits. What organizational relationships are likely to lead to such behavior? What organizational relationships can be devised to minimize pressure for or occurrence of such behavior?

6. The First National Bank is permeated with dignity, tradition, and conservatism. Of its 800 employees, 20% have more than 20 years of service, and many officers entered the bank years ago as clerks. The personnel department has long confined its attention to recruitment, records and payroll, cafeteria, medical service, and employee activities. A new president has just promoted a 40-year-old junior officer to a newly created post of personnel vice-president. In addition to directing the existing personnel department, the president wants the vice-president to "modernize the personnel practices of the bank" with respect to salary administration, training-on-the-job, systematic retirement, and executive development. What authority should be given to the vice-president for each of his activities?

7. A textile firm with several mills in the same vicinity has a director of quality control reporting to the general production manager. Under the director of quality control are inspectors who work in the various mills inspecting incoming raw materials, goods in process, and finished goods. What should be the authority relationships between these inspectors and the mill superintendents? the purchasing agent? the director of quality control? Should the inspectors tell operating foremen of defects and suggest ways of avoiding them?

8. "A good staff man must be able to *sell* his ideas." Why is this important? Suggest several ways a staff man might go about winning acceptance of his ideas from (a) a newly appointed foreman and (b) a tough district sales manager who has worked for the company twenty years longer than the staff man.

9. The concept of "composite relations" implies that an executive must wear several hats. What does this mean for the kinds of training he should receive and what difficulties might it signify for his individual actions?

CASE XVIII

The I.C.L.A. Construction Company

I was assistant to the president of a small, closely owned holding company that specialized in highly profitable operating units with minimum capital needs. One of our enterprises, The I.C.L.A. Construction Company, did a general construction business with gross sales of about $15 million a year. The firm had its central office in Memphis and originally had built houses and industrial plants in the Mid-South for its customers. Shortly before the time of this case, the trustees of our holding company authorized a new department to enter into highway construction. Until then, I.C.L.A. had really been run by four people—two civil engineers, a treasurer and general manager, and a purchasing manager. These four people, nominally directed by the treasurer and general manager, were responsible for the entire operation of the firm and had wide leeway in their freedom of decision. When the trustees decided to open the new highway construction department, my boss, the president, hired an experienced civil engineer. The organizational structure of I.C.L.A. was modified only to the extent that another department was added (see the organization diagram on page 472).

The managers were each on a fixed salary and, in addition, received a percentage of the net income of I.C.L.A. Each manager also had an opportunity to buy up to a 10% share of the stock of I.C.L.A. The equity capital was not traded on any stock exchange, and the managers were required to sell the stock back to the trustees of the holding company if they left the firm. The price of the stock for these purposes was established by an arbitrational provision involving three banking and brokerage houses.

I.C.L.A. COMPANY
PARTIAL ORGANIZATION DIAGRAMS

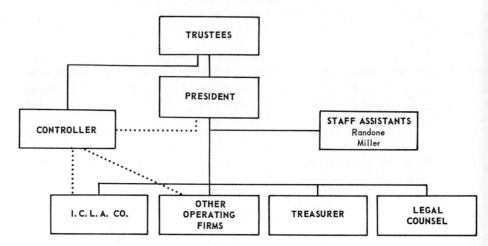

I. C. L. A. COMPANY

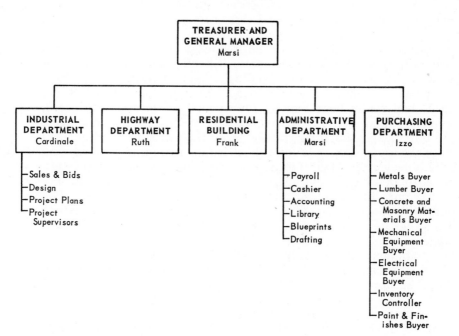

Our firm had a very good reputation and was therefore highly successful in its bids against competition.

Engineers in the various building departments prepared lists of materials and labor necessary for each bid and a time schedule for the completion of each part of the job. This information went to the purchasing department for the materials prices and cost estimates. Finally, the combined information was sent to the treasurer and general manager for control purposes. The treasurer supervised the financial aspects of the work done and gave his opinion on the budget from the point of view of the firm's capacity to profitably handle its overall construction program without endangering its solvency. The final bid was set by the chief engineer of the department and the treasurer with the participation of the purchasing department. If the firm's bid was successful, the budget served as the background and the control for the work.

Everything was explained in the budget. Generally, labor—and at times labor and materials—was subcontracted to other firms. As much as possible and except in the very largest cities, we bought the necessary materials—more to control the quality of the job than to gain any added profit. So we set up temporary divisions to coordinate the different subcontracts for each project. Typically, a department engineer both worked on the bid and then supervised or helped supervise a project.

The firm had much flexibility and few risks involving equipment or labor force. To obtain better performance and a higher profit margin, the timing of the beginning of the work of each subcontractor was scheduled in advance, and any delay affected costs because the subcontractors were often paid on the basis of time. Also the firm usually had to pay a penalty to the customer for delayed completion of construction.

After two months, the new department won a contract for building a new state highway link. The bid was $20 million for a two-year job. As always, the budget was ready. A new on-the-job supervisory division was set up for the project and the work began.

After a few months, complaints from all the other departments came to our holding company's central office. Materials were delayed in arriving, and in some cases the wrong material arrived. At the beginning we thought that this was merely the inevitable but temporary penalty the firm had to pay for its new organization. But the inefficiency of the purchasing department under the new arrangement continued and affected all departments. Efficiency of purchasing had been one of the main reasons for the previous success of the firm. The purchasing department tried its best to correct the situation, but something remained wrong.

To learn more about the situation, I made a tour of the construction divisions. For a week I listened to the on-the-job supervisors' complaints, but they could not tell me what the specific trouble was.

They gave me a long list of complaints, including delay in delivery and mix-up of materials among their divisions. Also, many of them wanted more independence, and it was suggested that each construction division be allowed to buy its supplies directly. Upon my return, I asked for a meeting with Mr. Cardinale, Mr. Frank, Mr. Ruth, Mr. Marsi, and Mr. Izzo. Mr. Cardinale was chairman.

Meeting

Cardinale: "The delay of materials has become our big problem and I don't like to speak of inefficiency in the purchasing department. I knew that with the new department to handle highway work the firm needed an adjustment period; however, we continue to have trouble. We must face the situation and try to find some way to relieve it."

Randone: "The situation must be solved as soon as possible. The organizational setup until now has been satisfactory, and I don't want to give more independence to the on-the-job supervisors. The purchase of materials is *our* concern, and if they are allowed to order, we will lose control. Therefore, our suggestions should be toward solving the problem without changing the present communication line of one organization."

Marsi: "The delay in the delivery of material has caused an immediate financial loss of $50,000 to $80,000, but the reputation of our firm may soon be threatened. The inefficiency of the company in handling the situation is now known to outsiders—bank, customers, and suppliers. Fortunately they do not know its effect beyond the new department on our whole internal organization. Our credit is still good, and next week I will go to sign a new credit line for the purpose of financing the needs of the new department. But we must clear up the situation and begin operating at our former high level of efficiency."

Frank: "I don't have many complaints, but some mix-up on deliveries of materials has occurred. Since the construction in my division was in advance of the date scheduled, the damage was fortunately small from a monetary point of view.

"Psychologically speaking, however, the on-the-job supervisors don't trust the purchasing department anymore. They feel that the residential building department will become only the little brother and they ask more decentralization in the big construction division at Houston, where we have that 200-house project.

"They want to order the material as stated in the budget directly from suppliers, sending only the bills to the Central Office."

Ruth: "In my department, many materials were delivered with delay. I don't understand why. We found that we needed a supply of bituminous concrete and crushed rock for reinforcement when we discovered that the ground along part of the route was softer than we had thought. The purchasing department was told about this change, but the materials arrived late. The highway was in advance of the original time schedule so the delay did not matter."

Izzo: "Although, as you say, the construction of the highway is now ahead of schedule, you have changed our original planned sequence of construction that we expected you to follow at all times. There are three separate stages of the job—earth leveling, first stratification, and laying of asphalt—and a certain amount of each of these should be achieved at any given time. We know that your percentage of the overall plan is ahead of schedule, but you have changed our plan of operation by finishing more of the earth leveling than is necessary at this time, and you have not completed enough of the stratification."

Ruth: "The construction division must work. I can't stop the work and wait for the material. The leased equipment for earth leveling costs about $10,000 a day. I can't stop it. The burden would be too great. We were able to work faster in leveling because we didn't find as much rock to blast as we expected; but we know that there is rock ahead in the route and the job will be harder and slower later."

Cardinale: "Technically speaking, you are right. Did you advise the purchasing department of the change?

Ruth: "I can't tell in advance what obstacles we will find. The obstacles are forecast in the budget, but they are spread over the whole period as an average. I can't follow the program strictly. I need to change the plan every day in order to obtain the right overall percentage of the planned program. The purchasing department must follow me. I can't follow the purchasing department."

Cardinale: "Estival, no one is accusing you. Speaking as the manager of my department, I have a long list of complaints and I think that my department suffered the most. We did not complain about the delay, but rather about the mix-up of materials. A delay is a delay, but getting wrong material makes everybody angry and nervous. Delays are often not anyone's fault, but we know that delivery of wrong material can only result from inefficiency. Two industrial plants are behind their planned time of completion. The money is nothing. The problem is that in one of the plants the machinery has arrived but it cannot be installed.

"The good name of the firm and *my* name as manager is beginning to decline. I trust the organization, but something must be done and quickly. I don't know what, but I want the right material at the right time, as before."

Izzo: "My department is not inefficient. My men are trying their best, but they can't work in peace. Calls and more calls come, and everyone is blaming us. Everybody thinks that we are playing favorites. We expect the on-the-job supervisors to ask us for special delivery if there is really an urgency; but now everything is treated as an urgent case. Nobody is cooperating. Everybody is only blaming us."

Randone: "During the next month the four managers will be the only ones who will be permitted to have authority to decide what is urgent and what is not. Perhaps this will help to alleviate this situation. Mr. Izzo, what do you think is the real problem and what do you suggest for solving it?"

Izzo: "The purchasing department is the only one that has a big concentrated job. From the moment the materials began arriving late, I exercised closer supervision. Everything must pass over my desk. I need two new men to . . ."

Cardinale: "Two years ago, the company had . . ."

Izzo: "I know it. Two years ago, the company had 20% more volume than it now has, but the variety of materials ordered and delivered was not so wide as now. We only had two operating departments then. I need two new people in the department. There are only seven men, eight counting me.

"I need only a month without pressure, and the department will be the same as before and the company will be as efficient as before. I will start a more rigid control and the budget will be checked again to see if we made any mistakes; but I am asking that any change you make be called to my attention."

Cardinale: "Bob, if you really need the two new employees, everybody agrees that you should hire them. What do you need? Two more specialists?"

Izzo: "No. Each of us needs some help. We are all somewhat overloaded. I need two people to help with the total work."

When I returned to our central office and reported all this to the president, he said: "It looks as if I.C.L.A. is getting organizationally too big for us. Should I recommend to the trustees that we sell it?"

REQUIRED: (a) Analyze the organizational relationships of the holding company and I.C.L.A. Consider at least such matters as the hiring of executives, the stock holdings, the form of the organization, the usefulness of the work done by Randone, and the decision about a new highway department.

(b) Appraise the carrying-out of the central management tasks in I.C.L.A.

(c) How can the purchasing tasks issue be resolved?

(d) Would you recommend selling the subsidiary? Is it organizationally too large for the holding company? (Consider such questions as what information should flow to the holding company, who can make the key decisions, and whether the holding company can maintain effective control.)

BALANCING THE
ORGANIZATION STRUCTURE

Sound administrative organization involves more than dividing activities into departments, divisions, and other sub-units and then defining the relationships between the heads and members of such units. In addition to these problems, which have been considered in the preceding chapters, central management should give attention to:

A. The role of committees in the organization.
B. The distinction between operating departments and service divisions.
C. Maintaining a balanced structure.
D. Recognizing the personal side of organization.

These aspects of organization are important in welding the several parts into a coordinated, overall structure.

ROLE OF COMMITTEES

Administrative organization is primarily concerned with the duties and relationships of single persons. The work of an enterprise is divided among the various employees so that each one has specified duties to perform as a supervisor or an operator. This concentration on the individual as the basic operating unit is necessary for efficiency in action and for purposes of control. When each person has a clear-cut job, he knows what to do and can be given praise or blame for the results achieved.

There are situations, however, when several individuals acting as a group can do a particular task better than a single individual. When an administrative task has been assigned to a group, rather than parceled up among several individuals, a *committee* has been formed.

Use of committees is a widespread practice; in fact some astute students of administration believe that committees are so widely used that they become a serious drawback to efficient operation.

477

Some executives use committees to avoid making difficult decisions; whenever they are in a tough spot, they "appoint a committee." All too often the committee is "a group of men who keep minutes and waste hours." Consequently, we should be careful just how and where committees are fitted into the organization.

Effective use of committees. *Management committee in a small firm.* One small plant employing less than 200 people formed a committee composed of the executives in charge of production and engineering, sales, auditing, finance, purchasing, and inspection. This committee met twice a week to discuss general problems affecting the entire business. Each member was supplied with full information regarding the financial condition of the company and the results of its operations. Thus, each of the executives was able to consider the problems of his department in the light of the general condition of the company.

If a difficult competitive condition arose in the market, the factory personnel were told of it. Likewise, men in sales knew of the production problems. This *interchange of information* enabled all executives to work together as a harmonious unit. The committee also served as a good clearinghouse for troubles. Moreover, all departments were informed of reasons underlying policies.

Salary committee. The setting of initial salaries and granting pay increases is a highly important task. It affects the morale of the individual employee and should be related to his whole work and personal situation; it should be kept in fair relationship with other salaries; it often is a major item of expense for the department or the company. A number of firms have concluded that this type of decision should not be left to the judgment of a single executive. There is always the possibility that personal prejudice will result in discrimination in favor of, or against, a particular person. Consequently, a salary committee composed of the senior operating executive, a representative of the personnel department, and the supervisor of the men whose salaries are being reviewed is given the responsibility for deciding upon all changes in salaries.

In a majority of cases, the recommendations of the immediate supervisor are approved by the salary committee. Nevertheless, the need for committee action may make the supervisor review his recommendations more carefully than he would otherwise have done. A further advantage of such a committee is that employees are more likely to accept the decision as fair and equitable if they know it represents the joint views of several individuals. In other words, such salary committees add an element of *safety* and *acceptability* to the decisions.

Community Chest campaign committee. Another common purpose of committees is to *secure cooperation* of members in carrying out a program. For example, often companies appoint a special committee of employees to help secure contributions to the Community Chest or the Red Cross. Usually such committees are composed of representatives from each major division. The committee may take a small part in planning the campaign but its major duty is to help get the job done.

The reason the committee is formed, rather than assigning the task to the various persons individually, is primarily a psychological one. People like to feel that they have at least an opportunity to share in the planning of the venture, and the feeling of joint endeavor that often develops in committee meetings may help boost morale. Recent studies of the use of committees in business situations indicate that "winning cooperation" is fully as important as "combined judgment."

Committees may be useful in many other situations. The foregoing cases merely illustrate how committees may be helpful in promoting coordination, providing integrated group judgment, and securing cooperation in the execution of plans. Committees can also be effective training devices. Through participation on committees, executives become aware of major company objectives and of effective ways of achieving these objectives. They can learn how problems arise, the point of view of several departments, and possible ways of dealing with the difficulties. Training, however, is a secondary benefit because rarely is it practical to set up a committee primarily for the purpose of training its junior members.

Situations where committees are ineffective. One drawback of committees is that they are often *slow* in reaching a decision. This was well illustrated by a pricing committee in a metal cabinet manufacturing company. The committee had been established to make sure that the views of the production manager, purchasing agent, controller, and sales manager were all taken into account when changes in prices were made. One summer, a competitive condition developed that led several of the company's competitors to cut their prices substantially. Two of the committee members were busy the day after the cut was announced, and the sales manager had an appointment with an important customer the following day. Immediately thereafter the controller went on vacation, and although the committee met in his absence, the final decision was not made until almost three weeks after the competitor's action. During this interval the company lost several orders and also created the impression in the minds of some customers that its products were high priced. This company continued to use a pricing committee, but as a result of its experience the sales manager has been authorized to make changes in prices under certain conditions without consulting the committee.

Another company drastically modified its use of committees after the board of directors found it almost impossible to place responsibility for some poor investments. The decision to make these investments had been made by a committee. When the decision turned out to be unwise, each member of the committee said that he had not really been in favor of the action but had simply gone along with the others. Even the man who made the original proposal said that he merely presented the idea as a possibility and that he had relied upon the judgment of the group. The net effect was that *no single person could be held accountable* for the action that was taken. This company now has fewer committees and they are definitely advisory. A single individual, often the chairman of the committee, is personally responsible for the action taken, and if he doubts the wisdom of the advice of the committee, he is at liberty to turn it down.

When decisive action is important, committees are often of little help. The balanced, tempered decision that presumably comes from committee consideration may, in fact, be simply a *compromise* that is neither "fish nor fowl." The management committee of a furniture company, for instance, could not agree on how much to spend for advertising. After long discussion, they decided on about half of the amount originally requested by the sales manager. Unfortunately, this drastic cut made the advertising campaign ineffective. It would have been better either to have cut the advertising to a nominal figure or to have undertaken a campaign large enough to impress retail buyers. Decisive action in either direction would have been better than the compromise that was finally followed.

In still other instances, political logrolling interferes with effective committee action. Members, knowing that they will want committee approval for some of their projects at a later time, support the position of other members' pet projects. Under such circumstances, committee approval means little so far as sound administration is concerned.

Committees are a relatively *expensive* way of arriving at a decision. If half a dozen men spend from 9:00 to 10:20 in a committee meeting, a whole man-day of time has been used up. Outside preparation time and the effect of interrupting other work add substantially to the time actually spent in meeting. This consideration of expense means that committees should not be used to consider relatively small matters, that is, issues on which a committee's decision is unlikely to result in much more profit than a decision made by a single individual. Unfortunately, a great many committees become bogged down in relatively small matters that do not warrant such an expensive way of handling.

Benefits and limitations of committees. No standard answer can be given to the question of the nature and number of committees that should be established in a particular company. The most common advantages and disadvantages of committees have already been illustrated and are summarized briefly in the diagram below. In addition, before establishing a committee, thought should be given to the social setting in which it will work. This will include such things as the availability of competent members; their training, background, and personality; previous experience with committees and the prevailing attitude toward them; the techniques of supervision normally used; and the general operating climate. It is safe to conclude that the appointment of committees should *not* be the standard answer to difficult problems, nor a standard device to cover over weaknesses in administration.

IMPORTANT FACTORS IN DECIDING WHEN TO USE COMMITTEES

Benefits		**Limitations**
Better coordination		Slow action
Cooperation with plan		Divided responsibility
Group judgment		Danger of compromise
Training of members		Expense

Guides for successful committee operation. If a committee is set up, several steps may be taken to increase the chances of its success. The following points are pertinent.

1. The duties and the authority of the committee should be defined clearly. Unless all members have a clear idea of the purpose of the committee and the subjects it is to cover, considerable time is likely to be lost in irrelevant discussion. The committee should know whether it is advisory or whether its decisions are to be final. When decisions are final, there should be an understanding of who will carry them out because it is obviously impractical for an entire group to be responsible for executing any plans.

2. Members should be selected in terms of their ability to help fulfill the purposes of the committee. A salary committee, for example, should be composed of a few highly respected and objective individuals, whereas a coordinating committee should include operating executives from the several divisions to be coordinated. When representation is important, committees may have to be large. In most other situations it is desirable to have only a few members and then to invite other people to sit in when subjects of interest to them are being discussed.

3. Often committees waste a lot of time determining the facts and the issues in a given problem. This can be avoided by designating someone to serve in a staff capacity, as described in the preceding chapter, for the committee. Such staff work can do much to overcome the disadvantages of expense and slowness of action that are typical of so many committees.

4. Work of standing committees that meet regularly can be expedited by a few simple procedures. Advanced preparation of an agenda, agreement on the types of information needed to make a decision, and summary of this information on a standard form are examples of procedures that greatly expedite the work of a committee.

The success of a committee depends to a considerable degree upon its chairman. The wise chairman will seek to avoid votes on important subjects. Instead, he will seek the opinions of members and attempt to summarize these in a way that all members will feel that they have contributed to the conclusion. Members are much more likely to agree with such a plan if they have not already voted for some other proposal. The committee chairman also plays an important part in seeing that discussion is kept on the subject, effective staff work has been done in advance of the meeting, and standard procedures are observed.

If committees are appointed only when they have a significant role to perform, and if the preceding guides for effective operation are followed, committees can become an important part of the organization structure of a company.

OPERATING DEPARTMENTS vs. SERVICE DIVISIONS

Need to distinguish service divisions. Grouping activities into departments, divisions, and other administrative units has already been discussed in Chapter 17. Frequently, all such units are not of the same type. Some will be performing basic steps directly concerned with providing services to the company's customers. Other units will be concerned with activities that aid the basic operating departments. Recognition of the difference between these operating departments and service divisions is important to an understanding of the overall organization structure.

The distinction between operating departments and service divisions has been very helpful in one of the large rubber companies. After careful study, this company decided to establish separate organizational units dealing with the following activities:

1. Tires
2. Footwear
3. Mechanical
4. Chemicals
5. Crude rubber
6. Exports
7. Advertising
8. Industrial relations
9. Public relations
10. Engineering
11. Research and development
12. Purchasing
13. Traffic
14. Legal

This is an imposing list, and if all units were treated alike, the president would have a difficult task of securing coordination. To overcome this difficulty, the company has identified the first six as "operating divisions" and placed a vice-president in charge of each. These are the units in which the basic consumer services are created. Most of them are large enough to have their own production and selling units, and each is responsible for showing tangible operating results.

All of the other units in the foregoing list are called "auxiliary departments." Each of these units is headed by a director and has relatively few employees compared with the operating divisions. There is a clear understanding throughout the company that the purpose of these auxiliary departments is to help the operating divisions do their jobs better. Only in this way can the existence of the service units be justified. In this particular company, finance and accounts are treated as a third category and report directly to the board of directors; most other companies with large product divisions, however, consider these functions as services.

The facilitating, supporting role of service divisions should never be overlooked. There is a tendency, particularly on the part of people in the service divisions, to recommend the transfer of more and more duties and control to the service division. Up to a point, this may be quite desirable. Members of the service division may have special skills and knowledge about such matters as traffic, real estate, or engineering. Moreover, they will not be so involved with operating details and will be able to give adequate attention to these functions. However, the activities are not ends in themselves. Any increase in the size of a division must continually meet the test: "Is this work adding to the overall effectiveness of the company, and can it be done better by separating it from operating activities?"

The general structure of a company in which service divisions are distinguished from operating departments is indicated in the accompanying chart. Of course, many other activities, such as telephones and messengers, real estate, warehousing, or traffic, may be set aside as service divisions under particular circumstances. It is not the type of work but its relation to the rest of the activities in the enterprise that makes it a service division.

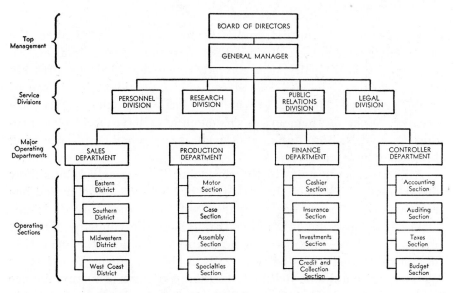

Organization structure of an electric clock company.

While this discussion has emphasized divisions serving the entire company, the same general idea is often found in the organization within a large department. A production department, for example, often has its own production scheduling, tool room, stockroom, quality control, and other auxiliary units that serve the production shop. Similarly, a large sales office may have units dealing with travel, customers' correspondence, display material, and the like.

Relationships with operating departments. Many service units simply perform certain work for the benefit of the operating departments. This is usually work that the department itself would have to perform if it had not been assigned to the specialized service unit. For example, a filing section may relieve the sales department of the bother of keeping all records pertaining to each of its many customers; a garage may take over the job of housing and maintaining salesmen's automobiles; and a warehouse may relieve the sales supervisor of all problems connected with the physical handling of goods.

In situations such as these, the relationships between the service units and the operating departments are relatively simple. There should be a clear understanding of (a) just what services are to be performed, including questions of speed and quality of work, and (b) how the service unit is to be notified as to what is needed. Of course, supervision will be necessary to make sure the work flows as planned, but the organization is simple and clear cut.

When a service unit is expected to give advice on how operations are to be performed, the relationships become more delicate. A sales promotion division, for example, may not only prepare advertising and display materials, but may also advise salesmen how to present new products to customers or when to start pushing for Christmas orders. The industrial engineer may be in a similar advisory position in the plant. Here we find the service unit operating in a *staff* capacity. As pointed out in the preceding chapter, the scope and nature of staff relationships needs to be understood and observed if the advisory unit is to be really effective. Even more complex relations arise if the service unit is given functional authority with respect to certain kinds of work. In this case, the service unit has quite a different relation to operators than the garage or the warehouse. The relation has shifted from an auxiliary worker to a spokesman for the boss.

Occasionally the service units have still another relation with operating people. A legal division, quality control section, or expense control unit may be given *concurring authority*. In other words, they cannot direct operating departments what to do, but they may have to concur, or approve, before activities can progress beyond a given point. For example, the quality control department may inspect raw materials or goods in process and hold up further production if quality standards are not met. The legal division may have to approve sales contracts, union agreements, or other contracts with outside parties before they are ratified by company executives. Occasionally an expense control unit will be given veto power over certain types of expenses, particularly if they exceed budget allotment. In most cases, the service units with concurring authority will also act in an advisory capacity, and the need to secure their "O.K." may be a relatively small aspect of the total relationship. Nevertheless, if concurrence is required this should be clearly understood by all people involved.

An important feature of organization structure, then, is to set up appropriate service divisions and define the relationships of the divisions to the basic operating units.

Drawbacks of separate service units. In the preceding discussion we have taken for granted that at least some service units will be useful. This does not mean that service units are always desirable. Particularly in small companies, and in many operating departments, the nature of the work may be such that no service divisions at all are needed.

As pointed out in Chapter 17, and re-emphasized in the preceding pages, the chief reasons for setting up service divisions are to get the benefits of specialization and adequate attention. The drawbacks of service divisions should not be forgotten, however. Most obvious is additional overhead expense. Salaries of specialists in the service divisions must be paid, and usually offices and equipment must be set aside for their use. Unless the service division can create significant economies in operations, these overhead expenses may absorb all the benefits from a separate division.

Less tangible but often more important is the added complexity that service divisions create. More units are involved in day-to-day operations, more relationships must work smoothly, and the task of coordination may be complicated. Sometimes members of a service unit become so interested in their particular activities that they lose sight of overall company goals.

Consequently, we should guard against the assumption that separate service units are always desirable. If careful analysis does show that a particular activity can be performed better in a separate unit, then, and only then, questions as to status and relationship that have been discussed in this section need to be considered.

BALANCED STRUCTURE

After major committees have been set up and the place of service units clarified, central management should take a look at the administrative organization as a whole. Has the net result of the many considerations affecting organization produced a balanced structure? For example, an attempt to relieve the span of supervision of one vice-president may have pushed too great a load on one of his subordinates or led to unjustified expansion of another department. The growth of sales of one product or a particular territory may have made a structure that was formerly balanced quite lopsided. Important among the features of balanced structure are (a) adaptation to crucial business factors and (b) possible use of parallel departmentation.

Adaptation to crucial factors. Balanced organization structure does not necessarily mean that there are an equal number of employees in each of the departments and sections under consideration. Instead the crucial factors in the success of the enterprise should be the focus. For every company there are certain activities that are particularly important to its success. In a chemical company, for instance, research is likely to be one of the crucial activities. In a mail-order company, advertising assumes great significance. An electric utility company must give particular attention to public relations. Even within the same industry one company may be more dependent upon low-cost production, whereas a competitor stresses service.

Often each of such crucial activities is placed in separate departments. Where this is not feasible, responsibility for these activities should be clearly assigned to a key executive. Normally, the chief executive himself will want to have direct contact with the individual who personally supervises crucial activities. The final result of this type of analysis should be a structure balanced more in terms of the importance of activities than in the size of the payroll (although, of course, payroll will be one of the factors that determines importance).

Use of parallel departmentation. Some manufacturing companies have two or more plants performing similar operations. Chain store companies typically have a considerable number of retail outlets doing similar work. Finance companies, and some banks, operate a whole series of branches rendering similar services to customers. Department stores and wholesale companies normally have a series of sections whose activities differ only in the product with which they deal. For companies such as these, the feasibility of using parallel departmentation should be examined.

Parallel departmentation simply means that the organization within several branches, plants, or departments doing similar work will be set up on a similar or parallel basis. This arrangement is indicated in the accompanying chart, which shows three

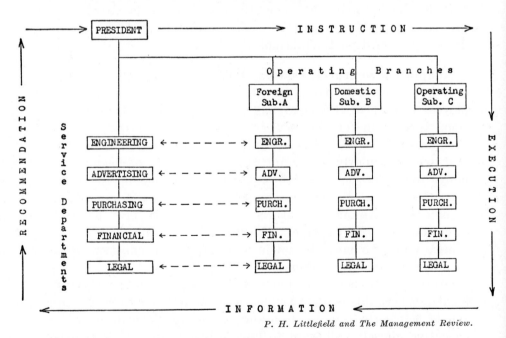

P. H. Littlefield and The Management Review.

Diagram showing parallel departmentation. This chart emphasizes only the general concept; it does not show all the units of the company, nor all the relationships.

operating branches, each of which is organized into the same five subdivisions. In addition, in this case, central staff units covering the same five functions have been established at the headquarters level. A similar concept is followed by a food chain that insists that each of its retail outlets shall have four main subdivisions— groceries, meat, produce, and finance. Parallel departmentation is also used by companies that have a single operating subsidiary or branch; the subsidiary is then set up with the same major divisions as are found in the parent company.

Direction and control is made easier when each of the operating units is organized on a parallel basis. Executives throughout the company know who to contact for information and who to hold accountable for activities in each area. Moreover, by having the units organized on a similar basis, it is easier to compare the results of one with another; this comparison may provide a useful standard for control. Some companies also find that parallel departmentation makes transfer of personnel from one operating unit to another easier.

The principal disadvantage of parallel departmentation is its lack of adjustment to local needs. Customer demands, operating conditions, volume of activities, physical facilities, capacity of executives, and other factors will vary from branch to branch. When a standard pattern is used, it is much more difficult to adjust the local organization to the particular circumstances in each unit. Also, the benefits of parallel departmentation become less significant in companies that operate with a high degree of decentralization.

These considerations suggest that considerable judgment should be exercised in deciding how far to carry the idea of parallel departmentation.

PERSONAL SIDE OF ORGANIZATION

Still another vital consideration in designing an organization structure is that of human relations. The effectiveness of any organization structure depends in part upon availability of people to fill positions. On the other hand, the organization will have a bearing on the morale of the people who work under it.

So far, we have discussed administrative organization in an impersonal way, as though human beings could be molded like metals to fit a particular place in a business machine. In practice, the people who occupy the positions provided in the organization plan are distinct personalities, and they can be fused together as a working unit only by taking account of their individual characteristics and idiosyncrasies. An organization, no matter how well designed, cannot operate effectively unless the men who fill the positions understand and are enthusiastic about the work assigned to them. Therefore, central management must recognize the personal problems involved in every organization. Important considerations in this regard are:

1. Adjusting responsibility to the ability of individuals
2. Avoiding inflexibility
3. Appreciating the inevitable conflict between individual and collective action.

Adjustments to ability of individuals. As a first step in formulating an administrative organization, it is desirable to draw up what might be called an ideal form of organization. In application, however, this organization often must be modified to fit the capacity of the individuals who will occupy the positions.

Restricting the scope of responsibility. For example, in setting up a new administrative organization for a manufacturing concern doing an annual business of over $30 million, the president of the company was in hearty agreement with the recommendation that the position of personnel director for the entire company be established. When the study reached the point of selecting an individual to fill this position, the best candidate was the employment manager in the factory. This individual seemed to have most of the characteristics needed for a good personnel director and was already well known and well liked by many of the employees. His experience, however, had been somewhat restricted, and he had not had an opportunity to become acquainted with several broader personnel problems.

For these reasons the president decided that the job of personnel director for the entire company should not be established at that time, but that the employment manager should be appointed personnel manager for plant employees. This would give him an opportunity to secure experience in dealing with a wide range of personnel problems. In addition, he would be able to establish his work in the plant on a sound footing before tackling services for office, sales, and other employees of the company.

Adding another executive. There are many other occasions when the assignment of activities must be adapted to the available personnel. In a concern one tenth the size of the one mentioned above, the sales manager had considerable ability in hiring, training, and supervising salesmen. He was, however, an individual of the proverbial salesman type and lacked ability to decide what merchandise should be included in the line of the company and the probable volume of orders for each article. He also lacked judgment in planning the amount of inventory to be held at the branches of the company.

In a company of this size the sales manager often performs these activities, but, in this instance, a position of merchandise manager was created and those activities falling between the actual production operations and the sales supervision were placed under his direction. The merchandise manager relieved the sales manager of making decisions on merchandise to be carried, determining the volume of goods to be manufactured, maintaining detailed records of inventories of finished goods at all locations, directing the movement of inventory from the plant to the branches so that orders could be filled promptly, and supervising the actual filling of orders and shipping of merchandise to customers.

This form of organization enabled the sales manager to devote his entire attention to the activities that he most enjoyed and for which he was best fitted. At the same time, it provided for the supervision of an important and necessary group of merchandising activities that otherwise might have been mishandled.

Another possibility might have been to place in a position over the sales manager someone who would handle a wider range of activities, giving the new man such a title as "director of sales." Because of the personality of the sales manager and his relationship with the salesmen, however, putting a new executive over the man who was generally recognized as the head of the sales department was considered inadvisable.

Too much emphasis on personalities. Such modifications to the ideal form of organization are often necessary. A great many companies make the mistake of going to the other extreme and building an administrative organization around personalities rather than following a logical assignment of duties; then every time a shift in personnel occurs, the organization has to be reshuffled. Nevertheless, when an individual does have special value to the company, a modification of the organization structure may be the most practical solution to the problem.

Retention of flexibility. *Companies may be overorganized.* One writer humorously described a well-organized factory as one that functions as follows in case of a fire:

> " a. An employee detecting fire reports to foreman.
> b. Foreman reports to shop superintendent.
> c. Shop superintendent reports to departmental manager.
> d. Departmental manager gets in touch with factory manager.
> e. Factory manager gets in touch with president. (If in town.)
> f. President notifies the board, if sitting.
> g. Board records matter, instructing secretary that fire be put out.
> h. Secretary issues requisition to fireman for extinguisher.
> i. Fireman issues extinguisher to foreman of department concerned.
> j. Foreman signs for issuance of extinguisher.
> k. Foreman proceeds to scene of conflagration.
> l. Foreman finds fire has gone out.
> m. Foreman returns extinguisher.
> n. Fireman signs for return of extinguisher.
>
> You see that even in emergencies everyone knew exactly what to do—no rush, no flurry, no panic; a proper check on the issuance and return of stock; everything running with well-oiled smoothness; the situation completely under control from start to finish." [1]

This is an exaggerated statement of a tendency that often develops, particularly in large companies. If too much effort is spent on making a very sharp division between the activities performed by one department and those performed by another, and if detailed and rigid definitions of responsibility are used throughout the whole organization, inflexibility is likely to prevent adjustment to the many variations and to personal problems that inevitably arise in any form of cooperative human activity.

The organization does not deal with a static situation and consequently should not be too rigid. Changes in the competitive market, the necessity of peak operation of a factory in order to meet a large influx of orders, the conservation of cash in times of credit stringency, and many other conditions call for flexibility in the organization that adjusts itself to new circumstances. Moreover, there will be changes in executive personnel from time to time. Consequently, if there has been formal and rigid definition of

---

1 "How to Run a Bassoon Factory," originally appearing in *Punch.*

responsibilities of a position while it is occupied by one individual, difficulty may be encountered in changing these responsibilities for a new person taking his position.

Flexibility in assignment of duties. To attempt to allocate responsibility for all types of problems that may arise is often unwise. Instead, there may be a definite distribution of the more important activities, but the unusual and intermittent problems can be assigned by the general manager to the individual who is best able to handle them at that particular time.

For example, the finance manager of a publishing house might be expected to handle the leasing of office space along with other long-term contracts that are a regular part of his job. In one publishing house, however, the duty was assigned to the editor because he had a general knowledge of the activities of the company and the nature of the space required. Moreover, he was not overloaded with work at the time the company changed its location. In this instance, the finance manager had been with the company only two years, and at that particular time was very busy with other work. Clearly the editor should not take on financial responsibilities as a regular part of his activities, but the organization should be so established that such a special assignment might be made if conditions required it.

Collective versus individual action. Before leaving this discussion of the personal side of administrative organization, the inevitable conflict that arises between collective and individual action in every business enterprise should at least be recognized. This is not a new problem, nor is it confined to the business world.

The individual in the political organization. Since the beginning of history, there has been a continuous conflict between the rights of the group and the rights of the individual. Primitive man combined into groups for purposes of protection, and in order to secure efficient group action it was necessary to appoint leaders. These leaders, in a desire to increase their power, sought to increase the power of the group at the expense of the rights of the individual. Man soon found that the leaders he had chosen to protect his rights became the chief danger to the maintenance of these rights.

Down through the centuries this struggle has continued unabated. At present, in many foreign countries the rights and dignity of the individual are consciously and definitely being subordinated to the interests of the group, or at least to the dictators of the group. People in the United States revolt against the thought of dictatorship because of their traditions and because they place a high value upon individual integrity and self-respect. Even within this country, however, there are those who believe the freedom of the individual should be further restricted by the authority of the central government.

Individual freedom within a business organization. This problem, which is so significant in political life, is also present in industrial life. Our study of business operations bears out the fact that nearly all people depend to a great degree upon extensive, cooperative, human effort. Each business enterprise is, in effect, a cooperative effort. Nevertheless, a business enterprise must depend upon its individual executives and employees for the originality, the drive, and the creativeness that are so essential to the successful operation of every business organization. Thus, each business entity is faced continuously with the problem of how to secure through collective action the coordination of activities necessary for the achievement of common objectives and, at the same time, give to the individual that freedom of action necessary for the development of initiative. Since the individual executives and employees constitute the dynamic element in all systems of cooperative action, some way must be devised to make room within the group for that spark of individuality emitting from each member of the organization.

Of course, greater individual freedom can be permitted in some lines of work, such as research and personal selling, than in other departments where the action of each person is very closely tied up with the actions of other individuals.

Viewpoint of the supervisor and the supervised. This problem is of great importance both to potential employees and their bosses at all levels. An employee must recognize that in order to secure successful group action the degree of freedom of all employees has to be restricted. All employees, therefore, should make a conscientious effort to cooperate in the collective action. In the interests of collective action, an employee must be willing to see his ideas, his "brain child" perhaps, set aside by those who presumably have a greater appreciation of the entire problems of the company. On the other hand, the group should not be permitted to dominate the thinking of the individual. Employees should develop an independent and questioning attitude, always considering possible improvements in the actions of the company.

In the same way, the manager must not, in his eagerness to achieve quick results, develop a form of organization and a philosophy of management that will hinder the development of individual members of the group. The organization should be sufficiently flexible to give some leeway to the varying characteristics of the individual members of the organization. At the same time, it should be strong enough to challenge the loyalty of the individual so that he may see the benefits of working with his fellows toward the common objectives of the company. In seeking a balance between collective and individual action, the manager faces one of his most difficult but most interesting problems.

SUMMARY

Assigning duties and establishing relationships constitute the bulk of the task of administrative organization. Several other aspects are vital, however, in welding the parts into a balanced structure. Four of these have been discussed in this chapter.

1. Committees can often be used to supplement and strengthen individual effort. In the right situations, they aid in securing coordination and cooperation. They also may be used to obtain group judgment on important problems. As an administrative tool, however, they are expensive and slow; responsibility is diffused and hence control is more difficult. For these reasons, care should be exercised in using committees to strengthen the organization structure.

2. Distinguishing between operating and service units helps to clarify the structure. This aids in defining relationships and also is useful in allocating manpower and in resolving jurisdictional conflicts. Fundamentally, a service division exists only to facilitate the work of operating departments (and their supervisors), and its performance may be judged in these terms.

3. Still another aspect of overall organization is that of emphasis and consistency. Running through the entire organization process is the recurring question of whether a change in one area will upset or cut across the organization in another area. Parallel departmentation sometimes helps to keep the numerous activities of a large concern in line, but inevitably some local adaptability is sacrificed. As a guide in securing good balance, we have sug-

gested that attention be focused on provision for crucial activities, that is, those activities that are likely to make the greatest difference in net results.

4. Finally, the organization structure should be considered in terms of its suitability to, and effect on, the people who will fill the jobs created. Usually the dictates of good organization should determine the work assigned to each executive, but some modifications may be necessary if a talented and long-service executive does not fit the positions in the ideal organization. There should be enough leeway in job assignments, and willingness to adjust duties, to permit as much individual freedom as is consistent with coordinated action.

QUESTIONS FOR CLASS DISCUSSION

1. Several research studies have identified one of the key tasks of central management to be coordination of the functional departments or operating divisions of a company. Can this task of coordination be assigned to a management committee or an executive committee, or should it better remain the responsibility of the president or chief executive officer? What kinds of issues can a single executive resolve that a group could not?

2. "Committees within a company should serve in a *staff* capacity." What does this statement mean? Do you agree?

3. (a) Do you think every major department of a company is entitled to a representative on each standing committee? (b) Would you consider the same factors in deciding on the size of and in selecting members for a (1) budget committee, (2) shop grievance committee, (3) salary committee, and (4) safety committee?

4. In a study of 31 leading companies, Holden, Fish, and Smith found four types of service units that they call (a) advisory agencies, (b) coordinative agencies, (c) service agencies, and (d) control agencies. Using the service units mentioned in the last three chapters, or others you have observed in actual operation, give examples of each of these four uses of the service unit concept.

5. Wide use is made of parallel departmentation in the Army. Do you think it is more suitable for the Army than for a large business concern? Explain.

6. State three important ways in which *size* of company affects the administrative organization best suited to its needs. Consider, for example, the organization needed for a small dress shop, a department store, and a dry goods chain; or think of a small town weekly newspaper, a large city daily, and a chain of newspapers. A manufacturing concern with 30, 300, 3,000, or 30,000 employees is still another illustration.

7. For several years the only activity of the Olsen Engineering Company was research and development work on missile parts, mostly on contracts for the government. Now the company has decided to manufacture some of the parts developed in its research. How is this change in objective likely to affect the administrative organization of the company?

8. "If every administrative organization must be adapted to individual executives sooner or later, why not start out by building the organization around the existing executive personnel?" How would you answer this question? Give reasons for your answer.

9. "An employee of a company gives up much of his freedom. On the job he has to do what his boss says; and if he hopes for promotion he has to dress, talk, join clubs, entertain, and live according to the pattern set by company executives. He becomes an *organization man.*" What should a company do to counteract this tendency? Should the company exercise any influence on behavior of an employee except while he is at work? Is your answer the same for a clerk and for the company vice-president?

CASE XIX

A.B.C. Corporation

The A.B.C. Corporation produces and distributes packaged food products, such as cereals, spices, puddings, jellies, crackers, salad dressings, etc. The company sells nationwide and conducts a very large national advertising campaign. It has 75 plants located throughout the United States and markets 65 different products, each under its own trademark. These are all food products, but are not otherwise closely related. They vary from long-margin specialities with comparatively small volume to larger-volume items with smaller profit margins. Different raw materials and commodities are used in their processing. All products, however, have the common factor of being sold through retail grocery stores. Gross sales are $250,000,000 and total assets are $125,000,000.

Management is centralized. The chairman of the board, the president, and four vice-presidents with responsibility for sales, production, purchasing, and law make up the executive top of the company and operate as a committee on all general policy matters.

Sales, advertising, and sales promotion are all under the jurisdiction of the sales vice-president. All plant operations, as well as research and engineering, report to the production vice-president. Purchasing is the responsibility of its vice-president, who also governs traffic. Public relations, law, and corporate functions are under the general counsel. Financial responsibilities are handled by the president, and employee relations are covered by each vice-president in his own area of responsibility.

The company was established as a combination of several food companies and has acquired others since. One of the theories of the organizers was that there would be great advantage in wholesale distribution if one salesman could cover an entire line on one call as against a number of salesmen each calling to sell a single line. Saving in time alone would be of great value to the distributor. This principle has been retained and proved successful as the company has grown. One sales organization handles all of the products. Each product is given specific time and attention by the sales organization in accordance with its demands. A product manager "buys" sales efforts and is charged with the cost of his particular use of the sales organization.

The head of the field sales organization reports to the vice-president. The advertising manager and the sales promotion manager take care of advertising and sales promotion for the entire line, but each product has its own advertising campaign and appropriation. The sales promotion manager is in charge of the missionary salesmen who contact retailers.

To assure protection from neglect or error, single products or a group of products are assigned to one of 20 product managers. Each product manager is responsible for seeing that his product receives the attention necessary for its success from the sales organization, the production department, and the advertising and promotion department. He specializes in the pricing and sales appeals questions of his product. He reports, however, to the sales vice-president, who has the overall say. The sales vice-president can curtail any efforts of the product managers if he is using his sales force for special effort on some other product or products. There is no institutional advertising. All advertising is coordinated and placed by the advertising manager with final authority in the sales vice-president.

Each plant is operated by a superintendent whose authority is over wages, maintenance cost, output, quality, hiring, inspection, and the other normal plant operation responsibilities. Superintendents report to 8 regional production managers who are responsible to the production vice-president. The volume of production in each plant is scheduled by the production control group reporting to the operating vice-president. Final schedules are set after consulting the sales vice-president.

The business has more than doubled in the past 10 years and profits, both gross and net, have increased. The number of plants has grown from 35 to 75. Dollar purchases have increased proportionately. New taxes and new reports to the government have added complexity. The management feels certain problems are potential dangers that should be solved before they become serious.

There have been periods in which a product has gotten into difficulty because of loss of favor with the public, bad management, or even neglect. Attention of the sales vice-president to the problems of some products has caused him, at times, to fail to recognize difficulties in others even though the product manager of such products has recognized them and has brought them to his attention. The burden on the present officers is becoming too heavy to insure proper attention to all of their responsibilities. Employment of assistants apparently causes loss of the close touch of the top group that is necessary to insure success.

Opportunities for increasing the line of products and expanding the business are being lost because of lack of executives' time to study them or to manage new products. In any business where specialties sold under trademark brands are the major business of a company, it is necessary for that company to continually bring out new products and to study old ones to determine, in their case, the point of no return with regard to promotion and advertising expenses.

Once the top executive group has approved the idea of a new product, it is put under the responsibility of any one of the vice-presidents. He develops an organization and brings it along. At first the advertising appropriation for a new product is not the responsibility of the sales vice-president but of the developing vice-president. Eventually, if the product proves out, it is turned over to the regular line of organization. With new products and growth in the old, the weight, complexity, and number of decisions that have to come up to the very few men at the top mean a heavy burden for them.

The A.B.C. Corporation management feels that, in addition to lost opportunities for sound expansion, profit opportunities in present products are not being fully recognized. The business may have grown too big for the form of management. Executives desire more responsible attention for each product.

At the same time they desire to keep the advantages of central management in purchasing, traffic, institutional reputation, and minimum sales approach and to maintain the high-caliber advice and experience now present in law, advertising, accounting, and public relations.

REQUIRED: Top executives conclude that A.B.C. has a problem of organization.

(a) How have changed conditions in this company affected the appropriateness of its organization structure?

(b) What changes do you recommend be made in the company organization structure? In your answer be sure to indicate (1) how the desired product responsibility can be achieved, (2) any changes in line authority, and (3) the use, if any, of staff, functional authority, or committees.

BOARD OF DIRECTORS AND
CENTRAL-MANAGEMENT
ORGANIZATION

Vital to success of every enterprise is the organization for central management itself. We have just examined major issues that central management should consider in organizing the total enterprise, but we touched only briefly on arrangements for the small group of key people who decide on such matters as company objectives, policies, and organization structure. The need for a workable understanding of "who is to do what" is fully as important for activities of senior executives as it is for people in a plant or a branch office.

First, let us summarize central-management tasks, noting especially the distinctive aspects of the work. Then we shall consider how the board of directors, the senior executives, and other groups can contribute to the performance of these functions.

DISTINCTIVE TASKS OF CENTRAL MANAGEMENT

Members of central management—president, vice-presidents, general managers, chief financial officer, and others charged with running the company as a whole rather than one segment—have supervisory duties just like every executive. They must guide, motivate, and control their immediate subordinates; and they will have some ordinary tasks like signing papers or greeting visitors that do not differ significantly from activities of many others in the company.

These duties are not unimportant. They should be done well because they contribute to the effectiveness of the company and because they will be regarded as examples for others to emulate.

Critical issues. In addition, central management has an array of pivotal duties it cannot delegate. Subordinates or consultants may assist, but the judgments are so critical to long-run success or the impact is so pervasive that the actions must be taken by the senior executives. The following brief description gives the flavor of these distinctive tasks of central management.

Setting company objectives. When the W. R. Grace Company decided to diversify into chemicals and other activities not associated with its steamship business, the company sharply altered its course. Accompanying the expansion of product lines was a new spirit of aggressiveness and risk-taking.

Ideally, objectives are set on the basis of a long-range forecast. Thus, when a leading manufacturer of bowling alley equipment foresaw a saturation of its traditional market, it moved into the school furniture field where growth could be confidently predicted on the basis of population statistics. Of course, long-range forecasts may also indicate that an enterprise should stick to its present business. Such was the conclusion when a medium-sized oil company decided not to become involved in international operations; diversion of the company's limited financial and personnel resources in foreign activities might well have undermined an attractive and safer development in the particular domestic market the company served.

Establishing major policies. A selection of policies also calls for broad judgment. The J. C. Penney Company, for example, built its nationwide chain of stores partly on a cash-and-carry policy. A common joke in the company was that Mr. Penney established the policy because his middle name was "Cash." Whatever its origin, the policy worked well. However, a dramatic shift in consumer financing occurred in the 1950's. The Penney company decided that a policy which had been an asset for over half a century had now become a liability, and it reversed its position on granting credit to customers.

In other instances, central management may decide to stick with a basic policy. General Foods Corporation provides a dramatic example in its decision to stick with a policy against the union shop. The company was confronted by a very strong union on the West Coast, its position in the frozen food business was in jeopardy, and only half a dozen employees did not want to join the union. Mr. Clarence Francis, then head of General Foods, felt that the integrity of its entire personnel policies was at stake, so the company stuck with its policy. Fortunately, Mr. Francis was able to convince the union that the company's record did demonstrate fairness and liberality, and the union shop demand was dropped.

In deciding to maintain its former policy, the board of directors had to match up the possible losses in an important segment of its business against the ramifications of a shift in policy on future employee relations throughout the company.

Long-range planning and strategy. In addition to objectives and policies, long-range programs typically incorporate the timing and the magnitude of future actions. These are major decisions, as executives in every airline that has shifted to modern jet planes can readily testify. In fact, several major lines found themselves in serious financial difficulties because their long-range planning for new equipment was faulty.

Strategy often enters into long-range planning. For example— shifting the illustration from airlines to aircraft manufacturers— Boeing invested several million dollars designing a large jet cargo plane at a time when neither the Air Force nor the commercial airlines showed any interest. The company's forecast of aircraft trends proved to be correct and Boeing not only secured large military orders but won a major position in the commercial aircraft field. In contrast, Convair Division of General Dynamics Corporation overcommitted itself in an attempt to catch up in the jet race and lost $350 million (probably the largest civilian mistake up to that time).

Changing organization structure. When Mr. Ralph Cordiner became president of General Electric Company, he accepted the position only after the board of directors agreed to support a major reorganization. He recognized that the change would cause temporary disruption, risk of loss during the transition, and opposition by members of the old guard. Such a rocking-the-boat while a company is profitable takes foresight and courage. At about the same time, the president of a much smaller chemical concern chose an evolutionary approach to the organization structure he believed the company needed. Even though he moved slowly, the changes were recognized by central management as having a profound effect on the company's ability to expand in the future.

Selecting key personnel. A delicate, and in some ways the most critical, task of central management is the selection of a chief executive and the men who report to him. These men not only dominate the success or the failure of existing policies and objectives, they also typically are key figures in formulating new plans. Often the man selected reflects a judgment of what the company most needs at that time. For instance, a large insurance company that had been highly successful in expanding its position in the industry selected a conservative financial man as its new president. This move came as a surprise because another younger, dynamic vice-president was much better qualified to continue the successful practices of the retiring president. Actually, in the expansion process expenses had gotten out of line and the older man was selected because it was anticipated he would insist on a tightening up that was needed at that time. He was due for retirement in a few years, and then the younger man was placed in the top post. If the older, conservative man had been president for ten or fifteen years, the company might have lost much valuable momentum; but a shakedown for a much shorter interval probably added long-run strength to the company.

Approving large capital expenditures and contracts. When a company commits, say, 3% or more of its total assets to an investment that will be recovered only over a period of years, central management should take a good hard look at the soundness of the venture. For example, when a department store invests in a new branch in a suburban shopping center, someone must double-check not only the ability of the store to manage such a branch, but also the specific location, capacity, and design of the building to be constructed. Since capital expenditures are relatively easy to identify and control, some central managements insist on reviewing small as well as large projects. The question then arises whether such a review is the most effective way to use the time and the talents of these men.

Fully as important to long-run success, though less tangible, are long-term contracts. Thus, a highly successful manufacturer of detergents quite properly gave long consideration to the granting of an exclusive franchise to sell its products in Europe. Often a purchase contract or a retirement plan may involve as much money over a period of years as a new building. We have already noted in Chapter 14 that long-term leases are an alternative way of acquiring the use of fixed assets. The length of such commitments, as well as their amount, makes their review by the same group of people who are thinking in terms of long-run objectives and policies desirable.

Negotiating mergers and major agreements. Typically, members of top management are active participants in major negotiations. The railway merger movement of the 1960's, for example, probably absorbs more time of the senior executives of the lines involved than any other problem. Such agreements are always complex, and other matters seem insignificant when a merger is in the offing.

Other major agreements may be of such significance to the company that its senior officers personally devote important blocks of their time to negotiation. The president of a company seeking to install pay television, for instance, spent more than half of his time securing the necessary approvals from federal and state regulatory commissions and companies affiliated in the venture. Similarly, the president of a nonscheduled air freight line made government approval of transatlantic flights his top priority task for over two years. Subordinates could do the spadework, but the importance of the agreement and the attitude of outside parties required that the company be represented by a senior executive.

Officially representing the company. Many people represent a company—salesmen, purchasing agents, union negotiators, and others. On some occasions this representation must be done by a member of central management. When a congressional committee calls upon a president to testify, he rarely sends one of his lieutenants. Likewise, security analysts much prefer to quiz the president —and to contribute to the company's financial standing, he usually meets with them. Charitable and civic groups also much prefer to deal with senior executives who can speak officially for their companies. The benefits of such activities are intangible and perhaps small, yet they are an inescapable part of business citizenship.

Approving annual budgets. Annual budgets can be a primary device for guiding and coordinating company operations. The budget presents, in condensed form, the financial aspects of an overall company program. Because of its terseness and comprehensiveness, many central managements use the annual budget— within stipulated limits—to control a whole array of more detailed plans. Review of the budget provides an opportunity to check the integration of short- and long-range plans, to iron out unresolved differences in emphasis, and to set short-range targets. Central management endorsement is necessary if the budget is to serve these purposes well.

Coordinating and controlling. Although central management is predominantly concerned with the future, it must maintain a guiding influence on current activities. Any firm with a group of vigorous executives will occasionally encounter sharp differences of opinion. Central management has the task of "umpiring" so that action may proceed.

Finally, as stewards for the entire enterprise, central management must keep a watchful eye on current results. If operations are unsatisfactory, someone must be objective enough and tough enough to insist on remedial action. The decision of Ford Motor Company to admit that the Edsel car was a flop and should be discontinued— even though millions of dollars had been invested in its planning and initial production—was certainly difficult to make. Pride and personalities were involved. By decisive action, continuing efforts on a losing proposition were checked and resources were redirected to projects that held much greater promise. Hindsight tells us that the Chrysler Corporation would have fared better by similar decisive action with respect to the De Soto five or ten years sooner than it was actually taken.

Most of the preceding examples of critical central management problems deal with large firms. Small companies also face similar issues that to them are just as crucial. The aim of the above review has been merely to emphasize the nature of the central management task, the organization of which is the theme of this chapter. Since the entire book takes a central management viewpoint, a more systematic and complete list of problems that may land on the desk of a senior executive can be obtained from the outline of each of the chapters.

Characteristics of central management problems. Emerging from this review of critical issues faced by central management are four characteristics that appear again and again. These do not describe the total job, but they help to identify its distinctive nature. In general, central management is concerned with problems that are:

1. *Important.* Importance, here, may be tested in relation to (a) income, (b) survival, and (c) other basic objectives of the enterprise.
2. *Long-range.* In an established, ongoing, social institution, central management can influence today's actions only slightly. By contrast, it is in a unique position to shape long-range objectives, policies, and actions bearing fruit in the future.
3. *Company-wide.* Due to its position, central management can appreciate the impact of action in one department on other parts

of the enterprise. It must seek strategic emphasis and balance in the total effort.

4. *Qualitative.* Many judgments of people, events, pressures, risks, and other intangibles must be made, and relative values must be attached to predicted outcomes.

On another dimension, if central management is to deal with problems having these characteristics, it needs a high degree of objectivity and wisdom, coupled with decisiveness and courage. We are not claiming that senior executives are, in fact, paragons; we are only identifying the qualities that appear to be especially important to provide in an organization for central management.

ROLE OF BOARD OF DIRECTORS

Although corporations make up only about one tenth of the total business firms of the country, they contribute nearly three fourths of the income produced by business firms. Most business concerns with a hundred employees or more are incorporated, as well as a very large number of nonprofit enterprises; consequently, it is appropriate to inquire how top management functions should be organized in a corporation. (Later discussion of the use of executives and staff applies to proprietorships and partnerships as well as to corporations insofar as such enterprises organize for central management functions.)

Legal theory. Stockholders of a corporation are not expected to perform management functions, and typically they are even more passive than they need be. Except for rare insurrections, stockholders do little more than vote for directors, approve recommendations submitted by management, and hopefully collect dividends. Normally they simply sell their stock if they don't like the way the corporation is run.

Large stockholders may be active, to be sure, but this is almost always done as a director or perhaps as an officer of the corporation. Once in a while, when a corporation is badly mismanaged, a group of dissident stockholders will wrest control from the existing management. However, they too pass management responsibility to a "new" board of directors. So, the stockholders *per se* do not provide central management.

According to legal documents, the board of directors establishes objectives, sets policies, selects officers, approves major contracts, and performs many of the other functions describe in the preceding section. Unquestionably the board has the power to do these things. The practical question is, Can we expect the board to perform these functions well or should most of the initiative and activity be delegated to executives of the corporation?

An inactive board. The activities performed by a board of directors vary widely. Until recently, most boards left the entire administration of the firm to executives.

The rationale for such an arrangement is that operating problems can be settled best by men who have an intimate acquaintance and long years of association with the company. These men can dispose of problems in their normal daily contacts without bothering with a meeting of the directors. The directors then confine their attention to formal action on dividends; to the election of officers; to the approval of any public reports; and to decisions on various minor matters, such as the approval of a given bank to be used as depository for funds of the company or the granting of a power of attorney to some trusted employee. Most of these actions are taken upon recommendation of the executives, and consequently the meetings of the board of directors are perfunctory affairs.

Membership of the board. Recognition that the board of directors can and should perform a more vital role has been growing. However, the nature of this role depends upon the composition of the board.

An inside board. Often a board of directors consists largely, if not entirely, of executives of the company. Such directors are well informed about internal operations, the success of the company is of great importance to them, and they are readily available for discussion when critical issues arise.

Unfortunately, an operating executive has difficulty taking a long-run, objective view of his company. He is inevitably immersed in day-to-day problems and is emotionally committed to making certain programs succeed. Moreover, he cannot disassociate himself from social pressure of his colleagues and particularly of his boss; he is naturally concerned with maintaining the goodwill of these men because they can make life easy or hard for him. To assume that this man can change his perspective and his loyalties when he walks into an occasional board meeting is unrealistic.

A board of directors composed of executives can function as a top management committee. Under favorable conditions, as we shall note later, they do contribute a valuable point of view to central management problems. Rarely can they unaided develop an objective, independent and tough-minded view of the company as a whole.

A few conspicuous exceptions exist; the Standard Oil Company (New Jersey) is probably the best known. In this instance, most directors are full-time employees of the company, but they are relieved of all operating responsibilities and focus their attention solely on central management problems. Very few companies can afford such a full-time board of high calibre executives (the direct expense of this board is over $2 million per year). A modified version is to have an executive committee of the board composed of men who devote their full time to central management. This arrangement is also rare because of the expense involved.

An outside board. As the name implies, an outside board of directors is composed of men whose principal interest is in some other company or profession. A banker, a prominent attorney, and senior executives of companies in other industries are commonly used as outside directors.

The advantages and the disadvantages of outside directors are just the opposite of those for inside directors. The men coming from the outside have independence of judgment and objectivity; they can see the company from a different point of view, and they are not wrapped up in short-run problems. On the other hand, they lack an intimate knowledge of the company operations and its relations with outside groups. More serious, they lack time to become fully informed; having major commitments in their principal line of activity, they cannot be expected to devote more than a few hours a month for the nominal directors' fee that is customarily paid. All too often a man accepts a directorship for the prestige attached or as a friendly gesture. He is willing to give advice, but he cannot be expected to exercise initiative in seeking directions for the company to expand or in weighing the likely consequences of a change in policy.

Typically, though not always, the least useful outside director is a "watchdog." This is a man placed on a board to protect some special interest—bondholders, major customer or supplier, minority stockholder, a labor union, or the like. The reason for his appointment gives him a divided interest; and while he shares a desire for the success of the enterprise, he may not be fully objective in appraising major proposed changes. Fortunately, able men are often nominated by such interest groups, and over time these men "identify" with the company fully as much as with their original constituents. If the reverse occurs and the watchdog function predominates, meetings of the board of directors will probably cease to be a forum for frank discussion of central management problems.

Slow growth is occurring in the use of professional outside directors. These are usually men of broad experience, either as former executives or as consultants, who devote a significant amount of time to any directorship they accept. In return, they are paid a fee (often $5,000 to $10,000 a year) to compensate them for their services.

Since outside members and inside members each have their advantages and limitations, progressive companies now attempt to get a balance between the two groups. The aim is to get a board of directors with varied experience, talent, and viewpoints.

Feasible duties for a board. Because of the membership problems just discussed, it is unrealistic to assume that a typical board of directors will perform the functions assumed in the legal theory. The board, as such, cannot be expected to provide the initiative and the creative drive needed in central management. In fact, a company will be fortunate in attracting to its board a group of men who can provide wise counsel. We do not mean to underrate the value of a strong board of directors; the point is that even a good board cannot be expected to do the total central management job.

What, then, should be the role of the board of directors? A practical assignment for a typical board should include these duties:

1. *Approve major changes in objectives, policies, organization structure, and large commitments.* This assumes that carefully prepared recommendations on such matters will flow up from the senior executives. Even if the board approves a large majority of the recommendations made, the necessity for developing a thoughtful justification of the proposals stimulates executives to think through such changes from all angles. This careful preparation of a recommendation may be as valuable as the combined judgment of the board.

2. *Select top executives, approve promotions of key men, and set salaries for this top group of executives.* This assignment is both delicate and highly important. It requires independent and yet informed judgments. The board of directors is in a better position to perform this task than anyone else.

3. *Share predictions of future developments, crucial factors, and responses to possible actions.* Here the board is contributing to planning in the formulative stage. The benefits of the broad experience and the diverse points of view are made available to the executive group. Outside members of the board can provide this sort of counsel without unrealistic demands on their time.

4. *Evaluate results and ask discerning questions.* The board should appraise operating results both for prudent control and to obtain background information. This evaluation process should include the asking of a variety of penetrating questions. Most of these questions will be readily answered, but a few may set off a line of thought previously overlooked. Both directors and executives should recognize that the prime purpose here is to see problems from new and useful angles.

5. *Provide personal advice informally.* Already familiar with the company, a director may be an excellent source of advice to executives. The treasurer may call a banker-director about a recent change in the money market, or the marketing vice-president may call another company executive about a new advertising agency. Perhaps the president will want to test out an idea before a formal recommendation is presented to the board as a whole. The informality of these contacts encourages a free exchange of tentative ideas and intuitive feelings.

A board performing the functions just described is particularly valuable because such a check and independent viewpoint can rarely be developed within the executive group.

SENIOR EXECUTIVES

Legal titles. Officers of a corporation—president, vice-presidents, treasurer, secretary, etc.—are formally elected by the board of directors in accordance with provisions of the company's bylaws. Occasionally, the bylaws also contain a realistic job description for these officers; but typically the bylaws simply make some sweeping statements about the duties of the president and the treasurer and say little or nothing about other officers. Often a senior executive such as general manager is not a legal officer at all, whereas an individual performing perfunctory duties in the secretary's office may be formally elected by the board. Common practice is to leave the legal authorization quite general, because this is difficult to change; instead, the actual working relationships are developed orally, by exchange of memoranda, or possibly in a company organization manual.

Legal titles, then, give us only vague clues about how a top management actually functions. Usually the role of the various executives is developed first and then any necessary legal formalities are performed later. It is entirely possible for a vice-president or even a president to have no operating duties at all. Consequently, from the viewpoint of the actual management of the business, legal titles tell us little.

Tasks to be performed. However the legal titles may be arranged, senior officers have vital duties to perform. They are the men who must work out operational definitions of objectives and policies based on a careful appraisal of trends, company strengths, obstacles to be overcome, impact on the rest of the company, and the like. The executives, with rare exceptions, negotiate major agreements for the company. They are the ones who represent the firm to congressional committees. A review of the annual budget with an understanding of its implications is an assignment senior executives are best able to perform.

A quick review of the distinctive tasks of central management presented in the beginning of this chapter will reveal that much of the work must be performed by full-time, thoroughly informed company executives. If the company is to be strong, these executives must provide initiative and leadership. Others may help, but in a typical enterprise the senior executives must provide the dynamic force.

Of course, a senior executive may also be an owner and a director; but as we have seen, they are not in an optimum position to provide strong leadership in those capacities.

The chief executive. Normally, the chief operating executive also serves as the focal point for central management. This man usually holds the title of "president," but for diplomatic reasons he may be named chairman of the board, executive vice-president, or perhaps general manager. Ideally, he has vision; lays plans for 5, 10, or 20 years ahead; is a master of strategy and a negotiator; has ability to pick able men; stimulates and leads both immediate subordinates and employees throughout the company; is a popular and effective leader in civic and industry affairs; expects high standards of achievement by his subordinates; and courageously takes remedial action when all is not well.

Again, realism forces us to admit that no single man can excel in all these respects; and even if he had the ability, he would not have the time to do all these things personally. Consequently, the wise chief executive tries to see that important activities he cannot perform himself are done by someone else in the company. This conclusion leads us to the question of how the chief executive's "office" can be organized.

Dual executive. The most common way to relieve the central management burden on the president is to share the job with another senior executive. Various combinations of titles are used: chairman of the board and president, president and executive vice-president, or president and general manager are examples. Whatever the titles, the two men have to develop their own unique way of splitting the total task. The division is likely to reflect the particular interests and abilities of the two individuals. One man may handle most external relations while the other works with executives within the company. One may focus on long-range development, and the second may deal with current problems. Sometimes the division is along functional or product lines. Perhaps no continuing pattern exists; each works on whatever seems most pressing at the moment. Regardless of how the work is shared, an intimate and frequent interchange is desirable so that the two men function as a closely integrated partnership.

Occasionally, three men work together as peers, but the integration of their thoughts and activities into a single president's office view is difficult.

The dual executive arrangement works better in the top job than in other executive positions—probably because a higher proportion of the total work involves planning and deliberation and less time is involved in supervising daily activities. Nevertheless, it is a delicate arrangement and depends on getting the right combination of personalities.

Management committee. Another sharing device is the management committee, perhaps called policy committee or planning committee. Here all senior executives serve on a committee that deals with several central management tasks. Establishing objectives and policies, building long-range programs, appraising capital expenditures, and reviewing annual budgets are typical activities.

A top management committee has all the inherent advantages and limitations of any committee, as discussed in the preceding chapter. It clearly is a good coordinating mechanism; but if it is just an added assignment for executives who are already fully occupied with managing their respective departments, not much creative central management work will be accomplished in committee meetings. The firms with best success with a genuine central management committee have deliberately relieved its members of a significant part of their supervisory burdens, often by placing a single deputy under each member. The members are then expected to devote a quarter to half their total time to central management problems assigned to them by the president.

Central management staff. Another well-recognized way to assist the chief executive with central management tasks is the use of a staff. Several leading companies, for instance, have a staff group working on *long-range planning*. These men study future trends, explore possible additions to the product line, project requirements for buildings and for training personnel, and prepare similar data and recommendations for consideration by the president. The organization for long-range planning is a special problem in itself because central staff should tap the ideas of thinking people throughout the company. A few firms rotate young executives in and out of the long-range planning group for this purpose. Decentralized companies may select a long-range planning man in each operating division; the ideas of these men are then funneled up to a coordinating staff, the chief executive, or to the management committee if one exists.

The use of an *organization planning* staff reporting to the president is becoming more common. Such a unit assists in adapting the company organization structure to changing needs. A related task sometimes combined with organization planning is *executive personnel development*. Of course, executive development may simply be part of the training activity of the company; but in some cases the personnel staff advisor to the president shares in the selection, development, and compensation planning for senior executives.

The role of the *business economist* is often confined to making cyclical forecasts of volume and prices in the industry; however, in a few instances he has become an active participant in central management discussions. Similarly, *financial analysts* occasionally become advisors on central management issues.

These are merely illustrations of the kinds of problems the top staff may handle. Such men do more than assemble information specifically requested by the president, helpful though this may be. To be a really significant member of the team that assures that central management tasks are performed well, a staff man must be a respected, intimate advisor of the senior executive. Such staff men are hard to find, and not all chief executives know how to use staff effectively on difficult, intangible problems.

SUMMARY

In addition to the many—and important—problems of current daily management of an enterprise, an array of distinctive tasks must be performed by central management. Important among these tasks are setting company objectives, establishing major policies, developing long-range planning and strategy, changing the organization structure, selecting key personnel, approving large capital expenditures, negotiating major agreements, officially representing the company, and coordinating and controlling the overall company actions.

Most companies can handle such issues best by a combined effort. The board of directors has an essential role of objective evaluation, independent approval, and injection of varied ideas and viewpoints. To perform this role well the board usually should consist of both inside and outside directors.

The major burden for central management, however, must be carried by full-time executives. The chief executive serves as the focal point, but he needs assistance. This may be provided by having dual top executives, a management committee, staff assistants, or a combination of all three. All such arrangements are delicate and call for men of outstanding ability. The particular organization adopted in a specific company will depend both on the personalities involved and the issues that are critical.

Small firms cannot support so many participants. Nevertheless, two or three outside directors can be carefully chosen, and one of the executives—the president or perhaps a vice-president—can be assigned a light enough supervisory load to permit him to give concentrated attention to the longer-range, broader issues of central management.

An established business may coast for several years with weak central management. For long-run success, however, nothing is more crucial. Through some kind of organization, the job should be done and done well.

In the preceding chapters on organization, we discussed grouping of activities for effective operation, organizational relationships, and organization structure. We have now emphasized another vital element—the provision of some kind of organization to perform distinctive central management tasks. Of course, sound organization alone is not enough; it must be manned by good executives. The next chapter is devoted to this related topic of executive personnel.

QUESTIONS FOR CLASS DISCUSSION

1. A new, young president of a rapidly growing chemical and agriculture products firm in which one family held a dominant—but not a majority—interest stated that his actions needed to reflect the spirit of aggressiveness and risk-taking required in such a firm. He said: "My job is to constantly jack-up the organization with new ideas. I am always on the search for new processes, new cost-control ideas, and new ways of organizing and operating. I pass these along, see how they are accepted, and then, if they are put into practice, check up to see how they have worked out." Under what circumstances would this be an effective view of a central manager's job?

2. The new executive offices of an aerospace company with $800 million in sales and 40,000 employees were designed with no individual offices for the chief executives and the corporate staff. Instead they all had desks on an open floor—an executive bullpen. The purposes were to increase the contact among the 90 officers and 70 secretaries, to remove barriers to discussion, and to reduce artificial status symbols. Closed consulting rooms were provided for occasional talks or telephone calls. The president said: "This arrangement works for us but is no panacea for all management problems." Under what circumstances might this idea be translatable to other companies or to other parts of an organization?

3. A National Industrial Conference Board Study of boards of directors showed some significant differences between the boards of directors of manufacturing and nonmanufacturing companies. Manufacturing company boards averaged 11 members of an average age of 58, had fewer compulsory retirement provisions, had larger numbers of committees, and had 46% of their board seats held by employees. Boards of directors of nonmanufacturing firms (utility, transportation, and financial firms) averaged 14 members (an even number) of an average age of 62, had fewer committees concerned with stock options and executive salaries and bonuses, met somewhat more often, and had 25% of board seats held by employee directors. What explanation can you provide?

4. "Directors of a company should be selected to represent major stockholders or other groups concerned with the operation of the firm. In a sense, they are trustees or agents to make sure the interests of their respective principals are protected." "Directors should be selected for the contribution they can make to the success of the company." Which of these viewpoints do you advocate? Can they be reconciled? How will the operation of a board of directors be affected by the principle guiding the selection of its members?

5. If you held an important position with a manufacturing concern and were asked to be a director of another company that sells raw materials to your concern, would you accept? Aside from intercompany relationships, is there any information regarding the company you would want to have before agreeing to serve as a director?

6. Special studies of the membership of the Young Presidents' Organization (president before age 40 of a firm with 50 or more employees and sales of $1 million, or $2 million for a nonindustrial company) have indicated that the men are typically "unabashed egoists" who demonstrate daring, initiative, and rugged individualism and have an urge to build rather than to manipulate. "The . . . compulsion and obsession is not to make money, but to build an empire." Do these findings have any relation to the tasks and the duties of chief executives stated in the chapter? What do they indicate about the problem of who should take responsibility for the major duties and critical issues of central management?

7. Public utilities (telephone companies, natural gas companies, electric companies, and the like) are closely regulated as to accounting and financial practices, areas served, prices charged, and the kind of product or service sold. With these crucial matters taken care of by regulating bodies of the state, is there any need for a set of directors of such firms?

8. "The description of the duties performed by the officers of a corporation as given in the bylaws is so general that it is quite inadequate as an outline of the responsibilities they actually exercise in the operations of the company." Should the bylaws be more specific and conform to the administrative organization followed in the daily operations?

9. At one point the president of a firm whose sales had grown from $12.6 million to $194 million in ten years said: ". . . it hasn't been much fun. When a small company grows this quickly, you're under constant strain making sure you get out of small-league thinking and learn how to handle the problems thrust on you. . . . I don't feel elated. Our big growth just created a responsibility to keep all the additional people we hire employed. . . ." How can he fulfill that responsibility? What is required to "learn to handle the problems thrust on you"?

CASE XX

Koch Electronics, Inc.

Shortly before the quarterly meeting that followed a reconstitution of the board of directors of Koch Electronics, Inc., a group of directors wrote to the other members. Their letter (Exhibit 3) was in reaction to the agenda drawn up for the board's next meeting (Exhibit 2) and included a proposal that would considerably affect the activities of the directors.

Koch Electronics manufactured electrical communications equipment for sale to other industrial firms, to the federal government, and to the general public. Sales were approximately 50 to 60% to industry, 30% to the government, and 10 to 20% to retail customers. The industry's sales were on a rising trend and had some cyclical fluctuation but no seasonal pattern. Sales were generally steady from month to month.

The company was about forty years old and had been run by a stable management under the leadership of only two presidents. Within the past year, however, unsatisfactory financial results (see Exhibit 3) had brought pressure from the company's investment banker and a group of stockholders. This resulted in some resignations among the directors and the addition of others to the board (see Exhibit 4).

Mr. John Walters, president and general manager, remarked: "I was sorry to lose those men. Mr. Husband was an outstanding electrical engineering consultant who had, at one time, headed his own firm. He helped us greatly with technical matters about which he and I or Mr. Sansone (engineering vice-president) conferred directly. Similarly, Mr. Pugh advised us on plant construction and location questions, and Mr. Bible helped with financial policy and bank relations. Nevertheless, I am looking forward to working with the new board members. We trust they will be able to provide advice to the management based on their special competence."

Stock ownership was diverse. No one stockholder, except Mr. Walters, held more than 2% of the outstanding shares. The stock was actively traded on one of the smaller stock exchanges. Mr. Walters had built up his holdings of between 5 and 10% through the exercise of stock options awarded under various contracts. The present contract reserved 75,000 shares of the authorized but unissued stock for purchase by Mr. Walters over the next five years at the market price existing when the option agreement began (July of the previous year).

REQUIRED: (a) Do you agree with the letter from the three directors? Explain.

(b) What position would you, as a director, take toward the items on the agenda? Explain your reasoning.

EXHIBIT 1

Members of the Board of Directors
of Koch Electronics, Inc.

Mr. Robert Smith, Chairman—President, Smith and Associates (an investment counseling firm)

Mr. James A. Allen—Treasurer and Vice-President, Koch Electronics, Inc.

Mr. Hartley C. Ashford—President and Director, Middle State Insurance Co.

Mr. Robert Barlow—Vice-President and Sales Manager, Koch Electronics, Inc.

Mr. Hultgren Berg—Senior Partner, Chauncey, Gray and Berg, Certified Public Accountants

Mr. Weston R. Brown—President and Director, The Sales Advertising Co., Inc.

Mr. William F. Butcher—Wallace, Summers, Easton & Co.

Mr. John R. Saylor—Secretary, Koch Electronics, Inc.

Mr. Robert Sansone—Engineering Vice-President, Koch Electronics, Inc.

Mr. Leonard Smith—Production Vice-President, Koch Electronics, Inc.

Mr. John A. Baker—Five Persons Bank and Trust Company

Mr. John Walters—President, General Manager, and Director of Research, Koch Electronics, Inc.

Mr. Robert A. Weiss—Goldner Wax and Candle Company

EXHIBIT 2

Agenda

Second Quarterly Meeting,
April 20, 1 to 5 p.m.

Koch Electronics, Inc.

Item One —Tour of the plant to view production changes and to inspect product modifications.

Item Two —Review of company operations and results—Mr. Walters. Review of industry and general economic conditions—Mr. Robert Warren, consulting economist.

Item Three—Gift of shares to Midwest University and other organizations. For the past five years the company has issued a total of 1,000 shares each year to Midwest University and certain charitable organizations. The market value on date of issuance is deductible for tax purposes.
(Midwest University specialized in scientific and engineering education. Mr. Smith and Mr. Walters were alumni. Mr. Walters had been prominent in university and alumni affairs for some time.)

Item Four —Authorization of dividends on the common stock.

Item Five —Stock option agreements.

Item Six —Two executives resigned recently. It is proposed that the board authorize agreements with their replacements—Mr. Robert Sansone, engineering vice-president, and Mr. Leonard Smith, production vice-president—that 25,000 shares in total of unissued stock be made available for purchase by these executives at the present market price with a limit of five years to the agreements.

EXHIBIT 3

The Board of Directors
Koch Electronics, Inc.

Gentlemen:

We are sending this letter to all of you—since we believe that these matters need more serious attention than they will receive at the next quarterly directors' meeting. Our observation is that the conduct of the meetings is such as to preclude major attention to items not already developed in detail on the agenda.

First, we propose that an executive committee of the board be established. It would meet monthly to review the course of operations under existing policy as approved by the board. It is our opinion that too little attention has been devoted in the past by the board to general matters of the direction of the company. Members of this committee should receive substantial compensation of about $1,000 per meeting plus expenses rather than the current payment for expenses only.

Second, we believe that the Development Investment Account now capitalized as an asset should no longer be so regarded, that the net amount remaining after amortization should be written off in a reasonably short period, and that no more charges should be made to this account. We recognize that patents that still have over ten years' remaining life have been secured from development work whose cost was charged to this account. However, we believe that the development work is mainly for product improvement and for maintenance of the firm's market position. Thus it is a current activity whose cost is properly a period charge.

We have requested that the secretary include these items on a revised agenda. Our letter is to acquaint you with our serious concern.

> Very truly yours,
>
> William F. Butcher
> Wallace, Summers, Easton & Co.[1]
> John A. Baker
> Five Persons Bank and Trust Co.[2]
> Robert A. Weiss
> Goldner Wax and Candle Co.[3]

---

[1] A Chicago investment banking firm that had undertaken stock sales for Koch Electronics.
[2] A large Chicago bank.
[3] Mr. Weiss was president of this firm, which manufactured candles and paraffin waxes.

EXHIBIT 4

Stock Prices, Koch Electronics, Inc.

	High	Low	Average
Current Year	22⅛	21¼	
Preceding Year	42	25	32
" "	47	36	40
" "	52	38	44
" "	38	24	32
" "	30	26	27
" "	29	18	24
" "	27	15	18
" "	19	11	14
" "	16	10	12½
" "	16	8	12

EXHIBIT 5

Selected Annual Financial Information
Koch Electronics, Inc.
First Quarter of Current Year and Ten Past Years
(All figures in thousands except dividends per share)

Sales	Net Profits After Tax	Dividends Total	Per Share	Retained Earnings Year End
$ 3,600 [1]	$ 70 est.[1]			
13,200 [2]	(600) [3]	$120	$ .40	$2,700
15,500	300	480	1.60	3,400 [4]
16,200	650	465	1.60	3,600
15,800	450	440	1.60	3,400
17,100	650	425	1.60	3,400
17,500	680	400	1.60	3,200
15,400	540	240	1.20	2,800
13,900	420	240	1.20	2,500
12,800	310	200	1.00	2,310
8,400	150	100	1.00	2,200

[1] First quarter, current year.
[2] Last year.
[3] Net loss.
[4] Certain minor adjustments, in addition to dividends, affected the retained earnings.

Notes to the Last Annual Financial Statements

Note D—The accumulated cost to the Development Investment Account was $1,980,000. Amortization (based on patent life) amounted to $600,000. The balance was carried as an asset to the amount of $1,380,000. Current research and development costs of $262,000 were accumulated in the Development Investment Account.

Note E—Authorized capital stock consists of 800,000 shares of common stock. At the year end there were 300,000 shares outstanding leaving 500,000 of the authorized shares unissued. No stock options were exercised during the year.

Of the unissued shares, 75,000 were reserved in favor of Mr. Walters in accordance with a management contract between the company and Mr. Walters adopted by a resolution of the stockholders.

INTEGRATING CASES
Organization

TOWN SHIRT COMPANY

In 1937, executives of the Town Shirt Company were convinced that their basic task of organizing a major company with nation-wide sales was completed. Shirts, ties, and underwear, marketed under the Townleigh brand, were sold in better department and men's furnishings stores throughout the country and sales were rising steadily, indicating wide public acceptance of the company's products and its brand name.

More than two decades later another group of executives realized that the organizing task was never completed and that more problems faced them.

Early history. When the Town Shirt Company was formed by the merger of three small shirt and collar manufacturers in the early 1920's, its goal was to seize upon the change in trends in men's attire and to ride with this to become a leader among companies selling men's wear.

Following World War I, men, who had in service become accustomed to soft collars, drew the line at donning again the old reliable starched choker. Soft and semi-starched collars and shirts with collars attached became the vogue.

Presidency of the new concern was filled by A. R. Alcott, sales vice-president of one of the predecessor companies. He and his associate officers believed the company could benefit from large-scale selling and advertising economies and that it could salvage much of the goodwill accrued to the merged companies. There was a large market for quality shirts ranging in price from $2 to $5, and the new officers believed they could style and produce a line for that market more effectively than could small manufacturers. The company had contacts with many men's-wear dealers. It had good plants located in communities of skilled needleworkers.

Finally, the officers deemed the company's financial condition strong enough to stand the outlay during the four or five years that would be required to rebuild the company on a new basis.

Among the steps in the expansion sparked by Mr. Alcott were:

1. Organize a merchandising department for effective styling and designing. Develop the ability to schedule and control production with a large percentage of style merchandise. Improve fabrics and basic product patterns. Avoid fads but keep ahead of shirt makers generally with all conceivable developments in good style and quality.

2. Imbue the production organization with pride in quality workmanship. Thereafter improve routines and methods to effect all possible manufacturing economies consistent with uniform high quality. Evolve a method of allocating work and controlling production in all factories so that inventories would not be excessively large, but yet so that various product lines would be available as required by the sales department.

3. Organize sales methods—use a system of selected dealers. Use a few salesmen; weed out and replace the less effective men. Carry on intensive shirt advertising.

4. Bring about harmony between departments. Abolish "product executives." Have one production manager for all products. Create close cooperation between the sales and merchandising departments. Give all executives a company rather than a department point of view. Give them more unhampered responsibility, and encourage freedom of discussion and creative suggestion.

By 1937 this program had been successfully put into operation. The following points were significant aspects of the revitalized organization.

Merchandising department. A key to the early success of the company was its merchandising department, which determined what should go into the line, how much should be manufactured, and when it should be manufactured.

The department selected weaves, fabric designs, and garment patterns. It did some original creating and made adaptations from high-priced wear seen in European and American fashion centers. Choosing patterns involved such matters as determining the type of collar for a shirt, or the form and dimensions of the shirt itself. The final styling job involved deciding which cloth designs to make up in the various garment patterns.

The merchandising manager, the production manager, the sales manager, and the president of the company estimated sales and determined the general rate of operations for the next year at the beginning of each season. The four main seasons were Easter, spring, fall, and holiday; and the probable size of each seasonal line was determined by past experience.

An assistant to the merchandising manager took care of much of the detail. He handled the routine work of making sure that lines were put into production schedules, that cutting orders were given, that salesmen had sample swatches, that delivery dates were set and adhered to, and that orders for cloth were placed when patterns were selected. Regular purchases of fabrics were made by the merchandising department. That department was therefore responsible for seeing that fabricators were properly instructed and controlled.

In addition there was a liaison man between the sales and merchandising departments. He watched for slow moving numbers, watched stocks of staples, looked for any apparent deviations from quality or style standards, and kept the merchandising manager in close touch with the sales department's point of view. Further, to foster close cooperation between these two departments, the sales and merchandising executives met together once a month. In this meeting the merchandising officers explained new ideas and developments and the sales officers were given a chance to suggest and criticize.

While merchandising efficiency was being developed, the size of the line had been growing. The fall shirt line for 1936 contained 300 patterns in 1,400 styles, an increase of nearly 100% over 1928. The spring tie line for 1937 contained 250 styles. The handkerchief line increased to about 100 patterns and was believed to represent a great improvement in selections.

Manufacturing and production control. The general offices as well as the main factory, were located in New York City. Here the company made plain and fancy shirts, collars, and ties. Three plants in Pennsylvania made staple shirts, one in Massachusetts made underwear (shirts and shorts), and the Georgia plant made handkerchiefs and staple shirts.

Each plant had its distinctive characteristics, due to differences in products manufactured, size, equipment, etc. Nevertheless, central staff departments, because of their specialized knowledge, exercised considerable influence over the plant managers.

The engineering section selected buildings and equipment, purchased all operating supplies, designed some equipment, and kept in touch with all new machine developments. It allocated factory space to the departments and it set work routines. The personnel section was in charge of welfare and training of personnel and was a clearing house for employment. Plant managers did their own hiring and firing, but only after consulting with the personnel section and giving reasons for proposed changes. Labor troubles, of which the company had almost none, were settled through this section.

Quality maintenance was an essential part of the company's program, and it was emphasized by various educational and control devices. Inspection was carried on for some operations by persons who did nothing else; for others, it was done by working foreladies.

The merchandising department gave the production department its order for a week's cuttings. That order listed by dozens the fabrics and styles to be used, ordinarily in multiples of 48 dozen, a number best suited to cutting and other operations. The production control section then "scaled" the various lots into collar sizes and sleeve lengths, and it assigned the work to the various plants. Each plant manager reported daily on the stage of production of each lot assigned to his plant.

In ordinary practice the heads of the engineering, personnel, quality control, and production control sections worked with and through the plant managers directly. They visited the plants three or four times a year and kept in touch with them by post and phone the rest of the time. The plant managers were familiar with company standards; nevertheless, the quality of their work was regularly inspected.

The addition of further products, such as pajamas or socks, was not undertaken in the pre-World War II period. Experimentation with pajamas convinced officers that nightwear offered too little opportunity for styling and tailoring leadership; and sock manufacturing had nothing in common with the company's experience. Moreover, company officials judged that the salesmen had a large enough line and that the addition of other products would reduce sales efficiency and thereby defeat the fundamental objective of low-cost selling.

Sales reorganization. The plan for building up a shirt business entailed revamping the sales organization. Surveys in several areas revealed that gross sales to many small customers were not sufficient to pay for the salesman's calls. The new officers decided to select leading men's shops and department stores as authorized Town institutions. They should be reputable firms, financially strong enough to meet credit standards, and large enough to carry a fairly complete line of Town merchandise. The company desired these stores to promote its products actively.

This new program involved real selling and not simply order taking. The sales organization was reduced in size by eliminating the least able men. It was strengthened by some replacements, and the whole group was reeducated in sales technique. This was done by means of literature, sales meetings, and personal instruction. The whole sales program had to be synchronized with the developments in the merchandising department. By the end of 1935, the company deemed the job to be about finished.

Internal relations. As a part of its plan, the new management adopted definite methods to effect harmony and cooperation among all officers. The relations between the sales and merchandising departments have been indicated, as has also the simplification of production management for all products under one man. The board of directors, composed of all the key executives of the company, continued to meet once a month. The president welcomed suggestions and urged the members to be free and frank with constructive criticisms. As a consequence, the meetings became an increasingly productive source of useful ideas. A New York management group, including local superintendents, met weekly to discuss production problems. Twice a year a general meeting of all administrative and operating officers was held. At that time juniors and seniors alike were urged to make recommendations and offer criticisms. The company had a policy of making promotions from within the organization, and it was felt that these meetings helped develop the younger men by giving them a broader view of the company's operations.

All officers were urged to use their own judgment and resourcefulness in handling departmental problems. Mr. Alcott regarded it as his job to train other officers to do their work and not to do it for them; to determine and carry out general policies without involving himself in routine detail; to set standards for all departments and watch their performance; to keep in close touch with business conditions, particularly as they affected the company's industry; to diffuse a sense of loyalty and active interest throughout the whole organization. Associate officers praised his success in achieving these objectives.

Continued growth. The organization which evolved by 1937 is shown in Exhibit 1. This formal grouping of jobs and titles proved its effectiveness during the period of attainment of national recognition and distribution of quality shirts.

In the succeeding years modifications in the organization structure accompanied the expansion of sales and output and the addition of new products until the present organization (shown in Exhibit 2) was developed.

Following World War II pajamas were added to the product line so that the company would not lose out on a men's-wear item for which styling and tailoring had become important. New plants and research facilities were built to take care of existing demand and promote company leadership. A research building and another plant were added to facilities in Georgia, and two new factories were located in Missouri. This expansion sparked a sales increase of 100% from 1943 to 1950.

New president. When this rapid rise in sales had convincingly demonstrated the vitality and endurance of the company, Mr. Alcott retired. His successor, C. W. Barker, moved up from the sales vice-presidency.

With Mr. Barker as president, the company continued to change and expand. A new line of shirts, the Townleigh Executive, was introduced to keep the company in touch with the best styles and to serve as an entreé into fashionable shops that might later carry other Town Company products. Growing consumer interest in sports and leisure clothes was recognized by the addition of swim trunks, strolling shorts, cabana sets, and leisure slacks to the merchandise line.

A major step in product policy was the addition of a line of boys' wear, including dress and sport shirts, ties, underwear, handkerchiefs, and swim trunks. This line was marketed through regular channels to department stores and boys' specialty stores. In the past, boys' wear had typically been made and sold by small

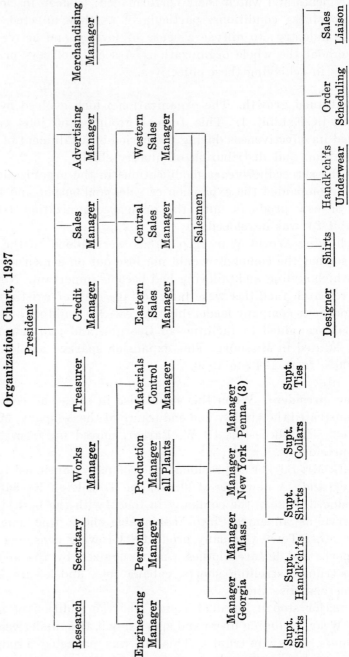

EXHIBIT 1
TOWN SHIRT COMPANY
Organization Chart, 1937

EXHIBIT 2

Current Organization Chart

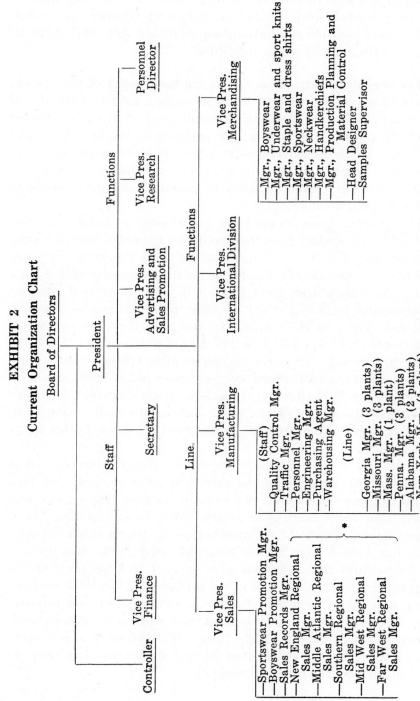

* Reporting to the five regional sales managers are a total of 100 general line salesmen, 20 sportswear salesmen, and 10 boyswear salesmen.

specialty manufacturers. The Town Shirt Company had avoided entering this field until the postwar baby crop fattened the market. The 1- to 6-year-old population had increased 70% over 1940 by the time the new line was introduced.

The organization problem. It is the basic belief of the present group of executives that Town Shirt cannot afford to stand still but must increase its sales through additional effort on its existing products and through adding new products to the line. The company has now reached the point where the executives feel that they must thoroughly examine company organization structure to obtain maximum potential with the present lines and perhaps to add new product lines.

The existing lines of products are shown in Exhibit 3. For each of these product lines the executives have determined a sales volume goal that they feel must be met over the next five years in order to continue the healthy growth and success of the company. As can be seen from Exhibit 3, this set of goals implies substantially increased effort on some product lines well beyond that now given to these lines. In the past, company executives have noted that there has been difficulty in putting what they deem to be proper sales emphasis on the smaller volume items. Company salesmen and perhaps even company sales managers have tended to put their effort on the sale of dress shirts to the neglect of some of the other product lines. This can be easily understood, for Town Shirt Company's big reputation has always been in its dress shirts.

Some of the other products appear to require different kinds of selling effort than does the shirt line. For example, the consumer appears to purchase ties more on impulse than on any predetermined basis as he does shirts. Also, in selling ties, brand names do not seem to be as important as in selling shirts. Sportswear has a much more marked seasonal pattern than does the sale of dress shirts and sportwear also appears to have some of the impulse characteristics noted in the sale of ties. For these reasons, there appears to be a need for the salesmen to call on retailers very frequently in selling ties, much more so than in selling shirts, underwear, and handkerchiefs. Some competitors who sell neckwear exclusively call more often on each dealer than has been the custom for the Town Shirt Company.

EXHIBIT 3

PRESENT LINES OF PRODUCTS AND SALES GOALS

(The figures used in this table are not exact company figures and are used for illustration only)

Product Line	Time to Show Line	Present Volume	Goal
Dress Shirts [1] .... Staple Fancy Townleigh Executive Full Dress Synthetic	2 hours	$30,000,000	$40,000,000
Underwear .... Cut and Sewn Knitted	½ hour	5,000,000	15,000,000
Ties	1½ hours	4,000,000	8,000,000
Handkerchiefs	½ hour	3,000,000	8,000,000
Sportswear [2] .... Swim Trunks Cabana Sets Bermuda Shorts Leisure Slacks Sport Knits Sport Shirts	3 hours	15,000,000	30,000,000
Boyswear .... Sport Shirts Dress Shirts Swimwear Sport Knits Neckwear Handkerchiefs	3 hours	3,000,000	15,000,000

[1] Dress shirts include over 2,000 items due to variety of fabrics and collar styles.
[2] Sportswear includes over 1,500 items due to variety of fabrics, colors, and models.

Top executives of the company have also noted a tendency for the sales management to be well satisfied with overall results and overall averages and not to look for distribution within these results by products. Thus, if sales increase in any one year, this is regarded as a healthy sign by the sales department and no further examination is made of what has happened to sales of each product line.

Duties of most executives reflect the prewar organization, although additional specialization such as the following has been introduced. The manager of sales record is responsible for records of production control and sales. That is, he maintains the paper work dealing with the control of production. Until recently, the company had general line salesmen only. During the past two years, the sportswear salesmen and the boys'-wear salesmen have been added. However, to date they approach customers in big cities only. The merchandising managers are in charge of styling, pricing, and purchases of raw materials for their particular lines.

With the exception of the New York plant and one Georgia plant, each factory specializes in one product line.

There are naturally some differences of opinion among executives as to the need for a reexamination of the company's organization structure. The vice-president of merchandising, one of the older executives in terms of service with the company and a prime mover in the success of Townleigh dress shirts, is least convinced that the present structure presents any difficulties.

Other executives have seen several recent failures to move quickly into developing markets for such products as button-down shirts and Bermuda shorts. Sales were lost and some retailer ill-will incurred. By the time the program for making and selling walking shorts came to the president for approval, the company was one year late in seizing its opportunity in this field. Since Mr. Barker alone had the ultimate responsibility for profits, many such problems came to him for decision. This used up much of his time and slowed company operations.

Mr. Grobe, director of personnel relations, feels that any plan that is worked out will not be of much value unless the people in the company believe that whatever is decided is the right thing to do.

REQUIRED: (a) Explain how the current organization structure was devised. Analyze its relation to the objectives of the company. Explain why the changes were made in the organization structure from 1937 to the present.

(b) State how the company should go about deciding what changes to make in its present organization.

(c) State the modifications, if any, that you believe should be made in the formal organization.

NATIONAL SPONGE RUBBER DIVISION OF NATION-WIDE RUBBER AND CHEMICAL CORPORATION

Some three years after Nation-Wide Rubber and Chemical Corporation had purchased the former National Sponge Rubber Company and had merged the two organizations, Chester Williams, general manager of National Sponge (also a vice-president and director of the parent company) remarked: "Aftermaths of the merger and subsequent organization changes have affected us in interesting ways. I am about to recommend that we recapture our sales and research functions and become pretty much an independent unit."

Before the merger, National Sponge had operated three plants in a town near Muskegon, Michigan. Its original product lines had been sponge rubber fishing floats and, later, weather stripping for automobiles. When foam rubber came into prominence, National Sponge had expanded rapidly through its early technical competence and developments in the technology of foam rubber. It soon became a leading private brand manufacturer of foam rubber pillows and mattresses. About the time of its acquisition by Nation-Wide, National Sponge was moving rapidly into production of polyurethane foam mattresses, pillows, and upholstery materials.

Since National Sponge's research efforts supplemented or duplicated some of those of Nation-Wide, the two departments were combined and located in a major research campus near Galveston, Texas. National Sponge's sales effort had emphasized large accounts (400 accounts were served by 55 salesmen—4 in Boston, 12 in New York, 8 in Philadelphia, 5 in Chicago, 2 in Minneapolis, 4 in Houston, 8 in Los Angeles, 4 in San Francisco, 3 in Denver, 2 in St. Louis, and 3 in Detroit). This had meant spotty market coverage. With the sales function taken over by Nation-Wide's major sales organization and only a sales liaison function left at National, the number of accounts sold to had increased substantially. The account managers were added as one group to the marketing organization. In addition, the line was sold by the field sales organization that handled all other company products. The field sales group was set up by territories, districts, and regions.

Production at National Sponge Division was carried on in three different plants. However, the volume of sponge rubber products had declined and that of polyurethane had increased so that all

Nation-Wide Rubber and Chemical Corporation Organization Chart

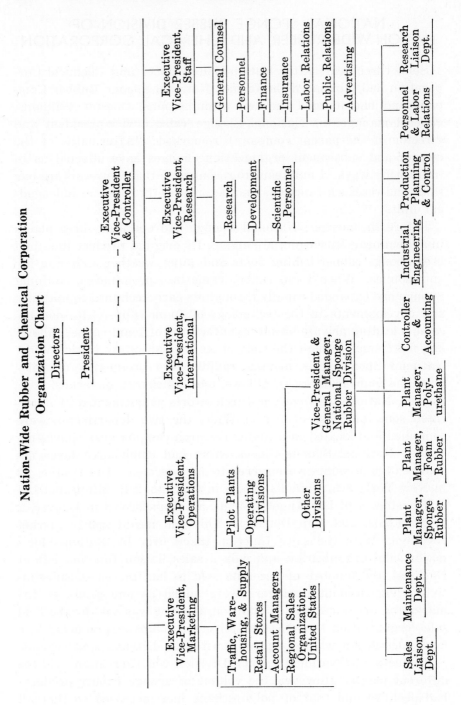

materials and finished goods storage, as well as shipping and receiving of urethane products, was done out of the sponge plant. This created some labor troubles because many of the women working at jobs in the sponge plant earned—on the basis of historical rates—several cents an hour more than did men on the polyurethane jobs for work that the men regarded as physically more demanding and in poorer working conditions. The personnel department at National listened to such complaints but did not think much could be done about them. The process and machinery used for production in each plant differed substantially from that of the other plants.

Chester Williams had formed no conclusion one way or another on the sales matter, but he heard often from production planning about the difficulties of the new organization structure. In summary these were: that the sales liaison department merely passed on information from corporate marketing and that it did not adequately represent Sponge's point of view on debatable matters; that production schedules were constantly being upset by changed shipping demands from the corporate warehousing and supply division; that warehousing and supply had once or twice been known to ship back carloads of mattresses for temporary storage, thus clogging the yards at Plants 2 and 3; and that the sales liaison people came late in the morning or held irregular hours, thus disrupting the morale of other office workers. He did know that shipping costs had been cut 25% under the new arrangement.

Industrial engineering was a problem of a different kind. The department manager, John Pugh, had once managed the foam rubber plant, but Mr. Williams believed him to be incompetent and had insisted that Pugh be reassigned when Williams was promoted from head of the polyurethane plant to general manager. Williams said: "Right now he should be looking at the foam plant, but I don't think he even sees the problem. For a long time their practice has been to rotate the men and the foremen among the shifts. This goes from section foreman to line foreman all the way to the shift foreman. The trouble is that the men and the foremen rotate in opposite directions. This is no way to build stable work groups. I don't think a man's system can adjust to these rapid time changes. (Each man worked on one shift for one week, then rotated to the next.) Also, with the little we know about work groups and productivity, we should be able to predict that the foam plant is a low-output shop. But Pugh is in here trying to sell me on time studies for the sponge plant. With output decreasing there, he's wasting his time."

In the urethane plant, where he spent most of his time and effort, Williams believed in what he called "task-force management." "When we have a problem—and we have a lot of them because this is a relatively new technology and a relatively new process— I assemble the team that can work best on it. This means I have to choose men from various organizational levels and indicate to them that they have to work together until the job is licked. As an example, a team I assembled recently was pulled together for a seating job for a new Douglas jet. The people I had to get together were a chemist, a pillow-line foreman, a woman who is a chief sewer in an assembly operation, and the head of the assembly operation. Together they had the technical know-how and the operating contacts to solve the job right and to do it fast. Our competition from other manufacturers on prices and from other divisions on profits is so keen that we need all the managerial tricks we know to keep ahead.

"This kind of management does not go over well in the foam plant. In fact, the general foreman actively resists it. He prefers that problems come right down the line. The sponge plant no longer has any problems that need rapid or specialized attention. Its major problem is an equipment one. If we can't get some new equipment that we have designed for automobile weather stripping to operate satisfactorily, we'll be out of that business."

Mr. Williams continued: "There is one real organizational structure problem—the research work—and I guess what you would call an organization problem—the controller's position. To take up the latter first, a couple of times I have had the executive vice-president and controller from headquarters call me for an explanation on some cost or operating data just about the time I have seen these data. Once I checked immediately with the operations executive vice-president and he was just being brought into the problem. One of these incidents concerned some hot costs on a new product we had test-marketed and were about to introduce and the other was a tabulation on the causes of some labor troubles we were having here. Each time there was a clear answer that I could give, but some time there is not going to be a clear answer and then someone will be on the spot.

"As to research, formally it is all done in Texas. Our liaison department takes problems to them and brings results back. They have a magnificent set of laboratories and hundreds of Ph.D.'s. But we aren't so dumb here. (Mr. Williams held a Ph.D., an honorary Sc.D., and several patents on basic processes for making foam rubber.) We have some very bright chemists and chemical engineers whom I have brought in under industrial engineering for work on process engineering. Actually they are doing what Texas might well call development work. Also I have some ideas of my own on a polyurethane automobile tire that I am sure the boys in Texas haven't thought of yet. But it would take a sizeable operation to carry these ideas out. In my opinion, to do them effectively we have to have a research organization, a pilot plant, and maybe even a production plant in close conjunction and cooperation. We have urethane production here, but we certainly don't have anything like a pilot plant or an authorized research activity. The problem isn't money—Nation-Wide is loaded with funds—but agreement on who should or can do what best.

"That reminds me of the running argument we have about maintenance. Each plant manager wants his own maintenance section so that he can schedule work as best suits his production needs. I've had the maintenance department head work out a cost study on this. His figures, which I believe, show that maintenance costs would be doubled if we formed three sections—extra men, equipment, and so forth. The plant managers argue that it would save them downtime, but their studies on this aren't very convincing. The foam plant, as an example, lost some time on various jobs waiting for maintenance; but, as far as I can tell, the direct man hours wasted were few. The cost of those man hours was no more than 10% of the total maintenance man-hour bill.

"To go back to that one research problem on polyurethane, I'd need an absolute minimum of 8 men here for that. This would cost about $400,000 to $500,000 a year. It is not the money that counts but the work the men have to do and their associations. Scientists need laboratory time to do their jobs effectively, but they also need contact with other people in labs and in the company. They need quick and constant face-to-face communication or, at a minimum, verbal communication with people in their own laboratories, their specialties, and their fields. This, of course, is in addition to the libraries they have to have available. The work that I have in mind for scientists to do needs a relationship with a production facility or with a pilot plant at the very minimum. There may be other factors or variables that need to be looked at in thinking about such an organization problem as this one of the research people, and there may be bases for a solution that I haven't thought of— but that's part of your task."

REQUIRED: (a) Should National Sponge recapture its sales and research functions? Explain your reasoning and the implications of your recommendation for both National Sponge and Nation-Wide.

(b) What internal (that is, within the National Sponge Division) organization problems does Mr. Williams have? How have these arisen?

(c) What do you think is Mr. Williams' problem with the controller? What, if anything, should he do? (Be specific in your answer. State the exact words you would use if you were in Mr. Williams' position and if *you* decided to talk with any other executive.)

PART

4 ⋮ **DEVELOPING MAJOR RESOURCES**

Ch. 21 · Executive Personnel

Ch. 22 · Facilities

Integrating Cases—Resources

CHAPTER

21 : EXECUTIVE PERSONNEL

Importance of executive personnel. Without good executive personnel, sound objectives and policies and a clear organization plan soon become idle hopes and unrealistic aspirations; with good executive personnel, they provide the guidance and the structure for a purposeful enterprise.

The development of a competent group of immediate subordinates is a duty that can never be fully delegated. Larger companies may have a service division that provides assistance in dealing with executive personnel problems, but each executive still carries primary responsibilities for having competent people in the supervisory and key positions under his direction.

The typical manager is concerned with only a relatively few executives and other key personnel. These are likely to be people he has worked with and known intimately over a period of years; they may well include many of his best friends. As an executive he is responsible for seeing that they not only perform today's tasks effectively but develop so that they can assume the larger responsibilities of tomorrow. This development involves habits, attitudes, and skills that may take years to develop. Except for filling unexpected vacancies arising from death or resignation, executive personnel is a long-run problem. Because of these *personal, intangible,* and *long-run* characteristics of executive personnel, general policies are inadequate to deal with specific situations. In addition to using policies, the manager should give his personal attention to the delicate and highly personal situations in his company or his department.

Wide variation in company practice. Since executive personnel involves close personal relationships, considerable difference occurs in the way executive selection and development is handled in various companies. A few examples will indicate the wide variation.

A president who evaded his responsibility. In one relatively small company with eight key executives, the president had been for many years the key figure in coordinating operations. Each subordinate was given considerable latitude within his own department, but he was expected to concentrate his attention in this area. The executives were very friendly with one another, and the president himself had a personal interest and deep loyalty to each of the members of the group. There was a general understanding that the sales manager would probably be the next president, and beyond that the matter of executive succession was given little thought.

The cold facts of the situation were that the sales manager was an excellent salesman but not a very effective executive. He was indecisive and preferred not to assume administrative responsibility. As long as the president was active, these traits were not a serious handicap to the company. All the salesmen were experienced individuals who were glad to accept the kindly suggestions of the sales manager and who were able to proceed with a minimum of supervision.

When the president died and the sales manager succeeded him, the latter's lack of executive ability created an acute problem. Other executives found it difficult to get positive decisions from the new president, and in his effort to please everyone he was likely to reverse himself. Coordination, or lack of it, was largely a result of the voluntary contacts between the several executives. The new president could not adjust to his new responsibilities and suffered a nervous breakdown within three years. The man who was next appointed as president had considerably more ability but had been given virtually no training for the job as chief executive. Six to eight years elapsed before the company really recovered from the shock of the death of a president who failed to provide adequately for his replacement.

Looking back on this case, one wonders why a successful president for so many years failed to anticipate the difficulties upon his withdrawal from the company. Perhaps he never faced the question squarely. More likely, he recognized the limitations of the sales manager but could not bring himself to take the drastic action that would have been involved in the selection and training of another executive to be his successor. This would have created strain and upset personal friendship. Since no immediate action was necessary, he probably evaded the issue and hoped it would work out all right somehow. Had he taken the necessary action when he was still president, the company would certainly have been better off and the sales manager spared a nervous breakdown. This would have taken considerable courage, however, because there was no assurance that all the people concerned would have recognized the need for the action.

An inadequate beginning. Another firm recognized the need for a good supply of executive talent in the organization, and employed eight to twelve college graduates each year for a period of more than ten years. These young men, together with several promising young people already employed, were given a six-month training course embracing all activities of the business. At the conclusion of the course, the potential executives were placed throughout the company wherever there was an opening. The staff people who were responsible for the program then concentrated on recruiting another group of promising young people.

Over a third of the executive trainees left the company within a year after they had been assigned to regular work, and fewer than 5% were with the company after ten years. A few important posts of the company are now filled by men who came through this "executive program," but many more came from other sources.

Many of the young men quit because, after being treated as an exceptional individual and being invited to examine the innermost operations of the company, they could not stand the shock of taking an ordinary job where they were expected to "earn their keep." The company had an announced policy of giving these young men no preferred treatment after they had completed the training course, on the assumption that if they had outstanding ability they could earn their promotions in competition with other employees. Many of the "old timers" among the executives held the view that every young man needed four or five years' experience before he was ready for promotion, and this naturally led to poor morale among the ambitious young "potential executives."

In this case the whole task of executive development had not been adequately thought through. The company certainly put more men through its "executive program" than the operating organization was prepared to absorb. Even more fundamental was the lack of systematic attention to executive needs at all levels and the processes by which these needs might have been fulfilled,

Informal development program. More thought is given to executive development in many companies than appears on the surface. Frequently these concerns have no announced program or procedure but do give the matter of executive personnel regular attention. One company, for example, has a "little green seedbox" that contains a card for each key man who is a present or potential manager of one of the concern's principal operations. Each year the work of these men is reviewed by a senior executive along with the man's supervisor, and when a man is assigned to a new position his performance is watched closely. Then, as opportunities open, they are moved into positions of increasing executive importance. Of course, if it is decided, after watching a man for several years, that he has reached his maximum his card will be removed from the file.

Wide variations exist in this type of approach. Typically, the cards or the pages in a loose-leaf notebook contain little information other than a record of the positions a man has held, his salary, and perhaps notations on his outside civic or educational work. If the president or a senior vice-president is the one who directs the activity and he makes sure that each man's performance is reviewed at least once a year (though not necessarily in a formal review session), then it is likely that considerable executive development work will take place and that the selection of men for promotion will be based on a broad view of the man's experience.

Where the activity is treated more casually or where the reviews are sponsored by an individual who lacks prestige with other executives, the attention given to executive development will probably be substantially less. In any event, the kind of training on the job that occurs depends almost entirely upon the interest and ability of the supervising executive. Given the proper company tradition, backed by the necessary inspiration and guidance of the chief executive, such informal plans for executive development have worked remarkably well in some companies.

Formalized executive programs. Positive and systematic attention to executive personnel has led several companies to put the work on a formalized basis. For example, one large concern has a plan that provides for the preparation of detailed organization charts, written job descriptions, and man specifications for each supervisory and executive job throughout the company. Along with this analysis of executive requirements goes an annual appraisal of executives on a carefully prepared six-page form. From these records of needs and available talent, replacement schedules are prepared showing which individuals are ready for immediate promotion and which ones probably will be qualified for promotion within a few years. Potential candidates for each executive position are listed on these tables. Finally, a plan is prepared for individual development for each individual who is not qualified for immediate promotion.

The personnel department provides assistance and guidance for this program, but the work of appraising individuals and providing for their future development and promotion is done by the operating executives. The company admits that considerable time is necessary to make the plan work effectively. Nevertheless, the top officials believe development of executive personnel is so important that the time required to do a systematic job is worth the trouble.

Essential elements in a sound program. The examples of executive development just given range all the way from almost complete neglect to a highly formalized plan. They indicate that current practice is far from standardized. Nevertheless, there is increasing agreement on certain basic elements that every manager should keep in mind when dealing with his executive personnel problems. Even if he decides not to use elaborate forms and procedures, his thinking should embrace the following steps:

1. A prediction of the types and number of executives his company (or department) will need for successful operations in the future.
2. A review, or inventory, of the executive talent now available.
3. A tentative promotion schedule, based on the two preceding steps, that provides for manning each of the positions in the anticipated organization and, insofar as possible, for a potential replacement for each of the key executives.
4. A plan for the individual development of each person slated for promotion, so that he may be fully qualified for his responsibilities.
5. Compensation arrangements that will attract and hold the executives covered in the foregoing program and provide incentives for them to put forth their best efforts.

The significance and nature of each of these steps will be considered in the following sections. A detailed analysis of techniques, however, is beyond the scope of this book.

ANTICIPATING EXECUTIVE REQUIREMENTS

The basis for any long-range planning for executive personnel is an understanding of what kind of men will be needed. Surprisingly, this obvious first step is sometimes overlooked. In one company, for example, the top administrator held the view that "we always have room for good men around here," and on several occasions he brought competent men into his organization with no clear-cut idea of what they were to do. These men either got bored waiting for a significant assignment or they created friction by interfering with activities that other executives thought were under their direction.

A more common failure in anticipating executive requirements is to assume that a title provides an adequate guide to the kind of man that is needed. As we have seen in the preceding chapters, the duties of a vice-president or a controller, for instance, vary greatly and there is a corresponding range in the abilities needed to fill the position. A hard-driving, enthusiastic sales supervisor is quite a different individual than an analytical and imaginative planner of merchandising campaigns, and yet either of these men might have the identical title of product sales manager. Before sound executive development can be done, a clear understanding is needed of (1) the jobs to be filled and (2) the characteristics of men needed for these jobs.

Jobs to be filled. A study of organization, along the lines indicated in the preceding part of this book, will result in a long-range organization plan with descriptions of each key position needed in the future. These position descriptions are not necessarily put in writing, but if there is clear-cut organization there must be an understanding of the duties and relationships of each executive position. If plans for the future administrative organization have not already been clarified, then organization analysis becomes a first step in the executive personnel program.

Position descriptions prepared for organizational purposes differ in emphasis from those used in an executive development program. The more ticklish aspects of organization involve defining the borderline between the various units and spelling out interrelationships when activities must closely coordinate. Such divisions of responsibility are not so important for executive development purposes. Here, interest centers on the major duties to be performed, the degre of decentralization and hence the judgment that must be exercised by people at different levels in the organization, the importance of initiative and enthusiasm, and similar matters. In other words, we need to sense the role the person in the executive position will play in the operation of the enterprise.

Characteristics of men needed for these jobs. The second phase of this analysis of executive requirements is to translate the duties into *man specifications*, that is, the personal qualities a man needs to fill a given position effectively. We can describe the duties of a football quarterback or a plant superintendent, but it is another matter to set up a list of qualifications that we think a man should have to fill such a position successfully.

These man specifications may be stated in terms of knowledge, supervisory skill, emotional stability, judgment, dependability, ability to deal with outsiders, social attitudes, and the like. Unfortunately, it is difficult to define requirements for positions in such terms because experience shows that men with quite different makeups may be successful in the same kind of a job. Another way to draw up man specifications is to list the principal things he will be expected to do, such as build customer goodwill, control expenses, plan for future expansion, stimulate and develop his subordinates, etc. This kind of a list is easier to prepare but is not entirely adequate when a man is being selected for work that is quite different than he has already done. For instance, it is hard to appraise the ability of a crack salesman to be a sales supervisor because there has been no opportunity to observe him doing the kind of activity required of the sales supervisor.

In the establishment of man specifications, then, we find one of the first reasons why executive development cannot be reduced to fixed procedure. Specifications for the end product are not exact. Nevertheless, if there is to be any careful planning, it is necessary to build up reasonably accurate and useful descriptions of the kind of executives that will be needed to man the organization.

One additional point regarding executive requirements should be emphasized. Most executive personnel work pays off only in the future. Executives are being trained to do their present jobs better tomorrow, and they are being groomed for future positions of high responsibility. In fact, much executive development work cannot be expected to show results in less than three to five years and some of it may take much longer. Consequently, the organization structure five years hence is more important than the present one.

The outlook for the company must be studied to forecast the volume and nature of activities. These will throw light on the organization structure that will be needed and hence on the requirements for executive personnel. Moreover, the existing organization may be far from ideal. Shifts in executive personnel are a logical time to realign duties and correct organizational weaknesses. If this is to be done, plans for executive development should, of course, be based on the new, rather than the old, organization structure.

INVENTORY OF EXECUTIVE TALENT

The second basic step in planning an executive personnel program is appraising the executives already in the organization. The organization and position analysis just discussed shows what executive talent is needed; the appraisal of executives, considered in this section, shows what talent is available to meet these requirements.

Generally an inventory of executive talent is taken to discover weak spots in the normal flow of executives through the promotion channel. It indicates where additional development work is needed to assure that satisfactory replacements are available when necessary.

A good inventory will also bring to light the competent executives who are not being used to their fullest capacity. For example, the president of a pharmaceutical company was shocked when his nephew resigned, along with two key salesmen, and established a competing firm. Evidence clearly indicated that these men had not been assigned to challenging positions and they considered their prospects for promotion so remote that they preferred to take the risk of establishing a new enterprise. A good plan of executive appraisal would have shown the president that these men were prepared for additional responsibilities. He should then have tried to find positions that would more fully utilize their ability, and if this was not possible, he should at least have openly examined the situation with each of the men. In other words, an executive inventory would have been useful even though there was no immediate need for replacing key men.

Different uses of executive appraisals. Executive appraisals may be used in several different ways, and their value will be improved if these are recognized at the outset.

(a) The primary purpose of executive review may be to *select* a man for an existing or anticipated vacancy. For this purpose a critical and objective appraisal of the man's future potential is needed.

(b) Executive appraisal may point to the need for training and development when abilities of executives are matched against the man specifications for a given position. Deficiencies may come to light and individual *development programs* can then be built around these deficiencies. When the emphasis is on personal development, the appraiser can identify much more closely with the man being reviewed and together they can seek out opportunities for improvement.

(c) Executive appraisal may be used to establish bonuses and pay increases or other forms of *compensation.* Here attention centers on past achievements rather than future potentials. Objectivity is needed here, as it is when considering men for promotion.

When a company uses its executive appraisal for several different purposes, as is usually true for those companies that have a well-rounded executive development program, it is important to maintain a balanced point of view. Objectivity is vital, while at the same time a sympathetic interest in the individual is needed for planning for individual growth.

Informal appraisal of executives. In a great many companies no systematic appraisal, or inventory taking, of executive ability is made. Nevertheless, considerable informal appraisal typically takes place. This was the method followed in a financial company, for example, that had about 800 employees. In addition to the 12 senior officers and 20 junior officers, there were approximately 85 first-line supervisors and other key employees. The size of the company permitted each of the senior officers to know personally all of the executives as well as some of the outstanding operating persons.

The president and the senior vice-president made it a practice to "keep their eye on the boys." They asked questions and otherwise followed the work of the various executives closely enough to have a clear impression of what most of the men were doing. In addition, they occasionally talked with each of the officers about the men under their supervision and what might be done to assist them in their development. The officers feel that more formal ways of inventorying executive talent are unnecessary in their situation.

Informal executive appraisal, such as that just described, is a natural and continuing process that should be used by everyone in a managerial position. The more formal appraisal techniques, discussed in the next paragraphs, supplement rather than substitute for this type of evaluation. The informal appraisal is done at convenient times, in connection with other work; consequently, it creates no special burden on executives.

Limitations of this method are: (a) some executives who are primarily interested in technical problems may fail to size up the men with whom they come in contact; (b) the appraisals may be incomplete, with emphasis on past performance and little attention on future potential; and (c) in larger concerns where no one man can know personally all of the present and potential executives, it is extremely difficult to compare candidates in one department with those of another and to exercise any measure of guidance and control over an executive development program.

Systematic evaluation of executives. To overcome the limitations of informal executive appraisals, several companies have definite procedures for executive personnel reviews at least annually. In their simplest form these evaluations consist of only an annual memorandum written by the supervisor of each executive outlining the man's outstanding accomplishments, weaknesses, steps taken for his development, and future potential.

At the other extreme are rather elaborate evaluation forms that record an overall appraisal of the man's work during the past year, a rating of his personal qualities, promotion possibilities, and plans for individual development. The Armed Services use a similar technique; in fact, the file of fitness reports is the primary basis on which Navy officers are selected for promotion.

These formal evaluation plans build up a record covering each executive, which is very helpful when he is being considered for transfer or promotion. Usually several different people have submitted appraisals and the total record is not dominated by some single event, as may happen when sole reliance is placed upon informal appraisal. Moreover, the formal procedure tends to make the evaluation more thorough and consistent.

On the other hand, standard forms and procedures by no means insure that appraisals will be made carefully and honestly. Unless the executive making the appraisal believes that the whole process is worth while, he may fill in the form hastily and with answers that he thinks will lead to the promotions and transfers he would like to see made. Evaluation procedures do, of course, use time of busy executives and they add a formality to highly personal relations among executives. Consequently, before such formalized evaluations are introduced, it is important to make sure that the process will significantly improve executive development and that executives throughout the company recognize its benefits.

Senior executives are primarily interested in results rather than in arguments as to the advantages of particular appraisal methods. In some manner suitable to the enterprise, a review or inventory of executive talent should be made. This knowledge of the capacity and the weaknesses of the executives is essential for building a sound executive development program.

PLANS FOR FILLING EXECUTIVE POSITIONS

Need for planned executive progression. The treasurer of a medium-sized manufacturing company recently told the president that he wished to retire within a year. This was no great surprise because the treasurer was already 68 years old and his health was forcing him to slow down. Two years earlier a young man had been brought in to assist the treasurer in his daily work, but this man had displayed more energy than judgment. Consequently, the president recommended to his board of directors that the company immediately employ a new assistant treasurer.

In the discussion that followed, it soon became apparent that there was no consensus as to the type of man that was needed. The difference in opinion was due largely to differing ideas as to what the treasurer of the company should do. The president and other executives of the company thought of the position largely as it was currently being carried out, whereas several of the board members felt that a new treasurer should play a much more vital role in overall company operations.

Agreement was reached that no one within the company had the necessary experience, so a new assistant treasurer was brought in. This man appears to be capable in financial matters, but still missing is a clear definition of duties he should follow when he becomes treasurer.

This example shows a lack of forward planning with respect to executive replacement. The president had failed to recognize the coming retirement of one of his key executives as an opportunity to strengthen his organization. As a result, he had no clear-cut specifications for the man who should be selected as a trainee to replace the treasurer. Moreover, the lack of advance planning made it almost impossible to train anyone in the company for this post.

Development of executive personnel, as already noted, is largely a long-run problem. Men need time to develop the knowledge, skills, and judgment required in most executive posts. On the other hand, having the right man in the right position at the right time is of supreme importance in administering a business. Here is an area, then, where long-range planning is of supreme importance —even though human behavior is hard to measure and to predict, and results may not turn out just as planned.

Replacement table approach. Transfer and promotion of executives is a normal occurrence in a typical business concern. Deaths, retirements, and resignations create vacancies. If these are filled by promotions, additional vacancies are created in the lower ranks. In fact, one vacancy at the vice-president level may result in shifts of half a dozen men. New positions, resulting from expansion, have a similar effect. The problem is how can a company plan to meet such changes.

The replacement table approach rests on three ideas we have already discussed. The first is anticipating executive requirements in terms of positions to be filled and the man specifications of executives needed in such positions. The second is a policy of promotion from within. Third, assuming promotion from within, the inventory of executive talent discussed in the preceding section provides the personnel data needed for concrete planning. Replacement tables are simply a device for weaving this information into a tentative plan.

REPLACEMENT TABLE

JOB NO.	JOB TITLE	JOB INCUMBENT	AGE	SENIOR CANDIDATE	JOB NO.	AGE	JUNIOR CANDIDATE	JOB NO.	AGE
	MANAGEMENT LEVEL GROUP "A"								
2C21	Service Manager	K. L. Foster	47				G. E. George C	5C64	38
							A. A. Day C+	3C23	35
2C52	Sales Engineer	B. C. Johnson	65	C. D. Dewey C	3C24	42	L. M. Mason D+	5A28	38
2C77	Const. Manager	E. E. Bryant	49	No Senior			E. F. Burnes C+	6B16	37
2C12	Accountant	F. G. Bray	55	No Senior			No Junior		
	"B" Office Managers								
3C22	Loc.	G. H. Miller	63	)			)E. D. Hill C	6F41	42
3C23	Loc.	A. A. Day	35	)G. E. George C	5C64	38	)M. N. Johns C+	7B18	33
3C24	Loc.	C. D. Dewey	42	)L. M. Mason D+	5A28	38	)W. X. Hobbs C	4A72	35
	Local Service Mgrs."A" & "B" Offices								
5C31	"A" Office	R. R. Colby	62	)					
5C64	Loc.	G. E. George	38	)M. N. Johns C+	7F21	35	X. Y. Bell C+	6A57	37
5C65	Loc.	R. S. Williams	41	)W. X. Hobbs C	4A72	33	E. D. Hill C	6F41	42
5C66	Loc.	S. T. Fuller	57	)					
4C12	Zone Maint. Prom.	T. U. Webster	51				R. S. Williams D+	5C65	41
							X. Y. Bell C+	6A57	37
9C31	Zone Modern. Prom.	"Vacancy"		No Senior			T. V. Dodge D+	7D41	32
9C46	Zone Maint. Super.	V. W. Gary	58	F. E. Hyde C+	7F46	39	No Junior		
9C18	Zone Field Eng.	P. T. Monroe	39				T. U. Olson D+	7A81	48
							U. V. Larsen C	4B29	41

Sample sheet from replacement table of Otis Elevator Company. "Senior candidates" are qualified to take over position without further training other than normal job indoctrination; "junior candidates" need one to five years more training. Letters after names tie in to annual executive appraisals. Note that some men, such as Hobbs and George, are listed as candidates for more than one position.

Replacement tables show, for each executive position, one or more persons who might replace the present incumbent. The preparation of such tables requires that the man specifications for each position be used to select the best candidate available within the company. Some companies distinguish between candidates who are already qualified to move into the positions and those who need a year or more training before they would be prepared to take on the new duties. To be useful, such a chart should be realistic. Thus, if some contemplated positions are now vacant, they should be shown in this way. If there are no real candidates for a given position, this too should be frankly revealed. Of course, one individual may be considered as a candidate for two or more positions.

Ideally, every senior post in the company should have one or more potential replacements listed on the replacement chart. Some people contend that there should be a replacement for every executive throughout the organization. Such an ideal is often very difficult to achieve in practice, and there is serious question as to how much money and effort a company should spend training a replacement for a man who, in all probability, will stay in his present position for ten or more years. On the other hand, having replacements for executives who are likely to retire or to be promoted to other positions is highly important. Some replacement tables attempt to show this timing; but more often the likelihood of a shift, and consequently the need for a fully prepared replacement, is left to the judgment of the people reviewing the replacement table.

Such replacement tables are subject to frequent revision. Unexpected changes in company operations or in the personal lives of executives may shift requirements. Some men will develop faster and others slower than anticipated; in fact, as time progresses some men will be added and others dropped as candidates for particular positions. Not infrequently, an understudy is moved to still another position and a new understudy must be found. Nevertheless, preparation of a replacement table serves a very useful purpose in pointing up where available replacments are lacking. Moreover, it forces realistic review of the men who are likely to be promoted, and if they need further development immediate steps may be taken to start the necessary training.

Replacement tables are, of course, confidential documents because they reflect highly tentative promotion plans that may have to be revised later. For this reason, some executives prefer never to put their ideas down in writing. For smaller companies or for a single department this may be satisfactory *provided* the same basic thinking takes place. The chart is merely a device to help an executive think through a very "iffy" subject. It is the systematic analysis of executive replacement, rather than the particular pieces of paper, that is important.

Methods of selection. Planned replacement of executives modifies, but by no means eliminates, the need for wise selection of individuals to fill executive positions. Possible candidates must first be identified, later one of these may be designated as an understudy, and when the vacancy occurs, the final selection must be made. This sifting process should improve the selection because judgments are made at different times, often several years apart, and this provides opportunity to reconsider earlier impressions.

In addition, there will, of course, be unexpected vacancies for which final selections must be made quickly.

The use of periodic appraisals to provide data on individuals and the matching of such data against position descriptions and man specifications have already been recommended. The suprising thing is how often these basic steps in selection are disregarded. Many executives are inclined to substitute their intuitive likes and dislikes of individuals for the analytical approach suggested.

Selection will also be improved generally if *group judgment* is used. The appraisal of individuals involves so many intangibles and personal bias is so difficult to remove that the views of at least two or three people should be considered in making executive selections. The final decision usually rests with the immediate supervisor, subject to approval by his boss. In addition, the views of other executives who have worked with the candidate, and of the central personnel man who has studied all available candidates, should be considered. Often the views of all these people will confirm the wisdom of the proposed selection. If there is a difference of opinion, then a warning has been raised and further observation on the points in question can be made. Probably in no other phase of business administration is group judgment more valuable than in executive selection.

When tentative selections of one or more candidates for a position are made several years before the actual vacancies occur, *trial on the job* may be possible. A candidate may pinch-hit in the job when the present incumbent is off on vacation or on special assignment. This is not an adequate test because usually the interval is too short for the new man to exercise much initiative, but it may throw some light on his capabilities.

A more likely arrangement is to assign the candidate to work in a department or a branch where he can demonstrate ability to do certain phases of the work. Such assignments typically serve the purpose of both training and selection. If time permits, a man may be tried out in several different positions. What a man does in the past is no definite assurance of what he will do in the future, but it is probably the best evidence we can obtain.

No mention has been made of psychological tests for selecting executives. A few companies are experimenting with this approach, especially at the foreman and other first-line supervising level, simply bcause executive selection is such a crucial problem. Also, when a quick selection has to be made from individuals outside the company, such data may prove to be a useful supplement to other sources of information. However, when careful appraisals of men already working for the company are possible and group judgment and trial on a series of different jobs can be utilized, there is serious doubt whether psychological tests, in their present state of development, can add much that is useful.

DEVELOPMENT OF EXECUTIVE TALENT

Plans center on individuals. Executive training cannot be accomplished well *en masse*. As already noted, executive training deals with a relatively few individuals each of whom is typically in a different stage of development and is prepared for a different job. Consequently, executive training should be approached on an individual basis.

The planning for executive progression, already described, points to the areas where each individual needs further development. Any gap between the specifications for a position and the abilities already possessed by the candidate should receive attention in the development plan. Likewise, if a man's performance on his present job does not measure up to what is desired, these weaknesses should be corrected.

One company asks the following questions in designing a development program for each executive.

1. What are his executive qualifications, his strengths and weaknesses? In brief, WHAT IS HE?
2. What are his possibilities, his growth potential? WHAT MAY HE BECOME?
3. Knowing what he now has and the requirements of the position he may aspire to, it is possible to make an estimate of WHAT HE NEEDS TO GET THERE.
4. With these facts in hand, try to fill the gaps in his experience by A PLANNED COURSE OF ACTION.[1]

One aspect of individual development plans deserves emphasis. Most of the initiative and the work must come from the individual himself. To be sure, the company has a vital stake in the matter and typically does a number of things to assist in the process. Nevertheless, a good executive cannot be developed unless the man

---

[1] Formulated by George B. Corless, Standard Oil Company (New Jersey).

himself does a large share of the work. In this chapter we are primarily concerned with what managers can do to guide and aid in executive development, and consequently the discussion centers around things done by the company. It is well to remember that a company cannot make executives as it can make a physical product; instead, its role is to help the man help himself.

Training-on-the-job. By far the most important and lasting training an executive receives is on-the-job. In all types of work there is no adequate substitute for actually doing the operation; this applies to executive planning, direction, and control fully as much as it does to selling or operating a machine.

A supervisor or other executive close to operations can make work experience much more valuable if he will *coach* the man being trained. Just as an athletic coach makes suggestions, watches performance, points out weaknesses, and encourages the athlete to do better, so may an executive help his subordinates to learn on the job. The good coach needs to understand the emotional as well as the intellectual makeup of his protege, and use discretion in the time and the manner in which he makes his suggestions. He needs to cultivate mutual respect and a desire for improvement. Conceived in this manner, the combination of work experience plus coaching can become powerful tools for executive development.

When a man has been selected as a candidate to fill the position of his immediate boss, the *understudy* method may be employed. The younger man not only performs his own duties but seeks to learn all he can about the work of his supervisor. He takes every available opportunity to put himself mentally in his boss's situation and think through what action he would take if the responsibility were his. The senior man, in turn, welcomes suggestions and wherever practical permits the understudy to participate in action or even to carry out particular projects on his own responsibility. By such a process, the understudy can be really prepared to take over the new position when the final promotion is made.

Often an executive cannot get all the training he needs on a single job. For example, in preparing a man for the position of sales manager, it may be desirable that the man spend several years as a salesman, two or three years in the sales promotion division, perhaps five years as a branch manager, and at least three or four years as an assistant sales manager. Many companies make a regular practice of such *job rotation* for purposes of executive training. The replacement table described previously may provide for transfers and promotions that do not immediately put the best man available in each vacancy but uses some of these vacancies as training spots for men who are thought to have high executive potentials.

The job rotation described here is to be distinguished from the relatively brief indoctrination tours in which a man spends a few weeks or perhaps a month in each of a series of departments becoming acquainted with what is going on. Instead, job rotation for executive development normally assumes that a man will fill a given position for a few years and will show that he can handle that job well before he is moved on to the next position.

Training off the job. A variety of activities are useful supplements to training-on-the-job. The following list, while by no means complete, indicates some of the possibilities.

Committees. Committees are rarely established solely for the purpose of training. Nevertheless, they often do provide fine opportunity to sense the viewpoints of other departments and to become acquainted with problems outside the normal scope of one's position. Consequently, men may be assigned to committees partly for the training they will get from participation.

Company conferences and courses. When a company undertakes a new activity or a new approach to some function such as budgeting or foreman training, conferences or perhaps even a whole course on that subject may be desirable. Some executives hold monthly meetings with their key subordinates partly for the training they provide. The difficulty of finding a subject and a time when enough executives can attend such courses places a definite limit on how far this type of training can be carried.

Industry contacts. Literally thousands of trade associations hold meetings and make studies on various problems relating to their particular industries. Work with such trade associations, or with professional associations, provides a range of new ideas and an opportunity to explore problems with men who are not indoctrinated with the same company approach. Trips to other offices or plants often have the same broadening effect.

University courses. Universities are giving increasing attention to adult education and often provide a variety of courses on business subjects. Many companies encourage their executives to take courses in areas where they have limited background. Also, several universities are offering intensive 4- to 12-week courses in top-management problems; these are particularly valuable for men who are moving from departmental positions to jobs demanding wider perspective.

Individual reading. Few executives have the time or energy, after a busy day, to study long and difficult books. They often do gain much information from regular reading of trade periodicals and professional journals. Also, if they are assigned some special project, they may do considerable outside reading.

Adaptation of off-the-job training to individual needs is particularly important because the executive has only limited time to devote to such purposes. He has a major job to perform and, if he is trying to get the maximum benefit from training-on-the-job, he does not want to slight this major assignment. Consequently, the off-the-job training should have real significance for the individual to justify the additional effort it entails.

EXECUTIVE COMPENSATION

Plans for executive selection, promotion, and development, which have been discussed thus far in this chapter, will not be successful unless the executives believe that their compensation is reasonable and fair. To round out the picture, then, we need to take a brief look at such issues as base salaries and pensions, executive bonuses, stock options, and nonfinancial compensation for executives.

Base salaries and pensions. The setting of executive salaries may be approached in the same way as was recommended for lower-level salaries in Chapter 12: (a) The different positions may be compared one with another in order to establish a reasonable internal alignment. Usually salary grades are not necessary, but the several positions should be at least ranked and some means used to determine the approximate spread between the different positions. (b) Relating executive salaries to outside compensation is much more difficult because comparable jobs in different companies are hard to find. Usually it is possible, however, to set the president's salary in some reasonable relationship to companies of similar size in the same industry. Also, salaries of junior executives frequently tie into, or overlap, those established under the employees' salary administration plan. With both ends of the "salary curve" established, a general curve for the entire group can be drawn. (c) Allowance for individual differences can be made by establishing a range from starting salary to maximum for each position.

This approach to executive salaries is far from exact. The relative importance of positions is hard to measure and is likely to be colored by the efficiency or inefficiency of the particular incumbent. Nevertheless, a decision as to salary has to be made and the approach is as fair as anything yet devised.

Because of the uncertainty in evaluating individual positions, and also because there can be a wide difference in the individual performance of men holding the same position, a wide salary range often with a 50% spread from the minimum to the maximum for a given job is customary. For example, it might be determined that the president should be paid somewhere between $20,000 and $30,000 per year, whereas the sales manager should be paid between $12,000 and $18,000 per year. This still leaves room for considerable judgment regarding the specific salaries, but there are at least some general guides from which to work.

If a company has a pension plan for its employees, executives are usually included. Not infrequently, however, there is a maximum on the amount of salary to be considered or on the pension that will be paid. When this is true, the pension provides relatively limited protection for the executives in their old age. Under existing regulations of the Federal Internal Revenue Service, it is extremely difficult to give top executives more favorable pension treatment than other employees. Consequently, pensions generally cannot be used to meet the special compensation problems of executives.

Executive bonuses. Many companies use bonuses for their executives. In fact, one recent study shows that approximately 50% of all companies use this method of compensation in one form or another. Bonuses enable the company to vary executive compensation in good times and bad times, and they also serve as an important incentive.

The use of a bonus plan is illustrated by a manufacturing concern that recently received stockholder approval for an executive bonus fund. A 6% return on the total stockholder investment is first set aside from net profit; 20% of any profit in excess of this amount is put into the executive bonus fund. The division of the fund among the several executives is determined by the board of directors. Actually, percentage shares amounting to approximately three fourths of the total fund are assigned at the beginning of the year, at the same time that base pay for the executives is set. The remainder of the fund is kept in a "kitty" and is used to reward special performance during the year.

There are many variations on this general pattern with respect to both the size of the total fund and also the division of the fund among the several executives. But the general idea of a fund somehow related to profits is fairly common practice. Of course, many special bonus arrangements are designed to meet particular situations. For example, the manager of a single product department may be paid a bonus on the showing in his department, regardless of the results of the overall company. Likewise, a sales manager may receive a bonus on total sales volume. Whenever such special arrangements are made, care must be exercised to make sure that the executive works as a member of the total management team, even though his bonus may be directly affected by only one or two factors.

If an executive has an opportunity to earn a large bonus, the size of his base salary is usually cut. In general his base salary plus the average bonus he will earn over a period of years should about equal the total amount that would have to be paid a comparable man earning salary alone. Bonuses, like most other aspects of executive personnel administration, need to be carefully tailored to fit the particular situation.

Stock options. Executives may be given an opportunity to buy stock in their company for several reasons. Some people believe that stock ownership will significantly increase an executive's interest in company welfare. In other cases the company may not be able to pay an executive a cash salary and bonus large enough to retain his services, and some form of stock bonus or stock option is used to supplement the cash compensation. By no means the least important reason for using stock options and similar schemes is an attempt to help executives meet their personal income tax problems.

Since income taxes rise sharply as the amount of the annual income increases, many executives find that a large portion of their bonus has to be paid to Uncle Sam. Consequently, an executive would prefer to have his income relatively stable, rather than large in some years and small in others. Even better, he would like some arrangement to have his financial returns from the company classified as a capital gain on which the income tax is substantially less than on current income. Stock option plans, which give an employee the privilege of purchasing the company stock at some stipulated figure, may help an executive meet these personal income tax problems.

The laws and rulings on such matters are highly technical, but in general they provide that if an executive buys stock below the current market value, he has to consider the difference between his purchase price and the market value as current income. Under special circumstances, he may be given an option to buy stock at close to the market price prevailing when the option is granted, then wait for the price rise before exercising his option, and still count his profit as capital gains. If he holds the stock over a period of years and the market value rises in the meantime, he can, of course, sell the stock at the higher price and treat the rise in value as a capital gain. In general, then, stock options do not enable the executive to avoid personal income tax. They may, however, give him more flexibility in adjusting the time when the income is considered to be earned, and possibly the income from a stock option may be treated as a capital gain.

Stock options and stock purchase plans are too complicated to be used as an ordinary method of executive compensation. Instead, they should be regarded as a possible means of meeting particular situations.

Nonfinancial compensation. In thinking about executive compensation, it should be recognized that virtually all businessmen are motivated by nonfinancial considerations as well as the cash payment for their services. In fact, after a man's salary enables him to live comfortably, the nonfinancial factors become increasingly important. For example, some men respond to the urge for power, others desire social prestige, and some will sacrifice additional income for security. Improving the company's position in its industry or otherwise "winning the game" is often a strong spur, and the desire to create something and to render social service is a more common motive than is generally realized.

The ability of a company to provide such nonfinancial compensations usually is not a matter of deliberate decision by the board of directors; nevertheless, they are vital forces in enabling the company to attract and retain competent executives, and they should be recognized when decisions are being made regarding financial compensation.

SUMMARY

An able corps of executives is crucial for the long-run success of any enterprise. The selection and development of executive talent often is given inadequate attention, however, because problems are not diagnosed far enough in advance and because personal relationships may make an administrator reluctant to take the necessary action.

A systematic approach to building the needed corps of executives includes: (1) anticipating executive requirements through advance organization planning and forecasts of the positions to be filled along with specifications for men needed to fill them; (2) taking an inventory of executive talent available within the company; (3) developing tentative plans for using the available talent to fill the anticipated positions, and noting needs for further training or additions; (4) developing men to meet their current and planned responsibilities through on-the-job and off-the-job training, and (5) providing compensation that will attract the quality of executives required and keep their morale high.

Larger companies may find printed forms and standardized procedures helpful, whereas the central managers in smaller firms may use the same method of attack with no formal paper work. In fact, there is always danger that the use of forms will become a substitute, rather than an aid, for the careful thought that good executive personnel demands.

Flexibility in the use of this systematic approach is necessary to adapt it to individuals. Developing executive talent is always a personalized matter, and no standard approach will fit exactly all situations. Application to a particular group of persons, or to a single department within a company, calls for ingenuity and judgment.

QUESTIONS FOR CLASS DISCUSSION

1. "The competition of company recruiters for the good college seniors is undesirable. Pay rates are bid up so high that the embryo executives are overpaid relative to other employees; this upsets morale, puts the new man in a tough spot, interferes with sound training, and makes salary increases during the first five years small. Also, the seniors get such an inflated idea of their importance that they aren't worth much when you do hire them." Relate this statement to executive personnel practices described in this chapter. What should a company needing a reservoir of potential executives do about this kind of a situation?

2. Review your answer to the A.B.C. Corporation case following Chapter 19. How does your recommended organization structure help resolve the first, third, and fourth of the elements of a sound program for executive development summarized earlier in this chapter?

3. Should two or more men be kept in active competition for an executive position that will be vacated by retirement, or should a single "crown prince" be selected several years in advance? What are the advantages and the disadvantages of each system?

4. Executive job descriptions may be used (a) to clarify the organization, (b) to aid in selecting men to fill the jobs, (c) to help in setting executive compensation, and (d) to show executives the objectives and goals of each position. Explain how job descriptions may be useful for each of these purposes. Do you think a single description can serve all purposes well?

5. Executive appraisals may be used (a) to help in making selection and promotion plans, (b) as a basis for bonus and salary changes, and (c) for guidance in individual development programs. Explain how appraisals may be useful for each of these purposes. Do you think a single appraisal can serve all purposes well?

6. Give at least four important ways the problems of executive compensation differ from those of compensation for operative employees and suggest methods for dealing with each of these distinctive aspects of executive compensation.

7. The president of a large company says, "We make it clear to each of our executives that he will not be considered ready for promotion until he has trained a man to take over his present duties. This puts the initiative for training squarely on the shoulders of those who want to get ahead." Do you think this is a wise plan? Is it adequate?

8. How do the executive personnel problems and the practical ways of dealing with such problems differ in (a) small companies and (b) large companies having several thousand employees?

9. Job descriptions, man specifications, individual appraisals, promotion tables, and salary ranges for each position are among the personnel devices recommended in this chapter. Under what conditions should each of these be (a) put in writing and (b) shown to incumbents and candidates for a given position?

CASE XXI

Blakeman Textiles, Inc.

Blakeman Textiles, Inc., is a manufacturer of cotton grey goods. The company makes mainly plain print cloths in standard widths of 38½ inches and 39 inches, but it also weaves cheese cloths and tobacco cloths. Grey goods, as they come from the loom, are made from uncolored yarn and must be put through further finishing operations (dyeing, bleaching, printing, etc.) by the customers before usage.

The Blakeman family owns the major share of the company and is active in the management. Herman Blakeman, son of the founder, retired after 40 years of service and was chairman of the board of directors until his recent death. Irving Blakeman, 60, succeeded his father as chairman of the board and, at the same time, retained his position as president. He is very active in managing all the affairs of the company, but he finds that the double load is tiring and looks forward to stepping out of the president's job in the near future. Samuel Shepheard, Irving's son-in-law, is assistant sales and production manager, while Samuel's wife, Irving's daughter, is promotion and advertising manager.

The wide print cloth division of the cotton goods industry is very competitive. There are several hundred manufacturers all making similar cloth of standard width and construction. Purchasers adapt their needs to standard construction (number of threads per inch, lengthwise and across the goods) in order to have enough sources of supply to assure competitive prices. Mills prefer to make standard cloth since this assures them a ready market as well as low costs from mass production. While cloths from every mill meet width and construction standards, not all mills produce cloth of the same quality. Variations exist because of the use of better yarn, better machinery, or better production techniques. Quality differences lead to either slightly higher prices or more easily attained sales.

Marketing is concentrated in the Worth Street district in New York City. This concentration intensifies competition by making quick price adjustments possible. Much of the cloth is sold by selling agents who meet buyers and pass on bids to the mills. There are no list prices and the price for each order is set by bargaining between the buyer and the mill or its selling agent. Blakeman sells its grey cloth either to converters, who do the finishing and thus take the style risk and responsibility for pattern selection, or direct to manufacturers. The company sells through brokers and also has five salesmen who work on commission.

During and since World War II, the entire textile industry has seen widespread vertical and horizontal integration. Some of the larger and stronger companies have undertaken complete operations from yarn production to sale of finished cloth, while others have added more mills of the same type. Blakeman has recently completed one new Southern mill; but a Northern mill, of 25% less capacity, is being shut down. Machinery shortages and large sales during World War II, alleviated the overcapacity that plagued the industry during the 1920's and 1930's. Since 1940, machinery and plant efficiency have generally increased. Managements have become more skilled in adapting output to the market, in making changes in machinery and techniques, and in control over inventories.

The Blakeman Company has, so far, been successful in meeting competition, both price and quality-wise, and in keeping up with changes in production techniques and machinery. Sales have tripled over the past fifteen years.

The positions of members of the Blakeman family in the management have already been described. A more complete organization chart is shown on page 568. (The company has no formal organization chart or manual, and the diagram is merely an attempt to picture relationships that exist in practice.) Ages of the various officers are given in brackets following their names. Irving Blakeman has had 39 years of service with the company and has been in active charge for some time. His ability in all branches of the business is widely recognized, and the recent success and expansion of the company has been due in no small part to his personal efforts.

Mr. Pearson has been with the company for 25 years and has responsibility for production scheduling and inventory control as well as being sales and production manager. In an industry noted for keen competition and for sharp bargaining between buyer and seller, he has performed well. Mr. Pearson began his work in the selling part of the business and became a successful salesman. He works very well with the president and the treasurer, but he has shown little interest in the detailed financial problems of the company. On occasion he has stated that he preferred to stay away from the headaches associated with financial matters, since he had enough of his own.

The treasurer, Mr. Ezekiel, is looking forward to an early retirement. He has been with the company for 42 years and has handled the difficult financial problems associated with expansion and seasonal requirements. The company's profit margin is too low to be a major source of funds for expansion and the Blakeman family has required that a large portion of profits be paid out as dividends. The treasurer has thus been forced to deal actively with banks to obtain both short-term and long-term loans. The resulting problems of keeping interest costs low and repaying and refinancing loans have required a good deal of skill. Finally, the company's net working capital has been relatively low during the course of expansion and the treasurer has had to watch carefully over the trade accounts receivable and accounts payable in order to maintain liquidity.

Mr. Fisher, the superintendent of mills, has charge of production operations in the company's four plants. Company products have always been of good quality as the result of good production techniques. The layout of the company's newest mill permits most of the materials handling to be done by machinery and, in connection with the use of the latest equipment, enables the company to use operators of lower skill on many jobs than is possible in other mills. Employee morale is uniformly good.

Samuel Shepheard, after graduation from college, spent three years in the Army and has been with the company for the past three years. He has become well acquainted with the production scheduling and inventory control systems used by the company and has relieved Mr. Pearson of most of the detail connected with these jobs. He has also assisted Mr. Pearson in dealings with some major buyers, but he has done no selling on his own. As the result of summertime work in the mills while in college and his production scheduling work, he is familiar with the production techniques and problems of the company. He seems to get along well with the company salesmen and is well liked by Mr. Pearson.

Mr. Yule, the secretary, has had no responsible supervisory positions in the company. The board of directors consists of Herman Blakeman (recently deceased), Mr. and Mrs. Irving Blakeman, B. Ezekiel, D. Yule, and one outsider, S. Kendall. Mr. Kendall has given some thought to the desires of Irving Blakeman and Mr. Ezekiel to retire. He recognizes that the company can continue to succeed only if financial problems as well as sales and production problems receive adequate attention. Since he is satisfied with Mr. Pearson's performance and feels that Mr. Pearson will continue to do an adequate job of handling sales and production problems, he has recommended to the board that a man with extensive financial experience be hired to become both president and treasurer. As president he will lean heavily on Mr. Pearson for conduct of sales and production problems. Having the new executive responsible for the two positions will enable the company to pay a large enough salary so that a capable executive can be attracted to enter this family-owned company.

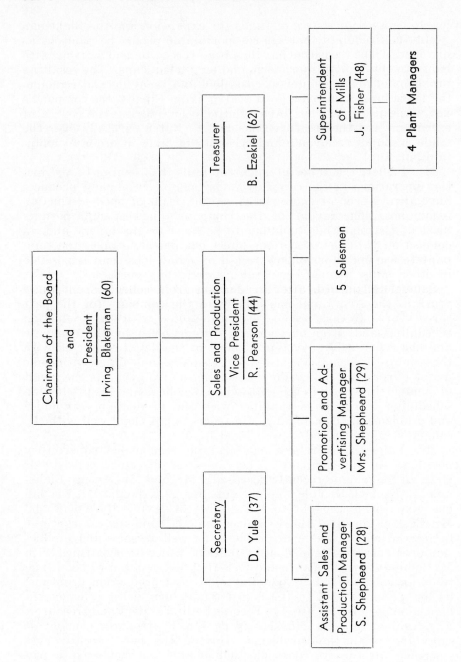

Chairman of the Board
and
President
Irving Blakeman (60)

Secretary
D. Yule (37)

Treasurer
B. Ezekiel (62)

Sales and Production
Vice President
R. Pearson (44)

Superintendent
of Mills
J. Fisher (48)

4 Plant Managers

5 Salesmen

Promotion and Advertising Manager
Mrs. Shepheard (29)

Assistant Sales and
Production Manager
S. Shepheard (28)

Mr. Irving Blakeman is not sure that this is the correct solution for the company's executive problems, since he himself wishes to get away from close attention to the company and he feels that the president's position should be filled by a man who can success-fully administer all aspects of the business. He is also concerned about the possibility of having to pay large salaries to two new executives, a president and treasurer, since this additional expense might well affect the amount that could be paid to the family in dividends. The company's profit margin is not wide enough to support a large number of highly paid executives. Furthermore, Mr. Blakeman wants to do all he can to bring his son-in-law, Samuel Shepheard, along toward eventual overall management of the com-pany. Mr. Blakeman is not sure that Samuel Shepheard is ready to become president as yet and believes that further training is necessary for him. During this additional training his performance in all aspects of the business could be judged.

REQUIRED: What steps do you recommend that Mr. Blakeman take regarding executive personnel in Blakeman Textiles, Incorpo-rated?

22   FACILITIES

The term "facilities" is used here to include the office equipment and the office space of a professional firm; the store building, furniture, fixtures, and delivery equipment of a retail establishment; and the factory building, machinery, tools, offices, and warehouses of a manufacturing company. Facilities are the things used in performing the activities of a company.

Adequate facilities are essential for quality goods to be manufactured and for intangible services to be performed efficiently. On the other hand, the ownership of facilities imposes serious burdens. Large amounts of capital, often 25% to 50% of all assets a company owns, are needed for facilities, and capital so invested cannot be quickly converted into cash. Consequently, improper investment may so deplete the working capital as to hamper operations and perhaps lead to bankruptcy. Also, the depreciation, repairs, insurance, taxes, and interest costs resulting from an investment in facilities create a fixed annual charge on operations that may become a heavy burden.

The relative importance of facilities will, of course, vary from company to company. Nevertheless, their impact on successful operations and on the financial soundness of the enterprise requires that virtually every top executive and department head give at least some attention to assembling the proper facilities.

Facilities as a part of business administration. The type of facilities required by any company will depend upon such things as the product line of the company, its methods of sales promotion, its policy regarding the use of capital, and its personnel program. We have discussed capacity and production processes in Chapters 9 and 10. It will be assumed that these policy questions have been decided, and consequently the company knows the activities in which it will engage. The problem then becomes one of securing satisfactory facilities for the performance of the activities.

Many of the questions that arise in connection with facilities involve technical problems, the discussion of which has no place in this book. The manager will ordinarily rely upon the advice of an engineer so far as the technical aspects are concerned. Nevertheless, a number of very important questions remain that a manager must decide. Such problems involve:

1. Location of facilities.
2. Building construction.
3. Selection of equipment.
4. Layout.

LOCATION OF FACILITIES

The dynamic nature of our economy keeps location a live issue for most companies. Shifts in markets, new sources of raw materials, changes in freight rates, new laws on price differentials, and modifications in wage and labor conditions all affect the desirability of a particular plant location. In retailing, too, population shifts and changes in buying habits often call for reappraisal of store locations. Especially in growing companies, questions as to where new facilities should be located will arise.

A sound approach to the location of facilities includes the following steps:

(a) Determine for the specific company or operation what *factors* are most important in selecting a location.
(b) Focus attention on a limited number of areas and sites by *successive narrowing* of the locations being considered.
(c) Consider advisability of *deconcentrating* operations to two or more locations.

Factors influencing location of a hosiery mill. A specific example will highlight issues in selecting a location. One of the leading manufacturers of women's and men's hosiery in a midwestern city found itself increasingly embarrassed by the lower prices that southern mills were able to quote. This company, therefore, made an intensive study of the desirability of moving to the South.

Analysis of industry figures showed no reduction in the number of machines located in the northern area, although there had been some shifting away from the highly unionized cities to rural districts. On the other hand, most of the growth had occurred in the South. Some of the new plants were branches of northern mills, and others were newly organized firms with all their facilities in the southern region.

Reasons for moving to the South. Investigation showed that the primary reasons for the development of industry in the South had been: (a) low labor rates; (b) freedom from union restrictions regarding hours, number of machines per worker, overtime use of help, and similar questions; and (c) the inducement offered to northern capital by southern cities in the form of lower taxes or tax exemptions, low building costs, favorable arrangements regarding power and fuel, and sometimes free sites. These favorable conditions, plus the use of up-to-date machinery and efficient methods, enabled the southern mills to have significantly lower costs than most of the northern mills.

Disadvantages of the South. On the other hand, a number of factors tended to detract from the desirability of a southern location. The largest markets for hosiery are found in the industrial and business areas of the North, and southern hosiery mills incur a greater expense in providing satisfactory delivery service to customers in these large markets.

Another disadvantage is difficulty in securing satisfactory personnel. The southern workers generally have not developed experience in hosiery operations, and as a result the costs of supervision and inspection may be substantially higher than are corresponding costs in an efficient northern mill. Furthermore, there has been difficulty in securing foremen who are familiar with the hosiery industry and who also know how to handle southern labor. This factor tended to offset, in part, the lower labor rates in the South.

Moreover, some of the advantages of the South were diminishing. In 1929 the hourly earnings of southern hosiery workers were as much as 45% lower than those paid by companies in northern locations. The wage differential, however, had almost disappeared as a result of the federal minimum wage law, war shortages of manpower, and union activity. Also, the freedom from union restrictions was also diminishing as formal collective bargaining was extended through the South.

The company concluded that although a southern location was more desirable than a northern one, the existing differences in costs and the possibility that these differences might be significantly reduced in the future did not justify the expense of moving facilities from the North to the South at that time.

Factors affecting choice of location. The preceding example has indicated that many factors need to be considered in selecting a location. The most important of these are:

A. *Markets.*

The importance of being located near customers depends largely on the nature of the product or the service sold and the type of customer it is desired to reach. The doctor who is a general practitioner usually locates in residential communities, whereas the specialist will locate in a central business district where he can serve more conveniently patients drawn from a wide territory.

Drugstores and other retail establishments that sell convenience goods are greatly interested in buyer traffic. Few customers will bother even to cross the street to buy merchandise such as cigarettes or candy bars. Buyer traffic is also important to wholesale firms in New York City. Retail store buyers like to be able to inspect merchandise of several companies without traveling long distances; so definite wholesale districts have grown up for carpets and rugs, bedding, women's ready-to-wear, and similar groups of products. A salesroom located outside the established district is at a definite disadvantage.

For those products normally sold in the customer's office, a good marketing location is simply one that enables the firm to give customers quick delivery service and that decreases the cost of transporting merchandise from the plant to customer. For perishable and bulky products, a location near the customer may be quite important.

B. *Materials.*

Nearness to raw materials is usually a minor consideration for retail stores and service establishments. The importance to a manufacturing plant, on the other hand, depends largely upon the ratio of raw material transportation cost to total production costs. For example, the cost of transporting iron ore and coal are significant in the total cost of steel.

As is often true, materials needed for steel production are rarely found in the same location, and a steel company must decide whether it prefers to be close to iron ore or to coal. Recently, steel facilities have been expanded on the East Coast where iron ore may be delivered easily from new South American and Labrador mines, even though coal is less accessible than, say, in Pittsburgh.

Occasionally, convenience of getting materials is as important as transportation costs. For instance, one reason dress manufacturers locate in New York City is to secure quick and easy access to cloth of a style currently popular.

Access to both selling markets and material markets is, of course, a matter of cost, time, frequency, and ease of transportation rather than distance. Thus, for practical purposes, Denver, Colorado, is more accessible to Chicago than is Fort Smith, Arkansas, even though Denver is 200 miles farther away.

C. *Labor.*

A service or retail firm usually finds a satisfactory supply of labor wherever sufficient customers to constitute an adequate market are located. Not so with manufacturing. Many industries require highly skilled labor, and most firms cannot undertake the expense and the time to develop an adequate supply of skilled labor where it is not already available. Firms subject to wide fluctuations in volume seek locations where meeting peak requirements will not be a major obstacle.

In addition to *availability* of satisfactory workers, attention must be given to the *prevailing wage rates* and the *nature of labor organizations.* The intelligent manufacturer today knows he cannot avoid some form of labor organization. He also knows that labor leadership in some areas is militant and uncooperative as contrasted with leadership that follows the philosophy that the employees must seek to secure efficient and low cost production, which will react to the benefit of both the employees and the employer.

D. *Power.*

Electrical power will probably be available in any location considered—except for remote mines and lumbering activities. The cost and the dependability of supply, however, do vary and should be checked when a location is selected.

E. *Climate and physical conditions.*

Those companies wishing to locate beside rivers to secure transportation or a sufficient water supply have to weigh the possibility of flood against the dependability of an adequate flow of water. Some factories must dispose of waste materials or obnoxious gases, and they must locate where this disposal is not unduly burdensome or offensive. Many cities have zoning laws that restrict the location of both retail and manufacturing establishments. With air-conditioning, climatic conditions are less likely to influence plant location than formerly. Textile mills, for instance, no longer have to be located in areas having high humidity because ideal spinning and weaving conditions can now be carefully controlled with automatic humidifiers. On the other hand, good flying weather that makes testing easy has aided the growth of the aircraft industry in southern California.

F. *Special factors.*

Communities occasionally offer special inducements to companies to locate within their borders. The community expects to obtain substantial commercial benefit from purchases made by plant and office employees. A city may donate land or reduce taxes on new facilities. During depressions, local governments may acquire buildings through nonpayment of taxes, and these properties may be donated to a company that agrees to employ a minimum number of workers for a stipulated period. Such inducements as these are rarely important enough to justify selecting an otherwise poor location; but if several locations offer approximately equal advantages, these special concessions may affect the choice.

Narrowing choice of locations. After the important factors affecting the choice of a location for a given plant, store, or office have been determined, there are, of course, innumerable places that might be considered as the new location. Some means of simplifying the choice must be followed. A useful approach is to narrow down the places considered by successive limitations, as was done by a firm manufacturing heavy machinery.

This company faced the necessity of making improvements in its existing buildings. These improvements had been postponed because the company had been experiencing a series of labor difficulties that had accumulated considerable bitterness as well as inefficient practices. The directors of the company did not care to make further investments in fixed assets where possible labor complications might prevent the earning of a satisfactory return on the investment. They finally decided that the only way out of the difficulty was to move the plant to a new location with a new building and a fresh start in its labor relations.

In selecting specific cities that might provide a favorable location, the company proceeded by the following steps:

1. The country was divided into a number of large geographical areas, and the relative desirability of these areas was determined.
2. Specific regions within the areas worthy of detailed consideration were selected, and the relative economies of operation in the selected regions were determined.
3. Cities were selected within the most favorable regions, and the relative advantages and disadvantages of each of these cities were compared.

Following this procedure, the company first determined that it should be located within the general territory east of the Mississippi River and north of the Mason and Dixon line. This territory produced practically all the raw materials required by the company, and it furnished the market for the bulk of its output. The skilled labor that was needed for manufacturing operations was available in a number of localities, and transportation facilities were generally superior to those in other territories.

The next step was the selection of specific regions, and, after careful consideration, the following regions were determined to be worthy of consideration:

The Mohawk Valley in New York.
Southern Michigan.
Central Indiana and Northern Ohio.

The Naugatuck Valley in Connecticut and the Schuylkill Valley in Pennsylvania were also considered at some length, but they were eliminated because of the comparatively high labor costs in these regions.

Cities providing a possible location within these regions were carefully appraised with respect to:

1. Proximity to market for company's products.
2. Availability of raw materials.
3. Availability and costs of labor.
4. Availability and costs of power, light, and fuel.
5. Type of public regulations, including taxes, workmen's compensation, and restriction of hours of work.

Several of these factors were not capable of arithmetical measurement, but estimates of differences in costs were made for the remaining factors. The study showed that the following cities were all worthy of consideration: Richmond, Indiana; Lima, Ohio; Rochester, New York; Elyria, Ohio; Kalamazoo, Michigan; Battle Creek, Michigan; Alliance, Ohio; and Syracuse, New York. Appraisal of some of the more intangible factors resulted in the elimination of Alliance and Elyria, Ohio, and Syracuse and Rochester, New York. Final selection of one of the remaining cities was determined by the availability of a desirable site and building that could be purchased at a favorable price.

The cost of moving to a new location was greater than the cost of repairing and modernizing the old facilities of the company. Nevertheless, officers of the firm were convinced that the lower operating cost of the new location would more than justify this additional investment.

One aspect of this approach, the successive narrowing of locations to be considered, deserves emphasis. The importance of factors shifts as attention moves from broad geographical areas to cities and to sites. Proximity to markets, sources of raw materials, and supply of labor are likely to be controlling in selecting areas. Once a single area or several of roughly equal attractiveness have been chosen, other factors assume greater significance.

In the selection of cities or districts such factors as state and local taxes, community attractiveness, attitude of local leaders, labor laws, and labor organizations become more important. Then when choosing specific sites, the price, shape, terrain, water, waste disposal, zoning, fire protection, utilities, accessibility for workers, railroad connections, highways, and similar specific considerations become dominant. Valuable time and money will be wasted if these factors affecting sites are studied before the problem has been narrowed down to a limited number of areas and districts.

Deconcentration of operations. In the preceding discussion, we have assumed that each company operates in only one location. As companies grow in size, consideration should be given to using two or more locations. Many manufacturing concerns, retail stores, banks, and insurance companies are opening branches and taking other steps toward deconcentrating their operations.

External benefits of deconcentration. Examination of the reasons for dispersing operations shows that most of the location factors already considered have a bearing on this issue. One of the main advantages of having plants or stores in two or more locations is to be close to several segments of the market. Bakeries, bottling plants, and industrial gas (oxygen, acetylene) plants, for instance, must be close to their customers. Other companies find that several locations enable them to give better service, cut shipping costs, and enjoy the reputation of being "a local firm."

When raw materials are expensive to transport, as in the copper or meat packing industry, locations close to each major source of supply will be an advantage. Several different locations also enable a company to tap different reservoirs of labor. When the labor supply in one location is fully utilized, going to a new area may be easier than inducing men to move to the present plant. Also, it may be healthy for both company and community to avoid a single employer dominating the area's economic life.

Most companies with decentralized activities find that they are better fitted to their economic environment in at least one of the above ways.

Economic size of operating unit. The major restraint on deconcentration is the need for an economical size of operation at each location. The technology of some industries requires a large volume for efficient performance. Thus, in oil refining or steel making tremendous quantities of production at a single plant tend to lower costs. Once a point is reached, however, when duplicate facilities are used to handle added volume, then a separate location will be at no disadvantage so far as technology is concerned. Also, if two or more products call for independent production operations, no technological loss will arise by having them manufactured in separate plants.

A related aspect to economic size of units is the cost of specialized services such as power, personnel, accounting, shipping, and the like. The volume of activities at each location should be large enough to support a full complement of such services. For example, the cutting and sewing of men's shirts can be done in quite small units, as far as actual processing is concerned; but the economical shirt plant must be large enough to justify skilled service units.

When deconcentration is first undertaken, duplication of buildings, specialized equipment, and service divisions often entails greater expense for these items than would be necessary at a single location. With increasing volume, this disadvantage diminishes and at some point the extra expense will be more than offset by the external benefits mentioned above. Part of the job of the central manager is to forecast whether the business available for an additional plant or store will carry such a local unit beyond this minimum point.

Management consideration. Deconcentration of operations creates both disadvantages and advantages from a management viewpoint. Without doubt, physical separation interferes with communication and in this way complicates the tasks of supervision and coordination. Also, leveling out employment and making personnel transfers is more difficult.

On the other hand, smaller operating units have distinct advantages for local management. Local executives can comprehend and keep track of the entire operation. Moreover, the personal acquaintance of most of the workers with each other and their supervisors helps build morale. Usually, a local plant will not be involved in unlike activities, and this further simplifies the job of management. Businessmen often summarize these factors by saying that dispersed units are a "manageable size."

The discussion of executive development in the preceding chapter brought out the need for good training spots. Deconcentrated plants and stores serve this purpose well because even junior executives quickly see the entire operation, and there are positions where men may be tried out before being promoted to senior jobs.

Training will be especially valuable if deconcentrated operation is coupled with decentralization of authority (discussed in Chapter 18).

Location, then, is not quite so simple as may appear at first glance. In addition to deciding where the main establishment is to be situated, the administrator must weigh the possible advantages of separate locations for parts of his company's activities. Retail stores may need separate branches, warehouses, or garages. Financial institutions likewise may branch out. Manufacturing concerns may use separate plants for production of parts, distinct products, assembly, or local supply of a common product. As we have seen, decision on such matters requires attention to external factors, technological questions, and managerial considerations.

BUILDING CONSTRUCTION

Difficulties in selecting a building. Building construction should not be considered separately from other decisions regarding facilities and general policies of the company. For example, some construction engineers think that a building three stories high provides the cheapest construction from the point of view of enclosing the largest cubic area within four walls and under one roof. The desirability of such a building, however, will depend upon the type of operations performed, the weight of materials, methods of handling materials, and the value and the availability of the land on which the building is erected.

Further complicating the selection of a building is the fact that even in this age of standardization very few buildings are identical. Almost every business building is specially designed to fit the location and the use for which it was originally intended. Obvious variations include single versus multiple stories, shape and arrangement of areas, type of construction material, and innumerable other features. The problem is to obtain a building with characteristics suited to the needs of a particular company.

Distinction between new and old buildings. In general, if a company is constructing a new building, it may proceed with a complete plan for its facilities. First, a decision must be reached regarding the location, the capacity, the equipment, the type of production, and the layout to be employed. A building must then be constructed to house these various operations. This building should be regarded more or less as a shell into which the other facilities, ideally designed and arranged, are placed.

Few concerns are in a position to follow this convenient and comparatively simple procedure. Often they own or purchase a building already in existence, and then facilities must be arranged within the building in a way that will require the smallest outlay for alterations. Under such circumstances, the building will probably be carefully appraised before detailed plans for layout are prepared so that revisions in plans and new construction work can be reduced to a minimum.

Problems requiring the attention of the manager. Although engineers must be employed to deal with technical matters of building construction, management should give attention to such significant problems as:

1. Cost of construction.
2. Effect on operating cost.
3. Expansion possibilities.
4. Appearance.

Cost of construction. For financial reasons, management naturally seeks to limit the amount of capital invested in facilities. Often, if such a policy is followed, architects and engineers, who regard high standards of construction and performance as of first importance, become provoked and disgusted. Although management must rely on the architects and engineers for technical and engineering advice, it should reserve the right to exercise practical judgment in determining the amount of funds to be invested in the construction or purchase of a building. Management must balance the marginal utility of each special feature against its incremental cost.

Effect on operating costs. Material handling costs. A building should be constructed to permit the use and the satisfactory layout of efficient equipment. An efficient flour mill, for instance, requires that the material be moved from one operation to another by the force of gravity; consequently, milling operations should be conducted in a multiple story building. On the other hand, if the direct-line method of production is to be employed by a concern manufacturing heavy products, a one story building will probably permit substantial savings in material handling costs.

Heating, lighting, and other service costs. The expense of heating a building will be affected by its construction. Because of the failure of walls and windows to provide adequate insulation, and also because stairways, skylights, walls, and other features may affect the circulation of air, certain parts of the building may be hard to heat adequately without overheating other parts. Furthermore, with the rising popularity of air conditioning in the summertime, this question of adequate insulation takes on a year-round importance. The building must also be provided with adequate lighting, water, and toilet facilities. Unless all of these features are satisfactory, there is likely to be an increase in operating costs.

Maintenance of buildings. Building repairs are necessitated by (a) the action of the elements and (b) the wear and tear caused by operations. Stone, brick, and special compositions are only slightly affected by rain, sunshine, freezing, and other weather conditions. As a result, the cost of maintenance for a building constructed of one of these materials is usually much less than for a building constructed of wood. On the other hand, the original cost of a building made of these more durable materials is substantially higher. The cost of maintaining the interior is also affected by the type of construction.

Depreciation charges. The construction of a building will likewise affect the rate at which the original investment is depreciated on the company's books. The economic life of some buildings made of durable materials may be considered to be 40 or 50 years, thus requiring an average depreciation rate per annum of 2% 2½% of the original investment. Other buildings of less durable construction may be considered at last only 20 years and must be depreciated at an average annual rate of 5%.

Also important to the business administrator is the possibility of loss in event of sale. If the building is designed so that it may be readily used by other business enterprises and is located in a place where there is a demand for that type of building space, it is reasonable to assume that the economic life of the building will be determined primarily by its physical construction. If the original company does not have use for the building during its entire life, it may be rented or sold to some other concern.

On the other hand, if the building is of a special construction suited only to a particular type of operation or is located in an out-of-the-way spot that would not be attractive to some other company, then its economic life might be shorter than has been anticipated in setting the depreciation rate. Sometimes buildings are intentionally constructed so as to be more salable in event the original owner does not wish to continue to use them throughout their economic life. Incidentally, sale-and-lease-back of such buildings is easier to arrange.

Reducing risks by building construction. Hazards such as fires, floods, and explosions, may be reduced by the proper designing of a building. For example, when a building is constructed of cement and brick, the possibilities of its destruction by fire are greatly lessened, and it may even be termed a "fireproof building." The cost of insurance on such buildings is substantially less, which results in lower operating costs as well.

Following a disastrous flood, one of the leading retail stores in Pittsburgh constructed doorways and showcases so that flood waters could be kept from its merchandise for a substantial period of time. In addition, movable showcases were installed so that they could be taken to the second floor in the event such action became necessary. The likelihood of explosion can also be minimized by the construction of proper ventilation facilities and the use of proper storage facilities. For particularly dangerous products, it is usually preferable to construct detached buildings so as to reduce the possible damage in case of accidents.

Many of the operating expenses—materials handling, heat, light, maintenance, depreciation, insurance—can be reduced by a higher initial investment in the building. The engineer can provide estimates and advice on what is desirable, but the manager must make the basic decision on how far the company should go in attempting to cut operating expenses in future years through improved building construction.

Provision for expansion. Provision may be made for the expansion of a building in its original construction. This can be accomplished by providing heavier foundations than are necessary for the original building, and by reserving space for additional elevators and stairways so that additional stories can be added on top of the building at some future time.

In anticipation of horizontal expansion, a wall may be constructed with no windows so that additions can later be made on that side of the building without requiring any change in the original structure other than cutting through the necessary doorways.

Appearance. The importance of appearance of a building varies greatly. Appearance is not as important to a manufacturing concern as to a retail establishment or professional firm, but manufacturing companies have realized that appearance may have an important psychological effect upon their employees. The attractiveness of factory buildings has also become more significant since improved transportation has increased the likelihood of customers seeing the plant of a company.

In retail establishments and offices visited by customers, the appearance is much more significant. The outward appearance of a roadside refreshment stand may account for a large part of its popularity. Many stores operating in old buildings erect modern, flashy fronts so as to present an attractive impression on potential customers. Even banks woo potential depositors with impressive structures.

The effect on customers and employees of the appearance of a building is an intangible thing that cannot be measured accurately. The manager must use his judgment in deciding the extent to which this factor, as well as construction costs, operating costs, and provision for expansion, should influence the construction of a building for his company.

SELECTION OF EQUIPMENT

Numerous kinds of equipment. In a general consideration of central management such as this, we cannot discuss specific types of equipment for different classes of industries. Numerous and varied operations must be performed in each industry, and the equipment needed for these operations is likely to differ materially from that used in any other industry. Often special-purpose machinery is designed for use in a single plant or office, and many technical problems are involved in their design and construction.

Some indication of the possible variety of equipment needed in a manufacturing plant can be secured when one thinks of all the machinery required for each of the following activities:

1. Production operations.
2. Material handling and storage.
3. Plant services, including power, light, heat, ventilation, and similar services.

An almost endless variety of facilities will be needed under any one of these headings.

Factors affecting choice of equipment. The business executive normally relies upon engineers for advice regarding design of equipment, estimates of operating performance, and of cost factors. Nevertheless, there is still need for a business decision as to what equipment will be used. The executive must take the basic data provided by the engineer and, with his knowledge of the company as a whole, make a decision on what equipment to install. Important among the factors to be considered in this connection are:

1. Investment required. To calculate the investment, the cost of installing the equipment and getting it ready for operation should be included as well as the amount paid to the manufacturer. Sometimes firms have old, unused equipment that may be repaired in their own shop, in which case the investment is the scrap value plus the outlay required to get the new machinery ready for operation.

2. Direct operating costs. This includes the cost of materials and labor. If the spoilage of one machine is greater than another, or if one machine can use cheaper raw materials, the calculation will be affected. Some machines require less labor to operate than others, and often there is a variation of skill required.

3. Indirect costs. Indirect costs are those that do not vary in proportion to the output of the machine. Included in this item are such expenses as depreciation, interest, maintenance and repair, and rental of space if the company does not already have the area needed.

4. Quality of product or service. The quality of the product often varies and this may be a determining factor in the selection of equipment. Usually improvement in the quality of a product requires higher investment or higher operating cost, in which case the administrator must determine whether the improvement in quality is worth the extra expense.

5. Adaptability of equipment. Most equipment is durable, and its purchase is often justified on the assumption that it is to be used over a considerable period of time. Before the equipment is worn out, however, the design of the company's products, its volume of operations, or some other production factor might change. It is desirable, therefore, that the equipment be adaptable to other uses. If it is standard equipment and a change in the company's operations eliminates the need for it, it may be sold to some other concern. If the equipment is not adaptable to new products or to other uses, conservative managers will select equipment only if the gross profits from its use are adequate to recover the investment within a period when use can be confidently predicted.

Choice of new equipment. In most business situations there are two or more kinds of equipment that might be used to perform a given operation. The task of the business executive is to make a *choice* between these alternatives, and consequently he should concentrate his attention on the *differences* between the alternatives.

This approach to selection of equipment by comparing differences in alternatives is illustrated in the following simple case. A wholesale company was building a new warehouse and, among other features, was considering whether to use belt conveyors or small electric trucks and trailers. A comparison of the engineering estimates showed:

			Differences	
	Conveyors	Trucks	Conveyors	Trucks
Investment	$185,000	$75,000	$110,000	......
Average annual operating costs	12,000	44,000	......	32,000
Average annual indirect costs (excluding interest)	14,000	8,000	6,000	......
Average annual net difference in costs				$26,000

Rate of return before income tax: $26,000 ÷ $110,000 = 23.6%.
Rate of return after income tax of 50%: $13,000 ÷ $110,000 = 11.8%.

These figures indicated that the conveyor system would require a much larger investment but its operating expenses would be lower. To bring the figures into sharper focus, the average rate of return was computed. This showed that the ratio of cost-saving earnings to added investment would be 23.6% before income tax or 11.8% after income tax. The management then had to decide whether this return was high enough to justify the extra $110,000 required by the conveyors.

The quality of work under the two methods was considered to be about equal.

Two considerations led the management to decide to use trucks. The company was investing a large part of its *available capital* in the warehouse, and the directors felt that investments in equipment should be made only when there would be a substantial return in the near future. In this instance, it looked as though the after-tax return would average 11.8%—a rate below the company's 15% standard for such investments. Moreover, the operations of the company had been shifting rapidly. The trucks were highly *flexible*, whereas the conveyors were stationary and would have lost much of their value if they had to be torn out to make room for new requirements.

A few brief comments on the estimates used in this example will be helpful in applying the approach to other situations. Most significant is the absence of any attempt to cover all costs of the warehousing operation or to stick rigidly to conventional accounting practices of recording such costs. Only those costs that would be different because of the choice of one or the other type of equipment were considered. Interest was excluded because management wanted to know the rate of return; to have included a portion of, say, bond interest would have been counting cost of capital twice. If management had been interested in the *pay-out period* (the time required for savings to recover the investment), then interest on the average investment would have been treated as a cost but depreciation would have been excluded.

Replacing present equipment. A manager often has to decide whether to replace existing facilities with new equipment. This poses a problem similar to one just discussed except that one of the alternatives is the continued use of the present machines. Here, again, the sound approach is to concentrate on difference between the alternative courses of action.

With existing equipment there is the question of what value to place on it, that is, what "investment" is involved in continuing to use old facilities? There are, of course, several values for any asset including appraised value, sales price, earning value, book value, and replacement cost. Each of these values is a valid figure for its particular purpose. The question is which to use in considering the desirability of investing in new equipment. For this purpose, the price at which the equipment could be sold is the significant figure. This is the amount the company gives up in order to continue to use the asset, just as the purchase price is what the company gives up to get a new machine. So, in computing the difference in investment, it is the sales value of the present equipment that should be deducted from the cost of the new equipment.

Incidentally, the sales value of an asset at any given time is almost never exactly the same as the accounting book value. Machines may be fully depreciated and still have sales value. Likewise, many facilities cannot be sold for their current book value, especially if they have high installation costs or are of special-purpose design. This does not mean the accounting figures on fixed assets are wrong; they simply are not intended to show sales value.

Sometimes new equipment is so much more efficient than present machines it pays a company to replace even relatively new facilities. One manufacturing concern, for example, had five engine lathes that were only six years old and in good running condition; each could be sold for $3,600. It considered replacing these with two new turret lathes costing $21,000 each. The turret lathes could turn out fully as much work as the present equipment and would cut labor costs substantially as shown in figures below.

| | | | Differences | |
	Engine Lathes	Turret Lathes	Engine Lathes	Turret Lathes
Investment (amount currently given up to get or keep equipment)	$18,000	$42,000	......	$24,000
Annual expenses:				
Direct labor	$16,000	$ 6,900		
Power and supplies	1,800	800		
Taxes and insurance	500	1,200		
Depreciation [1]	2,000	2,800		
Total annual expenses	$20,900	$11,700	$ 9,200	......

Rate of return before income tax: $9,200 ÷ $24,000 = 38%.
Rate of return after income tax of 50%: $4,600 ÷ $24,000 = 19%.

---

[1] Depreciation assumes engine lathes have 9 years of remaining life with no scrap value; turret lathes, 15 years life with no scrap value.

This company had adequate capital to make a net investment of $24,000. Its cutoff level for investment in new equipment was 16% after income tax. Moreover, because of the general outlook for skilled workers in its area, the company was following a policy of mechanizing its operations wherever practical. Consequently, the engine lathes were replaced with the turret lathes.

The approach to selection of equipment that has been discussed in this section is applicable, at least in broad terms, to many management decisions. Attention is focused on *differences* in investment, operating costs, and results for each of several alternatives. To simplify the analysis of these differences, all items that can be reduced to reasonably accurate dollar estimates are combined together, and the net investment and the net savings or payout period is computed. Then the more intangible factors such as risk of obsolescence, shifts in volume of business, alternative uses of capital, improvements in quality of product or service, flexibility in operations, and the like are weighed. On the basis of these considerations, the executive must decide whether the tangible dollar figures are attractive or unattractive.

LAYOUT

Layout deals with the arrangement of equipment for purposes of operation. In a plant, for instance, the various machines, storage bins, conveyors, and other apparatus should be placed so that volume and economy objectives are met.

Process versus direct-line production. One basic decision that will have a major effect on layout is the choice of direct-line or process production. In many industries equipment can be grouped according to *processes*, having all equipment related to a given process located in the same area. A second alternative is to arrange machinery by *products*, or in a *direct line*, so that the product flows directly from one machine to the next with a minimum of handling.

The layout adopted by a manufacturer of breakfast foods illustrates the main factors in deciding on basic flow of work. Production of these foods involves the following operations:

1. Mixing the ingredients used in the product.
2. Cooking the product.
3. Rolling or otherwise shaping the product.
4. Toasting the product.
5. Packaging the product.
6. Packing the product in cartons.

This concern manufactures several different cereals and quickly recognized the advantages in having mixers, rollers, ovens, and packaging machines for each product. This would permit the use of specialized machinery, and automatic conveyors could be installed to move the product from one operation to the next. The conditions under which production operations were performed might be standardized, and any variation from these standards that affected either quality or production costs could be readily detected. Consequently, the company constructed a building devoted entirely to the production of corn flakes.

The other alternative was to have all of the mixing equipment in one place, the cooking equipment in another department, and the ovens in a third department. By such a grouping, the same equipment could be utilized for several different products. Thus, if the volume of one product was low, the equipment could be employed in producing another product that was in greater demand. Under this arrangement, each process department would have several machines, and should a breakdown occur in any one of these machines, the entire line of production would not necessarily be stopped. The other machines could be run at a higher capacity or overtime in order to secure the necessary output.

Actually, the company did use the process method of production for some of its products that were sold in comparatively small volume. The size and the irregularity of the demand for these products did not justify the investment in direct-line method facilities.

Direct-line production in the automobile industry, packing plants, and other large-scale operations has received wide publicity. There are, however, many situations such as a typical cotton cloth mill where a process layout is preferable. In some concerns the two methods are combined. For example, a process layout may be used in the early stages of manufacture, while a direct line will be employed for assembly of the finished product.

Benefits of direct-line production. The more important advantages of direct-line production may be briefly summarized as follows:

1. Handling cost is often reduced. The distance that materials must travel is usually shorter, and automation is more readily adopted.

2. Economy in the use of space is often possible.

3. A lower investment in inventory may result. With direct-line production, the time needed to change raw materials into finished merchandise is usually shorter, and this permits a reduction of in-process inventory. Since the quantity of finished goods inventory is often based upon the length of time it takes to replenish it, this inventory may also be somewhat reduced.

4. Production control is facilitated. There are fewer lost orders, and the expense of following up orders is reduced. The inevitable bickering and buck-passing that arises between shops performing one process on a variety of goods is also eliminated.

Reasons for using process arrangement. The process type of production also has certain distinct advantages that may make it more desirable in some situations. The more important of these are the following:

1. It is more flexible and can be adapted to products of changing design and specifications. A concern operating on a job-order basis or producing only a limited quantity of a product of one specification usually finds that the flexibility of the process basis outweighs the possible advantages of the direct-line basis.

2. The investment in machinery may be lower because the machinery for each process is used for several different types of products. Moreover, the machinery is likely to be utilized nearer capacity than is possible under the direct-line method in which the machinery usually is idle unless the particular type of product for which it is designed is in demand.

3. A breakdown of one machine will not, in most cases, tie up the entire production of the process group. The flow of production can be diverted from one machine to another much more readily than is possible in a plant that is set up on the direct-line basis.

4. Supervisors and workmen develop a skill in handling a variety of products. The direct-line type of production tends to develop skill on a product basis, whereas the process type trains men in performing a particular operation on a variety of products. In those industries in which products vary from time to time, the latter type skill is desirable.

Interrelation of buildings, equipment, and layout. Although direct-line versus process production has been discussed under layout, a decision on such matters will also have an important bearing on the type of equipment that is most economical for a particular operation. For instance, if a given machine is to be used for a widely different group of products under a process setup, it will have to be of greater size and flexibility than any one of several machines that might be used in each of the production lines under a direct-line method. Furthermore, the type of building needed for the process method will probably differ from that best suited to the direct-line method.

In a few industries, machines are moved about. Companies producing heavy products such as locomotives or ships, for example, typically move machines to the materials rather than vice versa. This obviously affects equipment, layout, and buildings as well. Clearly, then, a decision as to type of production should be made early in any study of facilities. After this has been settled, equipment selected and building space made available, detailed layout can be considered.

Steps in improving layout. An approach useful in developing detailed layouts of plants—and offices and stores—is as follows:

1. The area needed for each machine group performing one operation, sometimes called a production center, is first determined. This includes not only the area occupied by the machine, but also the space necessary for the workmen and for the materials moving to and from the machine.
2. In a similar manner, the area required for storage and service facilities may be determined.
3. The arrangement of the production centers must be made, with a consideration for the flow of productions through the plant. This arrangement will, of course, be affected materially by the company's decision as to process versus direct-line production.
4. The storage and service departments must be fitted into the layout at points convenient for the production unit that they are to serve.
5. A final step consists of juggling the location of the equipment so that the arrangement will either minimize the space required or fit the equipment into the available area. For this purpose it is often useful to cut out small pieces of cardboard in the same shape and proportionate size as the actual equipment and move these pieces around on a cardboard drawing of the floor plan until the most satisfactory arrangement is found.

A diagram of a carefully studied layout for a woodworking shop is shown below.

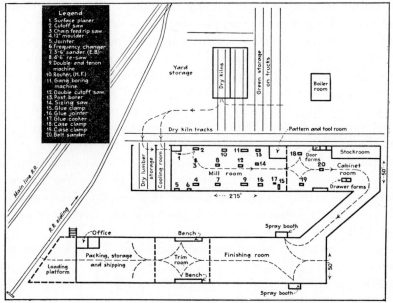

Factory Management and Maintenance

Layout of woodworking shop.

Retail store layout. Thus far, our discussion has centered around the layout of manufacturing facilities. Many of the same problems as those already discussed will be found in the layout of office space. Layout of retail stores and consumer service establishments raises a further consideration not found in office and production layout. Since facilities are used for display and service to customers, the effect of the layout on sales volume becomes of major importance.

In a department store, for example, the number of customers passing near the entrances and the main aisles, particularly on the first floor, is much greater than those passing through the less accessible parts of the store. Consequently, goods more frequently demanded by customers or merchandise with high gross profit is placed in these more convenient locations. Some types of merchandise, however, customers wish to spend much time in selecting. The sale of such merchandise will not benefit from heavy customer traffic to nearly the same extent as will small standard products that the customer spends little time in selecting. Moreover, merchandise that appeals to a customer's fancy and may be purchased on impulse without previous consideration will reap large benefits from heavy customer traffic.

Still another factor is that many customers like to purchase the same type of products or supplementary products together. It is advantageous therefore to have curtains, draperies, rugs, pictures, and other household furnishings in the same area. Women's coats, dresses, and hats will also probably be placed in adjacent areas.

These considerations have primarily to do with convenience for the customer, but they also aid in selling merchandise. Obviously all departments cannot have choice locations; consequently, the management must give special attention to the response of each department to a given location and the effect one department may have on the sales of other departments. In this regard, gross profit rather than sales volume is the primary consideration. Moreover, the management must preserve the favorable appearance of the store as a whole.

Retail store layout is not entirely a matter of facilitating sales. Merchandise must be moved in and out of the store, provision must be made for storage, and service facilities are necessary for both the customer and the employee. There are questions of economy of space in retail stores just as in manufacturing establishments.

In a retail establishment the problem of facilitating sales assumes major significance, but other layout issues should not be disregarded, particularly in nonselling areas.

In any layout problem considerable ingenuity is required to balance the relative importance of each factor to the enterprise. The result is almost always a compromise, particularly if the layout must be fitted into an old building with dimensions, pillars, windows, and other features not well suited to its present use. Here, again, the difficulty of the job makes the arrangement no less important.

SUMMARY REGARDING FACILITIES

Every manager, from president to section chief, must give at least some attention to providing the space and the tools needed by his subordinates to carry out their duties. Major issues encountered in this connection are (1) location of facilities, (2) building construction, (3) selection of equipment, and (4) layout. While the manager must often look to the engineer for technical advice and estimates, many basic questions can be answered only through the exercise of business judgment. The nature of these questions, and suggested ways of dealing with them have been presented in this chapter.

Substantial changes have occurred in the design of manufacturing establishments during the last half century. The nineteenth century factory was likely to be a dimly lighted, poorly ventilated place in which layout was haphazard and materials followed a dubious path from one process to another. In contrast, the modern plant reflects the influence of functional design. The very style of modern architecture emphasizes light, simplicity, and usefulness. All through the modern factory, facilities show evidence of study as to how each unit can be suited to its task and placed in the best position to perform that task.

The retail store has also changed greatly in appearance. A visit to a modern, high-class store is a study in aesthetics. Both the exterior of the building and the fixtures within present a pleasing, harmonious appearance, and merchandise is displayed in a way that makes the customer glow with the pleasure that may be secured by its purchase.

The change from the old to the new is by no means complete in all business concerns; but this much is certain, the efficient manager has learned that a careful study of his facilities and the use of modern, well-designed equipment are requisites for successful operation in present-day competitive conditions.

QUESTIONS FOR CLASS DISCUSSION

1. (a) How do the factors that are important in selecting a *city* in which to locate the plant of a vacuum cleaner company differ from those to be used in locating a cement plant? (b) For the same two plants, compare the factors that would be important in selecting plant *sites*.

2. Louisiana offers a 10-year property tax exemption for new industrial investment, and governors of northern and eastern states make apoplectic remarks about piracy when delegations from southern states make visits to lure industry. A recent study in Louisiana concludes that only 7% of new industrial development there would have gone elsewhere if the taxes had not been forgiven and that the tax gimmick is "vastly over-rated." Why do the southern governors bother to make the trip, then, and why the apoplectic remarks?

3. In light of the management problems considered earlier in this book, what advantages do you think a company might secure from leasing a building rather than owning one? What conditions may make it necessary for a company to construct its own building?

4. A manufacturer of small household appliances is building a new plant to manufacture electric toasters and broilers. One major issue to be resolved is facilities for the sheet-metal stampings and first subassembly of the stampings. Model numbers and sizes have increased substantially so that production flexibility has to be provided to take account of changes in demand and style. There are essentially three ways to do this:

(a) Subcontract the work mentioned at an estimated annual cost of $8,500,000.

(b) Invest $15,000,000 in equipment for three semi-automatic production lines with specialized presses, dies, and transfer equipment on each line. The lines would run, depending on demand, at rates that varied from 2½ shifts to ½ shift. Estimated annual average labor costs (assuming present wage levels) would be $2,500,000 for direct operating work, $1,000,000 for set-up work, and $500,000 for retraining, and annual indirect costs would be $500,000.

(c) Invest $24,000,000 in "Detroit automation" or "flexible automation" equipment—one line with one set of bolster presses, interchangeable dies, and some idle stations in the transfer machines. Estimated annual average labor costs would be $1,500,000 for direct operating work and $250,000 each for set-up work and retraining. Annual indirect costs were estimated at $1,550,000.

Property taxes and insurance expenses of the company average 4% of total assets; the cost of borrowed capital is 6%. Purchase of the new equipment would not change the tax and insurance expense outlay. Physical life of the new equipment for high-grade service was expected to be 15 years. The economic life was more uncertain since it depended on changes in consumer habits and tastes and on the development of new or substitute appliances. The company's desired rate of return on new investment was 20% before income taxes and its minimum rate was 15%. Financial and managerial risks were such as to make investments yielding less than 15% unattractive.

Which of the three ways would you recommend and why?

5. How might (a) the land value, (b) the rate at which sales have been growing, (c) the financial condition of the company, (d) the desire to have a high salable value for the building, and (e) the manufacture of heavy products that require railroad shipment affect the type of building a company would construct?

6. Discuss the relationship between the choice of machinery and (a) production policies and (b) financial policies.

7. Give several ways in which a plant set up on a direct-line production basis can make provision for rush orders and repair work on regular products.

8. The layout of the woodworking shop shown on page 591 was adapted to the building already on the site. Suppose a new building were being constructed for the shop on the same site. Prepare a simple diagram showing the shape of the new building and the arrangement of equipment you would recommend.

9. What are the principal differences in basic layout between (a) an automobile manufacturing plant, (b) a flour mill, (c) a job printing plant, (d) a department store, and (e) a shipyard? How do you explain the differences? What kind of building is best suited to each?

CASE XXII

Blair Plastic Company

The Blair Plastic Company manufactures a variety of molded plastic parts. Most of these parts are sold to other manufacturers who use them in motors and a wide variety of equipment. A few of the parts go into toys and similar articles but, as a rule, such products do not call for the precision and quality which are important selling points for Blair products. Sales have been expanding and the present plant is no longer adequate to handle production efficiently. Machines are crowded, good layout has been sacrificed in order to utilize available space, and storage of work-in-process and finished goods is quite inefficient. For these reasons the management has decided that it must obtain additional space for its operations.

A construction engineer recommends that the company either (1) build an addition to its present plant or (2) build a new plant for its entire operations. The proposed addition would cost $225,000 and would be attached to the present building. It would comfortably house not only present operations but also a 20% increase in volume.

The proposed new plant would cost $600,000 and would have a capacity approximately equal to the present plant and the new addition. It would also be capable of further expansion, whereas a second addition to the present plant would be much more costly. The new plant would be located in a suburb of the city where the present plant is situated. The Chamber of Commerce of this suburb is anxious to attract new industries and will donate the land for the new plant. Most of the present employees would probably continue to work for the company in this new location, and its ready accessibility by automobile gives it a large potential labor supply. Insurance and taxes (combined) on the new plant will average $21,000 per year; on the present plant and addition they will average $15,000 per year.

The present building of the company was constructed 10 years ago for $515,000; it has been depreciated on the company books at the rate of 3% per year and has an estimated remaining life of 23 years. This property could probably be sold for $250,000.

Company engineers have been studying the way operations would be fitted into either the new addition or the new plant. They have become convinced that the new plant would be considerably more efficient because of better layout and materials handling. Their estimates show that operating costs in an entirely new plant would be $27,000 per year lower than in the present plant with the addition. They believe some new equipment would be desirable but this could be installed either in the new addition or the new building. Both the new plant and the addition to the present plant would have an estimated, useful life of approximately 33 years.

The treasurer of Blair Plastic Company urges caution in thinking about the proposed move to a new building. In the first place, he points out that the cost of moving equipment from the present building to the new one, and the operating losses that would occur during the transition, would amount to at least $25,000; this sum, he feels, should be considered as an additional cost of the new building. The preferred and common stock of the company is owned by a relatively few individuals who do not have additional capital to invest in the company; consequently, the new building would have to be financed with outside capital.

The treasurer believes $400,000 should be obtained to cover the difference between the cost of the new building and the sales price of the present one and moving and other costs incident to the transition. An insurance company has indicated its willingness to make a loan of this amount to the company, repayable in equal amounts over a 15-year period, at an interest rate of 5% per annum. Due to the possibility of technological changes in the industry and other uncertainties, the insurance company would probably insist on having a first mortgage on the plant and equipment as security for a loan of this duration. Although such a loan would be amply protected by assets and earnings it would make a marked difference in the balance sheet of the company.

Present Balance Sheet

Assets		Liabilities and Capital	
Cash	$ 121,000	Accounts payable	$ 283,000
Accounts receivable	309,000	Accrued taxes and	
Inventories	471,000	expenses	114,000
Current assets	$ 901,000	Current liabilities	$ 397,000
Building, net	360,000	Preferred stock	600,000
Equipment, net	645,000	Common stock	400,000
Other assets	86,000	Earned surplus	595,000
Total assets	$1,992,000	Total liab. and capital	$1,992,000

The treasurer points out that the company would be saddled with a big debt, whereas it is now free from any long-term obligations. Moreover, the loss on the sale of the present building would result in a reduction in earned surplus of approximately $110,000. The cost of moving would probably be offset on the company's books by the value of the land donated by the local Chamber of Commerce.

The president of the company believes that sales will probably continue on an upward trend. He recognizes, however, that the company would be seriously affected by any business depressions and that continuing research work will be necessary to protect the company against technological changes in the plastic industry.

REQUIRED: Should the Blair Plastic Company build the addition to its present plant or build an entirely new plant? Explain how you arrived at your answer.

TRIBORO TEXTILE EQUIPMENT COMPANY

The Triboro Textile Equipment Company operates three plants in Massachusetts in which cards, shuttles, heddles, and heddle frames are made. The three Winton brothers own equally all the capital stock of the company. The company has no long-term debt and earns a moderate profit in good years.

The Triboro company was first established by M. S. Winton, the great-grandfather of the present owners. Mr. Winton erected, in 1845, a frame building that is still the main part of the Triboro factory at Dighton, although five extensions have since been added.

The Dighton plant produces twin wire heddles and cards. Employees normally number 50. The headquarters and general offices are maintained here, housed in a new brick building.

The Taunton plant, bought in 1890, produces heddle frames and shuttles. This factory employs 100 to 150 men and produces 80% in value of the company's products.

The Hudson plant, bought in 1913, is an ordinary sawmill with the usual types of woodworking equipment. There are about 40 employees. It supplies the other plants with boxing and crating stock, makes wooden backs and handles for cards, which are shipped to the Dighton plant, and sells some custom-cut lumber to local dealers.

Products. I. *Cards* (a special kind of wire brush).

    A. Hand cotton and wool cards, used for combing cotton and wool fibers.
    B. Tow cards, used mostly by western Indians for combing wool before it is put into blankets.
    C. Blanket cards, used by individuals and laundries for fluffing up wool in blankets.
    D. File cleaners, used by machinists in cleaning files.
    E. Dog brushes, used for brushing dogs, cats, foxes, and other animals.

The principal card product at present is the common hand card made from a piece of leather, with staples inserted, tacked onto a wooden back with a handle. The staples are inserted in the leather on automatic machines. The tacking of the leather onto the wooden backs is a hand operation. These cards are sold chiefly to African natives. The Triboro factory is the only one left in the country that makes hand cards. The other forms of cards are made only in very limited quantities.

II. *Heddles* are the wires that hang on heddle frames to hold the warp threads during the weaving operation. The company manufactures heddles for making every kind of textile fabric from silk and rayon to duck and tire fabrics. One type, the flat heddle, is purchased from another concern and resold. About 90% of the heddles now used are of the flat type.

Heddles are made at Dighton on automatic machines developed by Triboro. Manufacture is mostly for stock, although some odd sizes are made only on special order. All heddles made at Dighton are trucked to Taunton and shipped from there.

III. *Heddle frames* are required in many sizes, from 20 to 540 inches, and are of two types: (1) The *iron end,* used in weaving cotton, silk, rayon, and other fabrics. The wood for the sides of this type is usually of western pine or spruce. (2) The *wooden end,* used in weaving woolen, worsted, and a few other fabrics. The wood used in this frame is ash, birch, beech, or maple.

Parts, as well as complete frames, are manufactured at Taunton, on special order only.

IV. *Shuttles.* The shuttle carries the bobbin of filling thread used in weaving. Triboro makes shuttles for weaving cotton, woolens, worsteds, silks, rayons, and other fabrics—all types except the carpet shuttle. About 90% of all shuttle bodies are made of dogwood; the balance of persimmon wood. Sometimes as many as 50 operations are required in the manufacture of a shuttle.

The company manufactures the wooden body of the shuttle and sand-casts metal eyes. Other metal parts used on the shuttle, such as the spindle, spring, tip, and die cast and forge cast eyes that are gradually replacing sand-cast, are purchased locally.

Shuttles of standard styles and sizes are made for stock. Special styles and sizes are made on order only, except as they may be partly processed up to a certain point beyond which processing is suspended until the order is received.

There is little standardization of shuttles in the industry. The shuttle manufacturers and the government have tried to get together on such a program but with no result. Weavers and mill men often want their own ideas incorporated in the shuttles they buy. The manufacturers of shuttles themselves are constantly trying to make some change that will individualize their product.

The Triboro shuttle business is secured for three main reasons: product quality, prompt shipments, and the close personal relationship between Henry Winton, Triboro general manager, and the firm's customers.

Quality is due principally to skilled workers and to the technical ability of the management, especially that of the plant superintendent at Taunton. This technical ability is evidenced by the highly efficient machinery designed and built by employees that make the firm one of the best equipped in the industry. The need for shuttle quality is indicated by the fact that they are passed back and forth in some looms at the rate of 210 times per minute.

Service to customers is made possible by anticipating their requirements. Many production orders are stated in the factory on the basis of Henry Winton's knowledge of what certain customers are likely to want. Although orders may not yet have been received, he knows that these customers will want about so many shuttles each month. Another aspect of service is the Taunton plant's ample capacity to make all the shuttles that can be used in the country, provided extra shifts are put on.

Management and organization. The directors (the three owners, their stepmother, a public accountant, a Taunton banker, and a retired textile executive) hold four regular meetings a year at which general policies are discussed and other matters requiring the attention of the board are acted upon. Such matters are setting salaries for the owner-managers and their assistants, fixing a bonus rate for the officers, purchasing new equipment, the purchase or consolidation of plants, and the advance purchase of large amounts of raw materials. The officers' bonus plan is based upon the supposition that $100,000 of sales per month represents the break-even point. In any month in which sales exceed this figure, 10% of the excess is divided among the three brothers equally as a bonus. This procedure possesses the incidental merit of reducing the combined income taxes of the company and the owner-managers. The three brothers also have equal salaries that were originally set by their father and have not been changed since his death seven years ago.

President and Assistant Treasurer—Theodore Winton. Theodore, 44 years old, as the oldest of the brothers in age and in service, was made president. His active duties consist largely of supervising production at the Taunton plant. As production manager of this plant, he is in charge of manufacturing effort from the receipt of an order through shipping.

Vice-President and General Manager—Henry Winton. Henry, 40, as general manager is in charge of the operations of the three plants. Actually he has little contact with any except the Taunton factory. He is actively in charge of sales, follows orders through the shop, and issues biweekly summaries of orders in process and orders not yet started in production. Whenever a special order is received or one for a shuttle not made before, he works out the manufacturing process in consultation with the superintendent, follows the progress of the order through the plant, and makes final inspection of the finished product before shipment. He also serves as credit manager and as purchasing agent for the Taunton plant. As sales manager, he spends much of his time out of town, making contacts with customers.

Henry has built up an unusually fine personal relationship between the company and its customers. The large volume of business with the southern mills has been secured by a salesman whom Henry has developed and who is especially popular with these mills. Most of the important contacts were originally made by Henry himself, and he makes it his business to keep in close association with them by frequent calls. He believes that the buyers of the various mills appreciate the opportunity to do business with one of the "bosses" rather than with an ordinary salesman. In this way, he has been able to learn the habits of each of the principal customers, who really counts in the securing of orders, and how they are placed. Henry acknowledges all orders received by a personal rather than by a form letter.

Treasurer—Benjamin Winton. Benjamin, age 32, the youngest of the brothers, beside his duties as treasurer, is actively in charge of the Hudson and Dighton plants and performs the purchasing function for these establishments. He is also in charge of the general offices at Dighton and is responsible for the financial records, billings, and collections for the whole organization. A head book-keeper and one assistant keep the financial records, and a woman, assisted by a few clerks, performs the other office functions.

Factory supervisors. 1. The plant superintendent at Hudson is in charge of labor relations and production under the general supervision of Benjamin Winton. He is largely responsible for the conduct of the plant.

2. The general foreman at Dighton practically runs the Dighton plant under the general supervision of Benjamin.

3. The plant superintendent at the Taunton plant is in charge of personnel, factory organization, and operations under the immediate supervision of Theodore and the general supervision of Henry Winton. There is also an assistant superintendent—(Theodore's son-in-law), a cost accountant, and foremen of the following departments: machine shop, frame, maintenance, brass foundry for eyes, four shuttle shops (woodworking, sanding, oil and shellac finishing, and assembly), raw material storage, and finished goods storage and shipping.

Raw materials. The principal and most expensive raw materials are blocks of dogwood and persimmon, which are purchased in the South, normally a year in advance of use, and which are usually delivered to the Taunton plant at the rate of a carload a month. Advance purchase and delivery are necessary for thorough drying.

Lumber for heddle frames is now mostly California pine. A year's supply is shipped from the West Coast at one time.

At Hudson, native wood bought as logs from local sources is used. Wire for heddles and cards is bought direct from manufacturers. All materials, other than lumber, and major mill supply items are carried in stock, and purchases are made from the balance of stores records when minimum quantities are reached.

Production orders and control. No formal system of production orders and control is in use at the Hudson and Dighton plants. The superintendents are able to follow production personally through knowledge of the rate of use of the products. They initiate and control production in accordance with their general knowledge.

At Taunton, a formal production order system is used to schedule production, provide authorizations for shipping, billing, and record copies for sales and production.

The economic lot in which shuttles should be made is between 100 and 1,000. When possible, shuttles of like types are grouped in lots amounting at least to this minimum quantity. Special shuttles are made nevertheless in quantities of less than 100, and are sold at no advance in price.

In making shuttles, about 10% more are started in process than the order calls for to allow for spoilage. It is general practice, in the case of special orders, for customers to accept the delivery of the actual quantity made.

Labor relations. The workers are above-average in intelligence and skill. All jobs are time-studied, and piece rates are set. All jobs are rated on the same basis, there being no difference in base pay according to skill. It is expected that the standard task will be exceeded so that employees will earn 15% more than the base rate.

There are no labor organizations in any of the plants. Taunton employs a large number of men of long service, but more recently has employed younger men to replace the older men retired. There are seasonal layoffs of younger men. The company does attempt to keep the older men employed the year round.

Personnel relations are handled largely by the plant superintendent. Occasionally Theodore is consulted, and at times difficulties arise in which Henry has to take part, due to the fact that some of the men whom Theodore has brought into the plant appeal to him for assistance and in some cases his decisions have been out of line with general practices, resulting in difficulties that have to be settled by the general manager. In general, however, the employee relations are satisfactory. There has developed a degree of strained relationship between the newer employees and the management because the latter has been anxious to avoid any act that could be construed as coercive.

Proposed consolidation of plants. For a number of years Henry has advocated the consolidation of the Dighton and Taunton plants and the sale of the Hudson plant. He is satisfied that continuance of the Hudson plant is entirely unjustified since in no year is it able to pay the cost of operation including fixed expenses. The other brothers, however, maintain that, because the out-of-pocket expenses are covered and the fixed expenses are there anyway, the plant is breaking even. Because of the disappearing market for cards, Henry feels the Dighton plant also should be closed or sold and its manuafcturing equipment moved to Taunton where there is ample space and land is available for expansion if needed. He would like to eliminate the unprofitable and slow-selling lines and to avoid the duplication of supervisory personnel and other expenses incident to the operation of both plants. He thinks it an unsatisfactory situation to have 40% of the personnel manufacture only 20% of the product. He has been overruled, however, in all of these matters by the other directors.

Competition. Triboro has one competitor in the stripper card field and one in twin wire heddles. There are three or four competitors in heddle frames and eleven in shuttles. Triboro does about one half the heddle business of the country and one sixth of the shuttle business. One competitor does about one third of the total business of the country.

Market. Most of the cards manufactured by the company go into export, largely to Africa. A good part of the cotton card business is with South America. Sears Roebuck and Montgomery Ward buy some cards for the farm trade. Shuttles are sold largely to northern and southern mills. Sales are made to a few mills in the Middle West and Southwest, although these mills are not visited as regularly as are those in the northern and southern territories. Over 80% of the business is with southern mills. Most of the woolen and worsted shuttles are sold through a tie-up with a loom manufacturer. Triboro obtains most of the original equipment business of this concern and much of the replacement business.

Organization for accounting. Mr. Benjamin Winton is responsible for financial and accounting matters. At the Taunton office there is one cost accountant and one assistant. The company's auditor, a Boston public accounting firm, has served for 13 years. Its functions include closing the books each year, making the annual audit, and preparing financial statements. To a large extent, matters of accounting policy are decided by this firm. All questions of capitalizing expenditures, depreciation, inventory adjustments, year-end adjustments, and all matters relating to the preparation of annual financial reports and federal tax returns are determined by the public accountant. Company officers are not familiar with these matters, and details about them are contained only in the accountant's working papers, which are kept at Boston. The public accountant thus actually assumes the function of a company accounting officer. A member of the accounting firm is also a member of the board of directors and thus extends his influence further by means of this participation in the formulation of major policies.

General accounting proceeds independently of the cost accounting carried on at Taunton and the other plants. Manufacturing costs are not used during the year to calculate monthly profit or loss, and at the end of the year the annual profit or loss is determined by the use of year-end inventories. In the valuation of these final inventories, however, use is made of costs developed by the plant cost accounting departments.

The objectives of the company's cost accounting at Taunton appear to be:

(1) To provide current data for payroll purposes.
(2) To provide unit costs usable at the end of the year for pricing physical inventories.
(3) To provide data regarding quantities of raw material, semifinished products, and parts on hand during the year.

The first of these is regarded as the major objective by the company personnel.

Overhead is added at the rate of 150% of the labor cost of factory operations. This rate has been used for many years. An inspection of profit and loss statements indicates that this rate is too low, but it is not possible to draw very definite conclusions from this examination because of the uncertainty as to the basis of the expense classifications.

Immediate difficulties. Since the settlement of the estate and the division of stock equally among the three brothers, the plan of equal salaries and bonuses initiated by the father of the present owners has been continued regardless of the contribution of each to managing the business. This plan has caused dissension because Henry Winton feels that he is largely responsible for the success of the company and that he should therefore receive larger compensation than his brothers. He also feels that, in the interest of efficient operations, the Hudson plant should be sold and all operations should be concentrated at Taunton, but his brothers disagree. Consequently, he is considering what action he can or should take under the circumstances.

If nothing can be worked out, he is considering the alternative of engaging in the manufacture of shuttles, either independently or by joining a competitor. Customers accounting for about 60% of sales have given assurances that they would stand by him should a split develop. Also, the sales force and many in the production force would go with him if he stays in eastern Massachusetts or Rhode Island.

REQUIRED: (a) What do you recommend that Henry Winton do?

(b) The Taunton banker has asked you, a member of his staff, to explain the problems you see in the operations of the company and to recommend to him the position he should take at the next directors' meeting.

WESTERN NADIR MARKETS, INC.

A proposal to expand the operations of Western Nadir Markets —a local chain of retail grocery stores—by taking over the financing and the operating of 4 discount supermarkets has been forced on the board by the ambitious president of Western Nadir. Since adopting the proposal would mean a considerable change in the kind of store operated and a greatly increased task for the company, some directors were bitterly opposed. Others thought the proposal deserved a thorough hearing.

Nadir Markets, a family-owned concern, operated 20 conventional supermarkets in West Coast City. In addition, it owned and operated 2 stores in Pacific City, whose rapidly growing suburbs were within a hard commuting distance of West Coast City. The last 2 stores had been opened within the past year at the urging of Calhoun Marks, the new president. When the directors decided that no one in the Nadir family had sufficient executive talent to be president, they brought in Mr. Marks from a distinguished career with the discount food operations of E. J. Korvette and Shop-Rite on the East Coast.

Nadir Markets had a solid reputation as a sound grocery firm, based in part on its excellent merchandising of meats and in part on the design and the location of its stores. These all served the wealthier areas of West Coast, were laid out attractively with wide aisles, no cut-case or tray-pack displays,[1] paneling on interior walls, occasional art exhibits by local artists, and complete air-conditioning. Exterior decor ranged from pseudo-Colonial to modern and was varied by location and surroundings. Each store had a special-order meat cutting service and an unusual layout that allowed direct access of the customer to the butcher. The procedure for meats provided a part of the policy on perishables explained by the president as: "Perishable products are over half of the housewife's regular food purchases. Quality can vary substantially and is hard to judge. Consider that the lady's reputation as a homemaker can change with the succulence of her roast beef or the tenderness of her steak. Here at Nadir she has learned to have absolute confidence in our perishables."

Last year's sales were $40,000,000 and profit after taxes was $375,000. Nadir Markets was one of the two largest chains in the city and had a significant share of its geographical market. The company's financial position is shown in Exhibit 1 and further financial data are given in Exhibit 2 on page 608.

Of the 4 discount supermarkets, one had very recently been built in West Coast City. Two of the others were planned for Pacific City, but their specific locations were as yet undecided. Location of the fourth was still uncertain. The West Coast City store had a weekly sales volume of $100,000 from a selling space area of 18,000 square feet in a total store space of 28,000 square feet. The decor was modern, meat processing was carried out in a separate area not exposed to the public, and the store was completely tray-packed.[2] The store also had a parcel-pickup system rather than the carry out service of Nadir Markets. Store hours were 9 a.m. to 9 p.m. Monday through Saturday.

Gross margins in this discount supermarket were:

Groceries	— 12.5%	Meat	— 16.0%
Frozen Food	— 18.0%	Produce	— 27.3%
	All Other	— 25.1%	

---

[1] More economical displays than unpacking all items from a carton and restacking them individually on the shelf.

[2] Merchandise was displayed still in its original carton with the top and part of the sides of the carton cut away to expose the contents.

Exhibit 1

Western Nadir Markets, Inc.
Condensed Statement of Financial Position
(in thousands)

Cash and Securities	$2,200	Accounts Payable and Accrued Expenses	$1,150
Accounts Receivable	100	Income Tax Due	125
Merchandise and Supplies	1,750		
Equipment and Improvements (Net)[a]	375	Total	$1,275
Other Assets	150	Common Stock	1,000
		Retained Earnings	2,300
	$4,575		$4,575

[a] All store buildings were leased.

Exhibit 2

Sales and Gross Profits by Department

	Nadir Markets		Industry Data [b]	
	Sales, % of Total	Gross Profit, % of Departmental Sales	Sales %	Gross Profit %
Grocery [c]	63.0	17.0	52.91	17.34
Frozen Foods	...	...	4.70	25.00
Produce	9.1	28.2	8.84	30.66
Meat	27.9	23.2	24.38	21.38
All Other	...	...	9.17	31.51
Total	100.0%		100.00%	

[b] Industry data for food chains with annual sales volume from $20 to $50 million.
[c] Includes frozen foods and all other items.

The store was night-stocked on Saturdays and Mondays in contrast to Nadir Markets, which were shelf-stocked during business hours.

Space allocations to departments varied slightly from one Nadir Market to the next, but, as a general rule, the division was as shown in Exhibit 3.

Exhibit 3

Percentage Space Allocations

	Nadir Markets	West Coast City Discount Supermarket
Grocery	47%	53%
Meats	18%	8%
Produce	12%	10%
Dairy	5%	5%
Frozen Foods	10%	4%
Bakery	5%	5%
Nonfoods	3%	15%

The effect of the West Coast City Discount Supermarket was substantial on two of the Nadir Markets and slight on a third. It was located 1 mile from one, $1\frac{1}{4}$ miles from a second, and 2 miles from the third. Sales volume losses had been 20%, 15%, and 10% respectively, but all those stores were still running at a slight profit.

A further check of operations at the discount supermarket showed that its reduced variety of items, tray-packing, cut-case displays, night-stocking, and parcel-pickup service had some effects on labor productivity.

	Discount Market		*Typical Nadir Market*	
	Labor Cost as % of Sales	*Sales per Man-Hour*	*Labor Cost as % of Sales*	*Sales per Man-Hour*
Groceries	4.2%	$40.20	6.4%	$30.10
Produce	6.5%	35.10	9.5%	23.20
Meat	5.9%	45.80	5.0%	48.90

Of the existing Nadir Markets, 5 had severe or above-average competition from large chains or large combination food and general merchandise discount stores; 10 had average competition; 5 had below-average competition, including one in Pacific City; and the other, including the second store in Pacific City, had very little competition.

Each store had an individual manager. Beyond this Nadir Markets was run by Calhoun Marks and a small central management group. One buyer handled all items but meats, and another bought and merchandised meats. An assistant to the president acted as a roving troubleshooter, helping out in or appraising stores that were having trouble. All store managers reported directly to the president. There were no field or regional supervisors—an uncommon happening in the grocery business. A warehouse manager, personnel manager, chief engineer, and controller rounded out the executive organization. This was commonly recognized to be a thin management. It was also a reason for the success of the firm, since executive salaries were 0.25 percentage points less than industry averages for comparable chains (each percentage point was 1% of total sales).

The controller and the meat buyer—both members of the family that owned Nadir Markets—had commented to other board members that, while they were busy before, the addition of the

Pacific City markets had brought them to the limit of their available time. "I used to burn the candle at both ends, now I've lighted the middle too," claimed R. A. Peyton Sheraton, controller.

REQUIRED: (a) How are company resources—executive personnel, facilities, and capital—related to company objectives, policies, and organization in this case? That is, to what exent are decisions in one area dependent upon decisions in the others?

(b) What do you infer are Mr. Marks's motives in recommending the absorption of the 4 discount supermarkets?

(c) If the discount supermarkets were taken over, what changes, if any, in Western Nadir Markets, Inc. activities and management would you recommend?

(d) Assume that you have been asked by the board of directors of Western Nadir Markets, Inc. to make a recommendation regarding Mr. Marks's proposal. Prepare a statement of your conclusions supported by reasons.

PART

5 GUIDING THE EXECUTION
OF PLANS

Ch. 23 · Short- and Long-Range Programming

Ch. 24 · Activating

Ch. 25 · Controlling Operations

Ch. 26 · Budgetary Control

Integrating Cases—Execution

SHORT- AND LONG-RANGE PROGRAMMING

Establishing objectives and policies, building organization, and assembling resources are all vital to the management of any enterprise. Still another group of activities requires executive attention if the firm is to achieve its goals. Steps must be taken to "get things done." This group of managerial duties we shall call *execution,* which is used here to cover:

    I. *Short- and long-range programming,* which deals with what actions are to be taken when.
   II. *Activating,* which is concerned with direction and motivation.
  III. *Controlling,* which seeks to assure that the results actually accomplished correspond with plans.

A large part of the time of junior executives is devoted to execution, that is, detailed programming, motivating, coordinating, and controlling. Central managers also must give a significant portion of their energy to getting things done. Policy formulation and organization planning set the stage, but no services are rendered and no profits are earned until action by first-line operators actually takes place.

Again, a word of warning about these three steps in execution is appropriate. In practice, they are not watertight compartments that take place in just the order listed. Management is a continuing and complex activity in which the various phases are often mixed up. Facilities are acquired and investment is controlled before detailed programs for production are completed. A program for putting a major policy change into effect may cut across minor policies, organization, and control procedures. Data developed in day-to-day control often is used in preparing long-range programs. Nevertheless, for purposes of understanding management, the division of execution into phases is essential, and the outline puts these various parts into logical relationship and perspective.

Nature of programming and scheduling. Our preceding discussion of managerial tasks has put primary emphasis on *what* should be done and has given little attention to deciding *how much* and *when.* Modern life is full of schedules—railroad schedules, class schedules, shipping schedules, and numerous other plans that regulate the time when certain activities are to occur. This prevalence of schedules has made punctuality one of the modern virtues.

Most schedules, including those in business, typically break the total operation up into parts and set a time for each of these parts. Often a starting time and a finishing time is shown for each part. Obviously, realistic schedules of this sort cannot be prepared unless a lot of previous attention has been given to just what is to be done, who is to do it, and the materials and equipment that will be available for the work. In other words, scheduling is based upon a lot of other management plans, and unless these other plans are sound, the schedules are likely to be difficult to achieve.

Programming, as the term will be used here, is somewhat broader in scope than scheduling. It typically deals with an area of operations that has not been so well planned out; instead, once an objective or "mission" has been established, the executive making the program first decides what principal steps are necessary to accomplish the objective and then sets an approximate time for each. When an entirely new activity is involved, the program may also indicate who is to undertake each of the steps.

While central management can delegate most detailed scheduling work, it should take an active part in shaping broader programs. Key issues faced in this important task will be examined in terms of:

    A. Short-range programming.
    B. Critical path analysis.
    C. Long-range programming.

SHORT-RANGE PROGRAMMING

Programs are useful to direct major projects and also to guide and synchronize the operations of an entire company. Here are examples of each type.

Company-wide programs. A clear example of programming that embraces an entire company, is found in the operations of a firm manufacturing men's shirts. This particular firm sells shirts throughout the country under a nationally advertised brand. The line includes staple shirts, fancy shirts (color, stripes, etc.), full dress shirts, sport shirts and related items. These shirts are made in several price ranges and within each range there is a variety of collar, cuff and front styles. In addition, for each of these numbers a complete range of collar sizes and sleeve lengths is required. When all these variations in model, style, fabric, pattern, color, price ranges and size are taken into account, the company manufactures in a single year over 30,000 items.

Salesmen of the company take orders directly from large and small retailers whom they call on at least three or four times a year. To maintain this extensive distribution, the company watches closely the quality of its shirts, including construction and finish of the cloth and care in manufacturing. It maintains warehouse stocks in several parts of the country to assure prompt delivery to its customers; and the merchandise is backed up by a substantial sales promotion program. The shirts are manufactured in several different plants located in four different states.

The programming in this company can be understood best by separate consideration of merchandising, sales promotion, production, and selling.

Merchandising. Programming begins with decisions as to the styles and colors of shirts that will be offered for sale. For staple shirts this poses no serious problem because styles change infrequently and decisions to drop or add a particular item can be made at any time. Staple shirts are carried in stock continuously and a high inventory of a particular number can be carried over into the following year. Fancy shirts and sport shirts, however, which vary with respect to fabric, color, and design are distinctly style items. There are two selling seasons; the spring line is released in October and sold in the succeeding months for January through June delivery, and the fall line is released in April to be sold in May, June, and July for August through December delivery. Actually, selection of the styles must be made about 18 months before the merchandise is on the retailer's shelf. If the styles selected are not in accord with public fancy, both the company and its retailers will suffer from slow-moving stock.

In addition to styles, quantities to be produced must be budgeted. In this company, fancy and sport shirts are broken down into about 50 groups (stripes, checks, novelty, solids, etc.) and then a decision is made on how many dozen of each group should be manufactured. On the basis of these budget limits, the number of specific styles can be determined and the specific patterns and colors can be selected. The patterns must, of course, be translated into detailed specifications of fabrics and construction. A final step in setting up the line is to select the three or four patterns that will be featured as style leaders in the sales promotion campaign.

Setting up the line, just described, results in specifications and a budgeted quantity for each style of shirt to be manufactured. On the basis of these budgets, orders are placed with textile mills for the cloth that will be needed. Only a limited number of textile mills are considered satisfactory sources for this cloth because of the company's insistence on high quality standards. In other words, the company cannot delay its commitments for cloth and then buy grey goods in the open market. It is true that the company can make adjustments in the quantities of a particular color when the cloth is sent to converters for dyeing and finishing. Also, if it finds itself with excess grey goods, the material may be sold in the open market. Such sales, however, are apt to result in losses because downward revision of company budgets is likely to occur at the same time the entire textile market is depressed. Nevertheless, losses on the sale of grey goods are usually substantially less than the potential losses on forced sale of excess inventories of finished shirts. In other words, commitments are made for cloth as soon as the line is set up, and there is only limited flexibility as to colors and quantities after this point.

Sales promotion. Advertising and other sales promotion of the company is designed to have its main impact on men and women who buy shirts from retailers. This means that the advertisements will appear in magazines and newspapers during the retail selling season. However, in order to secure retailer cooperation in this sales promotion program, copies of ads, display material, etc. must be placed in the hands of salesmen when they go out to solicit orders—by October for a spring line. This material can be in the hands of the salesmen only if planning of the campaign has commenced nine months earlier. Actually, work is begun on the sales promotion program just as soon as the line has been set up and the particular styles to be featured in the advertising have been selected.

Sales promotion activities of the company include: (a) a substantial national advertising campaign in magazines such as *Life,*

Time, and *Good Housekeeping* (women purchase about 50% of the men's shirts sold in this country); (b) local newspaper ads giving the names of dealers; (c) window displays, which convert street traffic into store traffic; (d) counter and interior displays, which make it easy for the customers to find and buy the merchandise shown in the window; and (e) direct mail inserts and circulars sent out by retailers to their customers. All these types of sales promotion must be closely coordinated so that they may have a cumulative effect. For example, statistics show that window displays timed and designed to tie in with national advertising have increased the sales of a store from 25 to 40%.

The national advertising program is developed in cooperation with the company's advertising agency. First, ideas and the theme for the campaign are selected; then an advertising schedule showing the timing and the amount of space for each magazine and other mediums is established. These six-month advertising schedules must be carefully prepared so that each feature of the program and each segment of the market receives adequate emphasis. After the national campaign has been scheduled, the agency is given samples of materials, information on prices, etc., and it proceeds to develop specific advertising for each medium to be used.

The theme and other distinctive features of the national campaign are carried over into direct mail pieces, window displays, counter displays, and local newspaper advertisements. Of course, the national campaign has to be designed early enough to permit preparation of copy and illustrations in these other sales promotion pieces; moreover, time must be allowed for the actual printing of at least samples of this material before the salesmen go on the road.

Except for the national advertising campaign, the actual use of sales promotion material depends upon cooperation of retailers. Responsibility for obtaining this cooperation rests upon the salesmen. Consequently, the effectiveness of the entire sales promotion program requires coordination with the selling effort as well as with the initial merchandising plans.

Production scheduling. The scheduling of production really takes place in three stages. The sales budget for each type of shirt, described under merchandising, serves as a general guide to level of activities. On the basis of these budgets, facilities can be expanded or rearranged, and plans can be laid for hiring and training new workers. Past experience with production at different levels provides a guide to facility and personnel adjustment that will be necessary.

Specific production schedules for each plant are prepared about a month in advance. Staple shirts are scheduled so as to assure adequate inventories of all styles and also to stabilize production to some extent. At the beginning of a selling season, limited quantities of fancy and sport shirts are put into production. For the most part, however, production of these items is not undertaken until orders are actually in hand. All orders received by salesmen are carefully tabulated by item, and a comparison of orders received with production previously authorized indicates the need for additional production. Weekly schedules are prepared showing the number of dozen of each style and color of shirt to be cut. At the same time these cutting schedules are issued to the plant, instructions are sent to the cloth converter regarding the shipment of cloth, and the buyer of "findings" (buttons, threads, etc.) is also advised.

The third stage in production scheduling is still more detailed. The weekly schedules just described indicate the style and the color of shirts but do not state the sizes to be manufactured. To determine this, a more careful analysis of inventory on hand and sales orders is necessary. Moreover, economy in the cutting of cloth dictates that cutting of fancy shirts must be done in piles of cloth 4 dozen thick. Some sport shirts, on the other hand, can be cut in piles 20 dozen thick. Consequently, in making up the production orders that actually go to the cutting floor, it is necessary to define the weekly schedules in terms of sizes and economical lots. At the same time consideration is given to daily work loads. This detailed scheduling also provides opportunity to adjust the cutting schedule for spoilage, discrepancies between schedule and production, slow delivery of materials and findings, and other minor changes.

Selling and shipment of goods. Mention has already been made of the key importance of salesmen in the sales promotion program. At the same time a salesman is showing the line for the following season, he should also be explaining the sales promotion campaign and securing the dealer's cooperation in local advertising, window displays, counter displays, and direct mailing. The whole campaign is keyed into the national advertising on a monthly basis and features such important selling seasons as Christmas, Easter, Father's Day, and the like.

We also noted that the scheduling of the production of fancy and sport shirts both precedes and follows the selling activities. Sales budgets provide the basis for buying cloth and making general sales plans. However, actual production of these products, with minor exceptions, awaits receipt of customers' orders. Thus the general programming provides the basis for the selling activities, and the selling activities in turn provide the data needed for more detailed programming and scheduling.

Close coordination between production scheduling and the handling of customers' orders is also needed. As a general practice the company holds a customer's order until all of the merchandise requested is in the warehouse; the entire order is then filled and shipped as a unit. This procedure works easily when orders are received well in advance of the requested delivery date and when all items are in stock or about to be produced. Some dealers, however, delay ordering until close to the selling season, and many written orders are received for merchandise to replenish stock during the retail season. If the desired goods are not on hand when an order is received, it is necessary to (1) hold the order until the requested goods are manufactured and sent to the warehouse, (2) ship part of the order immediately and the balance when the particular items requested are manufactured, (3) substitute shirts very similar to those ordered on the assumption that the retailer would rather have some merchandise than wait for the exact style requested, or (4) advise the retailer that at least part of his order cannot be filled.

The choice of one of these alternatives requires an intimate knowledge of the retailer's needs, and all doubtful questions are referred to the salesman covering the particular account. The company has approximately 150 salesmen with about 8,000 active retail accounts, so the task of handling each order in a way that will give the retailer good service is substantial. Without reliable information on production schedules and on the total provision of cloth for particular styles of shirts, this proper handling of retailers' orders would be almost impossible.

Throughout this sketch of overall company operations the need for programming and scheduling has been apparent. The activities of the various departments—merchandising, sales promotion, production, and selling—are closely related, and the quantity and the timing of actions must be closely synchronized. Financial budgets are used for expense control and for financial planning, but the basic programs and schedules are stated in units of specific products. Only in this way can the necessary coordination be achieved.

Programs for special purposes. For most operating purposes, programs can be fairly specific as to the steps and the timing involved. The same basic approach is useful, however, even though specific answers on some points may not be practical.

Expansion program. The operators of the hotel facilities at the Grand Canyon, for example, wished to develop an expansion program that would enable them to give better service to the many people who want to visit this scenic spot. Investigation revealed that three types of changes were needed in the physical facilities —maintenance, betterments that would improve the service in the existing plant, and major expansion of room and restaurant facilities. Any significant addition to total capacity, however, would have required more water; additional water could be secured only by investing $1,500,000 to run a pipeline to a spring several miles up the canyon. Pumping water from the bottom of the canyon to the brim would require additional electric power. This would probably mean bringing in a new power line. Moreover, a new sewage line would have to be laid in a ditch blasted out of rock.

The investment in these new facilities would not have been justified if they were to be used only two or three months of the year. Consequently, serious attention had to be given to attracting visitors to the canyon in the spring and the fall when, in fact, the weather is more desirable than in the summer. There were additional factors involved, but enough have been listed to indicate the need for some kind of a program that would divide the total problem of expansion into logical *parts* and indicate a *sequence* in which these parts should be attacked.

In this case, a time schedule probably could be established only for the first two or three steps, but the program should at least provide a systematic approach to a very complex problem. Since the desirability of expanding facilities depends so largely on extending the tourist season and building other off-season business, changes in facilities were restricted to maintenance and betterments until the practicality of the promotion program was tested.

Tax revision program. The desirability of a special purpose program also became apparent to a company that sought to reduce the federal excise tax on its products. The company quickly recognized that the chances of success would be materially improved if the industry as a whole presented its case rather than each manufacturer operating independently. Clearly, the newly formed industry association should make contacts with all of the influential congressmen and senators. To be most effective, however, the pleas of the manufacturers needed to be backed up by significant pressure on the part of local constituents. This meant that the retailers, and to the extent possible the consumers, should be enlisted in the overall campaign.

Clearly, if the efforts of all these people were to be most effective, there was need for a common program in which the role of each group could be clarified and some attention given to the timing of the several efforts. In a situation such as this, involving many independent enterprises and people, a detailed program and schedule covering an extended period probably would be of little value; but at least a general program was essential to get coordinated effort. Since the program was basically concerned with public opinion, there was great need for personal leadership and flexibility as the work proceeded.

Programs for special purposes, such as the two just discussed, are often difficult to project very far in the future. Forecasts of future needs and of operating conditions may be unreliable because the activity is so new and different. This unreliability of forecasts makes it hard to set dates and to estimate volume of work. Moreover, strategy in meeting competition or winning support of people often plays a key part in such programs, and it is difficult to decide on strategy very long in advance.

Basic steps in programming. The examples of programming given in preceding pages indicate that skill is needed in fitting the general concept to specific situations. Nevertheless, six elements or steps are found in the majority of instances. A manager will do a better job of programming if he is fully aware of the nature and the importance of each of these steps.

1. Divide the total operations necessary to achieve the objective into parts. The division of an operation into parts is useful for planning, organization, and control. Planning is improved because concentrated attention can be given to one part at a time. Organization is facilitated because these parts or projects can be assigned to separate individuals, if this will give speedier or more efficient action. Such division also aids control because the executive can watch each part and determine whether progress is satisfactory as the work is carried on without waiting for final results.

If the division into parts or projects is to be most effective, the purpose of each step should be clearly defined. The kind of work, the quality, and the quantity should all be indicated.

Often a single part of a large program is itself again subdivided; in fact, this process of subdivision may be continued for three or four stages. For example, an anniversary program of a department store may include as one of its parts a sale of men's suits. This sale in turn may be divided into buying, advertising, displaying, selling, etc. The advertising project may be divided up into selection of merchandise to be featured, writing the copy, preparing illustrations, scheduling the days and the newspapers in which the ad will appear, and integrating the suit sale ads with other advertisements of the store. Thus the concept of programming is applicable to situations ranging from large operations down to the work of a single individual.

2. Note the necessary sequence and the relationship between each of these parts. Usually the parts of a program are quite dependent upon each other. The amount of work, the specifications, and the time of action of one step often affects the ease or difficulty of performing the next step. Unless these relationships are recognized and watched closely the very process of subdividing the work may cause more inefficiency than it corrects.

Any necessary sequences are particularly significant. For example, in the shirt company already described the themes and designs to be used in a national advertising campaign had to be settled before window and counter displays and mailing inserts could be prepared because they were expected to tie into the impact of the national advertising. These necessary sequences have an important bearing upon scheduling. They tend to lengthen the overall time required for the operation, and since a shorter cycle gives a company more flexibility, the necessity of delaying one action until another is completed should be carefully checked.

3. Decide who is to be responsible for doing each part. If the operation being programmed is a normal activity for the company, the assignment of responsibility may already be covered by the existing organization. In the shirt company, for instance, the programming and scheduling of a new line was done twice every year, and the responsibility for merchandising, sales promotion, and other activities was clearly established by the organization structure. However, if the program covers a new operation, then careful attention should be given to the question of who is responsible for each part. These special assignments do not necessarily follow regular organization relationships and create only a temporary set of authorizations and obligations. In a very real sense, a special team is formed to carry out the program.

4. Decide how each part will be done and the resources that will be needed. The amount of attention that must be given to each step in setting up a program will depend upon the circumstances. Sometimes standing methods and standing procedures will cover almost all of the activities (as is true of military programming), and in other situations questions of "how" will be fully delegated to the persons responsible for each part. Nevertheless, the executive building the program must have enough understanding of how each part will be performed to appreciate the difficulties in the assignment and the obstacles that may be encountered. In particular, he needs some understanding of the *resources* that will be necessary to carry out each part of the program.

For realistic programming the need for (a) materials and supplies, (b) facilities, and (c) people must be recognized. Then the availability of these necessary resources should be appraised. If any one of them is not available, another project to obtain the resource should be set up; this may be treated either as an additional part of the original program or a subdivision of the project needing the resource. For example, if necessary personnel is unavailable, then plans should be made for hiring and training new employees. Many programs break down because the executive preparing them does not have a practical understanding of how each part will be carried out and the resources needed to carry it out.

5. Estimate the time required for each part. This step is, of course, closely related with steps 3 and 4 above and really involves two aspects: (a) the date or hour when the part can begin, and (b) the time required to complete the operation once it is started.

Possible starting time will depend upon the availability of the necessary resources. The work already scheduled to a machine, the time when key personnel can be transferred to a new assignment, possibility of getting delivery of materials from suppliers, the possibility of deferring work already in the shop or subcontracting part of the work, all have a bearing on when it is possible to begin any given part of a program.

The processing time once the activity is begun is typically estimated on the basis of past experience. For detailed scheduling of production operations, time-study data may permit a tight scheduling of activities. For a great many activities more time is consumed in conveying instructions and getting people actually to work than is required for the actual work itself. Unless this "nonproductive time" can be eliminated, however, it should be included as part of the estimated time.

6. *Assign definite dates (hours) when each part is to take place.* This overall schedule is, of course, based on the sequences as noted under Step 2 and the timing information assembled under Step 5. The resulting schedule should show both the starting dates and the completion dates for each part of the program.

Sometimes considerable adjustment and fitting is necessary to make the final schedule realistic. A useful procedure is to work backward and forward from some fixed date that is considered to be controlling. In the shirt manufacturing operation, for example, the importance of the selling season was so great that these dates were taken as fixed and the schedule was extended back from these dates. In other situations the availability of materials or of facilities may be the controlling time around which the rest of the schedule is adjusted. It is, of course, necessary to dovetail any given program with other commitments the company may have. Another important qualification is to make some allowances for delay. It is not desirable as a general practice to have such allowances all along the line as this may tend to create inefficient performance, but there should be safety allowances at various stages so that an unavoidable delay at one place will not throw off the entire schedule.

Programs may have to be revised, of course, to take account of unexpected opportunities or difficulties. If the initial job was well done, these revisions do not usually require as much executive effort as the initial planning.

CRITICAL PATH ANALYSIS

Development of PERT. Critical path analysis is a special technique for studying and controlling complex programs. It was developed in its more elaborate form as an aid in the design and production of Polaris missiles, and it has been used for many space age projects. The particular technique applied to the Polaris program was called PERT (Program Evaluation and Review Technique); many variations of the basic ideas have been used before and since PERT received wide publicity. The technique is of interest to us here because the central concepts can be helpful in many programming problems.

The design and production of Polaris missiles involved a staggering number of steps. Specifications for thousands of minute parts had to be prepared, the parts had to be manufactured to exact tolerances, and then the entire system had to be assembled into a successful operating weapon. And, *time* was of the essence. The basic steps in programming, just discussed in the preceding pages, were applicable; but the complexity of the project (and the fact that many different subcontractors were involved) called for significant elaborations.

Major features of critical path analysis. The basic ideas involved in this refined programming technique are:

1. All steps and their necessary sequences are placed on a diagram (see chart on page 626) so that the total *network* is explicitly set forth.
2. The estimated *time* required to complete each step after the preceding step has been finished is recorded.
3. Then by adding the required times for each step in any necessary sequence—or path—the path having the longest time can be identified. This is the *critical path*.
4. If desired, the difference between the total required times of the critical path and other paths can also be computed. Such differences are *slack times* or margins in which delays would not hold up the final completion.

Now, having identified the critical path, management can focus its attention on either reducing the time of steps in this path or at least watching closely for any delays. Also, management knows from slack time data where high pressure to meet estimated processing times may be unwarranted.

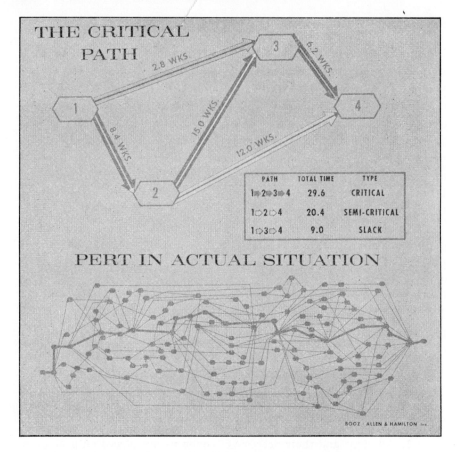

The upper chart contains:

THE CRITICAL PATH

PATH	TOTAL TIME	TYPE
1→2→3→4	29.6	CRITICAL
1→2→4	20.4	SEMI-CRITICAL
1→3→4	9.0	SLACK

PERT IN ACTUAL SITUATION

BOOZ · ALLEN & HAMILTON Inc.

Critical path analysis

The upper chart shows, for a very small segment of the total network, how the critical path is computed. The lower chart indicates how complex the networks may be.

The calculation of the critical path should, of course, be repeated as work progresses because some steps will be completed faster than anticipated and others will be delayed. This new data will certainly change slack time estimates, and a different critical path may arise.

With careful thought, the total network of steps and sequences can usually be prepared with reasonable reliability—at least for programs dealing with physical products. Time estimates prove to be less reliable, especially for new and unique activities. To deal with this uncertainty regarding time, often three estimates are obtained from the men who will be doing the work: optimistic, most likely, and pessimistic. Then a weighted average of these three elapsed-time estimates is used. *Refer to supplimentary dia.*

In critical path analyses of complex programs, such as Polaris, computations are sufficiently involved to make use of an electronic computer very helpful. In simpler programming situations, such as building construction, a computer is by no means essential.

General applicability. The main features of critical path analysis have application to many programs that are not sufficiently complex to warrant the complete PERT treatment. Often just the preparation of a network chart of sequences of steps will clarify the interconnections between actions taken by various departments. The launching of an additional magazine by a publishing firm, for example, was aided by such a chart.

Moreover, the concept of a critical path can be used in many programming problems even though an entire network is not charted. In the shirt company discussed earlier in this chapter, for instance, the critical path runs from the steps in line-building through sales promotion to plant scheduling and on to order filling. Acquiring grey goods, training personnel, and similar steps have to be done, but they are not "critical" from a timing viewpoint because of the early leads necessary in sales promotion. Programming in other companies may be geared to erection of new facilities or perhaps training of personnel. In all these situations, a recognition of what steps are part of the critical path will direct management efforts in "getting things done" to the crucial spots.

A word of caution is in order. Critical path analysis focuses on time, and few companies have data that enable them also to fit costs into the same framework. We would like to know how much speeding up or slowing down each step will change costs. Usually such cost estimates—even rough ones—are prepared only after critical steps are identified and an executive is trying to decide whether to make a change in plans. Similarly, critical path analysis does not deal with alternative ways of reaching a goal. The network is presumed to be settled. Of course, if the analysis identifies a serious bottleneck, then management may resort to a different method and may establish a new network.

Nevertheless, for many programming problems, timing is the major consideration. And for such problems critical path analysis can be a valuable refinement.

LONG-RANGE PROGRAMMING

Nature of long-range programming. Programming increases in difficulty as the time-span covered is extended, yet such extension is well worth the trouble in some circumstances. We have been discussing program cycles ranging from a few months to perhaps two years. Long-range programming seeks to extend the period to, say, five to ten years.

Underlying any long-range program should be well defined objectives. Basic objectives, such as those examined in Chapter 4, provide the general targets toward which the program is directed. And, basic policies, considered in Chapters 5 through 16, provide the guides and the limitations within which action is to fall. Establishing these is, of course, part of the total process of long-range planning. The *program* introduces a time schedule—the how much and when aspects—and thereby sets the intermediate objectives (which in turn become the targets for more specific and detailed short-range programs).

Applications. One of the best-known examples of long-range programming is the conversion of the Bell System to dial telephones. Forecasts of telephone usage—based on population growth, higher gross national product (GNP), and telephoning habits—indicated that manual switching could not handle the load. Besides, automatic dialing would improve service and hopefully cut costs. So the goal was clear, but the magnitude of the task was tremendous. Design of equipment had to be refined for recording calls, relaying long-distance calls, tieing in with independent companies, and the like. Completely new exchanges had to be built, millions of dollars of switching equipment manufactured, and millions of consumer units produced. Before any of this physical equipment could be installed, people—engineers, installers, and operators—had to be trained. Incidentally, company policy dictated that the transition was to be made with only seconds of interruption in service and no layoffs of regular employees. The public had to be prepared for the switch and educated to use the new equipment; utility commissions had to be kept advised. And the multimillion dollar investment had to be financed.

This incomplete list suggests the range of elements in the program. Many of the preliminary steps were taken ten years before the conversion in that area was finished. And with new developments in technology and markets, the process is still going on.

The Bell System example is enlightening because (a) a whole series of interrelated steps were programmed years in advance, and (b) the programming was done in terms of several elements— markets, engineering, facilities, personnel, and finance—not for just a single element such as finance.

The magnitude and the predictability of the Bell System is unique, of course. Nevertheless, quite different companies can use a similar approach. The Suburban Fuel Company, for instance, did long-range programming even though it was a small-town firm with net worth of only $100,000. For many years the family owning Suburban Fuel had been in the retail coal business. When fuel oil began replacing coal, the company also became a fuel oil distributor. Finally, when the grandson of the founder became president, he decided to withdraw from coal altogether and he set up a long-range program to do so. The program involved: (1) gradual disposition of coal facilities—no new equipment, sale of some trucks, and sale of the coal yard as a plant site in 5 years; (2) strengthening the fuel oil distributorship—adding trained burner servicemen, leasing more trucks, closer tie-in with sale of oil burners, and more systematic promotion of annual service contracts; and (3) withdrawal of most of the capital invested—the fuel oil distributorship to be "spun off" as a separate company, and liquidation of the original coal company at favorable tax rates. Initially a 5-year program, it actually was completed in $4\frac{1}{2}$ years because a good opportunity to sell the coal yard turned up.

In this example, we again see (a) a series of interrelated steps extending over a period of years and (b) a plan that embraced several different elements. The timing of the various steps was subject to adjustment, as was also true in the telephone conversion, and no attempt was made to spell out detail several years in advance. But the master plan provided a definite guide for actions all along the way.

The preceding examples may be misleading because only a small portion of business firms actually prepare long-range programs in a clear-cut fashion. The main reason is simple. Most companies cannot, or do not, forecast the nature and the volume of their activities 3, 4, 5, let alone 10, years ahead. Perhaps they know the direction they would like to go (their objectives); but uncertainties about competition, technical developments, consumers' actions, political and economic changes, and the like make timing hard to nail down.

Because of the difficulty of precise long-term forecasting, we need to examine carefully the benefits the typical company can reasonably hope to obtain from long-range programming and problems that must be overcome if it undertakes this management device.

Major benefits of long-range programming. A central management that embarks on long-range programming usually seeks these advantages:

1. Long-cycle actions are started promptly. An automated plant takes at least 2 or 3 years to design, build, and get in operation. A bright idea for a new product often requires 3 to 5 years for research, development, testing, and process engineering before it is ready to be marketed. Recruiting and training salesmen for electronic computers takes several years—assuming they cannot be hired away from established competitors. Raising a new crop of timber for lumber may consume 25 years.

Long-term programming indicates when such actions should be started. Opportunities will be missed or crises in servicing customers may develop unless early action is taken. To fail to act is equivalent to a decision to postpone entry into the contemplated operation. Even though predictions of need are uncertain, there may be no feasible alternative to starting down the road.

By preparing the best program that available knowledge will permit, a company increases the probability that it will be aware of when long-cycle actions should be initiated.

2. Executives are psychologically prepared for change. Many actions embraced in a long-range program need not, and should not, be taken immediately. They can await a year or more of actual experience, and by then some modification in the original plan may be desirable.

Nevertheless, even though the program is changed, the process of preparing it aids adjustment to new conditions. As a result of preparing the program, the idea that some kind of change in response to shifts in the environment must take place is already accepted. And, probably the nature of the adjustment will have been thought about—for example, transfers of personnel, refunding a bond issue, or local production in a foreign country. Then, when conditions are ripe, executives are prepared to move quickly. Good news or bad news may arrive unexpectedly, and the company response may differ from the program; but the ability to recognize the opportunity, to appreciate the range of actions that are necessary, and to get in motion has been sharpened by the mental exercise of preparing (and revising) a program.

The pace of technological and economic change is quickening. Product life cycles are shorter and competitors move into profit opportunities more quickly. Consequently, the ability of a company to adjust promptly to shifts in its environment is crucial to getting ahead and staying ahead in modern competition. So this psychological preparation for change that we have been discussing is more vital to central management today than it was a generation ago.

3. Actions having long-term impact are coordinated. Often an action taken to meet an immediate problem also significantly affects future operations of the company. For example, to get quick coverage of the West Coast territory, one firm gave exclusive distribution rights to an agent who also sold related products. The agent was successful in establishing himself as the local representative and the immediate problem was resolved. However, the firm soon expanded and diversified so that it needed a strong, national sales organization of its own salesmen; and the successful independent distributor on the West Coast proved to be very difficult to supplant.

The selection of executives for key posts, the licensing of a company patent, and the purchase of a warehouse for immediate needs are further examples where short-run solutions may prove troublesome in the future.

Now, if a company has a long-range program, central managers will be able to sense more easily whether current decisions do, or do not, fit into a consistent pattern of long-term development.

Note that in this list of benefits of long-range planning we do not include "a blueprint for future action." Only rarely are prediction and control of conditions several years hence sufficiently accurate to permit close adherence to a 5-year plan. But such a program does help identify actions that should be initiated now, it lays a psychological base for prompt adjustment to opportunities in the future, and it provides a pattern so that action on today's problems can be compatible with long-range plans.

Problems involved in long-range programming. Preparation of a long-range program of the type we have been discussing needs guidance. Key problems are what topics and period to cover, how revisions will be made, and who will do the work of developing the plans.

Topics covered. Too often so-called "long-range programs" are merely financial estimates conjured up by a bright young man in the controller's office. Such estimates take the form of annual profit and loss budgets for perhaps the next 5 years.

For operating purposes, dollar sales estimates have little meaning unless someone has thought in terms of the products that will be sold, the customers who will buy them, the prices obtainable in face of competition, and the selling effort necessary to obtain the orders. Similarly, the projected volume of goods must be conceived in terms of the resources necessary to produce them: plant capacity, trained workers, flow of raw materials, engineering talent, etc.

Therefore, long-range programs should be stated in physical terms. But it is impractical to spell out such plans in full detail; instead, management should identify the crucial factors and build the program in these terms. One of the keys to successful programming is this identifying of topics to be used; omission of vital factors will make the program unrealistic, whereas too many factors will make it unwieldy.

The long-range program should also be translated into dollar results: revenues, costs, profits, and capital requirements. Dollars are the best common denominator we have, and the financial results are an important aspect of any program. The point is that dollar figures alone are not enough.

Period covered. Five years is the most common period covered by long-range programs. There is no magic in this figure, however. Logically, long-range plans should be based on the necessary elapsed time for such important actions as product development, resources development, market development, or physical facility development. Three years may be long enough, or perhaps 10 years will be needed.

In fact, the necessary time varies. Resource development may have to be started 8 years before materials will become available, while 2 years may be adequate for market development. To deal with this variation, several companies (a) plan an action *in detail* only when a start is necessary, or (b) prepare a comprehensive program for 3 or 4 years ahead and then extend the period only for those areas requiring longer lead times.

Revisions. As results of first steps become known and new information about external conditions is learned, long-range programs need revision. The typical procedure is an annual review when near-term actions are planned in greater detail, a new year is added on the end, and adjustments are made in plans for the interim period.

Under this scheme, programs are revised several times before the period to which they apply finally arrives. This provides flexibility in long-range programming. It also entails a lot of work, and executives may become cavalier about plans for 5 years hence since such plans will be revised over and over again. These disadvantages of several revisions are strong reasons for restricting the period covered and making sure the benefits listed on pages 630 and 631 are actually being obtained.

Who prepares long-range programs? Central managers will certainly participate in long-range programming, as noted in Chapter 20. Equally clear, however, is the fact that they cannot do the job alone. They will need help obtaining ideas and specific data. Moreover, if the programs are to guide current commitments and to have the desired psychological effect on executives throughout the company, all major executives should participate —research directors, plant managers, sales managers, and the like. Since these executives have other pressing duties, they probably will ask a staff assistant to help with the planning.

Altogether, then, central managers, operating executives, and their staffs probably will contribute ideas, data, judgment or approval. A bit complicated, yes, yet necessary if the programs are to be carefully prepared and are to serve their intended purposes.

SUMMARY

Through programming, a manager formulates an integrated plan covering what, how much, when, and who.

Six basic steps should be taken: (1) divide the total operations necessary to achieve the objective into parts, (2) note the necessary sequences and relationships between each of these parts, (3) decide who is to be responsible for doing each part, (4) decide how each part will be done and the resources needed, (5) estimate the time required for each part, and (6) assign definite dates when each part will commence and end.

When faced with complex programming problems, a manager can use critical path analysis to identify those parts of the total activity that must be watched most closely if the final objective is to be met on time.

Long-range programming follows the same steps as any other programming. However, because of the great difficulty in forecasting accurately several years in advance, long-range programs have to be revised several times. While long-range programs must not be regarded as fixed, they do help flag actions with long lead times that should be started immediately, prepare executives to act promptly when opportunities or difficulties do arise, and provide a basis for reconciling short-run solutions with long-term plans.

QUESTIONS FOR CLASS DISCUSSION

1. Explain the relation, if any, between a company's policies and its short-range programming work. For example, do policies on sales promotion or on the timing of procurement affect production scheduling and financial cash budgets?

2. How does the provision of a balanced organization structure affect the task of short-range programming, if at all? What aspects of the programming task relate to the problem of design of the formal organization structure?

3. For some activities, such as engineering, product development, and sales promotion planning, many executives would argue that the creative aspects of the work make time estimates very unreliable. In view of this difficulty, do you think programming should be applied to this kind of work?

4. What influence does the increase in automation of a factory have on (a) the difficulty and (b) the desirability of careful programming?

5. Who should prepare short-range and long-range programs: operators, first-line supervisors, top executives, staff men reporting to the chief executive, or staff men reporting to department managers? Does the size of a company and the nature of its operations make any difference in your answer to this question?

6. Develop, as best you can, a PERT network for the program of the shirt manufacturing company discussed in the chapter.

7. Three "elapsed-time estimates" are often used for each step in a PERT network and weighted average is calculated. What weights might be assigned under what conditions of short- and long-range programming to the various estimates?

8. Sharp changes in business conditions because of business cycles, wars, and other factors put companies with long "lead times" (the interval between the initial design of a product and final sales to customers) at a serious disadvantage. What steps can a company take either (a) to reduce the total lead time or (b) to avoid some of the losses resulting from sales actions that are out of tune with current economic conditions?

9. Using the form of long-range programming explained on pages 628-633, work out such a program for your recommendations for the Island Creek Coal Company case (pages 70-80) or the National Lumber and Plywood Corporation case (pages 41-48).

CASE XXIII

William E. Berry Company

The William E. Berry Company, manufacturer of washing machines and related appliances, has decided to bring out an automatic clothes dryer that is to be a companion piece of equipment with a new model of the company's automatic washing machine. Moreover, the company has decided to build a new plant that will house the manufacture of both of these products. The new plant is to be financed through a long-term loan from an insurance company. These basic decisions have just been approved by the Berry Company board of directors, and the president is now concerned about a program for putting them into effect. A considerable amount of work has already been done by various executives of the company, but detailed plans have awaited board action on the general idea.

Assume you have been asked by the president to prepare for his approval a program covering the major steps that should be taken to get the new plant constructed and ready for operation. You were expected to talk to various executives concerned and have gathered the following information.

The sales manager believes that the new model of the automatic washing machine should not be put on the market until the new dryer is also ready. The company can then undertake a big promotion campaign in which the advertising of each product will lend support to the other. However, the sales manager stresses the importance of getting both products on the market as rapidly as possible. He believes this is essential for the company to maintain its competitive position in the industry. The Berry automatic washing machine has enabled the company to improve somewhat its total percentage of industry sales, but the sales manager believes that this ground may be lost if the company does not get its dryer on the market within the next year. Seven or eight months will be needed to develop the consolidated promotion program. The sales manager says there is no point in developing this program until the date when machines will be available is known because the advertising theme should be adapted to the economic and competitive situation prevailing at that time.

The treasurer stresses that the new long-term loan should cover all capital requirements connected with the new plant; that is, it should cover both the building and the necessary equipment. He points out that recent expansion of the company's business has already used capital made available from retained earnings. Moreover, if the new model and new product are as successful as anticipated there will be need for additional capital invested in accounts receivable, inventories, and related items. Earnings during the next year or two should provide capital needed for these purposes, but according to the treasurer's estimates there will be comparatively little margin left over for investment in fixed assets. The treasurer explained that the company operates with semiannual cash budgets, and consequently no detailed estimates of the financing of the new plant have been prepared. There have, however, been general discussions with an insurance company and a commercial bank, as indicated below.

The chief engineer of the company and his staff have given considerable thought to the new plant. They have decided that all sheet metal work, painting and enameling, and assembling of the automatic washers and dryers should be performed in the new plant. Company manufacture of parts, assembly of controls, and the assembly of the older style washing machines, wringers, and other products are to be performed in the old plant. In this connection it is planned to add some forging and electrical assembly operations that have previously been performed by suppliers rather than by the company itself. Since all painting and enameling will be transferred to the new plant, there will be considerable opportunity for revisions and improvement in layout in the old plant.

The chief engineer reports that plans for equipment and layout in the new plant are still tentative. He explains that several changes have been made in the estimated sales figures suggested by the sales department and that the treasurer has asked for estimates covering several different assumptions of work to be performed in the new plant. Because of these uncertainties, it has not been practical to attempt refined plans. Now that board action has been taken, the chief engineer believes it quite desirable to re-estimate the work load, make careful selection of the type and capacity of equipment necessary, and then study the most efficient layout of this equipment. He estimates that this engineering work can be done within three or four months and points out that if this work is carefully performed before the new building is started, costly changes in building specifications can be avoided. It is possible, of course, to make changes in the building specifications while the work is progressing, but the chief engineer estimates that making these changes after the original contract has been let may add from $15,000 to $100,000 to the cost of the new building.

Some contacts have already been made with suppliers of equipment. The salesmen from these firms are, of course, eager to give advice regarding the advantages of their equipment, and to submit bids on specific proposals. Indications are that most suppliers will be able to make delivery of equipment within twelve months. However, certain types of presses that would have to be manufactured to order may require as much as eighteen months for delivery.

The personnel director has considered staffing the new plant and especially filling the new supervisory and executive positions that will be created. He believes very strongly that these positions should be filled by people already in the organization, and the president has agreed to this general policy of promotion from within. The general plan is to pick the men who will be supervisors in the new plant far enough in advance so that they can help in planning the layout, procedures, manpower requirements, and other aspects of the new organization. This will have the double advantage of providing a practical operating view to the plans as they are being prepared and it will also be excellent training for the new men who will have responsibility for running the plant. The men who take such an active part in the early planning will be relieved of their present duties and assigned full time to planning operations of the new plant. It is expected that some men may spend as much as a year in this planning work and that all supervisors will be relieved of their other duties at least two months prior to the opening of the new plant. It is hoped that these men will have opportunity to study any new equipment that is to be used and perhaps observe it in operation in some other company.

An architect for the new building has already been at work preparing rough sketches and assisting the company in making estimates of the total cost of the new building. Considerably more work is necessary, however, to draw the detailed plans and prepare the specifications in the detail necessary for the placement of contracts for construction. Approximately two months will be required from the time the general size of the building is agreed upon until the detailed plans for the major part of the building are completed, and this would not include additional detailed plans that can be worked out after the original construction is under way.

The construction of the new building will be undertaken by some general contractor who is fairly familiar with the construction business and can arrange for subcontracts for particular types of work. Preliminary contacts have been made with three such contractors, each of whom has indicated an interest in bidding on the job. One man thought the building might be erected within a year after the contract is let, but the other two thought that it would be much safer to allow fifteen months. All of them indicated that these time estimates assume that steel would be available when needed.

A life insurance company has investigated the financial status of the William E. Berry Company, and has indicated a willingness to make a long-term loan up to a total of $2,000,000. The insurance company would expect to receive a first mortgage on all of the plant and equipment of the company, and probably would insist on other protective clauses such as maintenance of a sound current ratio, limitations on other long-term debts, and the like. The insurance company will enter into an agreement to extend the credit as soon as final plans for the building are completed. The actual cash, however, would not be advanced until the new assets are in place. Part of the money can be obtained as soon as the building structure itself is completed and the balance when the plant is actually ready to operate.

The legal counsel of the company has indicated that a loan agreement such as this must be carefully drawn, since the loan will extend over a period of twelve to fifteen years and many contingencies may arise during that interval. Also care must be taken with respect to the legal aspects of the actual construction itself. For example, it is necessary to secure completion bonds from the general contractor and to take out special insurance during the construction period.

The commercial bank with which the William E. Berry Company has been doing business for many years has indicated its willingness to make a short-term loan to finance construction while building is in progress. In other words, it is willing to make a loan to the company of any money that must be paid to the contractor prior to the time the long-term loan is obtained from the insurance company. Before advancing any money, however, the commercial bank will insist that the company have a firm agreement with the insurance company that the long-term credit will be granted. There are, of course, many details regarding the interest rate, repayment period, protective clauses, etc., that must be negotiated with the insurance company and the commercial bank before the financial arrangements can be completed. The new building will be constructed on the present site where there is ample space.

REQUIRED: Prepare a program for getting the new Berry plant erected and ready for operation. If there are any major decisions that the president must make before the program can be settled, be sure to indicate them.

24 ACTIVATING

The wisest objectives, policies, organization, and programs come to naught until they are put into action. This need to translate ideas into action has been a recurring theme throughout our discussion, but it warrants further recognition in a separate chapter. Central management plays an important role in activating an enterprise by:

1. Setting the *leadership tone*.
2. Fostering good *man-to-man communication*.
3. Providing an appropriate, viable *incentive structure*.

Controlling is also necessary in achieving results and will be explored in the next chapter.

LEADERSHIP TONE

Relations with immediate associates. Men in central management positions cannot escape being public figures, at least throughout their organization. Their behavior is closely watched for cues. The vice-president who jokingly said, "Guess I'll walk through the office in my shirt sleeves just to start a rumor," was well aware that many people would try to infer meaning from even his casual actions.

Usually central managers influence the tone of an enterprise primarily by the way they deal with their immediate associates. These associates, in turn, have contacts with many more people, and the influence radiates on out.

Significant here is optimism (or pessimism) about the future, confidence that the company can achieve intermediate and long-range goals, aggressiveness in tackling tough problems, fairness in dealing with outsiders and insiders, and similar attitudes that affect morale. A senior executive conveys his feelings on such matters partly by what he says, but even more by his decisions and actions. The men who work closely with him are naturally very sensitive about these attitudes because such viewpoints have a direct effect on their own futures.

No one has yet found a single formula that will generate good morale in all circumstances. The beliefs and the ideals of one's associates as well as the demands of the current situation influence the effectiveness of a particular leadership pattern. The hard-driving, risk-taking leadership of Henry J. Kaiser, for instance, would play havoc in a large New York bank. Within the limits of his own personal flexibility, each manager must seek a leadership pattern that seems appropriate to the needs of the situation. In making this choice he should recognize that his behavior will be extended to some degree throughout the company.

Contacts throughout the company. A spirit of optimism, conviction, or caution and other aspects of company viewpoint are also conveyed through direct contacts of senior executives with various groups of employees. Such contacts are inevitably brief and often superficial. Nevertheless, employees like to see, and better to talk with, the men who make the major decisions in the company they work for. Political leaders know well the value of a personal handshake, and military commanders do not underestimate the need for personal visits to combat troops. Merely to have established some personal identification is valuable. If, in addition, senior executives can generate enthusiasm for company policies and programs, the effect may be substantial.

MAN-TO-MAN COMMUNICATION

A wholesome attitude and spirit—discussed above—helps activate plans, but it does not remove the elementary need to communicate such plans clearly. Here central management sets an example in dealing with immediate subordinates and promotes a general pattern for clear boss-subordinate communications throughout the enterprise. Important means toward this end are workable instructions, consultative direction, and goal-centered performance appraisals.

Workable instructions. Giving instructions appears to be so simple that it should not present a significant problem in activating plans. Experienced managers know, however, that faulty directions often do create trouble.

Example of inadequate instruction. The textile division of a large manufacturing company having several semi-independent operating divisions had experienced a rapid expansion in sales in one year and was preparing for even greater sales in the following year. Unfortunately, retail store buying slowed up and signs indicated that the industry was about to enter one of its frequent cyclical declines. At this time the company president and the division vice-president discussed the outlook and agreed that the division should trim its sails and inventory should be reduced rather than expanded. This agreement was in effect an order from the president to the vice-president.

Difficulty arose because the order really was not clear. The vice-president took immediate steps to cut off new orders for raw materials, to stop or reduce the size of production runs wherever this could be done without jeopardizing orders already on the books or leaving materials in a semifinished state, and to push the sale of finished goods by granting price reductions wherever this could be done without completely demoralizing the market. These steps undoubtedly cut the inventory below what it otherwise would have been, but the in-flow of materials already on order and in process resulted in continued receipts and manufacture considerably in excess of the sale of finished goods. Financial reports were not completed until two weeks following the close of a month and so it was six weeks before the president learned that inventories actually went up half a million dollars instead of down. He then called the vice-president to task for failing to follow instructions.

The vice-president explained that he was in the process of carrying out the instructions and that he assumed the president had in mind "an orderly liquidation." Cancellation of orders from raw material suppliers would have created bad relations and probably claims for damages; forced sale of finished goods could have been made only at very substantial reductions inasmuch as retail stores did not want to increase their inventories. On the other hand, the president pointed out that the conditions in the industry had become steadily worse and that it would have been easier to get rid of the inventory six weeks ago than it was then. Again the president said, "Inventories must go down." The vice-president proceeded to take what he considered to be drastic steps, but he naturally was concerned about keeping the operating loss at a minimum because he would be considered responsible for such losses by the Board of Directors. Many of his assistants argued that time was needed to work off the inventory and that cancellation of orders with suppliers would cause them trouble just at the time they needed help and consequently would injure the division's long-run reputation in the industry.

The president grew impatient with the time it was taking to carry out his instructions and finally resorted to putting the division under close cash control. Bills for wages and raw materials were paid only out of funds collected from customers of the division. This drastic action finally succeeded in getting inventories liquidated about seven months after the original decision to "trim sails." In this instance there was no question as to the general intent of the directions given by the president. There was, however, considerable doubt as to how fast, how much, and at what expense the action should be taken.

Tests of a good instruction. The effectiveness of giving directions can be improved by making sure that the following simple tests of a good instruction are met:

1. The instructions should be *complete,* indicating what is to be done, the quality of performance desired, and the time when the assignment is to be finished.
2. Compliance should be *reasonable,* that is, within the capacity of the person receiving the instructions under conditions prevailing at that time.
3. The instructions should be *clear,* that is, the executive giving the instruction should make sure that the ideas in his mind are actually transmitted to the person being directed.
4. Key points of all major instructions should be put *in writing.*

In the textile division example, the intent was clear but the instruction was incomplete with respect to time and cost. Also, had the president's order been complete, the vice-president probably would have questioned its reasonableness. If the president had consciously thought of the tests of a good instruction—or observed them out of habit—serious confusion involving hundreds of thousands of dollars would have been avoided.

In practice, wide differences exist in the extent to which orders are put in writing. It takes time and effort to reduce instructions to writing, and many executives feel that at least for simple instructions this work is unnecessary. However, written instructions often add a certain definiteness to the direction and they reduce the occasions for argument when memories are faulty. As a general rule, instructions should be written when (a) several individuals are affected, (b) considerable time will pass before the work is completed, (c) complex and detailed information is involved, or (d) the matter is of such importance that special steps to avoid the possibility of misunderstanding are warranted.

On the other hand, routine instructions can be terse. For repetitive activities, often custom or standard operating procedures dictate how work is to be performed and the executive needs only to fill in the missing gaps. In other words, all the tests of a good instruction should be met, but some aspects are covered by previous orders and training.

One further qualification should be noted. The amount of detail in an instruction should be consistent with the delegation of authority to make decisions. For instance, if a president has given his chief accountant authority to establish the accounting system for the company, the president's instructions regarding, say, changes in salaries will not deal with recording such changes. Of course, the president and the chief accountant should have a mutual understanding about the results the accounting system is to achieve. In other words, delegations that are part of the established organization are like customary procedures noted in the preceding paragraph; they are part of the total behavior structure assumed when a new instruction is given. Obviously, if this assumed behavior structure is not understood by all people involved, the instruction will be ambiguous.

Follow-up on instructions. After instructions—complete, reasonable, clear, and perhaps in writing—have been issued, sound practice requires that they be followed-up. This is necessary not only to see that the particular instruction is carried out but also to cultivate the proper attitude toward instructions. Employees soon learn whether their boss "means what he says." If instructions are issued but not followed-up, employees naturally will postpone or disregard the work that they find unpleasant. The executive will then never know whether he can count on performance, and will have to spend much more time finding out what really happened. On the other hand, if the executive is careful to see that all instructions are complied with, then any new assignments will be considered as something that must be done. There will be a sharpness and positiveness about the administration in place of a casual, indifferent attitude.

This principle of follow-up on instructions imposes a burden upon the executive. He must be careful to issue only those instructions that he is sure he wants to be carried out, for otherwise he will have his subordinates performing work that is not contributing the maximum to the broad objectives of the enterprise. He should distinguish between minimum standards of satisfactory performance and goals that are desirable but not necessarily essential to the successful operation of the rest of the company. Moreover, if for some reason the instructions are no longer applicable, the executive must be sure that he modifies or withdraws them. Occasionally this may embarrass the executive because it may appear that he made a mistake in issuing the instructions in the first place. However, employee attitudes and morale will probably be better if the instruction is revised than they would be if the instruction were disregarded or employees were made to perform what they probably would recognize as unnecessary work.

This suggestion that an executive should always follow-up on instructions he issues does not mean that he is an autocrat in his administration. Subordinates may be given ample opportunity to participate in formulating the plans, and considerable authority may be delegated to them. Instead, it simply means that when instructions are issued they should be taken seriously.

Consultative direction. One of the most promising means of overcoming the difficulties of communication is called *consultative direction*. Under this technique the people responsible for executing an instruction are consulted about its workability and better ways of accomplishing the same result. Usually the executive will call in one or more of his subordinates and lay before them the facts of the situation that he faces; then these men together will explore possible courses of action. The subordinates may have some additional information and often will have suggestions on what should be done. The various suggestions will be examined, and finally an agreement will be reached on what appears to be the wisest action to take.

Among the advantages of this method of giving instructions are the cooperation and enthusiasm generated on the part of the people who have to carry out the instructions. Since they helped form the plan, they take a personal pride in carrying it out. The skillful executive will be quite willing to let his men feel that they originated the solution, even though he, too, had thought of it, because of the added incentive they will then have to make it work.

The instructions resulting from consultative supervision may be more practical than the ideas that the executive would think of alone. Moreover, consultative direction provides an excellent occasion for developing executives through coaching, already discussed in Chapter 21.

Consultative direction is not without its drawbacks. Theoretically, the agreement reached in the discussion becomes the instruction from the executive, and as such it should meet all the tests of a good direction that are listed on page 642. There is a risk that the discussion may terminate before the conclusions are fully crystallized and that each of the executives will be left to make his own interpretation of what was agreed upon. The second drawback is that the subordinates may feel that it is within their province to modify the course of action inasmuch as they helped formulate the plan in the first place. Both of these risks, however, can be minimized if the executive insists that the conference conclude with a succinct summary of what is to be done and he then makes it clear that these instructions are to be carried out unless he personally approves of some modification. The third drawback is that consultative direction does take considerable time of several executives; consequently, its use should be reserved for people and problems that will really benefit from the process.

A recent study of joint consultation in British industry confirms American experience, and difficulties, with consultation. While this study dealt primarily with relations between an executive and formally designated representative of the workers, the findings that are summarized in the accompanying table throw light on the en-

Effect of Relation with Executive on Employee Response

MEETING	RELATION-SHIP	METHOD	STATUS AND AUTHORITY	SENSE OF RESPONSI-BILITY	DECIDER
Deputation	Dominant-servile	Dictation	Rank	"His"	He decided
Negotiation	Competitive rivalry	Compromise	Strength	"No one's"	It was decided
Consultation	Collaborative	Integration	Function and qualifications	"Ours"	We decided

From a report of the British National Institute of Industrial Psychology.

tire supervisory process. The relationships range from deputa-
tion, in which the employees make a request of the executive,
through negotiations, or bargaining, to consultation. This British
report brings out again that the manner in which the plan is agreed
upon has much to do with the attitude of the people who have to
carry it out.

Goal-centered performance appraisals. Our discussion of workable instructions and consultative direction has focused largely on
communication regarding separate, unique operating problems.
Often an executive performs a myriad of interrelated problems:
he may supervise a dozen salesmen who contact hundreds of customers, or he may direct a variety of engineering projects. To
activate such work effectively, managers need a simple procedure
to discuss plans and results with each of their subordinates. Goal-
centered performance appraisals is such a technique.

The process begins with an employee (of any rank) agreeing
with his manager about the results he is expected to achieve during
an ensuing period—three months, six months or perhaps a year.
Such an agreement on results expected should be based on a
mutual understanding about several things: (a) the sphere of
activities the employee is concerned with, that is, the organization;
(b) the desired goals for these activities, both long-run and short-
run; (c) how achievement of these goals will be measured and the
level of achievement expected by the end of the period being planned; (d) the help the employee may expect from the manager and
others; and (e) the freedom and the restraints on how the employee pursues the goals.

Then at the end of the period the manager and the employee
again sit down to review what actually was accomplished, to
determine why deviations—both good and bad—from goals occurred, and then to agree on a new set of goals for the next
period.

At each review there is grist for a new discussion because a new
set of results are available for appraisal and a new set of goals
need to be agreed upon. As the process proceeds, the manager
has repeated opportunities for counseling the individual and for
relating individual performance to company objectives, policies,
organization, and programs. Hopefully, these discussions will be
carried out objectively and frankly, as already suggested in con-

nection with consultative direction. As a minimum, the employee should know what is expected of him and how his performance will be measured.

One of the advantages of goal-centered performance appraisals is that they set the stage for frequent interchange about goals and their achievement. In fact, when men work on distinct projects, the review may occur at the close of one project and the beginning of another. In other instances they become a part of programming discussed in the preceding chapter. If a man's total job and total performance are covered in such project or programming discussions, an additional period appraisal serves little purpose. Often, however, these discussions are sharply focused on a particular end result, and an annual examination of overall performance picks up loose ends and gives balanced direction. Whatever the timing, the important thing is that open communication take place between each employee and his boss on the array of factors involved in setting goals and their achievement.

Members of central management are directly concerned with workable instructions, consultative direction, and goal-centered performance appraisals only with their immediate subordinates. Nevertheless, in addition to setting a good example in these relationships, they can encourage this type of man-to-man communication throughout the enterprise.

INCENTIVE STRUCTURE

Important as leadership and communications are in activating employees, central management still has to provide a persuasive answer to his subordinates' question, "What do *we* get for our efforts?" An indifferent person will probably do the job poorly and slowly, whereas a properly motivated individual will try to exceed the expectations of his boss. Broadly speaking, a manager can influence this eagerness to cooperate through:

1. Indirect motivation.
2. Positive incentives.
3. Disciplinary action, or negative incentives.

Indirect motivation. Any individual will perform at his best only when he finds the working environment to be satisfactory. People differ in what they consider to be important and they are frequently willing to put up with conditions that they find far from ideal. Nevertheless, there are a whole group of things central management can do, not as rewards for good behavior, but rather as a sound investment in good employee morale. In this connection, central management should try to create within the company a situation that provides employees with (a) security, (b) attractive work, and (c) good treatment.

Financial security. One of the most striking shifts in social values during the past generation is the greater emphasis on security. Many people, including a large number of college students, now are more interested in a safe job than one that offers a chance to achieve wealth and fame. Of course, they like a position that offers both security and great future potential; but if one feature has to be sacrificed, it is probably the potential. Many of us have a dulled spirit of risk-taking and adventure.

This quest for security means that the energies of men may be sapped by a haunting worry about unemployment, accidents, illness, old age, and other possible troubles of tomorrow. It is quite possible for a man to be so upset from worry that he is inefficient in his job. (A small amount of uncertainty may be a good thing if it serves as an incentive for a man to make sure that he comes out on the right side of the fence.) As noted in Chapter 13, many companies have established plans that help their employees meet problems of financial insecurity. For these plans to have their full effect, it is often necessary for a manager to explain and remind his men of the protection they offer. Also in stable companies a manager can remind men that they need not worry about a job if they continue to do efficient work.

Psychological security. A sense of security involves more than financial matters. For example, there is a sharp difference between the self-confidence of a man who is "on top of his job" and the one who is not sure what it is all about. A manager can help to build confidence by taking time to make sure that each of his people know what they are to do, how they are to do it, and how well they are doing it. The goal-centered performance appraisal, discussed above, is one means of providing this type of psychological security.

Moreover, people will feel insecure if they hear through the grapevine about possible changes that will affect them. Here again a manager can often help by telling subordinates as far in advance as possible about changes that will affect them. Even better, if these people can have a share in planning the change, their increased knowledge and interest in the situation will go a long way toward removing the sense of insecurity.

Attractive work. A readiness to cooperate is also fostered by giving men work that they like. Attractiveness of a job depends partly on whether the man considers the work worthwhile. If an executive can help his subordinates to feel that the objectives of the company are desirable and that the particular job makes a significant contribution toward these objectives, then doing a fair day's work will become a rewarding experience for the man. On the other hand, if the job is regarded only as a way to get a pay check, the task of motivation will be much more difficult.

Most jobs call for skill, intelligence, and craftmanship of one type or another. If people can be assigned jobs that call upon their particular abilities, they typically will take pride in their work. Through proper work assignments and personal recognition, a manager can do much to cultivate such a sense of accomplishment.

Good treatment. . There are several different aspects in what most employees regard as good treatment. Prompt and considerate handling of grievances is certainly one of these. Even though the grievance be a minor annoyance or injustice, it can cause a gnawing discontent that seriously interferes with an employee's effectiveness on his job. Closely related to grievances is the positive action of a supervisor to look after the interests of his men. In the ebb and flow of company activities the manager should be on the lookout for opportunities for promotion, improvement in working conditions, adjustment in pay, and similar points of concern to his men. Diligent attention to such matters can contribute much to loyalty and morale.

Still another aspect of good treatment is recognition as an individual. Each man brings to his job a background of personal interest, hobbies, family relationship, religious beliefs, obligations, and personal health, which are inseparable parts of the total individual. A sympathetic recognition and interest in these off-the-job problems and aspirations makes a man feel that he is more than just a wheel in a large machine. Also, consultative direction, which has already been discussed, builds a man's self-respect and adds to his interest in the operation.

The foregoing suggestions for indirect motivation are, of course, simply good human relations. They cannot be used sporadically, such as prizes for a sales contest; rather they should become a normal part of the work situation. If a man can say of his job: "I like the work, they treat me well, and I don't have to worry," the foundation is laid for his enthusiastic cooperation in carrying out directions.

Positive incentives. Indirect motivation, which has just been discussed, creates a cooperative attitude but it does not provide a positive spur to greater effort. Most of us will put forth extra effort if we believe there is a reward for so doing. Without some form of positive incentive, there is a strong human tendency to "coast," to be satisfied with work that is just "good enough." Consequently, management adds to the indirect motivation some form of positive incentive.

Financial incentives. Sales commissions, production bonuses, and similar types of direct financial incentives have already been discussed in connection with compensation policies in Chapter 12. Also executive bonuses were briefly considered in Chapter 21. Compensation plans such as these provide clear-cut incentives and are used effectively by many companies. Nevertheless, they do have definite limitations. For many positions, operating conditions are so variable and output so difficult to measure that it is impractical to attempt to pay a financial premium that is directly related to the effort and the skill of the individual.

An alternative arrangement to commissions and bonuses is to give "merit" increases in base pay to employees whose performance is highly satisfactory. Unfortunately, merit increases are generally inflexible because the base pay rate is rarely cut back after it is once raised even though the work of the employee may no longer be outstanding. Nevertheless, merit increases are very widely used in American business and the possibility of earning them provides a strong financial incentive to many people.

The possibility of promotion to positions paying higher salaries likewise provides an important financial incentive. Promotions cannot, of course, be made solely on the basis of outstanding performance in a given job because of the different qualifications needed in the higher paying jobs. (The bookkeeper who is both accurate and fast is not necessarily qualified to be office manager.) While demonstrated competence, energy, and loyalty may not be the only factors considered in promotion, they certainly are important. In this connection central management can insist on careful review of promotions because the whole spirit of a department will be affected by "who gets ahead around here."

Respect by fellow men. Virtually every man responds to many incentives that are not financial in character. One of these is the attitude of associates and neighbors. In fact, social pressure to do certain things and not to do others is often more compelling than financial reward.

Recognition as a star salesman, as superintendent of the local plant, or being a "member of the palace guard" provides a strong spur to action for many men. Whatever the field of achievement, recognition of success gives most of us important inward satisfaction. Titles, citations, membership in honorary societies give clear-cut recognition; but there is also the less definite respect of fellow workers, friends, and neighbors. An executive cannot, of course, pass out social status and respect as he sees fit. However, through public praise, assignment of work, granting of titles, and in other ways, he can contribute to the stature of an individual in the eyes of his associates. The skillful manager will be careful to give this type of recognition only when it is deserved. So handled, it can often become an important incentive.

Influence and power. Individuals often will work hard for positions of power and influence. There is an excitement and a thrill that comes with making large purchases for a company, watching a plant operate partly as a result of one's own guidance, seeing a new product that includes one's own choice of design or color, or supervising a pension plan that one piloted through to final adoption. By changing assignments, an executive can add to or take away from the influence of his subordinates, and he makes these changes on the basis of the subordinate's ability and energy in getting results. This means that in a well-run company a man must continually win the right to hold an influential position.

These brief comments on nonfinancial incentives by no means exhaust the various means of providing positive motivation. The skillful executive will analyze the attitudes and the aspirations of each of his subordinates and then try to arrange operations so that each man will be challenged to put forth his best effort. There is even more room here than there is with financial incentives to design a pattern of opportunities and rewards that will build enthusiastic cooperation with the company program.

It is well to note that the doctrine of positive incentive necessarily requires some differentiation between individuals. Sometimes there is a single prize; that is, only one man out of several gets the promotion or a coveted trip to an international convention. And even where bonuses or prestige are available to all men, there must be objective determination as to who qualifies and who does not. As a result there will be some disappointments and perhaps some hard feelings, which will be unpleasant for the manager as well as the men concerned. This is simply part of the price that must be paid for the use of positive incentives.

Disciplinary action. Reprimands, probations, temporary lay-offs, demotions, and discharges all have their place in a total scheme of motivation. They are disciplinary actions usually used only when an employee has violated a company regulation or has failed by a wide margin to do satisfactory work. Experience has shown that such negative incentives do not bring forth the best efforts from people. Consequently, these negative incentives are almost always used only to maintain certain minimum standards of performance, whereas the positive incentives, already discussed, are more effective in getting people to put forth extra effort.

Almost every supervising executive will have to take disciplinary action from time to time, although the majority of cases will be with rank-and-file and new employees. It is important that this discipline be given in a constructive manner and not in a spirit of anger or retribution. The primary purpose of disciplinary measures is to influence the *future* behavior of (a) the offending person and (b) other employees.

Such a favorable effect on future behavior will be obtained only if the disciplinary action is regarded as fair. Fairness, in turn, requires first that there be a full knowledge of the rules of conduct and the penalties for breaking them. For example, smoking in an oil refinery may be sufficient basis for immediate dismissal, whereas smoking in a machine shop may be no violation at all. Secondly, fairness requires that full consideration be given to the provocation of the undesirable action and also the attitude, previous conduct, and personality of the individual concerned. In the third place, after full consideration of all the facts, disciplinary action should be consistent between individuals. This is particularly important to secure acceptance of the decision by fellow workers.

For key executives, disciplinary action is more likely to be prompted by failure to perform well than by breaking of rules. The main cost of a weak executive is that his occupancy of a key position prevents a more able man from doing that work well. A baseball team cannot afford a rightfielder who bats only .100. Such men must be transferred to jobs they can perform or be discharged. Reluctance to clean out "dead wood" from an organization tends to undermine the determination of other employees to exert themselves.

Often the disciplinary action has a widespread influence on other employees. Too harsh an action may make the man a martyr and cause discontent throughout the department. Treatment that is too lenient, on the other hand, may be interpreted as meaning that the supervisor considers the matter of minor consequence.

Negative incentives that are provided through disciplinary action are unfortunately a necessary phase of motivating subordinates. They must be combined with personal leadership, positive incentives, and indirect motivation, however, if the company is to be really efficient and dynamic in its operation.

SUMMARY

Central managers play a dual role in activating an enterprise, that is, "putting the show on the road." They must work with their immediate subordinates just as every other executive must initiate and stimulate action of people assigned to him. In addition, central managers strongly influence the activating process throughout the enterprise, partly by the examples they set and partly by establishing certain practices as standard procedures all executives are expected to observe.

Important elements in this activating process are (1) leadership tone, (2) man-to-man communications, and (3) a viable incentive structure. Central managers in their daily contacts and in their "field" visits can do much to generate a spirit of optimism, confidence, aggressiveness, fairness, or other attitudes—often called leadership tone or climate.

Man-to-man communication between executives and subordinates will be aided by making sure that instructions are complete, reasonable, and clear; by resorting to consultative direction on major problems; and by regular use of goal-centered performance appraisals. The aim in following these methods is to increase mutual understanding and also to gain acceptance of assignments that are made.

Coupled with climate and communication must be a pattern of incentives that encourages cooperation with company plans. This may be secured partly by providing employees with security, attractive work, and good treatment; that is, by creating a job situation that promotes a willingness to work. Positive incentives are also needed. These may take the form of financial incentives, increased social status and respect, or greater personal influence and power. Even when such incentives are provided, there will be a few people whose work is so unsatisfactory that disciplinary action is necessary. The discipline must be fair and consistent because it will have an influence on the future behavior of other employees as well as the one being disciplined.

Control, a step closely related to activating in the management cycle, is discussed in the following chapter.

QUESTIONS FOR CLASS DISCUSSION

1. The president of a rapidly growing but not very profitable food manufacturing company was described by his subordinates and by a researcher as: "He keeps this place going at a pretty determined pace . . . we can disagree with him in meetings and really slug it out . . . he is informal but quite demanding . . . he wants plans, memos, and written communications from us . . . he likes people to take the initiative in suggesting things . . . he held many two-and three-person conferences in his office during a typical day . . . he encouraged some competition among his executives . . . he expected other executives to come to see him and never dropped into their offices . . ." How would you characterize the leadership tone set by this president? How does it relate to the possible objectives of survival, growth, and profits?

2. "Men just won't work as hard as they used to, and when you ask them to do something they talk back," complained an office manager. Do you agree? How have higher wages, more education, social security plans, restriction of immigration, and similar social changes affected the task of supervision?

3. Explain how experience, beliefs, and attitudes of a man affect the task of giving him instructions. Should these same individual characteristics be considered in motivating him to carry out instructions?

4. Do you think consultative direction is more, or less, applicable if authority is centralized than when authority is decentralized?

5. The policy manual of an integrated and diversified textile company stated: "The objective of this company is to increase the intrinsic value of the common stock. It is not to grow bigger for the sake of size, nor to become more diversified, nor to make the most or best of anything, nor to provide jobs, nor to have the most modern plants, nor to have the happiest customers, nor to lead in new product developments, nor to achieve any other status that has no relationship to the economic use of capital. The company is in business solely to improve the inherent value of the common stockholder's equity in the company." Given this statement and acting as president, develop for your chief financial executive the set of results, goals, and measurements you would use for "goal-centered appraisal" of his performance. As a suggestion, use the outline of financial policies developed in earlier chapters.

6. Review the outline of personnel policies used in Chapters 11 to 13. Explain what bearing, if any, each of the policies discussed may have on (a) indirect motivation, (b) positive incentives, and (c) negative incentives. Which policies should cover all employees alike, and which should permit adaptation to individuals for purposes of motivation?

7. The executive vice-president of a soft-drink company said: "Watch the wet paint . . . What do you think of the four windows and my view of the park and the lake? (He laughed) With four windows I won't need a resume or any references—I can just tell people I'm a four-window executive. . . . I don't go much for these status symbols. If someone can't tell that you know what you are talking about unless he sees a rug on your floor, or lamps and end tables, or how many windows you have, then I don't want to spend my time talking to him . . . . The office move is symbolic . . . . I used to be a freight-forwarding clerk and before that just a kid from the wrong side of town . . . . The move here from the factory offices symbolized one kind of thing we have tried to build from selling more and increasing our size—acceptability or approval of the world around us . . . . Now that that I'm up on the 34th floor, I am beginning to realize there's a lot more to it . . . ." What is he saying?

8. In the television program *Patterns* (later made into a motion picture) the president and chairman put pressure on his labor relations vice-president by berating him in staff meetings, by ridiculing some of his ideas, by hiring a new man to work for the vice-president without consulting him, and by assigning the new man duties for which the vice-president had been responsible and which he had not performed well. Yet the president refused to fire the vice-president who, in turn, refused to resign. Why did the three men act this way, in your opinion, and how did their behavior affect the rest of the organization?

9. What part, if any, should a man with staff duties (as defined in Chapter 18) play in the different steps in activating? If you wish, in your answer assume that the staff man is concerned with sales promotion, or production scheduling, and that we are interested in the activating of salesman, or plant foremen.

CASE XXIV

Service Drug Wholesale, Inc.

Six months ago Samuel Chase was sent hastily from the home office of Service Drug Wholesale, Inc. to be manager of the Carrollton branch. His predecessor, Thomas Stone, had died of a heart attack. Mr. Chase was at the time staff operations manager for the company and had previously been manager of the company's smallest branch. (See Exhibit A on page 662 for an organization diagram of the company.) Carrollton was a large branch, and the city in which it was located has been growing rapidly for the past ten years.

Service Drug Wholesale, Inc. is, as its name indicates, a wholesale distributing firm that sells about 30,000 items to retail druggists in several Mid-Western states. Company headquarters are in Central City, and five branches are located in other large cities.

After six months in Carrollton, Mr. Chase became concerned about the effect of a threatened truckers' strike, both on the operations of the branch and on his attempts to improve the performance of the house. He wondered more specifically what he could say to Richard Stockton, the operations manager, who was responsible for shipping.

Background of the house. Mr. Chase was aware of the general feeling that Carrollton had never realized the potential volume that existed in its territory. Competition was keen both from the two other full-line wholesalers in the city and from five to six other wholesalers in the surrounding territory. Industries in the area were highly unionized, and an aggressive local was currently leading a fight to increase wages paid by wholesalers in the city. The presence of heavy industry and several large manufacturing companies led to a general high level of wages. In addition, help shortages were severe.

Mr. Chase had known his predecessor, Mr. Stone, only slightly through his general reputation and through a few recent dealings with him on warehouse layout and stock arrangement problems. Stone was ordinarily reported to be a very hard worker who had practically pulled the house through earlier troubles by his personal efforts. He was supposed to have been well versed in the drug field and to have known all the angles of internal operations. Mr.

Chase had found that Stone knew the most intimate details of routines and procedures.

Mr. Chase himself stated that he walked into the house cold. He found on arrival that service to the country customers was much poorer than that of competitors. The house customers were split about evenly between city and country. City deliveries were satisfactory, but country deliveries were generally made on the fourth to fifth day after receipt of the order. The house had about 18 employees in excess of standard. In spite of this, a goodly amount of overtime was being worked. The shipping clerks were working 3 to 4 hours extra every night, and everyone in the warehouse was working at least an hour overtime daily. Output was 15.7 lines an hour. (A "line" is one item on an order from a retail druggist. Each item is listed on a separate line of the order blank. Houses with average operating records have an output per worker of 20 lines per hour. Operating standards are developed from the average experience of many drug houses in similar situations.) Personnel turnover in the the past year had been 27%.

The first day. Three incidents occurred on the first day of his tenure as branch manager that caused Mr. Chase concern about the operations. In the morning, the receiving clerk came to him and said: "A carload of Kleenex has just arrived. Where do you want me to store it?" On the same day about noon, the sample room attendant came down and said: "I have a customer and will have to stay 30 minutes past 12 o'clock. Who do you want to take over when I go to lunch?" Mr. Chase later stated that he merely pushed the problems back in the laps of the receiving clerk and the sample room attendant since it would have been impossible for him to give a satisfactory answer.

In the afternoon, the operations manager, Richard Stockton, came to him and asked him what he, Stockton, should do in operations. "Mr. Stone had me responsible for the warehouse while he took care of the office." Mr. Chase's answer was: "Well, you're it. You know right from wrong. Go ahead and do it." As Mr. Chase said later, "At that stage of the game he knew the duties and the job description. He also had the operations manual." (The operations manual is a loose-leaf book containing many standard procedures for the warehouse as well as descriptions of common problems and suggested solutions. Manuals have been worked out by the company for all departments and state in fine detail procedures to be used and solutions to common problems.)

About 15 years before, Mr. Chase and Mr. Stockton had worked together as pricers in Central City. The two of them were both bucking to be head pricer and Mr. Stockton had been made head pricer first. (Pricers entered on each order the sales price of each item and then totaled the bill. This was later sent to the customer with his order.) In relation to that incident, Mr. Chase said: "We both knew that we were trying to get the job ahead of the other, but I could see that Stockton always had a slight edge on me and could do a good job of supervising the pricing." Mr. Stockton had later been promoted through other jobs and, after two years in the operations manager training course, finally had become assistant operations manager in Central City. There he had worked well as a member of that famous management team.

Action by Mr. Chase. Mr. Chase immediately started to take vigorous action in an attempt to pull the Carrollton house out of its difficulties.

For example, when the claims man came in with a claim from a retail druggist on a shortage, put it on his desk, and asked him "What do you want me to do with this?" Mr. Chase told him to pull out the original charge sheet (bill sent to the customer) himself, check the number of parcels delivered, and then see whether the claim was for a large or small number of items. The clerk did this and soon came back with the statement that two items amounting to one sixth of a dozen each were missing and suggested that the claim be allowed since there was no way of ascertaining exactly whose fault the shortage was.

In conjunction with Mr. Stockton, he planned a stock rearrangement that would move some of the heavier items and also fast-moving items to the end of the conveyor line. The two of them also worked out changes in the packing system that were designed to increase the number of baskets a packer could handle in a day. Several short conveyors were installed that eliminated much lifting and manual moving of baskets being checked and packages being sent to the shipping room. (One basket for each order is sent through the warehouse, and "pickers" fill the basket with appropriate items from the stations that they man. When the basket comes to the end of the conveyor line, the items are packed and the package is sent to the shipping room.) Mr. Stockton's desire to shift some people in the warehouse to different jobs was put into effect immediately.

Mr. Chase noticed that inventories were in excess of standard and were also out of balance, the buyers were in the habit of buying only from stock cards instead of also checking the inventory in the warehouse, and their work had evidently not been coordinated with sales. Mr. Chase was somewhat surprised to find this, since he knew that Mr. Stone had been a buyer for a long time before becoming division manager and had always dealt closely with the buyers even to the extent of doing a good deal of buying himself at one time when no personnel could be hired. To deal with this problem, Mr. Chase worked directly with the buyers, tried to inform them of expected sales of staples and of special promotions in order to bring their knowledge up to date, and reviewed their orders each night with them so that the inventory could be most quickly reduced and brought back in balance. The house was at the time delinquent in its cash payments to the home office. Two months later the head buyer was brought into the planning committee meetings and also a merchandising committee was set up. Planning meetings, attended by the five department heads plus Mr. Chase, were held monthly to prepare for special events such as introduction of a new line or display of Christmas merchandise and to discuss other important matters. The merchandising committee, with Mr. Chase as chairman, included representatives of the sales and buying departments. Meetings of this committee replaced the daily consultation of Mr. Chase and the buyers.

Within a few weeks, Mr. Chase sensed that there was some confusion among the staff as to just what they were supposed to do. He surmised that he had moved too far in pushing the people off and that he should attempt to pull them back. He talked this problem over with the sales manager, the only executive who was running his department effectively.

The sales manager, Roger Sherman, explained that Mr. Stone had been a very hard worker, energetic and aggressive. He had known so thoroughly what was to be done inside the house that he could either do it very quickly himself or tell other people specifically what should be done and could put his finger very quickly on the source of most trouble. Stone had been an old-timer in the business. Sherman had found it necessary to take away his own responsibilities from Mr. Stone and had even had to be quite vehement about it at times.

Roger Sherman stated: "Stone operated on the squeaky wheel principle. He spent less than half his time at his desk and his desk was always full of order sheets, invoices, claims, and purchase orders. Sometimes he used to come down on Saturdays and price the invoices. This was particularly common when we were short on pricers. When we were short of sundries at one time and Coca Cola another time, I had to tell him that the best system would be for the salesmen to allocate the supply among their own customers and not for him to hold the reins on the allocated goods. I argued that this kept him much too busy in dealing with the individual druggists. Stone liked to argue with you and talk the problem out. He would not just assign you a task, but you had to come up with the idea of what should be done or you had to raise objections to what was being done currently and you had to thrash out a plan with him. If you didn't do this, then you were not able to get a satisfactory answer out of him.

"Stone often stated that he did not want yes-men in his organization. He knew the business from top to bottom and you had to prove to him that you knew what you were talking about. Our omits (item ordered but not in stock) were usually over 12% (10% is standard), and if I took up the problem with Stone, he would sometimes try to be cooperative and work it out with the buyers. At other times, he would jump down your throat. He would say: 'No one else is doing any better than we are.' You couldn't do anything but walk off.

"I suppose he felt that he had been in the house for a long time and had been manager for a long time and that he knew what the problems were and was going to run the house his own way."

The credit manager was a particular problem. He was constantly at Mr. Chase's desk on one proposition or another. Mr. Chase felt that he brought in anything that was unusual or out of the ordinary. One day the credit manager said: "What can I do with these salesmen? Lewis will follow the decisions that we have agreed on for particular druggists but Morris won't. Morris came in with an order from Whipple Drug this morning and he didn't bring a check. I have told him many times that we can't accept any orders from Whipple without cash in advance." Mr. Chase said: "What are you going to do about it, Harold?"

"Well, I don't want to ship it without the money."

"What do you intend to do?"

"Well, it's a big order and we shouldn't send it out without the cash in advance."

"Well, what are you going to do? It's up to you to decide. Whatever you say, we'll go over and talk to the salesman and I'll back you up 100%."

Problems with operations and the operations manager. After a few months, although inventories were close to standard and omits were 10%, Mr. Chase noticed that delivery service was not improving markedly, that the amount of overtime work was the same, and that no reduction had been made in the work force.

Mr. Stockton, the operations manager, had been moved over from Central City three years before. There were rumors that Mr. Stone had opposed his coming since Mr. Stone had felt that he did not need any operations manager. However, the president of the company and the current staff operations director had felt that Mr. Stone needed an operations manager to at least install the changes in procedures that they felt might be valuable.

Mr. Stockton stated that he had several times suggested changes in the arrangement of the stock and also some shifts in personnel from one job to another. Not much was done about the suggestions. Sometimes Mr. Stone did not agree with them; other times he would not say anything. Mr. Stockton felt that he couldn't get any answer at all. On those occasions he would walk away and wonder what he was supposed to do. The question had really been left hanging in the middle of the air.

Mr. Stockton had also suggested a change in receiving facilities. This would involve spending about $5,000 for opening new doors in a blank wall and extending the dock. He took this up with Mr. Stone and Mr. Stone only said: "Hell, I know we can't get an appropriation for that:" At the time, the receiving dock was so located that only one truck at a time could come in. This caused other truckers to wait until the first truck was unloaded or to go elsewhere on their rounds and come back later in the day. Mr. Stockton remarked: "Well, under Stone the house was not making any money; therefore, he felt that it would have been hard for him to get approval to spend this $5,000."

At the time there were rumors that a city-wide strike was to be called against all contract carriers. (The company did not own its own trucks, but hired the services from outside trucking firms.) These rumors had been reported in the paper for a week and it appeared that the strike might well be called before another week was out. Mr. Chase called in Stockton and asked him about his preparations to meet this threatened strike. Stockton said: "I don't know what I'm going to do. I haven't really been able to think about it. This Carrollton is a tough place to do business. Something is always going wrong that prevents you from making any plans and carrying them out. In the past six months, we have caught 13 people stealing and this has wrecked production. Lines have dropped back off again from 18 in the last month. I had planned to put on the production bonus plan and sold it to the union, but we haven't had any pay-offs and now the union is really bitter about it and the stewards are always complaining. That kind of thing goes on all the time in Carrollton. You no sooner show some progress toward ·getting the warehouse running smoothly than there is a transit strike and half the force can't get to work and the other half comes late. This management group is not like Central City. Stone tied my hands all the time. I don't know what I'm going to do about the truckers' strike. These Carrollton people are different."

REQUIRED: (a) Analyze the supervisory methods used by Mr. Stone and Mr. Chase. Look at their relations with each of their subordinates, state how they acted and the effect of this on each subordinate. Explain the similarities and the differences in their actions and the differences in the behavior of the department managers..

(b) Explain, as best you can, why Mr. Stone and Mr. Chase acted as they did.

(c) If you were Mr. Chase, what would you say to Mr. Stockton now? State the exact words you would use.

EXHIBIT A

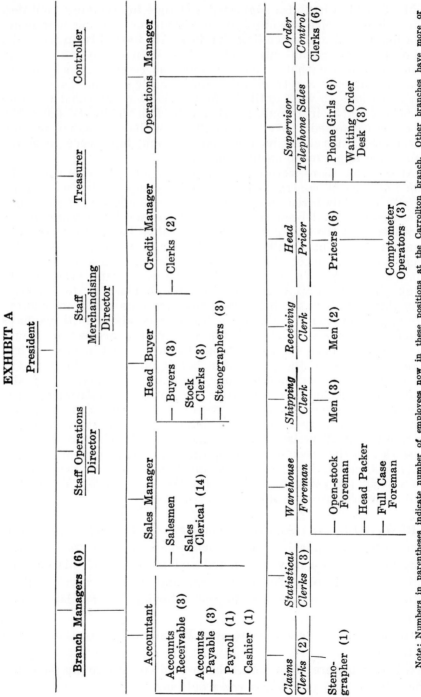

Note: Numbers in parentheses indicate number of employees now in these positions at the Carrollton branch. Other branches have more or fewer, depending on over-all volume.

25 ∴ CONTROLLING OPERATIONS

"Control" like so many other business terms may be used to cover a multitude of sins. We speak of control of a union president or a local politician, referring to the power these men wield. Financial control is often used to designate the person or the institution that has the determining voice in selecting the board of directors of a company. We speak of automatic control, remote control, voice control, and self-control with equal abandon. The discussion in this chapter, however, will be confined to means for controlling activities within a business.

Even after plans are carefully laid and employees are instructed what to do, the executive's job is not yet finished. There remains the need for watching what is actually happening, evaluating this performance, and changing instructions to fit conditions. The aim of this phase of management is to assure, insofar as possible, that plans are actually carried out and objectives achieved.

We shall examine first the nature of the control process. Then the control task that should be performed by central management will be explored in more detail. Finally, in the next chapter, the advantages and the limitations of budgetary control will be explored.

NATURE OF CONTROL PROCESS

Three basic elements will be found in every control procedure:

1. Standards of acceptable performance will be established.
2. Actual performance will be appraised in terms of these standards.
3. When actual results are found to be unsatisfactory, corrective action will be initiated.

Many problems arise in the application of this simple sequence: what should be covered by the standards and how tough they should be; who will do the measuring of performance and how this information will get transmitted to the people who evaluate it;

and what types of corrective action will lead to improved performance in the future. Let us look at a few illustrations of these problems.

Representative control problems. *Quality control in a food plant.* A manufacturer of cornflakes is concerned that his product not only be pure, but also have color, flavor, and crispness that will be maintained until the product is actually consumed. In a large measure, such quality is achieved by having the right processes and facilities and by standard procedures for both manufacturing and packaging. Nevertheless, control is necessary to assure that the plans are being carried out properly.

A key question is where to exercise such control. In this company checks are made at the following points: (a) occasional samples of raw materials are tested to be sure that they meet industry standards; (b) moisture tests are made every half hour during the cooking process, since this is a key factor in the final texture in the product; (c) all cornflakes passing from the oven to the packaging room are inspected visually for proper color; (d) a roving inspector sees that processes are being performed as specified and that cleanliness standards are observed; (e) an inspector opens samples of packages ready for shipment to see whether the final product comes up to standard.

Note that several inspections are made early in the process to avoid expense and confusion of rejecting substandard merchandise at a later stage. Heavy reliance is placed on sampling; this cuts the costs of inspection, and it is feasible because the entire operation is highly standardized. The visual test for color (the only 100% inspection in the entire process) really works with a *symptom*; improper color may be caused by several different things, which are immediately checked as soon as a deviation is detected. These particular features of the control system—control in the early stages, use of sampling, and watching a symptom that responds to several different causes—have possible application in all sorts of control problems.

Control of sales volume. For many years a chemical company had kept track of its sales in terms of dollars and physical units for each major line of products. Trends in these figures were the cause of rejoicing or dismay, but a new sales manager felt that they did not enable him to pinpoint difficulties and to take specific corrective action. Consequently, he expanded the sales control system in two ways. First, he kept track of sales results in much greater detail; all orders were analyzed in terms of salesmen, types of customers, geographical areas, and products, and cross-classifications of each category were charted. Second, he tried to develop some criteria for what sales should be in each category. For this purpose, he developed an index of activity for types of customers (consumer industries), geographical regions, and long-term trends for products. From this information and data on past sales, he developed quotas for subdivisions of the sales analysis. These quotas were adjusted up or down as changes occurred in the market.

These two steps generated a mass of statistics. However, with the aid of a sales analyst, the sales manager could identify particular areas or industries where orders were falling behind quota. Often the salesman concerned had a good explanation for the deviation, but in other instances remedial action was obviously called for. The salesmen grumbled about spending a great deal of their time with the new statistics. The sales manager, on the other hand, was convinced that the expanded controls brought to light difficulties that might have remained buried in the large totals formerly used. Experience also indicated that the salesmen, who received the control data as soon as the sales manager, became more diligent about covering each part of their assigned territory.

This example raises the question of how detailed controls should be. The previous controls of the chemical company were too general to be useful for operating purposes. On the other hand, if the company had pursued the pattern of control to very small territories and fine industry divisions, the mass of statistics would have been overwhelming and the variations of doubtful significance.

Another notable feature of the system was a variable standard. If industrial activity in a salesman's territory was booming, he was expected to secure higher sales, whereas a decline in the market he served was also taken into account in appraising his results. The assumption here is that the factors causing the expansion or the contraction in the market were beyond the salesman's control.

Inventory control. One way to achieve control in considerable detail and still not swamp executives with masses of information is to have measuring and corrective action taken by the men who are performing the operation—or perhaps done automatically. This possibility is illustrated by the inventory control system of a cash register manufacturer. This firm has to keep on hand 65,000 different parts so that finished machines can be assembled rapidly as customers' orders are received.

Briefly, the control system involves: (a) Establishing the minimum stock for each part (the standard). Whenever the supply on hand falls below this minimum, a standard order for additional stock is placed. (b) Maintaining a perpetual inventory record of each item and comparing this with the minimum standard. Formerly, this record and its examination (appraisal) was done by stock men on tags attached to the front of the bin containing each part. More recently, maintenance of the inventory record and comparison with the ordering point has been assigned to an electronic computer. (c) Whenever the stock on hand falls below the minimum standard, a requisition for additional materials is issued (corrective action). Of course, as demand and technology change, the standards have to be adjusted, and periodically a physical inventory is taken to make sure that the records are accurate.

This rather conventional inventory control system suggests two possibilities for many other controls. Once a clear-cut control is designed, it often can be operated by men close to the operation, perhaps the operators themselves. Upper management then can limit its attention to design of the system and checking to be sure that it is being properly utilized. And, in the extreme, when both the standards and the corrective action are clear-cut and current performance can be measured in quantitative terms, the entire control process can be automated.

Control of large capital expenditures. Typically, large capital expenditures must be approved by the board of directors before they can be advanced beyond the planning stage. Often all projects contemplated for a year are assembled together in a capital expenditures budget, as explained in Chapter 14, and specific approval is given for those projects the board considers most desirable. Once approved, the project becomes the control standard, and subsequent steps are checked against this standard.

In terms of the basic control process, this procedure differs significantly from the controls we have been examining. It is *pre-action control*. Action may not proceed until approval is given. The board of directors may have some standards it uses in deciding what will be approved, but it reserves the function of comparing specific proposals against its standards before any damage can be done. This holding a tight rein is in sharp contrast to a control system that operates routinely, if not automatically.

Every executive maintains control over some activities by withholding permission to act until he gives his approval to the specific act. Appointment of key personnel, signing large contracts, selling fixed assets, and starting a sales campaign are often treated in this manner. Progress is slowed, but the executive feels the particular subject is of such importance that he is unwilling to rely upon such standards as he can define with appraisal after the action is underway or completed. Obviously only a limited number of activities may be treated in this manner in a large, vigorous enterprise.

Control of executive development. The examples of control discussed thus far have all dealt primarily with objective data. Many important aspects of business operation are not so clear-cut. Nevertheless, control of these intangibles may be even more crucial to long-run success than things that are easily observed and measured. Executive development falls into this intangible category.

One well-managed company measures its progress in executive development in two ways. Annually, each key executive must report executive development activities undertaken by men in his department. The report covers special training assignments, appraisal reviews, training meetings, civic and trade association activities, and the like. The company recognizes that such reports omit perhaps the most important training that takes place on the job and also that the activities reported may not have resulted in any significant executive development. However, the hope is that emphasis on training activities will encourage executives and men alike to give attention to the basic process.

The second measure used by this company is the number of people considered to be ready for promotion. Data for this purpose are assembled from an executive inventory, such as described in Chapter 21. Again the unreliability of the data is recognized, but they are used simply as the best thing available.

Two control techniques are illustrated in the case just cited. One is the use of activities rather than end results. This is done because the company cannot afford to wait until the end of the process (5, 10, or 20 years in the case of executive development). Moreover, actual measurement of progress is difficult if not impossible. Basic research, legal work, and public relations are further examples of business functions posing this sort of measurement problem.

The case also illustrates the use of danger signals—or advance warnings—as a control device. If the number of men classified as promotable is inadequate to meet projected requirements, a danger signal has clearly appeared. In fact, more promotable men may be present than the inventory shows, or conversely, the estimates of employees' capacity to take on added responsibilities may be over-optimistic. Nevertheless, the warning is sufficiently serious so that more careful consideration and probably corrective action is called for. Every good control system makes wide use of danger signals because they help to identify trouble in the early stages.

The attempts to control executive development just described also illustrate a danger. Executives can become so absorbed in making the measures look good—for example, lots of training meetings and high evaluations of subordinates—that they fail to accomplish the underlying objective. In other words, because the controls do not deal specifically with desired end-results, they may misdirect effort.

Standards of performance. The cases discussed above illustrate various kinds of control problems. Now, let us turn to a more general review of the three basic steps in the control process—setting standards, appraising results, and corrective action.

Some standard or guide is essential in any form of control. Even informal control requires that the executive have some plan or standard in his mind by which to appraise the activities he is supervising. These standards should come directly from the objectives, policies, deadlines, specifications, and other goals established in earlier stages of the management cycle.

Satisfactory performance, of course, has many aspects, and it is impractical to set control standards for all of these points. Instead, strategic control spots are picked out for regular observation. Important considerations in picking these strategic points are: (a) catching important deviations in time to take corrective action; (b) practicality and economy in making observations; (c) providing some comprehensive controls that consolidate and summarize large blocks of detailed activities; and (d) securing a balance in control so that some aspects of the work, such as developing executives, will not be slighted because of close controls on other phases. What to watch is vital in every simple and effective control system.

"How good is good" is the next question. For each control point, an acceptable level of performance must be set. How many sales orders per month do we expect Joe Jones to obtain? What level of absenteeism is considered dangerous? Is a labor cost of $13.95 per unit satisfactory for our deluxe model? The answers to such questions become the accepted norms—the par for the course. One of the best ways of providing flexibility in a control system is to devise acceptable and prompt ways of adjusting these norms.

Appraising performance. Some comparison of actual performance with control standards may be done by a manager himself. A foreman in a plant, for example, exercises much of his control by direct observation of each worker and by examining the finished work. A sales manager may occasionally travel with salesmen to observe their performance and the attitudes of customers. Typically, however, control observations are made by someone other than the executive—an inspector, a cost analyst, market research man, and the like. Also, some control data is derived as a by-product of other record keeping. Expense data, for instance, may come from payroll and inventory records; sales data may be gleaned from a file of customers' orders.

Such separation of measuring performance from its evaluation and corrective action necessitates *control reports*. The information must be communicated from person to person, and this raises a host of questions: What form should be used? How much detail should they contain? To whom should they be sent? How often should they go? Can reports be simplified by dealing only with exceptions to standards?

The effectiveness of a control is usually increased by prompt reporting. If some undesirable practice is going on, it should be corrected quickly. Moreover, the cause of trouble can be learned better if people have not had several weeks to forget the circumstances. Also, employees, knowing that a prompt check on deviations from standards will be made, are more likely to be careful in their daily work. Consequently, the sooner a control report reaches a manager, the better the control will be.

Another practical issue in appraisal is whether sampling will provide adequate information. Perhaps refined statistical techniques, such as statistical quality control, can be used to decide the size of the sample and the inferences that can be drawn from it.

In some operations—aircraft manufacturing, for example—100% observation is essential. And, we have already noted that for certain key actions—capital expenditures and executive appointments are typical—a manager may insist on giving his personal approval before performance continues.

The engineering term "measuring and feedback" provides another way of describing this appraisal step in the control process.

Corrective action. Real control goes beyond checking on work performed. Unless corrective action is taken when standards are not met, the process amounts to little more than a historical record.

As soon as an unfavorable deviation from standard is detected, the causes of the trouble should be investigated. Perhaps the difficulty will be due to a lack of supplies, a breakdown of machinery, a strike in a customer's plant, or other hindrance in operating conditions. In such situations, the executive will take immediate steps to remove any obstructions he can.

At other times, the difficulty will be personal in nature. Perhaps there is a simple misunderstanding, a failure in human communication; this may be quickly corrected. More troublesome is inadequate training of persons assigned to do the work. As a rule in such cases, help is provided for the person until he has received the training he needs. Of course, if investigation reveals that the person simply does not have the necessary basic ability—and never should have been selected for the job—transfer of the work or a replacement of the individual may be the only satisfactory remedy. All too often, the gap between performance and standard reflects a lack of effort. The person may be able to do the work, he may understand what is wanted, and the operating situation may be satisfactory, but the needed incentive is lacking. This, then, calls for additional motivation by the manager.

Corrective action sometimes leads to a revision of plans. The check on operating conditions and on selection, training, direction, and motivation of the operators may reveal that the standards themselves are unrealistic. If control is to have any meaning in the future, such standards should be revised. Also, the delay in work may have been so serious that schedules need to be rearranged, budgets revised, or customers notified. These changes in plans should give operators and executives a new set of standards that are reasonable criteria for future actions.

CENTRAL MANAGEMENT CONTROL TASKS

In a going concern, many controls exist within a single department, and some of these may be used by a single individual. Central management obviously should not try to follow all of these detailed controls. It is vitally concerned that adequate and balanced control be exercised by someone, and it will also follow results in selected key areas. Thus, central management is concerned with:

1. The design of the company control structure.
2. Exercising control of overall results and at particularly crucial points.

Company control structure. The control structure of a company is more than the simple aggregate of the various controls used by different executives. These controls should be examined to be sure that no important considerations are missing; balance and emphasis should be examined to be sure it is in harmony with basic company objectives; and the compatibility of the controls with company planning, organization, and supervision should be assured.

Assuring adequate coverage. The table on the following page suggests a way to examine a company control structure. In the left-hand column should be listed all those result areas that central management believes should be controlled by someone in the enterprise. The areas listed in the table are merely suggestive. In practice, the management of any single company will undoubtedly want to be much more specific on some points and to omit others.

With the result areas identified, senior executives can discover a great deal about control in their company by filling in the rest of the table. Usually a company will have very good controls in some areas and only vague and informal systems in others. This may be due to historical custom or to the relative ease of obtaining certain kinds of data. As a result of the analysis, central management will know where to try to devise additional controls that will fill in the missing gaps.

Relation of controls to decentralization. In thinking about who should set specific norms, appraise current performance, and take corrective action, organization structure should be related to control structure. The greater the decentralization of authority to make decisions, the further down the hierarchy should be the short-run control activity. It is simply inconsistent to tell a man

Approach to

COMPANY CONTROL STRUCTURE

	System Design		Exercising Controls		
Result Area to be Controlled	Control Points	Form of Measurement (Indexes)	Set Specific Norms (Pars)	Appraise and Report	Take Corrective Action
General Management:					
Profitability	———	———	Who?	Who?	Who?
Market Position	———	———	"	"	"
Productivity	———	———	"	"	"
Technical Research	———	———	"	"	"
Personnel Dev.	———	———	"	"	"
Employee Relations	———	———	"	"	"
Public Attitudes	———	———	"	"	"
Sales:					
Output	———	———	"	"	"
———	———	———	"	"	"
	———	———	"	"	"
Expenses	———	———	"	"	"
———	———	———	"	"	"
	———	———	"	"	"
Resources used	———	———	"	"	"
	———	———	"	"	"
———	———	———	"	"	"
Other	———	———	"	"	"
Production:					
Output	———	———	"	"	"
———	———	———	"	"	"
	———	———	"	"	"
Expenses	———	———	"	"	"
———	———	———	"	"	"
	———	———	"	"	"
Resources used	———	———	"	"	"
	———	———	"	"	"
———	———	———	"	"	"
Other	———	———	"	"	"
Research & Eng.:					
Output	———	———	"	"	"
———	———	———	"	"	"
	———	———	"	"	"
Expenses	———	———	"	"	"
———	———	———	"	"	"
	———	———	"	"	"
Resources used	———	———	"	"	"
	———	———	"	"	"
Other	———	———	"	"	"
All Other Divisions:					
———	———	———	"	"	"
———	———	———	"	"	"

that he has freedom to run a division or department and then have some outside person make frequent detailed checks of just what he is doing and suggest corrective action. In fact, control of routine activities is often performed further down the line than decision-making.

On the other hand, the manager who makes a delegation needs some reassurance that his authorization is being wisely used. Consequently, summary reports of results are submitted monthly or quarterly to senior executives. Also, the senior executive may wish to watch a limited number of "danger signals" both for control and as a basis for future planning.

In addition, the senior executive may want to be sure that adequate controls are being used by his subordinates, even though none of the reports come to him. A simple example is insistence on tight controls on cash disbursements in a branch office with no further attention (except the annual financial audit) being given by the supervising executive. Quality controls and production controls are frequently handled on the same basis. In effect, a pattern of control is stipulated when the subordinate manager is appointed, but exercise of this control is a part of the delegation made to him.

Integrated data processing. A total view of the control structure for a company emphasizes the large number of control reports that must pass through the organization. Original data have to be compiled and then analyzed, and reports must be sent to the operator, his boss, and perhaps a staff group. In addition, summaries or reports of exceptions probably go to a senior executive. The total of these reports in a large company is staggering.

Electronic data processing equipment can speed up the analysis and the distribution of this control information—*if* it is in numerical form. Perhaps such equipment can also cut the expense of report preparation, though the usual result is a substantial increase in the number of reports (better control) for hopefully the same expense. However, to achieve this speedier, elaborated flow, the procedures for handling data have to be revised. Potentially, all original data will be fed into the computer, and there it becomes available for planning as well as control purposes. We then have integrated data processing.

This new speed and ready availability of data should be utilized in the company control structure. It may make certain controls in headquarters, *or* in the field, more feasible. At the same time, a danger should be recognized—a plethora of numerical reports will increase the tendency to overemphasize those factors that can be expressed numerically. Consequently, integrated data processing should be regarded as an aid and not as a determining factor in the design of a company control structure.

Relation of controls to other phases of managing. In stressing the desirability of central management carefully shaping the company control structure, we are not suggesting that a lot of controls be superimposed on other management activities. For example, the target dates set in programming of normal operations automatically become norms in the control process; quality control standards are simply the logical extension of product policies dealing with quality; and so on. Controls are the means for assuring that such plans are fulfilled.

Similarly, goal-centered performance reviews include agreeing on personal goals for the next six months or a year and then comparing accomplishments with the goals at the end of the period. Many of the goals thus established will simply be norms for factors already included in the control structure, and control reports will be used in the discussion of results. Of course, additional unique goals may be agreed upon and a temporary control cycle set up. But if the company control structure deals with crucial areas, a factual basis will already exist for much of the performance appraisal discussion.

Controls exercised by central management. Design of an effective control structure is a major central management task. But even an ideal structure will not relieve central management from exercising some controls itself. Several attempts have been made to identify a limited number of key result areas that central management should watch. The most suggestive of these is a list used by the General Electric Company. According to this approach, the effectiveness of overall management can be appraised in terms of:

1. Profitability, in both percent of sales and return on investment.
2. Market position.
3. Productivity, which means improving costs as well as sales.
4. Leadership in technological research.
5. Development of future key people, both technical and managerial.
6. Employee attitudes and relations.
7. Public attitudes.
8. Balance of long- and short-range objectives.

Note that this list places considerable emphasis on strength for future growth as well as on current profitability.

In addition, the General Electric Company and others expect senior executives to single out crucial problems in their particular industry or function and to watch these closely. Incidentally, what is crucial shifts from time to time—union relations may be especially sensitive at one time, foreign competition at another. So, the attention of top management shifts, leaving for subordinates the task of continuing vigilance.

As emphasized in Chapter 20, central management has a particular responsibility to be alert to *new* developments that may create opportunities or obstacles. Consequently, much of the data examined by central management is not for routine control but a source of possible cues to future changes.

SUMMARY

Objectives, policies, and organization provide the broad guides and the framework for the activities of a company. Executive personnel, facilities, and other resources are means needed to make this structure a reality. Planning is then extended to detailed methods and procedures, and on to programs and schedules. The manager turns all this preparatory work into action as he issues operating instructions and motivates men to execute the plans. Even then, the task of managing is not complete; there remains the vital step of control.

Control is necessary to insure that actual performance conforms to plans. The specific measures for control should, of course, be adapted to the particular activity. Nevertheless, three basic steps must always be present: (1) Standards of satisfactory performance should be set up at strategic points—points that will provide timely, economical, comprehensive, and balanced checks—and, for each point, a norm or level of achievement should be agreed upon. (2) Actual performance should be compared with these standards by sampling, 100% inspection, or perhaps required confirmation, and appraisal reports should be sent to all persons directly involved. (3) When deficiencies are detected, corrective action is necessary—that is, adjusting operating conditions, improving competence of assigned operators, motivating, or perhaps modifying plans.

Most control in a company is exercised close to actual operations. Central management, however, is vitally concerned that a comprehensive and effective set of controls is being utilized and that the company control structure is correlated with other phases of management. Also, senior executives must exercise selective controls themselves. While not the most time-consuming task of central management, the ingenuity in design of a company control structure, coupled with skillful exercise of selected central control, does contribute substantially to company success.

One of the most useful forms of planning and control is company-wide budgeting—the subject of the following chapter.

QUESTIONS FOR CLASS DISCUSSION

1. Scientific management devoted much attention to motion and time study, production scheduling, selection and training of workers, preventive maintenance, material specifications, and other features of shop management. What bearing, if any, does each of these facets of scientific management have on the job of a plant superintendent in controlling operations in his plant?

2. What strategic control points (as defined on page 668) would you recommend to the president of Orient Magnetics Company (page 325) to help him insure that the major problems he saw were resolved satisfactorily?

3. Inspection to insure quality may take place (a) when raw materials are received, (b) during the processing, or (c) when goods are finished. What are the advantages and the limitations of controlling quality at each of these points in the production process? Can a similar breakdown of inspection points be established for controlling the quality of sales work? of purchasing?

4. Does the grouping of activities into departments and sections affect the ease or the difficulty of control? Use the organization of a department store and a meat-packing company to illustrate your answer.

5. What connection is there between control of output and (a) "method of payment" discussed in Chapter 12 and (b) "motivation" discussed in Chapter 24?

6. The statement of objectives given in Question 5 of Chapter 24 stresses return on investment. Since it is a number and also encompasses all the results of the activity of the firm or a major division, would it not be possible to use this ratio alone for central management control purposes in place of the elaborate table on page 672? Explain how the return on investment idea could be extended to divisions or major functional departments such as sales or production.

7. The nation's fifteenth largest bank (measured by capital) found itself ranked ninety-fifth in profits because it specialized in trust work and large corporate loans and had avoided complete bank wholesaling or retailing banking with local customers. To change the profit picture, the directors introduced a cost control system based on automation of all paper work and month-by-month reports of volume and expenses from each new "profit center." When cost cutting raised the profit ranking to ninetieth after the first year, the directors were pleased. In the second year, general business activity declined, the projection of commercial loans could not be attained, and investment policy was switched to tax-exempt municipals. Profits and ranking rose again for the total bank, the municipal and trust departments showed spectacular gains, and all other departments dropped except for the stock custody and transfer departments which showed further cuts in cost. Should the directors be pleased with their efforts at control?

8. A major central management control task, as explained on page 675, is to be alert to new developments and crucial problems. Based on your recommendations for the Silas Oates Company, or the Island Creek Coal Company, or the National Lumber and Plywood Corporation, or Western Nadir Markets, Inc., explain what data and data sources you would seek—as a chief executive—to insure your fulfilling this key responsibility.

9. Marks and Spencer, Ltd., a large British clothing-store chain, follows marketing policies of "quality first," tasteful design, and the lowest possible price. The company realized international fame and attention when it eliminated one million time cards, all time clocks, and all reports of illness and absenteeism. For these it substituted supervisors' direct observation. Half a million complaint reports were eliminated by a new policy of accepting exchanges without question. Stock requisitions were done away with, and salesgirls entered stock rooms directly to get items they needed. (Stock room losses remained at prior levels.) Documented reports on sales trends were eliminated. Visual observation of sales activity and stock levels replaced the reports. Elaborate and extensive laboratories and designing rooms were set up to state exact specifications for suppliers and to test all merchandise. The laboratories emphasize close cooperation with manufacturers. News reports stated that the British War Office, the United States Third Air Force, and numerous big business enterprises have studied the control methods introduced by Marks and Spencer. Why were they interested? What were they likely to learn?

CASE XXV

Auberge Hotels, Inc.

"I can't imagine a duller task than your taking a look at our system of controls," said William Herbert, the executive vice-president of Auberge Hotels, Inc. "A lot of the information that the system turns up is interesting and necessary for managing as well as for reports to our stockholders. But reviewing the system as a system is an activity that delights only our most sheltered and dedicated bureaucratic types. However, if you are determined to see what we do, I'll turn you over to Robert Lee, an assistant of mine. He will give you whatever you need."

With that bracing introduction, Mr. Herbert led me to an adjoining office to meet Mr. Lee. After explanations had been given, Lee said: "Essentially we have two reporting systems—one for the eight hotels in the Mid-West and another for our chain of inns and motels. There are enough differences between the motel business and the big-city downtown hotel industry to warrant separate systems. However, the differences are not so great that you need to understand more than one to see the basic ideas.

"Let's begin with the overall document, our ten-year summary by hotel (see Exhibit A on pages 680 and 681). We enter on this only the most significant information. By reviewing it you can see some interesting events—Chicago as compared to Indianapolis, for example."

We talked about this table for awhile. Mr. Lee then continued, "There are two kinds of perspectives important to us. One you see in the trends over time that we have just discussed. Another is in the comparison to industry results. Here is an old example (see Exhibit B). A review of it will show you what I have in mind even though it is only one instance from many.

Exhibit B

Hotel Operating Trends [1]

Year	Percentage of Occupancy	Average Room Rate	Total Revenues per Available Room	Percentage Gross Operating Profit	Net Profit after Income Taxes per Room
1941	67.5%	$ 3.66	$1,996	20.5%	loss
1946	92.0	4.73	3,936	22.8	$270
1951	78.4	7.03	4,463	20.7	178
1956	73.2	9.12	5,240	22.6	252
1961	65.8	11.13	5,581	21.1	148
1962	64.4	11.28	5,550	19.4	106
1963	62.6	11.27	5,378	18.1	49

[1] Averages for a nationwide sample of 400 hotels (which had 11% of total available guest rooms). Source: Harris, Kerr, Forster and Company, *Trends in the Hotel-Motel Business*, 1960 and 1963 editions.

"Beyond this we get a lot of data on each hotel. Most of the data goes into the files here, although it is used carefully by the hotel general manager. Occasionally we will dig it out for a review of a special problem. I am talking mainly about the monthly statement for each hotel, which shows its actual revenues, costs, and net for the month as well as comparisons with the same month of the year before and with the forecast budget figures for that month. (As part of the planning process in the company, each hotel general manager submitted a twelve-month advance budget twice a year.) Here is a sample (Exhibit C) so that you can see what I mean. The figures are for one of the heavy months.

Exhibit C

The Indianapolis Auberge

Monthly Data

Item	Forecast	Actual	% Variation	Last Year	Variation from Last Year
Revenue:					
Room Sales ...	$264,785	$254,255	4.0 R	$257,044	1.1 R
Food Sales	187,306	173,136	7.3 R	192,500	10.1 R
Beverage Sales .	80,000	70,370	12.0 R	74,517	5.6 R
All Other Revenue	35,875	38,122	6.3	42,517	10.3 R
Gross Operating Profit	$173,689	$181,117	4.3	$182,408	.7 R
Profit Before Rent, Depreciation, Interest, and Income Taxes .	$160,425	$167,776	4.6	$182,408	8.0 R
Deductions:					
General & Admin.	$26,000	$ 21,197	18.5 R	$ 19,961	6.2
Payroll Taxes and Employee Benefits	21,300	18,639	12.5 R	14,542	28.2
Advertising	14,850	12,206	17.8 R	13,618	10.4 R
Heat, Light & Power	23,000	20,735	9.8 R	21,345	2.9 R
Repairs & Maintenance ..	25,300	25,373	.3	32,217	21.2 R
Rooms & Dept'l Profit %	73.00%	74.57	1.57	74.27	.30
Food Dept'l Profit %	15.00%	18.05	3.05	18.37	.32 R
Beverage Dept'l Profit %	47.00%	52.25	5.25	50.47	1.78
Cash Payroll % to Operating Income		31.99%		31.45%	.54
House Profit	30.60%	32.66	2.06	32.19	.47

Exhibit A

Ten-Year Summary (all dollar figures in thousands)

	1955	1956	1957	1958	1959	1960	1961	1962	1963	1964
The Congreve, Chicago										
Revenue	$ 8,700	$ 8,700	$ 8,800	$ 8,800	$ 8,830	$ 9,120	$ 8,960	$ 9,000	$ 8,600	$ 8,500
Percent occupancy	71.4	69.6	64.2	62.4	62.4	61.8	60.3	59.8	58.3	58.1
Gross operating profit	2,340	2,390	2,350	2,410	2,430	2,440	2,220	2,000	1,940	1,980
Profit before income taxes	782	900	790	845	795	675	571	422	344	425
(998 Rooms)										
The Addison, Chicago										
Revenue	$10,800	$10,900	$11,100	$11,000	$11,420	$11,300	$11,210	$11,220	$11,230	$11,150
Percent occupancy	77.6	77.6	73.5	71.8	73.2	69.3	67.2	67.1	66.4	66.2
Gross operating profit	2,910	3,000	2,950	3,020	3,150	3,030	2,800	2,620	2,510	2,600
Profit before income taxes	975	1,130	1,000	1,050	1,030	835	698	512	450	565
(1003 Rooms)										
The Milwaukee Auberge										
Revenue	$ 3,610	$ 3,800	$ 3,700	$ 3,500	$ 3,580	$ 3,660	$ 3,500	$ 3,200	$ 3,000	$ 2,860
Percent occupancy	72.3	69.5	65.1	58.8	59.6	58.3	54.6	51.1	50.0	48.5
Gross operating profit	975	1,070	975	961	980	1,000	860	730	670	680
Profit before income taxes	325	392	334	333	322	270	240	180	120	143
(500 Rooms)										
The Columbus Auberge										
Revenue	$ 4,850	$ 4,810	$ 5,000	$ 4,980	$ 4,950	$ 4,900	$ 4,880	$ 4,800	$ 4,850	$ 5,040
Percent occupancy	65.6	64.7	63.4	60.4	59.4	56.7	56.2	55.9	55.4	56.0
Gross operating profit	1,310	1,320	1,320	1,362	1,358	1,310	1,230	1,120	1,090	1,210
Profit before income taxes	436	496	450	474	446	362	300	250	194	252
(800 Rooms)										

Exhibit A (Concluded)

Ten-Year Summary (all dollar figures in thousands)

	1955	1956	1957	1958	1959	1960	1961	1962	1963	1964
The Cleveland Auberge										
Revenue	$ 6,200	$ 6,100	$ 6,600	$ 6,850	$ 6,550	$ 5,750	$ 5,400	$ 5,300	$ 5,280	$ 5,100
Percent occupancy	71.5	69.2	66.4	65.0	58.3	51.7	49.2	48.3	48.0	47.1
Gross operating profit	1,680	1,675	1,740	1,880	1,795	1,540	1,400	1,310	1,180	1,220
Profit before income taxes	558	630	592	650	580	424	380	280	210	260
(900 Rooms)										
The Detroit Auberge										
Revenue	$ 6,200	$ 6,150	$ 6,180	$ 5,810	$ 6,090	$ 5,720	$ 5,600	$ 5,680	$ 5,880	$ 5,920
Percent occupancy	77.4	74.3	70.8	65.4	65.1	61.8	59.1	59.2	60.3	61.2
Gross operating profit	1,650	1,690	1,615	1,600	1,661	1,530	1,420	1,360	1,320	1,420
Profit before income taxes	560	635	556	555	545	423	334	254	234	301
(730 Rooms)										
The Indianapolis Auberge										
Revenue	$ 7,260	$ 7,230	$ 6,980	$ 6,410	$ 6,810	$ 6,500	$ 5,785	$ 5,500	$ 5,280	$ 5,320
Percent occupancy	72.3	71.5	65.2	57.0	57.5	54.3	51.0	49.0	47.9	48.1
Gross operating profit	1,960	1,990	1,840	1,760	1,832	1,740	1,430	1,280	1,182	1,260
Profit before income taxes	650	750	630	610	612	480	321	250	212	265
(1,000 Rooms)										
The Pittsburgh Auberge										
Revenue	$ 3,810	$ 3,980	$ 4,040	$ 4,010	$ 3,850	$ 3,810	$ 3,660	$ 3,590	$ 3,510	$ 3,640
Percent occupancy	66.8	67.3	66.6	62.4	57.2	56.7	55.1	54.3	53.8	54.5
Gross operating profit	1,020	1,095	1,060	1,100	1,055	1,020	920	830	790	870
Profit before income taxes	344	415	365	381	346	292	202	160	140	182
(600 rooms)										

Gross operating profit = Total revenues less cost of goods sold, departmental wages and expenses, and administrative and utilities expenses.

Profit before taxes = Gross operating profit less fire insurance, franchise taxes, real estate taxes, depreciation, interest, and other capital expenses.

"For more effective control through figures, we rely at head-quarters on a quarterly summary of the profit and loss for each hotel as well as comparisons with the same quarter of the previous year and the budget forecast for the quarter. I look at this very carefully and note special points that Mr. Herbert should pay attention to. In turn he looks at all the data so that he can answer to directors who also review these sheets at their regular quarterly meeting.

"The final kind of numerical reports we use for control over all cost-producing activities is a special study. At odd intervals we may look into or call for anything from a study of maintenance costs by hotel to a study of restaurants. Here is an example of the most recent of these special studies. (See Exhibits D and E.) I think you will find something interesting about the returns for entertainment and for the various hotels in this one. Also here is a list of special reports over the past year (Exhibit F).

"I don't know for sure what you consider to be a control activity, but my definition includes two more things that we consider quite important. The first is the work of the Space and Resources Com-

Exhibit D

Food Department Comparison

Year to Date — October

(all dollar figures in thousands)

Departmental Sales	1964	1963	1962
Congreve	$ 2,429	$ 2,412	$ 2,372
Indianapolis	1,434	1,464	1,491
Pittsburgh	861	852	853
Addison	1,527	1,471	1,414
Cleveland	2,718	2,427	1,889
Columbus	2,501	2,534	2,508
Detroit	2,329	2,130	1,990
Percentage of Dept'l Profit			
Congreve	4.7%	6.5%	7.5%
Indianapolis	2.4	6.1	5.7
Pittsburgh	12.0	12.1	9.2
Addison	6.1	4.0	2.5
Cleveland	9.9	9.0	1.1
Columbus	5.8	7.4	7.0
Detroit	12.0	14.2	9.0
Average Check			
Congreve	$2.06	$1.99	$1.84
Indianapolis	2.51	2.41	2.37
Pittsburgh	2.60	2.53	2.54
Addison	2.65	2.52	2.49
Cleveland	5.44	5.13	4.79
Columbus	4.45	4.38	4.36
Detroit	2.53	2.49	2.33

Exhibit E

The Congreve

Restaurant Study

Year to Date

	Cafe Blanc	Sky Room	Coffee Shop	Banquets
Revenue				
Food	$428,804	$703,760	$111,801	$1,061,092
Beverage	195,907	74,086		
Cover Charge	95,492			81,448[1]
Miscellaneous				11,198
Cost of Sales	194,656	275,833	38,100	297,458
Salaries and Wages	124,224	222,788	38,592	203,081
Supplies	53,500	45,000	25,685	68,882
Other Employee Costs	28,000	60,859	8,773	38,879
Music and Entertainment ..	156,696	13,714	......	....
Indirect Expenses	88,732	90,438	27,854	146,237
Advertising	45,552	351	34	458
Room Profit	$ 28,833	$ 68,863	($27,237)	$ 398,743

[1] Room rental.

Exhibit F

Index to Special Studies for the Past Year

1. Payroll taxes, 10-year review.
2. Trade association dues and contributions.
3. Charitable contributions.
4. Complimentary rooms.
5. Write-offs and accounts turned over to collection agents.
6. Productivity report.
7. Repairs and maintenance—comparative costs.
8. Utility cost and consumption comparison.
9. Jewelry vault thefts.
10. Personnel turnover study.
11. Vacant rooms and out-of-order rooms.
12. Food and beverage—average checks.
13. Private label beverage report.
14. Other expense—Food Department.
15. Comparative laundry costs.

mittee. This is a group made up of our three most experienced hotel general managers, our operating vice-president, Mr. Phillips, and our executive vice-president, Mr. Herbert. Their role in this committee is to look at the space available in each hotel and to attempt to find ways to maximize the profitable use of that space. As an example, they recently sliced a large ballroom in two horizontally. The ballroom had an unusually—excessively—high ceiling. The committee retained the ballroom, but put another meeting room on top of it to serve group gatherings of all kinds. The money these days for large, downtown hotels is in group and convention business, so you can see the value of using the space this way. Another example—a barber shop was moved from the main floor to a mezzanine and was replaced by an airlines reservations office. This tripled our revenues from the space.

"The second activity I had in mind was personal visits by Mr. Herbert and Mr. Phillips to each hotel. They spend two days every six months in each hotel for the major purpose of reviewing what is going on in that property with the general manager. They talk about everything related to expenses from local wage rates to air-conditioning. The content of the talk varies with each hotel and depends upon the situation at the time. My view of this is that it is a major way for the chief executives to gather information about what is occurring in the chain. Since it involves all their senses, I think it is an even better way than formal reports to form an estimate of the behavior of the firm.

"I suppose there is one more activity I should mention. We have a group of internal auditors checking on various accounting matters and reviewing our fraud-detecting procedures. Our public accountants insist that this work is necessary, but I have never seen it result in anything that had any significance for managerial action. From that view, their salaries are a waste of dollars. We don't have too many to waste.

"This completes what I believe to be our control procedures. I think it answers what you had in mind as you explained it when we began. If you come up with any ideas from reviewing what I have said or from looking over the reports, I should certainly be glad to hear them. Good luck."

Mr. Lee opened the door of his office. I walked out into the corridor.

REQUIRED: (a) Analyze each exhibit to ascertain the information useful in it for central management purposes. Explain the conclusions you draw from appraising the data.

(b) Appraise the control system of the company. In doing this, look at (1) the kinds of information and reports needed to fulfill company objectives and to assist in the major tasks of central management; (2) the kinds of information provided by the control system; and (3) how complete the system is in satisfying the needs you see.

CHAPTER
26 BUDGETARY CONTROL

Budgeting involves the statement of future plans in specific numerical terms, usually financial accounts. Although commonly called "budgetary control," the process also aids planning and coordinating as well as control. In fact, when used on a company-wide basis, it often becomes one of the basic tools executives use to manage operations. This chapter first reviews the underlying techniques of budgetary control and then considers some of the problems in using budgets for central management purposes.

Essential features of budgetary control. Good budgeting involves:

(1) *A statement of plans for a given period in the future expressed in specific, numerical terms.* Sales plans, for example, must be reduced to an estimate of the dollar and the unit sales volume that is anticipated. Other departments must follow a similar procedure and restate their plans in numerical estimates.

(2) *Coordination of these estimates into a well-balanced program.* The production department must plan to manufacture the kind and quantity of products that the sales department hopes to sell, and the plans of the purchasing department must be adjusted so that raw materials will be available when required by the production department. Should the plans of these and other departments require more cash than will become available during the normal course of operation, either the plans must be readjusted or the treasurer will have to plan to secure additional funds from some outside source.

(3) *Preparation of reports showing a comparison between actual and estimated performance, and revision of the original plan when such reports show that a revision is necessary.* If the budgets are to be an effective control device, actual performance must be compared with the estimates so that reasons for failure to meet the plan can be determined and a revised plan agreed upon.

685

Examples of nonfinancial budgets. Not all budgets are in dollar terms. For instance, a raw materials budget may be expressed in pounds or yards of specific commodities. Similarly, a personnel budget may show the number of men or man-hours of each type of skill needed to carry out a given activity. Finished goods budgets are often stated in terms of quantities of each product, as was done by the shirt manufacturer described in Chapter 23. Such nonfinancial budgets are vital for detailed planning and control.

General company-wide plans, on the other hand, can rarely be stated in physical terms because so many different things are involved. For overall planning, some common denominator is needed. This common unit is dollars. The specific plans are translated into dollars, as far as possible, and then the plans are more easily compared, added, and condensed into estimates that can be quickly reviewed by anyone concerned. There is danger, of course, that dollar estimates will be used without giving thought to the more specific physical units they represent, and also that the intangible factors that cannot be expressed in dollars will be overlooked. For comprehensive budgets, however, the dollar is the most satisfactory unit we have yet devised.

BUDGETARY CONTROL IN A BUSINESS

Any firm that budgets its entire operations must prepare numerous estimates and subsidiary budgets before a plan for the entire company can be combined into the master budget. For our purposes, a few condensed samples of such budgets will illustrate how the process works.

Sales budget. The Nonskid Tire Company produces only one product. For purposes of simplification, let us assume that this product is sold to wholesale dealers at a constant price of $13 a tire, with credit terms of 30 days after shipment. On the basis of experience and anticipated market conditions, the sales department estimates that the sales next year will be 890,000 tires distributed monthly as shown in the table on the following page.

Finished goods budget. The sales budget does not necessarily represent the production schedule. To have tires ready to meet the spring demand and to keep plant operations fairly stable, the production manager planned to produce 5,000 tires above shipments

Sales Budget

	Number of Tires Shipped	Value of Shipments
January	65,000	$ 845,000
February	65,000	845,000
March	70,000	910,000
April	75,000	975,000
May	85,000	1,105,000
June	90,000	1,170,000
July	85,000	1,105,000
August	80,000	1,040,000
September	75,000	975,000
October	70,000	910,000
November	65,000	845,000
December	65,000	845,000
Total for year	890,000	$11,570,000

each month during the first 4 months of the year and then to level off at 80,000 per month through August. Once the production rate was set in physical terms, it was converted into dollars for overall budgeting.

Materials purchase budget. From the production schedule, monthly material requirements were estimated, and these provided the basis for purchasing plans. For example, each tire requires 8 pounds of rubber, and the Nonskid Tire Company has a policy of carrying crude and synthetic rubber inventory equal to requirements for the next 3 months. With this information the following purchase budget for crude rubber was prepared:

Crude Rubber Budget
(in thousands of pounds)

	Opening Inventory	Purchases	Required for Production	Closing Inventory
January	1720	640	560	1800
February	1800	640	560	1880
March	1880	640	600	1920
April	1920	640	640	1920
May	1920	640	640	1920
June	1920	600	640	1880
July	1880	560	640	1800
August	1800	520	640	1680
September	1680	520	600	1600
October	1600	560	560	1600
November	1600	560	520	1640
December	1640	600	520	1720
Total		7120	7120	

Purchase requirements for other materials were estimated in a similar fashion. The company found substantial savings could be secured by contracting to purchase its fabric requirements for an entire year. The company agreed to pay one third of the purchase price in March and the balance in monthly installments of $200,000. The fabric was to be delivered as paid for.

These material budgets had to be stated in terms of physical units for purposes of the purchasing department. In addition, two conversions into financial terms were needed. Using estimated prices per unit, *cash disbursements* could be calculated, the time of disbursement being determined by the date of billing plus the normal credit period. Dollar estimates of *expenses,* on the other hand, depended on when the material was to be used.

Budgets for personnel and other expenses. For a complete budgetary program, estimates of personnel requirements are needed. Here again it may be desirable to prepare budgets in physical units as well as in dollars, because the personnel department must adjust its selection and training program to provide for the type and the quantity of labor required.

Every company has expenses other than materials and payrolls that often amount to a substantial part of the total. Insurance, taxes, interest, electric current, depreciation, professional fees, and many other items must be recognized. For the Nonskid Tire Company it was estimated that miscellaneous factory overhead items would amount to $55,000 a month, and in addition there would be a charge of $20,000 a month for depreciation on machinery. The advertising program called for monthly expenses varying from $35,000 to $43,000, and administrative expenses were about $26,500 per month. Semiannual interest payments on the bond issue were $25,000.

Note that the payroll expenses are based on people employed and the other expenses on actual activities in the month when they are expected to occur. (They are *not* based on *averages* per unit of output.) This practice is necessary if budgets are to be used for coordinating purposes; it also shows up the effect of fixed expenses when volume is high or low.

Cash budgets. One of the most important types of budgets shows the estimated receipts and disbursements of cash and the resulting fluctuation in the cash position of the company. To prepare such an estimate, the planned receipts and disbursements of each activity must be consolidated into a single statement.

Care must be exercised to include only those items that involve cash. The production of additional inventory and the selling of merchandise on credit may increase the assets, but until the inventory is sold for cash and the merchandise sold on credit is paid for by the customer, neither of these activities can result in an increase in cash receipts. There are also a number of items that are not normally considered expenses of the company that do require cash outlays. When a company invests cash in new equipment or buildings, for example, these items are not charged directly to expense but are treated as assets that will serve the company over a period of time. The Nonskid Tire Company, for example, plans to make capital expenditures of $10,000 a month for miscellaneous machinery in addition to the investment of $212,000 for the contemplated expansion in capacity. The company is also obligated to retire bonds amounting to $100,000 at the end of the year, and it plans to pay regular dividends on its preferred stock quarterly. The depreciation charges on fixed assets, however, are merely bookkeeping estimates which reflect the fact that the assets have given up some part of their value during a brief period of operation, but there is no cash outlay involved in such charges. It has been a policy of this company to buy in December enough government notes to cover its income tax for the year.

The resulting cash receipts and disbursements budget for the Nonskid Tire Company is shown on page 690.

The preparation of this cash budget discloses the need for the second basic step in budgetary procedure—the development of a workable program. The budget shows that the cash balance at the beginning of the year would be entirely depleted in March. Consequently, the company would either be required to secure additional capital or to change its plans. The budget shows, however, that this need for additional capital is only temporary.

Since the company already had established a credit line with a bank, the treasurer proposed to meet this cash deficiency by a bank loan. No company can operate without at least some cash, and, consequently, it is necessary to borrow enough money from the bank to keep the cash balance at a reasonable figure, which the

Monthly Cash Budget

(in thousands of dollars)

	Jan.	Feb.	March	April	May	June	July	Aug.	Sept.	Oct.	Nov.	Dec.
Receipts from Sales	845	845	845	910	975	1105	1170	1105	1040	975	910	845
Disbursements:												
Purchases	403	429	1121	639	639	639	623	597	571	526	377	387
Payroll	192	192	202	213	223	228	223	218	208	197	187	187
Factory overhead	55	55	55	55	55	55	55	55	55	55	55	55
Advertising and selling	35	35	37	39	43	43	43	41	39	37	35	35
Administrative	26	26	27	28	27	27	27	27	26	26	26	26
Interest on bonds and bond retirement	...	...	...	...	...	25	...	...	...	...	...	125
Preferred stock dividends and income tax notes	...	...	24	...	...	24	...	24	24	...	...	221
Capital expenditures	10	10	222	10	10	10	10	10	10	10	10	10
Total	721	747	1688	984	997	1051	981	948	933	851	690	1046
Cash Gain or (Loss) from Operations [1]	124	98	(843)	(74)	(22)	54	189	157	107	124	220	(201)
Opening Cash Balance	445	569	667	507	433	411	465	514	531	498	482	562
Cash Gain or (Loss) from Operations	124	98	(843)	(74)	(22)	54	189	157	107	124	220	(201)
Bank Loan	...	...	683	...	...	...	(140)	(140)	(140)	(140)	(140)	...
Closing Cash Balance	569	667	507	433	411	465	514	531	498	482	562	361

[1] Cash gain or loss is figured prior to borrowing from the bank so that the amount of money needed and the time when it might be repaid will be clearly shown. For purposes of computing profit or loss, the interest on the bank loan should be included with other operating expenses.

NOTE: Figures in parentheses indicate a cash loss.

treasurer estimated should be about $400,000 for the Nonskid Tire Company. It was planned to borrow $700,000 in March to be repaid in five installments of $140,000 each in July, August, September, October, and November. Interest at the rate of 5% per annum was to be discounted from the original amount received. The resulting monthly cash balances are shown on the bottom line of the table.

Budgeted profit and loss. The detailed information developed in the preceding budgets provides the basis for a monthly and annual profit and loss budget for the entire company. The yearly totals are given in the budgeted profit and loss statement at the top of page 692.

Now, if a net profit of approximately $204,000 is the best that can be expected by this company under prevailing conditions, the preceding budget will probably be approved. The management may take the attitude, however, that a return on common stock of only $108,000, after allowing for preferred stock dividends, is unreasonably low. In that case the management must review each of the supporting estimates to see if there is not some change in plans that might lead to improved results.

Estimated balance sheet at end of period. It is often desirable, particularly if the company is borrowing money from a bank, to estimate a balance sheet for the end of the budget period. This will indicate to all those dealing with the company's financial problems the probable financial status of the company. Moreover, such a balance sheet may have considerable bearing on the source from which the company secures its funds, or it may influence any decision to revise the program in order to conserve cash. The comparison of the balance sheet for the Nonskid Tire Company at the beginning of the year with the estimated balance sheet, based on the information already presented, at the end of the year is shown at the bottom of page 692.

Comparison of actual results with budget. Comparing actual results with the budget and making necessary adjustments in future plans to correct any difficulties revealed is largely a matter of thorough analysis to discover causes for variations from budgeted figures and the formulation of revised plans. To illustrate,

Budgeted Profit and Loss Statement for the Year

Net Sales			$11,570,000

Cost of Goods Sold:
  Materials:

Rubber	$2,848,000		
Fabric	2,047,000		
Other Materials	1,780,000		
Total Materials		$6,675,000	
Payroll		1,550,000	
Supplies		192,000	
Depreciation		240,000	
Overhead Items		660,000	
Total Cost of Goods Sold			9,317,000
Gross Profit			$ 2,253,000

Operating Expenses:
  Selling Expenses:

Payroll	$ 800,000		
Supplies	48,000		
Advertising and Selling	462,000		
Total Selling Expense		$1,310,000	

  Administrative Expenses:

Payroll	$ 120,000		
Supplies	36,000		
Other Administrative Expenses	319,000		
Interest	67,000		
Total Administrative Expenses		542,000	
Total Operating Expenses			1,852,000
Operating Profit			$ 401,000
Income Tax			197,000
Net Profit			$ 204,000

Budgeted Balance Sheet at End of Year Compared with Actual Balance Sheet at Beginning of Year

Assets	Actual Beginning of Year	Budget End of Year
Cash	$ 445,000	$ 361,000
Accounts Receivable	845,000	845,000
Finished Inventory	262,000	262,000
Raw Materials	1,158,000	1,158,000
Fixed Assets (net)	2,420,000	2,512,000
Total Assets	$5,130,000	$5,138,000
Liabilities and Capital		
Accounts Payable	$ 403,000	$ 403,000
Bonds	1,000,000	900,000
Preferred Stock	1,750,000	1,750,000
Common Stock	1,500,000	1,500,000
Retained Earnings	477,000	585,000
Total Liabilities and Capital	$5,130,000	$5,138,000

suppose that the Nonskid Tire Company operated according to its budget for the first ten months of the year, but in November a softening of material prices precipitated a "price war" in the industry, and the company was forced to lower its selling price to $10 a tire in order to maintain the planned volume of sales. In December prices were stabilized at $12 a tire, but many dealers and consumers had built up stocks in November so the volume of sales dropped to 50,000 tires. Moreover, an 8% drop in material prices and a 5% drop in finished goods costs necessitated a downward adjustment in the book value of company inventories.

As a result of these conditions, the profit and loss statement and the balance sheet at the end of the year compared with the budgeted figures are as shown on the following page.

The first striking difference between the budget and the actual performance is a decline in sales of $440,000, which can be explained by the reduction of $3 in the selling price during November and the reduction in the number of tires sold during December from 65,000 to 50,000 coupled with a $1 reduction in selling price. The cost of goods sold in December was also lower to the extent that costs were variable, but the gross profit still showed an unfavorable variance from the budget of $314,000. In addition, the company took a loss of $105,000 on inventories on hand at the end of the year. Income taxes were reduced, of course, but the net loss for the year was $8,000 compared with a planned profit of $204,000. Thus, by the examination of a single table and an analysis of the conditions reflected in the figures, an executive could understand why the company suffered a loss.

An explanation of the differences between the actual and the budget balance sheets for the end of the year requires an understanding of the inventory and financial policies followed. As far as possible the executives tried to secure a closing inventory of materials and finished goods of the same size as planned. This meant that production had to be reduced by 15,000 tires in December because of lower sales, which in turn reduced the raw materials purchased during that month. Fabric was already purchased for 65,000 tires so that an extra supply of this material was on hand at the close of December. The physical inventory of other materials and of finished goods, however, remained as budgeted.

More than offsetting the increased inventory of fabric was the decline in the value of goods on hand, causing a net reduction in

Comparison of
Actual Profit and Loss for Year with Budget

	Budget	Actual	Difference
Net Sales	$11,570,000	$11,130,000	—$440,000
Cost of Goods Sold:			
Materials	$ 6,675,000	$ 6,560,000	—$115,000
Payroll	1,550,000	1,538,000	— 12,000
Supplies	192,000	189,000	— 3,000
Depreciation	240,000	240,000	....
Overhead Items	660,000	664,000	+ 4,000
Total Cost of Goods			
Sold	$ 9,317,000	$ 9,191,000	—$126,000
Gross Profit	$ 2,253,000	$ 1,939,000	—$314,000
Operating Expenses:			
Selling Expenses	$ 1,310,000	$ 1,300,000	—$ 10,000
Administrative Expenses.	542,000	542,000	....
Loss on Revaluation of			
Inventory	....	105,000	+ 105,000
Total Operating			
Expenses	$ 1,852,000	$ 1,947,000	+$ 95,000
Operating Profit or (Loss) .	$ 401,000	$ (8,000)	—$409,000
Income Tax	197,000	....	— 197,000
Net Operating Profit or			
(Loss)	$ 204,000	$ (8,000)	—$212,000

Comparison of
Actual and Budgeted Balance Sheet at End of Year

Assets	Budget	Actual	Difference
Cash	$ 361,000	$ 396,000	+$ 35,000
Accounts Receivable	845,000	600,000	— 245,000
Finished Inventory	262,000	249,000	— 13,000
Raw Materials	1,158,000	1,100,000	— 58,000
Fixed Assets (Net)	2,512,000	2,512,000	....
Total Assets	$5,138,000	$4,857,000	—$281,000
Liabilities and Capital			
Accounts Payable	$ 403,000	$ 310,000	—$ 93,000
Bonds	900,000	900,000	....
Preferred Stock	1,750,000	1,750,000	....
Common Stock	1,500,000	1,500,000	....
Retained Earnings	585,000	397,000	— 188,000
Total Liabilities and Capital	$5,138,000	$4,857,000	—$281,000

the value of raw material inventories of $58,000. Finished goods inventories also had to be reduced $13,000 in order to reflect the new costs. The reduction in accounts receivable and accounts payable reflects the reduction in December sales and rubber purchases respectively.

The story behind the change in cash involves several factors. First, a large part of the operating loss was caused by a revaluation of inventory; this was a book entry and involved no outflow of cash. Second, several disbursements were reduced; no income tax provision was needed and preferred stock dividends were omitted in December. Third, the reduction in money loaned to customers in the form of accounts receivable was a source of cash. These factors more than offset the loss in operating revenues so that cash was actually $35,000 higher than budget. This situation illustrates the point emphasized in Chapter 14 that losses and need for cash are not necessarily correlated.

This analysis of actual results compared with budgets shows clearly that the plans for the following year must be reviewed and probably altered to fit the change in competitive conditions that developed at the end of the current year. We now find ourselves back at the point where the discussion of the Nonskid Tire Company began—the formulation of budgets—ready to follow through the budgetary process for another year.

Flexibility in budgeting. The budgets for the Nonskid Tire Company already described, like any other budgets, should not be regarded as a final and unalterable plan that cannot be adjusted to meet different conditions than those anticipated when the plans were prepared. Each month, actual performance should be compared with the budgets. If this comparison indicates that the budget cannot be followed in the future or if one of the executives discovers a better plan, then corresponding adjustments can be made in the budget estimates.

For example, if the sales manager should decide that the anticipated sales will not materialize and recommends that the sales budget be reduced, this fact will be of immediate interest to several other executives. The production manger may want to make adjustments for reductions in operations, the purchasing agent may decide to purchase a lesser amount of raw materials, and the treasurer must revise his plans in the light of the changes as estimated by the other departments. The budget is a tool designed to assist management, and its achievement must never be permitted to become an end in itself when the management believes a different course of action to be more desirable.

Many companies make budget revisions regularly. One common way is to (a) revise the budget for one month on the 15th or 20th of the preceding month, and (b) make a new budget for the month twelve months off. In this way the company always has a budget for a year ahead, and the detailed operating plans for the month immediately ahead are revised in light of current operating conditions. All sorts of variations of this idea are possible; a company may use quarters instead of months; or an annual budget may be set up in general terms only and monthly budgets may be revised and extended as suggested for a three-month period.

If budgets are to be used only for purposes of expense control, then the so-called *flexible budget* may be helpful. Under this scheme, expenses are estimated for different levels of operation. Then after the budget period is over and the level of actual operations is known, the amount that expenses should have been for that level of operation can be determined. This gives an expense standard adjusted to rate of activity and is very useful in expense control. However, since flexible budgets deliberately do not set a level of operations until after the work is done, they are of little value in planning and coordination. Neither the purchasing agent who is buying materials nor the treasurer who must arrange bank loans can wait until until the month is over to decide what must be done. In other words, flexible budgets serve a special purpose, but they are not suited to comprehensive budgeting as it is discussed in this chapter. Periodic revisions are a much better way to get flexibility in budgeting for general management purposes.

CENTRAL MANAGEMENT USE OF BUDGETS

The impact of budgets on the operation of a firm depends upon how central management uses them. Planning, coordination, and control may all be aided if budgeting is made an integral part of the management process.

Effect of budgets on planning. *Benefits.* The preparation of budgets for several months or a year ahead encourages operating executives to anticipate problems—opportunities as well as obstacles—and to prepare to deal with them. Today's problems always seem pressing, and a busy executive naturally has difficulty finding time to lay careful plans for tomorrow. However, the need to submit budget estimates that will be fitted into a total plan for the company creates a pressure to think about future action and results. Moreover, the estimates have to be specific dollar amounts, usually on a monthly basis. This encourages care and concreteness in forward planning. And, since *all* expenses and incomes are included, the coverage of the planning is wide.

Budgets can easily be reconciled with most other forms of advance planning. For example, the effects of programs of the type discussed in Chapter 23 can be stated in financial terms and can become part of the budget estimates. Capital budgeting, considered in Chapter 14, is a means for selecting investment projects, and the estimated receipts and disbursements for the projects selected can be incorporated into the overall budgets.

Need for central management support. Budgeting encourages but does not guarantee careful advance planning. Some budget estimates are merely predictions. Predictions and plans are quite different psychologically. A prediction of an expense item or an income may involve no positive determination of what should be done; it may be merely a passive guess of what will happen.

Also, budget figures can be prepared by staff assistants who have little influence over actions taken. The busy boss may simply want some figures to turn in to the budget director and may give little thought to what they portray. In such a case, obviously the budget does not reflect careful planning and the operating executive has taken no self-imposed obligation to make the plans work.

To avoid these dangers, central management should itself use the budget as a planning mechanism. Senior executives should spend enough time with their subordinates reviewing estimates, asking about alternatives, and pressing for justification to assure that the budget figures do reflect careful plans. Insistence that financial figures be supported by plans in physical terms is a means toward this end. Staff men may help both central and departmental executives with the routine aspects of preparing estimates; but unless the key executives themselves actively participate, the planning benefits listed above will not be attained.

The amount of work necessary by important executives does suggest a limitation of budgets for long-range programming. Many activities reflected in a budget estimate need not be planned three to five years ahead, as revised estimates will undoubtedly be required when action is more imminent. Consequently, rough approximations are acceptable for parts of a budget for five years hence, whereas careful planning should lie back of those parts calling for immediate preparatory action. Confusion about which parts of a budget should be prepared with care and which can be mere predictions has led several companies to use budgets for only one or two years ahead, with longer range plans confined to a few key elements.

Budgets and coordination. Since budget estimates of one department are often dependent on activity of another department—for example, production on sales, purchasing on production—the process of putting together company-wide budgets stimulates a lot of interdepartment exchange of plans. Specific monthly plans can be cross-checked for consistency, especially if back-up figures in physical terms are exchanged.

Aside from the budget figures themselves, other information helpful to coordination typically is passed along in budget meetings. The sales manager, for example, may comment on competitive developments, and this information may dampen or whet the production department's interest in a new process. This sort of information, and the awareness of imbalance between departments, is likely to be disclosed early in budget discussions. Such early discovery of potential trouble is valuable because adjustments to secure coordinated company action are easier to make if the nature of the imbalance is known before one or more departments embark on a course of action.

Here again, central management support of the budgetary process is needed. Lack of balance may be spotted by the men who carefully review plans of several departments. Also the intercommunication and the attention to synchronization of plans is much more likely to occur if top management clearly demonstrates that budgeting is to be taken seriously.

Control via budgets. The most distinctive advantage of budgets as a control device is their comprehensive coverage. Normally all important accounts in the profit and loss statements are covered, and many of these figures will be subdivided by departments. We have no other index of performance that permeates an entire company so completely.

Also, budgetary control is simple in one important respect. Accounting records are already being compiled, so comparison of the budget plan with actual results entails no new measuring system. The entire mechanics—though not substance—of the compilation, measuring, and reporting of budgetary control data can be grafted onto a good accounting system with relative ease. These two advantages—comprehensive coverage and ease of installation—account for much of the popularity of budgets as a control device.

Unfortunately, the close tie of budgets with accounting is a mixed blessing. Financial accounting serves several masters. It pictures the condition of the company to the public; it serves as a basis for income tax returns; it guides financial planning; and lastly it aids in the general management of the firm. To fulfill the function of objective, conservative reporting to the public, a variety of rules have been established—notably the nonrecognition of intangibles. And, to provide data for tax returns, rules of the Internal Revenue Service are followed. Coupled with these restraints is the need for annual reports even though a year may not correspond to the cycle of operations of the industry (for example, aircraft building). As a consequence, financial accounts do not— and should not try to—reveal several aspects of company operations that vitally concern management, such as new product development, public relations, and specialized training of employees. We should recognize that budgetary control operates within the same limits as regular accounting and, comprehensive as it is, does not deal adequately with intangibles.

Also, no control device—including budgets—will have much impact on operations if it is not used regularly by key executives. If central management does not insist on an explanation of marked deviations of actual results from the budget, subordinate executives will probably also disregard the budget as a standard. Contrariwise, the executive who knows that a deviation is sure to be on the agenda of the next executive committee meeting will try to prevent the deviation or at least start corrective action before the meeting takes place. In other words, central management can determine how vital budgets will be as a control by its own behavior with respect to them.

SUMMARY

Good budgeting requires three steps: (1) the statement of plans for a given period in specific, numerical terms; (2) coordination of these estimates into a well-balanced program; and (3) comparison of actual results with the budget figures so that revision of plans can be made when necessary. While this process may be applied to a single type of expense or a separate department, the greatest value of budgeting comes from comprehensive budgets which cover the entire operations of a company.

Comprehensive budgeting provides several benefits: (a) Planning is improved because each executive must clarify his plans early and must think in concrete, specific terms. (b) Coordination is aided through dovetailing of plans prepared by several different departments, and through an early exchange of information among executives. (c) Control is facilitated by the provision of a comprehensive standard of performance; actual results can be readily compared with this standard since it is typically stated in terms of financial accounts.

Comprehensive budgeting is a supplement to, and not a substitute for, other aspects of good administration. For instance, clear-cut organization is needed for the preparation and the enforcement of budgets; policies serve as guides in drawing up plans that are then expressed in the budgets. Detailed programs and controls are still necessary if overall results are to be satisfactory. Budgeting encourages the use of these other managerial tools, and it makes a distinctive contribution in pulling diverse plans and activities into an integrated program of action.

For budgeting to achieve these results, however, central management must make it a vital part of the entire management process. Budget mechanics and reports are not enough. In fact, there is danger that a great deal of time will be wasted, especially by staff men, in preparing insignificant estimates if budgeting is treated as an afterthought to the main stream of decisions, instructions, and appraisals. But if central management insists that budget figures reflect concrete plans rather than casual estimates, that revisions be made in all interrelated budgets when one department modifies its plans, and that deviations of actual results from budget standards be dealt with aggressively, then "budgeting control" can serve as a major integrating mechanism for overall company administration.

QUESTIONS FOR CLASS DISCUSSION

1. A report of a recent meeting of the Budget Executives Institute concluded: "There was a disquieting feeling that few of those assembled ever would agree on just what a budget is." Why might there be disagreement among such men as Campbell Soup Company's vice-president for corporate planning, ITE Circuit Breaker's controller of financial planning, the Reading Railroad's superintendent of budgeting and cost control, Ampex Corporation's assistant treasurer, and the comptroller of a city-owned rapid transit system?

2. A company president, before going to a director's meeting to review the company's new budget, said that he could throw away the book containing the complete budget before the meeting and no practical harm would be done. Do you agree?

3. (a) Is there any reason why budgets cannot be used within the sections or departments of a department store even though these budgets are not a part of a general program for the entire store? (b) What are the advantages of having a consolidated budget for the entire store?

4. Suppose you have been placed in charge of budgetary procedure for a company just installing budgetary control. Outline step by step how you would work back from the sales estimates (a) to the schedule of purchases by the purchasing department and (b) to the monthly profit and loss budget.

5. In other parts of this book emphasis has been laid on sound forecasts, clear-cut organization, good executive personnel and facilities, and well-designed programs. In what ways will the presence of any one of these factors assist the management of a company to secure effective budgeting control?

6. In a company that places heavy reliance on operating executives and supervisors for the preparation of budget figures, one executive contends that since he makes up estimates for his department he should be permitted to revise them whenever operating conditions necessitate. What answer would you give this executive?

7. On page 699 it is stated that financial accounts do not reveal several aspects of company operations that vitally concern management. How can these activities be expressed in numbers or dollars so that they can be included in the budgeting framework?

8. (a) Does the establishment of budgetary control mean that all operations must be kept within the appropriations of the budget for the period? (b) Under what conditions should the operating executive make commitments and incur expenses larger than those provided for in the budget? (c) What procedure should be established to provide flexibility in the budgetary program?

9. The operating vice-president of the Rutland Railroad once commented on budgeting procedure. "When we first started the budget, we used a revenue estimate from the traffic department. Now I make my own estimate based on past experience and general forecasts of business conditions. From this revenue estimate and using a 78% operating ratio—which is what a sound railroad should have—I can tell the total of operating expenses I can allow. This year I broke this 78% among the departments. This gave them a total expenditure goal to hit. I tell the fellows, 'This is what it has to be!' They scratch around and say they can't do it. We work over what they have come up with and base our final figures on the very best thinking as to what we can do. We cut the original estimate of the maintenance of way department from $1,000,000—which we could not afford—down to $895,000. Our force now, however, in the shop or on the track, is at a minimum.

"If we have to cut, I figure out the total, consult with the chief engineer and the division superintendents, and they figure out where it can be done. A track gang might be cut from 6 to 5. The mechanical division might rearrange assignments—or not recondition old boxcars. Retiring the cars stops this kind of expense. The transportation division has to make working agreements with the unions. We attempt to get train units (engineer, fireman, conductor, trainman) down to a minimum. Occasionally, by negotiation, the locals will overlook national rules. It takes a constant review of operating expenses to see where we can save a little here and there.

"In the budget meeting of the chief executives we get together on the two revenue forecasts—that of the traffic department and that of the operating vice-president. We could handle increased revenue with very little trouble."

Results for the past two years have shown actual revenues ½ of 1% above the budget and actual expenses 3% above the budget. Appraise the vice-president's actions.

CASE XXVI
State Telephone Company

John Rogers, Assistant Vice-President (Commercial), had before him a consultant's report, "Forecasting and Budgeting for New Terminal Demand" (see Appendix A on page 710). He now had to appraise this report to see if it provided any useful ideas or recommendations. Rogers had been given the report by the Vice-President (Staff) who asked him to look it over and report back what there was in it that might be worthwhile.

The consultant, a specialist in economic statistics and operations research, had recently completed some four months' observation of the forecasting, budgeting, and planning work of State Telephone Company. He had been called in by the Vice-President

(Staff) as a matter of general routine. The Vice-President (Staff) was not dissatisfied with the budgeting work of the company, but he occasionally liked to have it reviewed and appraised by outsiders. The consultant's assignment was "to appraise the budgeting procedure to see how well it served the company as an instrument for control and coordination."

Organization structure. The State Telephone Company was a large independent firm (that is, not owned by American Telephone and Telegraph Company) that served a diversified area. Within its operating boundaries were one major city, several smaller cities, some large towns, and rural sections with small towns and diversified agriculture.

The formal organization is symbolized in the diagram on page 705. Responsibility for operations was divided among four regions and then among districts within each region. For example, there were eight districts in the Central City region. In addition, complete staff groups reported (1) at the company level to the Vice-President (Staff), and (2) at the region level to the various managers of the operating functions.

The five operating functions were: commercial, traffic, plant, engineering, and accounting.

A general commercial manager was responsible for selling telephone services to individuals and commercial enterprises, for public telephones, for establishing rates for the various kinds of customers, and for forecasts of market demand within his geographical segment. A traffic manager supervised all switchboard operations, both local and toll; was responsible for routings of various kinds of special calls; and was responsible for servicing the calls to and from public switchboards. A plant manager was responsible for maintaining and testing all central office equipment, for methods of installation and operation used in central offices, for maintaining buildings, and for constructing central office buildings and equipment. A chief engineer was responsible for all plant and transmitting equipment outside the central offices, such as cable, poles, and building connections, and for equipment on customers' premises. The engineer was also concerned with devising plans for new buildings and equipment and with maintenance practices for all kinds of equipment such as radio, teletype, public switchboards, central office switching equipment, and cables. A general accounting manager was responsible for accounting methods, accounting training, payroll accounting, plant accounting, accounts payable, and customer accounts receivable.

At the two top management levels, the company level and the regional level, one man was centrally responsible for the five key functions and for overall operations within a given geographical segment—the President for the entire company and the four regional vice-presidents for the Central City, the Northern, the Southern, and the Western regions. This division of formal responsibility had not been carried to the district level. There was no general superintendent responsible for all five functions in the Charonia district, for example. The company had, however, established at the district level what were called "district teams." These teams were visualized as being analogous to the operations of a small telephone company with responsibility for results in the particular district. Each "district team" was composed of a district commercial manager, a district accounting manager, a district plant superintendent, a district traffic superintendent, and one or more district engineers. The operations and the planning duties of the "district teams" had considerable significance for the company's budgeting procedure.

The regional commercial staff men concerned with markets, rates, personnel, and methods reported to the general commercial manager in their individual regions, but they also reported to a staff man at the company level whose responsibility paralleled theirs. Thus we find an Assistant Vice-President (Commercial) in charge of the company's commercial staff. This assistant vice-president had reporting to him a general rate engineer, a general marketing superintendent, and a general commercial operations supervisor. The last named three spent a great deal of time collating and working on the plans and ideas submitted to them by their three counterparts at the regional level. The Assistant vice-president (Commercial), together with two other assistant vice-presidents who were responsible for staff work in the functions of traffic and of plant and engineering, reported to the Vice-President (Staff), who in turn summarized all staff work for the Executive Vice-President (Operations).

This staff organization, which existed in parallel throughout the company, carried heavy responsibilities for developing plans and budgets for the various operating functions (traffic, plant, commercial, engineering, and accounting).

Economic forecasts in staff planning and budgeting. Each quarter, company economists who forecasted general business conditions for the entire company met with the company staff members who were responsible for seeing that plans were developed for specific parts of the telephone business. The general marketing superintendent, the four regional market forecast supervisors, the four regional superintendents of commercial staff, engineers of plant extension planning for the four regions, and the program engineer for the company attended each meeting. Past forecasts, recent results, and forecasts for the coming two years of station gain (net number of new telephones added) were reviewed.

State Telephone Company
Partial Organization Diagram

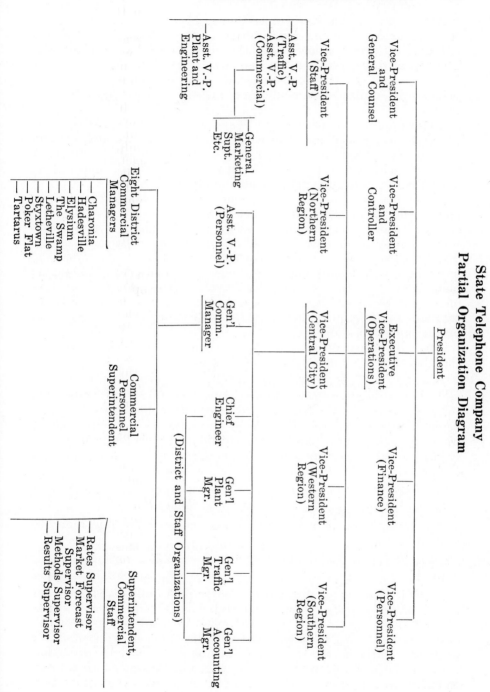

After such a quarterly meeting, each man then passed on conclusions to his counterpart on the district teams and assisted the district teams in developing the next forecast of station gain. The actual forecast of station gain was worked out at the district meetings, not at the staff meeting mentioned. The staff met primarily for discussion and to extend their own thinking.

General planning forecasts. These were two-year forecasts of net main terminal demand in each district. Once worked out and agreed upon, they were passed on to other staff men who used them for engineering plans, building plans, revenue estimates, personnel plans, cost budgets, and plant planning.

While market forecast staff men participated in the district team meetings as advisors, the decision as to the level of the forecast was the sole responsibility of the district team. The decision was not only a forecast but also an order for equipment for the district. The consolidated orders from each district provided the basic data for all equipment planning for central office and outside plant additions. In addition, this forecast was used by all departments for all budgeting purposes—estimating revenues, messages carried, force requirements, space requirements, expenses, net profits, and cash flows.

Each district team member had specific responsibilities toward the general planning forecast, as follows:

District Commercial Manager. Chairman, gathered information on local business conditions, analyzed past performance. Presented sales programs and their anticipated effect on main terminal demand. Presented the attitude of business people generally toward current or future economic conditions. Presented information gained from real estate agents on new and proposed commercial construction.

District Plant Superintendent. Recorded connections and disconnections. Estimated future losses from demolition.

Plant Engineer. Forecasted all new construction and counted that underway.

District Traffic Superintendent. Furnished data on net terminal gain.

District Accounting Manager. Had the major responsibility for transmitting knowledge of general business conditions to these district team meetings. Presented general business conditions as developed by Vice-President and Controller's office. Presented any pertinent information on local business conditions developed through meetings or interviews with banks or other institutions. Summarized the important factors that may influence future telephone demand.

Hadesville District Meeting

(An abstract to illustrate a typical procedure)

The Agenda:

1. General business conditions.
2. Analysis of past performance.
3. Review of future main terminal demand:
   (a) New construction.
   (b) Loss from demolitions.
   (c) Sales stimulation.
   (d) Normal demand forecast.
   (e) Miscellaneous events.
4. Review of future residence extension demand.

The district accounting manager analyzed economic expectations for the state and for the city's business activity. He foresaw a further decline from current levels and an upturn beginning within six to nine months. He expected a slow pace of recovery over the succeeding year.

The district commercial manager said: "This district is heavy in textile loft operations and textile workers. There have not been many layoffs, but lost overtime means the people are slower to pay telephone bills and will make partial payments. This increases work for the business office. The small retail establishments are optimistic in this district. No resistance has developed to sales of additional telephone business to them."

The review of results of main station gain for the past year showed "200 under the estimate." The plant engineer explained this as "a slowdown on Washington No. 2. It leveled at 42% filled when other apartments have been giving us 60%."

The group then turned to the forecast for the next two years. It used a form showing, by months, new construction at each address to aid in preparation of the forecast. The plant engineer explained that he had built up a 50% filled as the basis of his forecast. "Negroes and Puerto Ricans are moving back in. They are returning from Elysium. Earlier demolitions had forced them out, but now they can return. They are moving into these new buildings from congested areas elsewhere."

One man asked, "Is there any information from installers on the kinds of people moving in?"

The engineer said, "No, but we have had information from them in the past on row reconversions."

"We forecast for 50 new stations on A Street."

"Will it be finished by then?"

"No, ground is not broken yet. The observer reports it 55% sold, but the plans are not even finished. We have put it in on an optimistic basis to keep it on the list. Fifty won't hurt us much."

"You can put it in for the second year. It is possible to get it built by then, but not probable."

"Okay. We'll put it in the first quarter and take it out of December."

"On Jefferson No. 3 we expect 60% fill."

"What is the rental status?"

"I'm not sure."

"Ray (Berg, the district commercial manager), what influence of business changes did you use in distributing these?"

"We took a little longer than usual to get the expected 60% fill. In the past we have had this in six months, but now we put it in over the entire year.

"For normal demand (which is that which cannot be accounted for by known or expected construction and demolition) we had a poor November and December, expected 320 and only had 14. We don't know why. So we are cutting normal from 1,550 to 1,160 and are putting more of this in the second half than in the first half."

"Are we all in agreement on this?"

"Well, it is only down 50 from last year's actual."

"Yes, but it is down considerably from the earlier estimate of 2,450. New construction and demolitions are easy to account for. It bothers us all not to be able to pin down 'normal,' so we are trying to find out about it. Last year we were below the main station gain forecast in part because building completion slowed due to the cement strike and because the federal government would not accept one project. But most of it was in the decline of 'normal', and we're not sure here. This is the factor where changes in business conditions hit."

In discussing the forecast for net station gain, the team members reviewed the status of construction projects address by address. The chairman then asked the staff men present as observers if they had any questions.

"It is possible that new construction may be low. You have 825 next year and 400 the year after. Why the drop?"

The chairman answered, "There is nothing in the picture that is going to start. If there are going to be completions in two years, then we must have demolitions now and nothing is going on there. We have several indefinites from the Dodge reports, which we have listed on the plant engineer's report. The people are moving out slowly from 309 Polk Street. This is about the only one that could be completed."

The plant engineer said, "All these people seem to be feeling their way along at the present time. They won't state anything definite."

A staff man said, "Well, two years is the critical time for this forecast and we don't want to be low for the engineers."

"Right, we could put in 130 for Polk Street and bring the forecast up to 1,900. But this will be offset by the drag in the Blair Street houses."

The engineer said, "Don't forget how tight we were at the end of last year on equipment. We only avoided trunking down to Letheville because demand was not quite up."

The market forecast supervisor summarized, "Look at the net overall; it is not bad." He quoted the figures for four years.

The group then turned to developing the forecast for residence extensions. The district manager said, "The girls continue to do a good selling job, but resistance will be up next year, so we don't look for more than 1,300."

The market supervisor said, "Now we have to spread this out by months. Let's slow down some in the first half of the year and bring it up more in the second half to take account of general business conditions."

The district manager said, "Things look better for the following years, so we put down 1,400 for the first and 1,450 for the next for extensions."

The market supervisor asked, "Why is it reasonable to show an increase? You said there would not be so many new houses."

The district manager said, "Yes, but there will not be so many demolitions and move-outs then and the forecast is for better business on the whole."

Meetings in other districts followed the general pattern that has just been illustrated. In districts in which large projects were involved, close attention was paid to the specific circumstances of each project. In the Charonia district, for example, there were many changes by business firms.

The district forecasts and orders were consolidated into a forecast of total station movement and gain. This was used for all other budgeting. As an example, the company revenue superintendent said: "I predict any changes in rates that may be forthcoming. Then, with the knowledge of how many stations will be in service and with other forecasts of the amount of use of each station, I can readily prepare the revenue estimate that goes to the president for approval." The company program engineer remarked: "Once we know how many new stations will be added and how many will be changed, it is relatively easy to plan the central office equipment needed and the outside plant equipment needed. We get cost estimates from various sources and then have an equipment budget ready for approval." Similarly, other staff men developed projections of labor, supplies, and materials needed to provide the number of telephones called for. With the proper wage and cost projections, these were consolidated into the operating budget, which also went to the president for approval.

Appendix A
State Telephone Company
FORECASTING NEW TERMINAL DEMAND—
STUDY AND RECOMMENDATIONS

(An abstract of significant parts of the consultant's report.)

Economic Analysis and Telephone Demand for Small Areas

The assumption that must be made in formulating a forecasting program is that the forces affecting telephone demand in small areas are identifiable and are subject to rational analysis. In some cases this assumption is untenable when a large firm or government agency creates or discontinues or modifies greatly an installation because of noneconomic factors that may be political, personal, or purely fortuitous. State Telephone Company has experienced difficulties recently in connection with the closing of military installations and the changing policies of certain large corporations. The final decision, in such cases, could hardly have been predicted on rational or even other grounds.

If, on the other hand, the relevant forces are subject to study and if they will yield to assiduous disciplined attack, much can be done toward arriving at reasonably accurate forecasts of telephone demand for the required periods into the future. . .

The task of performing the economic and sociological analysis and of evaluating its implications should be performed by full-time personnel on a team basis, with teams of three persons consisting of an economist, a sociologist-demographer, and an experienced telephone demand forecaster.

The people who, under this program, actually create the forecasting procedures will become familiar with the various types of problems and situations to be analyzed. Their experience with these analyses, and the natural trial-and-error process of watching the forecasted future become the present, will help them attain a level of ability far beyond that which any of us now possess.

They will, in approaching a region, first decide how the region should be divided into forecasting sections. In some situations, such as Ahab's Island, a single central office are stands alone in its economic distinctiveness. In other regions, several central office districts may together constitute an area of relative economic homogeneity. *The size of the region to be considered should depend upon the economic characteristics of the region rather than on the administrative division of the State Telephone Company.*

There is no specific technique that can be applied to all localities. Rather, within the framework of a general technique or approach, each small area as defined above must be considered separately and a program for forecasting must be evolved that will be designed specifically for that area.

Thus, we must know not only the population of persons, households, and business firms, and the telephone penetration of these populations, but we must also know *why* these are as they are and *how* they been changed and *why* they have been changing. The factors that must be analyzed include: the economic base, births and deaths of firms, characteristics of local business firms, personal income, zoning, patterns of residential construction, ethnic factors, habits and customs, availability and suitability of land for development or redevelopment, enabling facilities such as transportation, water supply, and sewerage, and possible changes in all of these. In addition, there must be some understanding of the influence of changing business conditions, both general and local, on local telephone demand. This last may serve as a mechanism for fuller utilization of the currently available economic conditions analyses. . .

Although not essential, it may be desirable to attempt to establish objective numerical aids to forecasting. These might be expected generally to take the form of time series or correlation analyses. It may well be found that, in small areas, such statistical analyses may be more useful than they have been on a company-wide basis. Particularly, this may be expected to be the case when the telephone characteristics of the locality are dominated by a small number of measurable economic or demographic forces.

The Economic Expediters

To supplement the general program for detailed analysis of small areas, an economic troubleshooting task force should be available for consultation and analysis on specific problems. This task force function should be performed by the same three-person teams described above. Their job should include both the expediter function and the regular economic base analyses.

Throughout the company, there are situations where local personnel are aware that something is in prospect that may have an important effect on telephone demand, but they are not able specifically to take it into account in their forecasting. This generally results from the fact that, while the known event is related to new telephone demand, the relationship and the effect are not direct, and careful analysis of intermediate steps must be considered.

Does a new plant in a town mean that residential development will take place near the plant? Will there be residential development at all? Why? The answers depend on number of workers, geographical distribution of available labor force, transportation facilities, availability of suitable land, habits and customs of the potential work force, etc. When information about a new plant is obtained, a summons for the economic expediters may well provide a sound basis for forecasting the effect on future telephone demand.

How can the "do-it-yourself" conversions in the Charonia district be forecast? How long does it take before there are two or more families in the "single family" house? (In one block in the Swamp district, there are 23 "single" homes with 65 main stations.) What is the sociological basis for this pattern of development?

A Program for Improving the Budgeting

(1) Forecasts will be improved. The three-man teams will be more expert in their work than are the district teams because of their training and specialized experience. As an example, it is my judgment that revenue estimates for the next two years are understated by 5 to 7% through excessive conservatism on the part of the district teams and their failure to take the generally expected upswing in business into account. Investment costs should rise 2% more and operating costs 4 to 5% more than is implied by the current forecast of total station movement and gain. On an index basis, this means that profits are seriously understated.

	Current Forecast	*Improved Forecast*
Revenues	100	105-7
Variable Costs	65	68
Fixed Costs	30	31
Net Profit	5	6-8 (+20% to 60%)

(2) Coordination will be aided. A general forecast can be developed for approval by the president or the board of directors. Once approved, it can be used by all forecasting teams and applied with consistency to each forecasting area. Present procedure allows a forecast to be diluted as it moves from economists to market forecast supervisors to accountants to district teams.

(3) Control will be more accurate. With more proficient forecasters giving full-time attention to the estimates of telephone demand, more accurate standards will be developed. This will allow the later comparison of results to be more meaningful.

Clearly the program is expensive. However, it can, with reasonable certainty, be expected to improve the forecasts. The costs of the program can easily be computed. It is altogether likely that the costs of improving the forecasts will prove to be very small with respect to the potential benefits of better forecasts. In that case, the entire program will be a profitable investment.

REQUIRED: (a) Explain the present procedure for developing budgets, including the responsibility of the district teams and of the staff members at company and regional levels.

(b) Explain the consultant's proposals and how they differ from the present procedure.

(c) Evaluate the consultant's statement that present revenue estimates are too conservative.

(d) What would you tell the Vice-President (Staff) about the consultant's report?

INTEGRATING CASES
Execution

SOLIE BAKERIES, INC.

Several months after the acquisition of bakeries in Maryland had completed the expansion plans of Solie Bakeries, Inc., the president of the company turned over to the controller the task of recommending a system of controls that would make available more adequate information than was currently being received about the operations of the branches and that would improve company planning. The controller, Mr. James, had only recently been added to the company staff. Before this he had been a senior accountant in a large public accounting firm.

History of the firm. The original bakery in Newark, New Jersey, conducted a retail door-to-door business selling cakes, pies, bread, and other products to housewives. This company gradually expanded and branches were opened in nearby New Jersey towns. After a number of years of profitable operations in Newark and northern New Jersey, a major expansion program was undertaken. New branches were opened throughout New Jersey, Southern New York, and Eastern Pennsylvania, and existing bakeries, carrying on the same type of business, in Delaware and Maryland were purchased. The purpose of the expansion and mergers was to realize the purported advantages of large scale operation.

The current organization. Headquarters of the company have remained in Newark, and all chief executives, with the exception of the Southern operations director, are located there. The current organization can be visualized by referring to the diagram on the next page.

Authority over operations has been decentralized to the branch managers, and each branch manager is held responsible for the profit and loss realized in his particular territory. The work assigned to the operations directors is confined to giving advice

713

on current problems to the branch managers and suggesting possible ways for improving operations. These directors have all been successful branch managers in the past. The central functional officers have authority over their particular fields, and the branch managers are expected to carry out the general policies established by these officers. In some cases the authority of the central officers is exercised concurrently with that of the branch managers.

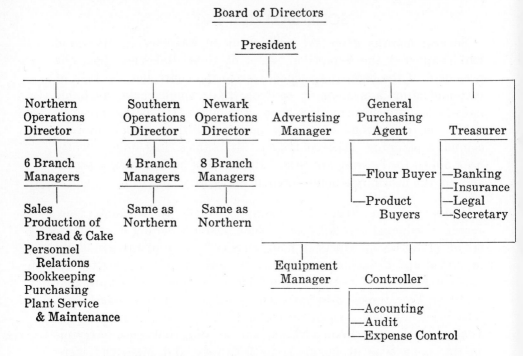

Board of Directors

President

Northern Operations Director	Southern Operations Director	Newark Operations Director	Advertising Manager	General Purchasing Agent	Treasurer
6 Branch Managers	4 Branch Managers	8 Branch Managers		—Flour Buyer	—Banking —Insurance
Sales Production of Bread & Cake Personnel Relations Bookkeeping Purchasing Plant Service & Maintenance	Same as Northern	Same as Northern		—Product Buyers	—Legal —Secretary

Equipment Manager   Controller

—Acounting
—Audit
—Expense Control

Policies affecting operations. Although authority over operations is decentralized, the president has established certain policies that are followed by the branch managers. The first policy is that of a limited line of products. Each branch is expected to decide upon "specials" for each day of the week and publicize these in advance in order to help reduce the number of items made on any one day. Fancy items that might have only a limited market are discouraged. The branch managers report to the regional operations directors the number of different items baked during a month and are asked for explanations if the number of bread items exceeds 100 or if the number of cake items exceeds 150. Emphasis in production is on volume output at relatively low cost.

Branch operations. Since much of the recent expansion of Solie Bakeries, Inc., was brought about through purchase of existing bakeries with established lines of products, there are differences in the formulae used in the local plants even for such items as bread and rolls. Pies and other pastry have still more local variation. Suggestions of the regional operations directors tend to bring some uniformity, but local bakers make their own final decisions. This policy is necessary in order to adapt the formulae to changing local temperature and humidity conditions, both of which affect fermentation and baking. Quality control is a local responsibility.

Branch managers are in charge of the arrangement of equipment and manufacturing procedures. They receive some help from the operations directors if it is requested. The central equipment manager is in charge of equipment purchases and maintenance routines, but some weight is given to the local managers' opinions when changes are made.

The products to be made on any particular day and the amounts are decided by the branch manager in conjunction with his sales manager. Sales are made direct to consumers from door to door. Each salesman has an assigned route and calls on his customers every day or every other day, depending on the territory. Responsibility for the merchandise rests with the salesmen and they are charged each day for the amount of goods they take out. The men make most of the sales for cash, but extend weekly credit to some customers. Collection is done by the salesmen. The average number of customers per salesman is 200. Orders for the following day's load are given by the salesman on the basis of orders taken from customers in advance and of average sales expectancy for the particular route. A total is then arrived at for the branch by the sales manager and an order given to the production department for the following day's output. The accuracy of the estimates of the following day's sales determines the losses from sales missed or from stale returns. Bread or cake products not sold on the route are returned by the salesmen. Some items can be redistributed or sold at the branch at a reduced price. Most items, however, are a complete loss because of product perishability. Keeping stale returns low is felt to be a key factor in the success of branch operation. Stale returns and profit together generally make up about 6% of the sales volume.

The rate of turnover of salesmen in some branches is excessively high. These men are paid on commission, and new salesmen realize only about 50% of the earnings of older, established salesmen. The company is currently trying to overcome this difficulty by hiring only married men who can pass certain physical and personality tests. Wages are set by the branch manager as a part of his general responsibility for personnel in his branch.

Minutes of any meetings held at the branches are sent to the operations directors and to Newark headquarters.

Purchasing. Items purchased by this company fall into three general classes. The first class consists of standard raw materials on which substantial savings can be made through volume purchasing. These are flour, sugar, milk, yeast, lard, and eggs. Flour is the largest single item bought and is purchased from several sources on contracts running about 90 days. It is delivered in carload lots from mills to the various branches as needed. The second class consists of raw materials not customarily bought in large quantities such as nuts, fruits, jams, and jellies. The types and amounts of these ingredients used varies somewhat because of differences in local tastes. The third class consists of items not used directly in the manufacture of bread products. Some of these, such as wrappers, printed boxes, and stationery, have been made standard for the entire company and can be bought in fairly sizeable quantities. In addition, delivery equipment and baking machinery must be purchased. The company uses trucks for route deliveries, and purchases these in addition to operating supplies such as tires, oil, and gasoline.

The general purchasing agent for the company supervises buying of all classes of products except equipment and operating supplies. These are purchased by the equipment manager, but he usually confers with the general purchasing agent and the branch manager affected on any major purchase. Authority for emergency purchases with a limit of $100 has been given to the local managers. Some of them continue to buy regularly nuts, fruits, jams, and jellies in order to, as they explain, have products adapted to local tastes.

The purchasing department is organized on a product basis. Flour is the largest item of purchase and the general purchasing agent confers weekly with the flour specialist as to purchases.

Equipment. Vehicles, machinery, and buildings are under the general responsibility of the equipment manager. He consults with each branch manager on important questions concerning baking equipment. The branch manager is responsible for maintenance work and repairs on trucks. Original purchases of delivery equipment are made by the equipment manager. Mr. Johnson, the equipment manager, spends a large part of his time visiting the branches and talking with the local branch managers and their garage foremen. During these visits he attempts to check on whether or not the maintenance routines that he has specified for trucks and baking equipment are being followed.

Accounting. Monthly profit and loss statements and balance sheets for each branch are filled out by branch bookkeepers according to a system established by the controller. Separate profit and loss statements are made for bread and for cake products. In these statements expenses that cannot be directly assigned are charged on the basis of sales volume. Copies of all statements are sent to the regional operations directors and to the Newark office. In addition weekly sales reports for each branch are distributed to these officers. Monthly reports on advertising expenditures and flour consumption are given to the president.

Bookkeepers at the local branches have all been trained in the Newark office at one time or another. The controller has established all their procedures and does his own hiring and firing. Several traveling auditors are also employed to check on the accounting and cash-handling routines at the branches.

Treasurer. Duties of the treasurer are outlined on the organization diagram. He takes care of all banking arrangements and negotiates all insurance contracts. Each branch has a payroll account and a general account at a local bank so that funds can be disbursed for the payroll and regular local expenses. All cash receipts are deposited daily and each month the branch manager is required to send the surplus cash arising from operations to the Newark office. Bills for local purchases have to be approved by the purchasing agent or equipment manager before they can be paid.

Existing controls. Some of the current controls and control procedure have been illustrated in preceding paragraphs. During his investigation of these procedures, Mr. James found that control over inventories varied from branch to branch.

Physical inventories are taken at the end of each month, except in those plants that maintain perpetual inventory records. Inventories are valued at LIFO. Changes in the amounts of finished goods on hand are nominal, so it is simple to compute a ratio of materials expense to sales for each plant. At present, no further detail is reported to the headquarters office; reports do not show expenses by kinds of raw materials.

The practice regarding the withdrawal of materials from inventories varies considerably between plants. At several of the plants, stockmen simply take materials from storerooms upon the oral requests of the bakers. These withdrawals correspond roughly to actual materials usage, but a limited supply of sugar, salt, powdered milk, and the like are kept on the mixing floors. In most of these plants at least a few of the items, such as nuts, are kept locked up to prevent "snacking" and pilferage; all other materials are in storerooms open to any of the men handling receipts or withdrawals of materials. A few of the plants have a storekeeper who maintains a perpetual inventory record on all items in stock, and must be given a written requisition for any withdrawal.

Quantities to be bought by the purchasing department are estimated on the basis of average requirements in the past adjusted for special promotional efforts. Each branch notifies the purchasing department one month ahead of its "specials" for the coming month.

Recommendations of the controller. Mr. James submitted this report to the president of Solie Bakeries, Inc.:

> "The recommendations made in this report are designed to fulfill the objectives of providing more adequate information than is currently available about branch operations and of improving company planning.
>
> "(1) *Cash*—In some branches checks are being issued with only one signature. Since correction of this procedure is within the province of the controller's office, instructions have been issued to all branches that signatures of both the bookkeeper and branch manager will be required. It has also been found that bank accounts are reconciled and verified by the local bookkeeper or one of his subordinates who is also responsible for daily deposits. Since most branches do not have a large enough staff to separate these two tasks, the auditors of the controller's

office have been instructed to give special attention to a review of bank reconciliations as part of the internal audit procedure.

"(2) *Accounts Receivable*—It is recommended that the amount of accounts uncollected after two weeks be deducted from the salesman's commission.

"(3) *Inventories*—It is recommended that each branch adopt a perpetual inventory system. Minimum and maximum stock limits and reorder quantities can be prescribed for each raw material item and a requisition sent to the central purchasing department when materials are needed. A physical inventory should be taken every six months to verify the stock records. This count of inventory should be under the supervision of the branch bookkeeper in order to minimize fraud. In all branches the storekeeper should be made responsible for admission to the storeroom and should designate who is to countersign the stores' requisition. Jams, jellies, nuts, candied fruits, etc., should be kept locked up.

"(4) *Fixed Assets*—Control of these assets is currently the responsibility of the equipment manager. The only improvement that appears to be necessary is clarification of the minimum expenditure that must be approved by the board of directors. There is no adequate statement at the moment of the extent of responsibility of the equipment manager for initiating and approving expenditures. It is therefore recommended that the board establish these limits. It is also recommended that a form for the requisition of capital expenditures be designed. This will be initiated by the equipment manager and sent to the board of directors for approval. On it can be designated the reasons for the request for expenditure, the amount to be spent, and a description of what is to be purchased.

"(5) *Expense Control*—No uniform cost classification or reporting of expenses exists at present. It is therefore recommended that a cost classification and standard costs be worked out for bread production, cake production, branch selling expenses, branch total costs, regional total costs, and for each of the functional fields, advertising, purchasing, equipment, accounting, and finance. Costs should be reported monthly and be given to all officers at Newark as well as the Southern Operations Director. In the case of production and selling costs, the reports should show dollars of expenditure for each cost item expressed in terms of output units; for example, direct labor costs per pound of bread, or heating costs per pound of cake. This information will allow company officers to analyze results three ways: branches can be compared with each other, current and past periods can be compared, and actual results can be compared to standard.

"Costs of operating equipment should also be reported in more detail than is done at present. These expenses should be reported in two ways: first, each branch should report costs per mile for gasoline, oil, repairs, etc.; and second, actual expenses charged to each truck and for maintenance of other equipment should be reported.

"Since production formulae are not standard for all branches, interbranch comparisons of materials expense will be difficult. It is recommended that each branch manager write down the formulae actually in use and send copies to the home office. Company auditors can then prepare reports of adherence to these formulae by using information from sales reports and raw material requisitions. Auditors' reports should be sent to the regional operations directors for action. Control over prices of raw materials is made difficult because of random market variations. It is recommended, however, that actual prices by products be reported by the buyers to the general purchasing agent and regional operations directors weekly, and that a monthly summary be sent to the president together with an analysis of trends in materials prices and explanations of significant price changes. It is also recommended that company auditors check the evidence of request for and receipt of bids on purchases of raw materials.

"(6) *Sales Information*—Regional operations directors should receive monthly reports of sales by products and by salesmen for all branches. Weekly reports of total sales by product line should also be sent to the operations directors and the president.

"It is felt that the system of reports and controls recommended in this report, when added to those currently existing, will provide adequate information for company planning and sound control over operations."

Copies of Mr. James' proposal have been circulated to branch managers and the reaction has been anything but enthusiastic. Several of the managers of branches acquired by merger are already finding it difficult to adjust to "Newark control," and these men are opposed to any further interference with their activities. One of them says, "We should decide whether we are running our bakeries for profits or to pay overhead. I've run this plant for twelve years without so many reports, and nothing has happened to baking bread that makes them necessary now."

Another commented, "If those fellows at Newark would come out here and find me a couple of good salesmen, they would improve profits more than a whole carload of statistics ever could."

The operations directors have been noncommittal about the proposal, although one did remark, "Looks like I'll have to hire a new man to tell me what all these figures mean."

REQUIRED: (a) What role do you believe the executives in Newark (and the Southern operations director) should perform? That is, what should they do to help build company profits?

(b) What are the crucial activities of the branch managers?

(c) In view of your answers to (a) and (b), what controls do you recommend be established in Solie Bakeries, Inc.?

PARKER GEAR COMPANY

A few months after he was promoted to president of the Parker Gear Company, Mr. John Sheffield became disturbed at the size of company inventories. Inventories, when expressed as a percentage of sales, were then more than twice the industry average, and the company also had a large backlog of orders. The president also knew that some customers were dissatisfied with deliveries, since only partial shipments had been made.

To assist him with these problems, Mr. Sheffield called on a friend, Mr. A. O. Billings, who was currently with a firm in another industry but who had previously been associated with the Parker Gear Company. Mr. Sheffield was able to persuade Mr. Billings to return to the Parker Gear Company because Mr. Billings preferred to live in Weston, a large city in the northeastern part of the country, and because of the challenge that he saw in the problem posed to him, even though returning to the Parker Gear Company meant an immediate decrease in his salary.

The exact problem posed to Mr. Billings by the president was:
To bring about the following changes:

(a) Decreased inventories (raw material, work in process, finished goods).
(b) Improved forecasting of customer demand and closer tie-in of forecasts to manufacturing schedules.
(c) Maximum flexibility of scheduling procedures.
(d) Better control of finished goods inventories and their distribution to district warehouses or individual customers to provide the greatest possible customer satisfaction.

The Parker Gear Company is one of a group of firms, each of which manufactures a general line of gear and speed reduction units and sells these through a nationwide distributing organization to customers in many different industries.

In order to have an exact basis for recommendations that were to be made, Mr. Billings and one assistant spent several months reviewing the forecasting, scheduling, control, and coordination procedures then in effect at the Parker Gear Company.

Sales. Sales volume of the Parker Gear Company amounted to about 7% of the industry total. Customers in many industries were served, either directly or through distributors. Close to 100 distributors made up the largest group of immediate customers.

They resold in turn to all kinds of customers for replacement and maintenance as well as original equipment purposes. These distributors were not captive but carried competing lines of products. The sales division also had 16 district offices in various cities throughout the country in which stock was carried. In addition to sales to distributors, direct sales were made to original equipment manufacturers of farm implements and tractors, aircraft, power shovels, hoists, diesel engines, machine tools, etc.

The Sales Division, one of four main divisions of the company (the others were Engineering, Production, and Accounting) had the following departments: Advertising, Research, Industry Sales, Parts Sales, Distributor Sales, Foreign Trade, Sales Contracts, Order Department, Finished Stores, and Shipping.

Products. The Parker Gear Company produced 8 basic types of gears, which were generally differentiated according to the type of teeth on the gear, plus speed reducers, sprockets, universal joints, and transmissions. When the various combinations of sizes and special features were considered, the product line had about 3,000 items. This line was constantly being increased as adaptations of old items were brought out by the Parker Gear Company or as customers called for special items to suit their particular needs. Although the company was very willing to develop special items for particular customers, it had an expressed policy of expanding the use of such items to other customers so that each item would have as wide a market as possible.

Orders. Mr. Billings found evidence of difficulty during his examination of the Sales Order Department. All orders received from customers during one 5-day period were audited and the following information was developed:

Table A

		Average	Range
Total number of orders	470		
Calendar days for processing:		*Average*	*Range*
Sales and Engineering		4½ days	2–124 days
Order Department		2½ "	1–33 "
Sales Pricing		1½ "	0–7 "
Accounting		1½ "	1–3 "
Total		10 days	

Time for processing 19 orders (with 2,500 items each) each of which required more than 2 weeks to process:

	Average
Sales and Engineering	43 days
Order Department	8 ”
Sales Pricing	3 ”
Accounting	3 ”
Total	57 days

A study of one product group in one particular day revealed:

Initial Information	*Final Information*
Warehouse requisitions for 208,-009 items, required to cover 6 months' field requirements and 6 months' schedule beyond.	Field requirements overstated by 70%.

Customer orders specified many different combinations from the line of 3,000 different items. A typical order was received first at a district sales office, where it was edited and acknowledged and then teletyped to the head office Sales Order Department in Weston. The order was registered, sent in turn to the Pricing and Credit Departments, and then back to the Sales Order Department. At this point it was the practice of the head of the Sales Order Department to review the order. He routed selected orders for unusual items to the Industry Sales Department and to the Engineering Division. On other orders he determined what shipping promise he wanted made on the basis of the customer's request, his own knowledge of the production program, and his file of inventory information printed out daily by the computer room.

The decision on the shipping promise and the customer's order were then passed on to one of several order department schedulers. Each scheduler handled a particular range of sizes and types of gears. He ordered shipments of finished items or called for production of such items, utilizing again the inventory and production records issued by the computer room. The schedulers' main job was to reassign priorities among orders—a judgment that could not be delegated to the machine system used at Parker Gear. (The firm had two computers, one for engineering and scientific purposes, the other for commercial purposes such as production scheduling, payroll calculations, inventory records, assembly and fabrication standards, parts lists, and the like.)

The Sales Order Department reported monthly to the president on the estimated sales value of production, using the following form:

Estimated Sales Values of Production, Month_____											
Production total for Type	Type	Size Groups									
		1	2	3	4	5	6	7	8	9
Quantity Value	Herringbone	Quantity Value	Quantity Value	Quantity Value	etc.	etc.	etc.	etc.	etc.	etc.
Quantity Value	Spur									
etc.	Helical									
	Universal joints									
	etc.									
	Total									

Customers who had inquiries, special problems with particular orders, requests for information on the timing of an order, cancellation requests, or complaints about delivery ordinarily took up these matters with the salesman in their district. The salesman, or his sales manager, would then call the Sales Order Department. Depending upon whom the salesman knew, he might talk to the head of the Sales Order Department or to one of the schedulers or perhaps to one of the production control schedulers to obtain information to answer the customer's request.

During his investigation, Mr. Billings found some dissatisfaction and complaining among the people in the Sales Order Department. Some of this he felt was due to technical reasons, such as the looseness of the controls of items that entered into finished stock. Returned goods were frequently placed directly in finished stock, and special reserves were authorized at various times by company officers and others. An investigation of the availability list as compared to customers' orders during February revealed the following information:

Table B

Product	In Stock	Remarks
EE3	128	5 orders in house. Oldest is of 8/5 for 7,000 items specifying delivery in Feb. On 2/25 assigned all 128 to a new order.
J62	43	1 order in house for 400 items. Stock on 1/5 was 63. On 2/9 all 43 assigned to new order but still on availability list on 2/10.
R5	35	1 order in house specifying delivery "at once" of 952 items.

Summary of 2/10 availability list versus actual customer orders file: on a sample of 16 sizes, 4,604 units assignable that could be shipped without substitution; 32 orders, of which 8 could be completely filled and 24 partially. $3,542 sales value of the 4,604 items.

New products. As mentioned before, new items were added to the line either following their development by the Engineering Division or at the request of a customer. The Sales Division often found it necessary to take on a particular item in order to meet competition or in order to satisfy a customer who ordered large quantities of other items. It was frequently felt that the Parker Gear Company could not fail to produce a special item for a customer or otherwise it would lose all of that business. Machinery designers, in bringing out new machines or adaptations of old machines, were constantly calling for special gears to be used in their product. The Sales Division willingly aided the customers in development of such special gears, since this meant that gears made by the Parker Gear Company would be used for replacement as well as for the original equipment and that demand would extend over a considerable period of time.

When the Sales Division received a request for a new item, the general sales manager circulated a request for review of the possibility of producing the item to the product engineer who would be concerned with the particular item (the Engineering Division was organized by product departments), the manager of nonproductive planning (who was in charge of estimating and methods in the Production Division), and the cost accountant. After a review by these men, the decision to add a new item was made by discussion between the general sales manager and the product engineer.

Decisions to discontinue items in the line were made by the general sales manager and the product engineer concerned acting together.

Production. The Parker Gear Company had three plants, two (Plants A and B) in Weston and a third in a smaller town nearby. The first half of the processing of almost all orders was carried on at Plant A where rough machining, preliminary heat treating, and some finish machining operations were performed. The balance of the operations—hardening, grinding, inspection, and assembly—were performed in Plant B.

Forged blanks, bar stock, and castings were purchased from outside suppliers and were used as raw materials for the gears.

Production work in gear manufacturing was not simple. For example, a typical straight bevel gear went through 34 different operations on 23 different pieces of equipment before it was ready for the magnetic particle inspection on a Magnaflux and final testing and wiring in sets in the Test Room.

At Plant C some gears were made in large quantities to special order for the aircraft industry. Cases for speed reducers were also made here.

Production control. Production was scheduled through Plants A, B, and C in job lots. Many items were manufactured only to order, but the majority of the gears were considered standard and were carried in stock. The stock items were cataloged and advertised as quickly as available. All plants were currently producing to capacity, and the Production Division was constantly seeking ways to increase output.

The complicated nature of the production control process can be understood when it is realized that one customer's order might be filled from inventory at either of two plants, from production at any of the three plants, or from branch warehouse inventory. Since one part might be used on any one of several finished items and since a process layout was used, it was common practice to have a substantial parts inventory at various stages of the process.

Regular production scheduling was done by computer. Experienced programmers and industrial engineers spent all their time keeping the system up-to-date. Schedules for special items, however, depended upon lot-size calculations made by a separate group of schedulers who used information from engineering design and from the computer for their decisions. They frequently found it necessary to make adjustments in the schedules implied by the promises of the Sales Order Department.

Even after this it was necessary at times to make changes in a production order as it went through the plant. Customer requests for modification of an order as relayed through a salesman or rush orders from the Sales Order Department made such changes necessary. Therefore, what was shipped out might not be what was specified by the customer. For example, six shipments might be made rather than one. Changes such as these were entered directly on the shipping ticket. Daily delivery sheets (Finished Stock Movement Notice) were sent to the Production Planning and Sales Order Departments.

An unsolved problem noted by Mr. Billings was the scheduling of parts and orders so that changes of setup were far less frequent and took account of a series of orders and not just the next part to come through.

Annual production program. Operating rates for the coming year were approved each fall by the president after consultation with his chief subordinates. These operating rates covered fairly broad groups of products, not individual items. They were estimated and approved each year in advance so that general plans could be made for purchasing raw materials, hiring labor, and replacing equipment. Detailed scheduling of individual items was done day-to-day by computer and by production schedulers as has been explained.

Development of the production program began with a forecast of dollar sales volume built up in two ways. Salesmen estimated dollar volumes in their territories. This was reviewed by the district sales managers and finally was consolidated by the general sales manager. The company statistician, a subordinate of the treasurer, made a second estimate. He projected general business conditions and translated this into an estimate of industry sales and of company sales. The two estimates were presented at an executive staff meeting of the financial, production, sales, and engineering vice-presidents and the major staff officers—the director of industrial relations, the general counsel and secretary, and the vice-president of manufacturing methods. After some discussion, the president decided what the final estimate of sales volume was to be. This was expressed in monthly dollar totals.

After the sales estimate had been determined, the production vice-president used it to decide the operating rate by product groups. Members of his production control staff presented recommendations for operating rates by product groups. This department had analyzed, for each type and group of product, past performance of the purchasers. The recommended operating rate for each product group was developed on a card that had the following form:

Type and Group of Product						
Unfilled Orders	Total Finished Stock	Daily Operating Rate	Overdue Orders	Manufac- turing Delivery to Stock	Branch Warehouse	
					Demand	Shipments
		by months				

When the recommended daily operating rates had been developed, the production vice-president submitted the recommendations to the president for decision.

Finance

The financial vice-president played a major role in recommending fixed and working capital investment for the coming year and in developing operating and cash budgets. In addition he was responsible for the accounting activities of the company.

The recommendations for capital investment and investment in inventories were made by the financial vice-president. He made an analysis of inventory and capital expenditure requirements based on past balance sheets and profit and loss statements and combined this analysis with his knowledge of the estimated sales volume (which had been approved earlier) in order to come up with his recommendations. These were presented to the president for his approval.

In developing the operating and cash budgets, the budgetary staff worked closely with the personnel of the various divisions. Each department and division head discussed his expenditures for previous years and his projected expenditures with members of the budget staff. The resulting projected expenditures were then combined by the budget staff and worked into final budgets, which the financial vice-president discussed directly with the president. Once the president had approved the budgets, then the amount of expenditure allocated to each department or division head was circulated to him.

The Accounting Division circulated three reports on inventory and sales to the other divisions and to the chief executives for informational purposes. The form of these reports is as follows:

Monthly Inventory Report					
Product Classes	Location		Total	Over and Under	
	Plants A, B, C	Branch Warehouses		Last Month	Year to Date
1					
2					
3					
etc.					

The product classes reported were differentiated on the basis of gross profit; that is, Product Class 1 contained all individual items having a large gross margin while Product Class 8 contained individual items having a small gross margin.

Monthly Sales Reports					
Product Classes	Quantity	Net Sales Value	Year to Date		% Gross Profit to Sales
			Quantity	Value	
1					
2					
3					
etc.					

Sales Report This Year Compared to Last				
Product Classes	Quantity Shipped	Net Sales		Gross Profit
		Volume	% of Total	
1				
2				
3				
etc.				

The inventory exhibit for December was received by the other department heads during the first week in February. The December dollar value of production figures were released on February 27.

Since the president had been concerned about the size of company inventories, Mr. Billings spent some time investigating results for the past year. He found a differential of $1½ million between the projected finished inventory and the actual finished inventory. The work-in-process inventory goal had been $3.1 million, but actual work-in-process inventory was $3.9 million at the balance sheet date. Further analysis of Type C, Group 9 product showed that its inventory goal had been calculated on the basis of a production cycle time of 7½ months, whereas a large order for that product which had been needed for the end of May had started into scheduling on January 15 and was shipped on May 30.

To deal with the problem of excessive investment in inventories, the treasurer recommended that an arbitrary cut of 10% be made in all inventory goals for the coming year and that this be reflected across the board in the daily operating rate. This was felt to be the quickest and most impartial way of reducing inventories and making a start toward getting them to a more reasonable size.

The sales vice-president vigorously opposed any decrease in inventories since he was sure that the current level was, at best, barely adequate to maintain the current level of sales. Any decrease could mean customer dissatisfaction through longer waits for items not in stock.

Recent balance sheets follow:

Balance Sheets, December 31

(All figures in thousands)

Assets:	Current Year	Preceding Year
Cash	$ 960	$ 650
Accounts Receivable	2,370	2,580
Inventories	10,550	9,580
Plant and Equipment (Net)	6,530	6,140
Other Assets	300	550
Total Assets	$20,710	$19,500

Liabilities and Capital:		
Accounts and Notes Payable	$ 6,170	$ 4,720
Accruals and Taxes	4,110	4,480
Common Stock	3,000	3,000
Earned Surplus	7,430	7,300
Total Liabilities and Capital	$20,710	$19,500

The company had followed a consistent policy of financing plant expansion through retained earnings and had been able in this way to avoid any burden of fixed debt charges. Earnings in recent years had been substantial and had allowed the company to maintain a good record of dividend payments.

A recommended solution

The solution proposed by Mr. Billings was as follows:

"There is a major company matter that needs specific attention over the long haul. The gathering together, auditing, and analysis of the detailed data to formulate a clear picture of the past and present is a full-time, permanent task that is too much to ask of any operating officer in our company. Such analysis and planning cannot be limited to any individual division of our business, for it comprehends every primary division in the business—Sales, Production, Engineering, and Accounting.

"We are proposing that a central administrative staff have responsibility for installation and direction of detailed planning and control methods and procedures, and for coordination of general company planning. We inject a primary responsibility for company inventories.

"The central administrative staff shall report to the president. See the following chart:

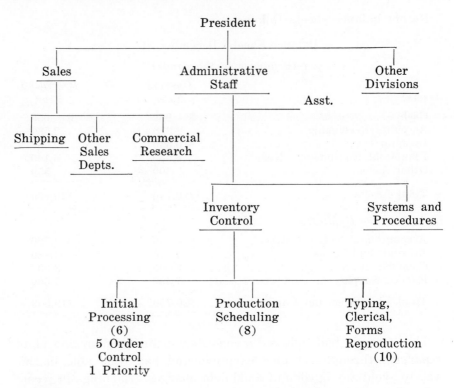

President

Sales

Administrative
Staff

Asst.

Other
Divisions

Shipping   Other
Sales
Depts.

Commercial
Research

Inventory
Control

Systems and
Procedures

Initial
Processing
(6)
5 Order
Control
1 Priority

Production
Scheduling
(8)

Typing,
Clerical,
Forms
Reproduction
(10)

REQUIRED: (a) Do you agree with Mr. Billings' recommendation?

(b) Appraise the usefulness of the information contained in the reports circulated by the accounting department.

(c) What should Mr. Sheffield say to Mr. Billings about his proposal for a central administrative staff?

(d) What steps do you recommend that Mr. Sheffield take to improve coordination in the Parker Gear Company?

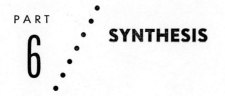

PART

6 SYNTHESIS

Ch. 27 · Company-Wide, Integrated Approach
to Central Management

COMPANY-WIDE,
INTEGRATED APPROACH
TO CENTRAL MANAGEMENT

Need for integrated approach. The variety of problems facing every central manager can be approached in several different ways. One method is to analyze each problem by itself, without regard to others. Such separate treatment has several advantages; it aids in a concentrated and detailed study, and it "clears the deck" of one issue before starting with another. This approach is likely to be most useful when the structure of administration is well established and the problem being studied is clearly defined and falls distinctly in a single area.

Many of the major problems of management have been discussed in this book, and reference to a particular chapter or section may be helpful in solving individual problems of a business executive. In other words, for someone using the approach noted in the preceding paragraph, this book may be regarded as a handbook, that is, as a convenient collection of ideas about central management.

There are serious limitations to "handbook" thinking about central management, however. Although a ready source of ideas and possible solutions to specific problems is unquestionably helpful, most management situations call for something more. Action on one problem or in one department of a company is likely to affect other activities. A solution that appears desirable from a narrow study of the problem may prove to be impractical because of limitations imposed by facilities, objectives, or other controlling factors of the situation; consequently, it is often necessary to consider a particular problem as only a part of the whole. Central management thinking requires that problems be considered from a company-wide point of view and that any course of action chosen be integrated into the total picture.

This broad integrated viewpoint, which is essential for a good central administrator, is also of value to departmental heads, staff men, and many other employees of a company. Many departmental problems can be solved satisfactorily only if the full ramifications of a proposed course of action are recognized. Men in staff positions must ever be aware of the interlocking nature of company operations if their advice is to be really constructive.

Steps in integration. Granting that an integrated approach to business administration is desirable, how can it be achieved? Can anything more be said than that the executive or the analyst should take a company-wide point of view?

The process of integration in business administration cannot be expressed with a mathematical formula. The number of situations and variables is so great that a generalized formula would have little practical use. It is possible, however, to indicate a number of steps that, if followed conscientiously, will help anyone reach an integrated judgment. Simply stated, these steps are:

1. Be sure to recognize all the important factors and issues related to the problem being studied.
2. Note interrelationships and interdependence among these factors and issues.
3. Decide upon the relative importance of (that is, attach weight to) the various factors as they exist in the particular operating situation.
4. In the light of Steps 1, 2, and 3 above, decide upon a practical course of action that will accomplish the objective.

The last two steps in this list must be taken in terms of a specific situation. Cases can be presented for practice in creativeness and the use of business judgment, but the skill thus developed must remain a personal attribute. Fortunately more help can be provided for the first two steps. Here the outlines and the discussions contained in the earlier chapters of this book can be put to good use. A broad survey of the problems facing a business administrator has been made, and this survey outline may be used as a suggestive check list for Step 1, the recognition of important factors and issues. Moreover, the survey outline and the accompanying discussion have brought out many interrelationships that are of value in Step 2.

Consequently a quick review of the general structure of the book will be of value. For present purposes this review need cover only the highlights and suggest some of the more important interrelationships. The purpose of the review is to indicate how the general survey outline may be used as a tool of integration; it is not intended to be a complete summary of all the points made.

Outlook and basic objectives. A review of the industry outlook and the position of a company in that industry (as outlined in Chapters 2 and 3) gives a picture of where the company appears to be headed. This is a passive study of the background in which the central manager must operate. The manager must first conceive of an enterprise that will operate successfully in this setting.

The general character of such a company will be shaped by its basic objectives. The place or niche the company seeks in its industry should be defined. Some thought should be given to the speed with which this position will be sought and the sacrifices one is willing to make to get there. An attitude toward social responsibility and a general philosophy of management will go further in rounding out the concept of the ideal company. These objectives probably will not all be achieved immediately, and as the firm becomes a going enterprise, some objectives will take precedence over others. Nevertheless, these objectives, along with the outlook, provide a background in which all plans for integrated action will be tested.

Sales policies. Every enterprise, large and small, private and public, must decide upon the products or the services it will provide. Policies regarding type, number, and quality of products affect directly or indirectly virtually all other plans of the company. Materials, personnel, and facilities needed, the operating methods employed, and the controls established are all affected by product policy.

Intimately associated with plans for products are policies covering the customers to whom these products will be sold. In fact, a careful analysis of the needs and the buying habits of the company's customers may have a controlling influence on what products are in the company line. Type, size, and location of company customers and the channels of distribution employed further define the economic service provided by a company. Whenever a significant change in company activities is contemplated, the wise administrator will consider whether the action will have a favorable or adverse effect upon the ability of the company to give the selected customers the products and the service they want.

If the company is to survive, it must establish pricing policies that will be attractive to customers and at the same time provide more than enough income to cover all expenses. Some aspects of pricing policies, such as discounts and price lining, must be closely tuned to customer markets; but wide changes cannot be made without repercussions on product design, volume of production, facilities needed, and production methods. These repercussions of the more detailed aspects of pricing carry even more force when policies regarding the general level of prices are under consideration. The central position of pricing becomes clear when we recognize that any action that has a major effect upon cost is likely to prevent or require a change in prices, and contrariwise a change in price has a direct bearing on the ability of the company to undertake different kinds of activity.

The right goods offered to the right customers at the right price come close to being a winning combination. It is still necessary to use some form of advertising, personal solicitation, or other kind of sales promotion if the company is going to reap full benefits of its other activities. Effective selling will indirectly aid all other departments of the company. Consequently they will be concerned that any proposed changes do not seriously interfere with quality, service, and other sales appeals used by the company.

Although this brief review of the relations between sales policies and other management plans is incomplete, the value of a company-wide, integrated approach to such problems is evident.

Production and purchasing policies. Just as it is impossible to conceive of a company without some form of product, customer, pricing, and sales promotion policies, so too is procurement essential to the very existence of every enterprise; and production and purchasing policies, like sales policies, are closely related to many other aspects of management.

An ever-present question is what should be made and what should be bought from someone else; and even if the company decides to manufacture its finished product, this raises the issue of whether to make or buy its raw materials. The answer to this question will, of course, have a major effect upon the need for facilities and other resources and upon the financial structure of the company.

Policies regarding the timing of procurement also affect many other activities of the company. The amount of working capital needed, for example, will be influenced by a decision to manufacture for stock, make large production runs, anticipate price increases, or maintain large inventories to assure service to customers. A decision to stabilize production, to cite another example, will affect not only the personnel policies but also the capacity of production and storage facilities needed and perhaps product line and sales promotion policies. Comprehensive budgets will, of course, reflect these procurement policies and may be one of the principal means used to assure that timing of procurement is coordinated with other company activities.

Not all companies have much choice regarding the production processes used. The choice, if there is one, may have a marked effect upon facilities, capital requirements, organization, and personnel needs. Policies regarding the extent of specialization, automation, and decentralization will also influence executive personnel requirements, methods, procedures, programming, and other phases of company activity. Clearly, company-wide thinking is needed in dealing with such problems as these.

Personnel policies. To a large extent personnel policies should be designed to provide the manpower needed to carry on the activities called for by the sales, production, and purchasing policies. In some situations, however, the predominant influence runs in the other direction, that is, a sound personnel policy may require adjustments in sales and procurement activities. Delivery service or store hours, for instance, may be curtailed so that employees can have convenient working hours.

Moreover, personnel policies, particularly those dealing with promotion and discharge, are closely connected with supervision and motivation. If these policies are not accepted as fair by the employees, executives will have a difficult time getting enthusiastic cooperation from their subordinates. The tie between compensation policies and activating is even closer. One of the principal ways of securing indirect motivation is to have satisfactory policies regarding arrangement for work and employee services, so here again is a close connection between policies and operations.

Selection and training activities are, of course, geared to personnel specifications for the various jobs. These specifications, in turn, are determined by the production processes and equipment of the company. For instance, a change from selling to many small customers to concentration on a few large ones will require a shift in the selling methods used; this shift in selling methods will change the type of man who should be selected as salesman and the training he will need. The change in size of customer may also lead to modifications in selling organization, size of production runs, prices, and delivery service, and these changes, in turn, may further modify personnel selection, training, and compensation.

Union relations will have an important bearing upon other personnel policies, particularly compensation, arrangements for work, and employee services. Moreover, good union relations will have an effect on the ability of a company to give customers dependable delivery of goods. Under some circumstances, union relations will have enough bearing on total cost so that a company may have to withdraw from certain markets. There is no doubt that difficulties with unions have encouraged some companies to push forward on a policy of mechanization and occasionally to either move or open new plants in other locations.

Financial policies. Financial policies, like personnel policies, tend to be adapted to the needs of the business. Thus, policies on the use of capital in a utility company will favor high investment in fixed assets, whereas in a department store a much larger portion of the capital will be used for inventories and accounts receivable. In other words, the uses of capital are determined largely by the kind of assets that are needed to carry out the sales, production, and personnel policies.

Following this line of thought, the sources of capital will be adjusted to the kind of assets the company has. A company with large amounts invested in fixed assets is more likely to secure capital through bonds than a company with assets largely in inventory. Similarly, the possibilities of obtaining bank loans will depend largely upon the use to which these funds are to be put. On the other hand, if the company must look to stockholders as a source of additional capital, dividend policies will be affected. Thus, the ratio of dividends to earnings may be kept low so that more of the earnings will remain in the business; or if the company is concerned about creating a favorable market for its securities, special attention may be given to a stable dividend rate over a period of several years.

The preceding paragraphs suggest that financial policies play a passive role, being a handmaiden to the other policies of the company. Sometimes just the reverse is true. A limitation of the amount of capital that can be obtained from different sources often leads to strict policies regarding the uses of capital. These policies in turn set limits on the volume of business that can be undertaken, the inventories that can be carried, and the new buildings and equipment that can be purchased. Under these circumstances, it may be argued that the other policies are subordinate to the financial ones. However, even where this is true, the role of the financial policy is more a matter of outside limits on the various uses of capital than it is positive and specific guidance.

This brief review of policies has not attempted a systematic summary of all the policy issues covered in Part 2 of this book; a summary chart has already been given on pages 410 and 411 and more detail may be found in the individual chapters. Instead, the review has mentioned some of the ways in which each of the types of policies are interrelated with other phases of company opration. This emphasis on the interlocking aspects of policy formulation shows the need for an integrated rather than a piecemeal approach to company management.

Administrative organization. Many activities are necessary to carry out the policies of a company. For purposes of efficiency, these activities must be grouped together into jobs suitable for a single individual, the jobs must be combined into sections, and the sections must be combined into divisions or departments. Since the work of one man or department is often dependent upon the work of other parts of the organization, relationships between the various units must be defined. In this way an organization structure for the company is established, as explained in Part 3.

Policies and methods lead to activities that are the grist for administrative organization. In special circumstances the relationship may run the other way, with organization limiting the policies that may be adopted. For example, the inability of an organization designed to sell domestic fuel oil to handle also industrial lubricants may prevent a company from adding the latter group of products to its line. Or, the cost of setting up an organization to supervise activities in southeastern United States may be so great that the company will decide not to sell to customers in this territory.

Decentralization of authority has an impact beyond the organization structure. It influences the techniques of activating and control that are appropriate, it changes the kind of people needed to fill positions at lower levels of the organization, and it often results in a modification of the programming and budgeting activities of a company. The flexibility and the improved motivation that are sometimes achieved through decentralization may enable a company to take on different products or to manufacture some raw materials that would be unwise extension of activities in a highly centralized organization.

Consequently, as these illustrations show, it is unwise to make organization changes without also considering how other management plans may have to be adjusted to conform to the new organization setup.

Resources. In actual administration, the design of an organization structure and the selection of executives to fill positions in that organization are almost inseparable. Ideally the best possible organization is designed and then executive personnel are selected to fill the positions created (see Part 4). This assumes complete freedom in the selection of executives, a condition that almost never exists. If the executives already within the company and those who can be recruited do not fit the jobs in the ideal organization, then the only practical thing to do is to modify the organization.

The capacities of the existing and available executive personnel may affect other company plans. An ample supply of technical and management know-how may encourage a manager to take on new products or to expand his activities. On the other hand, the lack of the right men may lead to postponement of actions that would otherwise be desirable. In a similar manner the quality of executive personnel will influence the type of motivation and control used within the company. Of course, abilities of executives are not a static quality, and executive development programs may be designed so that the company can in the future improve its organization, expand its activities, or simplify its controls.

Facilities may be regarded simply as the tools necessary to carry out the company policy. In this sense the location, design, and layout of facilities should be determined by the policies and other operating plans.

For an established company, however, the administrator must think in terms of the facilities already on hand. In the short run

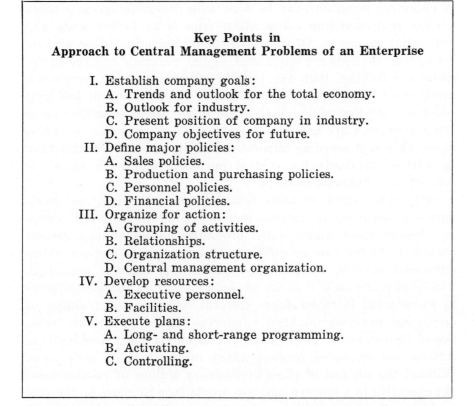

Key Points in
Approach to Central Management Problems of an Enterprise

I. Establish company goals:
  A. Trends and outlook for the total economy.
  B. Outlook for industry.
  C. Present position of company in industry.
  D. Company objectives for future.
II. Define major policies:
  A. Sales policies.
  B. Production and purchasing policies.
  C. Personnel policies.
  D. Financial policies.
III. Organize for action:
  A. Grouping of activities.
  B. Relationships.
  C. Organization structure.
  D. Central management organization.
IV. Develop resources:
  A. Executive personnel.
  B. Facilities.
V. Execute plans:
  A. Long- and short-range programming.
  B. Activating.
  C. Controlling.

he does not have time to build new buildings and buy new equipment; instead he must limit the products and the quantity he plans to make to the capacity of the facilities available to him. Even in a longer period the cost of new equipment and buildings, compared with the cost of continuing to use the existing facilities, may prevent the adoption of an otherwise good program. Consequently, the wise administrator does not make final plans until he has assured himself that the necessary facilities will be available at a reasonable cost.

Execution of plans. By their very nature the manager's tasks of execution are linked with objectives, policies, organization, and resources. The closeness of these relations will be clear in a quick review of the management problems discussed in Part 5.

Good programming calls for a broad and integrated understanding of administrative action. The timing of work, as expressed in operating programs, can be done with dependability only when a clear understanding exists about who is to do the work and with what resources. Of course, if the organization is not already set up, the methods are unplanned, or the materials and the equipment are lacking, then the process of programming assumes a much more important role; it becomes the management tool that promotes detailed planning in these other areas. Realistic operating programs are also closely related to later phases of operations; they will serve as important aids in securing coordination, in setting standards for control purposes, and as a basis for constructing financial budgets.

Activating, which includes leading, communicating, and motivating, is obviously an essential step in getting the work performed. As already noted, many of the preceding phases of management contribute to the ease or difficulty of activating. Clear-cut objectives and policies, well-defined organization, realistic programs, and other plans make it easier for both executives and subordinates to know what is to be done. Careful selection and training of employees provides qualified employees to carry out the tasks. Sound compensation policies and provision for good working conditions and employee services assist in the task of motivation. Without the support of these preliminary actions of management, the executive in a modern business would face so many on-the-spot problems that it would be almost impossible for him to keep operations running smoothly.

Control is the final step in the cycle of management. It checks actual results against standards to see whether the plans have been carried out as intended. Control is built upon previous planning because the standards of performance come from these plans; it provides the basis for subsequent planning in its appraisal of what has been successful and what has failed to meet the mark. There are, of course, many technical questions of inspection, reports, and special techniques such as budgetary control; but these have no real value except as they help to achieve past plans and to lay a basis for future plans. In other words, control has significance only when it is tied in to the other steps in managing.

Value of general survey approach. The preceding brief review of the central management problems covered in this book has made it abundantly clear that these problems interlock and that action in any one area should be taken only after the impact this action will have on other areas is checked.

What, then, is the value of the general survey approach that serves as the framework of the book? Since the problems are all interrelated and a company-wide viewpoint is desirable, does it make any difference how the problems are classified and in what order they are considered? In other words, how does the outline help us with an integrated approach to central management?

The approach is useful for three primary reasons: (1) It provides a reasonably complete *coverage* of the problems facing the central management of a company. For any specific company the outline should be varied, of course; some topics will be unimportant, while other topics, such as transportation or research policies, may have to be added. But if used with discretion, the approach gives considerable assurance that no major factors have been overlooked in analyzing the overall administration of a company.

(2) The approach also assists in integration because it suggests key *relationships* that should be kept in mind in planning action in any one phase of administration. The grouping together of closely related topics, the logical sequence of problems, and the movement from general to specific management issues all help in sensing a company as a whole. It would be quite impossible to indicate all interconnections in any arrangement of ideas simple enough to be usable, so the most we can expect is one that is suggestive. Familiarity with this particular approach will enable an executive to spot most of the important relationships quickly.

(3) Moreover, some help is provided on the third and fourth steps in integration, listed at the beginning of this chapter. Formulation of a practical, integrated course of action requires that each proposal be checked for its workability from many angles. Thus a proposed policy change should be checked against other policies, its effect on organization, the availability of key personnel and facilities, and the problems of control created. At any one of these check points, the proposal may have to be revised or further plans be made; and there will always be some moving back and forth. This checking process can be described as one of *"successive adjustments and refinements."* The general survey approach is helpful in this process because it provides a useful sequence in which this cross-checking can be done.

No approach to business problems can substitute for personal judgment in a specific business situation. A logical approach can, however, be of immense help in sizing up the situation quickly and bringing out those issues that do call for business judgment. The approach to problems of the central manager, which provides the structure of this book, has been applied to a wide variety of companies; and it has proven to be of unique value in obtaining an integrated view of company-wide activities.

PART 7 • COMPREHENSIVE CASES

Case 1 • Norris Paper Company

Case 2 • Robbins Lawn Mower Company, Inc.

Case 3 • Barber Ice Cream Company

Case 4 • Jones Joints, Inc.

Case 5 • Rocklyn Corporation

Case 6 • Eastern States Iron and Steel Company

Case 7 • Novins Wallpaper Company

Case 8 • Frederick & Frank

CASE

1

NORRIS PAPER COMPANY

BACKGROUND OF COMPANY

"Where should we go from here?" is the question bothering Frank
Norris after six years as the third generation president of the Norris
Paper Company. In the early 1900's, Mr. Henry Norris established the
company in Chicago, Illinois, to provide "a permanently profitable investment for himself and his family through the distribution of wrapping
papers and allied products."

Nature of business. As a wholesaler of coarse papers and allied products, the firm has sold throughout its history to laundries, dry cleaners,
candy stores, specialty clothing stores, grocery stores, bakeries, restaurants, butchers, department stores, drugstores, florists, and industrial
concerns of all sizes and kinds. There are many thousands of both active
and possible buyers when all the various consumers of coarse papers are
taken into account. Although lacking exact statistics, the executives of
the company are confident that Norris Paper Company sells to 15% of
the potential buyers in its trading area. This makes the company one
of the four largest distributors of coarse papers in the Chicago area.

The company distributes over 3,000 items when differences in sizes
and qualities of its products are taken into account. The company provides a complete range of wrapping materials for its customers. In
addition to papers, it sells bags, boxes, tapes, labels, and a full line of
twine. It also distributes to small retail stores a variety of items for
resale, including paper napkins, towels, plates, cups, and related items.
Cleaning supplies—brushes, brooms, cleaners, insecticides, gloves, and
mops—are offered to all customers. Salesbooks, mailing tubes, shredded
packing material, and even sawdust are carried to round out the service
to particular types of customers.

The product line has, of course, been changed with shifts in retail
distribution. In the early days of Norris Paper Company's operations,
retailing was carried on through large numbers of small, individually
owned establishments known in the trade as "Mom and Pop stores." The
owners took merchandise out of boxes and barrels according to customer
requests, wrapped it, and put it in a bag for the customer to carry while
she walked home.

Salesmen of Norris Paper Company built steady patronage for themselves and the company by fostering close personal relationships with

749

the owners of these retail stores and by performing such services as taking inventory of paper products whenever they called on a customer. The salesmen, who worked hard and made 15 to 20 calls a day, could count on a dozen orders given on the spot and constantly knew of the satisfaction that comes of making a successful call.

Indeed, the relationship between salesman and customer was so sound that often the salesman could count on the customer's remaining with him if he moved to some other firm than the Norris Paper Company. This kind of opportunity appealed to some of the successful salesmen. Over the years, Norris Paper Company sired several competitors as salesmen started their own distributing companies.

Small competitors are particularly troublesome to Norris Paper Company when business is slack. These firms are more flexible in their pricing and attempt to attract business by making special price deals with customers. They frequently have little administrative staff and often the owners do most of the selling as well as the management. They are willing to cut heavily into their gross profit to attract business.

In the past, Norris Paper Company has tried to meet such competition by utilizing its financial strength and its warehouse capacity. The ability to invest heavily in inventory and to store large quantities of paper allowed the company to make special deals with mills and thus to reduce its product costs. These deals were negotiated by the chief executives of the firm and depended upon their free-wheeling and imaginative contacts with the major executives of the paper mills.

In recent years, many of the Kraft paper mills have gone into converting, thereby having a controlled outlet for much of their capacity. As a result, Norris executives have found it much more difficult to buy advantageously even in periods of business recession.

The company has always sold paper and other products to industrial concerns as well as to retail stores. Until the mid-40's, industrial sales amounted to about 25% of the total for the company. Since then, the proportion of industrial and retail sales has reversed, and now industrial sales provide about 75% of the total volume. These customers typically buy through a purchase order, which is mailed to the distributor. A salesman calling on a purchasing agent usually has to wait to see the buyer and then has 15 minutes to make a presentation. Even if the buyer is interested, he sends his order through the mail at some later time. A salesman can make an average of only 8 calls per day on industrial accounts, and the relationship between the buyer and the seller is substantially different from that in the retail trade.

The move to industrial accounts has, on the whole, not been voluntary on the part of salesmen; they have had to seek new customers as their grocery business dwindled.

Increasingly, the foodstuffs coming to the grocery stores have been prepackaged, thereby reducing the retailer's need for wrapping materials. Moreover, independent grocery supermarkets have banded together with wholesalers in voluntary chains in order to minimize their purchasing costs. Buying cooperatives in the grocery field generally sell at mill cost plus 1 to 5%, depending upon the quality of the item ordered. The cooperatives have taken over most of the distribution of nationally advertised retail items such as napkins, towels, and tissues. Norris Paper Company still manages to sell to some stores supply items that are not resold, such as paper bags. The grocery retail business that has been retained despite the efforts of the cooperatives has been kept primarily because the older salesmen have personal contacts going back 25 years or more. In addition, Norris Paper Company gives 30-day credit and its salesmen call on the store managers. The cooperatives do not give credit and make no sales calls.

To help offset the decline in its wholesale business with retailers, Norris Paper Company entered the folding box business in 1946. The aim was to get a manufacturing profit as well as a wholesaling profit on this part of the business. Actually, the box plant has done little better than break even and company executives are still trying to find just the right niche for this part of their total activity, as will be explained more fully later.

Shift in management. Frank Norris' father was the sparkplug and dynamo for Norris Paper Company for many years. Energetic, personable, with a wide acquaintance in the trade, he personally sold the largest customers; attended to the major buying problems, especially the deals with mills for particular lots or special prices; encouraged, trained, and directed the sales force; provided most of the ideas for new products, new customers, or new sources; and acted as the general support for the entire organization.

In 1959, Frank Norris, grandson of the founder, became president when his father died unexpectedly. The company started as a family business and has remained in that tradition to a considerable degree. Frank's great-uncle, Francis G. Norris, is chairman of the board, and his uncle, John B. Norris, is chairman of the executive committee and treasurer. Several of the salesmen with the best accounts are members of the family, as are several people in the office. Most of these people regard the company as a small, warm, family corporation that provides a haven and an opportunity at various levels of responsibility.

Frank Norris was only 35 years old when he became president and he moved cautiously at first, partly because of his own uncertainty and partly because he was surrounded by men who had been with the company much longer than he and felt free to challenge any proposed change. Many of the employees remembered Frank as a small boy.

During the six years of Frank Norris' tenure as president, three executives have emerged as the central figures in the administration of the firm—Frank Norris, Philip Freneau, and Royall Tyler. Philip Freneau has been with the company almost as long as Frank Norris, and before that he was in accounting. Royall Tyler had considerable sales experience with two different paper concerns before joining Norris

Paper Company two years ago. Together these three provide most of the drive and the initiative in the central management of the business. Frank G. Norris is completely retired from active work and John B. Norris is semiretired.

One of Frank Norris' first major changes was a physical move of the warehouse and office. For years, the company had owned two buildings in downtown Chicago. They were multistory structures not well suited to rapid handling of merchandise and possessing only limited loading facilities. After considerable search, a two-story building was found on the west side of Chicago. This building contains 105,000 square feet of total floor space (compared with 55,000 feet in the old buildings), is of modern fireproof construction, and is leased for 30 years with an option to renew for 15 more. The first floor can contain any warehousing or manufacturing operation, and the second floor, about 12,000 square feet, is suitable for offices or warehousing. Frank Norris and Philip Freneau decided that this building provided an opportunity to accomplish operating efficiencies and to bring all operations under one roof with centralized management control. Warehousing activities were moved early in 1961 and the folding box plant was brought in from its separate location a year later.

A basic company objective developed by Frank Norris and Philip Freneau back in 1961 calls for "dual efforts of consolidation and expansion." An early step toward consolidation was the move of box-making operations into the same building as the coarse paper distribution operation. This allows closer top management surveillance of both companies and facilitates joint use of accounting and sales personnel.

The other part of company strategy has to do with expansion. According to Philip Freneau: "Growth of one of the companies will mean that it will probably move from the west-side building. This will take place, however, only after a period of demonstrated proof that the division management has the capabilities of running an expanded operation. Thus, it would move out on a substantial foundation."

Problems of implementing this basic strategy are indicated in a more detailed analysis of company operations.

WHOLESALE OPERATIONS

Salesmen entrepreneurs. On frequent occasions the executives of Norris Paper Company say: "The major strength of our company is the ability of our sales force. A group of strong, resourceful salesmen enabled this company to grow." These men are "commission salesmen" and an understanding of the way they operate is essential to a grasp of the nature of Norris' wholesaling operations.

The company establishes a salesmen's cost for each item in the line. Then the company and the salesmen split the gross margin between the selling cost and the selling price. The company does also suggest a selling price, but the salesmen may and do frequently adjust this price as they feel is necessary to get business from their customers.

Each salesman picks his own customers in any location he wishes and decides how often he will call on them. As long as an account is active, another Norris salesman may not solicit business there. The salesman pays all his own expenses.

This method of selling means that, in effect, each salesman is in business for himself. The amount of his earnings depends upon the gross margin on his sales, and the gross margin depends upon how many customers he succeeds in selling and the prices he charges. Obviously, this kind of an arrangement has a strong appeal to salesmen who like to be independent in their activities.

Customers. Norris Paper Company operates a warehouse in Rockford, Illinois (about 90 miles west of Chicago), as well as the main operation in the city. The 20 salesmen working out of each of these warehouses cover the metropolitan area and the north-central counties in Illinois. The selection of individual customers is indicated in the following comments by successful salesmen on the way they have built up their particular accounts.

A Rockford salesman describes his job. "Rockford is not so competitive as Chicago. I have about 100 customers, 15 industrial and 85 retail. The industrial customers buy towels and tissues, the retail customers buy 35% for their own use and 65% for resale. I developed the territory myself by making 30 calls per day and gradually building up a group of customers. This rate was necessary when I was trying to get established. Now I make about 6 calls per day on the industry route and 10 to 15 on the retail route. My time is divided one week to each.

"The move now is toward industrial customers, and to build new sales I will work an item. That is, I'll take something newly brought into the line or a hot item such as a seasonal item and push it for 10 to 12 calls per day. Recently, I have made a few sales to laundries. My first effort was to call on one to show the owner how he could save some money by a different method of wrapping. Success with this led me to check the phone book for other laundries and to attempt to build up this trade. Of course, the backbone of my business is with established customers.

"One week I call through Cherry Valley, Marengo, and Belvidere and then spend 2½ days in Rockford. I estimate that I sell to about 65% of the potential retail accounts in the first three towns. Of course, other Norris men are in the same territory. The next week I highlight Winnebago, Seward, Byron, and Mt. Morris, calling on perhaps 30% of the accounts, and then spend a day in Rockford.

"I am never home before five in the afternoon. Plenty of days in this business are discouraging, but I make it a firm rule to stay out and often find that I pick up a good order in the last half hour.

"Each of us at Rockford has towns that he hits regularly, except one man who is 100% industrial. Most of the industrial accounts are in

Rockford. I have about 40 customers there, but there is a lot of volume left in Rockford."

A Chicago salesman describes his job. "I cover mostly the West—Oak Park, Maywood, and the western suburbs. As my customers moved, I followed them. Retail markets are 95% of my business and I specialize in meat markets and bakeries. Since I have been in this business for 38 years, I have gotten many customers through recommendations or calls from people who used to work for customers and are starting on their own.

"For meat markets I specialize in butcher's paper of high quality. For bakeries I sell boxes, poly bags, shopping bags, cash-and-carry bags, cordage, and twine. My best success is by personalizing each bakery's printing.

"I have been a director for about 10 years. I attend meetings, give opinions, and try to see malfunctions in the warehouse. If there are dangers in excess stockpiles of a few items, I call this to Tyler's or Frank Norris' attention—or I may note that a truck has been parked and waiting for an excessive time."

Another Chicago salesman describes his job. "I sell Kimpak, Kraft, tapes, twine, tissues, towels, nontarnish paper, wrapping papers, and coffee cups mostly to electronic, motor, and farm equipment manufacturers. I built my list customer by customer, locating them in the telephone red book by industry and by referrals from other customers. I know what they will buy from the products they ship—based on past experience.

"The customers are lined up by territory and I call on 6 per day on the average. As a commission man, I can't shoot too much of my time waiting. For each customer I keep a record of each item bought, each date he purchases, and the price quoted."

Products. As already noted, the company carries a variety of products in addition to a complete line of wrapping papers and related products. A continuing problem is finding new products that can be sold in profitable volume and dropping old products. With respect to this problem, Royall Tyler remarked:

"In adding new products we need to judge the direction in which we are going. We took on an industrial cellulose wadding line because this is a technical, industrial product. We had been trying to get the line for several years. They held off because our reputation in the trade was: 'Oh, hell, they sell grocery stores. You don't want to fool with them.' After five months they finally gave us the line. It is sold on a suggested resale price and in small units, so it fits in with a warehouse operation.

"A big responsibility is to keep abreast of the changing nature of the business. The cellulose wadding line is good for the men as they move into the industrial field. It provides an entry for them to the industrial purchasing agent beside just Kraft and toilet paper. Any purchasing agent buys these, but he does it on price. We need something to be able to continually feed the purchasing agent with new items to build him up in his own concern. He can go to his boss or to production with a new idea and thus get some credit in his company. For example, a fellow who was packing marble had never been satisfied with his packing materials and we were finally able to come up with a special laminated paper that did the job. This kind of selling calls for creativeness on the part of the salesmen in helping the purchasing agent.

"Four years ago we took on bagged charcoal. One of our Kraft paper suppliers made it. It was a resale item for our retail men. At the time I was bent on new items. I took a flier on something that had a dynamic market. We bought it in carloads of 30,000 pounds at $1,500 a carload with 5% off for preseason buying before March 1. We sold it in 10-pound bags (prepacked by the supplier), mainly from the Rockford warehouse. Two years ago we sold 6 carloads and last year 10 carloads. It went out to the salesmen at 53 cents per bag selling cost. Last year, at first retailers were getting it for 55 cents on a minimum order of 50 bags. Then Jewel Tea began to use it as a leader and sold it at 49 cents per pag and, at the end of the season, our price to the retailer had dropped to 51 cents.

"Now, we have a half-car carryover. Should we buy more for the next season? How much? At what price? What is the cost of the few broken bags in the car and the warehouse—say 5 to 10 bags per car? How does the product affect our corporate image?

"We have records, of course, on the volume and the profit margin of each item each year. However, these are difficult to interpret because some items are carried as a service to a particular group of customers. Normally, once an item is in the line we keep it there until the volume is very small or the profit margin highly narrow. Then we check with salesmen to be sure that dropping the item will not seriously hurt their standing with important customers. Pruning the line is a continual task, but more important to our future success is finding new items that our salesmen can sell at a good profit margin."

Shipments. While a great majority of the orders taken by Norris salesmen are for shipment from the company warehouses, about half of the dollar volume is shipped directly by the manufacturer to the customer. From Norris' point of view, both the mill drop shipment and the full carload shipments are desirable because no inventory is carried and no physical warehousing is involved. Of course, the margin of profit on this type of business is smaller, and a customer who buys paper in carload lots very often will start going directly to paper manufacturers, eliminating Norris altogether. The importance of these various types of shipments last year to the men selling out of Chicago is indicated in the following table; warehouse sales are a much higher percentage of the total in Rockford.

Type of Shipments
Sold by Chicago Salesmen

	Warehouse Sales	Mill Drop Shipments	Full Carloads
Dollar sales	$1,281,000	$869,000	$541,000
Number of orders	20,458	3,952	187
Average value of order ...	$ 63	$ 220	$ 2,891
Rate of earnings for salesmen (% of sales) ..	7.2	5.3	2.9

The company has not been successful in selling products other than paper and twine in carload lots. For example, Frank Norris attempted to sell cellophane in large quantities to big customers. The margin he was able to obtain over the manufacturer's price was too small to warrant the effort in getting the sales and tying up capital in accounts receivable.

Pricing. The specific prices charged a given customer are determined by the salesman. He knows most about the customer's needs, the service Norris Paper Company is rendering to that customer, and the competition he faces. The other data with which the salesman works are salesman's costs, which are developed as follows:

A. Carload shipments—cost to the firm.
B. Mill drop shipments—cost to the firm plus 2%.
C. Warehouse shipments—cost to the firm plus 5 to 15% (the percentage depends upon warehousing cost and the size of the specific order).

For both warehouse shipments and mill drop shipments, the salesman gets 50% of the gross margin above his selling cost. On carload shipments he gets 45% of the gross margin. The gross profit that the company retains from this pricing and commission process, unfortunately, has been too narrow to yield the company a profit in recent years. Philip Freneau states: "Our markup has not kept up with our warehousing cost, and the company split of the difference between price and salesman's selling cost is not adequately covering our general administrative expenses."

Industry statistics compiled by the Paper Merchants Trade Association support the belief that Norris Paper Company's gross margin is low. While the figures are not strictly comparable because of differences in accounting and in competition in the Chicago area versus the country as a whole, the following table does indicate that the trading margin of Norris Paper Company is at least 1% below the industry average (the margins for the Rockford warehouse are more nearly in line with the industry as a whole).

Gross Profit Margin—Norris versus Industry
(Selling price minus actual cost)

	Warehouse Sales	Mill Drop Shipments	Mill Carload Shipments
Norris Paper Company	20.8%	12.8%	6.3%
Industry averages:			
All merchants	21.8	11.9	
Merchants earning less than 1% on sales after taxes [a] ...	21.7	11.7	
Merchants earning between 1% and 2% on sales after taxes [b]	22.0	11.9	
Merchants earning over 2% on sales after taxes [c]	23.0	13.2	

[a] 40% of total reporting.
[b] 54% of total reporting.
[c] 6% of total reporting.

Philip Freneau has suggested that the company add 1% to the markup between actual cost and salesman's cost in order to cover the increase in warehousing and administrative expenses. Frank Norris is reluctant to make this move because he believes that the salesmen are trying to get the best price they can already; consequently, Philip Freneau's suggestion would merely decrease the earnings of the salesmen. Frank Norris points out that the average earning of salesmen has already dropped well below $9,000 and that it is becoming increasingly difficult to attract good salesmen for this compensation.

Purchasing and warehousing. *Purchasing.* Norris Paper Company deals with 186 suppliers. Annual purchases from any one source range between $4,000 and $1 million. Two thirds of the buying volume is done with 10 mills. Executives of the company regard relations with suppliers as second in importance only to those with customers. A long-standing relationship with a paper supplier is particularly important in times of general shortage, when larger quotas are assigned by the mills to old-time customers. However, the importance of tonnage discounts have been minimized in recent years.

Royall Tyler observes: "The days of the superduper deal in purchasing are over. There was a time when Frank's father could fly to a mill and get 20% off for buying a hundred tons of Kraft. Norris Paper Company could do this with its capital and warehousing strength. There are no more price concessions of this kind. Earlier this year we bought $50,000 of Kraft—a side-run from a northern mill. We wound up selling it at 20% below cost because of the working capital squeeze."

During Frank Norris' tenure as president there have been several changes in purchasing responsibilities. A brother-in-law insisted on an office job in 1960 and was appointed purchasing agent. Two years later, dissatisfied with his progress in the company, he left to manage a variety store. The manager of the twine and cordage department then was tried out in the job. He lasted 30 days. The present purchasing agent, Mr.

Cable, was then brought in from Rockford where he had been serving as sales manager. Reporting to Mr. Cable are three people: a typist, a stock buyer, and a drop shipment buyer. The stock buyer does most of the purchasing of warehouse items, maintaining the perpetual inventory of the goods in the warehouse and doing some expediting at the request of the salesmen. The drop shipment buyer quotes prices to the salesmen, occasionally surveys mills for a price when requested by a salesman, and handles the details of purchasing from the mills.

Mr. Cable spends about 50% of his time attempting to find mill sources for new items brought in by the salesmen. On repeat orders he follows the long-standing company practice of ordering from a source that had originally supplied the item. Mr. Cable also approves invoices for discount terms and the f.o.b. point; talks to mill representatives; and signs or initials all purchase orders (about 500 per month). Negotiating with mills on standard items is not difficult, since each mill has a published price list and Mr. Cable can tell from these the price to pay.

One of the problems in purchasing is the tendency of some mills that sell direct as well as through wholesalers to solicit business for their own account when they note that they are making repeat drop shipments to a Norris customer. About 75% of the coarse paper mills sell both directly and through wholesalers. At times, there have been difficulties between Mr. Cable and several of the salesmen. Mr. Cable attributes this to the salesmen's constant pressure for a lower price and for "what they call special deals; they always want 5% off and want the mills to ship more quickly than they can."

An attempt was made in 1963 to consolidate the purchasing of Chicago and Rockford, but this did not work satisfactorily. There was difficulty in communicating from Rockford to Chicago the specifications of just what was wanted. Since both Chicago and Rockford typically buy in large enough quantities to get the highest quantity discounts, the intangible advantages of one man placing more business with a supplier did not seem to warrant the confusion created by consolidated buying.

Warehousing. Warehousing has posed no significant problem to Norris Paper Company since it moved from its old quarters in downtown Chicago. The new building has almost twice the space of the former quarters, and its construction permits much easier receipt and handling of goods. In fact, with the increasing proportion of goods shipped directly from the mills, the warehouse space is not being utilized to its full capacity.

The move to the new warehouse, coupled with greater use of pallets and forklift trucks, has permitted a reduction in the warehouse personnel from 13 to 8 men; however, the space cost is much higher. Delivery, which is done by contract trucker, costs somewhat less, partly because of the improved loading and unloading time. The net effect of these differences in costs balances out, and the 1964 charge for warehouse and delivery was $189,000 compared with $192,000 in 1959. Of course, during this interval wages increased, so that costs are certainly below what they would have been if the move had not been made. Service to customers probably has been improved. So, while the move has proven to be a wise one, it has not yet given the company any marked advantage.

Personnel. Top executives of Norris Paper Company agree that, in the wholesaling operations, having the right salesmen is the major personnel problem. Warehouse and office personnel can be hired and trained as needed, but salespeople take longer to develop and are more difficult to find.

The Chicago sales manager points out: "In Chicago, 50% of the sales force has been with the company more than 15 years. The average age is 51 years. We have two groups with only 5 men in between. The 7 older men have been here 20 to 30 years, and the younger group of 8 have been with us 2 years or less. Ordinarily, we don't have so many new salesmen. This is some of our own doing, since we have forced turnover to a certain extent in view of the advanced ages of 4 or 5 men and the incompetence of 2 who were wasting good accounts. Normally, there should be 2 openings a year in the entire sales force.

"It is almost impossible to hire an experienced paper salesman. We certainly would make an opening if an experienced man wanted to come with us. In finding new salesmen, we look for someone who has been in other kinds of industrial selling, if an industrial route is open. For a retail route, we look for someone who has been selling cookies, or meats, or some retail product. Normally, we hire in the 28- to 38-year age bracket. Young men have not been successful with us.

"Training a man in this business is not easy. First, we have so many items. I could spend a month alone with any new man. Second, the best way to learn is on the street—getting questions on specific things. We have tried several times to hire a man and put him inside at various desks. He learns the names but not the specifics of the product. A drawback of this is that we are limited on the salary we can pay, so we could only hire a 21-year-old for such a spot. It would be hard to determine just when he would be capable of going outside, and we can't have him inside for 5 years. Furthermore, a good young man won't wait 5 years."

Some adjustment may be necessary in the way the company develops future salesmen. Royall Tyler observes: "The prevailing philosophy in Norris Paper Company has been that men were on their own. They did their own pricing, set their own routes, and developed their own customers. We have difficulty pursuing this kind of effort now. First, who is going to plod for $100 a week to build his own empire? No one has to do this now; there are too many other opportunities. Second, for low-pressure selling we need high-caliber men. Third, the emphasis in industrial companies and the large retail accounts is on technicians and purchasing. The man our salesman talks to is no dope. The glad-hander does not get the business."

Norris salesmen earn between $7,500 and $15,000 per year. For experienced salesmen, this income comes from their commissions—based on the split of the gross margin earned on their sales as already explained. In addition, each December the company gives salesmen 1% of the commissions they earned during the preceding year to be used for gifts for their customers. The difficulty of making profitable sales affects the salesmen's income as well as the company's net profit; currently the average annual compensation for salesmen is about $8,500.

New salesmen are paid a guaranteed minimum commission of $150 per week. Their earned commissions are not expected to equal this amount until probably a year. However, after the first six months both the company and the man carefully review his progress and he is kept on only if it appears likely that he will be earning the minimum guarantee during his second year. In the past year, the company paid new salesmen a total of $19,000 in excess of their commissions. This total is disturbing to the senior executives, who feel that the "excess draw" should be about half as large.

The Paper Merchants Trade Association recently made a study of salesmen's compensation and came up with a proposal that is more complicated than the Norris plan but that also gives a company more control over the activity of salesmen. Most Norris executives believe, however, that the unique strength of the company sales force is related to the system of compensation. "Changing our compensation method for the sales force," Royall Tyler observes, "is like an Act of Congress to the salesmen. I got absolutely nowhere a year ago when I suggested we might study the matter. Good paper salesmen—and we have them—can go anywhere. An officer left us just a few months ago to go into business for himself. He can buy almost as cheaply as we can from the same source."

Financial results of wholesale operations. The sales, expense, and profit figures for Norris Paper Company wholesaling activities during the period 1958 through 1964 are shown on page 761.

The very narrow profit margin on which Norris Paper Company works is clearly indicated in the results for the past 7 years. Over the period the gross profit margin has been squeezed, and at no time during the period has the company earned a net profit after tax of 1% of sales. When allowance is made for the change in the date of the fiscal year in 1963, it is noted that the dollar sales volume moved up from 1960 through 1963, but the balance between expenses and gross profit remained very narrow throughout the period. In 1964 both sales volume and gross profit margin dropped; expenses were also trimmed compared with the annual rate in 1963 so that the company was barely able to break even.

Actually, the wholesaling operation is not so cleanly separated from the folding box operations as the financial statement implies. There is a substantial amount of joint action in selling, warehousing, and administrative work, and the allocation of these expenses between the whole-

Norris Paper Company
Income Statements—1958-1964

	Year Ending Sept. 30 1964	9 Months Ending Sept. 30 1963	Year 1962	Year 1961	Year 1960	Year 1959	Year 1958
	(Figures in $1,000's)						
Net sales	5,628	5,074	6,344	5,831	5,215	5,461	5,113
Cost of goods sold	4,689	4,176	5,335	4,868	4,315	4,450	4,152
Gross profit	939	898	1,009	963	900	1,011	961
Expenses:							
Selling	346	329	393	369	356	407	388
Warehouse and delivery	189	157	194	213	177	192	173
Administrative and general	398	361	361	344	338	355	340
Total expenses	933	847	948	926	871	954	901
Operating profit	6	51	61	37	29	57	60
Other income and deductions (net)	1	—9	—7	—3	—9	—22	—1
Net profit before income tax	7	42	54	34	20	35	59
Income tax	2	19	13	15	+ 3	25	13
Net profit	5	23	41	19	23	10	46
	(Percent of Net Sales)						
Net sales	100.0	100.0	100.0	100.0	100.0	100.0	100.0
Cost of goods sold	83.3	82.5	84.1	83.5	82.7	81.5	81.2
Gross profit	16.7	17.5	15.9	16.5	17.3	18.5	18.8
Expenses:							
Selling	6.2	6.3	6.2	6.3	6.8	7.5	7.6
Warehouse and delivery	3.3	3.2	3.1	3.7	3.4	3.5	3.4
Administrative and general	7.1	6.8	5.7	5.9	6.5	6.5	6.7
Total expenses	16.6	16.3	15.0	15.9	16.7	17.5	17.7
Operating profit	0.1	1.2	0.9	0.6	0.6	1.0	1.1
Other income and deductions (net)	0.1	—0.1	—0.1		—0.2	—.4	
Net profit before income tax	0.1	1.1	0.8	0.6	0.4	0.6	1.1
Income tax		0.4	0.2	0.3		0.4	0.2
Net profit	0.1	0.7	.6	0.3	0.4	0.2	0.9

saling and the folding box company is necessarily somewhat arbitrary. To understand the total picture, then, we should take a close look at the folding-box activities.

FOLDING BOX OPERATIONS

Norris entry into folding box industry. Folding Box Corporation is a subsidiary of Norris Paper Company. It manufactures and sells folding boxes to department stores, bakeries, candy stores, dry cleaners, and speciality clothing stores both in Chicago and throughout the Mid-West.

This company was started in late 1945 when Norris Paper Company decided to diversify and enter a manufacturing field. Frank Norris' father persuaded John Trumbull to leave his post as production superintendent at another folding box company and to come to Norris Paper Company as general manager of its box subsidiary. Mr. Trumbull had some sales accounts that came with him to Folding Box Corporation. For several years before this, Norris Paper Company had been distributing stock boxes to its customers.

In 1945 and 1946 the market was very strong for stock boxes, especially among the "Mom and Pop" stores. Paperboard was in short supply generally, but Norris Paper Company was able to get some board through its regular paper suppliers with whom it had long-established and firm relationships. Through the acquisition of used machinery and with the hiring of John Trumbull, Folding Box Corporation was ready to operate.

Although the machinery was old (some executives of the Norris Paper Company called it "castoff"), it was suitable for making stock boxes and was adequate in its location, for the building structure was such that high-speed presses could not be used.

Stock boxes are used by many different customers and are made in a few standard sizes. As a result, they can be made in long runs, stored, and sold in dribs and drabs. Meeting customer requirements for service is no problem since the boxes are taken from storage and shipped immediately.

Salesmen of Norris Paper Company have carried much of the selling burden for Folding Box Corporation. They sell to small accounts for the most part. John Trumbull and Paul More (production manager) sell to large customers. These men compete with salesmen from 20 other folding box manufacturers in Chicago and from approximately 200 such manufacturers in the rest of the United States.

During the 8 years of its operation on the South Side, Folding Box Corporation was run pretty much as a separate company with only its financial policy subject to control by Norris Paper Company. Products, production methods, purchasing, prices, and sales promotion were all directed by John Trumbull and Paul More. In addition to providing Norris salesmen with an additional product and additional sales commissions, Folding Box Corporation earned a fair rate of return on the initial investment of about $120,000. Sales and net profits for the first 6 years of operation are shown below.

	Sales	Net Profits
1951	$591,000	$16,000
1950	594,000	20,000
1949	591,000	23,000
1948	454,000	—13,000
1947	472,000	10,000
1946	303,000	19,000

Industry trends. The folding box industry is a segment of the much larger packaging industry. Since World War II, packaging by manufacturers has been a rapidly growing and dynamic field. Packages are not only designed to protect the product until it reaches the final consumer; they also are an important element of the sales promotion by presenting the product in an attractive manner to the consumer. Color, fancy printing, new plastic materials, and novel designs have all contributed to this great growth in packaging.

Manufacture of folding paper boxes is not complex. They are run through presses for printing and for cutting and creasing. Then, after stripping the unused corners or cutouts, those boxes that will have a cellophane window are run through a machine for this purpose. The boxes are then either glued or stapled, after which they are tied into large bundles for shipment to customers. Substantial production economies are possible if the boxes are produced in long runs on highly automated machinery; consequently, cost control is an important element in the industry. Also, wide difference exists in the quality of the printing and the precision with which the boxes are made.

During the 1950's several of the major producers of paperboard went into the production of folding paper boxes. These companies make boxes for products such as soapflakes or frozen foods by the millions; they are interested in selling the tonnage of their paperboard plants as well as making the converting margin. At the same time, many of the large consumers installed box equipment of their own. As a consequence, large tonnage business is not available to an independent converter such as Folding Box Corporation.

Numerous manufacturing concerns, however, either have diversified products or are small in total capacity. These companies often buy from 1,000 to 100,000 boxes of a particular size and design. Pharmaceutical companies, for instance, need a different box for each size bottle of each product they sell. These boxes must contain a printed message regarding the contents, and usually they will fit into an overall color and style that characterizes a particular line of products. Suit boxes, purchased by department stores, involve much less converting effort, often having only the name of the store printed on the top of the box. The independent paper box manufacturer makes his money, not in buying and reselling paperboard, but from the converting work he performs on the board. Of the total selling price, the converting margin ranges from less than 30% for suit boxes to 80% for tricky, multicolor display boxes.

Because of the trend toward vertical integration mentioned above and the competition from plastic packaging, the independent folding box manufacturer has had to be quite resourceful to make a good profit margin during the last 10 to 15 years.

Products. Since Folding Box Corporation was first established, stock boxes have been a primary product. For example, Folding Box Corporation carries in its warehouse:

> Cake boxes
> Sausage boxes
> Two-piece clothing boxes
> Laundry boxes
> Envelope boxes
> Men's hat boxes

All of the above stock boxes are made up in quantities of 25,000 to 100,000 of each size and are carried on hand for sale in smaller quantities. They are sold plain or are printed with the customer's name.

Actually, for the industry, stock boxes account for less than 7% of the folding boxes produced. Most folding boxes used for food, beverages, hardware, tobacco, soap, cosmetics, medicine, textiles, sporting goods, and toys are manufactured to the specifications of the customer.

Folding Box Corporation is in the process of shifting its sales away from standard boxes. By 1956, only 33% of its sales were in this line, and by 1958 the percentage had dropped to 25%. Both the executives of Folding Box Corporation and the sales division of Norris Paper Company recognized that higher profit margins are potentially available in special boxes. But difficulties must be overcome in both production and sales if the volume of this kind of business is to be increased.

Sales arrangements. About half of Folding Box Corporation's sales are obtained by Norris salesmen. Most of the other half come from "house accounts" handled by John Trumbull and Paul More. John Trumbull says: "One of the great advantages we have over competitors is the many, many contacts of the Norris salesmen. Our competitors may spend months just to get in to see a man, whereas the Norris salesman is already doing business with him and can approach him on folding boxes without any special introduction. We haven't yet really learned the best way to take advantage of this great asset."

Most of the house accounts handled by John Trumbull are department stores and other large retail chains. This type of customer is more interested in price than in unique design, and Philip Freneau remarks about John Trumbull's sales, "He gets the volume all right, but it usually is low-margin stuff."

Two years ago, Folding Box Corporation hired a man to sell only folding boxes. He had been working as a salesman for a competitor, and when the competitor closed down its Chicago plant, Folding Box Corporation was able to hire him. John Trumbull felt fortunate to find someone with the requisite technical background and experience. His record with the company indicates that he is a plugger, not a real salesman. He does have one account that buys about $100,000 worth of boxes per year. "If that were lost, he would be in real trouble," says Paul More.

Royall Tyler, in commenting about the possibility of increasing sales, says: "Folding Box Corporation is the hardest place to get a man for. John Trumbull is looking for a second full-time man, hopefully with experience. A salesman there should be talking not only to the purchasing agent but also to the packaging engineer and the advertising people. He is competing with Robert Gair, Container Corporation, and Marathon. In this kind of selling, you are selling a source of supply— a dependable, reliable producer of part of the customer's entire sales package and sales message.

"The biggest opportunity for selling is in the specialty box field, but it is a terrific problem. The way to sell is to come up with a design or construction that is unique, to understand the customer's needs and relate these needs to art and design work. For example, one customer with a new automatic packaging line required 12 calls by John Trumbull in addition to those made by the Norris salesman who had the account."

Production. *Cost reduction.* In the production phase of Folding Box Corporation, Frank Norris and Philip Freneau have been concerned primarily about reducing costs and improving quality. An early step to get control of these two aspects of the business was moving the box plant from its South Side location to the new warehouse where top corporate officials could watch the operations more closely and some economies in the flow of materials could be realized. Unfortunately, the benefits of these changes are difficult to measure, and on the other side of the ledger is an increase in annual rental from $12,600 to $25,500.

After the operation was well established in its new quarters, Philip Freneau installed a job order cost control system. The general feeling now is that the operating costs are reasonable in terms of the equipment in the plant and the size of the orders being run. In 1962, a new, high-speed printer was purchased for $40,000. This was particularly suited for long runs of stock boxes.

Even with these measures, however, Folding Box Corporation's costs for stock boxes were high. A Michigan company that does a large volume of business in stock boxes offered to sell boxes to Folding Box Corporation for 5 to 10% below the latter's production costs. After some negotiation, Folding Box Corporation agreed to buy at least $100,000 of such products during the ensuing year at the quoted prices. Also included in the deal was the sale of the high-speed printer to the Michigan firm. As a consequence, Folding Box Corporation purchased rather than produced most of its stock boxes starting in June, 1963.

At the end of the year, the Michigan company reported that it had suffered a loss and consequently was obliged to increase its prices to Folding Box Corporation. Paul More has been looking around for another source and is now negotiating with a Chicago firm that sells only to jobbers. Prices quoted by the Chicago firm are as good as those originally set by the Michigan company and on some items are 10% lower. Philip Freneau, who currently is general manager of Folding Box Corporation, feels, "If somebody else can sell them to us cheaper than we can make them, it is better to use our plant for other items."

John Trumbull is not so sure what the final effect will be of having a large portion of the stock boxes produced by someone else. "At least we now know that our costs are in line with our competitors' costs, and that should help us get a satisfactory margin on this part of our business. However, we won't really be ahead until we get some new volume in the shop to take the place of the boxes we are now buying. A lot of our overhead is fixed, and we need a 50% increase in the work going through the shop to absorb it."

Product quality. Folding Box Corporation has been able to produce satisfactory quality for the kind of orders that have been going through the shop. Most of these have been standard one-color print jobs. To improve its ability to do specialty work, the corporation purchased a two-color press and a window-cellophaner in 1964. Even with this equipment, however, the company is fundamentally set up to produce standard type boxes. An additional investment of at least $200,000 or $300,000 would be necessary to equip the shop to do precision four-color work on a competitive basis, and if the company does move in this direction, the workers will have to adjust their methods accordingly.

Key personnel and organization. For most of its existence, Folding Box Corporation has been run by John Trumbull and by Paul More, who joined the corporation in 1948 after working several years with a large integrated paper and box manufacturing company. The two men both handle inquiries from customers, schedule production through the plant, and estimate new quotations for special orders. In addition, a plant superintendent directs the printing, cutting, and gluing, as well as the dye room foreman, two materials handlers, and the shipping clerk.

A year ago, Frank Norris became concerned about the control of costs and the financial results of Folding Box Corporation, and he asked Philip Freneau to take on the assignment of general manager in addition to his other duties with Norris Paper Company. Philip Freneau encouraged John Trumbull to focus most of his attention on new sales and Paul More to concentrate on purchasing and production. All three men work closely together and the division of duties is not sharply drawn.

Much of the sales direction is working with the salesmen of Norris Paper Company and assisting them when they run into technical problems. John Trumbull also does personal selling himself and supervises the one full-time box salesman.

All the accounting and financial work for Folding Box Corporation is done by the office staff of Norris Paper Company under Philip Freneau's general direction. Deliveries are made by the same trucking firm that handles Norris Paper Company shipments. In actual operations, then, Folding Box and Norris Paper are closely interwoven.

Financial results. The comparative income statement for the last six years (given on page 768) shows that Folding Box Corporation had a significant increase in sales between 1960 and 1962, and has been holding at about this level during the last two years. The net profit picture, however, shows that Folding Box Corporation is barely breaking even and lost over 2% of sales in the last year.

Folding Box Corporation has never paid dividends on its common stock. It has paid a small dividend on the preferred stock since it was issued in 1962 to finance the purchase of the high-speed printer.

Folding Box Corporation never has had a long-term debt, and until last year it never borrowed from the bank. This strong financial position was possible because the investment in fixed assets was quite low in relation to the total volume of business done. When the first major addition, the high-speed printer, was made in 1962, Norris Paper Company purchased newly issued preferred stock to finance the deal. Then, in the past year Folding Box Corporation purchased additional equipment for approximately $39,000, but this purchase was financed by short-term loans—$25,000 from the bank and $14,000 from the supplier of the equipment. This method of financing is noteworthy, partly because it reduces Folding Box Corporation's current ratio below 2 to 1, and also because it represents the first time Norris Paper Company or one of its subsidiaries has gone into debt to finance expansion.

Folding Box Corporation
Balance Sheet as of September 30, 1964
(in $1,000's)

Assets		Liabilities	
Cash	4	Notes payable to bank	25
Trade receivables (net)	64	Equipment contract payable	14
Inventory	108	Trade accounts payable	52
Prepaid expenses	16	Accrued salaries and payroll taxes	9
Recoverable income tax	3		
		Total current liabilities	100
Total current assets	195	*Equity*	
		Preferred stock (6%, $100 par,	
Accounts receivable from Norris		395 shares held by Norris Paper	
Paper Company	10	Company)	40
Cash surrender value of life in-		Common stock (1,220 shares out-	
surance	6	standing; 96% owned by Norris	
		Paper Company)	122
Total other assets	16	Retained earnings	64
		Total equity	226
Equipment (net)	115		
Total assets	326	Total liabilities and equity	326

Folding Box Corporation
Income Statements—1959-1964

(Figures in $1,000's)

	Year Ending Sept. 30 1964	9 Months Ending Sept. 30 1963	Year 1962	Year 1961	Year 1960	Year 1959
Net sales	825	631	846	761	663	666
Cost of products sold	737	536	711	656	569	569
Gross profit	88	95	135	105	94	97
Expenses:						
Selling	77	42	50	38	34	41
Administrative and general	34	56	67	55	53	46
Other deductions less other income	+ 3	+ 1	7	23*	...	...
Total expenses	108	97	124	116	87	87
Profit before income tax	+ 20	− 2	11	− 11	7	10
Income tax	+ 3	...	4	+ 4	3	3
Net profit	− 17	− 2	7	− 7	4	7

*1961 other deductions included $23,000 moving expense.

(Percent of Net Sales)

	Year Ending Sept. 30 1964	9 Months Ending Sept. 30 1963	Year 1962	Year 1961	Year 1960	Year 1959
Net sales	100.0	100.0	100.0	100.0	100.0	100.0
Costs of products sold	89.3	85.0	84.0	86.2	85.8	85.5
Gross Profit	10.7	15.0	16.0	13.8	14.2	14.5
Expenses:						
Selling	9.3	6.7	5.9	5.0	5.1	6.1
Administrative and general	4.2	8.8	7.9	7.3	7.9	6.9
Other deductions less other income	+ .3	+ .2	.9	3.0	.1	...
Total expenses	13.2	15.3	14.7	15.3	13.1	13.0
Profit before income tax	− 2.5	− .3	1.3	1.5	1.1	1.5
Income tax	+ .4	...	.5	+ .6	.5	.5
Net profit or loss	− 2.1	− .3	.8	.9	.6	1.0

PROPOSED PURCHASE OF DUPLICATING PAPERS, INC.

To increase volume and improve profit margins, the senior executives of Norris Paper Company are currently considering the purchase of a small company in the *fine* paper business. This company, Duplicating Papers, Inc., is a subsidiary of a much larger company, Northern Industries. It distributes paper, supplies such as inks and cleaners, and duplicating materials such as carbons, stencils, and master sheets that are used in offices for various duplicating processes including mimeographing, Xerography, Bruning Copyflex, spirit (alcohol) duplicating, gelatin duplicating, etc.

Duplicating Papers, Inc. maintains a sales office and a warehouse in Chicago and has branch sales offices in Pittsburgh, Detroit, Grand Rapids, Milwaukee, and St. Louis. There are four salesmen, including the sales manager in Chicago and one agent who may have another line in each branch office. Shipments are made directly to all customers from the Chicago warehouse, which is manned by a foreman, a shipping clerk, a cutter, a materials handler, and a packer. The Chicago sales office and warehouse is in a different section of the city than the Norris Company's offices—about forty-five minutes to an hour's drive away.

Frank Norris says: "The same purchasing agent in many industrial and retail concerns buys fine papers and office supplies as well as wrapping paper. This would then be a new arm to our operation and would present our salesmen with another opportunity to make more money from the same customer. It may be a method of opening the door to new accounts. The disadvantage, of course, is that the purchasing agent might have allocated 15 minutes to the salesman for his coarse paper presentation and might then make him go to the end of the line to wait for another 15 minutes for his fine paper presentation. Or he may have determined that just so much business and no more was going to the Norris Paper Company.

"In general, the fine paper business is more profitable than the coarse paper business. This is especially true since more and more coarse paper mills are going direct to customers. This may be an opportunity for us to move into greener grass.

"The market for duplicating papers is any business office that has a duplicating machine. This includes insurance companies, advertising agencies, employment agencies, and industrial concerns. There is no profit in selling to universities or schools since these are a bid proposition—except for a few small rural schools.

"In selling duplicating papers and supplies, the salesman can build a story—'romance the product.' He can talk about the care that goes into making the paper, the sizing, and the coating. There is some product differentiation that results from the papermaker's skill. There is also some branding identification. Promotion with a purchasing agent can rest heavily on the manufacturer's promotions. This can also be done with the supply items, since they are branded.

"Northern Industries wants to sell because the general manager of Duplicating Papers, Inc. is retiring and it has no one to move over into that position."

Philip Freneau has looked into the financial aspects of the proposal. He reports: "Northern Industries proposes to sell us all the assets of Duplicating Papers, Inc., except cash, for their book value. According to the latest balance sheet these total $96,000, most of which is in inventory and accounts receivable. Half the total price would have to be paid in cash and the other half in a demand note to Northern Industries at 5% interest. If we buy, we'll probably set Duplicating Papers up as a subsidiary like Folding Box Corporation. Norris Paper Company could lend the new subsidiary $48,000, and then the new subsidary could turn this cash over to Northern Industries along with a note for $48,000 and get all the assets in exchange. We would also pay the subsidiary $15,000 for its common stock, and that could be used for working capital.

"Frank thinks I should be president of the subsidiary, at least at the start, to provide general oversight. However, we would need two people to do the daily work. We've been thinking that the Chicago sales manager of Duplicating Papers could be made vice-president; his knowledge of the selling end of the business is something we very much need. He is earning about $12,000 a year now, and we might raise that to $13,000. Of course, he could continue to sell his good accounts. In addition, we need someone to do the buying and to handle contacts with suppliers. We've been thinking of using Bill Barron, who has been our Chicago sales manager for Norris Paper, for this job because he could also be a good link between the new subsidiary and the Norris salesmen. Obviously, one of the things we want to accomplish is to develop additional sales volume through the Norris contacts we already have. We would hope to keep on all of the present Duplicating Papers salesmen—although some of them are not making much money—and these men could sell all accounts that were exclusively for Duplicating Papers. They would be like the salesman who works for John Trumbull in Folding Box.

"Sooner or later, we would want to bring the Chicago operation over into our main warehouse. We have plenty of room here and could make some economies by consolidating the office activities. Besides, we'd save about $10,000 a year rent that Duplicating Papers is now paying; their lease expires in about a year. We would not make this move too quickly, however, because we do not want to lose the knowledge and the experience that the trained personnel of Duplicating Papers has, and some of those people might not be willing to either move or travel halfway across the city to go to work.

"The attractive thing about the whole deal is the nice margin that is available in this kind of business. Our salesmen haven't seen a 40% gross margin for a long time, and they'll have to learn about making sales that are small in dollar volume but that may have as much profit in it as an order for wrapping paper three or four times the size. We'll have quite an educational job to do; but getting into the fine paper business will be another direction we can expand, in line with our basic policy. In fact, this deal could be a way we could move on into processing and selling fine paper to printers. It's easy to get enthusiastic about the proposal until you begin to wonder where the capital is coming from."

Duplicating Papers, Inc.
Balance Sheet—9/30/64

Assets		Liabilities and Equity	
Cash and U. S. bills	$108,000	Accounts payable	$ 13,000
Accounts receivable (net) ..	21,000	Accrued taxes	6,000
Inventory	57,000		
Total current assets ...	$186,000	Total current liabilities.	$ 19,000
Prepaid expenses	4,000		
Equipment and furniture (net)	2,000	Capital stock	30,000
		Retained earnings	155,000
Leasehold improvements ...	12,000		
Total assets	$204,000	Total liabilities and equity..	$204,000

Duplicating Papers, Inc.
Comparative Income Statement

	Three months ending			
	9/30/64		9/30/63	
	Amount	%	Amount	%
Sales:				
Paper	$47,200	51.0	$ 65,500	53.6
Supplies	45,400	49.0	56,800	46.4
Total	$92,600	100.0	$122,300	100.0
Cost of sales:				
Paper	$32,300		$ 42,900	
Supplies	23,900		32,000	
Total	$56,200	60.7	$ 74,900	61.3
Gross profit	$36,400	39.3	$ 47,400	38.7
Shop expense	$ 8,000		$ 9,900	
Selling expense	10,000		14,200	
Administrative expense	12,300		13,900	
Total expense	$30,300	32.7	$ 38,000	31.0
Profit before income tax	$ 6,100	6.6	$ 9,400	7.7
Income tax	1,800	2.0	2,800	2.3
Net profit	$ 4,300	4.6	$ 6,600	5.4

TOP ORGANIZATION OF NORRIS PAPER COMPANY

If Duplicating Papers, Inc. or another company like it is added to the Norris Paper Company family, the top organization will become even more complex. Already the senior executives are faced with severe pressure on their time and energy. All agree that a clarification in organization is desirable if a workable plan can be devised in light of the work to be done and the people available.

Legal organization. The present board of directors of Norris Paper Company consists of the following members:

> Francis G. Norris, Chairman of the Board, not active in daily affairs.
> Frank Norris, President.
> John B. Norris, Treasurer, now not active in daily affairs.
> Philip Freneau, Secretary, Chief Accounting and Fiscal Officer, General Manager of Norris Paper Company, Executive Vice-President of Folding Box Corporation.
> Royall Tyler, Vice-President of Marketing.
> William H. Barron, Sales Vice-President, Chicago office.
> Charles B. Brown, Vice-President, one of the senior salesmen.
> George Brown, General Manager, Rockford operations.
> James F. Cooper, Assistant Secretary (head of law firm that serves as general counsel to the company).
> James A. Herne, General Manager, Twine and Cordage Department.
> Henry James, Sales Manager, Rockford.
> William V. Moody, successful salesman for over 25 years.
> John Trumbull, Vice-President of Sales, Folding Box Corporation.

No clear pattern for selecting members of the board exists, and once a man is named a director he is continued until he retires from the company. The practice of having senior salesmen on the board has been carried over from Frank Norris' father. Four members of the board are relatives of Frank Norris—Francis G. Norris is a great-uncle, John B. Norris is an uncle, and Charles B. Brown and George Brown are cousins.

The board is used as a place to discuss policy changes, and Frank Norris finds these discussions helpful because various viewpoints are represented. Most decisions, however, are made by Frank Norris with the close counsel of Philip Freneau and Royall Tyler. A real restraint on what these men decide to do is found in the control of common stock votes.

Some dissatisfaction, especially with respect to dividends, has been voiced by various stockholders. To assure continuity in management, a 5-year voting trust was established in 1963—after considerable discussion—with John B. Norris, Frank Norris, and Philip Freneau as trustees. The voting control is now divided as follows:

> 25%—Frank Norris.
> 25%—John B. Norris.
> 25%—A Chicago bank as trustee of one family estate.
> 25%—The voting trust mentioned above.

Operating organization. As already noted, the three senior executives —Frank Norris, Philip Freneau, and Royall Tyler—work closely together in performing the central management functions. Philip Freneau typically focuses on financial, accounting, warehousing, and other operating problems, while Royall Tyler gives most of his attention to purchasing, new products, and sales direction. Frank Norris deals with almost any problem of the business; in addition, he is active in civic affairs, entertains customers or suppliers a couple of evenings a week, and personally makes about 10% of the company's sales. All three are very busy.

Within Norris Paper Company, activities are divided on a territorial, functional, or product basis. The major division is between the Chicago and the Rockford warehouse. The general manager at Rockford is responsible for purchasing, warehousing, and sales, and has a Rockford sales manager and a warehouse foreman reporting to him. In Chicago, there is a sales vice-president, a purchasing agent, a warehouse foreman, and office manager. Since Chicago has no general manager, these functional executives report directly to the senior executive.

The manager of the Twine and Cordage Department occupies a somewhat unique position since he buys and promotes the sale of his particular group of products. He has a high degree of product knowledge, watches his inventory and pricing closely, supervises one salesman who concentrates on this line of products alone, does some selling himself, and takes the initiative in getting Norris salesmen to push his particular products. He does not have much versatility outside of his particular field, but Frank Norris feels he is a very competent executive in what unfortunately is a rather static product area. Because of his competence and specialized knowledge, the manager of Twine and Cordage has a higher degree of freedom of action than most second-line executives.

Folding Box Corporation, as noted earlier, has a part-time general manager—Philip Freneau—and then an operations executive and a sales executive who, in fact, overlap in their activities much as Royall Tyler and Philip Freneau do in the central management.

These comments on the executive setup of Norris Paper Company should not overshadow the vital role played by commission salesmen in Norris activities. The company has been built over the years on the concept of salesmen acting much as individual entrepreneurs. Each salesman is expected to take the initiative in building a profitable clientele of customers. Traditionally, the rest of the organization provides products and services that salesmen need to serve their customers. The present organization of Norris Paper Company can be understood only by keeping this way of operating in mind.

FINANCIAL SITUATION

The present financial condition of Norris Paper Company is shown on the accompanying balance sheet. Data for 1959 are also given so that the effect of recent operations on financial condition can be observed.

Norris Paper Company

Balance Sheets for Close of Fiscal Years 1964 and 1959

(in $1,000's)

	Sept. 30 1964	Dec. 31 1959
Current assets:		
Cash	$ 84	$ 74
Accounts receivable (net)	538	417
Inventories a	487	474
Prepaid expenses	14	13
Total current assets	$1,123	$ 978
Investments and other assets:		
Investment in Folding Box Corp.	$ 157	$ 117
Installment note receivable b	94	.....
Cash surrender value of life insurance	13	1
Miscellaneous	65	34
Total investments and other assets	$ 329	$ 152
Property and equipment (net)	$ 202	$ 192
Total assets	$1,654	$1,322

	Sept. 30 1964	Dec. 31 1959
Current liabilities:		
Notes payable to bank	$ 100	$ .....
Trade accounts payable	438	259
Accrued items and other current liabilities	60	101
Total current liabilities	$ 598	$ 360
Long-term liability on compensation contract	$ 24	$ 51
Stockholders' equity:		
Preferred stock—7%	$ 287	$ 287
Common stock c	395	14
Retained earnings c	350	610
Total equity	$1,032	$ 911
Total liabilities and equity	$1,654	$1,322

a Inventories in 1964 are valued on a last-in, first-out basis; if they had been valued on a first-in, first-out basis, the total would be $80,000 higher.

b Installment note, payable $6,000 per year, arose from sale of former office and warehouse. Capital gain of $118,000 was realized on sale. Amount shown is future amount due less reserve of $27,000 for income tax on payments when received.

c In 1964 common stock was split 55 to 1 and the stated value per share was cut from $5 to $2.50; the purpose was to create common stock that would be more marketable.

While not as liquid as in 1959, Norris Paper Company continues to be in good condition. The current ratio is almost 2 to 1; in fact, cash plus accounts receivable exceeds the current liabilities. Long-term debt is nominal.

The financial structure of the company reflects a long-standing tradition of avoiding debt. Both Frank Norris' father and grandfather did not want to borrow from a bank or incur other obligations that might force the company to liquidate inventory or other assets under adverse conditions. John Norris and Francis Norris hold this same view and would like very much to see the present bank loan paid off. On the other hand, they and other members of the family want regular dividends.

Virtually all the common and preferred stock is held by various members of the family. Since preferred and common stock were usually issued in a combined unit, ownership of the two classes of stock has similar distribution. Dividends have been paid regularly on the 7% preferred stock ($20,000 per year); dividends have not been paid on common stock since 1961 because of the company's need for additional capital.

A current problem facing the management of Norris Paper Company is how to obtain additional capital for expansion. Retained earnings have not been a source of capital in recent years. The increase in stockholders' equity between 1959 and 1964 arose almost entirely from a profit on the sale of the former office and warehouse, and this sum is not available for current purposes because it is tied up in a long-term sale contract.

Two proposals requiring significant amounts of capital are currently before the company management. One is the purchase of Duplicating Papers, Inc. described in the preceding section. The second is a proposal to buy the building that the company is now renting. Philip Freneau explains this proposal as follows:

"A short time ago the owners of our building came to Frank Norris with a proposition that we buy the building for $750,000. I told him not to listen until they got down to $500,000. Well, now the owners are down to $550,000 and Frank says, 'How about it?' The building was erected in 1954; it has 105,000 square feet of floor space, is of modern fireproof construction, is faced with brick, and fronts on three streets in one of the better light-industry areas of the city. The taxes are around $12,000 per year, and we already pay the maintenance.

"On paper this looks like a good proposition when you consider that we are required by our lease to pay $60,000 per year until 1991, with an option for renewal of another 15 years. Conservatively, the building has 30 years of remaining life, and the land is worth at least $50,000. That means depreciation would be $17,000 per year. Interest at 6% on the full price would be $33,000 per year. So, when you add taxes, interest, and depreciation, the total isn't much more than we're already paying in rent. But this figure is for the first year. If we use the depreciation to pay off the mortgage on the building, the average interest during the whole period would be only $18,000. Using that figure, the average annual cost would be only $47,000, or $13,000 less than we are now paying. We collect $25,000 per year rent from Folding Box, but that is all within the family.

"The catch, of course, is where to get the capital to swing the deal. We could borrow 80% of the cost of the building on a first mortgage, but we would still have to find $110,000 somewhere else. I know we're in the wholesale business and not the real estate business, but the return on that $110,000 looks pretty good when you consider the margin we make on selling paper."

QUESTIONS

1. Is the basic company objective of "consolidation and expansion" clearly understood? Is it successful? Is it wise? What changes, if any, do you suggest in basic objectives?

2. Trace the ramifications (effects) of using commission salesmen on other sales policies, purchasing policies, personnel policies, financial policies, and organization.

3. Should the concept of "salesmen entrepreneurs" be continued, abandoned, modified? Explain why.

4. How would you attract, train, and pay the salesmen needed to carry out your proposals made in answer to Question 3?

5. Do you recommend the purchase of Duplicating Papers, Inc.? Why? If so, do you agree with Philip Freneau's plan for organizing, financing, and staffing the operation?

6. Should Norris Paper Company buy the building it now occupies? What are the chief central management decisions (or premises) you had to make in arriving at your decision?

7. What should be done to improve the profitability of Folding Box Corporation? State the principal obstacles you foresee in carrying out this recommendation, and indicate how you propose to overcome them.

8. Do you have recommendations for improving the organization of Norris Paper Company and its subsidiary? What assumptions are you making regarding executive personnel? Are they realistic?

9. How should your proposals made in response to Questions 3 through 8 be financed? Include in your financing proposals any changes in the present financial setup that you believe should be made.

10. Prepare a five-year program for the Norris Paper Company and its subsidiaries, indicating the sequence and the timing of major moves and an annual financial projection of results you believe should be obtained. What provision should Frank Norris make for revising and filling in this program?

ROBBINS LAWN MOWER COMPANY, INC.

Casey & Bordinat, Inc.
Marketing Analysts & Consultants
100 Washington Blvd.
Detroit, Mich.

Mr. Don Robbins   April 15
18603 Warwick Drive
Royal Oak, Michigan

Dear Mr. Robbins:

This is in the nature of a follow-up to our recent conversation about the prospects for marketing your power lawn mower. Since you have applied for a patent and have spent a great deal of time and developmental costs thus far, we shall not discuss the engineering or legal facets of your problem.

Your lawn mower, we believe, has excellent prospects of gaining a foothold and of being a good profit maker. The exclusive "roto swirl" feature on a rotary mower should solve one of the consumer's basic objections to rotary power mowers; that is, that the mower does not give as clean a cut as does the conventional, or reel type of power mower. We have tested your mower, and the "swirl" literally makes the grass stand on end which should be a big sales feature.

The trend in power mowers is definitely to the two cycle engine. However, since the demand is so strong for these engines and the large manufacturers may in effect be paying a premium for them, we suggest that you use a gasoline four cycle, two horse power engine for the following reasons: These engines are more plentiful, liberal discounts are offered for quantity lots, mower manufacturers still offer similar mowers using either the two or four cycle engine, and there should be no sales resistance since the consumer at present basically does not know, and cares little, whether his mower engine is two or four cycle.

The trend in home lawn mowers is definitely toward color. Blue, green, red, and yellow appear to be the more popular colors to be used on the chassis, handle assembly, and wheels. We recommend that you include these color schemes in your production planning in order to take advantage of this trend.

The brightest spot of all appears to be in the potential demand for gas-powered lawn mowers. During recent years there has been an average increase of 850,000 new dwellings per annum and the trend should be upward. This means new home supplies, and certainly the garden tools industry is going to get its share. Obviously, the market is ripe for a product that has an exclusive feature such as yours.

Next, the power mower industry is growing by leaps and bounds. With the move to suburbia, the increase in the size of home plots, and the growing "do it yourself" movement, a power mower is becoming a necessity instead of a luxury item. It should also be noted from the figures enclosed that the replacement market is entering the scene and will play a big part in absorbing the production of 2 million power mowers in three or four years. Within a couple of years rotary mowers should outsell the reel type 2 to 1.

I hope that in the event you desire further information you will not hesitate to contact me at your convenience.

Sincerely,

John Sadler,
Research Associate

P. S. Hello, Don, may I add a personal note as your former neighbor and golf partner? The above looks pretty rosy from the product and total market viewpoint. However, one of the realistic points you will have to face is the tough competition in this game. Some of the large companies operate independent subsidiaries, mainly located in the midwestern states, and these are full-blown companies in themselves; good marketing channels, skillful sales forces, research staffs, production planning—with plenty of "know-how"; all this lies ahead of you. It's tough to get accurate figures on the number of companies in the game. 200 to 300 is probably as good a guess as any with many a producer going in and out the same year. Some of the giants may sell 75,000 power mowers per year. The independent may exist on 500 but he won't last long at that figure.

How many could you sell? If you're lucky it may look like this:

1st year	1,000– 1,200	mowers
2nd year	3,000– 3,600	"
3rd year	10,000–12,000	"

I know you've considered working with Jim Bennett on the production end. Obviously, you've got to sacrifice somewhere along the line; it's either freedom for the entrepreneur or profits. To go it alone could be rough from my observation. The marketing organization can either make or break you as it ties in with production. Also Jim can certainly swing the financial hurdles and that appears to be no mean trick in the mower industry.

Well, there it is, Don. We'll keep our fingers crossed. I will send the bill along after you've got the production up to 100,000 units. Say hello to Alice.

Best wishes,

Joe Casey

ENCLOSURE 1

OCCUPIED DWELLING UNITS IN THE U. S., 1920-1965		OWNER OCCUPIED, NON-FARM DWELLING UNITS IN THE UNITED STATES, 1920–1965	
YEAR	MILLIONS OF UNITS	YEAR	MILLIONS OF UNITS
1920	25	1920	7.5
1930	30	1930	10.2
1940	35	1940	11.2
1950	43	1950	19.8
1960	53	1960	25.5
1965	58	1965	29

ENCLOSURE 2

MARKET PROJECTION & BUYER ANALYSIS
POWER MOWERS

YEAR	TOTAL SALES UNITS	NEW SALES UNITS	% OF TOTAL	REPLACEMENT SALES UNITS	% OF TOTAL
Last year	1,100,000	950,000	85	150,000	16
This year	1,280,000	920,000	72	350,000	28
1 year hence	1,500,000	1,095,000	73	405,000	27
2 years hence	2,000,000	1,400,000	70	600,000	30
3 years hence	2,000,000	940,000	47	1,060,000	53
4 years hence	2,200,000	950,000	43	1,250,000	57

Source: *Garden Supply Merchandiser* (Trade Journal of the Garden Supply Industry).

Bennett Products Co. Inc.
13000 E. Nine Mile Road
East Detroit, Michigan

June 17

Mr. Don Robbins
18603 Warwick Drive
Royal Oak, Michigan

Dear Don:

This is to confirm our discussions at the Club house last Saturday afternoon. As I see it we can put your "roto swirl" on the market in the following three ways:

1. I will buy your patent rights for $5,000 and pay you a 2% royalty on all sales on which your "roto swirl" feature is utilized. I will produce, sell, and finance it as a separate division of my company. The 2% will be calculated on the sales price to the distributors.

2. I will buy 80% of the stock of your company and your patent for $3,000 cash; will offer you the position as Manager of the Lawn Mower Division at $8,000 per year salary, and will pay dividends on the stock beginning with the third year of operations. (These dividends will not exceed a 50% payout of net profits for each year of the division's operations.)

3. I will produce the chassis, rotor blades, handle assembly and accessory parts, whether they be of metal or plastic, on a contract basis per the following prices for your 21″ rotary mower:

	LOTS OF 100 (Per Mower)	LOTS OF 1,000 (Per Mower)
Chassis:	$4.00	$3.20
Rotor:	3.00	2.50
Misc.:	2.25	1.50
(Rods, Clutch Axles, Springs, Grips, etc.)		

Of the three alternatives, either (1) or (2) above are equal from my viewpoint. Naturally, I would prefer the second since you would then be able to join my growing organization and could participate directly in the profits based upon your successful performance. Also I could then count on a good man who knows lawn mowers to run the show for me.

The least desirable from my point of view would be on the contract basis. As you know, I've got a backlog of production orders now for plastic parts and band saws. Pretty soon I'll have to put on a third shift, if it keeps up, and that always causes headaches. However, Don, I'd still do it on a contract basis in spite of headaches, controller's included. Just last week Lee Johns was griping that he couldn't keep our accounts straight with the contract work. It makes more headaches trying to account for inventory, finished goods, who supplied what materials, etc. Obviously, Lee doesn't care for outside, spasmodic contract work. But then again he's not running the show.

If you go on your own, a couple of things to remember, Don. You'll need an assembly area, storage or warehouse space, at least one or two salesmen, and a whale of a lot of dough to carry you for a year. The lawn mower producers are making the mowers right now for sale next spring. The salesmen hit the wholesalers in the Fall and Winter, and so it goes. I can easily handle the financing since we've got a nice surplus. I don't know about your finances, of course. If you've got them licked, more power to you.

Let me know, Don, I think we can work out a deal together again.

Jim Bennett

Bennett Products Co. Inc.
13000 E. Nine Mile Road
East Detroit, Michigan

July 10

Wayne Oakland Bank
14290 E. Gratiot Avenue
Detroit, Michigan

Gentlemen:

Per suggestion of Mr. Bennett, I am enclosing a copy of our Income Statement and Balance Sheet for the year just ended on June 30. These are merely for purposes of your records and have been certified to by our Public Accountants, Beans, Bull, and Bittner.

Mr. Bennett has indicated that he desires to repay $30,000 of the $42,000 term notes due September 1. The $12,000 difference may be charged to our account at that time.

Thank you for your past services.

Sincerely,

Lee Johns
Treasurer-Controller

Enclosures: 2

ENCLOSURE 1 BENNETT PRODUCTS CO. INC.
Income Statement
Year Ended June 30

GROSS SALES:

Saws: Jig & Band	$ 75,000
Drill Presses	205,100
Plastic Accessories	242,000
Contract Sales	39,250
TOTAL SALES	$561,350
Less Sales Discounts	9,150
NET SALES:	$552,200

COST OF GOODS SOLD:

Materials (Metals, Plastics)	$ 85,321
Other Material Parts	22,356
Direct Labor	95,300
Indirect Factory Expenses	90,200
TOTAL COST OF GOODS SOLD	$293,177
GROSS PROFIT ON SALES:	$259,023
General & Administrative Expenses (See Schedule 2)	122,000
NET PROFIT FROM OPERATIONS	$137,023
Federal Income Taxes: (See Schedule 1)	68,502
NET INCOME FOR YEAR	$ 68,521
Dividends	$ 28,521
Added to Surplus	40,000

Schedule 1
Federal Income Tax Calculation
Year Ended June 30

Normal tax 30% on ½ first $25,000	$ 3,750
Normal tax 30% plus 22% Surtax on earnings over $12,500	64,752
Estimated Total Fed. Corp. Inc. Tax	$68,502

Schedule 2
Statement of General and Administrative Expenses
Year Ended June 30

Shipping Supplies	$ 4,213	
Shipping Labor	7,210	
Commissions & Salaries (Sales)	22,350	
Freight Expenses	802	
Advertising	7,890	
Misc. Selling Expenses	2,100	
Travel Expenses	3,223	$ 47,788
Office Salaries	$27,248	
Postage	300	
Telephone	1,155	
Office Supplies	3,221	
Donations	475	
Entertainment Expenses	703	
Taxes—Federal & State, Social Security	10,350	
Depreciation—Equipment, Office	300	
Employees' Profit-Sharing Contribution	30,460	74,212
		$122,000

ENCLOSURE 2   BENNETT PRODUCTS CO. INC.
Balance Sheet as of June 30

ASSETS
CURRENT ASSETS:

Cash	$ 24,000	
Accounts Receivable	87,395	$111,395
Inventories (Lower of Cost or Market)		
Raw Materials (Est.)	$ 83,200	
Work in Process (Est.)	6,300	
Finished Goods (Est.)	32,000	
Supplies (Est.)	3,000	$124,500
TOTAL CURRENT ASSETS		$235,895

FIXED ASSETS

Property, Plant, & Equipment	$305,220	
Reserve for Depreciation	155,200	$150,020
Prepaid Expenses		15,085
TOTAL ASSETS		$401,000

LIABILITIES AND CAPITAL
CURRENT LIABILITIES:

Accounts Payable		
Trade Creditors	$ 23,502	
Due Employees	6,325	$ 29,827
Notes Payable		
Short Term	$ 42,000	
Accrued Expenses	39,372	
Reserve for Taxes	63,000	144,372
TOTAL CURRENT LIABILITIES		$174,199

CAPITAL:

Capital Stock—Authorized 1,000 Shares Par Value $100 each, 1,000 Shares Issued:	$100,000	
Earned Surplus	126,801	
TOTAL CAPITAL STOCK AND SURPLUS		226,801
TOTAL LIABILITIES AND CAPITAL		$401,000

July 18

Mr. Jonathan Robbins
221 Juniper Blvd.
San Francisco, California

Dear Dad,

If this letter is a rather long one, I hope you will understand that I have a problem and need your advice. Our lawn mower company is organized as a going corporation. Alice and I own the stock. The patents are in process and I've gathered all the data I need. Since I have previously sent you copies of Joe Casey's and Jim Bennett's letters you are up on that end. In recap, then, here's what it looks like:

Product: 21" rotary cutting, "roto swirl" (exclusive feature); 4 cycle, 2 horsepower Power Parts gas engine. Wheels with pneumatic tires, plus chassis and other parts available in colors. Price $99.00 suggested to retailers. Price to wholesalers $75.00 if Jim Bennett manufactures it.

Production: 2 major alternatives:

(1) Have Bennett produce the parts and assemble, with motors and wheels purchased, in his subsidiary division.

(2) Have Bennett produce the parts by contract, I will purchase the motors and wheels, and assemble with the help of 2 part-time men.

The additional procurement costs will look like this under either alternative:

	ORDERS	
	IN 100 LOTS (Per Mower)	IN 1,000 LOTS (Per Mower)
Power Parts, 4 cycle, 2 hp. Engines	$35.50	$30.50
4 wheels, with pneumatic tires	6.00	5.30

Assembly, packing, etc. should add about $3.00 per mower.

Marketing: Again two choices are available, if I decide to assemble the mower myself: (1) go through wholesale houses, (2) sell direct to hardware stores in the area and eventually expand my own sales force.

The sales figures will look like this:

(1) *Through wholesalers:*

	RETAILER	DISTRIBUTOR	MANUFACTURER
Price by:	$99.00	$75.00	$60.00

(2) *Direct to retailers:*

	RETAILER	MANUFACTURER
Price by:	$99.00	$67.00

In relation to these distribution costs, Jim Bennett informs me that the mower industry works through large distributors who sell garden supplies. He would use his sales force that sells saws and other products to various distributors, to sell lawn mowers to garden supply distributors. This is not good in my opinion since they will not be lawn mower salesmen. I've worked, sweated, and dreamed over this lawn mower. As a matter of fact, I have talked directly with several hardware retailers who said they would buy machines from me directly. They like the idea of the added profit and the exclusive feature. There is another important consideration, that of service. The hardware retailers would like to be able to get service quickly if a machine doesn't work properly—and the factory salesman can do a better job than a disinterested distributor who has a hundred other articles to sell.

Jim also keeps hammering away about sales promotion, national advertising, warehousing costs, etc. I think I can lick these by producing in 100 lots and selling personally until we need to produce another batch. This may sound like shoestring operations. That's true—but at least it's all mine anyway!

Finances: This is the rough road to hoe. I think we can swing it though. I'm up to $12,000 salary and am now a senior Sales Engineer with Michigan Tool & Die. My fifteen years experience should come in handy. A few life insurance policies and a mortgage may give me another $6,000 beyond our present "corporate" assets (see our latest balance sheet attached). Obviously, I'd have to start this on a part-time basis if I decided not to sell out—and in the garage at that. No overhead!

What's this man Jim Bennett like? Quite a boy! He came from an Arkansas farm at the age of 19 and got a job with Chrysler in the production shops. In the evenings he and I repaired old washing machines, vacuum cleaners, and the like. He saved every penny, and a couple of years later he and his wife bought and operated a super service station. Within two years, Jim sold this and became a Plymouth-Chrysler dealer. Everything Jim has touched turned to gold. Later he formed his own machine shop and plastics operation. The auto sales agency was sold two years ago and since then he's invested heavily in large outlying tracts of real estate.

As a millionaire, his hobby is backing racers in the Indianapolis speed event. This guy is terrific. He always seems to make money and is in there at the right time. He has had quite a turnover of managers at his plant though—I know they have to produce for Jim or else! I think he's going to build a diversified financial and manufacturing empire the way he's going. He's certainly a go-getter and we get along well together.

Well, Dad, there we are. As a retired engineer you ought to have some thoughts on the problem. I'd certainly appreciate your frank opinions because I should take some action one way or another pretty soon if we hope to get in shape for next spring's business. Keep well.

Don

ROBBINS LAWN MOWER CO., INC.

Balance Sheet, June 30

ASSETS

CURRENT:

Cash		$900.00
Inventories:		
Office Supplies	$100.00	
Materials: Steel Rods	200.00	
Motors	210.00	
Finished Mowers	300.00	810.00
TOTAL CURRENT ASSETS		$1,710.00

FIXED:

Miscellaneous Tools	$252.00	
Furniture, Equipment, etc.	375.00	627.00
OTHER: Engineering, Development, Patent Application		3,500.00
TOTAL ASSETS		$5,837.00

LIABILITIES AND CAPITAL

CURRENT LIABILITIES:

Accounts Payable:			
Trade Creditors	$280.00		
Accrued Expenses	57.00	$337.00	
Notes Payable		500.00	$ 837.00

CAPITAL:

Common Stock		5,000.00
TOTAL LIABILITIES AND CAPITAL		$5,837.00

QUESTIONS

1. Do you agree with the consultant's conclusion that Mr. Robbins could sell 1,000–1,200 mowers the first year? What is the relationship between estimates of owner-occupied, non-farm dwelling units in the United States and market projection for power mowers?

2. What return could Mr. Robbins realize from Offer Number 1 in Mr. Bennett's letter? How would Mr. Robbins' annual income from Offer Number 2 in Mr. Bennett's letter compare to his present annual income?

3. How does Mr. Bennett's view of the kind of marketing effort needed for the mower compare with that of Mr. Robbins? With your own?

4. What is your opinion of the current and the long-term financial position of Bennett Products Co. Inc? Why is part of the term note being renewed? Do you agree with Mr. Casey that "Jim can certainly swing the financial hurdles"?

5. What is the potential unit profit, accepting Mr. Robbins' estimates of prices and costs? What total dollar return per year will this provide?

6. How would production facilities, production organization, equipment, labor force, and purchasing compare under the alternatives:

(a) Mr. Robbins goes to work for Mr. Bennett.

(b) Bennett Products produces the parts and assembles, with motors and wheels purchased, in its division.

(c) Bennett Products produces the parts under contract, Mr. Robbins purchases the motors and wheels and assembles.

7. What sales appeals and promotional efforts can be used to establish this new power mower if Robbins makes and sells it himself? If he works for Mr. Bennett?

8. Outline the program Mr. Robbins would need to undertake to make and sell the mower himself.

9. Develop the program Mr. Robbins would need to follow if he were to work for Mr. Bennett as General Manager of the Lawn Mower Division.

10. What were Mr. Robbins' objectives in developing the power mower? What other objectives does he appear to have from his letter? How would all these be served if he sold his patent? If he worked for Mr. Bennett? If he went in business for himself?

11. How would *you* answer Don Robbins' letter?

3 **BARBER ICE CREAM COMPANY**

During the two years after the acquisition of Barber Ice Cream Company by Great Lakes Creameries, Incorporated, revenues of the subsidiary rose but profits did not keep pace with the growth in sales. On the contrary, net profits declined. Now, in the winter lapse after the heavy summer selling season, the central executives of Barber Ice Cream Company are reviewing the management and direction of the subsidiary in an attempt to see how the profit trend could be reversed and how returns on sales and on investment could be restored to their former levels.

History. Barber Ice Cream Company had been started over thirty years before in Indianapolis as a street vending operation by Mr. Joe Barber, who, at the time, owned one ice cream truck from which he sold chocolate-covered vanilla ice cream bars and small cups of ice cream. With some aggressive selling effort by Mr. Barber, the firm expanded rapidly in Indianapolis. Within five years it opened a branch in Evansville, Indiana. After the opening of this branch, sales then became large enough so that the Barber Ice Cream Company built its own plant for manufacturing ice cream. Within another few years the firm opened another branch in Chicago, at which it had both a manufacturing plant and a street vending operation. Sometime later, a third operation had been opened in central Illinois with its base in Decatur. Two years ago Mr. Barber sold his firm to Great Lakes Creameries, Incorporated. He then retired as chairman of the board of Barber Ice Cream Company and turned his attention to his other business interests in real estate and grocery distribution.

Great Lakes was a large regional manufacturer of dairy products, based originally in Minnesota. Its operations had been extended through the years to Wisconsin and then to northern Illinois and northern Indiana. In addition to its own branded line in Minnesota and Wisconsin, it carried on an extensive private-label dairy products manufacturing business in northern Illinois and northern Indiana. The acquisition of Barber Ice Cream Company meant that Great Lakes Creameries moved further into direct sales to the consumer and to a new geographical area.

Great Lakes also purchased a street vending operation in St. Louis at the same time as its acquisition of Barber Ice Cream Company. The St. Louis firm, River Ice Cream Company, was a small, independent, street vending operation. The firm had 25 sales trucks, which sold throughout the city of St. Louis. It purchased its ice cream requirements from a large ice cream manufacturer in the city. After the acquisitions, River Ice Cream Company was discontinued as a separate entity and organizationally was merged with Barber Ice Cream Company to become another branch.

THE INDUSTRY

Sales and distribution. Manufacturers of ice cream products everywhere in the country also physically distribute them from point of manufacture to retail outlet. This is true almost without exception.

The number of ice cream manufacturers is diminishing. The current level of about 15,000 plants represents a decline in the past five years of some 15%. About 12% of the plants account for slightly over 90% of total ice cream production. The general tendency is for ice cream makers to merge to form more economical producing units. In some instances, large retail chain stores are acquiring local ice cream manufacturing companies to make their own ice cream and squeeze out the maximum profit.

Novelty items now account for about 20% of total ice cream manufactured (measured in gallons). However, they represent a higher percent of total industry profit contribution, since they have relatively higher margins than straight ice cream. Changes in the share of market attributed to ice cream novelties can be judged from the exhibits attached. Regular packaged ice cream is often "footballed" (sold below cost as a loss leader) to build retail store traffic. In contrast, in retail stores, novelty ice cream prices remain relatively stable and carry higher margins to offset the "losses" from high volume packaged ice cream price selling.

The precise laws, customs, and margins for ice cream manufacturing and distribution vary by geographical area. There are varying regional, state, and federal laws and regulations that apply to the dairy industry and to manufacturing, warehousing, and wholesale distributing of ice cream.

Most manufacturers operate a one- to two-week inventory at their plants. They hold and handle products from —30° Fahrenheit to —10° Fahrenheit. Recent experience seems to indicate that major ice cream manufacturers today have excess warehousing and trucking space.

Most major ice cream manufacturers also appear to be increasingly aware of the fact that consumer-accepted and well-promoted novelties are quite profitable. Most manufacturers further realize that there are large profits to be gained by maximizing the utilization of their plant, warehouse, and trucking capital.

Sales of frozen dessert (ice cream, ice milk, Mellorine) vary from region to region. The West, North Central, Pacific, and East North Central regions are highest per capita; the Atlantic and New England regions are average per capita; the Mountain, South Atlantic, and South Central regions are relatively low per capita. The relative share of ice cream to ice milk production also varies considerably by region and by state.

The standard pattern for distribution of ice cream through retail stores is to have each major retail outlet lined up with one ice cream manufacturer to supply private-label ice cream requirements and part of the branded ice cream requirements. Private-label makers also negotiate with novelty ice cream producers for a license.

There is a trend today for all retail stores to own their own —20° F. cabinets. This degree of cold is required to store ice cream successfully. In distributing to retail outlets, driver salesmen have traditionally operated on a straight commission in the delivery of ice cream products. There is a trend today towards straight salaries, however, with many of the major manufacturers already away from the commission system.

Generally, most novelty ice cream products sold in retail grocery stores are produced by different manufacturers on a franchise basis. A local novelty may be the invention of a particular ice cream manufacturer, which then makes and distributes it exclusively.

Ice cream manufacturers normally load long-distance trailers at their plants to service branch distribution points as far as 300 to 500 miles away over 1- to 5-day runs.

The industry's rising distribution costs are generally forcing manufacturers to consolidate plants and to seek more economical ways to service retailers. The industry is late in catching up with the times and is still saddled with servicing hundreds of relatively small-volume accounts.

Ice cream advertising, measured in a special test three years ago, amounted to $6 million. Only two brands, Sealtest and Borden's, spent over $1 million that year. Further data about market trends, geographic patterns, consumer attitudes, and usage are given in the accompanying tables.

EXHIBIT 1

Dairy Products, Entertainment Foods, and Desserts
Estimated Annual Sales Volume
(Millions of retail dollars)

Milk	$7,000	Cheese	$1,000
Eggs	2,600	Cookies	980
Soft Drinks	2,500	Potato Chips	600
Candy	2,400	Nuts	500
Baked Sweet Goods	2,100	Gelatin Desserts	110
Ice Cream	1,500	Pretzels	100
Butter	1,000	Prepared Puddings	55

EXHIBIT 2

Frozen Dessert Definitions

(Source: Ice Cream Review)

Ice Cream	Made with cream or butterfat, flavoring, and sweetening.
Ice Milk	Lower butterfat content than ice cream.
Mellorine	Same as ice cream, but vegetable fat instead of butterfat (coconut or cottonseed oil).
Sherbert	Milk-based, with juice, rind, or pulp of fruits and lower butterfat than ice milk.
Water Ice	Same as sherbert, but without butterfat.
Soft	Served immediately after being made.
Hard	Frozen for at least 12-14 hours.

EXHIBIT 3

Frozen Dessert Volume

(Millions of gallons annually)

	ICE CREAM	ALL OTHERS	ICE MILK	MELLORINE	TOTAL
Last Year	702	79	186	53	1,020
Preceding Year	697	78	163	50	988
" "	698	79	145	45	967
" "	699	80	134	42	955
" "	657	69	117	40	883
" "	651	68	111	34	864
" "	641	67	103	34	845
" "	629	69	90	32	820
" "	597	66	80	31	774
" "	605	67	65	24	761
"	593	61	54	11	719

EXHIBIT 4

Ice Cream Volume Trends

(Past ten years)

	DOLLARS PER CAPITA	GALLONS PER CAPITA
Last Year	$7.87	3.9
Preceding year	8.01	3.9
" "	7.67	4.0
" "	7.43	3.8
" "	7.55	3.8
" "	8.26	3.8
" "	8.09	3.8
" "	7.93	3.7
" "	8.38	3.8
" "	8.66	3.8

EXHIBIT 5
Trend of Ice Cream, by Production Categories

	BULK	PACKAGE	NOVELTY
Last Year	21.2%	59.7%	19.1%
Preceding Year	21.9	59.1	19.0
" "	23.0	58.9	18.1
" "	23.8	58.3	17.9
" "	25.6	56.9	17.5
" "	31.6	51.3	17.1
" "	34.9	48.7	16.4
" "	36.0	47.1	16.9
" "	39.8	43.7	16.5

EXHIBIT 6
Per Capita Production of Frozen Desserts, by Region

REGION	GALLONS PER CAPITA
West North Central	6.3
Pacific	6.0
East North Central	5.7
Middle Atlantic	5.6
New England	5.4
United States Average	*5.4*
Mountain	5.0
South Atlantic	4.8
South Central	4.5

EXHIBIT 7
Time of Day When Frozen Desserts Are Eaten

	AGE GROUP			
TIME	6-8 YEARS	9-11	12-14	15 AND OVER
Before Lunch	4%	2%	2%	3%
At Lunch	16	20	26	19
Between Lunch and Supper	28	30	26	21
At Supper	18	18	21	22
After Supper	34	30	25	35

EXHIBIT 8
Novelty Warehouse Withdrawal Data
Sample of 21 Stores—Class II
Average-unit movement per week, per store purchasing
(Report of a national market-sampling group)

	OCT.-NOV.	JUNE-JULY
Popsicles	50	105
Fudgicles	57	105
Eskimo Pies	60	124
Tropicana	24	39
Hawaiian Punch Bar	..	70
Drumstick	44	80
All others under 10¢	112	335
All other 10¢ and up	56	65

Field checks of retail store ice cream cabinets reveal an average pricing for most novelty ice cream products of 6 units for 59¢, with the exception of one recognized quality novelty ice cream product—Good Humor—which is found retailing at 4 for 59¢ (15¢ apiece), and higher priced novelties that are very seasonal in nature (for example, Christmas wreaths, bunnies, and turkeys made of ice cream).

General social and economic conditions. One of the central executives of the Barber Ice Cream Company remarked that anyone's faith in the long-run future of the street vending ice cream business had to be evaluated in the light of license restrictions. These were making it more and more difficult to sell on the street. In all cities, there now tended to be more enforcement of standing ordinances, with no more than 15 minutes allowed in one spot. In major cities, it was no longer possible to stand for an hour at a time outside of schools.

The second factor was availability of novelties in supermarkets. Without having looked at the exact data himself, he felt that this availability was increasing. In addition, as automobiles and trucks increased in number, there were the rising costs of mobile equipment and of garaging. These contributed to the major problem of keeping sales rising at the same rate at which costs increased.

This executive remarked that any new communities entered wanted each street vendor to be photographed and to have his fingerprints taken. Officials did not want bells rung loudly in the streets nor did they want their children upset by vendors' behavior. And they were very strongly against accidents. The executive remarked, "We have to ask ourselves whether the peddler concept is less acceptable year by year."

Consumer buying habits. General changes in consumer behavior affected street vending as well as the more abstract social, economic, and legal forces. As one executive put it: "I think house-to-house selling has a future because people are getting lazier every day. This fits the total trend toward convenience foods." In addition to this view, central executives of Barber Ice Cream Company expected that the "novelty idea," that is, the adaptation of a product to suit individual tastes through variety, would be beneficial to the company. Variety in itself—the fad notion—was also thought to be relevant to consumer buying habits. Finally, higher personal incomes were expected to mean desire for better products and the ability to afford higher prices. Given these ideas, there might well be a substantial future for street vending of novelty items. The general sales manager explained his view as follows: "Ice cream sales may not be increasing as fast as the population growth, but it is still a major food with sales well over a billion dollars. The fact that ice cream is 'footballed' and that it is privately labeled so much leads to the reason why it has not grown. It is because there has been so little incentive. That is why novelties with a higher profit per sales have to grow."

Competition. Very few firms were so successful in the street vending of ice cream that they remained a factor in the business from year to year. Only the Good Humor Corporation had succeeded on a large scale across the nation. Companies such as Howard Johnson had tried and failed. There were, however, some regional producers—of which Barber was one—that had been reasonably successful in a given area. In addition, there were a larger number of small competitors in each city. The numbers and the kinds of the individual enterprises changed rapidly from year to year. Some competitive efforts appeared to come in waves. For example, from 1958 to 1961 there was a major increase in soft ice cream selling. Many large trucks were put on the street. Their numbers and competitive efforts tended to raise problems of noise, accidents, and nuisance that aggravated local officials as well as consumers. After 1962, the numbers of these competitors tended to decline markedly. Stricter licensing laws helped to do this.

Ice Cream Sales by Type of Outlet

Outlet	Percentage
Food Stores	56%
Drug Stores	6%
Confectionary Stores	2%
Franchised Chain Outlets	12%
Street Vending	2%
Restaurants	13%
Home Delivery	3%
All Other (vending machines, variety stores, industrial feeding, and other) ..	6%
	100%

MARKETING

Product policy. The original items, first sold in Indianapolis, were a 10-cent bar on a stick—vanilla ice cream with chocolate covering; a 5-cent fruit ice stick; and a 20-cent cup with three flavors—vanilla, strawberry, and chocolate. The branches still sold these products. In the meantime, they had added many coatings and flavorings to the 10-cent bar, had extended the variety of fruit flavors of the 5-cent ice stick, had also extended the number of flavors in the 20-cent cup, had introduced 25-cent sundaes in a cup, and had notably increased the quality of the fruit ice sold as a nickel bar. In addition, some of the trailers parked in a fixed location, such as a recreation department concession in a park, carried other items like candy, pretzels, potato chips, and other food for snacks.

Barber ice cream was quality ice cream—so the company maintained. To carry this out, it insisted on a 14% butterfat content and a maximum overrun of 80%. Illinois law allowed ice cream to be marketed with a minimum butterfat content of 12%, but the Barber Bar was deliberately kept above this minimum requirement. All ice cream must be whipped with air so that it will be smooth. It is quite common for ice cream to have an overrun of 100%. This means that the mixture has been doubled in size from the solid ice. Through experiment, Barber Ice Cream Company had found that ice creams with more than 14% butterfat and with an overrun of less than 80% are not as easy to digest and do not have the taste characteristics desired by consumers looking for a quality product.

The notion of quality extends from the product to the service given. For example, the company has worked out detailed instructions as to the best method to serve the buyer, including always giving a napkin with each purchase and insisting that the vendor be the first to greet each customer and that he run, not walk, to any waiting car.

A third product policy is that of a limited line. The number of items in the line—flavors, coatings, and the like—are determined by the merchandising manager in Chicago. The existing policy is that the line of products should be uniform throughout the system. There are certain manufacturing as well as financial reasons for this. The merchandising manager constantly has new ice cream items under review. In addition, several proposals have been made for non-ice-cream products such as frozen candy bars and frozen food casseroles with precooked foods that need only be heated. Proposals of this nature have come from branch managers interested in increasing their sales volume.

Pricing policy. Prices and product policy have always been established at company headquarters. One purpose has been to avoid being pulled into a cheaper market (the 10-cent bar was changed to 15 cents some years ago). Under this thinking, the action of the merchandising manager has been to work toward introducing higher-valued products. As an example, his plans for the coming season include a 20-cent "Large Bar." With continued prosperity, he believes that product innovations should emphasize higher values and higher returns to the company. One problem from state to state or municipality to municipality has been varying and increasing sales taxes. The company has found through experience that it is necessary to absorb the increases in such taxes since there is great consumer resistance to paying a 1-cent increase on what had formerly been a 15-cent item. Sundaes that could be sold at 25 cents could not be sold at 26 cents, for example. Price changes also affected the products sold. For example, during the previous summer the price of sugar had been raised substantially. Analysis by the merchandising manager indicated that increasing the size of the fruit ice bar and raising its price from 5 cents to 10 cents would automatically increase revenues by several hundred thousands of dollars. Since the 5-cent bar would be unprofitable at the increased sugar price, it was necessary to make both the price and the bar size adjustment.

Distribution policy. Barber sold its ice cream almost entirely through street vending. At various times, individual grocers and grocery cooperatives had approached the company with a proposal that Barber Bars be distributed through these stores. The former management, cognizant of manufacturing, financial, and management problems, had always turned down such proposals.

Barber did sell a small proportion of its sales through machine vending. In two large industrial plants in Evansville, Indiana, it dealt through a separate wholesaler who installed, repaired, and stocked the vending machines. Each of these freezers cost $700 for each in-plant location. While the machine vending had worked well in the two large industrial plants, the company was not sure that the idea could be extended elsewhere.

Promotional policy. The advertising budget was set at company headquarters. Advertising was not a concern of the branch or district managers. Media were selected by the agency and the advertising manager, as were point of sales material on the sales car. The company advertised only in spot announcements on television and radio, and then only late in the spring and early in the summer. Its advertising was mainly directed at adults in order to gain general community acceptance for the idea of street vending by Barber Ice Cream Company. Major points emphasized were product quality and cheerful service.

Customers. Barber sold to anyone who was willing to come up to one of its cars or trailers. It had found through experience that children made up 65% to 70% of the buyers. A Barber Bar or a Barber Pole ice cream was one of the few things that a child, particularly a small child, was allowed to buy on his own. The company believed that small children put great store in the experience of carrying their own money, making their own decision as to the flavor they wanted, and paying for the purchase themselves. About half of the remaining customers were parents buying for children accompanying them. In the evening hours, typically it was the father who made the purchase. He could generally be persuaded to buy (within bounds) the most expensive item the child desired. During the day, mothers accompanied children and tended to be very price conscious. Most mothers were convinced that the fruit ices were quite satisfactory for their children.

Sales volume. The central management of Barber Ice Cream Company was concerned about the general problem of revenues. In their terms, the managers thought about attaining higher sales averages per car per day. The company average achieved during the past summer was $67 of revenue per car per day. Of course, this fluctuated from month to month and from salesman to salesman. It varied from $10 per day to as high as $200 per day. However, the focus was on the average and how to increase it. Company executives had varying ideas on this problem. It appeared to them to be difficult to increase efficiency overall by automating sales. "A man can't sell more ice cream now than he could twenty years ago." Sales might be increased if the caliber of salesman could be improved. The sales average might also go up with a more appealing price and product line. The central management believed that within every territory there were sections where the right price or the right products could get more business. It might also be possible to change the size or the shape of the bars to make them more attractive or to introduce new products. The concern with higher sales averages was general among the central management of the company.

There appeared to the central executives to be several variables that affected the daily sales average per car. One of these was a variable that went under the name of "sales force lethargy." The belief was that men often stopped selling when their daily revenues reached a certain point, $100 or $125, or when their take-home pay for the day reached a certain point. One executive said: "Why do they feel that way? It's mostly human nature. We don't get the best educated or most ambitious men. It's a matter of the kind of men they are. I don't know of any group pressures to limit earnings."

One thought was that it was the spring start that was really crucial. The company had to develop a pattern of getting the men out on time in the morning and getting them accustomed to bringing home a certain amount of money almost immediately. If this didn't happen, then the men began to feel pressures at home not to be away so much of the time and also to bring home a paycheck. The problem of early spring had not yet been resolved in general. One manager commented that the salesmen did not want to try unless they could see an hourly gross of $10.

During the summer, as has been said, many of the men appeared to reach a peak in total revenues that they did not attempt to exceed. According to some executives, this had been affected by increased commission rates that had been put into effect gradually within the last few years. With increased commissions and more benefits, the salesmen did not have to work as hard as formerly to be satisfied. The company had established bonus arrangements to persuade men to remain on the job during the entire month of September. In Indianapolis this amounted to 2% of the season's sales and in Chicago it amounted to 8%. About half of the men typically earned a bonus for staying the last four weeks.

A second major factor that appeared to affect sales averages per car was a basic trend toward more leisure time. As one executive put it: "The men now want more leisure time. This is a kind of general social attitude that is very difficult to modify. The salesmen now want to work 8 hours, not 12 to 15. There is more and more rebellion against the hours as new and younger men come in. The only answer I have found as a rule is to hire older men. Even the college boys—that is, those who don't need the money for tuition—complain about the hours and don't try to push as they should. We have been able to work out an agreement in one district that some men can work 5 days a week in June, July, and August if they arrange for this in advance."

The final major factor that was considered to affect higher sales averages was district sales supervision. Most executives felt that even the experienced men needed careful supervision to maximize sales from their territory. This took a close knowledge of the men as well as the territory. The ability to supervise closely depended somewhat upon the number of new men. These varied by branch from 30% to 50% of the total men. Those districts with fewer than one third new men could, of course, do a better job of training and supervising. The first effort of district sales management was to get the trucks out on the road—to see that all the available cars were loaded by 10 a.m., staffed with whomever was available, and sent out to a territory. Another requirement was to train the men whenever time was available. Getting the trucks out on the road meant taking some chances on the men, since turnover in the spring was typically very high. As one district manager put it, "If we can get them to shave and wash and put on a clean suit and white shirt, that's half the job."

Sales training had three phases. As the first phase, a district manager spent a whole day with a new man and showed him how to cover the route assigned to him. The emphasis in this phase was on learning the streets and the schedule. In the second part of training, the district manager spent half a day with the new man. During this time, he showed him how to strengthen his sales approach. The district manager also reviewed with the trainee his route and schedule. It was extremely important that a route man hit each street or each segment at a particular time. The children and the other buyers became accustomed to buying according to a time schedule. This half-day phase might follow the first phase by a week or 10 days. At that point the district manager would terminate the route salesman if he appeared unteachable or unproductive. The third phase of training was individual attention by the district manager during early morning hours—9 to 10 a.m. During this time, the two men went over the sales presentation used or the kind of greeting the salesman made. A district manager would do this two or three times with new men until he was convinced that an acceptable level of training had been attained.

One district manager reported that it was car days on the road that counted. His district increased 25% in sales by operating 25% more days. The dollar average per car went up $1 per day, but he insisted that the cars get out early in the spring and stay out late in the fall.

Another variable affecting sales was the kind of men recruited. Districts invariably had good success with college students who pushed pretty hard, but they were only available for 10 to 12 weeks. The men who worked for 6 months tended to pace themselves—"inevitably" as one district manager said. The district manager with the greatest success in recruiting had actively searched for milkmen who had lost their jobs when dairies discontinued home deliveries.

One additional variable that occasionally affected sales averages was a special competitive drive. A district manager maintained that he won the sales competition one month by asking "my guys to stay out long enough to collect extra money after they were exhausted." On the last day he wrote each of his men a note asking him to pull in a little extra. He said that although the other managers laughed at him, his district won by 7%. This manager said: "Examine any other sales organization. They all have contests or other sales motivators. I give out cigars as prizes. One time I quit this and I missed the bonus quota. The price of that cigar was $125 in lost commissions."

In summary, it seemed to the central management of Barber Ice Cream Company that higher sales averages per car, which vitally affected net profits, were governed by some major variables including a general social tendency toward desires for more leisure time, by a general lethargy of the sales force, and finally by actions on the part of branch management. Effective branch management could operate on a number of variables including recruitment, training, persuasion, seeing that the maximum number of cars was on the road, and, finally, covering the full period from April to the end of September.

Advertising other than displays on the cars was a recent phenomenon for Barber Ice Cream Company. The company had begun to purchase spot announcements on local television and radio stations. The influence of these on sales was undetermined as yet and probably could never be determined.

ORGANIZATION

Organization structure. The current formal organization structure of Barber Ice Cream Company is shown in the partial organization diagram on the opposite page.

The president of Barber Ice Cream Company remarked that several new jobs had been established at the headquarters in Chicago since the acquisition by Great Lakes Creameries. During the first year, the company had its old executive staff of president, sales manager, controller, and fleet manager, all of whom had moved up from Indianapolis, and a treasurer brought in from the Great Lakes organization. During the past year, there had been added to the executive group the purchasing agent, the general manufacturing manager, the plant engineer, the general merchandising manager, and the latter's assistant—the advertising and promotion director. These men had been added to the executive staff at the suggestion of Great Lakes Creameries.

The duties and the responsibilities of most of these managers are commented on in other parts of the case. The typical action of the new executives can be seen in the following comments by the plant engineer: "We are shuffling duties, but up until now my job has been to set up an engineering function. There was none here until I came. I began by establishing a capital budget. My responsibility is to handle all items in the budget, including relations with contractors and supervision of construction work. An added function is engineering service to our two branch plants. Before my coming here, they turned to outsiders. Now, they come to me.

"Another function should be to make studies on improving operating efficiency in the branches and plants. I want to work to develop ideas for incorporation in the budget. We have certain major crying needs in the Indianapolis plant that will require a considerable investment. My part in this is to appraise others' suggestions, to initiate some of my own, to arrange for outside contractors to do the work, and to super-

BARBER ICE CREAM COMPANY
Partial Organization Diagram

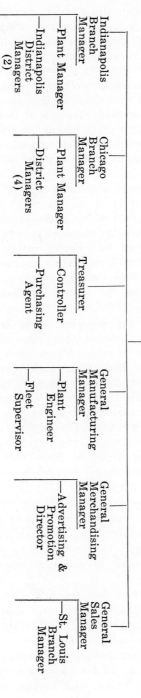

President
Great Lakes Creameries, Incorporated

President
Barber Ice Cream Company

Treasurer
— Controller
— Purchasing Agent

General Manufacturing Manager
— Plant Engineer
— Fleet Supervisor

General Merchandising Manager
— Advertising & Promotion Director

General Sales Manager
— St. Louis Branch Manager

Chicago Branch Manager
— Plant Manager
— District Managers (4)

Indianapolis Branch Manager
— Plant Manager
— Indianapolis District Managers (2)
— Decatur District Manager
— Evansville District Manager

vise it as it is put in place. I can also see opportunities for investigation for improvement. One example is truckloading. Perhaps we should have the cold room set up as a self-service supermarket for each driver to do his own loading rather than have him issue an order and then have the cold room loaders load the trucks. This would reduce labor cost, since the drivers' labor is free. It might well have other ramifications that I have not as yet thought of; therefore, at this point all that I can say is that the matter should be studied. To look at it effectively would require plant visits and talks with plant managers and district managers. In addition, I would have to do some thinking and studying on my own. Time taken at various intervals over a year would undoubtedly be necessary.

"Before I came here, one man was in charge of all facilities. Since there was a lot to do, he left it up to the plant managers to a considerable extent to take care of their own engineering problems. Without a technically competent specialist to consider such matters, other people from sales and finance entered into consideration of these kinds of problems. They still do this, based upon their past practice. I would say that it is going to take me some time to get this matter of technical competence and responsibilities for particular decisions worked out."

Problems and benefits of the merger. Since organization changes from the merger were still in process, there was no central agreement as to the implications of its results. There were, however, varying views. One vice-president said that in the past, because of the seasonal nature of the business, there had been reluctance to add any 12-month overhead to a 6-month business. Cost control in the past had been "very little staff." Another general manager remarked that Great Lakes was planning for expansion and growth. This meant more people at the top and more specialists—for example, the purchasing agent, the plant engineer, and the advertising director. These were able people who came in from the outside and were making a contribution as they learned the street vending business.

Another central manager remarked that he felt much better off being with Great Lakes in a large organization rather than with a small company. There were more opportunities for each man to prove himself and to strive for higher positions. A man who did a good job for Barber Ice Cream Company could move to other divisions of Great Lakes Creameries.

One branch manager remarked that the firm had not yet learned to make effective use of its organization. He said that if Indianapolis or Decatur wanted information, it would go directly through channels rather than send a memo or call the person who had the information. Decatur would go to Indianapolis and Indianapolis to Chicago for ideas on maintaining the trucks. In his view, this was a waste of time and it was not necessary. He felt that, with further experience, problems of communication of this kind could readily be overcome, but he was not sure just what action management should take to speed the process.

General views on branch management. The branch manager's job was generally considered to be a key one for the company and also a difficult one. The reason for this was the seasonal nature of the business and the very rapid expansion, within a 10-day period, during the spring from dormancy to perhaps 200 people working in one branch. Decisions had to be made by the minute in this spring season. Each branch went from a zero sales rate to about a one or two million dollar sales rate within a very few weeks. This meant that one man in touch and on the local scene definitely had to be in charge.

The major problem that branch managers worked on was the development of sales. They had general supervision over and responsibility for the support brought into this, such as vehicles and stock; but sales development was the key. Several branch managers remarked that if they had high sales they could cover up a lot of mistakes, so their effort was put there.

Sales development meant both internal sales management and a lot of personal contacts with commissions and officials. As one branch manager put it: "This takes years to develop. If you are well known and trusted, then a village official will not let a situation go sour."

The first emphasis in the spring was on getting enough help and on training them. Since the head loader, chief mechanic, and plant manager worked the year round and their functions could be reasonably well scheduled, there were not so many problems in the spring as with sales. In sales there were day-by-day crises—men out sick, no-shows, new routes to put in, and so forth. This meant 18-hour days and 7-day weeks stretching on into July. One branch manager said, "By August you are really exhausted; there's nothing you can do but live through it."

One organizational move that was being considered was adding a second manager to each branch to allow the branch manager to spend more time on sales effort. This second manager would take over the other functions of plant, fleet management, and cold room management.

One of the general managers in Chicago remarked that from the branch manager's standpoint the additions to headquarters staff were not all beneficial. First, their salaries added to the overhead allocated to the branches. The branch managers might well feel, "How do we pay for all these big company tactics we're following?" While specialists might eventually be useful, at the moment they were costing dollars and saving pennies. An added number of staff people also meant increased visits from the central office—additional new faces showing up and time taken from the major task of branch management.

District managers were primarily responsible for supervising the route salesmen. In addition, they had other duties that included handling their own correspondence and typing, making appearances in court on accident cases, handling public relations and community relations work for their district, acquiring licenses, making personal responses to customer complaints, and developing decent relationships with mayors and sheriffs. For the district manager, the basic spring's work was training the salesmen. The company had a considerable turnover of district managers; about half of them were new each year. Most of these men were promoted from route salesmen. A few came in from smaller districts to larger ones.

FACILITIES AND PROCUREMENT

The company made its ice cream and other products at two plants, one in Chicago and one in Indianapolis. It purchased ice cream for the St. Louis street vending operation from a large local manufacturer. Each of the two plants had its own plant manager and production staff. In addition, there was in Chicago a general production manager, a fleet manager, and a general purchasing agent, all of whom were concerned with some aspects of the problem of production, facilities, and procurement.

Manufacturing ice cream. To make ice cream, milk and cream delivered to the plant was first pasteurized by heating in special equipment developed for this process. It then moved to a chilling tank in which it was held both to reduce its temperature and to act as a reserve inventory for the ice cream freezers. Once chilled, the liquid was pumped to a battery of individual ice cream making machines called freezers. In these, it was mixed with certain additives, cooled rapidly, and whipped until it reached the proper temperature and attained the consistency of a very heavy liquid. From the freezers, it was pumped either to a bar-making machine or to other special forming machines for packaging. The bar-making machine, known as a Gram machine, contained a large number of individual holes or molds into which the heavy liquid was poured and into which the sticks were inserted. Once the bars were stripped from the molds, they moved through additional packaging equipment to be individually wrapped and then bundled in cartons. The cartons then moved by conveyor belt into the cold room or hardening room in which all the finished inventory was kept at a very low temperature. From the hardening room the products were later shipped to various districts or loaded onto the sales trucks at the manufacturing branches.

Chicago operation. The Chicago plant was generally considered to be well equipped and to be a low-cost operation. Although it was small and had the minimum equipment for manufacturing ice cream, relative costs were as low as those in many large companies. The Chicago plant manager attributed this to careful planning and scheduling. He said, for example: "In a small operation such as ours, it is necessary to make several changeovers each day; therefore, I have emphasized cutting down the changeover time. We have worked it out so that we have a changeover down to 2 to 3 minutes. We can do this by scheduling flavors properly. As an example, we always run chocolate last."

During peak operations for two shifts, the Chicago plant had 33 people altogether, including janitors, machine operators, packers, power plant engineers, and the like. The plant manager viewed his major problem as operating for only 6 months. This meant he had to rehire each spring. For skilled men, such as engineers on refrigeration machines and boilers, he hired moonlighters—men who worked for the city and who could work part-time in the evenings. They were both skilled and stayed with him for years at a time. The Chicago plant had been kept reasonably up-to-date by making small improvements each year as had proved necessary. The one major problem that the Chicago plant manager wanted to have improved was dry storage space. At present, he bought cartons and packaging material in less than carload lots because he often did not have places to store supplies. Cartons stored inside the plant would occasionally come unglued, or the lids would steam out of shape because of the high humidity. An investment of about $25,000 to $30,000 would alleviate this problem. An extension could be added to the present building. The plant manager stated that the central management was fully aware of the problem and had known about it for several years. His view was that the secret to his performance was close supervision and some luck in getting people to return for several years, as well as some competition between the two shifts. He did not see much possibility for reducing manufacturing costs in Chicago, since he already had as much automatic equipment as he could use. As a matter of fact, output could probably be increased 20% to 25% with the current equipment. In his view, increased profit had to come from added sales. The Chicago plant manager believed that the product line was wide enough currently. Any further move to something like chocolate fudge or a chocolate eclair would call for special equipment and special nozzles that not only had to be developed but would also be underutilized. Such special products would also run up manufacturing cost through additional changeover time.

Indianapolis. The plant situation in Indianapolis was much less favorable than that in Chicago and, particularly, equipment was quite old. There were several one-tube ice cream machines that had been purchased second-hand and for which the company could not now get parts. Although they were at the moment in perfect operating condition, their productivity was low and they were costly to repair. The hardening and storage room was also very old. It had been repaired last year at a cost of $7,500; however, these repairs were only temporary. The plant manager believed that in the very near future $100,000 would have to be invested to entirely replace the hardening and storage room.

The Indianapolis plant at present had no problem in maintaining the necessary output, but there were some problems with individual products or individual machines. For example, the plant manager said that

Indianapolis was making an ice cream sandwich this year by the same methods and equipment with which he had had considerable troubles in the past two years. He predicted that next year the scrap rate would exceed 35% on this machine. In addition, he wanted a bar stacker at an investment cost of $5,000. This would replace 3 part-time workers in total. There was an additional problem with an exit door from the icebox through which the cartons were taken for loading. The existing door allowed only a one-half inch clearance on each side of the rack, and the floor was slightly slanted. While the racks could be gotten through the door, the production manager claimed that a large number of cartons were torn. He wanted to widen the door at an expense of about $700 but had not as yet gotten approval from Chicago to do so. Should approval not be forthcoming within the next two weeks, then he would not be able to make the change since he would then be too close to the next manufacturing season.

Product quality was maintained through purchase of the finest raw materials and through careful supervision by the plant superintendent. The tests utilized were taste-sampling by the plant superintendent of products in process and of finished products. Other than this, the firm had no quality control procedure.

St. Louis. In St. Louis, unlike Chicago and Indianapolis, Barber Ice Cream Company purchased its products from an outside supplier. On his own equipment, the supplier used packaging materials and labeling materials supplied by Barber. This supplier also sold bars and small containers to independent competitors of Barber in the St. Louis area. The recent expansion of Barber Ice Cream Company meant that the supplier's specialized equipment for products purchased by Barber was now utilized at full capacity. It was estimated that an investment of somewhat over $400,000 would be required at a minimum for Barber to build its own plant in St. Louis. This included $100,000 for a 9-row Gram machine as well as related pasteurizing, freezing, packaging, cooling, and hardening-room equipment. Such a plant would be large enough to support a sales volume of $2,000,000 and over.

Plant personnel. The hourly people in the plant who worked the packaging machines and did cleanup work were 90% transient. A small percentage came back from year to year. The pay rates varied from area to area. In Indianapolis the women started at $1.40 an hour and the men at $1.55 an hour. The production manager remarked that in the entire plant during the last year only one of the employees was a high school graduate. He added that, although their educational background was limited, they worked hard; they had to. Most of the work was machine-paced. The people in both the Indianapolis and the Chicago plants seemed satisfied to do a good day's work from the plant superintendents' point of view. Both superintendents said they followed through on any complaints right away, and that they had particularly learned how to work with women. The major secret was to give them good close training and not expect too much from them at first. If they appeared not to be able to do one job, then they were transferred to another that they liked better. Generally, employees were not let go until other employees started complaining about them.

Fleet management. The central fleet manager in Chicago was generally responsible for maintenance, repair, and operation of all the trucks of the company. He viewed this as a major and important task, since a large percentage of the assets of the firm was invested in the street trucks.

From his view, the problem of maintenance was difficult because at least half the mechanics had to be hired new each season. The labor situation on mechanics was such that all good technicians worked the year round, so that Barber Ice Cream Company got only the dregs in hiring part-time workers. Drivers themselves had a very minimum of schooling in how to operate the trucks. This also affected how well the equipment was used.

The fleet manager purchased all automotive equipment, advised on the layout of the garages at the plants and outlying districts, and tried to spend as much time in the garages as he could. He viewed his major problem as taking a look at the trucks in the fall to advise what major overhaul was needed during the winter and then trying to troubleshoot as much as possible during the summer. In addition to this, he attempted to make sure that each garage was equipped with proper lift equipment.

The mechanics working in each branch were responsible to the branch managers. The fleet manager stated that his purpose was to give them as much technical advice as he could and in particular to make sure that their garage facilities were as adequate as was necessary. Major maintenance was done during the winter by district managers and by the few year-round mechanics. If major overhauls became necessary during the summer, they were usually subcontracted since the mechanics were then busy with minor maintenance, oil changes, washing, and so forth. The purchase of the additional new cars for St. Louis had been arranged for by the president of the company. The cars were supplied by the same major automobile manufacturer who had supplied the great majority of the company's trucks in years past.

Purchasing. The central purchasing agent was a new executive in the firm. He stated that his major function at the moment was establishing a formalized purchasing procedure. In the past, buying had been done by any one of the four central executives of the company or by branch managers. There had been little competitive bidding and no formal confirmation of purchase orders.

The purchasing agent had now worked out a procedure whereby only certain people, including the branch managers and all central executives, were authorized to purchase. All purchases over $25 had to be confirmed by an order with a copy to the purchasing department. A volume of more than $500 with any one supplier also had to be confirmed with a purchase order. Copies of purchase orders were now being sent to accounting; the function of approving invoices had been removed from the authority of plant managers and now rested in branch managers or central executives.

In addition, the purchasing agent had centralized the authority for buying packaging supplies, sticks, cartons, and corrugated shipping containers. It was still left up to each branch to buy its own sugar. This had to be done locally for shipping cost reasons. The purchasing agent stated that purchasing specifications on all products remained to be developed. In his view, the branch managers had not been much affected by the changes he was instituting. They had some more paper work in confirming purchases, but their time was saved on buying negotiations and on purchasing major items. He was sure that the number of items purchased by the branch managers would be reduced.

As yet, the purchasing agent had not been able to introduce forward purchasing and was still buying from week to week on demand. He said that while there was informal and intuitive history on minimum and maximum inventory levels (two weeks' supply in most cases), a formal procedure was yet to be developed. This was one of the projects he had in mind. The central purchasing agent stated that he had been able to save about $60,000 in purchasing costs. One way he had done this was by switching suppliers on printed cartons. This had reduced the carton cost by $10,000. He foresaw savings of the same order of magnitude in purchasing sticks. The central purchasing agent viewed his future as busy since he saw a large number of projects to carry out. Specifications on overruns and underruns by suppliers, write-offs on obsolete materials, effective buying of company cars and trucks, quality control procedures for all materials purchased, inventory levels, and re-order times were some of the projects he had in mind.

Manufacturing management. The central manufacturing manager explained that he had two major problems: (1) equalizing the cost of manufacturing among the branches and (2) getting facilities in shape for expansion. He felt that with the greater advertising of products and with broader markets the business was certain to expand and that expansion was necessary because profits had not been satisfactory. In his view there was always room for cost improvement in manufacturing through better scheduling of men and materials, less loss, less waste, and better quality control in the plant. The manufacturing manager viewed the expansion problem as being limited by the capital that was available.

He also stated that Indianapolis needed a certain number of improvements in order to take care of particular problems there. For expansion, he looked to the development of additional specialized equipment for new products such as sandwiches or ice cream eclairs. He felt that the labor force was satisfactory—a good organization of dedicated people who were conscientious, worked many hours willingly, and, in the summertime, put in 12 to 14 hour days without complaint.

PERSONNEL

The man and the task. While the duties of a salesman had been well worked out by the company, as was explained in the marketing section, the puzzle as to what kind of person made the best salesman had not been resolved. Executives had varying views. They felt that the general understanding of a route salesman's job was quite limited. By comparison, everyone knew what a plumber or a carpenter did. A man looking for a job in those fields could decide for himself whether or not he wanted it; but in contrast, the outsider had no idea of the real nature of a routeman's job. It might look easy, pleasant, and happy to spend your time lifting a 3-ounce bar. Most people seemed to feel that the route salesman's job was part-time. They did not realize that a man earned his livelihood with this job. One executive felt that few people applied because general understanding of the job was so limited. Some who had contact with better salesmen seemed to feel that they could make such a fortune in six months that they could retire for the balance of the year. Other outsiders assumed that the salesman made only pennies per sale; therefore, they could not see how he could earn a living. It was generally believed that the job had no status, even though a top salesman earned more than most white-collar workers or even many construction workers. People interested in white-collar jobs certainly never applied for a route salesman's job. The work itself called for long hours, 10 a.m. to midnight regularly during the summer, and usually seven days a week from April through September. This varied somewhat from branch to branch. During the winter months some men held other part-time jobs, some went south, and some went to school.

Turnover varied from branch to branch and from district to district. In some instances, 50% of the men were new at the beginning of the season and in some instances only 20% of the men were new. Of the new men, very few remained throughout the season, and it was common to have two or three different men on a truck that had been assigned to a new man at the beginning of the year. It was generally felt that the oldtimers were very good bets to return from year to year. If a man stayed with Barber Ice Cream Company more than three seasons, he was reasonably certain to return for the following season. Oldtimers seemed to enjoy the work, the contacts, and the people. It was generally agreed that the year-end bonus was attractive to these men.

As to the kind of man to hire initially, there were varying views and no central agreement. One branch manager reported that he had had the greatest success with men over forty. They weren't able to get a job outside; he welcomed them. Another man said, "I look for the steady plodding type—the southern man whose wages have been low. When he

comes with me, he is getting $125 paychecks and these are good to him."
Another branch manager who had thought hard about the problem reported: "Young men in their twenties are not satisfactory for us. They
tend to need steady jobs to support families. We should therefore avoid
trying to recruit them except in highly special instances such as ex-
bakery or milk truck salesmen. I have found considerable success with
school dropouts and war babies just coming into the job market. These
are men who sometimes can't get jobs because they have not yet had
military service. They have good physical stamina and they can be
motivated. With proper attention, they can be made into very good
competitors. They'll work hard against one another for the top dollar."

Compensation. The salesmen worked on commission, which varied
from branch to branch. In St. Louis and Indianapolis it was 24%; in
Chicago there was a sliding scale of 25% for new men, 30% for second-
year men, and 33% for men with over 5 years of service. In addition,
the men earned a bonus if they stayed through the year. The bonus was
2% of total sales in St. Louis and Indianapolis; in Chicago it was 8%.
The bonus was viewed as a problem, both from the standpoint that there
were differences among branches and because some managers felt that
it gave inadequate motivation. As one manager put it: "It is possible
for a man to be happy with a take-home of $80 a week, stay throughout
the season, and make an 8% bonus. He really has not done an adequate
sales job. Why should he get any bonus?"

Plant workers, as well as mechanics and loaders in the branches, were
paid on an hourly schedule. The rates were negotiated with the union
in Chicago and were established by branch managers in St. Louis and
Indianapolis. In practice, pay in the latter two cities was about $.70
an hour less than in Chicago.

Compensation for district managers was a base salary plus a 1%
commission on all sales. The average take-home pay for each district
manager was about $10,000 a year. The district managers worked the
same long hours as the drivers during the April to October season.
During the balance of the year they came in to perform maintenance
tasks on the trucks and in the branches. District managers, like all
other executives of the company, received 30 days' vacation during the
year.

The sales manager of Barber Ice Cream Company was convinced that
district manager compensation was a general problem throughout the
company. As part of this, he noted that, under the new union contract
in Chicago, certain men working in the plant could earn almost as much
money as a district manager who had been on the job for 10 years or
more. Furthermore, the man in the plant worked 40 hours during the
season, whereas the district manager went as high as 90 hours a week.
The sales manager was also not certain that a straight 1% commission
on sales was suitable for the problem of increasing marginal sales. In
his view, added marginal revenue always meant extra effort. At present,

a district manager got the same 1% for the last $20,000 as for the first $200,000. Therefore, the sales manager had in mind changing the compensation to a base pay plus an incentive for an increase over the previous year. He wanted district managers to be dissatisfied with the amount of sales that they made, but also to be satisfied in their relationships with the company and to be paid for their efforts.

Benefits. The company's sickness insurance policy was standard for all personnel. It included payment of a basic Blue Cross policy but not a Blue Shield or doctors' services policy. In addition to that, there was a major medical policy with a $600 deductible feature. As to life insurance, each route salesman was insured for $5,000 (this had been negotiated by the union in the last contract). All district managers and other executives were insured for $1,000. As to retirement benefits, there had been none prior to the acquisition by Great Lakes Creameries, Incorporated. Now, each executive earned retirement credit from the time of his employment under Great Lakes. The salesmen and plant people entered into the retirement agreement when they began a second season of employment. The retirement plan was noncontributory and nonvested.

Union relations. St. Louis and Indianapolis personnel were not organized. Chicago route salesmen and plant personnel were organized by a local of the teamsters' union. The last union negotiation had increased wage costs by 9% and had resulted in a contract with a 40-hour basic week with time over that at time and one-half plus double-time for Sunday and holiday operations. This, of course, pertained to the plant and branch personnel only and not the route salesmen. The drivers earned only commission. Head mechanics in the branches were paid slightly over $4 an hour and were guaranteed a year-round job.

According to the pension plan, a man received retirement benefits if he had worked a minimum of 15 seasons for the company. The retirement rate was $50 a month for a retiree with 15 seasons' service. It increased to a maximum of $100 per month for 25 seasons' service. Prior to the Great Lakes acquisition, the company had had no union in Chicago. However, Great Lakes plant people had always been organized, and Barber Ice Cream personnel came under the agreement at the time of the acquisition. The agreement called for one week's notice of layoff and a minimum of 4 days' work when plant personnel were called in.

FINANCE

The financial results of operations since the acquisition can be seen in Exhibits 9, 10, 11, and 12.

At the same time, some two years ago, that Barber was acquired through an exchange of stock with Great Lakes Creameries, Incorpo-

EXHIBIT 9

Barber Ice Cream Company
Division of Great Lakes Creameries, Inc.
Opening Balance Sheet

Assets		Liabilities	
Cash	$ 400,000	Accounts payable	$ 250,000
Inventories	100,000		
Plant	825,000	*Equity*	
Sales trucks	825,000	Stockholder's equity	2,050,000
Goodwill (B)	75,000		
Office equipment	75,000		
Total	$2,300,000	Total	$2,300,000

Note A—100% of the common stock (1,000 shares) owned by Great Lakes Creameries, Inc.

Note B—Goodwill account established from the acquisition of the assets of the former River Ice Cream Company.

EXHIBIT 10

Barber Ice Cream Company
Division of Great Lakes Creameries, Inc.
Current Balance Sheet

Assets		Liabilities	
Cash	$ 845,000	Accounts payable	$ 150,000
Inventories	200,000		
Plant (net of reserves) ..	660,000		
Sales trucks — (original cost, $975,000, less reserve)	395,000	*Equity*	
Goodwill	75,000	Common stock	2,050,000
Office equipment (net of reserves)	60,000	Retained earnings	35,000
Total	$2,235,000	Total	$2,235,000

EXHIBIT 11

Barber Ice Cream Company
Division of Great Lakes Creameries, Inc.
Sales and Earnings

YEAR	SALES REVENUE	NET PROFIT AFTER TAXES
Current	$4,050,000	$(33,000) [1]
Last Year	3,650,000	68,000
Preceding Year	3,200,000	207,000
" "	3,100,000	202,000
" "	3,150,000	192,000
" "	2,900,000	174,000
" "	2,890,000	173,000
" "	2,800,000	160,000
" "	2,750,000	160,000
" "	2,760,000	162,000

1 Loss

EXHIBIT 12
Barber Ice Cream Company
Division of Great Lakes Creameries, Inc.
Profit & Loss Statements
(All figures in thousands)

Account	Chicago		St. Louis		Indianapolis		Total	
	Last Year	This Year	Last Year	This Year	Last Year	This Year	Last Year	This Year
Sales	2,000	2,100	450	850	1,200	1,100	3,650	4,050
Cost of goods manufactured	660 [1]	670	202 [2]	349	450 [1]	450	1,312	1,469
Gross profit	1,340	1,430	248	501	750	650	2,338	2,581
Sales commissions	650	735	114	230	314	297	1,078	1,262
Advertising	20	42	5	16	11	22	36	80
Operating wages	38	38	20	20	46	46	104	104
Branch executive salaries	65	65	20	28	55	55	140	148
Branch executive bonus	10	..	2	..	6	..	18	..
Truck depreciation	166	166	26	56	83	83	275	305
Truck operating & repair	160	175	25	38	80	88	265	301
Garage lease	6	6	4	6	7	7	17	19
Office expenses	9	9	3	5	7	7	19	21
Interest	1	2	1	1	1	1	3	4
General & administrative expense	137	192	31	78	82	100	250	370
Central executive bonus	10	..	2	..	6	..	18	..
	1,272	1,430	253	478	698	706	2,223	2,614
Profit before taxes	68	0	(5)	23	52	(56)	115	(33)

[1] Includes all plant costs in Chicago and Indianapolis.

[2] Includes purchase costs in St. Louis plus costs of supplies furnished by Barber Ice Cream Company.

rated, the parent company bought for cash the assets of River Ice Cream Company of St. Louis. River Ice Cream had been discontinued and its operations were now merged with those of Barber Ice Cream Company. The price paid for the trucks, certain other assets, and goodwill was $150,000. The former owner of River Ice Cream continued as manager of the St. Louis branch under a 2-year contract at an annual salary of $20,000. Profits after tax of River Ice Cream had been $30,000 for the year before purchase by Great Lakes. In that year the owner had paid himself a salary of $10,000 and had charged $10,000 to depreciation of his trucks.

Barber Ice Cream was acquired by direct exchange of stock; 1,000 shares of Barber stock, all owned by the founder and president, were exchanged for 100,000 shares of common stock of Great Lake Creameries. The basis of the exchange was the book value of each stock at the date of exchange. Currently, Great Lakes Creameries had 1 million shares of stock outstanding. It was traded over the counter at a recent price of $28 per share. This price and the number of shares outstanding has not changed significantly in the past few years. Since the acquisition of Barber Ice Cream Company, all net profits have been retained in the subsidiary.

During the past year, the equipment account had been increased as a result of the purchase for St. Louis of 25 new trucks at an average price of $6,000 each. These new trucks were depreciated over a 5-year life. The trucks acquired originally from River Ice Cream and Barber Ice Cream were being depreciated over a 3-year life. The plant account had been revalued at the time of Great Lakes' acquisition. Depreciation of plant and equipment was now over a 10-year life.

Data relating to sales, expenses, and profit and loss by branches was now released to each branch. This had not been done in the past under the ownership of Mr. Barber. One reason was to help explain the discontinuance of executive bonuses for this year. In the past, it had been customary to pay such a bonus at Christmastime. The current fiscal year had just been concluded in January.

The executives of the company were aware that some rumors had spread through the division that the company was losing money. They believe this was based on an incorrect interpretation of branch profit and loss accounts. They also recognized that there were certain investment problems for the division based upon the age of equipment. The financial dimensions of this can be seen in the exhibits. Finally, they were unhappy about profit trends and were convinced that some action on prices or on costs was necessary.

CONTROL

Inventory control. Inventories were carried both on the sales cars and in the plant. The specific procedure for sales cars called for the driver to make up an order, which went to the cold room. The loader then filled a hand-push rack for each order. The driver signed for this order and packed his own sales car. He was charged for the order in dollars and cents. In a sense, this was a perpetual daily dollars and cents balance. If an order came in for over $200, then the branch manager was required to take a complete physical inventory of that truck to see if there were any shortages. The driver was told what he owed and was required to pay in cash. New drivers were given a standard load determined for the route they were to cover. After some experience, they were allowed to discuss modifying this load with the district manager. Old hands who had worked for several years seldom, if ever, needed to discuss their loads with the district manager.

Inventories in the plants were, of course, taken at the end of the selling season so that a final balance sheet could be drawn. Work during the selling season was generally so heavy that no physical count of inventories in the plant was made. The plant manager was expected to have the proper amount of supplies on hand to meet his sales needs.

Cash control. Branch managers were responsible for all handling of cash. According to generally worked-out procedures, 5 days elapsed between the end of one selling week and the drivers' receipt of a check for his commission. This allowed enough time for shortages to show up so that his check could be held if anything unusual occurred. When the driver came in at the end of each day, he turned his cash in first before filling out his order form for the cold room loader. Once the order for each truck was completed, a copy was sent to the cashier. Each order was numbered, and the cashier checked that sequence the following evening when cash was received. As the driver turned his cash in, he put it on top of a pink slip from the previous day that had been extended to show the amount of merchandise loaded on that previous day. Each morning the district manager checked the order forms and also the summaries of cash turned in for the previous day. At this point, he was presumably able to note any serious discrepancies.

Cash control was a problem at the beginning of the season. Fairly often, cash shortages built up because a route man might well take living money from his load during the first two weeks until he got paid. If the shortage was not discovered or was not paid up, then the district manager was held accountable. Several district managers had thought of bonding the men or of holding up on the first few weeks' paychecks until the problem of cash shortages could be cleared up, but such procedures were very difficult because of the financial situation of the men who could be hired.

Branch control. In the past two years a new practice had been instituted of developing accounting statements for each branch and circulating these to the appropriate branch managers. The branch managers generally favored this, since they wanted to see what was being accomplished and to know the results of their operations. Some of them were disturbed by what they thought were recent losses, since these were the reverse of what they expected from the time and the effort they put in on their operations. Several branch managers said it was the accounting that seemed to them to be the question. In their view, it was impossible to segregate the controllable expenses from the overhead expenses. They felt that they were working hard but had not been able to show good results although they had cut controllable costs. One branch manager stated that the costs of selling and the costs of carrying the investment should be separated so that he would not be held responsible for investment costs he could not control.

Expense analysis. The central managers of the company were, of course, concerned with cutting expenses so that profits could be increased. The treasurer remarked that before the beginning of the last year he had recommended that some of the overhead be cut by eliminating a plant engineer and a general production manager. He felt that it was not only the salaries of these personnel but also associated expenses that ran up central overhead costs. In his view, the branch managers in general did a good job of keeping costs down and the big target to be concerned with was sales per car per day. In his view, sales commissions were too high also. For the future it would be necessary to decrease these sales commissions by at least an average of 5 percentage points. This needed to be done in order to assure the future general profitability of the company.

The company's controller remarked that certain manufacturing expenses had also caused difficulty in the last year. Sugar, as an example, had suddenly jumped in price and had increased materials cost by some $50,000. In addition to that, some new products had production bugs in them that could not be worked out during the selling season. In his view, better cost control was needed for the branches—overall costs as well as manufacturing costs. For the future he foresaw a controllable expense budget for each branch manager. He had not completely worked out, however, the items to be entered into such an expense budget.

He further explained that the depreciation costs made the income statements before and after the acquisition hard to compare. To some extent, the assets had been written up at the time of acquisition according to an engineering survey made by competent outside engineers and appraisers. Both manufacturing equipment and sales cars were being written off in a fairly short period.

Additional control efforts. Central executives had in mind making some changes in existing control systems that they thought would increase profitability. One example was increasing sales by working out a new incentive plan for branch managers and district managers that meant "control before the fact." Such an incentive plan would be based on a quota system calling for a given percentage increase above this year's operation. All details had not as yet been worked out. The general principles were to give a bonus beginning with 95% of quota and increasing the amount of bonus so that the bonus eventually at some point would be as much as 2% of sales. It was felt that such a compensation system would lead to emphasis on the marginal sales in September, for example.

In addition, the controller proposed to require the district managers to work out sales figures by routes as well as car days by route. He knew that the managers would balk at the paper work involved, and therefore he proposed adding a record clerk at each branch. Such an extra office man would cost $5,000 and would require about $100,000 extra in sales to pay for his salary. In the controller's view, this would be quite possible. In his view also, the expense budget would help by requiring the branch managers to pay close attention to such things as the spoons and the napkins that the salesmen gave out. Branch managers could readily watch this kind of expense and see that it did not get out of hand because of waste. This was just one example of the possibilities of a controllable expense budget for each branch.

BRANCH OPERATIONS

Chicago. Chicago was currently the largest branch, with 4 districts, 160 sales cars or vehicles, and about $2,000,000 of sales each year. Competition in Chicago was quite substantial, both from the Good Humor Corporation and from a number of independents. The independents sold both hard ice cream and bars in competition with Barber's product line and soft ice cream from large-sized trucks. Good Humor Corporation's product line was analogous to that of Barber Ice Cream Company. In general, it sold in the same areas, although it had a larger number of trucks on the road in the Chicago area.

Barber Ice Cream Company's largest seller in Chicago was the Barber Bar. Generally, Chicago was viewed as a reasonably high-quality, high-price market. The Chicago branch manager remarked that a price reduction at the beginning of the previous selling season had not helped Chicago. His sales volume in units sold had not increased as a result of the price reduction. A later price increase was in his view the correct move.

He remarked: "Our cars average $75 a day. I wish it were $85. What do I need to do to get it up there? I need excellent weather, good managers, and good sales supervision. I have some routes that average over $100 a day. These are always in districts where the district manager has the fewest number of cars to supervise."

As to his duties as branch manager, he said that his time was pretty well used up on the office end. First, he made sure that he had ice cream for the day; second, he checked bills; third, he handled correspondence; fourth, he took care of any peddling license problems; and fifth, the telephone rang incessantly about accidents on the streets, organizations that wanted unit discounts and free goods, and so forth. From his view there were not enough hours in the day to do the job. Occasionally at night he got out and did a little riding around the city. The Chicago branch manager viewed the product line and pricing policy as "just about right."

"It is very important to understand that the branch manager's focus is on sales and that he must have the authority in his branch to bring everything to bear on this. He must be able to insist that as many trucks as possible be put on the road even though they are not in perfect operating condition on any one day. He must also be able to insist that the plant run on any one day in such a way as to give him the products he needs for that day."

Indianapolis. The Indianapolis branch was the oldest in the company; in fact, the Barber Ice Cream Company had been started in Indianapolis. The branch manager remarked that his greatest need was for additional sales supervisors. In his view, each district should have not only a district manager but also a route supervisor. Supervisors who constantly rode the trucks, trained and retrained the salesmen, made sure that the routes were covered in the most efficient manner, and filled in when men were sick were the keys to volume sales. He also stated that Indianapolis was a different kind of market than Chicago. It needed a low-priced line. With a longer selling season than Chicago, it was important to establish a competitive position very early in the season. The best was to do this was to equal or beat the independent competitors on a price basis. Once it had been established that Barber had a low-priced 5-cent stick, as well as 10- and 15-cent items, to appeal to all children, then it could cover the market adequately and "run the competition off the streets early in the summer."

The commission percentage paid in Indianapolis was less than that in Chicago. The branch manager remarked that this was in part historical accident and in part the absence of a union. He said also that the longer sales season and the cheaper living costs in Indianapolis meant that his salesmen could, overall, do just as well as those in Chicago even though they had a smaller commission percentage.

In the branch manager's view, the problem of 12 to 14 hours a day work for the district managers could in part be resolved by having a supervisor for each route. The two of them would complement each other and also provide some management relief. He stated: "The time-off idea has to come and the hours are now too long. The company needs a way to utilize the time and the energies of men over 50 effectively." The idea of added supervision and shorter hours should be easy to sell, in his opinion, but he didn't think it actually would be. There were too many men in central management and also higher branch managers who had been through the experience of long working hours and thought everyone else should also.

The consensus of the two district managers in the city of Indianapolis was that a raise to 7 cents of the "nickel-stick bar" hit their sales very hard. Until then the price structure had been excellent. They remarked that Indianapolis was a price-conscious town, so that when the price went up 2 cents, it was very hard to explain to the children. Their view also was that younger men of 18 to 22 and older men of 50 and over were the best salesmen. This seemed to have something to do with the way the children who did the major share of buying viewed people of these ages. "It's staying on a route for more than one season that really raises the average. There was one old guy—over 60—who built up a route from $7,000 to $16,000 by just staying with it and getting known."

In the branch manager's view, the problems of training and turnover of personnel would be resolved to a great extent if the company could get the right product and the right price, which would mean a decent sales volume and income per salesman. Then the salesmen would remain with the company and the turnover problem would lessen. The branch manager also wanted additional products to help carry the branch overhead and to extend the selling season. Anything from frozen candy bars to frozen dessert items or frozen food specialties seemed to him to be possibilities. "The only way we'll really know is by trying them out to see how they sell. With the overhead we have today, we need a year-round business. Although we do the best job possible in six months, that's just not enough time." He said in conclusion, "I guess my major point is that Indianapolis varies from the other branches and we need pricing and products adapted to our city. Street vending still has a solid future here."

Decatur. Decatur was a separate district with products supplied from the Indianapolis branch. The city of Decatur was not large enough itself to warrant a district, but trucks based in Decatur also operated in Springfield, Champaign, and Urbana, and the Decatur district has a year-round concession at Chanute Air Force Base. The district had 30 trucks and sales of about $450,000 a year.

The quality of product, especially during the middle of the summer, was at times a problem to this district. While the quality of manufacture was good, the problem was storage and shipment. Occasionally, the Indianapolis branch was short of hardening space and therefore shipped out bars or other products before they were completely hardened. The thought was that the product would harden while in shipment or while in the Decatur cold room. However, during the rush season there was not usually enough time to store the products long enough in Decatur to harden adequately. They then went out on the trucks too soft and broke down on the trucks.

The Decatur manager also said that he had no control over what was shipped to him. In his view this was unfortunate because tastes in central Illinois differed from those in Indianapolis. For example, special items like coconut or toasted almond were very big in the Decatur district, but the nickel stick of fruit ice was not. Incomes on the average were relatively higher in the Decatur district than in Indianapolis, and 10-cent and 15-cent items did very well. The manager remarked: "In quite a few instances the company acts as if all the branches are one. You see this at meetings where all the managers are together. I know that top-level has headaches, but all I want is my merchandise delivered in good shape, my cars out, and a free hand. Then I can go to town. I have increased sales steadily in this branch and can see very good possibilities of further expansion. One thing we certainly could do is get more vending machines on the University of Illinois campus."

The district manager remarked that he would like to come out with a 17-cent or 20-cent specialty item like chocolate eclairs. These could be sold to his public, since he had large sales in the evenings to adults for dessert after dinner. The Decatur district manager saw one additional need: a field supervisor in each city. He had one field supervisor to help him, but this was not enough to do a job adequately, especially since the trucks were scattered so widely geographically. The Decatur branch leased garage space and also storage space from a large cold storage warehouse. The leased garage space was more than adequate; the cold storage warehouse was occasionally inadequate at the very peak of the season. The district manager did not think this a serious problem, however.

Evansville. The Evansville district was also served from Indianapolis. It was about half the size of the Decatur district in sales volume and number of cars. The district manager remarked that Evansville was a much cheaper market than Chicago so he needed the nickel stick as a steady item. Discontinuing it last season hurt his tie-in sales badly. His main problem was a lot of turnover. He had been wracking his brains for years to think of ways to reduce the turnover. He had concluded that good men just would not stay with the company. "It's an in-between kind of thing." To get good salesmen, he looked for college boys to come in in June and depended on the 25% of the men who remained over from year to year. He stated that the average pay in his district was about $2,500 for the summer. He also commented on the hours: "As the season wears on, I am like the salesmen: I get a little tired—maybe a little grumpy. Then this feeds on down through the district."

The district manager said that he had increased his average $10 per day over the last 2 years by doing three things; scaling the size of the territory covered to the ability of the salesmen, supervising very closely, and being tougher with the poorer men and letting them go quickly. This was very hard to do in the spring but was necessary for the entire season's success.

He emphasized that the price structure in Chicago was not right for his market. He needed something for the poorer sections, which, he said, "all districts have." He also said, "Perhaps Chicago can sell pistachio; we can't. I'd like to see a 10-cent ice milk bar with a candy coating. This could be done in bright colors and fruit flavors with circus shapes: clowns, animals, and so forth. I get ideas all the time. If I could get together with 10 or 15 men from the company periodically, I'm sure a lot of good would come of it."

As to pricing, the district manager said further: "We lowered prices of a few items for a short period last season. I think it was a good move. We went into lower income areas with these items and sold there for the first time. Had we kept them, it would have paid off over the complete season. If we can't serve all the low income areas, our competitors will. This, then, gives them a base from which to operate, so they move into the higher income areas for a little cream. They skim off just enough of the market to trouble us. All we have to do is get a good start in the spring and then we are set for the summer. People like ice cream here."

St. Louis. The St. Louis branch had been added to Barber Ice Cream Company when Great Lakes bought out an independent operator, River Ice Cream Company, and retained its owner as the St. Louis branch manager. He operated successfully with 25 cars one year, and he doubled the number of cars the second year to 50 in total. His sales increased from $450,000 to $850,000 the second year. A route supervisor was added to the branch management to take responsibility for the increased number of salesmen.

This branch bought, as it had in the past, from a large local ice cream manufacturer. Quality of the product was fully satisfactory. The range of items that could be offered was less than that of the Chicago or Indianapolis branches. The St. Louis branch manager remarked that the job had very challenging good points and also some bad points. He had a great feeling of personal satisfaction from doing the job and found the monetary rewards pretty good. He also appreciated the wide latitude of handling his own branch. Visits by the general sales manager appeared to the St. Louis branch manager to be mainly for the purpose of acquainting the general sales manager with what was occurring in St. Louis. The St. Louis manager thought, however, that there was great waste in the winter because of the nature of the business. He said that the company could, for example, have at least monthly meetings during the winter to assemble district managers and branch managers at one point to talk over problems and to swap ideas on improvements.

The St. Louis branch manager believed that the key to sales in his city was close supervision. For the next year, he looked forward to adding a second route supervisor. He felt that this would increase sales by at least $200,000. "More supervision means higher volume. Get the volume and you'll make money. It's as simple as that."

St. Louis did not go along with the general price increase for the rest of the company during the past summer. It did not have to because of a yearly contract with the supplier. The branch manager viewed this as fortunate since his lower-price items were real leaders. He felt that if his prices had been raised, then his drivers would go independent. They would get ice cream from one of several suppliers and sell it from their own trucks. They could do this because they had built up neighborhood trades over 5- or 6-year periods. Barber Ice Cream Company would have a very difficult time competing against them.

The St. Louis branch manager felt that success in his city could be attributed in part to the better weather than that of Chicago.

The number of drivers returning from year to year had been very substantial—65% to 70% for River Ice Cream Company during the 10 years of its operation before purchase by Great Lakes. The manager remarked that he had done this by keeping in touch with his men. He sent out Christmas cards with a personal note and, beginning in February, had begun to write them, hoping they had a nice winter, looking forward to seeing them again, did they have a friend they'd recommend for a job, and so forth. This had always helped. He also stressed safety at the branch and thought his program was pretty good. As to comparison to other branches, he didn't know. "This bothers me. We should get together from different branches and get ideas from each other."

The St. Louis manager felt that the acquisition by Great Lakes was fortunate from his view. "The corporation invested in 25 new trucks in one year. I would never have been able to do this. It was a wise move. Street vending has plenty of future here."

THE FUTURE

Central executives of Barber Ice Cream Company were concerned not only with the problems of current operations but also with certain ideas that seemed more of a long-run nature. Over the past 5 years there had been a consistent policy of attempting to increase sales revenue by increasing the number of car-days on the road. The president and the general sales manager constantly dwelt on this subject in their discussions with branch managers. Each branch reported each day on the number of cars on the road and the number of cars not in service for one reason or another. Average car-days per branch per year had gradually increased from 120 to 160. By now, there was a general understanding throughout the organization that it was almost a sin to have a car inactive.

Products. Central executives interpreted events in the ice cream industry to signify a change toward greater sales of novelty items. This meant to them that basically what the company had was the Barber name, its quality reputation, and the ability to produce a reasonably large variety of ice cream products with imagination. What it needed, then, was a wider product line to accord with the general trend in the industry. The general merchandising manager felt that this had to extend not only to increased ice cream items but also to other products such as frozen desserts. He cited the large number of frozen standard desserts that one could see in grocery stores around the country and said that this indicated wide consumer acceptance of frozen dessert specialties. Certainly these could be carried on the Barber trucks. In his view, the major reason for additions to the central staff was innovation.

Another executive remarked that the introduction of a line of new and lower-priced items would provide the opportunity to reduce the sales commission, say from 30% to 20%. The men could be asked to take on lower-priced items at a lower commission, staying with the standard commission on older products. This would have to be negotiated with the union in Chicago. The company could go to the union with a plea of poverty, asking for certain changes in the contract.

Distribution. Central executives saw opportunities in distribution methods that were not as yet used. One suggestion made frequently but not yet thoroughly examined was automatic vending machines at a chain of gasoline stations. A second possibility that had been suggested was an institutional division to attempt to sell on a large scale to schools and hospitals that had cafeterias. While public schools were generally not open to individual selling, certain private schools and a few of the smaller rural schools purchased directly from ice cream companies. Beginning operations on a wholesale basis would require at least one salesman, a driver with a large truck, and probably a maintenance man for cold storage cabinets of the customers. The extent of this market was uncertain, but the Indianapolis branch manager had estimated that sales of $50,000 would not be hard to achieve in the first season and that $100,000 could be realized within two or three seasons.

These various ideas on widening the product line and selling by different methods meant that the sales management jobs of the branches would be increased in scope. To compensate for the other tasks in supervising a branch that the branch manager would have to spend less time on, central executives were thinking of changing the organization structure at the Chicago and Indianapolis branches to add a distribution manager who would be concerned with the physical problems of getting distribution with inventory control, with supervising loading and cold room operations, and, perhaps, with supervising the plant managers.

The President's View. The president remarked that one of the major problems facing Barber Ice Cream Company was rising costs. While this could be met in part with increased productivity in manufacturing, it appeared to be almost impossible to match it with increasing sales efficiency. He put it this way: "How can we offset increases in sales costs with increases in sales results? The trends are the other way." He felt that added cost controls had been introduced and further controls were necessary. Results varied from branch to branch. A technically oriented branch manager did a good job on maintenance. A sales oriented branch manager did little or no maintenance work. Variations in these were reflected immediately in fleet operating costs. These costs and sales volume problems meant to the president a financial squeeze that had to be resolved by basic planning.

QUESTIONS

1. Explain, from your analysis of industry events, why Great Lakes Creameries, Incorporated, had become interested in purchasing Barber Ice Cream Company and River Ice Cream Company.

2. Should price and product policy remain centralized as the responsibility of the general merchandising manager? What are the benefits and the drawbacks of this? How does it contribute to meeting the objectives of the company?

3. Do you have any recommendations for changes in distribution policy? What are the manufacturing and financial implications of any change you may recommend?

4. Can the company develop any work and hours arrangements that will help alleviate the "rebellion against long hours"? Be specific as to

the scheduling you have in mind, its effect on salesmen's pay, and its effect on the efficiency of selling.

5. Which of the various proposals for increasing revenues—product line changes, changes in distribution, changes in sales supervision—do you recommend that the company undertake? What are the cost and profit implications of your recommendations?

6. Should a second manager be added in each branch to be responsible for the nonselling work of the branch? If you recommend this, then explain the relationship he would have to the branch manager and to the central executives of the company.

7. Should the various improvements wanted at the Chicago and Indianapolis plants be made? Why have they not been undertaken before?

8. Should the company invest $400,000 in a plant in St. Louis now or at any time in the foreseeable future?

9. Appraise the work being done by the fleet manager and purchasing agent. Is it useful to meet the cost-reduction objective?

10. What can be done to meet the objectives stated by the general manufacturing manager? Do you have the same view as he does as to the company's problems?

11. What personnel policies do you recommend for hiring, training, and compensating the sales force, plant workers, and executives of the company?

12. Evaluate the two acquisitions by Great Lakes Creameries, Incorporated. How well did Mr. Barber do financially? How well did the former owner of River Ice Cream Company come out?

13. What do you recommend to improve the profit and loss reporting to each branch? Can the investment and the controllable costs be separated?

14. What answer would you give the president to the various questions he raised in considering the future of the company?

JONES JOINTS, INCORPORATED

BACKGROUND OF COMPANY

Through its history, Jones Joints, Incorporated has concentrated on the manufacture of pipe nipples. A pipe nipple is a short section of pipe, threaded on both ends. Such nipples are used primarily in plumbing installations and repairs.

The company was founded by Mr. Solomon Jones during World War I when there was a high demand for all kinds of pipe joints. It is located in an industrial city of approximately 50,000 population, about 40 miles outside of Chicago. The company weathered the depression of 1921 and provided Mr. Jones with a satisfactory income during the rest of the 1920's. By cutting down on all types of expenses during the 1930's, Mr. Jones was able to keep his company going. During World War II sales and profits rose. They then varied up and down, but on the average gave Mr. Jones more than a modest living.

Three years ago, Mr. Jones decided to sell the company. He was already past the normal retirement age and the company could be sold for enough to give him an adequate income for the rest of his life.

Mr. Jones sold the company to a small investment syndicate in Chicago, and retired completely from the management. The syndicate appointed as General Manager a Mr. Custer, whose business background consisted of twenty years' experience in a machinery and parts jobbing firm in Hong Kong. Mr. Custer was anxious to establish himself in the United States, and was very cooperative with the syndicate managers, looking to them for all major policy decisions.

Operating results were unsatisfactory during almost all of the period of syndicate ownership. Sales volume dropped off about 40%, partly as the result of the loss of Mr. Jones' personal friendships in the trade. The plant employees, who had been unorganized up to that time, joined an international union. A union contract was signed granting substantial increases in pay, but the following year when further increases were requested the owners pointed out that the company was operating at a loss and refused to do any more than maintain status quo. Whereupon the employees struck and the plant was shut down for a period of almost six months. During this period most of the company's customers turned to other sources for their pipe nipples.

For several months during this strike period the company continued to purchase pipe from its regular supplier and, because pipe was in scarce supply at the time, the owners were able to arrange for its resale at a significant profit. These profits helped to save the company during the time when the plant was shut down. However, when the steel company discovered that the pipe was being resold rather than processed, it cut off the supply.

Finally, enough of the employees indicated a willingness to come back for work to permit the plant to begin operations again. It has been necessary to reestablish sources of pipe and to get back sales. Fortunately, the demand for nipples has been good and sales have recovered to a rate of approximately $100,000 per year. While this volume would have permitted at least break-even operations in the 1930's, under cost and operating conditions now prevailing, Jones Joints, Incorporated, will lose several thousand dollars per year.

By this time, the investment syndicate decided to dispose of the company and after some negotiation has recently sold all of its interest to Mr. Walter Felton. Mr. Felton is a highly successful real estate broker in the city where Jones Joints, Incorporated, is located, and he has been active in the Chamber of Commerce and other local affairs. Mr. Felton gave the investment syndicate $75,000 for all of the common stock of the company and company bonds having a face value of $125,000. At the time Mr. Felton purchased these securities, the company books showed the balance sheet to be as follows:

Jones Joints, Incorporated
Balance Sheet at Time of Purchase

Assets			*Liabilities and Net Worth*		
Cash		$ 2,000	Accounts Payable		$ 4,000
Accounts Receivable		6,000	Accrued Expenses		2,000
Inventory					
Pipe	13,000		Current Liabilities		6,000
Nipples	9,000	22,000	Bonds		140,000
Prepaid Expenses		2,000			
			Total Liabilities		146,000
Current Assets		32,000	Common Stock (25,000		
			shares, $1.00 par value)		25,000
Land		20,000	Surplus		4,000
Buildings (net)		47,000			
Machinery and					
Equipment (net)		73,000			
Furniture		1,000			
Truck		2,000			
Total Assets		$175,000	Total Liab. and Net Worth		$175,000

In the purchase transaction, Mr. Felton was careful to have the records show that he was paying $74,500 for the bonds and only $500 for the stock. The bonds, which had been issued at the time the investment syndicate bought control, carry 5% interest and have seven years to run until maturity. Bonds having a stated value of $15,000 are still owned by Mr. Solomon Jones. Shortly after the purchase of Jones Joints, Incorporated, Mr. Felton wrote the following letter to his 15-year-old son who is away at school.

Dear Frank:

It may interest you to know that I have just transferred to your name all of the common stock of Jones Joints, Incorporated. You probably remember passing the plant on the way to the roller rink.

Now don't get excited and rush out to treat all the boys to double-chocolate sundaes just because you are the sole owner of a business. To be sure, the balance sheet shows that this stock is worth $29,000; but, as a matter of fact, it is worthless at the moment. The company has been losing money, and if we should try to sell the machinery and buildings, we would discover that they were greatly overvalued on the company books.

It so happens that I own most of the bonds of Jones Joints, Incorporated, and you, as the new proprietor, are going to have a tough time paying me off. So, instead of being a bloated plutocrat, you are likely to find yourself paying off a loan to your dad.

Just to cheer you up about this prospect, let me say that old Solomon Jones, whom you may remember seeing in town, has offered to sell me the $15,000 of Jones bonds he holds for $.70 on the dollar. My hope is that the company can make enough money to buy up these bonds. In fact, I too am willing to sell the company any, or all, of my bonds for $.70 on the dollar. Only time will tell whether the company will be able to make enough money to get rid of its debt in this manner. I intend to give the company a lot of personal attention the next year or two hoping to get it on its feet again.

So, the stock that I have given you is worthless at the moment, and any money the company might make in the future will be used to pay off bonds. You can see why I still advise you to hang on to your nickels. If you can get any psychic income out of being the owner of a company, go right ahead, but be careful about spending your hard cash.

Don't forget Betty will be home in three weeks and we expect you here for Saturday and Sunday.

Love,
Dad

PRESENT OPERATIONS

A general description of company operations at the time Mr. Felton took over Jones Joints, Incorporated is given in the following paragraphs:

Sales policies

Jones Joints, Incorporated, currently manufactures and sells a single type of product, steel pipe nipples. These nipples fall into three broad categories, depending upon the kind of pipe used: standard black nipples, standard galvanized nipples, and extra-heavy black nipples.

Prior to World War II, the company also manufactured brass nipples. During and since the war, however, brass pipe has been so difficult to obtain that it was almost impossible to assure customers of delivery of a range of sizes. Moreover, the greatly increased use of copper welding in plumbing installations has cut the demand for brass nipples substantially. Consequently, Jones Joints, like many of its competitors, no longer carries brass products in stock.

In concentrating on nipples alone, Jones Joints, Incorporated, is following the typical industry pattern. There are a few large manufacturers of pipe fittings who also sell nipples, but most of the nipples are manufactured by some 30 to 35 relatively small companies scattered throughout the United States. The product is highly standardized so that there can be very little quality or trade-name differentiation, and, at least to date, there have not been major production economies available to large companies that could not also be utilized by smaller firms. In recent years, Jones Joints probably produced approximately one per cent of the nipples used in the United States.

The company, like its competitors, sells its products in a wide variety of sizes. Its regular line of standard black nipples are made from pipe ranging from ⅛ of an inch to 12 inches in diameter while the length of the nipples range from ¾ of an inch to 12 inches. Galvanized and extra-heavy nipples are offered in corresponding ranges although the standard price list does not show pipe sizes above 6 inches. In addition to the standard sizes the company will make, on special order, nipples of other types of pipe lengths or threadings.

Because of this variety of sizes in three different qualities of pipe, the company is currently offering its customers over 700 different items. There is, however, very little call for the larger sizes and the company actually attempts to carry a stock of only the sizes indicated in the following table. For internal purposes, then, there are 363 standard items, and about an equal number that are offered for sale at no special premium although they are typically manufactured only on order.

The company sells all of its products to wholesale plumbing supply houses which in turn sell, primarily, to local plumbers. Most of these company sales are made by two manufacturers' agents, each of whom has an exclusive territory. One agent operates in Chicago and its suburbs to the west and north, while the other agent operates south of Chicago and as far east as Michigan City, Indiana. The latter agent has been affiliated with the company for only about a year and has not produced much volume. These agents normally receive 5% on all sales made to wholesalers in their territory. Each agent represents a variety of companies manufacturing plumbing supplies so that it pays him to maintain fairly frequent and close contact with the wholesalers in his area. Usually orders for nipples are placed only at the time the agent calls on the wholesaler although occasionally the wholesaler will call the company direct. The company has placed complete reliance on its agents to develop sales in their respective territory.

LIST PRICES FOR STANDARD BLACK NIPPLES, EACH

DIAMETER	CLOSE NIPPLES LENGTH	CLOSE NIPPLES PRICE	OPEN NIPPLES 1½"	2"	2½"	3"	3½"	4"	4½"	5"	5½"	6"
⅛"	¾"	$ .23	$ .23	$ .24	$ .25	$ .26	$ .28	$ .30	$ .32	$ .35	$ .37	$ .40
¼"	⅞"	.22	.23	.24	.25	.26	.28	.30	.32	.35	.37	.40
⅜"	1"	.22	.23	.24	.25	.26	.28	.30	.32	.35	.37	.40
½"	1⅛"	.23	.24	.26	.28	.30	.32	.35	.37	.40	.42	.44
¾"	1⅜"	.29		.31	.32	.35	.37	.40	.43	.47	.50	.54
1"	1½"	.42		.45	.49	.52	.55	.59	.62	.67	.71	.74
1¼"	1⅝"	.53		.57	.60	.64	.68	.73	.78	.84	.89	.94
1½"	1¾"	.63		.67	.73	.78	.84	.90	.96	1.02	1.08	1.14
2"	2"	.82			.90	.98	1.06	1.14	1.22	1.31	1.39	1.48
2½"	2½"	1.63				1.78	1.92	2.06	2.18	2.32	2.47	2.62
3"	2⅝"	2.06				2.21	2.38	2.54	2.68	2.86	3.04	3.23
3½"	2¾"	2.95						3.53	3.72	4.04	4.36	4.66
4"	2⅞"	3.36						4.03	4.25	4.62	4.98	5.34

NOTE: Prices for larger sizes increase sharply to $53.09 for a 12" x 12" nipple. Standard galvanized nipple prices are roughly 20% higher than figures given above, and extra heavy black nipple prices are approximately double.

For many years Mr. Jones had known personally the buyers in many of the wholesale plumbing houses in the central and north central sections of Illinois, and through personal contact he secured a significant volume of business from these customers. This business fell off after Mr. Jones retired and has been almost completely lost since the plant was shut down by the strike. Manufacturers' agents representing the three or four other manufacturers in the Chicago area are always on the lookout for business and were quick to pick up orders which Jones Joints could not fill.

Jones Joints follows the typical industry practice in its approach to pricing. First, list prices, which are used by plumbers in making out bills for their customers, are established. Most nipple manufacturers have approximately the same list prices, and these schedules are likely to remain unchanged over a period of several years. Second, the price actually charged a wholesale supply house will depend, of course, upon the discount from these list prices. Such discounts change more frequently than list prices, inasmuch as they serve as the mechanism for price competition. In recent months, Jones Joints has been offering discounts of 81% plus 10% to all recognized jobbers and distributors. The resulting net price is in line with the published price of competitors. In addition, it is industry practice to allow a 2% cash discount on all bills paid within 10 days after the first of the month in which goods were shipped.

The selling agents of the company have insisted that they find it difficult to secure large orders because competitors are offering an additional 5% or 10% discount on such business. Mr. Custer has taken the position that prices are already cut so low that the company is not making any money and, consequently, he has consistently refused to give more than the 81% plus 10% discount. He contends that agents who have the right relationships with the wholesalers will be able to get the big orders at established prices and that there is no use trying to match or exceed all discounts which the buyers for wholesalers allegedly can get because there is no way of knowing how much of this is bluff and the buyers will probably give the order to the man with whom he is most friendly anyway.

Jones Joints does not do any advertising or any other sales promotion directly to the wholesale plumbing supply houses. Mr. Custer believes that any action the company could take would be so small that it would make no significant impression on the wholesalers, and further, he feels that such sales promotion activities are the responsibility of the selling agents.

Production operations and facilities

The manufacture of pipe nipples is a relatively simple operation. Pipe is first cut into the appropriate lengths; then the threads are cut and the finished nipples moved to storage where they await shipment to companies. More specifically the operations being performed at Jones Joints, Incorporated are as follows:

(1) The pipe is unloaded from the open railroad cars on which it is received by two men standing in the car and throwing it over the side. The pipe is then placed in racks where it is stored until needed for production.

(2) Workmen take the appropriate number of lengths of pipe from the rack and carry them to a roller-cutter that can be set to cut the pipe to the desired length.

(3) These sections of pipe are shoveled into a wheelbarrow and wheeled to the threading machine where they are dumped into a bin on the floor. Extra lengths of pipe found around the cutters or in the bins are tossed into a barrel and later are sorted by pipe size. These lengths are often used for small, rush orders.

(4) Threads are cut on hand-operated or automatic threading machines that also ream the end of the pipe.

(5) The finished nipples are placed in wheelbarrows as they come off the machines and are wheeled to the finished stockroom where they are shoveled into bins. Incidentally, the pipe is sufficiently hard so that this type of handling does not impair the quality of the finished product.

(6) When a customer's order is received, the required number of each size nipple is counted out of a bin and is placed in either a small keg or a bag for shipment.

Production scheduling is done on quite an informal basis. For items carried in regular stock, the foreman keeps an eye on the number of finished nipples in the various bins. Whenever the stock in a given bin gets low, he makes a note that some more should be produced. The size of the run is varied according to how fast he has observed the item is moving. Large nipples, which are not carried in stock, are typically produced when an order is received. However, since there is an extra expense in setting up the threading machine to produce a particular nipple, it has been customary to overrun a customer's order and place these extra nipples in reserve. The company has a considerable inventory in these miscellaneous sized nipples and often is able to fill an order for a few such nipples if they can be located in the miscellaneous stock.

The company is usually out of stock of at least several of the 300 standard items it normally carries. This results either from receiving several customers' orders for a given size before it comes up on the foreman's list for production, or from a shortage of pipe of the proper size. When such shortages occur, it is customary to send customers only partial shipments, unless the work already assigned to the shop will make it possible to complete the needed nipples within a couple of days.

Pipe is purchased in a somewhat similar informal manner. Mr. Custer watches this inventory and places orders as particular sizes of pipe get low.

The facilities of the company are generally old and in only fair repair. The main plant building was purchased by Mr. Jones when he started the business and two frame additions were made in the early '20's. In the early '40's a good roof was constructed over the pipe racks but this area has not been enclosed on the sides. The floors in the plant are wooden and in rather poor condition.

The company has 6 roller-cutters for pipe of different sizes. They were purchased in the last few years and still are in good operating condition. Twelve pipe threading machines are currently in use, and several older machines along with a variety of other equipment are in the warehouse. These 12 machines vary in the size of pipes they can handle, with an overall range of ⅛ of an inch to 12 inches. There is some overlapping capacity for pipe sizes in most popular demands. Several of these machines were purchased in the 1920's, although some of the equipment was bought second-hand when business picked up in the '40's.

In addition to the foregoing, hand-operated threading machines, 2 automatic threading machines were purchased when the company was first taken over by the Investment Syndicate. On these machines a single operator can thread 180 two-inch nipples in an hour or as many as 540 half-inch nipples in an hour. These machines are the only really modern equipment in the plant.

Auxiliary equipment includes grinding machines for sharpening dies and reamers, air compressors, and miscellaneous hand tools.

All of the threading machines are driven by belts attached to an overhead drive shaft. Light is provided by an overhead bulb above each machine but the general effect in the shop is quite dingy. Except for the addition of the 2 automatic threading machines, the plant is about as Mr. Jones operated it for many years.

Personnel

Jones Joints now has 11 people on its payroll; 8 workmen in the plant, a foreman, a secretary-bookkeeper who works in the office, and Mr. Custer, the general manager. This number is considerably smaller than worked for the company during World War II and the years immediately following, when 30 or more people were often on the payroll.

All but one of the men in the plant are long-service employees who became disgusted during the long strike and came back to work for the company. As a result of this bitter experience there is a strong anti-union sentiment among the workers. These men know the plant thoroughly and are able and willing to perform almost any operation necessary. Typically, 3 or 4 of them work with the threading machine, 1 takes care of finished stock and shipping, and the other 3 do the less skilled job of handling pipe and cutting it into lengths. These men are paid on an hourly basis at rates that are neither particularly low nor high for that labor market.

The foreman is also a long-service employee who has had much of his factory experience at Jones Joints. He has shown considerable understanding and ingenuity in keeping the equipment operating and making necessary repairs with a minimum outlay of cash. He has had no formal training in production management, however. As already mentioned, Mr. Custer came to the company without previous experience in this type of business. Nevertheless, he has become familiar with operations, handles all contact with customers and agents, buys pipe and other supplies needed, takes care of all financial matters, etc. The secretary-bookkeeper is a recent high school graduate who handles the routine office operations very competently.

The company has given no thought to personnel activities, such as training programs or recreational activities, nor does it provide its employees with any special financial benefits. When business is dull there is a tendency to stretch the work out to provide continuous employment and the men are used for any repair work that may be necessary. There usually are some periods during the year, however, when men are working on short shifts.

Finance

Aside from the changes associated with transfer of ownership, Jones Joints has made no major financial moves in the last few years. Two automatic threading machines were purchased with cash on hand, shortly after the investment syndicate acquired control of the company. Since that time, however, operations have been unprofitable and capital additions have been held to a minimum. Some of the fixed assets, notably the machinery and equipment, probably are over-valued on the balance sheet, but the current assets are sound.

The company has not borrowed from the bank since World War II. It has had enough cash, partly as a result of low replacement of fixed assets, to pay its bills within the discount period. The relatively large bond issue which is outstanding was created at the time the investment syndicate purchased control of the company. These bonds did not provide any new capital, but were issued instead of stock because the investment syndicate preferred to have interest-bearing securities instead of equities. Also, a limited quantity of the bonds was used in making settlement with Mr. Solomon Jones. During the last couple of years when operating losses have been incurred, the investment syndicate waived interest payment on the bonds it held but payments were made to Mr. Jones. Consequently, there has been no technical default on the bonds, although it is evident from the balance sheet that had the full interest been paid, the company would have been forced to raise additional cash from borrowing, liquidation of inventories, or some other source.

Mr. Felton originally intended to make only a maximum investment in the company of $65,000. Since he has already exceeded this amount by $10,000, he is very much concerned that the company stand on its own feet with no more advances of cash from him. In fact, before concluding the purchase he talked with a local banker about the possibility of a loan to the company should this become necessary. The banker indicated that if Mr. Felton could develop a program that would enable the company to make at least a small profit, it would be willing to make a loan up to, perhaps, 80% of the value of the inventory, with one further and important qualification. The bank would make such a loan only if Mr. Felton would agree not to force the company into bankruptcy in event of default of bond interest payments and would subordinate his claims to that of the bank's.

Mr. Felton pointed out to the banker that his program for improvement of company operations might require the purchase of new equipment, and he knew that commercial bankers often frowned upon the use of short-term loans to finance additions to fixed assets. In the ensuing discussion it appeared that the bank would be willing to finance two thirds of the purchase price of new machines, which had a ready resale market, provided it received a chattel mortgage on such equipment and probably a preferred lien on other fixed assets. These discussions indicated that financial aid from the bank would be definitely limited. There was enough assurance, however, to make Mr. Felton feel that he would not be devoting most of his efforts to keeping the company out of bankruptcy, and he proceeded to purchase the stock and bonds described.

The profit and loss statement of the company for the year preceding its purchase by Mr. Felton is given below.

Gross sales		$108.000
Less: Agents' commissions	$5,000	
Freight out	4,000	
Cash discounts and allowances	2,000	11,000
Net sales income		97,000
Operating costs:		
Materials	$47,000	
Labor	30,000	
Depreciation	7,000	
Heat and light	2,000	
Factory supplies	3,000	
Repairs	2,000	
Office salaries	8,000	
Insurance, real estate taxes, and other administration	2,000	
Total costs		101,000
Operating loss		4,000
Interest paid		1,000
Net loss		$ 5,000

PROPOSED CHANGES IN OPERATION

Mr. Felton bought Jones Joints, Incorporated, with the firm belief that internal operations could be improved. His real estate business had involved enough industrial properties to give him a general background of how an efficient plant should be set up and operated. Consequently, as soon as he took over Jones Joints, he sought suggestions for improvement. The changes proposed to Mr. Felton by three different people are described in the following paragraphs. Mr. Felton is currently considering which of these suggestions he should adopt.

Mr. Weise's plan

From time to time, Mr. Felton had received through the mail letters and circulars from the George F. Lay Co., Management Engineers, describing the great savings and improvements in profits that both small and large companies had obtained by following the advice of these engineers. A letter from the Lay Co. with a return postcard came to Mr. Felton at the time he was negotiating for Jones Joints, Incorporated. It offered to send their representative to look over the company and discuss what improvements could be made, "with no obligation whatsoever on your part." Mr. Felton returned the card and a Mr. Weise from the George F. Lay Co., called on him a week later.

After discussing the problems of Jones Joints, Incorporated for about an hour in Mr. Felton's office, Mr. Weise said that he was sure that his firm could help Mr. Felton make substantial improvements in company operations. In order to develop a more specific plan, however, he wanted to spend two days in the plant and going over the records. Mr. Weise said that because of his wide experience in other companies and the comparatively simple operations of Jones Joints, Incorporated, he believed he could outline a course of action after this brief investigation. The survey would also give him a basis for determining the fee to be paid for any help needed from the Lay Co. Mr. Felton agreed to this plan and introduced Mr. Weise to Mr. Custer. Several days later he received the following letter from Mr. Weise.

GEORGE F. LAY COMPANY
Management Engineers

Dear Mr. Felton:

At your request, we have made a survey of Jones Joints, Incorporated for the purpose of determining what action should be taken to reduce costs and put the company on a profitable basis. The possibilities for improvement are large and this letter outlines a plan that will enable you to realize the greatest returns on the investment you have made.

It is only fair, at the outset, to tell you frankly that the company is now in poor condition. Rarely in our extended practice have we encountered a company needing improvement on so many fronts. Facilities are antiquated, methods are high cost, labor is inefficient, and the existing management is unable to cope with the situation.

Fortunately, such weaknesses are at the same time opportunities for great improvement, the hidden sources of future profit. By utilizing modern management know-how, which we have gained from our wide experience with many companies, you can correct these weaknesses, earn a handsome return on your investment, and demonstrate to your friends your keen judgment in buying up this company that appeared destined for the auction block.

We are listing below the major changes that we believe should be made in the near future. There then follows an estimate of the profits that will result from these moves. These suggestions need considerably more refinement before they can be put in effect, but our experience with similar problems will enable us to get the work done with dispatch and in a manner that will insure the greatest return. Briefly, then, the changes that should be made are:

1. *Major building alterations should be made.* These alterations are necessary to provide adequate housing for the modernized operations outlined below.

   The first need is to close in the sides of the pipe storage shed. You already have a good roof over this area and by closing in the sides the effective plant space can be increased almost 50%. You will then be able to handle your pipe inventory in a modern manner protected from the elements.

   The second major building alteration is replacing the wooden floor with a concrete floor and pouring a concrete floor in the present pipe shed. This new floor will give you flexibility in the location of machinery, ease in the movement of materials, and a reduction in accident hazards.

2. *Pipe threading equipment should be modernized.* This is necessary to bring your plant efficiency and labor costs in line with other manufacturers who have modern equipment.

   The first, and perhaps most obvious, change will be to remove the overhead drive belts and substitute individual motors on each machine. Individual motor drives have become standard in all modern plants because of the flexibility in operation and particularly in layout which this permits.

   More important, however, is the replacement of the present hand-fed threading machines by automatic machines. You already have two automatic machines and, in our opinion, should buy six more. Hand-operated machines should be kept only for production of large nipples or special orders. These new threading machines, along with probably four of your existing hand machines, will give you a capacity to produce approximately five times your present output if you operate on a two-shift basis, and enable you to undertake production scheduling as outlined below.

3. *There is need for a general plant clean-up.* In connection with building alterations and installation of new equipment, all parts for old machines no longer being used and other miscellaneous scrap in the warehouse and about the plant should be sold. The plant is

in need of a new coat of paint, and modern lighting fixtures should be installed.

4. *The unloading and handling of pipes should be mechanized.* A small electric hoist mounted on a rail running from the railroad siding across the pipe storage shed could eliminate most of the present unloading by hand.

The present pipe racks should be torn out and pipe stored in bays on the new concrete floor. Sections of pipe would be lifted from the railroad car by the hoist and then carried directly to the bay where they are to be stored. This change would eliminate two separate hand operations and substantially cut labor costs.

Moreover, the roller-cutters should be moved to the end of the pipe bays so that the pipe may be lifted from the bays and set directly into the cutters with a minimum of handling.

5. *Mechanical equipment for the movement of pipe lengths and finished nipples is needed.* If the lengths of pipe coming from the cutters are dropped into properly designed tote boxes, they could then be easily moved by a small fork-lift truck from the cutters to the threading machines.

Likewise, the nipples could be placed in tote boxes and the same fork-lift truck used to carry them to the finished stock storage bins. This truck could lift the tote box to a height that would make it easy to unload the nipples into the bins.

6. *A system of inventory control and production scheduling should be established.* Such a system is needed to avoid partial shipment to customers, rush production orders, and an irregular volume of work in the shop itself.

Sales of each item carried in stock should be carefully analyzed to determine normal rates of consumption and the quantity of inventory at which new orders should be placed must be computed. It is suggested that the bin for each item be divided in two parts, so that the order point quantity can be physically separated. As soon as the inventory falls to this level, requests for additional production can be sent to the central scheduling board.

The size of economical runs for all items should likewise be computed and a central scheduling board set up that shows the time when each item in short supply will be produced and the machine to which it will be assigned. Similar computations for minimum of each type of pipe should be established and a purchase control system worked out.

7. *Output standards and financial incentives for plant workers should be installed.* All of the preceding steps will contribute to a lowering of labor costs. The setting of individual output standards with financial incentives will insure that these savings are realized. To accomplish this, method and time study will be necessary. Output rates for each item on each machine that may be used will be com-

puted and these standards will serve as the basis for a well-designed financial incentive scheme.

As a result of these steps, we are convinced your labor costs can be reduced to approximately 20% of the selling price of your product. At the same time your service to customers should be improved and your employees will be receiving more take-home pay because of the bonuses they will be earning. Fundamentally, we believe it is the reduction in your labor costs that will serve as a key to long-run profitability of Jones Joints, Incorporated.

You will recognize, of course, that these important changes in company operations cannot be secured without some additional investment of capital. While it is impossible at this time to make accurate estimates of the new investment required, we have prepared some approximate figures because we know you will want to face squarely what is necessary to put your company on a sound basis.

Tentative Estimates of Capital Requirements

Building alterations		$ 5,000
Machinery:		
6 automatic threading machines	$24,000	
Motors and installation	6,000	30,000
Plant clean-up		3,000
Material handling equipment-pipe		2,000
Material handling equipment-nipples		4,000
Total		$44,000

If it were not for the substantial improvement in company operation that this investment will permit, we might hesitate recommending these moves. However, our estimate indicates that you will receive handsome returns from this additional investment. We have made some tentative estimates of the operating costs that, on the basis of our experience, we are convinced you will achieve when the plant is modernized as outlined above.

Estimated Operating Costs and Profits Resulting from Modernization Program

(Yearly Figures)

Net Sales Income	$100,000	$200,000	$300,000	$400,000
Operating Costs				
Materials	49,000	98,000	147,000	196,000
Labor	20,000	40,000	60,000	80,000
Depreciation	12,000	12,000	12,000	12,000
Heat & Light	2,000	2,000	2,000	2,000
Factory Supplies	3,000	5,000	7,000	9,000
Repairs	2,000	2,000	2,000	2,000
Office Salaries	8,000	8,000	8,000	8,000
Insurance, Taxes, etc.	2,000	2,000	2,000	2,000
Total	98,000	169,000	240,000	311,000
Operating Profit	$ 2,000	$ 31,000	$ 60,000	$ 89,000

To reap these profits, improved sales effort will be necessary. You now have only one good sales agent and are completely unrepresented in your local market. By securing two new agents, and selling to manufacturers as well as wholesalers, your sales should increase substantially. Moreover, the low operating cost that will result from our modernization program will permit you to make strategic price cuts on large orders; thus, if by making an average price cut of 5% you could bring your sales to $400,000 per year, you would still be earning an operating profit of almost $70,000.

In closing this letter, I wish to outline for you the financial basis, which I am sure you will agree is reasonable, for our carrying out this modernization program. One of my associates and I will do intensive work over the next three months to bring about the improvements outlined above. It is impossible at this time to state exactly how much time this work will require, so we prefer to base our fee on a per diem basis: $150 per day for myself and $100 for my associate, with the understanding that our total billing, during the next three months, will not exceed $5,000.

We will then work with you in meeting any problems encountered while the new set-up is in operation. This will, of course, require much less time on our part and I propose that my associate should spend one day a week with you, while I personally continue to exercise general oversight in this operational phase. My associate will be paid at his regular per diem rate, but I believe that the fairest arrangement for my services would be 20% of the operating profit as computed each quarter.

In this way you will continue to get the broad experience that our company can bring to bear on your problems and obtain a much needed supplement to your existing management personnel. At the end of two years, we can take another look at the arrangement and see what changes either of us wishes to make.

During this time we will, of course, have your assurance that any changes we recommend will be put into effect.

I am awaiting your confirmation of this arrangement so that we can proceed promptly with the work. The contract can be signed when I come. There is much to be done but the prospects for improvement are so bright that I am eager to get started.

Sincerely yours,

(signed) B. L. Weise

B. L. Weise, Engineer

George F. Lay Co.

Suggestions made by public accountant

Jones Joints, Incorporated, had had its income tax return prepared by a local public accountant. Since this man already had some background in the company, Mr. Felton asked him for any suggestions he had to improve operations.

The accountant stated that the accounting records of the firm were adequate for tax purposes but were not designed to be used by management for day-to-day decisions. He said that perpetual inventory records of each item in finished stock and for each type of raw material would provide the management with current information useful in making delivery promises to customers and in scheduling production.

Further, he stated that accounting records could be arranged so that the actual cost of manufacturing each type of nipple could be computed. This would require some type of job-order ticket on which the quantity of pipe and man-hours of work on cutting and threading were recorded. The accountant suggested that a single percentage of overhead be added to these direct material and labor costs rather than undertake any more refined method of allocation. Such costs, he believed, would be useful to the management in price setting and in calling attention to unusual delay or waste of material.

Once the system was established, it was the accountant's opinion that these records could be maintained by a single additional clerk.

Mr. Simon's proposal

A few months before Mr. Felton purchased Jones Joints, Incorporated, Mr. Custer had received a letter from a Mr. Simon who was seeking a position as sales manager. A follow-up on this letter disclosed that Mr. Simon was currently employed in a wholesale plumbing supply house in St. Louis. He was an energetic and aggressive individual and felt that his opportunities would be greater if he could obtain a sales position with some manufacturer of plumbing supplies.

Mr. Felton invited Mr. Simon to come for an interview, explained the company situation and asked Mr. Simon what steps he would propose for increasing company sales. Mr. Simon suggested a two-fold approach: (a) improvement of the product and (b) more intensive and extensive sales effort. He pointed out that he had no experience in the manufacturing end of the business and consequently would not qualify to make recommendations on production problems.

Mr. Simon recognized that it would be difficut to make Jones Joints pipe nipples distinctive in quality, but he did have a plan for packaging the product so that it would be more convenient for the wholesaler to handle. He said a number of plumbing supplies were now being shipped in standard size paper cartons and he believed the idea could be adapted to pipe nipples. He recommended that all standard size smaller nipples be packed 100 to a carton, while the fast moving larger nipples be packed either 50 or 25 to a carton.

The advantages to the wholesaler, Mr. Simon said, of receiving pipe nipples in cartons include the following:

> Inaccuracies in counting and sorting would be avoided.
> Mixing of sizes with the result "wrong size" complaints would be eliminated.

Bins could be replaced with neat open shelving.

Inventory could be taken easily.

A reorder slip could be placed on the box at the standard ordering point, thus providing a simple and automatic device for the buyer when new supplies were needed.

Cartons could be easily and more quickly handled than boxes or barrels and no carton would be heavier than a single man could easily lift.

No extra wrapping would be needed when the wholesaler sold by the carton.

Counting of nipples would be unnecessary when sold by carton lots.

The wholesaler could place a label with his own name on the box, thus getting some free advertising.

There would be a natural opportunity to sell plumbers larger lots at one sale.

Mr. Simon felt that the cost of the cartons would not be much more than the present barrels and boxes. Moreover, some of the economy available to the wholesaler would also apply to the finished stockroom of Jones Joints, Incorporated. Hence, he did not think that the use of cartons would significantly increase cost but would provide a distinctive selling appeal.

Mr. Simon also reported that wholesalers and plumbers often prefer fittings from which the cutting oil has been removed. He said it was his understanding that many companies pass their plumbing fixtures through an oil extractor because the recovery of cutting oil more than offsets the cost of the processing. (An independent check on this point indicated that use of an oil extractor is relatively simple and that oil recovered would offset at least a large part of the extra handling involved. A secondhand oil extractor can be purchased for approximately $1,000.) Removal of the cutting oil would also keep the cartons in neater and firmer condition.

"With something distinctive to sell," Mr. Simon continued, "the company should really go out after the business." He said that if he were made sales manager of the company he would make direct contact with plumbing supply wholesalers, not only in the area formerly contacted by Mr. Jones, but also in the South Chicago area where the manufacturers' agent was not now very effective. Since the other agent was doing a reasonably good job, he favored leaving this situation alone, at least for the present, while intensive effort was being given to the other territory.

Mr. Simon also recommended that the company expand the areas covered by manufacturers' agents; he suggested getting a man in the Minneapolis area, another in Milwaukee, a third in St. Louis, and possibly one in Cleveland. It is fairly common practice for pipe nipple manufacturers to pay freight on shipments of 300 pounds or more. To be competitive in the more distant markets, Joines Joints would probably have to absorb a larger amount of freight. Mr. Simon agreed that considerable study would be necessary to determine how much freight the company could afford to absorb, but pointed out that production costs on this additional volume of business would be lower than present costs. Delivery time would also be slower but he felt the use of cartons would offset this disadvantage.

Mr. Simon urged that the company adopt a more flexible pricing policy, because under certain competitive conditions the wholesalers will not place a large order for pipe fittings unless they receive an extra 5% or 10% discount. There apparently is no simple way to determine what discounts are necessary, and Mr. Simon stressed the need for somebody who had good customer contacts and a feel for the market. Mr. Simon believes that the manufacturer's agent often absorbs part of such extra discounts when a large order is involved.

As a further source of sales, Mr. Simon recommended that the company go to large equipment manufacturers who use pipe nipples in their products. This business is competitively priced because of the large volume of only one or two sizes. Here again, Mr. Simon felt that products in cartons might prove a strong selling point provided Jones Joints were willing to meet competitive prices.

Mr. Felton also raised the question of personal compensation. In his reply Mr. Simon said that he was confident that he could do the company considerable good and consequently was willing to take a low base salary with an opportunity to share in the results of his efforts. He proposed a base salary, plus commission on sales, along with an opportunity to buy some of the company stock. Although the discussion was purely exploratory in nature, the following figures were mentioned: $5,000 base salary, plus 3% of all sales made directly by the company to customers and one half of 1% of sales made through manufacturers' agents. Mr. Simon's traveling expenses on the road would be paid by the company. As to the stock option, when Mr. Simon learned the general financial structure of the company, he suggested that he be given an option to buy 4,000 or 5,000 shares of common stock at par value, but that this option could be exercised only as the bonds were retired. In other words, each time 10% of the bonds were retired he could buy 10% of the optioned stock from Mr. Felton's son.

Reaction of present management to proposals

Mr. Felton has discussed the various suggestions he has received with the foreman and Mr. Custer. Their reactions have been mixed. While they are quite cooperative about making some changes, they are not enthusiastic about doing all the things proposed.

The foreman quite naturally was in favor of fixing up the plant and getting new machinery. However, he did express a strong feeling that many of Mr. Weise's suggestions were "too damn fancy." "No use throwing your money around like that. The boys and I can fix the sides on that shed. There's enough lumber in them old racks to use for studs.

You buy some corrugated siding and we'll fix the place up ourselves. Same way with the floors. The boys have been complainin' about those floors for years. They'd be glad to rip 'em up and make a bonfire out of 'em. You just get the Nelson Construction Company to deliver us some ready-mix cement and we'll have concrete floors all over the place. As fer paintin' it and fixin' up the lights, we can do that in our spare time."

"Too fancy, that's what it is. Just take that electric hoist, for instance, it's a good idea not havin' to go liftin' that pipe all around, but that don't mean a man can't do any work. An ordinary chain hoist would do the job just as well. Maybe better, an' a man wouldn't have to do too much pullin' either. The same way with that fancy spoon-fed truck, or whatever it's called. We ain't cripples around here. Might be a good idea to put some tote boxes on four-wheel dollies. Might build a little rack to put 'em on, but the boys can push 'em around, especially if we get new floors. This place ain't so big we need sumpin' to ride around on. Just a waste of money, that's all."

Further conversation with the foreman about the possibility of the company making its own changes in the plant indicated that the foreman estimated that most of the things suggested by Mr. Weise could be accomplished by an outlay of about $4,000 to $5,000, in addition to the cost of the new machines.

The foreman was even more positive about the proposal for a production cost and production control system. "Well, Mr. Felton, if you want my opinion that paper work just takes a lot of time and don't do anybody any good. Least ways, in a place like this. If we were makin' airplanes, that'd be different. In a small place like this I don't need to do a lot of pencil pushin' to find out whether the boys are workin' or not. And it's plenty easy to tell when the stocks are low by just goin' and takin' a look. Sure we run outta sumpin' once in a while; but if you want us to bear down on that, it's not goin' to happen often, least ways if we got the pipe on hand."

"There's one more thing I just don't see. Now all this business about time study and incentive plans and that stuff. Just as sure as you get started with that stuff there's gonna be arguments. I don't think there's much chance of havin' a union around here, but there's nuthin' like a lot of lousy incentive plans to give the union boys sumpin' to stir up a fuss. Mr. Weise says in his letter that he thinks labor costs oughta be about 20%; the way I figure, that's about 50% better than we're doin' now. And with that new equipment we could get 50% more work out of the present men without half tryin'. Why, if you're satisfied with 20% labor cost, I'll tell you what I'll do. Now, this is assumin' we get the new equipment and the plant fixed up. Any time the labor cost gets below 20% you just give us the difference in foldin' money, to be divided up between me and the boys. We'll get the work out all right. As a matter of fact, if the boys know that's what you're gonna do, we'll get a lotta these changes done awful quick, too. You just guarantee us that 20%

and we'll get the work out. You'll get most of your repairs thrown in for nuthin', too."

"Oh, yeah, there's one other thing I wanted to mention. It says in here somethin' about cleanin' out all that old equipment in the warehouse. Well, you know I hate to do that because every once in a while I go over to the warehouse for an old part or to fix up another machine. Oh, I guess some of them old machines ain't much good, but its kinda handy havin' them around. You know that business about puttin' the nipples in the cartons, that'd be a lotta nuisance, seems to me. If it'd help sales, of course, we can do it all right; but it's mean changin' things around in the stock room. Now don't get me wrong; we'll do anything you say. Sure would like to have some of that new equipment."

Mr. Custer was not quite as definite in his view as the foreman. He said he thought there was much merit in the ideas, but each specific question would have to be given careful study. He stated most of his objections in terms of the expense and capital expenditure involved, but did make it clear that he did not like the idea of employing Mr. Weise to put in his proposed plan.

He reported that Mr. Weise had telephoned him a week after the letter had been sent and took the attitude that, of course, the company was going to carry out the plan. When Mr. Custer indicated the matter was still under consideration, Mr. Weise replied that he assumed that had been settled when Mr. Felton asked him to make a survey of the company operations. Mr. Custer also commented that he had heard in Chicago that the George F. Lay Company had a reputation for high-pressure selling. While no specific mention was made of the point, it was clear that Mr. Custer was annoyed by the uncomplimentary remarks made in Mr. Weise's report.

Mr. Custer was more favorably disposed toward Mr. Simon, but questioned whether the company should take on the extra expense of a full-time sales manager. He told Mr. Felton that he was greatly encouraged by the prospect of making some changes in the company operations. He explained that he had made several suggestions to the investment syndicate managers but that they had been very reluctant to make any changes particularly if capital expenditures were involved.

QUESTIONS

1. Outline the steps you recommend the company take during the next year to increase its sales volume.

2. What measures do you believe the company should follow to cut its production costs?

3. Briefly summarize the major steps you believe the company should take to improve its operations and then prepare a statement of the sources and application of funds for each year during the next five years.

4. Do you recommend that Mr. Felton make special effort to arrange his personal finances so that he can accept Mr. Jones' offer to sell the

$15,000 of bonds he holds? What alternative proposition do you think Mr. Felton might make to Mr. Jones which would be advantageous to both men?

5. Should Mr. Weise and/or Mr. Simon be employed by Jones Joints, Inc.? Should any other changes be made in the management personnel or organization of the company? Give reasons justifying your recommendations.

6. What are Mr. Felton's real objectives in owning control of this company? How does a recognition of these objectives affect your recommendations of actions that should be taken? Do you believe Mr. Felton's initial investment of $75,000 was a wise one?

7. Should Jones Joints, Incorporated, change any of its existing personnel policies? Justify your answer. What kind of an executive incentive plan, if any, should Mr. Felton set up for the general manager, and for any other key personnel you recommend be added to the company?

8. Assuming the recommendations you made in answer to questions 1, 2, and 3 were put into effect, would you personally be interested in buying company stock at $1.00 per share?

ROCKLYN CORPORATION

HISTORY OF THE BUSINESS

The Rocklyn Corporation was founded by its present president and owner, Mr. B. B. Barker, in 1927. Mr. Barker was an experienced businessman, having owned and operated another successful company which he sold in 1926. He then decided to enter the automotive replacement parts business, which was expanding rapidly in the latter twenties. The company has concentrated on the manufacture of a single steel part used (in various sizes and designs) in almost all motor vehicles, and involving a rather complete machine shop for its fabrication. The plant, located in southern Ohio about 50 miles from Cincinnati, is equipped to do work of good accuracy and has automatic screw machines, grinding machines, drill presses, milling machines, turret lathes, heat treating equipment, inspection equipment, facilities for simple assembly operations, and other related machinery.

The automotive replacement part business is a large industry in itself. Thousands of garages and repair shops throughout the country have to be supplied with replacement parts for the numerous makes and models of motor vehicles. Some automobile manufacturers sell replacement parts for their own cars through their own distributing organization—primarily to "authorized dealers" and "authorized service" garages. There are many other repair shops, however, and the "authorized service" man often repairs additional makes of cars; parts needed for this business are typically supplied by the automotive parts jobber who maintains an inventory of a wide variety of parts ready for immediate delivery to local repairmen. Replacement parts manufacturers, like the Rocklyn Corporation, sell most or all of their output to these parts jobbers. The larger parts manufacturers sell both to the automobile manufacturers for original equipment and to the jobbers for replacement.

The Rocklyn Corporation was just getting on its feet when the depression of the early 1930's occurred. After weathering this storm and the depression of 1937-38, it was, by 1940, a small but firmly established enterprise. During World War II three things happened that greatly expanded its business:

1. The demand for replacement parts was very high. No new cars were put on the road, and very few trucks; consequently the existing equipment had to be repaired and repaired again. The War Production Board recognized the vital importance of main-

taining existing equipment and allocated steel needed for the manufacture of replacement parts.

2. The Rocklyn Corporation increased its share of the replacement business. A number of the other manufacturers, including several of the large firms that had always considered the replacement business as secondary to sales of original equipment, withdrew from the market. In this situation, Rocklyn's reputation for quality and service enabled it to increase sales and also to develop close relationship with key jobbers throughout the country.

3. The company undertook, for its size, a large amount of war work. It started early in 1940, and thus was tooled up for prompt expansion. In the peak year this military business alone was four times as large as the company's entire production in 1939.

The effect of these changes on company sales is shown in the following table:

YEAR	CIVILIAN SALES	MILITARY SALES	TOTAL SALES	ESTIMATED RATIO ROCKLYN CIVILIAN SALES TO TOTAL INDUSTRY REPLACEMENT SALES OF THE PRODUCT
1938	$ 275,000	....	$ 275,000	4%
1939	330,000	....	330,000	4
1940	325,000	$ 80,000	405,000	4
1941	380,000	510,000	890,000	4
1942	645,000	980,000	1,625,000	6
1943	805,000	1,335,000	2,140,000	8
1944	1,145,000	890,000	2,035,000	11
1945	1,710,000	675,000	2,385,000	15
1946	2,815,000	....	2,815,000	21
1947	3,360,000	....	3,360,000	25

Sales in the immediate postwar period have been gratifying to the company. The demand for replacement parts remained high due to the continued shortage of new cars. More important to Rocklyn, its position in the industry continued to improve. This was largely a result of close jobber relationships developed in the latter years of the war; it also reflects the fact that Rocklyn was able to supply quality products on prompt delivery, whereas several of its competitors have been slow in making the conversion to peacetime operations—at least in this field. It should be noted that higher sales in 1946 and 1947 reflect some inventory accumulation in the distributive channels, and also price increases, following the removal of O.P.A. controls, of roughly 30%.

The financial results of operations in 1947, the best year in the history of the company, are shown in the accompanying profit and loss statement on page 846.

The management of Rocklyn is far from complacent, however. The number of old cars on the road is abnormally high, as is shown by the figures on page 846.

In prewar years the average age of cars on the road was 4½ years, whereas the average age now (1947) is 9 years. As a result of car age

Rocklyn Corporation

Profit and Loss Statement for Year, 1947

Net Sales		$3,360,000
Cost of Goods Sold		
Raw Materials	$850,000	
Direct Labor	340,000	
Indirect Labor	220,000	
Small Tools, Dies, Jigs, and Fixtures	80,000	
Depreciation	30,000	
Insurance and Taxes	20,000	
Other	90,000	
Total		1,630,000
Gross Profit		1,730,000
Selling Expenses		
Commissions and Warehouse Charges	$470,000	
Shipping Expense	120,000	
Sales Salaries and Bonus	30,000	
Advertising	20,000	
Other	30,000	
Total	670,000	
General and Administrative Expenses		
Executive and Office Salaries and Bonus	$230,000	
Miscellaneous Taxes	20,000	
Interest and Discounts (net)	50,000	
Other	50,000	
Total	350,000	
Total Expenses		1,020,000
Profit before Income Tax		710,000
Income Tax		270,000
NET PROFIT		$ 440,000

Estimated Number of Vehicles Scrapped

(Withdrawn from Registration)

1927 to 1931 yearly average	2,700,000
1932 to 1936 yearly average	2,100,000
1937 to 1941 yearly average	2,350,000
1942	2,147,000
1943	1,485,000
1944	775,000
1945	— 91,000*
1946	—416,000*
1947	478,000

* More cars were brought out of storage than were scrapped.

and conditions of supply, the wholesale sales of automobile parts and accessories rose from $553 million in 1940 to $1,753 million in 1946, or from about 19% to 54% of new vehicle sales. Sooner or later, as the old cars go off the road, there will be a drop in the automotive replacement parts business.

As the immediate postwar boom passes, competition will probably become keener; the automobile companies themselves will give more attention to the profitable parts business, the large manufacturers who make original equipment will take renewed interest in the replacement business, and new manufacturers may enter the field. Rocklyn's share of the total market is now sufficiently large so that it is more vulnerable and is quite sure to feel the effect of the increased competition. Consequently, there is serious doubt whether sales of the present product can be expected to keep the war-expanded plant busy in the future. In addition, the company must deal concurrently with a number of personnel and financial problems.

SALES POLICIES

Products

The duplication of original equipment for replacement parts is relatively simple in the hands of the highly trained engineering department maintained by the company. Each time a new car or new truck model comes out, the company purchases a number of samples of the particular part in which it is interested in order to determine if new design is involved or merely dimensional changes. If the former, the possibility of patent infringement is thoroughly investigated first. If the latter, chemical and physical properties, dimensions and manufacturing tolerances are determined. It then reproduces the original part in all essential characteristics. These can be produced and placed in the hands of jobbers by the time replacement demand develops. This item is then continued in the line as long as any significant number of vehicles of that model are on the road, roughly ten to twelve years.

The present product line of the company, then, is a single part; but this part is made in many designs and sizes. The company covers all principal makes of cars, even Fords (Ford's own price on replacement parts is so low that independent producers can make no profit on such items, and they carry them only if they wish to offer their customers "complete coverage"). To cover the different makes of cars and the model changes that actually affect motor parts, the company carries between 70 and 80 items in its line; these will fit over 95% of the cars and trucks on the road.

The company makes products of as high quality as the original equipment. A few of the competitors sell products of lower quality at a much lower price; but the company believes that, in the replacement parts business, dependable quality is more important in maintaining sales volume than a lower price and so has not attempted to meet this competition.

Because of the outlook for the company with its present limited line of products, Mr. Barker is seriously considering some form of diversification. Among the things that are being considered are the following:

(a) Subcontracting

Under this plan, Rocklyn would seek to do machine shop work for other manufacturers who lack adequate capacity in their own plants. This would be relatively simple to undertake since Rocklyn would have no responsibility for designing or for selling the finished product and would have none of its capital tied up in inventories. Fundamentally, the company would be merely selling a service. During the war such business was easy to get and profitable, whereas in the 1930's when many plants had idle capacity it was difficult to more than cover out-of-pocket expenses on such business as could be obtained. At present, the company probably could obtain some subcontracting work at prices that would cover all direct expenses and most of the average overhead, but competition again is keen because many other machine shops likewise have idle equipment.

(b) Original equipment sales

Rocklyn is not equipped to make large production runs needed for original equipment in the popular cars. It might, however, make original equipment for certain makes of trucks or for farm or industrial tractors. To get into this market, the company would have to take much more initiative in product engineering and design, the purchaser would probably obtain competitive bids on each new item he wanted, and new problems of selling and production scheduling would be involved.

(c) Other replacement parts

The company is equipped to make a number of other automotive replacement parts, but the outlook for such parts is, naturally, substantially the same as Rocklyn now faces. Investigation of prevailing prices and estimates of costs have failed to reveal any particular product where the margin is unusually wide so as to make it especially attractive to try to break into that field.

(d) Hand wrenches

The sales manager has proposed that the company make sets of hand wrenches. Parts jobbers usually carry such products for sale to garages and their mechanics, and consequently the company could use its established channel of distribution as well as selling through hardware jobbers and mail-order houses. Here, again, Rocklyn would have no distinctive advantage and would be competing with a number of established firms whose trade names are well accepted.

(e) Conveyor equipment

Contact has been established with an inventor who has a patent on a special type of roller conveyor that would be used for internal plant transportation. The inventor has had some of the equipment made at various shops and is now looking for a company that will undertake full responsibility for production and sale of the product. The patented features provide a talking point, but except in unusual circumstances the new product would perform substantially as other products now on the market. Rocklyn is well equipped to make the moving parts; considerable space would be required for assembly and storage.

The treasurer, with considerable support from the plant superintendent, does not believe the company should embark on any of the lines outlined above. He points out that present sales are the highest in the history of the company, that it has taken twenty years to build the company to its present position, and that effort can well be devoted to protecting the present business rather than diverting attention to some new line—unless the new line has outstanding possibilities.

Customers and sales promotion

Rocklyn Corporation sells its product to more than 4,000 automotive parts jobbers located throughout the United States. As already noted, special effort has been made during the last few years to building good jobber representation in each local area. These jobbers might, and some do, carry one or two competing lines of each product, but they generally prefer not to do this as long as the product of one company, such as Rocklyn, is well accepted by their customers because duplicate lines significantly increase their inventories.

Contact with these jobbers is maintained through a group of manufacturer's agents, each of whom represents Rocklyn along with several other non-competing concerns in an exclusive territory. Actually there are about 40 salesmen representing Rocklyn to the jobbers. Prior to the War, when the company's share of the market was much smaller, the cost of maintaining a company sales force adequate to reach jobbers all over the country would have been prohibitive, and agents provided a convenient and relatively economical means of obtaining sales. The commissions now being paid to agents might be enough to cover the cost of an exclusively Rocklyn sales organization. Its own sales force would concentrate on Rocklyn problems alone and would be more responsive to company controls. The sales manager has suggested that such a change be made, but Mr. Barker is reluctant to switch from agents to company salesmen at this time because present sales volume may not be maintained and in a number of instances the agent's relationship with the jobber is such that the Rocklyn line might be dropped if the agent represented a different firm.

The principal appeals used in the sale of Rocklyn products are quality, "coverage" of virtually all types of cars and trucks, prompt and dependable delivery, and the personal reputations of the various salesmen concerned. To assure delivery, warehouse stocks are maintained at fifteen points throughout the country in addition to the plant; public warehouse service is used at each point for this purpose. The company regularly carries advertisements in six of the leading automotive trade papers, at an annual expense of approximately $20,000 per year. The primary purpose of these advertisements is to assure familiarity with the company name and its product throughout the trade, rather than serving as a direct means of obtaining business.

The company does not attempt to sell to auto supply chain stores, as these concerns almost invariably want a cut price and are often willing to take lower quality to get it. The large mail-order houses, however, insist on top quality first and then are concerned with price; and Rocklyn has done some business with them, even though their retail price is somewhat below the company "list" price. These concerns serve the man who makes his own repairs and do not compete with outlets served by jobbers; consequently there is no significant undercutting of the principal channel of distribution. The volume of this business is not large, and is secured by direct, personal contact of the sales manager or the president.

Pricing

Pricing in the industry starts from a nominal list price for each item. It is standard industry practice for manufacturers to sell to jobbers at 60% off list, and for the jobbers to sell to garages and repairmen at 20% off list. Thus, of each dollar the car owner pays to the garage for repair parts, the garage keeps 20 cents, the jobber gets 40 cents, and the manufacturer gets 40 cents. Sales direct to large car dealers vary from 25% to 40% off list. To Mr. Barker, at least, these look like wide margins, but the trade practice is firmly established and he has thought of nothing he might do to narrow them and still obtain business.

Each manufacturer does determine what his list prices shall be. Here the choice is basically being in line with the large producers—often the suppliers of original equipment or cutting considerably below this general level in an effort to get business on a price basis. There are numerous variations of a few cents on individual items, but the general pattern is fairly clear. Rocklyn's present policy is to set its list prices approximately in line with those of other producers of first-quality products. A few times in the past the company experimented with cut prices but concluded that this raised such questions about quality in the minds of repairmen that it did more harm than good. Now that Rocklyn has become a major producer in its particular field, it is likely that any attempt of Rocklyn to cut prices would be matched by other competitors. So, if there was doubt as to the wisdom of cutting prices before the war, there is even greater argument for not doing it now.

The matter of freight charges is under current discussion. Prior to the war, the company paid all freight to the jobber's platform. In connection with O.P.A. price ceilings, this was changed during the war to terms of f.o.b. manufacturer's warehouse. Since the ceilings have been removed and the general price level increased, the jobbers have been complaining about paying freight—especially those located some distance from a warehouse point. Recently Rocklyn has agreed to pay freight on all shipments of over 100 pounds, but several of the company's agents are strongly recommending full return to the prewar basis.

PRODUCTION POLICIES

The company follows a policy of keeping its plant equipped with modern machinery, insofar as its finances will permit. When a machine is no longer able to do good precision work or when it becomes obsolete, it is sold rather than kept on the floor for occasional jobs. As a result of the large expansion during the war, most of the equipment is relatively new—over two thirds of it being purchased within the last six years.

The building is of conventional one-story, mill type construction, and is also in good condition. Early in the war a large addition was built to provide space for war work, and this increased the floor area from about 10,000 square feet to 40,000 square feet; and since VJ-Day an additional 20,000 square feet have been added. The expansion utilized all the unoccupied space remaining in the plot of land owned by the company, and since adjacent areas are already occupied by other plants, no further horizontal expansion is feasible at this location. The building was not designed for second-story additions and, at best, this would provide only storage space. Fortunately, existing space is ample for present production, and through a more concentrated layout up to possibly 2,000 square feet could be made available for additional activities if space had to be found.

These facilities enable the company to perform all operations from the time the rough steel is received until the finished product is shipped. The company has never made its own castings because its volume would not even approach that necessary for efficient foundry operations, but all subsequent work is done in the plant. Steel is purchased from five or six supply companies, depending primarily upon delivery terms which they offer. Castings are secured from two foundries, although no attempt is made to keep duplicate molds at the two plants.

Production scheduling and inventory control have posed a number of problems, especially in recent years. Prior to the war the plan was simple and crude. Order points were arbitrarily set up for each of the warehouses, and whenever one of these points was reached a new supply was shipped from the plant. At the plant, the superintendent watched finished stock on hand, and whenever a particular item looked low, he would make a new run that he thought would last three to six months. This worked reasonably well, although total inventories were fairly high relative to sales and emergency runs on specific items were not unknown. Wartime restrictions on inventories and shortages of materials gave rise to a set of complex and special procedures, most of which have been scrapped with considerable enthusiasm. It is now clear, however, that return to the prewar system would be unsatisfactory because one or two months' excess inventories now involve a considerably larger sum of capital; if a drop in sales and/or in prices should occur excess inventories would confound a difficult situation, and the confusion and inefficiencies resulting from special orders are now more clearly recognized.

A smart young inventory clerk, who has just completed a course in production management, has advanced the following plan to meet this situation. (1) A monthly record of sales by items will be kept for each warehouse, and an average monthly sales for the past 12 months will be computed currently for each item. (2) Forecasts of sales, by item, from each warehouse will then be made. For this purpose it will be assumed that sales in the future will be the same as the last average unless the sales manager and the president in reviewing the estimates decide that some different figure should be used. These forecasts for the several warehouses can then be totaled to obtain a forecast of company sales by items. (3) At the plant, at the beginning of every month finished inventory (plus work in process) of each item will be compared with the sales forecast, and if the inventory of an item is less than 6 weeks' estimated sales, it will be put in production that month. The plant superintendent will decide upon the order of work during the month, but he will be expected to produce items with the lowest inventory during the first week or two. (4) The standard production run will be 3 months' estimated sales. This means runs on slow-moving items will be much smaller than runs on fast-moving items, but it is contended that keeping the inventory within limits is more important than obtaining economies from the larger runs. (5) Minimum stocks at warehouses will be 2 to 6 weeks' estimated sales, depending upon the distance of the warehouse from the plant. Specific shipments to warehouses will be based on estimated sales, inventories on hand at the warehouse and the plant, and economic shipment lots.

PERSONNEL POLICIES

Selection and training

The personnel policies and practices of the company reflect the recent transition from a small nonunion shop to a medium-sized organized plant. Many informal arrangements are carried over from the prewar days, while in other areas formalized and often more complex practices have been adopted to meet specific needs.

The total number of employees of the company increased from around 50 in 1940 to a peak of over 300 when operations were on a three-shift basis in 1943. Due to labor shortages and other conditions at that time, the company found that better results could be obtained from two 10-hour shifts than three 8-hour shifts. The plant has been operated on a two-shift basis since that time, although overtime has been eliminated and some departments work only a single shift. This has permitted a reduction in number of employees so that at the close of 1947 the payroll showed the following:

Machine operators and other productive labor 165
Inspectors, maintenance men, and other nonproductive
labor 39
Foremen and supervisors 19
Office workers 25
Executive and other salaried employees 21
Total 269

These employees have been obtained from the local area, in which Rocklyn is a relatively small employer, without the use of written job qualifications or special tests. The management feels that the number of new workers hired before or since the war has not warranted elaborate employment standards, and during the war standards were not helpful because an employer had to take whomever he could get. The company has a strong tradition of promotion from within; so, typically, young and inexperienced (though often with some specialized training in high school) people are hired for simple jobs, and the more complicated, higher-paying jobs are filled from people already in the shop. Each new worker is given a trial period of 60 days, after which time he is considered a regular employee. Promoted employees are subject to a trial period of 30 days and are transferred back to their former jobs if they cannot perform satisfactory work on the new job within that period. No discrimination is made against women for jobs in the shop or in the office, and a number of highly skilled jobs in the plant and one of the supervisory positions in the office are held by women.

Seniority is considered for both promotions and for increases and decreases in the work force "only where (a) ability to perform the work, and (b) physical fitness are relatively equal." In practice, seniority plays an important part in layoffs, although the arrangement is flexible enough so that a worker with clearly lower efficiency is laid off first.

Training is entirely on an informal basis under the direction of a foreman or a skilled worker. In contrast to the elaborate and time-consuming apprenticeship rules in some shops, a worker is given 1 to 4 weeks' training for the normal work he will do on his new machine and then is expected to develop speed during the ensuing year. The typical worker, as a result, has comparatively little versatility unless he has been in the shop long enough to have worked on a variety of operations on several machines. Nevertheless, the results in terms of efficiency and quality have been satisfactory, and the speed of promotion has been fairly rapid for a number of workers. Training in the office is on the same informal basis.

Compensation

As a basic policy, the company plans to pay wages generally in line with rates of the "high-pay" firms in the area. There has been no announcement of such a policy and Rocklyn does not attempt to match the highest rate paid in the area for each job classification, but it is hoped the employees will feel that in general Rocklyn pays as well as anybody else. The union, of course, puts strong pressure on the company to match any blanket increases granted to large national unions by the big steel companies or the automobile companies. If these increases become a pattern that is followed by the principal employers in the local area, Rocklyn goes along; but fundamentally the company believes its wage rates should be tied to those in the local area rather than to a national pattern.

The *base* or hourly rate of pay for individual workers has always been influenced by the type of job and the all-round performance of the individual. When it became necessary to standardize these rates, due to increased size and union pressure against "paternalistic" wage setting, the management did not want to set a single uniform rate for all workers in a given job classification, for clearly a man who had only one month's training on a given machine was not as valuable to the company as the experienced worker who could do a variety of work and assist in general plant operations. Consequently, a rate-range has been established for each type of job. The beginner in a job classification is paid the minimum rate; then, if his efficiency is at least 80% of standard, he receives automatically four quarterly increases in base rate amounting to $16\frac{2}{3}\%$ of the difference between the minimum and the maximum for his job; the remaining increase to the maximum base rate for the job (one third of the difference between the minimum and the maximum) is awarded at the discretion of the company for such things as ability, safety, quality, care of equipment, attitude toward fellow workers and absenteeism.

Base rates have been set for 30 types of jobs. These rates have been determined partly by prevailing custom in the plant, partly by comparison with rates paid by other companies, and partly by collective bargaining. No systematic job evaluation has been used for this purpose. The range from minimum to maximum for each job varies from 10 cents per hour for the simple jobs on which comparatively little skill can be developed to 35 cents per hour for jobs where there can be a marked difference between the beginner and the experienced operator.

In addition to variation in base rates, the company has a financial incentive plan. This was installed during the war as a means of increasing output and of paying higher wages to outstanding workers. Output standards, in terms of hours per piece, have been established by means of time study for each operation on each item produced. (The "standard" is really an estimated normal time plus 20% for personal and fatigue allowance.) The daily efficiency of each production worker can thus be obtained by taking the ratio of standard time for the work he turned out to the actual time spent; the efficiency of the whole plant can be computed in a similar manner.

A bonus is paid to all production workers whose daily efficiency exceeds 80%. The total bonus is equal to 1% of base pay for each percent of efficiency above 80. Thus, if a man works at 92% efficiency, his total bonus would be 12% of his base pay; if he works at 110% efficiency, his total bonus would be 30% of his base pay. Actually he is sure of getting only one half of his bonus, because one fourth of it is paid only if the efficiency of the whole plant is at least 80% and the other fourth is paid only if the overall scrap (primarily rejects on quality) for the plant is less than 2%. All indirect labor is paid a bonus based on total plant efficiency; the bonus is $\frac{1}{2}$% of base pay for each percent of plant efficiency above 80.

Since the incentive plan was installed, the total plant efficiency has been between 90% and 105%, and never has fallen to 80%. A number of the more skilled workers have fairly consistently had efficiencies of over 100%.

The foremen, office workers, and salaried employees have no formal financial incentive plan. They do, however, share in the bonuses described in the next section.

Employee services and benefits

The company seeks to provide good working conditions but does not undertake recreational or other social activities. The washrooms are clean and have modern equipment, a dispensary with a registered nurse in charge is maintained, and there is a lunch room for employees where hot coffee is provided.

Vacations with pay are granted to all employees with 1 year or more of service. Those who have been with the company 1 to 5 years receive a 1-week vacation, and those with 5 years or more service have 2 weeks.

For the last several years the company has given two types of year-end bonuses. A Christmas bonus has been given to factory and office workers. Factory workers have been given approximately 1 week's pay, whereas office workers, who do not share in efficiency bonuses, are given 2 to 4 weeks' pay depending upon their quality of work, cooperativeness, and similar factors. Factory foremen, supervisors, and all salaried employees share in an executive bonus, which has been paid in the form of preferred stock in the company. The amount of executive bonus going to each individual is determined by the president after consultation with the immediate supervisor concerned. A number of the executives have pointed out that receiving this bonus has actually imposed an immediate hardship on them, inasmuch as they have to pay income tax on the total amount but receive no cash other than the 7% dividends. (To date, no one has refused to accept the bonus!)

In line with the present interest in old-age security, the company has been giving serious attention to setting up a pension plan and has consulted an actuary regarding the expense involved. Since the purpose is to provide for the permanent employees, and in order to simplify bookkeeping, only the 145 employees who have been with the company for 5 years or more have been considered in the cost estimates. The normal retirement age has been set at 65 years, and the amount of a pension will depend upon the employee's salary and his length of service with the company—both past and future. Costs have been estimated on two different bases: under the first, the employee would receive a pension of 1% of his salary for each year's service; thus a man who had 30 years' service at retirement age would receive a pension of 30% of his salary. The second basis gives less allowance for past service than for future service and also gives less credit for salary under $3,000 since this is covered by federal social security payments. Assuming that the size, age, salary, and length of service of the company workforce continues to be distributed as at present, the expense is estimated as follows:

PLAN	PENSION FOR EACH EMPLOYEE AT AGE 65 TO EQUAL:	ANNUAL COST TO COMPANY
A	1% of salary for each year of service	$66,400
B	For past service: ½% per year on salary up to $3,000, and ¾% per year on salary above $3,000	
	For future service: ¾% per year on salary up to $3,000, and 1% per year on salary over $3,000	49,000

Pension costs, then, would be in the range of 6 to 8% of total payroll. Reaction of the older employees to the proposal has been that a pension plan would be a fine thing, but with social security tax, income tax, and other deductions from their pay they are not in a position to share the expense; the younger employees have been indifferent to the plan, partly because many do not yet have the minimum 5 years' service.

Union relations

Prior to the war the number of employees was small, the relationships were personal and friendly, and apparently no one cared or did much about union organization. The large number of new employees taken on during the war naturally changed this relationship. The United Automobile Workers (CIO) formed a local at the Rocklyn plant and a large number of the new employees joined. Many of the older employees, if they joined at all, certainly were not active in the union.

The company, of course, recognized the new union, but treated it with as much indifference as the circumstances would permit. Actually the company was treating its employees as liberally as was possible under War Labor Board regulations, and under the circumstances the chief function of the union was to provide an outlet for "gripes." The union leaders engaged in some soap-box oratory, but meetings of the local were small and attended largely by a group that had an inveterate urge to let off steam.

Following removal of war restrictions on strikes, wages, and employment, Rocklyn management recognized that its labor relations were in a more fluid state. It had to decide whether to let the union situation coast along as it was or to take a more positive action. Fundamentally it decided that a strong, more-or-less friendly union was preferable to a weaker, chronically antagonistic union. So, in 1946, when the perennial demand for a union shop (that is, union or nonunion men may be hired but all must join the union if they are to be kept on as regular employees) was presented, the company granted the request but with the further provision that all employees should be required to attend union meetings (or pay a substantial fine for each meeting missed). Meetings were then well attended; the majority of the employees soon tired of the oratory and elected a new set of officers. The union is now truly representative of the workers, and management finds it advantageous to discuss with their Grievance Committee not only "gripes" but also layoffs, changes in scheduled hours of work, and similar adjustments. In 1947, not one grievance went beyond plant superintendent level.

FINANCIAL POLICIES

Uses and sources of capital

During the expansion of the company in the last decade, capital was very scarce and was used only for immediate operating purposes. A comfortable cash balance has been built up for the first time during the past year, as is indicated in the accompanying comparative balance sheets, but the policy of using it only for operating needs has been continued. Inventories have increased with the rise in sales and are being watched closely, as has already been discussed in connection with production scheduling. Accounts receivable have actually gone down, due

Rocklyn Corporation
Balance Sheets, as of December 31

	1947	1946
Current Assets:		
Cash	$ 470,000	$ 60,000
Accounts Receivable	270,000	360,000
Inventories	590,000	470,000
	$1,330,000	$ 890,000
Fixed Assets:		
Land	10,000	10,000
Building	150,000	140,000
Machinery and Equipment	520,000	460,000
	$ 680,000	$ 610,000
Reserve for Depreciation	270,000	240,000
	$ 410,000	$ 370,000
Total Assets	$1,740,000	$1,260,000
Current Liabilities:		
Bank Loans	....	$ 100,000
Accounts Payable	$ 60,000	50,000
Accrued Expense	90,000	80,000
Taxes Payable	290,000	220,000
	$ 440,000	$ 450,000
Equity:		
Preferred Stock	170,000	110,000
Common Stock	10,000	10,000
Capital and Earned Surplus	1,120,000	690,000
	$1,300,000	$ 810,000
Total Liabilities and Equity	$1,740,000	$1,260,000

to final settlement of accounts for war work. The company did invest $70,000 in building and equipment during the last year, in accordance with its basic policy of keeping the plant modernized; a significant part of the equipment purchased was war surplus and was obtained at very attractive prices.

There is question whether capital should be used to retire the preferred stock. This stock is 7% noncumulative, nonparticipating, and callable by the company at par. It has been issued to executives as a bonus in lieu of cash, and has unusual features (for example, high yield and noncumulative) designed for this purpose. The treasurer points out that it is not a good investment security for general distribution because dividend payments are so uncertain and, on the other hand, the company is not interested in paying out a high dividend except as an incentive to present executives. As executives owning the stock transfer it to their heirs or leave the company for other employment, this will become a more pressing problem.

Cash for operations was supplied initially by Mr. Barker, who owns all the common stock, and subsequently by the reinvestment of earnings. During the war, these sources had to be heavily supplemented by bank loans. It was possible to get the capital needed to finance the rapid expansion from the banks because of special governmental guarantees of construction and working capital loans needed for war work. If loans are needed for ordinary civilian operations in the future, the banks will be much more cautious.

Dividends

At no time in the history of the company have dividends been paid on the common stock. Mr. Barker has been more interested in the development of the company than in immediate cash income, and the only income he has received has been his salary. Of course, most of the profits during the war were subject to a 90% excess profits tax, and the remaining 10% was urgently needed in the business. Dividends have been paid regularly on such preferred stock as was issued; this has been considered necessary in order to make the stock attractive as a bonus.

Accounting reserves

Wartime regulations permitted the creation of depreciation reserves for war plant and equipment at a much more rapid rate than is allowed in peacetime. Rocklyn took advantage of these special provisions and substantially reduced the net book value of a significant part of its assets. Also, it has purchased some war surplus equipment at unusually low prices. The overall result is that the present net book value of its facilities is roughly $500,000 below the insurable value and the current depreciation charges are correspondingly low. These low depreciation charges contribute to low costs; this is no great competitive advantage, however, since most of Rocklyn's competitors have done the same thing.

From another point of view, there is question whether the current charges for depreciation are adequate. Not only are present book values low; in addition, the prices of new equipment are rising. Consequently, the present depreciation charge is failing to retain in the business the capital that will be necessary to replace equipment that is currently being worn out. Looking at it from this angle, costs are being understated and profits overstated (38% of which excess is being drained off into the federal treasury in the form of income tax). No accounting reserves have been created to deal with this situation.

Provision for transfer of ownership

Another financial problem is provision for the eventual transfer of ownership from Mr. Barker to his heirs. In a technical sense this may not be a company problem, but in fact it may have a profound influence on Rocklyn's financial structure. Federal and state inheritance taxes on an estate of this size will be substantial; if the estate has a value of $3,000,000 to $4,000,000, the tax will be about 25%.

There is, of course, no "market" value on shares of stock in the Rocklyn Corporation, so the Bureau of Internal Revenue or perhaps the court will have to establish a "fair value on the owner's equity that is being transferred to the heirs. For this purpose the Bureau of Internal Revenue may use "book value" if operations of the enterprise in question are stable and there is reason to believe that the assets are not overvalued or undervalued; or, whenever there is reasonable doubt as to the significance of book value, earnings of the enterprise may be capitalized. (War years might be considered abnormal, certainly deduction of excess profits taxes would not be recognized.) In a number of recent cases involving firms similar to the Rocklyn Corporation, the Bureau of Internal Revenue has used ten times the average earnings in postwar years as a reasonable value of the owner's equity. Using this formula, Rocklyn common stock would be worth $3,630,000.

If Mr. Barker were to die with circumstances as at present, a substantial part of his estate would consist of stock in the Rocklyn Corporation. More important, his liquid assets would be no more than enough to cover expenses and the tax on other personal assets. There is real danger, then, that the company would have to be put up on the auction block to secure cash to pay inheritance tax. To prepare for the eventual transfer of ownership, a number of alternatives have been considered:

1. Payment of large cash dividends so as to increase Mr. Barker's liquid assets.

2. Sale of the entire company for cash. Investigation indicates that the only people with enough cash and interested in buying firms of this type are seeking bargains. (If any or all stock is sold, Mr. Barker will, of course, have to include in his personal income tax approximately 25% on all "capital gains.")

3. Public sale of about 40% of the common stock. To an investment banker, this would be a small issue in a small and unknown company. Bankers contacted have said that they would undertake the sale only if it could be shown that there was a good speculative prospect of large increases in earnings.

4. Merger into a large company in exchange for stock. This would meet the tax problem only if the stock received from the large company could be readily sold for cash. The difficulty here is finding a large company that would benefit by entering a particular segment of the automotive replacement parts business; thus far no such company has been located.

EXECUTIVE ORGANIZATION AND PERSONNEL

The Rocklyn Corporation is small enough so that contacts between the executives is frequent and informal. Mr. Barker is clearly the key man in the operations. However, he does call the executive committee together regularly to review results and discuss problems ahead. Day-to-day supervision of production activities falls under the plant superintendent, and office activities under the treasurer. The accompanying chart, prepared by the treasurer, shows the executives reporting directly to the president and the principal functions of each.

The age, background, and outstanding characteristics of each of the executives is briefly summarized below:

The president, 62, has had broad business experience. He is thoroughly familiar with both the technical and business aspects of the company. The present policies and success of the enterprise are the result of his leadership. He wants to remain active in the company.

The plant superintendent, 51, has come up through the ranks. He can personally operate any of the machines, and knows the plant and at least all the older employees intimately. He is a hard worker, a good manager of men, and takes pride in "getting the work out."

The assistant plant superintendent, 32, is a graduate mechanical engineer and has had varied industrial engineering experience. He is analytical, energetic, and shows good judgment in applying new ideas to a practical situation. He gets along well with employees but has not had extensive supervisory experience.

The treasurer, 65, was associated with Mr. Barker in his preceding business venture and has cared for the "office end" of the Rocklyn Corporation activities for 18 years. Although basically conservative, he is always glad to consider new ideas for office operations or to prepare a new report. Through the long years of association, he has come to rely upon Mr. Barker for initiative and for decisions on major questions.

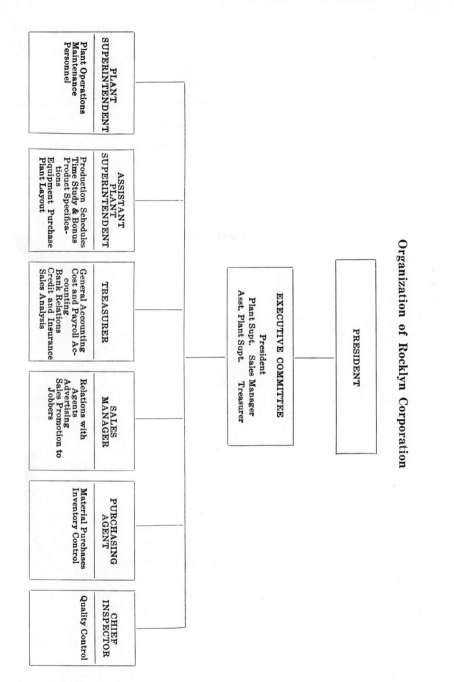

Organization of Rocklyn Corporation

The sales manager, 36, has had considerable selling experience, being employed by a manufacturers' agent in the replacement parts business prior to joining Rocklyn. He is optimistic, aggressive, persuasive, and has good ability in sizing up a total sales situation as a basis for deciding what course of action should be taken.

The purchasing agent, 37, did bookkeeping and accounting work before he got into purchasing. He is fully dependable and a good detail man. He tends to do work himself rather than delegate it, and he has not demonstrated much imagination.

The chief inspector, 41, was a skilled machine operator prior to becoming an inspector. While he is frank and does not hestitate to "call a spade a spade," he is respected and gets along well with the foremen and the workers.

QUESTIONS

1. Considering all facts relating to the company, do you believe a new product should be added to its line? If so, what and when? Justify your answer and explain how your plan will modify any other policies of the company.

2. Outline a program you would recommend for increasing the sales of the present product of the company, including any modifications you believe should be made in customer, sales promotion, and pricing policies.

3. Should the company establish its own sales force to make contacts with jobbers? Justify your recommendation, giving consideration to the outlook for replacement parts, modification in product line that you consider desirable, plans for transferring ownership, and similar matters insofar as they affect your proposal for selling activities.

4. Appraise the proposed plan for inventory control from the viewpoint of the sales manager, the plant superintendent, and the treasurer. Do you believe it should be adopted?

5. What "modern" personnel selection, training or compensation policies should the company install, and what modifications in present practice should be made? Give reasons for your answers.

6. A representative from the headquarters of the United Automobile Workers has commented that the Rocklyn compensation plan looked "complicated and subject to management manipulation." Do you recommend simplification or other modification of the present system? How would you justify your answer to local union representatives?

7. Do you recommend any modifications in the present executive bonus plan? Under what conditions, if any, should the preferred stock be "called" by the company?

8. What policies should the company follow to give its employees "security"? Justify your proposals, being sure to consider their ramifications with regard to various aspects of company operations.

9. To what extent do you recommend that management discuss with union leaders the company outlook, contemplated changes in policies, and transfer of ownership? Should the union be invited to help solve some of these problems?

10. Prepare a recommendation on present and future dividend policy for the company. State and support assumptions you have made regarding outlook for the company, alternative uses of cash, and similar considerations.

11. Do you believe the present policies of the company with respect to valuation and depreciation reserves for fixed assets are satisfactory? What changes, if any, do you recommend? Explain.

12. Outline a plan for meeting the inheritance tax on Mr. Barker's estate, which you think best fits this situation. What actions, if any, should be taken by the company now?

13. (a) Prepare an executive organization chart for the Rocklyn Corporation, assuming that executives needed for the positions you create will be available. Show at least the top two levels of organization, and on the chart or an accompanying sheet, list the major functions of each executive. State any assumptions you have made regarding *changes* in outlook or policies.

(b) What changes do you recommend be made in executive personnel of the company within the next year?

(c) Assuming the personnel changes you proposed in answer to (b) have been made, revise your answer to (a) to utilize the personnel you would then have.

EASTERN STATES IRON
AND STEEL COMPANY

Executives of Eastern States Iron and Steel Company, Incorporated, a medium-size, integrated manufacturer of flat-rolled steel products, are concerned both with reviewing the progress the company has made over the past several years in its expansion program and with attempting to appraise the future of the steel industry to see where the best opportunities might lie for a firm such as theirs. Eastern States has been an integrated steel producer for many years and is still actively engaged in the struggle to compete successfully in the domestic steel industry. The firm began a major capital expansion program several years ago and is also actively considering future expansion possibilities. Understanding the problems that have resulted from the expansion program as well as the opportunities that may lie ahead is of major concern to the central executive group of this company.

THE INDUSTRY

The iron and steel industry, in the United States especially, has often been in the public eye. Among the reasons for this are the glamour and the excitement of its production processes, its size relative to other industries, the homogeneous character of its basic products (the iron and steel industry can often be understood as such, which is not the case with many other industries), the spectacular effects of strikes in its industrial history, and the close attention paid to its pricing practices by academicians and government policymakers.

Demand. Until 1957, it was ordinarily assumed that demand for steel products showed wide cyclical fluctuations around a basic increasing trend. Since then, the consensus on trend has been less certain. An idea of the overall demand for steel products can be gained from looking at the chart on page 865 that shows the output index. The following table adds to the information on the chart.

Table 1

EMPLOYMENT	1960	1963	1964
All Employees	651	586.3	608 (est.)
Production Workers	528	476	498 (est.)
Index of Output	101.9	112.5	130.3
Expenditures on New Plant (in millions of dollars) ..	$1,500	$1,040	$1,600
Percent of Capacity Utilized —All Companies	66.8%	68% (est.)	77% (est.)
—Eastern States Iron and Steel Company	68%	69%	80%

IRON AND STEEL

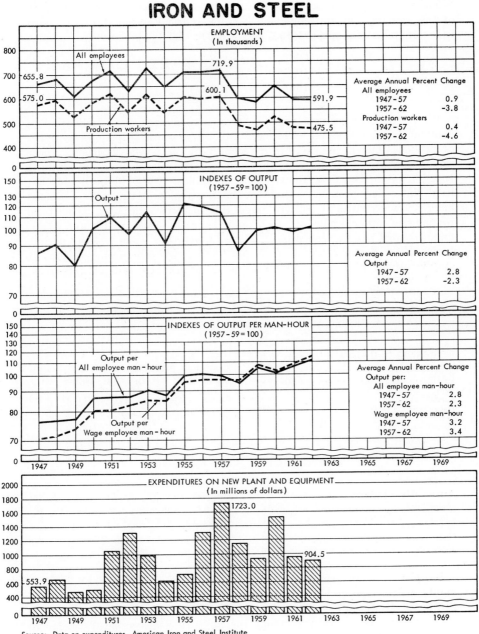

Source: Data on expenditures, American Iron and Steel Institute
       Indexes of output per man-hour based on AISI employment and man-hour data; not strictly
       comparable with BLS employment data shown.

The relative performance of the steel industry as compared to the rest of the economy can be judged by looking at the Federal Reserve Board index of industrial output (1957-59 = 100):

$$1962 \quad \ldots\ldots \quad 118.3$$
$$1963 \quad \ldots\ldots \quad 124.3$$
$$1964 \quad \ldots\ldots \quad 132.0$$

While these are output indexes, they give a very good indication of demand for the products. The next two tables show shipments by types of products and by markets in a recent year on a relative basis. These tables indicate generally who buys and what steel products are shipped. In addition to the data shown in these tables, it should be noted that light flat-rolled products (that is, sheet, strip, and tin mill products) have shown continual growth over the past two decades. The total tonnage of other kinds of steel, such as rails, bars, plate, and semifinished steel has increased little, if at all, over the same 20-year period. In recession periods, the demand for light flat-rolled products tends to stay relatively high, while that for the other products falls off rapidly.

Table 2

Shipments of Products by Type of Steel

PRODUCT	PERCENT	PRODUCT	PERCENT
Semifinished (ingots, blooms)	5.3%	Wire Products	4.2%
Structural, piling	6.5	Tin Mill Products	8.2
Rails	1.3	Sheet and Strip (hot rolled and cold rolled)	33.8
Bars	15.8		
Plate	9.1	Sheet and Strip (galvanized, coated, electrical)	5.9
Pipe and Tubing	9.9		

Table 3

Distribution of Steel by Market

MARKET	PERCENT	MARKET	PERCENT
Automotive Industry	22%	Appliances	5%
Construction	16	Oil and Gas	5
Steel Warehouses	15	Rail Transportation	3
Machinery	10	Shipbuilding	1
Containers	9	Export and All Other	8
Forgings, Bolts, Nuts	6		

Supply. The information that follows about technological [1] developments in iron and steel manufacturing is taken from a Bureau of Labor Statistics study called *Technological Trends*. The study was published in 1964, but the statements about the next 10 years generally refer to the 1962-1972 period.

---

[1] Readers who are unfamiliar with the technology of steel production processes will benefit from reviewing quickly information that can be found in general-purpose encyclopedias, in most libraries, or in the descriptive pamphlets that are generously made available to the public by the American Iron and Steel Institute or by most major steel companies.

Outlook. Advances in all departments of iron and steelmaking, including the introduction of new processes such as basic oxygen in steelmaking, indicate a steady increase in output per man-hour. Although a rising level of steel output is projected for the next 10 years, improvements in speed and efficiency from new methods and processes not yet widespread in the industry indicate that little if any increase is to be expected in the employment of production workers. Some rise may take place in the number of clerical, professional, and technical personnel.

Beneficiation and blast furnace operations. Upgrading or beneficiation of low grade ore into an ore concentrate of constant iron ratio is necessary, in part because ores of desirable physical and chemical characteristics are unavailable, in part because beneficiation results in reduced capital investment in coking and ironmaking facilities, and in some measure because of the higher quality requirements of steel customers. Beneficiation of ores is an important step toward automation of the blast furnace, which may mean reduced labor requirements. But possible economies may be offset in part by the greater labor and capital costs of beneficiation.

Injection of oil, gas, or powdered coal with oxygen enrichment, and higher top pressures, have brought higher production and lower coke consumption with a tendency to reduce investment in coke producing facilities. Despite a prospective decrease in the number of furnaces, these improvements may bring about an increase in blast furnace output between 1960 and 1970.

Use of oxygen in steelmaking. Oxygen injection, which reduces time for individual heats, has increased open-hearth capacity by as much as 30%. It is estimated that, by the use of oxygen, a 25% gain in open-hearth capacity is obtained from capital outlays of approximately 20% of the cost of equivalent new capacity.

Basic oxygen. It is estimated that one third of the country's steel capacity may be basic oxygen by 1970. Continuing improvements in the basic oxygen process—now about four to six times faster than the open-hearth—with capital and operating costs substantially lower than such costs in conventional open-hearth operation, suggests a rapid growth. The shorter heat time and the greater flexibility of the basic oxygen process appear to establish it as a better source of molten steel for continuous casting.

Introduction of continuous casting. Estimates of capital costs of continuous casting equipment range from 30% to 60% of the cost of primary mills, and recent improvements may effect additional reductions. Enormous time saving, lower operating costs, an increase in the utilization of steel—as high as 95% of the molten steel compared to 85% by the conventional process—and improvement in product result. Ten steps in the conventional ingot casting process from furnace to slab are reduced to 5 in continuous casting. Growing use of continuous casting appears likely, though not yet actually commercially applied as a high production item.

More instrumentation and automation. Increased instrument control has made possible the speedup of finishing mills, the achievement of closer tolerances in rolling, and more uniformity in products. Techniques for automating rolling and finishing operations are far advanced, and the number of mills adopting such controls is growing. Experimental studies are under way to develop data on blast furnace performance necessary to complete automatic control.

Greater adaptability of basic oxygen steelmaking and continuous casting to automatic controls, improvement of these innovations, and increasing knowledge of the blast furnace will undoubtedly augment the role of automatic controls. The manpower required for the additional conditioning and finishing of higher quality steel partly offsets the cost advantages of automation.

Higher quality, competitive products. Inroads of competitive materials in domestic markets and of steel products from abroad spur the development at lower costs of new and higher quality products such as thin tin, lighter weight structurals, and new coatings for many flat-rolled products. The demands of the space, defense, and atomic energy programs are resulting in the development of many new high quality alloy steels.

Foreign competition. Faced with an excess of capacity over their respective domestic needs and supported by some of the world's most modern steel plants and extensive research programs, foreign producers (West Germany, France, Great Britain, Japan) are concentrating on improving steelmaking processes and products in order to provide a greater variety of high quality steel products at lower prices. American steelmakers are confronted with the prospect of continuing foreign competition on a variety of steel products. Some steel companies are expanding their research activities for development of new and improved products.

MARKETING

Products. Eastern States was known in the industry as a "tonnage" producer rather than a specialty producer. This meant that it did not sell steels in a limited range of sizes with a concentration on the careful adjustment of the performance characteristics of its steels to needs of specialized users but, instead, made a wide range of general-purpose rolled and flat steels to high-volume users of standard products. Plain carbon plate, which is ¼ inch to 3 inches thick and up to 110 inches wide, had been a standard item of the company for years. Following the entrance into service of a new plate mill, Eastern States was now supplying the construction, transportation, and heavy equipment industries to a much greater extent than before. In the past, it had been mainly limited to steel warehouses as customers for its plain plate.

High-strength, low-alloy steels, with small percentages of columbium and other alloying materials, had recently been added to the product line. The automotive industry, especially truck builders and parts suppliers, was interested in these kinds of steels. After entering into a licensing agreement with one of the three largest steel companies, Eastern States was in a good position to supply all of its customers' low-alloy steel needs. Before the licensing agreement, the company had a limited range of such steels developed through its own efforts. Plate sales by Eastern States had increased from 135,000 net tons (12% of the total plate market for the sizes that Eastern States could formerly supply in its marketing areas) to 208,000 tons of plate (5.2% of the estimated plate market for the sizes the company could now supply in its market territories). The 110-inch plate mill was designed to produce plates from ¼ inch to ¾ inches thick. Plates of this thickness made up about 65% of the total plate sold. The balance of plates—¾ inches thick to 3 inches thick—were generally considered specialty items, particularly the 20% of the plate market that used plate over 1 inch thick.

A second major product of the company was hot-rolled sheet and strip. Sheet was ¼ inch or less thick and over 12 inches wide; strip was not over 12 inches wide. This kind of steel was normally used for making parts in which surface finish was not critical. Eastern States' hot strip steel was sold extensively to automotive manufacturers for use in frames and to automobile suppliers. The present hot strip mill was limited to rolling 30-inch widths, which could also be slit to narrower widths. Market studies indicated that purchases of hot-rolled sheet and strip followed this distribution of sizes:

SIZE	HOT ROLLED %	COLD ROLLED %
Under 25 inches	15%	2%
25-30 inches	3	7
30-36 "	4	9
36-48 "	52	56
48-60 "	23	14
Over 60 inches	2	12

Eastern States' market penetration in the widths it could supply was about 25% of the hot-rolled product and 33% of the cold-rolled product.

Cold-rolled steel was sold to customers such as tubing manufacturers, appliance manufacturers, and lamp manufacturers for whom the surface condition was important. To some extent also, the hardness and the tensile strength of the steel was important to such customers. The ordinary product of the company's cold mill had excellent surface finish qualities and enjoyed substantial acceptance by various customers. The major buyers at the moment were steel warehouses and one large manufacturer of small electrical appliances. About 30% of the total cold-rolled output went to this one customer. Other products of the company of somewhat less dollar importance but of long market standing were chemicals from the coke by-products plant and merchant pig iron. The chemicals benzol, toluol, xylol, naphtha, sodium phenolate, and pyridine were sold on long-term contracts to the chemical industry. Prices were negotiated by the head of the coke and chemical sales and were generally based on expected market prices over the life of the contract as well as volume needs of the various customers.

The blast furnace department, in addition to producing molten iron for use in the company's open-hearth operation, also produced pig iron for sale to grey iron and malleable iron foundries. Eastern States had been a major supplier of a large number of local foundries for many years. It carried substantial inventories of pig iron in order to be an assured supplier and a dependable source for prompt delivery on any size of order. At capacity operations, 7½% of blast furnace output was available for sale as merchant pig. Under operating conditions in the middle 1960's, about 15% was actually sold on the open market. The typical spot price for merchant pig was 60% to 65% above Eastern States' manufacturing costs; however, a substantial portion of its sales was not on the spot market but by negotiated contract.

Customers. Kinds of buyers for Eastern States' rolled products have been indicated earlier. As to their location, the prime market area served ran from near Boston to Richmond, Virginia. This area included the major share of customers. In addition, about 10% of sales were made on the West Coast from Los Angeles to Seattle, and a very small percent in the Gulf Coastal region, mainly near Galveston. Capacity on the West Coast for carbon plates had been above consumption for some time. This was not true of hot-rolled sheet and strip, for which capacity in boom years such as 1964 was less than consumption. It was especially not true of cold-rolled sheet and strip, for which consumption outran capacity by about 50%. Along the Eastern Seaboard, consumption of both hot-rolled strip and cold-rolled sheet and strip was generally higher than capacity to produce in that area. Plate capacity and consumption were more nearly balanced. This general pattern was also true in Texas.

While Eastern States thus enjoyed a transportation cost advantage for some of its products, its major means of competing was service and delivery. Some customers dealt with Eastern States because their trucks could load at the mill to pick up steel on the return trip to their home plants and then load with products to deliver to the Philadelphia metropolitan area. Trucking facilities were adequate enough so that customers' trucks could be scheduled out within an hour. Such a fast turnaround was not usually possible at very large plants. Eastern States' relatively small size left it at a disadvantage on rail freight shipments, but not on shipments by truck. In general, cold-rolled steel moved almost entirely by truck for quick delivery because its finished surface was susceptible to moisture damage. Hot-rolled steel and plate can be more readily shipped by rail; in fact, about 50% of Eastern States' plate shipments went out by rail.

The company used contract truck carriers entirely. One of the questions that concerns it is whether or not truck delivery will continue to be economical in light of the higher-volume, specialized cars that railroads are developing for steel shipments, such as the 100-ton type of coil car.

While fast service was a major competitive weapon in Eastern States' immediate market area, cost was the primary competitive factor in more distant market areas such as the Gulf Coast and the Pacific Coast markets. Eastern States could compete in these areas in one way by developing special finishes for its steels to serve small segments of the market. As long as these markets remained relatively small and as long as Eastern States' metallurgical work was ahead of that of competitors, such a strategy was feasible for competing in distant markets. As to the factor of cost delivered at the customer's mill, Eastern States could absorb as much of the cost of shipping as it desired. At one time, it had a substantial advantage in the West Coast market over Chicago competitors who shipped by rail. With the growth in production of West Coast steel mills, this advantage has disappeared on plain carbon plates. Remaining as a substantial supplier to Gulf Coast and West Coast markets will mean some ingenious consideration of transportation methods in the future. For example, if the piggyback plan did not have a mixture rule or if that mixture rule were changed, Eastern States might well open up a larger market in the southeastern states. As another example, foreign steel imported into United States coast cities provided substantial competition for Eastern States in 1963. To some extent, shipping rates from foreign countries are very low on certain steel products. These rates are set in conference agreements between United States shipping lines and foreign lines. If Eastern States could influence such conference rates, then it would improve its competitive position. In boom years such as 1964, however, foreign imports do not bother Eastern States particularly.

Competition. In the prime market area on the East Coast, Eastern States was in direct competition for all sizes of its products and all kinds with the Bethlehem Steel Company plant at Sparrows Point, Maryland, and the Fairless Works of United States Steel near Trenton, New Jersey. In the plate market it competed not only with Bethlehem but also with three other small to medium-sized integrated steel companies located not far from Philadelphia. Each of these competitors had certain characteristics that differentiated it slightly from Eastern States. Competitor A, for example, specialized in heavy plate and in clad plate for large reactors and pressure vessels. Competitor B was noted for its opportunistic pricing policy. It did not adhere to the oligopolistic pricing practices of the industry but instead charged high prices in boom periods and dropped prices under the market in depressed times. Competitor C turned to pipe production in very good times. During periods of relatively depressed conditions in the steel industry, Eastern States also faced considerable competition from the Pittsburgh mills of the major steel companies for all of its products but most especially for plate, for which price competition grew keen.

Channels of distribution. While Eastern States sold direct, for the most part, to manufacturers of industrial products, it also did a substantial portion of its business with steel warehousing companies. These were primarily wholesalers who carried substantial inventories and then sold to small buyers. Sales to warehouses varied between 25% and 30% of Eastern States' total sales. Dealing with warehouse customers had advantages in poor times and a certain disadvantage in boom times in the steel industry. These steel warehouses provided an outlet for steel and were relatively assured customers so that volume could be moved in depressed years. However, in boom years, they cut Eastern States out of one of the most profitable segments of the market —buyers who were distressed for inventory and were willing to pay substantial premiums for quick delivery even on fairly large amounts of steel. Prices to the steel warehouses could not be raised substantially or rapidly.

Pricing policy. For the past 10 years, Eastern States had followed the industry practice of selling its basic flat-rolled steel products at "posted" prices in both sellers' and buyers' markets. This meant that the company, like the industry leader, United States Steel, acted as if it belived that there was a kinked demand curve for its product and that it sold in an oligopolistic market. By following such a policy, Eastern States could live comfortably under the price umbrella of industry leaders. It also meant that the company could not break the price line during periods of very high or very low demand. One opinion held firmly by company executives was that its pricing policy improved long-run profits by better stability of operations through cultivation of customers who would buy in bad times as well as good. Since Eastern States occasionally operated its mills at times when other steel companies were shut down, there was some question as to the short-run economic feasibility of such a policy.

Marketing organization and promotion. The Marketing Division has several product sections devoted to selling rolled steel products, pig iron, and coke and by-products. Each of these three departments has its own sales force. The two latter ones are small and are operated entirely from the headquarters of the company. The rolled steel products department has district sales offices in Boston, New York City, Philadelphia, and Norfolk, Virginia. It operates through sales agencies in Portland, San Francisco, Los Angeles, Houston, Chicago, Cleveland, and Buffalo. These sales offices and agencies carry on the main promotional work of the company and are important factors in maintaining sound relationships with long-term customers. One of the company's basic objectives is to achieve a close relationship with customers who will buy consistently from Eastern States year in and year out.

The other departments of the Marketing Division are market research, customer services, and advertising and public relations. The market research department looks at economic factors that affect not only Eastern States but also its prime customers and concentrates on economic studies on long-term demand as well as guides for determining the optimum size of the product of the various mills. Customer services was set up particularly to process and expedite orders, to handle transportation, and to deal with other customer problems. It concerned itself with complaints and with prompt order handling. Advertising and public relations was pretty much a one-man department with the help of a secretary-assistant. This department published brochures that explained the facilities and the products of the mills and directed the advertising campaign developed by its agency. The goals this department worked toward were to represent the company as a reliable supplier of quality products and to "project the company's image" as a sound business and a substantial long-term investment.

PRODUCTION

Iron ore and ore mining. As can be seen from the product flow chart in Table 4, when measured at capacity of its operations, Eastern States used 400,000 tons per year of ore from its own mine. The mine was in the United States and produced a high-grade ore with 64% Fe. This amount of ore, however, was insufficient to provide all the ore needed for blast furnace operations, and the balance was purchased outside on long-term contract from sources in Venezuela and Liberia. The foreign ores came into the port of Philadelphia and were shipped by train to the Eastern States plant.

Since the foreign ores had a slightly smaller iron content and a less desirable amount of phosphorus and sulphur as impurities, and, in addition, since the foreign ores had a less desirable physical structure than the ore from the company's mines, the price of foreign ore delivered at the Eastern States plant had to be $2 per ton less than the delivered cost of Eastern States' own ore to justify its completely replacing Eastern States' domestic ore.

There was almost no spot market for iron ore. Practically all foreign sources as well as United States sources were controlled by large individual steel companies or by combinations of steel companies. Ore could be purchased from these firms on a long-term contract of 2 to 5 years in length, with the price for the longer term being somewhat less than that for the shorter term. Prices on particular contracts were set by individual negotiation. However, a good indication of the prices that Eastern States would have to pay at the present time can be obtained from the average values indicated in the table below.

Ore from Eastern States' mine was similar in structure and in iron content to the Mesabi ore for which a price at a Lake Erie port is quoted in Table 6.

With increases in wages and taxes, the cost to Eastern States of ore delivered from its own mine had increased until the current cost could be fairly represented by the average unit value of Canadian ore or the average price of Lake Erie ore.

Table 4

Product Flow and Sales
(Net tons at capacity operations)

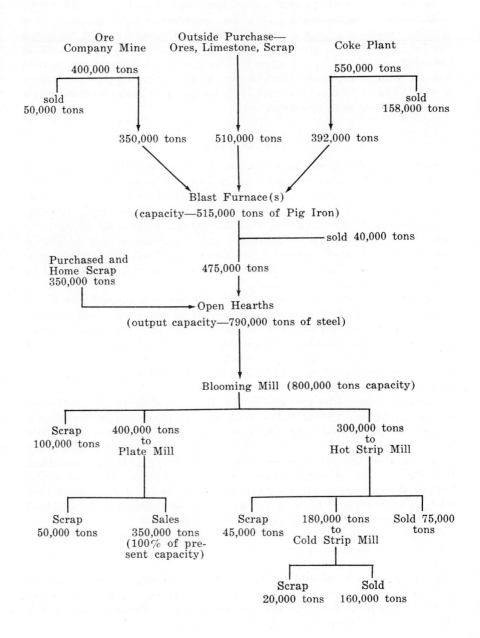

Ore
Company Mine

Outside Purchase—
Ores, Limestone, Scrap

Coke Plant

400,000 tons

550,000 tons

sold
50,000 tons

sold
158,000 tons

350,000 tons   510,000 tons   392,000 tons

Blast Furnace(s)
(capacity—515,000 tons of Pig Iron)

———— sold 40,000 tons

Purchased and
Home Scrap
350,000 tons

475,000 tons

Open Hearths
(output capacity—790,000 tons of steel)

Blooming Mill (800,000 tons capacity)

Scrap
100,000 tons

400,000 tons
to
Plate Mill

300,000 tons
to
Hot Strip Mill

Scrap
50,000 tons

Sales
350,000 tons
(100% of pre-
sent capacity)

Scrap
45,000 tons

180,000 tons
to
Cold Strip Mill

Sold 75,000
tons

Scrap
20,000 tons

Sold
160,000 tons

Table 5

Product Flow Key

1. Coke Plant	—Coal is converted to coke and by-product chemicals are collected.
2. Blast Furnaces	—Iron ore, coke, and limestone are continuously processed to obtain pig iron.
3. Open Hearths	—Molten pig iron, steel scrap, and other additives are heated 8 to 12 hours per batch to obtain steel, which is poured into ingots.
4. Blooming Mills	—Ingots are reheated and rolled into slabs.
5. Plate Mill	—Slabs are reheated and rolled into plates.
6. Hot Strip Mill	—Slabs are reheated and rolled into sheet or strip, which is coiled or cut in lengths.
7. Cold Strip Mill	—Coils of strip steel are cold-rolled and annealed.

Table 6

Iron Ore Prices

(Dollars per long ton)

YEAR	CANADIAN ORE AVERAGE ANNUAL UNIT VALUE	VENEZUELAN ORE AVERAGE ANNUAL UNIT VALUE	MESABI ORE AVERAGE PRICE, LAKE ERIE	WHOLESALE PRICE INDEX —ALL ORES USED IN UNITED STATES (1957-9 = 100)
1950	$ 6.85	n.a.	$ 9.36	70
1955	7.84	$6.37	9.36	91
1958	9.32	7.22	11.45	101
1959	9.58	7.71	11.45	96
1960	9.88	9.13	11.45	97
1961	10.24	9.46	11.45	98
1962	10.09	9.39	10.65	94
1963	10.56	8.34	10.65	93
1964	n.a.	n.a.	10.55	n.a.

n.a.—Not available.

The company's mine employed about 125 people in a location some 10 miles from a small town and about 35 miles from a city of 30,000 people. Mining the ore meant (1) drilling and blasting to release the ore, (2) some preliminary crushing but mainly loading and transporting to take the ore from the mine to the main crusher at the mine mouth, (3) crushing and separating to segregate sand and gravel and other tailings, and (4) loading onto railroad cars for the long journey to the Eastern States mill. The company's typical practice was to have the drilling and blasting work done well ahead of shipping requirements. At the present time, some 600,000 long tons of ore had been processed through this first stage. While drilling and blasting accounted for about 50% of the labor expense of the mine, these two stages collected only about 30% of the total mining cost.

Blast furnace department. The company has two blast furnaces and in the past has kept them both in operation, although not at full capacity. However, Mr. Howard Crichton, who came to the company from another firm some three years ago as general superintendent of primary production, became convinced that the furnaces could be run more efficiently. Following several studies, the top pressure was increased substantially and the physical structure of the charge to the blast furnace was changed. This increased the capacity of one furnace to 380,000 tons of pig-iron— enough to supply needs at recent operating levels.

Open-hearth department. The company operated 8 open-hearth furnaces capable of turning out at capacity almost 800,000 net tons of steel. Over the past 5 years the open hearths had been substantially rebuilt until they were all of about the same efficiency. The company attempted to operate with a 62% hot metal charge. With this percentage of molten pig iron coming in from the company's blast furnace and with 38% of the charge consisting of scrap and a minor amount of additive, each open hearth operated at its minimum time per cycle. It was possible, however, to vary the percentage of scrap charged to the open hearths from a minimum of 30% to a maximum of 70%. The economic feasibility of doing this depended upon the fluctuations in scrap prices. As the operating rate of the company increased toward 100% of capacity, it was possible either to use additional scrap purchased outside or to bring the second blast furnace into operation.

Table 7

Steel Scrap Price/net ton

(Heavy melting scrap, Pittsburgh)

YEAR	PRICE	YEAR	PRICE
1950	$35.05	1957	$42.44
1951	40.34	1960	29.44
1954	26.63	1962	25.80
1955	36.20	1963	24.10
1956	48.35	1964	30.80

One of Mr. Crichton's prime projects at the moment was studying the feasibility of using oxygen converters for manufacturing the company's steel. Experience in other companies had indicated that oxygen converters could produce steel at a cost of $10 to $12 per ton below that of steel made on open hearths when the price of steel scrap was about $30 per ton. In addition, this steel had some very desirable metallurgical properties and its quality could be closely controlled. These properties were most suitable for steel that would later go through the cold strip mill. Among the factors that Mr. Crichton was considering were the necessity of using about a 90% hot metal charge in the oxygen converters. Some firms used less than this; but, in Mr. Crichton's opinion, the maximum metallurgical advantage came from a high hot metal charge. In his opinion, experiments with the process over the next 10 years might lead to a somewhat lower percentage of hot metal charge (perhaps 60%). A new plant to produce about 500,000 tons of steel a year by the oxygen process would cost approximately $9 million. This would include an oxygen plant with two 40-ton vessels—one operating and one standby. Heats with such a vessel could be tapped every half hour. An oxygen process plant to produce 1 million tons per year would cost about $12 million.

With current labor costs, molten pig iron could be delivered to the open hearths at an intracompany charge of $40 per net ton. This charge included all variable costs and all overhead costs relevant to the blast furnace operations. About $4.20 of this represented a variable labor cost for the blast furnace operation.

The charge-to-tap time of the open hearths naturally varied with the percentage of hot metal used since the time to bring the steel up to the tapping temperature of about 3500°F. increased substantially as cold scrap was used. At a 62% hot metal charge, the charge-to-tap time was 8 hours. With a 30% hot metal charge, the charge-to-tap time increased to 12 hours. Variable costs from labor, fuel, power, and supplies increased by $3 per ton of output with the increase in charge-to-tap time from 8 to 12 hours.

Rolling mill department. It was the opinion of both the operating vice-president and the general superintendent of rolling mills that this department presented the major operating problems of the company. Of the four main mills, two—the plate mill and the blooming mill—were new and still not fully in operation.

Hot strip mill and cold strip mill. Both the hot strip mill and the cold strip mill had been installed new some 8 years before the time of this case. At present, their operators were highly skilled and their output was quite satisfactory. With some additional heating and finishing facilities, output of the hot strip mill could be increased by 50,000 tons for an investment of $1.2 million. The mill width would still be limited to its current size; however, total volume could increase. Both the hot strip mill and the cold strip mill had at least another 12 years of both economic and technically feasible life remaining without any major overhaul being necessary.

While the new blooming mill and the new plate mill were being considered several years ago, the company had also had under active consideration building a wider hot strip mill. This had been a favorite project of the operating vice-president. In its prime market areas, Eastern States' penetration of the market in the sizes it could provide averaged 24%. This gave it total shipments of hot rolled sheet of approximately 115,000 net tons per year. The operating vice-president's original proposal, which he still favored, was to build a wide hot strip mill with a capacity of 1,500,000 tons per year. This would require a steel production of approximately 2.1 million tons of ingots per year. Based upon the experience of several other companies with which the operating vice-president was familiar, such a mill would operate at a profit if output were over 1.2 million ingot tons. In addition to the mill itself, the capital requirement would include several heating furnaces, an entirely new building, and some additional storage space. The total estimates for capital requirements for the mill came to $32 million. At one point in its consideration of the proposed hot strip mill, the company had studied the feasibility of using a reversing mill rather than the continuous mill specified above. Capital requirements estimated for the reversing mill ran from $22 to $25 million. Metallurgical and marketability features of the two proposals are given in Table 8.

Table 8

Quality Characteristics

Question	Continuous Wide Mill vs. ES 30 Inches	Reversing Mill vs. Continuous
Gauge control of HR products	Better	Not as good
Surface quality	"	"
Drawability	"	Better
Quality of hot bands for CR	"	Comparable
Plates	"	"
Edge condition	"	"
Crown	"	"

Blooming mill and plate mill. Some 3 years ago, the company completed negotiations for the financing of a much larger blooming mill and a larger and higher speed plate mill than the 40-year old mills then operating. Construction and putting the equipment in place took about 18 months, and the new equipment has been operating for the past 18 months.

From the beginning customer reception of products from the plate mill has been favorable. The range of sizes available and the finished characteristics of the plate were superior to those of the former mills. Orders jumped rapidly so that it would have been possible in the first year to increase annual sales from 135,000 tons to 180,000 tons. The sales department claimed that the current rate of sales could be 90% of the plate mill capacity were the output available.

When the new plate mill was started, the old mill was shut down and dismantled and sold for scrap. Customer requirements then had to be met entirely from the new mill regardless of cost. During the first five months of operation, 50% of the plates rolled had to be scrapped for failure to meet customer specifications. This added considerably to cost and also presented a major problem of storage and handling. The rate of scrappage has since been reduced to 25% of output. The scrappage and start-up problems also meant that original delivery promises could not be met, and sales lagged some 30% behind the order rate.

As the new plate mill was started in operation, it became clear that much more retraining of operating personnel was necessary than had been foreseen. Old operating practices formed on the former mills were carried over to both the new blooming mill and the new plate mill and got in the way of efficient performance. Certain habits and practices of the crews on the final shear line and roll-out table limited output substantially. Plans for changing these practices had been inadequate, and various supervisory attempts since then had not been completely successful. At one point, the roll-out table and the cooling facilities were damaged. An additional $100,000 had to be spent in repairs, and shipments were further delayed while the repairs were made.

Both the operating vice-president and the rolling mill superintendent, as well as the superintendents of the blooming mill and the plate mill, were spending almost all of their time in attempts to bring these two mills up to the original expectations of cost and output. As the result of their intensive efforts, it was found that there were some errors in the original design of the mills and in the layout. These also contributed to restricted production. Some of these errors had been changed, some remained yet to be changed.

Capital expenditure projects proposed for the coming year included a $1 million expenditure on a new soaking pit to control the reheating of ingots before their rolling on the blooming mill. The installation of the soaking pit would improve the efficiency of the blooming mill since temperature evenness throughout the ingot and the temperature level could be more closely controlled by the new soaking pits. This would be particularly important when the operating rate was above 80%. The million dollar expenditure would then allow a substantial increase in the efficiency of the blooming mill. In addition, the firm planned to spend about $3 million on new finishing and shipping facilities for the plate mill. At the moment these facilities constituted a bottleneck and were a drag in meeting delivery promises. The proposed changes would result in a more efficient design and layout of the storage room for plates and in the various shipping docks. The result would be considerable improvement in the utilization of transportation facilities. It would mean quicker truck turnarounds and few or no delays for rail cars. While costs would be cut to some extent, perhaps 50 cents per ton of plate shipped, the major improvement would be in the company's ability to meet delivery promises and other customer requirements.

RESEARCH AND DEVELOPMENT

For many years, the company had had two departments in the operating division that were concerned with product quality and also with process improvements. The first of these, the metallurgical department, was responsible for internal quality control within the plant and also for working with sales representatives for proper application of products in the customers' plants. Service metallurgists from this department continually visited customers to help solve production problems and to assist in selecting the proper steel for the customers' needs. The plant engineering department worked on process improvements, on purchases of new equipment, and on design and installation problems of this equipment.

Several years ago, the top management of Eastern States felt a general alarm that was running through the steel industry as a result of increased competition from nonferrous materials. Many steel companies began then to accelerate their activities in the research area to develop new materials and new uses for old materials. Among these were stronger steels to meet customer requirements with less weight and perhaps less cost. Therefore, Eastern States set up a formal research and development department. A director was brought in from a technical research institute attached to a major university. At the university he had headed a considerable staff of people specializing in all aspects of metallurgical research. Shortly after coming to Eastern States, the new director, Mr. A. G. Berg, hired two research metallurgists, one to concern himself with alloy steels and the other with methods of direct reduction of iron ore using reducing gases of hydrogen and carbon monoxide. The eventual application of the latter might be to replace the blast furnace stage in steel production. The formal responsibilities of this department were stated as:

1. To develop new products and processes and to improve current products and processes.
2. To suggest research projects and to establish budgets for such projects.
3. To carry out research work on approved projects.
4. To provide technical assistance to other departments.
5. To advise management of possible areas for diversification.
6. To work closely with current and potential customers to develop products meeting their special requirements.
7. To work with the marketing department both in the introduction of new products and in establishing the probable future demands of customers.
8. To cooperate and participate in all technical matters throughout the company upon request of any department.

The first activities of the research and development department resulted within a year in the development of a low-alloy, columbium-bearing steel that had a high strength-to-weight ratio. This steel proved not to have all the performance requirements hoped for, but it was beneficial in certain rather narrow markets. Research work on the direct reduction of iron ore has continued; however, in the past year the importance of such work seems to have been reduced somewhat by the increasing efficiency of blast furnaces resulting from changes in blast furnace technology. When the research and development staff found itself substantially cramped for space and facilities during the first year of operation, a new research laboratory was built and all the necessary equipment for a physical metallurgy and alloy development laboratory was installed. In addition to its own activities, the research and development department has been instrumental in having Eastern States join in the support of a study in the use of electrical furnaces being carried out at a nonprofit research laboratory. The company contributes some $50,000 a year to this work. As a result of its interest in low-alloy, high-strength steels, the department suggested that Eastern States obtain a license from one of the three large steel producers to manufacture and sell a series of low-alloy steels used mainly in construction. After some negotiation, this license was granted by the large producer. It has enabled Eastern States to begin production of certain types of steels for the construction market in which Eastern States competed to only a very limited extent before.

PERSONNEL AND LABOR RELATIONS

The company's statements of objectives, principles, and basic policies included this paragraph:

> To provide our employees with good working conditions; to pay wages and salaries in line with those prevailing in the steel industry for similar work requiring like responsibility, experience, and skill; and to provide the most secure and steady employment possible within the risk conditions of the steel industry.

Some data that pertain to the carrying out of this statement of objectives follow in Table 9.

Table 9

YEAR	AVERAGE NUMBER OF EMPLOYEES	AVERAGE HOURLY COST OF WAGES & BENEFITS	TOTAL COST OF WAGES, SALARIES, & FRINGE BENEFITS	WAGES SALARIES, & BENEFITS AS A PERCENT OF SALES
Present	3080	$4.52	n.a.	37% (est.)
Previous	2910	4.15	$23,500,000	41%
"	2920	4.08	23,700,000	45%
"	2980	3.98	22,950,000	46%
"	3220	3.90	24,000,000	average of
"	3360	3.70	25,600,000	previous 10 years =
"	2960	3.51	20,200,000	36.4%

Table 10

EXECUTIVES	NUMBER	OVER 50 YEARS OF AGE	EXPERIENCE IN JOBS OUTSIDE EASTERN STATES (TOTAL YEARS)
President	1	1	11
Vice-Presidents ..	7	3	30
Sales	8	7	15
Operating	11	9	90
Purchasing	3	2	..
Control	5	4	..
Personnel	6	2	40
Research	1	0	20
	42	28	

Company policy was to negotiate its labor agreements with United Steelworkers of America (AFL-CIO) with terms almost the same as those negotiated by the larger steel companies. Eastern States typically waited until negotiation with the larger firms had been completed and then followed the "big steel" agreements with only slight modifications. Increases in fringe benefits and wages were universally granted to the nonsupervisory salaried employees following the pattern set by the nonexempt bargaining pattern.

Eastern States seldom, if ever, took a strike. It attempted to operate while other steel companies were on strike under the arrangement that any increases in wages and benefits would be retroactive to the beginning of the strike period. This personnel policy put it outside the usual behavior pattern of the industry. The use of such a policy as a competitive weapon was a constant source of discussion.

Shortly after some of the difficulties in putting the new rolling mills into operation became obvious, the personnel director recommended that the company establish a personnel relations committee that was to function in addition to the usual contacts between management and the union organization and to be a source of information and decision on personnel relations in addition to the regular line organization. During its first year of existence, the personnel relations committee concentrated on tackling some seniority matters that promised to be sticky in the next union negotiation. By the time the bargaining sessions came around, the seniority problems had been straightened out to everyone's satisfaction. The negotiations then became fairly routine. In its more recent activities, the personnel relations committee turned to analyzing the major problems of pay and security. It has come up with several ideas now seriously proposed both to the management and to the union. These ideas have mainly been borrowed from two other medium-sized steel producers, but have been modified somewhat to meet Eastern States' situation. The main ideas are: (1) Supplemental unemployment benefits (the money paid to a worker on layoff) will be increased so that in combination with unemployment compensation they will guarantee laid-off workers 80% of normal pay (up from the current 50%). (2) Such benefits will last 2 years rather than 1 year for younger workers and for the extent of the unemployment time for workers who have more than 15 years' seniority. (3) Sickness and accident benefits will be increased to 80% of normal pay against a present average of about 55%, these benefits to last up to 2 years for younger workers and as long as a man is out of work for men with more than 15 years' seniority. (4) A guarantee that a worker in any six-month period will achieve average hourly earnings equaling at least 90% of what he made in a previous base period. The base period is as yet undefined. The provision is designed to prevent severe wage reductions that might otherwise occur by changeover to new equipment and reduction in the skill ratings of jobs.

One consequence of the proposal is that total wage costs are likely to increase about 7 cents an hour although no direct increases in the basic rates are called for in the proposal. A second consequence is that the company's cost records will be much more widely open to the union than they have been in the past.

Training. Apprentice and on-the-job training courses have been established and operated by the company for some time. These courses were presumed to meet the constant requirements for relearning in light of the continual changes in operation that took place with both technological change and product change.

Managerial training was carried on both through a one-week course in the basic principles of scientific management for all company managers and by sending top managers to a similar but longer course given at a university. This training in managerial principles had been going on for some years. The great bulk of it took place some 5 years ago. It had been continued on a reduced level since. Following the initial formal courses, an on-the-job program known as the Management Job Analysis Project was begun. This project had as its purposes, first, developing clearly a definition of the various responsibilities for every person in management, and secondly, a continuing program to see that these responsibilities were measured, fulfilled, reviewed, and appraised. To supervise the job analysis project, the personnel department was carved in two and a new organization planning department was established. The director of the organization planning department worked for about two years to get the job responsibilities clarified and then moved on to developing an appraisal system.

The attempt to work out an appraisal system went on over several years. While none was developed, there were certain offshoots, such as an in-company course in organization and responsibility attended by every supervisor and the clearly expressed need for detailed and technical training programs in report-writing, metallurgy, and speed-reading. These last three courses were not developed in the company; instead, tuition was paid for employees who wished to take up such courses at nearby universities.

Twelve months ago, as part of a reorganization of the company's structure, the manpower planning department was brought back into the personnel department. A clerk was then assigned the task of reviewing the job clarification file each month to sort out any jobs that had not been rewritten for two years. These jobs were then reviewed and rewritten. Each supervisor was also directed to submit a schedule stating the times at which he held performance reviews with his subordinates. The personnel director then requested a written report of these reviews.

FINANCE

Tables 11, 12, and 13 contain data indicating the financial history and the current financial position of the company. The major financial

Table 11

Eastern States Iron and Steel Company
Balance Sheet at End of Last Fiscal Period
(All dollar figures in thousands)

Assets		Liabilities	
Cash	$ 2,400	Accounts Payable	$ 4,860
Accounts Receivable (net of		Income Taxes Due	90
doubtful accounts)	4,900		$ 4,950
Inventories (Note A)	7,900		
	$15,200	Long-Term Debt (Note B)	
		6% Bonds due 20 years	
		after issuance	$20,500
Property, Plant, and Equip-		6¼% Subordinated Convert-	
ment (at cost, less accumu-		ible Debentures due 25 years	
lated depreciation and de-		after issuance	6,500
pletion of $50,000)	$51,000		$27,000
		Stockholders' Equity	
		Common Stock ($20 par)	$12,000
		Capital Surplus	2,800
		Retained Earnings	15,450
			$30,250
		Reserve for Workmen's Com-	
		pensation and Supplemen-	
		tary Unemployment Bene-	
		fits	$ 1,500
		Deferred Income Taxes	2,800
			$ 4,300
		Deduct:	
		Treasury Stock (at cost)	300
Total Assets	$66,200	Total Liabilities & Stock-	
		holders' Equity	$66,200

Note A—Inventories are valued at the lower of cost or market. The LIFO method of determ-
ing cost was used for 80% of the total inventories. The balances are at average cost.

Note B—The 6% bonds are repayable over 15 years, commencing 5 years from issuance. The
debentures are convertible until due into common stock at $58 per share. Sufficient
shares of authorized but unissued stock have been reserved to meet this convertibility
provision. Cash dividends cannot be paid that will reduce retained earnings below
$16,000,000 nor net working capital below $8,000,000.

Table 12

Comparative Historical Record
(All dollars in thousands)

YEAR	SALES	NET INCOME	DIVIDENDS	PROPERTY & EQUIP- MENT (NET)	DEPRECI- ATION & DEPLETION	LONG-TERM DEBT
Present (at annual rate)	$68,000	$ 1,360	undetermined	$51,000 [1]	$4,100	$27,000
Previous	52,000	(1,100) [2]	none	53,000	3,700	27,000
"	49,000	(250)	$ 750	55,000	2,600	27,000
"	55,000	1,270	1,200	42,500	2,500	13,500
"	71,000	4,250	1,080	29,000	4,000	....
"	48,000	1,850	660	29,600	3,350	4,000
"	60,000	1,790	1,080	30,000	3,600	5,500
"	61,000	2,700	1,080	27,400	3,800	4,500
"	52,000	2,250	1,080	25,600	3,900	4,500
"	32,000	1,100	540	28,600	2,300	6,000

[1] At beginning of current fiscal period.
[2] Loss.

Table 13

Prices of Common Stock

Year		High	Low
Present	....	35½	21
Previous	....	28½	13⅝
"	....	37½	15⅛
"	....	42½	28
"	....	52⅛	25½
"	....	53⅝	28⅞

event of the past several years has been the assumption of some $27 million of debt taken on to finance the purchase of the blooming mill and the plate mill. The company placed this debt with several large financial institutions through the efforts of an investment banking firm. The event was significant in that it was, and is, rare in the steel industry to have a debt to equity ratio above 0.3. Improving financial results during the current year have allowed the company to pay off a short-term bank debt of $3 million.

Among the problems interesting the financial vice-president were dividend policy and the amount that it was wise for the company to spend on capital expansion over the next few years. The directors of the firm were considerably embarrassed by the necessity of foregoing dividends last year. The company had long enjoyed a reputation for paying some cash dividend on its common stock regularly for over 20 years. Eastern States is publicly owned and its stock is traded on one of the major stock exchanges. Among the questions to be considered in deciding funds for capital expenditure were, of course, the bond interest and the retirement payments due for the present debt and the amounts made available through the company's depreciation policy, as well as net income. The financial vice-president remarked that, were the company's mine closed, depletion allowances would decrease by about $750,000 a year. The company had for some years followed a policy of maximizing depreciation and depletion charges to increase the firm's cash flow. At present, it was charging the maximum depreciation possible. This charge would decrease steadily in the future as a source of funds—provided no additional investments were undertaken. Both the president and the financial vice-president stated that the new mills were an absolute necessity for survival of the company and that the debt financing, although risky, had to be undertaken. The financial vice-president's view was that the company needed to undertake whatever measures it could to get the stock price up, since any future external financing would have to be equity financing.

The effect on the company's financial position of delays in getting the new mills into operation can be judged from the following table. These data represent a forecast made at the time of refinancing when the mortgages were obtained.

Table 14

Schedule of Projections

(Dollar figures in thousands)

YEAR	PRESENT	FUTURE 1	2	3	4
Long-Term Debt	....	$13,500	$27,000	$27,000	$27,000
Plate Output (net tons)	125,000	154,000	208,000	256,000	275,000
Sales	$70,000	$70,000	$73,000	$79,000	$86,000
Net Income	$ 4,000	$ 3,100	$ 3,400	$ 5,750	$ 6,900
Working Capital	....	....	....	....	$ 7,900

Possibilities for future action. The company has currently underway an intensive study to determine the possibility of cost reductions by constructing basic oxygen steel facilities, either to supplement or to replace the present open hearths. It is not expected that the detailed studies will vary greatly from the approximate investment and savings figures mentioned earlier. However, the detail is necessary to justify financing arrangements.

The possibility of constructing a wide hot strip mill is also being reconsidered. In general, it is expected that the data given earlier would be reaffirmed.

Further possibilities were to increase the capacity of the blooming mill from 800,000 tons at present to 1,300,000 tons by adding more preheating facilities by an investment of $3,000,000 or to increase the capacity of the plate mill from 400,000 tons to 800,000 tons by investing $4,000,000 in preheaters and annealing furnaces. Both of these mills now have rolling facilities that would accommodate such increases in capacity.

One final action that has been proposed is to support very actively attempts to persuade Congress to pass legislation or the executive department to issue new administrative regulations that would prevent foreign steels from being sold in the United States at prices under those in effect in the country of origin. Whether the company should also recommend import quotas for steel products is a part of this question.

QUESTIONS

1. What market opportunities do you see for Eastern States Iron and Steel Company? Specify the kinds of products and the kinds of buyers you believe most suitable for the company.

2. What technological improvements are likely to be significant for Eastern States in the future? What influence would such changes have on the company's method of operation?

3. What can the company feasibly do about the possibility of increased foreign competition? Are there any actions open to it other than legal and political?

4. Appraise the suitability of the marketing organization and the promotional efforts of the company in light of the kinds of buyers it must sell to.

5. Appraise the existing pricing policy. Have you any suggestions for modification?

6. Would it be wise for the company to close its domestic iron ore mine for an extended period? (This has been done at times in the past.) (Iron ore was in plentiful supply around the world in the mid-sixties.)

7. With current scrap prices, should the open hearths be operated with less than a 62% hot metal charge? What scrap charge would lead to the minimum cost of steel?

8. Would you recommend that the company replace some of its current open-hearth capacity with oxygen converters or add to its capacity by installing oxygen converters? (Assume that the existing open hearths have no significant scrap value.)

9. Appraise the objectives and the work of the research and development department.

10. What recommendations would you make about the work of the personnel department? Consider such matters as wage costs, training efforts, the effectiveness of executive training, and the work of the personnel relations committee.

11. What bargaining posture do you recommend for the company in its coming negotiations with the union?

12. What capital expenditure programs do you believe the company should undertake this year and in the next few years? How much money can it afford to commit to such programs?

13. What recommendations have you as to the financial issues facing the company?

14. As a director of the company, what is your overall judgment as to the performance of the company in the past and its prospects for the future?

7 · NOVINS WALLPAPER COMPANY

COMPANY BACKGROUND

The Novins Wallpaper Company has been a prominent manufacturer of wallpaper for over half a century. For many years its only plant was located in the Mohawk Valley of New York State. In 1933 the Susquehanna Wallpaper Company, with a mill in eastern Pennsylvania, was merged into the Novins Wallpaper Company, and since that time production has been carried on in both states.

The financial structure of the company was reorganized in 1940, in order to provide securities which fitted the personal needs of the chief stockholders. Since then, the company has had a satisfactory sales and profit record except for the fiscal years ending in 1948 and 1950.

Novins Wallpaper Company
Sales and Profits—1940-1950

YEAR	NET SALES	NET PROFITS
1940-41	$2,100,000	$108,000
1941-42	2,500,000	187,000
1942-43	1,900,000	101,000
1943-44	2,000,000	152,000
1944-45	1,900,000	138,000
1945-46	3,100,000	205,000
1946-47	5,900,000	437,000
1947-48	3,900,000	98,000
1948-49	5,400,000	271,000
1949-50	3,300,000	(37,000) loss

The company recently built a new modern mill at a site about 100 miles from the old Susquehanna plant. Construction was started in 1947, but the acute inventory adjustment that characterized the industry in the latter part of that year lead to delays and the mill was not open for operation until the spring of 1949. The old Susquehanna plant has been dismantled and the property sold.

With its new mill, Novins Wallpaper Company is as well equipped as any manufacturer in the industry. Unfortunately, however, the new mill opened at a time when industry and company sales were declining. As a consequence, the company now finds itself in a difficult financial position and with a heavy overhead burden. The management of the company is now giving serious consideration to any ways and means at its disposal to overcome these difficulties.

OUTLOOK FOR THE COMPANY

Factors affecting the industry

Long run trends in the wallpaper industry are indicated in the following table:

Trends in Wallpaper Industry, 1899-1947

YEAR	NUMBER OF ESTABLISHMENTS	NUMBER OF EMPLOYEES	VALUE ADDED BY MANUFACTURE (000 OMITTED)	VALUE OF PRODUCT SHIPPED (000 OMITTED)
1947	58	5,462	$32,700	$58,900
1939	46	4,885	13,300	25,000
1937	42	5,171	14,900	26,800
1935	40	4,888	9,800	19,700
1933	39	3,706	8,900	15,800
1931	50	....	11,000	20,200
1929	56	5,420	16,500	30,000
1927	53	5,637	15,400	30,100
1925	49	5,806	15,100	30,100
1923	51	6,142	17,800	34,800
1921	43	4,623	12,800	29,100
1919	48	5,095	9,900	23,000
1914	48	5,684	7,400	15,900
1909	45	4,736	6,800	14,400
1904	44	4,410	6,000	12,600
1899	51	4,684	4,600	10,600

Source: U. S. Census of Manufacturers.

The wallpaper industry appears to have reached a state of maturity. When allowance is made for fluctuation in the general level of business, the number of establishments appears to be approximately stable, as does the number of persons employed. There has been a sharp increase in value of products, but to a considerable extent this reflects a rise in the price level rather than an increase in the total volume of output.

Year-to-year changes in wallpaper sales, however, have been substantial. Activity rose at a fairly stable rate from a low point in 1932 until the beginning of World War II, except for a setback in 1938. During the war years, conditions of supply and demand were both abnormal, and from 1943 through 1945 volume was curtailed through a 40% reduction in the allocation of paper stock. Paper continued in short supply into 1946, so it was not until 1947 that supply conditions enabled the industry to meet the full demand.

Wallpaper sales in the post-war period have been erratic, as shown by the following table:

Wallpaper Sales—1940-1950

(Figures in Millions)

SEASON (ENDING JUNE 30)	ROLLS	DOLLARS	SEASON (ENDING JUNE 30)	ROLLS	DOLLARS
1940-41	392	29	1945-46	356	38
1941-42	389	32	1946-47	439	64
1942-43	308	26	1947-48	269	38
1943-44	273	24	1948-49	327	55
1944-45	259	25	1949-50	206	32

The spread between the low point and the high point in both physical and dollar volume has been over 100% within the last five years.

The large volume of sales in the 1946-47 season included a substantial amount of inventory accumulation by wholesale and retail dealers. For many years they had been unable to maintain balanced stock and were inclined to "make sure" of their supply. At the same time a significant, though unknown, rise in the consumer demand for wallpaper was taking place. Wartime price controls had been removed and selling prices were rising briskly.

By the middle of 1947, it was generally recognized that the distributors were overstocked and that a cutback in manufacturing activities was necessary to permit the excess inventory to be absorbed by the ultimate consumer. General feeling throughout the industry was fairly optimistic, however, because it was believed that as soon as inventories were back to a more normal level, a high, post-war level of activity would prevail. The 1948-49 season appeared to justify this belief, with dollar sales volume by manufacturers rising to 55 million. The physical volume of sales, however, did not show as sharp a rise; manufacturers were finding it more difficult to pass on increasing costs; the underlying post-war demand for wallpaper began to be questioned and with a slipping of prices a policy of retrenchment became common throughout the industry.

These fluctuations in volume naturally make it difficult for a wallpaper manufacturer to achieve efficient operations. While considerable progress has been made in leveling out the seasonal fluctuations, it is necessary for companies to have a varying work force, or to pay overtime rates, in order to meet the changes from one year to the next. Wallpaper does not deteriorate much in storage, but it is bulky and, even more important, the style changes are sufficiently pronounced so that carrying inventory over a long period is risky.

Demand for wallpaper depends in part upon the level of the national income. In fact, as the table on page 891 shows, there was a close relationship between national income and industry sales from 1929 to World War II. Abnormal war conditions upset this relationship, but when sales rose in 1946 it was generally assumed in the industry that wallpaper sales would again be closely correlated with national income. Unfortunately, sales have not kept pace with rising income levels and the relationship between the two series is now uncertain.

Another factor that tends to increase the demand for wallpaper is the high level of residential building. There has been a building boom since World War II, as the accompanying figures show, and in the five years following the war over 5 million new dwelling units were constructed. Wallpaper has been used in many of these new houses, although for technical reasons it is not uncommon to defer papering until the house has had a year or two to settle. Moreover, new building far exceeds demolition, with the result that the total number of houses in the country has increased substantially.

Comparison of Wallpaper Sales and National Income—1929-1949

YEAR	WALLPAPER INDUSTRY SALES INDEX	NATIONAL INCOME INDEX	DIFFERENCE
1929	*100*	*100*	0
1931	67	67	0
1932	49	48	1
1933	53	45	8
1934	60	56	4
1935	66	65	1
1936	79	77	2
1937	89	84	5
1938	73	77	—4
1939	83	83	0
1940	91	93	—2
1941	108	119	—11
1942	88	156	—68
1943	81	193	—112
1944	83	209	—126
1945	127	209	—82
1946	216	206	10
1947	125	230	—105
1948	101	259	—158
1949	118	248	—130

Residential Building

	NUMBER OF NEW DWELLING UNITS		NUMBER OF NEW DWELLING UNITS
1935	216,000	1943	350,000
1936	324,000	1944	169,000
1937	336,000	1945	245,000
1938	408,000	1946	811,000
1939	515,000	1947	886,000
1940	603,000	1948	926,000
1941	715,000	1949	1,019,000
1942	497,000	1950	1,414,000

Housing alone does not create a demand for wallpaper. Demand also depends upon the frequency of redecorating and the type of material used. Home decorating competes for the consumer dollar with many other products. It is a postponable expenditure and tends to be deferred when consumers are hard pressed for cash.

An apparent trend toward amateur decorating is significant in this connection. During World War II, the scarcity and high cost of labor led many people to do their own home decorating. Having acquired a familiarity with the process, people are likely to think of home decorating as something they can do themselves. The continuing high cost of labor also encourages this amateur decorating. One wartime survey showed that 61% of homes in which wallpaper was used had one or more rooms prepared without the aid of professional paperhangers. The practice apparently varied considerably from one community to the other, inasmuch as postwar surveys show that wallpaper had been applied by a family member in 71% of the cases in Milwaukee compared with 44% of recently decorated homes in Omaha.

The chief competitor of wallpaper is, of course, paint. The statistics on the relative use of paper and paint are fragmentary and rather unsatisfactory. One survey of 1,800 homes found that approximately three fourths of them had wallpaper in at least one room. The specific rooms in which these 1,350 users had paper were as follows:

Bedroom	66%	Kitchen	20%
Living room	58%	Bathroom	19%
Dining room	52%	Study	13%
Hallway	48%	Playroom	8%

In a study made by the Chicago Tribune in 1946, it was found that for recent decoration paint had been used more than twice as frequently as paper.

Paint manufacturers have spent a great deal of money promoting the use of various types of paint for home decorating. Technical improvements have been made in water paints to improve their colorfastness and durability, and these have been particularly popular with amateur decorators. More recently there has been advertising emphasizing synthetic rubber emulsified products.

The wallpaper industry has been at some disadvantage in competing with the paint companies. Since the papers of a particular manufacturer typically lose their identity before they reach the consumer, advertising by manufacturers has uncertain value. Only two or three of the leading companies have attempted to establish brand recognition in the minds of consumers. The Wallpaper Institute was organized about 15 years ago, primarily to provide a united effort in the sales promotion of wallpaper. It has been active in working with home decorators, designers, furniture manufacturers, and other people influencing attitudes towards home decoration. Because of a limited budget and its limitations as a voluntary, cooperative effort, it has not been as aggressive in reaching the consumer market as have many of the paint manufacturers.

Many people in the home furnishing field believe that the typical housewife is becoming more sensitive to attractive home decoration. This interest, of course, includes furniture, draperies, curtains, floor covering, as well as wall cover. The wallpaper manufacturers have catered to this trend, and industry spokesmen point out that more attractive effects can be secured with wallpaper than with paint.

Very little wallpaper is being sold to apartment owners and other landlords for the purpose of redecorating space rented to tenants. During the 1930's, when housing was in ample supply, it was common practice in many areas to redecorate rented premises every two years. As a consequence, the "landlord" market accounted for about 23% of prewar sales. Since the war this market has virtually disappeared as far as the wallpaper industry is concerned. Such redecoration as landlords now do consists almost entirely of painting.

Position of the company in the industry

The position of the Novins Wallpaper Company in the industry is indicated in the accompanying table. This table shows that the Company sells approximately 10% of the total industry volume. The company has improved its position slightly during the last five years; from 1935 to 1945 its output accounted for between 7% to 8% of the industry total, whereas in the last few years it has enjoyed about 10% of the dollar volume of business and over 9% of the physical volume. Incidentally, the table also indicates that fluctuations in Novins' sales have been due more to total industry changes than to shifts in Novins' percentage of the total sales.

Sales Position of Company in Industry, 1934-1950

(Dollar and roll figures in millions)

| | SALES IN DOLLARS | | | | SALES IN ROLLS | | |
SEASON (ENDING JUNE 30)	INDUSTRY	COMPANY	COMPANY % OF INDUSTRY		INDUSTRY	COMPANY	COMPANY % OF INDUSTRY
1934-35	18.7	1.3	7.1		333	22.4	6.7
1935-36	20.7	1.4	6.8		355	24.0	6.8
1936-37	26.2	2.1	7.9		415	32.3	7.8
1937-38	23.6	2.0	8.5		345	28.5	8.3
1938-39	23.2	1.7	7.2		347	24.9	7.2
1939-40	27.0	2.2	8.1		391	32.1	8.2
1940-41	28.5	2.1	7.3		392	29.3	7.5
1941-42	32.4	2.5	7.7		389	29.9	9.7
1942-43	26.3	1.9	7.4		308	22.2	7.2
1943-44	24.4	2.0	8.1		273	22.3	8.2
1944-45	24.8	1.9	7.8		259	20.1	7.8
1945-46	38.2	3.1	8.2		356	27.8	7.8
1946-47	64.3	5.9	9.1		439	37.3	8.5
1947-48	38.1	3.9	10.3		269	26.1	9.7
1948-49	54.9	5.4	9.8		327	30.4	9.3
1949-50	32.4	3.3	10.1		206	19.4	9.4

Novins Wallpaper Company is one of the ten leading manufacturers in the industry. Its largest competitor, the United Wallpaper Company, enjoys a dominant position with approximately 25% of the industry's production. Novins belongs to a second group of companies, no one of which controls more than 10% of the volume. There are in addition about 25 small manufacturers, most of whom serve a regional or local market.

An indication of the scale of industry operation is given in the census figures in the table on the following page, which classify plants according to the number of employees. These figures show that the largest plant has fewer than 500 employees and that a typical plant has approximately 100 employees. Most of the larger companies operate more than a single plant, so while there are 58 separate wallpaper plants, there are fewer than 40 competing companies in the industry.

Size of Wallpaper Manufacturing Plants—1947

SIZE	NUMBER OF ESTABLISHMENTS	TOTAL EMPLOYEES IN SIZE GROUP	VALUE ADDED BY MANUFACTURER
1-4	4		
5-9	3	118	$ 544,000
10-19	6		
20-49	17	549	3,161,000
50-99	10	2,689	15,467,000
100-249	12		
250-499	6	2,106	13,560,000
Total	58	5,462	$32,732,000

Source: U. S. Census of Manufacturers.

Novins Wallpaper Company is comparatively unknown among consumers. In this respect it is typical of most of its competitors, except United and Imperial, which have a comparatively limited amount of consumer recognition. This absence of company or brand recognition by consumers reflects the marketing structure of the industry. Each wallpaper manufacturer designs a large number of wallpaper styles. From this wide selection of wallpaper jobbers select individual papers which they think will sell best, and then samples of each item selected are assembled together in sample books. These sample books are then distributed to retailers and paperhangers who show them to the final consumer. In this process the identity of the manufacturer is frequently lost. Even if his name does appear on the back of some of the samples, the consumer pays little attention to it. The consumer is more interested in color and design, and relies upon the local distributor for advice regarding quality. All of the larger manufacturers make papers in several different quality grades; this also interferes with building a distinctive reputation among consumers.

Wallpaper manufacturers are known among retailers and paperhangers. The leading manufacturers undertake trade promotions directed at the retail level; fastness of color, exactness of register and similar qualities are emphasized in these promotions. In this regard, Novins Wallpaper Company enjoys as good a reputation as most of the leading competitors. None of them has sufficient distinctiveness, however, to make a marked difference in sales on the basis of reputation alone.

The key to sales volume for a manufacturer distributing through the normal channels is held by the wallpaper jobber. A company's paper must be included in the jobber's sample books if it is to sell at all, and the jobber must be in close contact and be prepared to give 24-hour delivery service if his sample books are to be featured by the people operating on the retail level.

Styling, including design and color, is the key factor influencing the jobber in selecting papers to put in his sample books. Likewise, it is the key factor that attracts the attention of the ultimate consumer. The jobber is also concerned about other quality characteristics, delivery service, other aspects of his relationship with the manufacturer, and pricing that is in line with the rest of the industry.

Novins Wallpaper Company has done a good job of styling in recent years and has a good reputation in the trade with this respect. Its reputation for quality, aside from style, is satisfactory but not distinctive. Novin's service, however, is sharply criticized by jobbers. They feel that the company is slow and inaccurate in its shipments, that it is unreasonable in the way it handles requests for adjustments, that there are frequent errors in billing, and that company representatives are a little too dictatorial in their attitude. Some of this feeling on the part of jobbers must, of course, be discounted for jobbers are inclined to level the same complaints at the other large manufacturers. Nevertheless, it is clear that the company maintains its sales volume primarily because of the quality of its product rather than the loyalty of the jobbers.

The company's operating costs have been roughly similar to those of other manufacturers. Many of the wallpaper mills in the industry are fairly old and are located in cities where labor costs are not unusually high. Some of the small mills operate on very low overhead but usually the styling and quality of their product is not first class. Novins executives hope that their new plant will give them a distinct advantage but, as will be explained later, this benefit has not yet been achieved.

COMPANY POLICIES

Sales policies

(1) *Products*

The company classifies its wallpaper into six different lines, and for each of these there are a number of patterns and styles. A pattern is the basic design that is usually printed in a number of color combinations; each color combination is termed a style. In all there are approximately 500 patterns and 1,300 styles. In addition, the company makes approximately 200 styles of borders.

	PATTERNS	STYLES
Novins Standard	185	434
Novins Modern	48	225
Novins Mohawk	36	128
Acme	69	168
Susquehanna	142	326
Home Decorator	24	24
	504	1,305

The separation of company products into lines and the large number of styles in each reflects the company's policy to sell to a large number of jobbers and other distributors. Many of these distributors are in competition with each other and they prefer to have different patterns in their sample books. Moreover, some of the larger distributors insist on exclusive rights to a few of the patterns.

There is division of opinion within the company as to the desirability of such a multiplicity of patterns and styles. The sales manager believes that even a wider variety is desirable in order to build up sales volume. He stresses the need for at least minor variations of patterns in order to give competing distributors different products. Also he points to the difficulty in predicting consumer tastes and believes that the wider number of styles increase the company's chances of hitting upon numbers that will be popular.

On the other hand, the variety of styles increases production, storage, and shipping problems. The direct labor costs plus overhead of changing styles on a printing machine has been estimated at approximately $70.00. There are between 5,000 and 6,000 such changes a year, so that the total cost is substantial. The large number of styles also makes it difficult to keep inventory available for prompt delivery.

Several suggestions have been made for overcoming the problem of a large number of styles. One is that the style should be eliminated from the line promptly if it does not sell. In this connection, it is pointed out that a third of the styles actually account for a substantial volume of the sales. Another suggestion is to establish some minimum run, such as 5,000 rolls, and then hold the sales department responsible for disposing of this quantity if it agrees that the style should be run in the first place. Still another possibility is to attempt some pretesting of styles, probably by having proposed styles appraised by a panel of consumers or decorators, and in this way to eliminate a considerable number of items before they are even put into the line. Still others argue that the number of styles should be reduced, even if it does mean loss of sales volume, on the grounds that the company would make more profit by an attempt to concentrate on styles where large volume could be secured.

Serious consideration is being given to adding two special types of wallpaper. One is a plastic-coated wallpaper that is much more durable and readily washable. The price of such paper would have to be approximately double the price of regular paper and consequently its use would be limited to situations in which its distinctive quality was a decided advantage. One or two of the company's competitors are already making such a product, but as far as known the sales volume is not great.

Another possibility is paper that is given a coat of paste on the back and that may be hung by simply wetting the back surface. This type of paper has a special appeal to the amateur paperhanger who usually does not have regular equipment for mixing paste and applying it evenly to paper. One company has introduced such a line of ready-pasted paper and given it considerable sales promotion backing. In general, the regular wallpaper distribution channels do not think this type of paper has much promise. However, significant volume has been sold through department stores and other channels where people doing their own decorating are more likely to come.

The company has put out its "home decorator" line, which consists of paper trimmed along the edges and packed in a special carton containing two rolls. It is definitely designed for use by amateurs and is sold almost entirely through paint, hardware, and home furnishing jobbers. Unless some means can be found for increasing sales volume, it is likely that this line will be dropped.

In general, then, the company has not gone in for specialty wall covering products. To do so would require considerable capital both for product development and for promotion. Every year or two some new wall covering or wall finish comes on to the market, but company executives generally regard these as novelties that will have very limited use.

(2) *Customers*

The channels of distribution for wallpaper are not clear-cut because different distributors perform different functions. Generally speaking, marketing organizations may be divided as follows:

1. *Jobbers*—These leading wallpaper jobbers—or "master job-bers"—do a strictly wholesale business, reselling to sub-jobbers or to distributors.

2. *Subjobbers*—These firms, often called sample-book men, dis-tribute to retail stores and to paperhangers. They usually carry a limited inventory but rely upon the master jobbers for prompt delivery of most items. The distinction between a subjobber and a master jobber is not always clear.

3. *Retailers*—These outlets operate a direct-to-the-consumer busi-ness and they may also do some business with paperhangers.

In addition to such distributors—who are primarily concerned with wallpaper—paint stores, hardware stores, department stores, home fur-nishing stores, and even drugstores may sell wallpaper. These outlets usually sell direct to the consumer. They typically are supplied by wholesalers who handle the rest of their business, and these wholesalers in turn may deal either with manufacturers or with master jobbers.

Estimates of the quantity of wallpaper sold to paperhangers show wide variations, but it appears that less than half of it reaches the consumer by this ruote. The consumer may, of course, buy his own paper even though it is hung professionally.

Novins Wallpaper Company sells to all the types of distributors listed above. Its general policy is to deal with any customer who will buy in a large enough volume to warrant the trouble of shipping, billing, and collection. The bulk of its business, however, is secured from the master jobbers. There are approximately 250 such firms in the country, and Novins sells at least some paper to half of these. In addition, it sells to another 200 subjobbers, paint and hardware wholesalers, and occasionally to large retailers. This policy is followed in order to secure the maximum sales possible. Needless to say, it is not favorably regarded by the jobbers, who sometimes find the company competing with them. A similar practice is followed by other leading manufacturers, and the company contends that, as long as it maintains its discount schedule so that the jobbers are at no price disadvantage, the latter have no legitimate grounds for objections.

The company has made no detailed analysis of markets and customers. It has relied primarily upon its advertising agency for information secured in addition to that coming from its regular customers.

From time to time, the company has made some wallpaper for the large mail-order houses. It is currently considering entering into a contract with one of these firms under which Novins will manufacture a line of some 100 different styles and will carry some of the inventory, subject to order by the several distributing points of the mail-order company. The sales manager is quite enthusiastic about taking on this business because it will increase the total sales volume. Profit margins will be quite narrow and there is some risk that the company will either have to make uneconomical runs or find itself with excess stock at the end of a season. The principal attraction of this kind of business is that it provides volume and, consequently, would help absorb mill overhead.

(3) *Pricing*

Prices of the company's product are established in terms of the final sale price to the consumer. There is, of course, some difference in production costs of different types of wallpaper, reflecting differences in the types of basic paper stock used, the type of pigment, the number of colors and difficulty of obtaining clear register, etc. Nevertheless, the chief basis for establishing retail prices is the judgment of company executives on the appeal the paper will have to the consumer. The company intentionally designs papers in various quality ranges, and then adjustments are made in the final pricing in terms of "customer appeal." The overall result is that products of the company seem to be priced about in line with those of its major competitors. The company does receive a somewhat higher price than the average for the industry, as indicated in the table below; but this reflects success in reaching a somewhat higher average market rather than overpricing papers of a comparable quality and style.

Industry and Company Average Selling Prices, 1940-1950

(Per 100 Rolls)

	INDUSTRY	NOVINS
1940-41	$ 7.27	$ 7.17
1941-42	8.33	8.39
1942-43	8.55	8.57
1943-44	8.94	8.96
1944-45	9.58	9.48
1945-46	10.37	11.14
1946-47	14.67	15.81
1947-48	14.18	14.94
1948-49	16.78	17.75
1949-50	15.75	16.93

The company has established the following discount schedule to be used in determining the selling prices of different types of distributors. It not only follows this range of discounts in its own sales but encourages all firms handling its products to do likewise.

Novin's Discount Schedule

Consumer dollar:

Manufacturer	$ .20
Jobber	.14
Subjobber	.16
Dealer*	.16
Paperhanger*	.34
	$1.00

* In sales direct to the consumer, retailer typically gets the dealer and paperhanger margins.

For many years the discount allowed to paperhangers was 20% instead of 34%, whereas a wider margin was allowed to the jobber, subjobber, and dealer. All of the large wallpaper manufacturers made a similar change in their discount schedules at about the same time Novins Wallpaper Company did. This action resulted from pressure from the Wallpaper Institute to take steps that would encourage the local decorator to favor wallpaper over paint. As might be expected, the jobbers are not happy about the narrower margin and state that the cost and risk of carrying large inventories will have to be shifted back to the manufacturer if they are to operate under this new schedule. It has not been possible, to date, to ascertain the actual effect of the new schedule on either the jobber or the paperhanger.

(4) Sales promotion

The primary appeals used by Novins Wallpaper Company are good design and wide selection. As already noted, the company prices and quality of product are satisfactory but not distinctive and its service certainly cannot be called a "sales appeal."

For many years the company brought out a new set of designs each year; that is, new in the sense that many of the less popular styles were dropped and new ones were added. In the postwar period, Novins, along with most of the other leading manufacturers, has redesigned the line only every two years. This not only results in production economies but also has several market advantages. The task of preparing and distributing sample books is cut in half, the unsettling effect of price cuts on discontinued items is reduced, and the problems of small orders and short supply toward the end of a season are mitigated. Distributors, as well as manufacturers, now generally regard the two year cycle as desirable. However, small manufacturers who often imitate styles of leading companies are tempted to bring out annual "specials."

Sales of company papers are obtained primarily through sample books that are placed in the hands of thousands of retail dealers and paperhangers. The preparation of these sample books, which is typically done by the manufacturer to the master jobber, is an expensive job in itself.

The company makes a nominal charge for these books, which covers most of the out-of-pocket expense of preparing them. Jobbers, in turn, charge their subjobbers and retailers about $3 for a book of 300 samples.

The company uses salesmen to maintain contact with jobbers and subjobbers. These men also call on paint, hardware, and other types of jobbers who carry wallpaper as a minor sideline. They do a very limited amount of missionary sales work with retailers and other distributors. In general, the master jobbers and subjobbers do not look favorably upon this activity because they are suspicious that the company may be seeking direct sales. One or two competing manufacturers have salesmen who do missionary work with hotels and other large institutional buyers, but the Novins' management has felt that this market was too small to justify such effort.

The company uses several types of advertising and other forms of sales promotion directed primarily at the wallpaper and home decorating trade. It advertises in a variety of trade journals, takes an active part in various conventions, and uses direct-mail promotions to jobbers and subjobbers.

Advertising to wallpaper consumers is very limited. Company officials feel that they are not able to undertake a large enough campaign to build any real company reputation and, consequently, consumer advertising will benefit competitors as much as Novins itself. Such consumer advertising as is done is intended primarily to impress the retailer that "we too back our product with consumer advertising." In other words, it is a defensive measure designed to offset any advantage United or Imperial may enjoy in attracting jobbers and subjobbers to handle their paper.

The advertising agency of the company has raised serious question as to the soundness of this advertising policy and urges that consumer advertising be stepped up so that Novins will have some real company or brand reputation among wallpaper users. The agency has assembled some statistics that indicate that consumers who are thinking about doing their own papering for the first time are likely to be responsive to advertisements in the leading home magazines. Department stores indicate that well-known brands of wallpaper sell easier than other brands; this is particularly true of the ready-pasted paper. On the other hand, company executives point out that much of competitors' advertising features new types of wall coverings and that Novins spends as large a percentage of sales for advertising regular wallpaper as do most competitors.

The company recognizes that wallpaper in general competes with paint. Consequently, Novins officials have been active supporters of the Wallpaper Institute. Company contributions to support the Institute operations run over $10,000 per year. As might be expected, there is some difference of opinion in the wallpaper industry as to the activities the Institute should undertake and how much money each company should contribute to support this work. The Institute, of course, works on some industry problems in addition to sales promotion, although this is its primary function.

Production policies and facilities

Production of the company's 1,300 styles should be timed so as to provide good customer delivery service, economical production scheduling and production runs, a reasonable inventory of finished stock, and minimum problems of closing out discontinued numbers. This task is further complicated by difficulties of predicting both total wallpaper demand and the demand for individual styles.

It would be more descriptive to say that Novins has a man, rather than a policy, to deal with this problem. The production-planning manager, who works in the New York sales office, has been with the company for many years and has intimate knowledge of production and sales history. He personally establishes a weekly schedule of the styles and length of production runs for each mill.

This is a particularly complex task when the line is being redesigned and new sample books have to be prepared. The production-planning manager has at his disposal details of inventory and sales reports, but no formal procedures or policies have been established to regulate his decisions. He does, of course, discuss with senior company executives their opinions regarding the outlook for wallpaper sales.

The principal raw material used by the company is paper stock. This is a typical ground wood paper, largely No. 2 hanging stock, which is simple to manufacture and is available in satisfactory quantities from a number of different paper companies. Novins purchases over 60% of its paper requirements on a five-year, renewable contract that provides that the price shall be adjusted to competitive levels every three months. Over a period of time this type of contract has given the campany a small price advantage as compared with its open market purchases, although there have been short periods when open market purchases might have been made more cheaply. The balance of the paper requirements are purchased as needed from several different paper manufacturers.

Except for paper stock, which is purchased by the treasurer in New York, all other production supplies are purchased locally by the mill managers. Clay, color, and other materials needed for printing and finishing the paper are purchased as needed from well established suppliers. Cartons and other packaging materials are also purchased in a similar manner.

The production problem to which the company executives are now giving most attention is the most effective utilization of facilities and especially of the new plant in Pennsylvania. The new Pennsylvania plant is a completely modern, one story mill with approximately 250,000 square feet of space. It is well laid out and has a large 30,000 foot warehouse that will hold at least 4 million rolls. Wallpaper printing machinery has not changed in basic principle since the nineteenth century, so the advantages of the new mill do not lie primarily in the printing equipment. It does, however, have enclosed drying equipment, modern methods of handling raw materials and finished stock including packaging machinery, modern equipment for mixing and grinding clay and color, and special facilities for book making.

At present, the Pennsylvania mill has 10 printing machines installed, and these have been operated on a single shift. The mill was designed for 6 additional machines; if these were installed and the entire mill run on a two-shift basis, it would have an overall capacity of 32 printing machine shifts. Moreover, the plant site provides ample room for building additions to the present mill.

This new mill has created some serious financial problems for the company. When it was originally conceived, the estimated cost was $1,500,000. However, due to the rise in construction costs between 1946 and the completion date of 1949, and a number of changes in design, the investment to date in the mill has been $2,400,000. The 6 additional printing machines, using equipment already on hand, will cost approximately $500,000 installed. (If the New York mill were dismantled and certain equipment still in good condition transferred to Pennsylvania, these 6 additional printing machines might be installed for $400,000.)

The old Susquehanna mill has now been completely dismantled and the property sold. Much of its value had already been written off on the company books. A residual write-off of about $300,000 was charged directly to surplus in 1948. In addition there was about $150,000 moving and setup expense charged to the profit and loss in 1949.

The original Novins mill, located in upstate New York, consists of 2 buildings, the larger of which is over 50 years old. The old building is 4 floors high, and its layout and type of construction make adequate work spaces difficult to obtain. The equipment and work spaces are such that some of the rolling has to be performed as a separate operation and part of this is done by hand. Drying is slow because of air distribution difficulties.

The second building is now used primarily for warehousing finished stock, sample book assembly, and other auxiliary activities. Here again low ceilings and small bays make effective use of space difficult. Theoretically, 4 million rolls could be stored, but material handling costs would be high if the building were filled to this capacity.

There are now 20 printing machines in the New York mill. Due to inadequate space and work flow, only half of these can be operated on the second shift, which means that this mill has a theoretic capacity of 30 machine shifts.

The New York mill has a net book value of $500,000. Because both buildings and equipment are old, it is doubtful that the mill could be sold as an operating unit. If it were dismantled, the maximum salvage value would be $100,000. Members of the Novins family own some property in the vicinity of the mill, and this property might be difficult to sell if the mill itself were shut down.

The production cost per hundred rolls experienced during the last two years are indicated in the following table:

Average Production Costs—per 100 Rolls

	1949-50	1948-49
Materials costs	$ 6.32	$ 6.50
Direct labor	2.30	2.02
Factory burden	5.11	4.03
Design expense	.63	.58
	$14.36	$13.13

It will be noticed that costs jumped sharply the last year, primarily because of the increase of factory burden. This reflects the high overhead charges at the new Pennsylvania mill, which was operated at only a part of its estimated capacity. In fact, the accounting figures showed an unabsorbed "variance" of about $250,000 from estimated standards, due to the operation of the Pennsylvania mill at the low level. If activity at the Pennsylvania mill had permitted the achievement of the estimated standard, the average factory burden for all Company operations would be about $3.85 per hundred rolls instead of $5.11.

An economical level of operation at the Pennsylvania mill depends upon several things. In addition to obtaining the necessary volume of sales, the remaining 6 printing machines should be installed and the necessary increase in labor force recruited and trained. Because of the strained financial conditions, executives of the company are hesitant to make further investment in the new mill at this time. Problems of recruiting additional labor are discussed under *Personnel policies.*

Although there are difficulties to be overcome before the new mill can operate at a high level, the president of Novins is interested in exploring several possibilities. One possibility is to close down the New York mill and carry on all production at the new Pennsylvania mill. Preliminary estimates indicate net savings in overhead of $350,000 per year if the New York mill were shut down and completely disposed of. If the New York mill were shut down but held for a possible reopening later, savings in overhead would be approximately $300,000 per year. This figure is significant because several company executives question whether the new Pennsylvania mill could turn out as much product as the company sold in the 1948-49 year, even if it had 16 printing machines and operated on a two-shift basis (a third shift is impractical). Clearly, if company sales move substantially above 30,000,000 rolls per year, the Pennsylvania mill alone could not produce the total volume.

Another possibility is to transfer much, but not all, of the production to the Pennsylvania mill, thereby permitting it to operate at an economical level, and also to keep the New York mill in operation. Under such an arrangement, there would have to be a minimum level of activity at New York in order to justify the expense of running the auxiliary equipment, warehouse, etc.

A comparison of the estimated factory overhead under the three alternatives is shown in the table on page 904. Figures are given for both a 20-million roll and a 30-million roll level of operation.

Because of the poor profit showing last year, company management is anxious to take some steps that will cut its production costs.

Estimated Factory Burden per Year for Alternative Mill Usages

	20,000,000-ROLL PRODUCTION	30,000,000-ROLL PRODUCTION
A. Present set-up—both mills	$1,000,000	$1,200,000
B. Pennsylvania mill alone—16 machines, two shifts as needed	650,000	750,000
C. Both mills—most production in Pennsylvania:		
Minimum practical operation at New York mill:	$250,000	$300,000
Balance of production at Pennsylvania mill .... (16 machines)	600,000	650,000
Total burden, both mills	850,000	950,000

Personnel policies

Novins Wallpaper Company has not attempted to refine and write down personnel policies. Company executives point out that the peak employment of the company was about 500 persons and that currently there are fewer than 400 people on the payroll. Many of these employees, particularly in the New York plant, have worked for the company for many years, and in general company executives think of personnel problems in terms of individual personalities.

The task of recruiting and training employees for the new Pennsylvania plant has been the major personnel problem during the past year. Most of the jobs in a wallpaper plant are only semiskilled and wage rates throughout the industry are based on pay for this type of worker. Nevertheless, it is necessary that each man understand his own job and that the men work together so as to secure coordinated operations.

Several of the more skilled workers and supervisors moved from the old Pennsylvania plant to the new one, but over three fourths of the help consists of new employees. Since the wallpaper industry is comparatively small, none of these new employees had previous experience in a wallpaper mill. Partly because of the newness of the job, and also because the wages are pitched to the semiskilled level, there has been considerable turnover. When sales fell off and production was cut back in the New York mill, the company encouraged several of its employees who were laid off to transfer to the new Pennsylvania mill. The men have been reluctant to make the shift and only two of them took up this opportunity for more stable employment.

The company has a profit-sharing plan instituted over ten years ago. Under this plan, 10% of net profits, over and above a 5% return on preferred stock and a 6% return on common stock, is set aside for employees. This fund is divided equally among all employees who have worked over six months during the preceding year. The profits have not been large enough in most years to make the individual shares in the profit-sharing fund very significant.

Aside from profit-sharing, the company provides no direct financial incentives for its plant workers. Executives have given some thought to installing such incentives at the new Pennsylvania mill but abandoned the plan, at least temporarily, when the cost of setting reliable output standards was estimated. Moreover, it is recognized that for many of the jobs a group incentive would be more appropriate than an individual incentive. The possibility of setting up incentives for supervisors based on spoilage, quality production, labor costs, and perhaps other factors is still under consideration.

The company has a union shop agreement with the United Wallpaper Craftsmen and Workers of North America (A. F. of L.). This union has organized most of the large wallpaper companies. For a number of years, the basic company contract has been negotiated annually by the Wallpaper Institute Labor Relations Committee, which negotiates with the union on an industry-wide basis. Company executives favor an industry-wide contract because it tends to prevent any one company from being at a marked advantage or disadvantage with respect to labor costs. On the other hand, it may force the company to make concessions that it might not otherwise grant.

Grievances and other local matters are, of course, worked out between the union and the local mill manager. There was a strike for a few weeks at the old Pennsylvania plant four years ago. No significant stoppages have occurred since that time. The company has tried to secure friendly union relationships at the new mill, but the process of bringing in new help and establishing jobs in a new situation has given rise to a number of ticklish negotiations. Neither the local supervisors nor the union leaders have shown any interest in union-management cooperation with a view to cutting costs or stepping up production.

The company grants two-week vacations as well as the standard holidays in accordance with provisions in the industry-wide agreement. It has not gone beyond this agreement in making any provisions for retirement, sick benefits, hospitalization, and the like. The feeling of company executives is that they are already giving workers all they can afford under the union contract and that benefits in addition to those so required would not be particularly helpful.

Financial policies

The financial structure of the Novins Wallpaper Company before construction of the new Pennsylvania plant was started is shown in the balance sheet for June, 1946. At that time, the company fixed assets were largely depreciated and book value on these assets represented only 27% of the total. The company was in a highly liquid position, with current assets almost four times as large as current liabilities; in fact, the cash alone exceeded current liabilities.

Stock of the company has always been closely held by not more than about 50 stockholders. The present common stock and preferred stock represent equities in the two companies that were merged in 1933. Stock has not been used to secure outside capital for many years. Most of the expansion up to 1946 was financed through undistributed earnings, and bank loans were used only occasionally to finance seasonal inventories.

The decision to build a new plant has, of course, resulted in a major change in the use and sources of capital. As originally planned, this modernization of facilities was to be financed through a $1½ million, 10-year loan. This loan was obtained directly from an insurance company in the fall of 1947. The original agreement was somewhat complex and provided, among other things, for 4% interest, repayment of $150,000 a year commencing in 1949, and also a number of protective clauses such as a prohibition of pledging of any company assets for any other company debts, discontinuance of dividends if net working capital fell below $1,000,000, carrying of adequate insurance, etc.

Novins Wallpaper Company
Balance Sheets, 1946 and 1950

	JUNE 30, 1950	JUNE 30, 1946
Cash	$ 243,000	$ 689,000
Receivables (net)	526,000	611,000
Inventories	1,184,000	748,000
Total Current Assets	$1,953,000	$2,048,000
Deferred Charges	291,000	179,000
Land, Building & Equipment	3,082,000	804,000
Total Assets	$5,326,000	$3,031,000
Accounts Payable	$ 288,000	$ 261,000
Accrued Items	196,000	327,000
Bank Loan	800,000	....
Term-Loan—Current	150,000	....
Total Current Liabilities	$1,434,000	$ 588,000
Long Term Loan	1,350,000	....
Total Liabilities	$2,784,000	$ 588,000
Preferred Stock 5%	600,000	600,000
Common Stock	1,000,000	1,000,000
Undistributed Earnings	942,000	843,000
Total Liabilities and Equity	$5,326,000	$3,031,000

This financial plan did not prove to be adequate. As already noted, the cost of the plant proved to be almost a million dollars more than anticipated and then the sharp drop in earnings in 1947-48 put an unexpected strain on cash resources. These two factors forced the company to turn increasingly to its bank for financial help, and by the middle of 1949 the bank debt was $1,000,000 and the term loan was $1,350,000, making a total of $2,350.000.

Company executives had hoped that good profits in 1949-50 plus the depreciation charge of approximately $200,000 would enable the company to make the regular payment on the term loan and also reduce the bank debt. The sharp drop in sales and earnings made this impossible. After considerable negotiation with both the insurance company and the bank, the long term was again increased to $1,500,000 and arrangements made to borrow up to $800,000 from the bank. The interest rate on the insurance company loan has been increased to 5%; more stringent restrictions placed on the payment of any dividends (dividend payments of 1948-49 were possible under the term loan agreement only because the company was not technically liable for a substantial part of the building cost until it was ready for operation); and the bank loan is supposed to be further reduced as inventory is liquidated.

The effect of these and other financial changes is shown above in the company balance sheet for June 30, 1950.

Dividends were paid regularly on both common and preferred stock each year after the financial reorganization in 1940 until 1950. During most of this period the dividends were approximately 50% of the net profits for the year. An exception was made in 1947-48, when dividends exceeded profits by $12,000. The directors felt justified in this action inasmuch as payments for the preceding year had been very much less than the usual 50% division. The preferred stock issue is 5% cumulative with a further provision that the preferred stockholders may elect three fourths of the board of directors if preferred dividends are 3 years or more in arrears. A majority of the preferred stock is now held in trust accounts, with bankers or other individuals not connected with company management acting as trustees.

Dividend Payments, 1940-1950

	PREFERRED STOCK	COMMON STOCK	TOTAL
1940-41	$30,000	$ 30,000	$ 60,000
1941-42	30,000	50,000	80,000
1942-43	30,000	30,000	60,000
1943-44	30,000	40,000	70,000
1944-45	30,000	40,000	70,000
1945-46	30,000	80,000	110,000
1946-47	30,000	100,000	130,000
1947-48	30,000	80,000	110,000
1948-49	30,000	100,000	130,000
1949-50	—0—	—0—	—0—

No single person holds a controlling interest in the common stock. Through gifts, inheritance, and private sales it has been divided so that the largest block is now 12% of the total. Men now active in the company management own or control 23%. At no time has there been any challenge or serious question by stockholders of the existing company management.

The company profit and loss statement for the last two fiscal years is shown in the accompanying table.

Novins Wallpaper Company
Profit and Loss Statements, 1948-49 and 1949-50

	1949-50	1948-49
Net Sales	$3,321,000	$5,387,000
Cost of Goods Sold	2,797,000	3,964,000
Gross Profit	$ 524,000	$1,423,000
Expenses:		
Selling	241,000	301,000
Freight Out	96,000	134,000
Sales Promotion	89,000	147,000
Administration	210,000	228,000
Total	$ 636,000	$ 810,000
Operating Profit (Loss)	$ (112,000)	$ 613,000
Other Income and Expense, Net	34,000	(151,000)
Profit before Income Taxes (Loss)	$ (78,000)	$ 462,000
Income Taxes (Credit)	(41,000)	191,000
Net Profit (Loss)	$ (37,000)	$ 271,000

ORGANIZATION AND EXECUTIVE PERSONNEL

The administrative organization of Novins Wallpaper Company is indicated on the accompanying chart. The titles suggest the nature of the duties performed. One or two comments are needed to understand the main relationships between the several divisions and executives.

The company maintains its general office in New York City. The president, sales manager, and treasurer are all located in this office; all central accounting and financial matters are handled here, and sales work is directed from this central point. The manager of the New York mill and the designer are both located at the mill in upstate New York. The third center of company activity is at the new Pennsylvania mill. In general, these three offices operate somewhat independently of each other. The production-planning director and the cost accountant are in close touch with the mills, and the designer and the two mill managers frequently come to New York for conferences with other executives.

At first glance it may appear that the company has a rather complete organization with auxiliary and service divisions as well as operating divisions. In this connection this should be noted that there was a substantial reduction in staff personnel two years ago in an effort to cut down overhead expenses. The research department and industrial engineering department were completely eliminated and the number of people in the New York office and the auxiliary units at the mills were substantially reduced. Most jobs at the mill, such as production control, purchasing agent, personnel director, and inspector, are performed by single individuals. The treasurer at least believes that this cut in staff personnel has made it particularly difficult for the company to maintain good service with its customers. This service problem is, of course, complicated by having operations performed in three separate locations.

The board of directors is composed of the president, treasurer, vice-president (the New York mill manager), company attorney, and a man from a trust company that handles the estates of two deceased stockholders. This board meets only when necessary to perform legal functions. Policy and major operating decisions are really made by the company executives, and the legal counsel is called in for advice when legal issues are involved.

The following brief comments regarding each of the key executives will provide background for the present company policies and problems.

President

The president is 57 years old and has held this position since the company reorganization in 1940. He formerly was sales manager and has spent most of his life with Novins Wallpaper Company. He is a man of considerable personal energy, and his confidence and enthusiasm about the prospects of the company provide considerable stimulus to other executives. Having had most of his experience in the sales end of the business, he does not undertake detailed supervision of production operations.

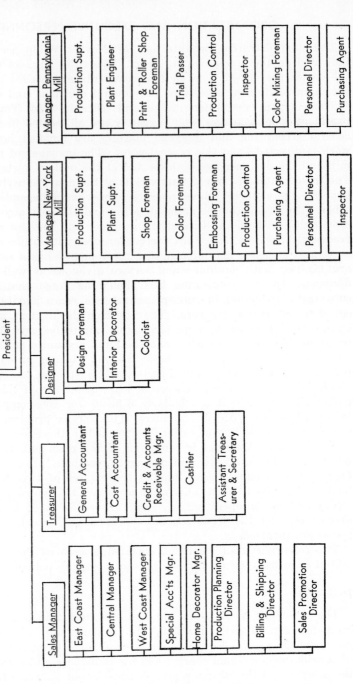

Novins Wallpaper Company
Administrative Organization

Sales manager

The sales manager, 52 years of age, is very well known in the wallpaper trade. He takes an active part in many conventions and spends a great deal of his time on the road. His personal charm and acquaintanceship is undoubtedly a major selling asset for the company. His thinking regarding selling activities reflects to a considerable extent the things that he does well personally.

Treasurer

The treasurer is a comparatively young man, 41 years old, who joined the company five years ago after experience in public accounting and in contract renegotiation for the Navy. He has shown a broad grasp of company problems, and the president uses him frequently as a man to handle special assignments or to make special studies. The treasurer has been active on several committees of the Wallpaper Institute. He does not, of course, have the years of background in either selling or producing wallpaper, but he knows enough about the business already so that he can discuss problems in both these areas effectively with other company executives and other men in the industry.

Designer

The designer, who is 49 years old, has had formal training in designing and worked in a number of different companies manufacturing furniture and draperies. He was brought into the Novins organization in 1943 when he worked under the New York mill manager. Two years later, the president decided that designing was such an important function that the man in charge of it should report directly to the chief executive; nevertheless, the New York mill manager continues to give him advice. It is difficult, of course, to appraise the ability of a designer, since a considerable number of the patterns are an adaptation of previously popular patterns or designs used by other wallpaper companies or in other interior decorations. Moreover, no designer is right all the time. The record and reputation of Novins during the last few years would indicate that this particular man is performing his duties very competently.

Manager of New York Mill

This mill manager, who also carries the title of vice-president, is 62 years old and the senior executive in the Company. He is a member of the Novins family and has spent all of his working life in and around the New York mill. At one time it was hoped that he would take over the new Pennsylvania mill, but he made it clear that he would not move from upstate New York. He is the largest stockholder in the company. While he was in full agreement regarding the construction of the new Pennsylvania mill, he feels strongly that the New York mill should continue to be operated. In general, he takes a production point of view regarding company problems; however, he has also been very much interested in design and gives frequent advice to the designer.

Manager of the Pennsylvania Mill

This man, 42 years old, worked for many years in the New York mill. He was then transferred to be assistant manager of the old Pennsylvania mill and served as its manager for the two years prior to the time it was closed down. He is thoroughly familiar with production of wallpaper. He personally is not particularly imaginative about new production techniques, but he seeks outside advice on these matters and has a practical view of what will and what won't work. His formal education was limited to high school, and his primary interest lies in the mechanical and technical end of the business.

QUESTIONS

1. Assume that the president of the Novins Wallpaper Company has asked you for an objective plan for increasing company sales. He tells you that he feels the company situation is critical and that he would be glad to have any practical suggestions which will aid sales volume and thereby increase profits. Outline your recommendations.

2. A home decorating consultant recommends that the company put heavy emphasis on sales of ready-pasted wallpaper. (a) Do you think this is a wise move? (b) What adjustment in policies, in addition to the changed product line, should be made if this recommendation is accepted? (c) Are there other types of wall covering which you believe should be added to the company line?

3. Should the company increase or reduce the types of customers to whom it sells products directly? For example, should it actively seek business from mail-order houses or other outlets not now solicited? Should it discontinue sales to subjobbers? Do you have other suggestions for dealing with the issues of multiplicity of types of customers?

4. Do you believe changes should be made in company pricing practices? What would your answer to this question be if the Antitrust Division of the U. S. Department of Justice charges members of the Wallpaper Institute with monopolistic price fixing?

5. The Novins Wallpaper Company, as one of the prominent firms in its industry, is in a position to influence to some extent the activities of the Wallpaper Institute. What type of program should the company urge for the Institute? What steps, if any, can the company take to get other wallpaper manufacturers to support this program? How much reliance should the company put on Institute action?

6. Outline the sales promotion program that you recommend Novins Wallpaper Company follow in 1950-51. If the company had no long-term debt, would your answer be the same?

7. What steps should be taken to stabilize production and/or sales? Should production planning be more formalized? If so, explain what you think should be done.

8. How are management problems of the company complicated by the fact that there are three centers of activity: New York City, upstate New York mill, and Pennsylvania mill? Do you agree with a proposal that the executive offices be located at the Pennsylvania mill? Why?

9. What actions should the company take to achieve more effective utilization of its new mill?

10. Outline a program to be installed in 1950-1951 for cutting production costs. If your proposals may have an adverse effect on other phases of company operations, explain why you think the benefits of your plan outweigh the disadvantages.

11. Assuming a decision were made to consolidate all production in the new Pennsylvania mill by July, 1952, what changes in personnel policies do you recommend be adopted (a) now and (b) when the New York mill is closed?

12. Do you think direct financial incentives for production workers should be installed in the near future? Justify your answer.

13. What dividend policy should Novins Wallpaper Company follow during the next few years? Be sure to state and justify important assumptions you have made in formulating your recommended dividend policy. What changes, if any, do you think preferred stockholders would insist upon if they elected a majority of the board of directors?

14. (a) Outline plans you recommend for the company to get out of its present financial difficulties. Be sure to consider whether these plans are workable in terms of company relations with its bank, the insurance company extending the long-term loan, preferred stockholders, common stockholders, and key members of management. (b) Express this plan in annual source and application of funds budgets for the next five years.

15. In view of the financial difficulties the company has gotten into during the last few years, should the treasurer be fired? Justify your answer.

16. What changes in organization do you believe are desirable to facilitate your program for the company? Explain. Do you believe new key executives are needed?

17. It has been suggested that Novins Wallpaper Company seek a merger with a paint company having distribution over at least most of the same territory covered by Novins. Do you recommend such action? Why?

8 ... FREDERICK & FRANK

Frederick & Frank, a management consulting firm with its main office in Cleveland, Ohio, was founded in 1923. By World War II a second generation of partners had taken over management of the firm. With a few changes, these partners continued to guide the business until a little over a year ago. At that time, the last two of the "old guard" completed arrangements to transfer their interests to a third generation of senior partners. Mr. Pendleton, age 51, has been the top man in the firm's work with the paper industry for several years. Mr. Buchele, age 41, and Mr. Corbin, age 43, are the key figures in the new management; they have the major financial interest in the partnership and, although younger than some other members of the staff, they are best known among potential clients.

Both Mr. Buchele and Mr. Corbin have engineering training. Mr. Corbin is the son of a former partner and has worked for Frederick & Frank all his business career. Mr. Buchele was an industrial engineer at Procter & Gamble for six years prior to joining the firm.

The transition to the new management has been completed, and all of the consulting engagements recently performed by the firm were obtained by present partners and staff members. The new partners feel that they have demonstrated that the firm can operate successfully under the present management, but they are far from satisfied with the results of the past year. Billings were maintained at about the same level as in the preceding five years, around $500,000 annually. Operating profit (net return before bonuses and distribution to owners), however, was only 8% of billings. The partners are naturally anxious to improve this result.

Competition in management consulting. Management consulting, while a fledgling compared with the professions of medicine, law, and engineering, has experienced a substantial growth in its fifty years of existence. For a time during and immediately following World War II, billings of the entire profession increased at a rate of about 10% a year. Recently, the increases slowed down to around 3% per annum largely because many clients expanded their internal staff to do particularly the more routine type of work. On the other hand, the number of companies using consultants and the variety of problems on which consultants give advice have risen. The Association of Consulting Management Engineers—the leading spokesman for the profession—estimates that industry currently is spending about $650,000,000 annually for outside consultants, and that nearly half of this total—about $300 million— goes to general management consultants. Scientific and technical specialists account for most of the balance. (These figures do not include legal fees, financing fees, or any commissions that are included as part of the cost of acquiring an asset.)

While the total volume of management consulting work is large and growing, the number of firms seeking business is also large. Management consulting is a highly personalized, intangible service, consisting solely of giving advice. No clear definition exists of just who is and who is not a management consultant, and the term is used quite loosely by people who occasionally give advice but may also earn their livelihood in some other manner. The Association of Management Consulting Engineers estimates that 2,500 consulting firms are active in the United States and Canada, in addition to several thousand individuals who devote full or part time to this work. Except for a dozen or more large firms doing annual business of over a million dollars, the vast majority of consulting firms are quite small. Most of these firms have developed reputations in a particular industry or special activity, for example, location of suburban shopping centers or company retirement plans. Other firms seek to serve small business in a locality such as Hawaii. Consequently, for any potential consulting work there are always several firms or individuals eager to serve.

Consultants may be used on all kinds of management problems—for diagnosis, for suggesting alternatives, for estimating costs and results of various alternatives, and for recommending a particular course of action. Frequently the consultant assists in the installation of his recommendation, but company management makes the basic decisions and carries responsibility for their executives. A recent survey of the Financial Executives' Research Foundation found the type of work performed in over a thousand engagements distributed as follows: [1]

General Management, Organization and Personnel	385
Financial	178
Marketing	188
Manufacturing	309
Technical	40
Office Systems	65

Large business concerns use management consultants more than small companies. For instance, in the survey just referred to, almost three quarters of the 364 companies replying to a questionnaire had used management consultants during the preceding three years. However, the ratio was 90% for companies with sales of more than $100 million, whereas it dropped to 60% for companies with sales under $10 million.

---

[1] Wilson Seney, *Effective Use of Business Consultants*, pp. 8–9.

Sales of companies surveyed (in $1,000,000)	Number of companies replying	Percent of companies that used consultants in previous 3 years
Over 100	90	90
10 to 100	162	74
Under 10	57	60
Total all companies, including 155 of unknown size	364	74

Typically, the use of management consultants is associated with *change*. Perhaps the company is in trouble, but more likely a fast-growing company wants expert assistance in moving more rapidly to its objectives. The following table, again from the Financial Executives' Survey, throws an interesting light on the reasons for using consultants. In written questionnaires, companies gave the pat reason for using consultants—special know-how and independent opinion. The more penetrating interviews, however, indicated that other motives are likely to be present. The fresh point of view of a consultant, his freedom to concentrate on getting the job done, his experience in putting changes into effect, and his capacity to train company personnel provide an important supplement to busy company executives.

Reasons Given for Using Consultants

	% of Total Responses	
	Questionnaires	Interviews
Stimulate change	2%	11%
Get results	8	13
Experience with implementing change .	3	22
Independent opinion	17	14
Special skills and know-how	64	23
Training	4	13
Confidential	2	4
Total of those using consultants ...	100%	100%

Frederick & Frank enjoys a well-established position in the growing, changing profession of management consulting. It is significantly larger than a great majority of firms in the field, although considerably smaller than the leading firms, several of which were established since the founding of Frederick & Frank. With a record of forty years of service, Frederick & Frank is much older than most of its competitors. It has long been a member of the Association of Consulting Management Engineers, which has a somewhat exclusive membership of about fifty of the leading *general* management consulting firms. Mr. Buchele and Mr. Corbin are well aware of the eminence of their firm and are anxious to take full advantage of their heritage.

Services and clients. Frederick & Frank started work in the production management field and for many years most of its engagements have been in this general area. The firm has had many engagements dealing with output standards, production control, inventory control, and all sorts of incentive plans for production and office workers. It is well known for its work with incentives for maintenance workers—a particularly tricky task. Plans for quality control are often associated with incentive plans. Layouts and materials handling studies are made for both plant and warehouses, and the layout work has been extended into office problems. At times the firm has been asked to make a production engineering study of an entire new plant, dealing with capacity, layout, and services, as well as various plant controls. On various occasions, clients have asked the firm to make overall cost and economy studies with respect to plant consolidations and to the opening of new branch plants. Related to this type of study have been economic analyses of markets and transportation costs.

To do effective work in the areas just described, Frederick & Frank has often become involved in related functions. For example, cost control has led to cost accounting. Frequently, new processes and new controls have required training of employees and supervisors, so the firm has engaged in this type of work. However, the firm does not get into psychological testing and morale surveys, nor is it active in the union relations field, partly because most unions think of the firm as "efficiency experts." The firm has conducted a number of job evaluation studies, although this work is largely confined to the paper industry. The firm has frequently studied plant organization. Often such organization studies involved the relationships of production with engineering and research and with physical distribution. Close contacts have been developed between members of the firm and managements of various companies, and in a variety of cases—mostly small companies—the consultant has been asked to become an overall management advisor to the client.

In a special category is the work of Frederick & Frank for the paper industry. Over the years the firm has done a great deal of work in this industry and has included on its staff several men who have intimate knowledge of the technology and other cost factors as well as acquaintanceship with executives in many paper companies. As a result, the firm is often called upon to deal with more diverse subjects in the paper industry than in other fields.

Most of the clients of Frederick & Frank are manufacturing concerns. Only occasionally has the firm been engaged by financial concerns or retail establishments. Normally its clients are located in the Mid-West or in the Middle Atlantic States, except in the paper industry where a client may ask Frederick & Frank to work in its Southern or West Coast mills.

During World War II and the succeeding readjustment, the services of Frederick & Frank were in high demand and the firm prospered. Clients were making many shifts in their product lines, capacity, and technology. Their own executives were hard-pressed and welcomed assistance with the special problems accompanying transition. Frequently a rapid change was called for, and this made installation costs relatively less significant.

After some ups and downs during the Korean crisis, the volume of work obtained by Frederick & Frank stabilized. Profits dropped. The principal explanations of this change in trend are not hard to find. (1) Potential clients were involved in fewer major changes in production operations, or at least there was not the same urgency to make these changes rapidly. (2) Many of the larger companies increased their internal staff to perform many of the activities done in preceding years by outside consultants. (3) Competition from other consultants increased, especially from one- or two-man firms. The war had produced many executives with substantial experience in changing production operations, and some of these men chose to become independent consultants. Typically, they worked with low overhead and concentrated their promotion effort on a few companies where they could establish close friendships. (4) More recently, the Management Services Divisions of eight of the leading public accounting firms have created additional competition.

Of course, as already noted, Frederick & Frank has the advantage of a long-standing reputation, and large clients may call upon the firm for special counsel. Often, however, these engagements involve primarily a principal or partner, with the client's own staff doing most of the "legwork"; the day of the big, long job involving months of continuous work for consulting staff men has largely disappeared.

Consulting fees. Frederick & Frank's basic method for establishing its fees is in line with usual practice in the management consulting profession. Fees are based on a per diem rate for all men who work on the engagement plus out-of-pocket expenses for travel, preparation of reports, and the like. For well-defined engagements, a client is given in advance an estimate of the total cost based on the projected man-days of work involved. Frederick & Frank would prefer to have the final fee based on the time actually expended, but clients frequently ask for a more definite commitment. In these circumstances, the firm states a maximum fee with the understanding that if the total per diem charge is less than the maximum, the lower figure will be used.

When price appears to be a significant factor in obtaining an engagement, Frederick & Frank may knowingly quote a low maximum, which means that its normal per diem rates probably will not be covered if the firm secures the assignment. Analysis of experience in a recent period indicated that the fee for approximately 30% of the engagements did not cover the standard billing rates. In most instances, however, the difference between the accumulated per diem charges and the fee actually charged was less than 10%. In several other cases the firm deliberately quoted a low figure because it was anxious to establish relationships with a new client.

The per diem rates used by Frederick & Frank are $250 for partners and junior partners, $200 for principals, and $150 for consultants. These rates are in line with those charged by other well-established consultants, although the rate for partners may be somewhat below the average.

(Broadly speaking, the earnings of a consultant are on a par with earnings of the upper-level executives they advise.) The smaller, less well-established firms may have per diem rates 20 to 30% lower. This comparison is hard to draw, however, because it is not clear whether an individual consultant should be compared with a partner or a staff consultant.

The senior partners of Frederick & Frank feel that price should not be the primary basis for obtaining engagements. Most clients that engage Frederick & Frank do so because they have confidence in the quality of work that will be performed. As with an individual selecting a personal physician, confidence that the work will be well done is more important than saving a few dollars on the fee. With this objective in mind, the partners feel that their present fee structure is "about right," particularly if they could reduce the number of jobs on which per diem rates are not earned.

Business development. The major way Frederick & Frank obtains new business is through personal contacts of members of the firm. About two thirds of the present engagements are with clients Frederick & Frank has served sometime in the past. To keep such business coming in requires an occasional lunch or some other kind of contact with key executives in client companies.

A large portion of the new clients are referred to Frederick & Frank by former clients, bankers, lawyers, or other influential people whose recommendation is sought by the potential client. Consequently, a favorable reputation with such individuals is important in obtaining new business. Of course, some engagements are obtained by direct contact of Frederick & Frank personnel with potential new clients. However, the number of such firms is so large that the firm has long followed a policy of attempting to be favorably known among influential people rather than by making numerous direct contacts with companies whose interest in services such as those rendered by Frederick & Frank is unknown.

All of these numerous personal contacts are made by partners and other members of the consulting staff. The firm never has maintained separate salesmen, believing that successful professional work depends heavily upon the confidence established between the client and the consultant who at least supervises the engagement.

As a member of the Association of Consulting Management Engineers, Frederick & Frank is bound by its code of professional ethics. Included in this code are the following provisions:

1. We will publicize our firm or services only in a manner upholding the dignity of the profession. We will present our qualifications to prospective clients solely in terms of our ability, experience, and reputation. We will not guarantee any specific amount of cost reduction or increase in profits from our efforts, nor will we accept

an engagement where fee is related to any cost reduction that may result.

2. We will neither accept nor pay fees to persons outside our firm for referral of clients. Nor will we accept fees, commissions, or other valuable consideration from individuals or organizations whose equipment, supplies, or services we may recommend in the course of our work with clients.

3. We will negotiate for possible work with a client where another firm is currently engaged only when we are assured there is no reason for conflict between the two engagements. . . . We will review for a client the work of another consulting firm currently employed by him only with the other consultant's knowledge.

The provision regarding publicity restricts Frederick & Frank to dignified announcements merely listing the kinds of work the firm undertakes, which may be sent by direct mail or inserted in newspapers and trade journals. As in the accounting and law professions, such announcements play a very minor part in attracting new business.

Actually, Frederick & Frank is subject to considerable competition that it considers unethical. Some management consultants promote their business aggressively. The most notable and successful of such competitors is George S. May Company, the largest management consulting firm in the world. This company violates not only the provisions of the Association code quoted above, but also other provisions relating to qualifications of personnel, etc. George S. May Company uses high-pressure sales promotion tactics and does not hesitate to promise substantial cost reductions. All management consultants seeking to make such consulting a "profession" suffer from the tactics used by George S. May Company and similar promoters. Frederick & Frank is particularly hard-pressed because its type of work lends itself to claims for immediate cost reductions.

Recently, Frederick & Frank has also suffered from competition of public accounting firms. In addition to making independent audits, for many years these firms have advised clients about systems and procedures. While there has been some overlap on matters such as cost accounting and budgetary control, in general the "appropriate sphere of activity" of public accountants and management consultants has been widely accepted. However, with the advent of electronic data processing, the public accounting firms greatly expanded their staffs to work on effective applications of the new equipment and also on operations research. Once launched, these management service divisions have expanded into almost all phases of management consulting. Promotional activities of the public accounting firms is professional, since it must conform to the standards of the accounting profession. Nevertheless, many management consultants consider this competition unethical on the grounds that (a) the public accountant has an inside track to the company needs and company executives as a result of his auditing work, and (b) an inherent conflict of interests exists between making an objective, independent audit and being an intimate advisor on management action. The contention is that an auditor may be less than objective reviewing his own handiwork (or potential handiwork), and that an outside auditor has undue potential power to get recommendations adopted, especially over middle-level executives.

For many years, Frederick & Frank described itself on letterheads and other publicity as a firm of "management engineers," a term widely used in the early days of management consulting. In fact, most members of Frederick & Frank's staff had formal training as engineers. Over the years, the term "management engineers" has become less common because (a) "managment consultants" became a respectable term and (b) professional engineering societies objected because often management consulting firms—especially those working in marketing and personnel—were not qualified to use the term "engineer." In keeping with this trend, Frederick & Frank changed its designation to "management consultants" five years ago. However, it still maintains a nominal firm of "Frederick & Frank—Engineers." This latter title is necessary in dealing with certain government agencies and in preparing certifications for financial and other documents. Engagements done under the engineering banner are performed by men qualified to use this designation, but no separate staff or separate office is maintained for this purpose.

To keep the firm's name before the public and to help establish reputations of the consulting staff, all professional personnel are encouraged to write articles for trade papers, to make speeches, and to become active in various professional and civic associations. Reprints of articles are mailed to many executives and serve as the primary impersonal promotional media of the firm. Essentially, promotion of new business follows a "Barkus is willin'" approach.

Organization. For many years, Frederick & Frank operated with its main office in Cleveland and a second office in New York, which over time became the center for work with the paper industry. In an effort to maintain closer personal contact with prospective clients, two additional offices have been opened: Chicago seven years ago and Cincinnati two years ago. Especially smaller clients who cannot afford large fees and often need help with fairly standard problems are contacted through these new offices.

Three levels are recognized within the professional staff: partners (including one junior partner), four principals, and ten consultants. Each engagement is placed under the personal supervision of a principal or a partner. Additional staff members are assigned according to the requirements of the job and their availability. Frequently men stationed in one office work under the supervision of a man from another office. A principal may serve as supervisor on one engagement and as simply a staff man on another. In effect, a new team is composed for each engagement, and a man finds himself on two or three teams at the same time. The aim, of course, is to assemble the kind of talent needed for each job but to keep the total time worked to a minimum consistent with quality performance. Often a client assigns one or more of its men to work closely with the Frederick & Frank staff, which means that the total team is composed of both consultants and client personnel.

Mr. Buchele and Mr. Corbin are located in Cleveland, Mr. Pendleton in New York, and the junior partner in Chicago. The Cincinnati office is still a one-man affair, a principal of the firm who calls upon Cleveland for additional personnel as needed. As noted above, all members of the professional staff are expected to participate in the development of new business, as well as serving clients. In terms of home base, the distribution of the firm's 28 employees is as follows:

	Professional	*Nonprofessional*
Cleveland	10	6
New York	4	2
Chicago	3	2
Cincinnati	1	—
	18	10

Professional personnel. Two thirds of Frederick & Frank's consulting staff have formal training in engineering. Most of these men worked for five or ten years with industrial concerns, often in a staff capacity, before joining Frederick & Frank. The partners continue to think of this pattern as desirable background for men joining the firm—an engineering degree plus at least five years of operating experience. Additional specifications are a keen mind, integrity of character, personal initiative and drive, and an ability to work smoothly and persuasively with other people. These latter characteristics are more important than the formal training, and not all men on the staff have college degrees. Recently, two men with MBA's have been employed and they are proving to be valuable additions to the staff.

Being a small firm, Frederick & Frank has no formal training program. New staff men are given a variety of assignments and have ample opportunity to secure counsel of other men working on the same engagement. In addition, staff members are encouraged to use unassigned time for personal study. Active participation in professional associations is also encouraged. The net effect is considerable personal development through an informal process.

Recruiting and training is a continuing task because Frederick & Frank, like all consulting firms, experiences considerable turnover of staff. The kind of men selected are attractive to clients and the very process of consulting and participation in meetings and other professional activities inevitably gives the men wide exposure. Job offers are sufficiently common so that staff men have a standard joke, "Don't even talk to the man unless he offers you twice what you are now making." The policy of Frederick & Frank is not to try to match each offer a staff man receives. Instead, the man is urged to consider whether he really enjoys consulting work, particularly compared with a more monotonous and often more political environment of a company. If a man chooses consulting as a career, then Frederick & Frank hopes it offers the freedom and opportunity for a man to advance as rapidly as his interest and abilities warrant.

Frederick & Frank's salary scale is geared partly to competitive salaries and partly to per diem rates that can be charged clients. When a man joins the firm, he is usually paid about what he has been earning. He is then given raises as his time becomes more billable to clients. The other side of the picture is the billing rate. A rule of thumb in the profession (often not achieved) is that the per diem should be approximately three times a man's daily pay. This ratio is based on the fact that a consultant often works only half or two thirds of his time on billable assignments and his employers must provide office space, secretarial help, and many other overhead items. At Frederick & Frank the average salary for consultants is $12,000, for principals is $16,000, and for partners is $25,000.

In addition to salary, all regular employees of Frederick & Frank receive a bonus. The total amount of the annual bonus fund depends upon the profitability of the firm during the past year. The distribution among the members of the consulting staff is based on (a) contribution to securing work and (b) gross profits earned, that is, per diem billed to clients minus salary. The first factor receives by far the greatest weight in determining bonuses. Under normal conditions, Frederick & Frank expects bonuses for the professional staff to average 20% of the salaries.

Financial results. The first full year of operations under the new management of Frederick & Frank resulted in income and expenses as follows:

Income Statement

Gross billings		$504,000
Expenses:		
Professional salaries	$279,000	
Nonprofessional salaries	61,000	
Rent	62,000	
Public relations	28,000	
Other expenses	32,000	462,000
Operating profit		$ 42,000
Bonuses		42,000
Income for owners		$ —0—

All the partners worked very hard developing the business after the "old guard" stepped out. They are not satisfied with results to date. Mr. Buchele has expressed his expectation of a normal year to be as follows: Operating profits to be allocated 50% for bonuses and 50% to the owners; the bonus fund to be large enough to pay 20% of the professional salaries and 10% of the nonprofessional salaries. He further observes that if gross billings had been $83,000, or 16% higher, this objective could have been met. As it was, bonuses were only 14% of professional salaries and 5% of nonprofessional salaries, with nothing left over for income to the owners.

The position of the owners is not quite as dark as the statement may appear, inasmuch as the partners are the sole owners and they receive salary and a participation in the bonus. Mr. Corbin also noted that he and Mr. Buchele decided to move the Cleveland and Chicago offices into new modern buildings, which raised the rent expense $20,000 annually. This was done for prestige purposes—to give the company a new look— and cannot be expected to pay off immediately in additional business. Incidentally, Mr. Pendleton doubts that clients care where the company maintains its office.

Mr. Buchele feels that a 16% increase in billings with its present staff is an entirely reasonable objective. He has prepared the following analysis of how the average professional man in the firm spent his time during the past year:

Total days—5-day week; 52 × 5	= 260	days
Vacations, holidays, etc.—6 weeks	= 30	”
Work days available	230	”
Public relations and training—about 1/5 of total time	50	”
Available for billing	180	”
Actually billed (at $186 average)	150	”
Slack time (20% of actual)	30	”

This analysis indicates that the staff could work 20% more time on client business and still have one day a week for self-development and promotion of new business. Some idle time is unavoidable in consulting because engagements cannot be fit neatly one after another. However, Mr. Buchele believes that the 50 days allocated to training and public relations should be used to obtain this necessary flexibility. He recalls the time when he and most other younger men in the firm were occupied at least 200 days a year on client business. Incidentally, those were the days when the ratio of consultants to supervisors was about twice the present ratio, which made the net profit available to partners even higher.

Possibilities for the future. None of the partners is satisfied with the results of the past year, but enthusiastic agreement is lacking on the directions to seek improvement and how fast to move. Several possibilities are under consideration.

1. Improve present practice. Mr. Pendleton has suggested that the firm continue to try to "do better what we are already doing" at least for a year or two. He feels that the firm has done well considering the shift in top management and that only a comparatively small improvement in billings is necessary to meet the profit objectives outlined by Mr. Buchele.

Mr. Buchele and Mr. Corbin are less sanguine about this approach because they are not sure what additional steps they might take that would significantly improve the firm's position in a highly competitive field. They recognize, however, that persistent plugging has been a major factor in the success of many consulting firms.

2. Aggressively promote Frederick & Frank. Two principals believe that the firm is seriously handicapped by observing the code of ethics of the Association of Consulting Management Engineers. With some of their competitors using the "hard sell" while Frederick & Frank uses the "soft sell" approach, often the former come away with the engagements. These two men particularly believe that their firm does better work and can legitimately make strong claims for results that will be achieved. They contend that Frederick & Frank's reputation is well enough established now so that membership in the Association is no longer essential in getting work. On the other hand, aggressive sales promotion they believe would easily and quickly increase the company's billings by 25 to 50%. If the firm started in this direction, several additional steps might be taken. New branch offices could be opened that would be used at least for sales promotion purposes, and in less industrialized areas the firm might pay "finder's fees" to carefully selected individuals.

The reaction of Mr. Buchele and Mr. Corbin to this proposal is both emotional and rational. Both prefer to think of management consulting as highly professional work, like law and medicine. On the other hand, they recognize that the firm could continue to maintain the same quality of performance even though methods of obtaining new business were modified. Future clients would be better served, they believe, by Frederick & Frank than they would be if they succumbed to the wiles of George S. May Company. "If we have a good product, why not sell it?" is the issue.

This approach does involve some risk. If Frederick & Frank discovered that it was not successful in aggressive promotion, return to the present status of a distinctly professional firm would be difficult indeed. A firm's reputation among influential people takes years to develop, and unless Frederick & Frank did something dramatic it would be an uphill task to convince people that—after a period of aggressive promotion—Association standards of conduct were again being observed. In other words, not only the chances of success but also the fact that it is a one-way street should be considered in weighing this alternative.

3. Expand into international field. Management consulting is expanding rapidly in many foreign countries. While wide variation exists, in general foreign countries are at least twenty-five years behind the United States in their adoption of the concept of using outside consultants on a wide array of management problems. European countries, of course, are thoroughly familiar with industrial engineering concepts, but United States companies opening plants in Europe have found local consultants circumscribed in their point of view. Consequently, these United States concerns have sought the aid of consultants familiar with United States practice. In addition, a change in viewpoint associated with the transition to the common market has led many firms to consider the use of consultants on problems formerly considered highly confidential.

In Latin America, the shift is even more dramatic. Use of consultants is regarded as one way to catch up rapidly on a half-century of industrial development. Many men, often accountants or engineers, with only limited training are now calling themselves management consultants. But there is no doubt that the total volume of consulting work is rapidly increasing.

Frederick & Frank have made a modest move toward participating in this foreign development. The firm has a reciprocal agreement with a group of Dutch consultants for the exchange of experience and techniques. In addition, the agreement provides for limited profit-sharing on business originating on one continent but performed by the affiliate firm on the other continent (the Dutch firm works throughout northern Europe). Thus far, only a few meetings between the partners of the two firms have taken place. This arrangement can be terminated on six months' notice by either of the firms.

Performing management consulting on an international basis is much more difficult than strictly engineering work that deals with things rather than people. To overcome problems of language, knowledge of local conditions, and development of personal confidence, local nationals have to be active participants in performing the consulting service. Consequently, a substantial amount of time is required for selection, training, and supervision of foreign affiliates, especially in the early stages. If Frederick & Frank were to pursue this opportunity for development, either Mr. Buchele or Mr. Corbin and probably one of the principals would have to devote most of their time to the undertaking for at least a year.

4. Invest in research on "product development." Mr. Corbin observes that: "The concept of product life-cycles—early development, rapid growth, maturity, and decline—also fits management consulting. An embryonic idea may kick around for years, and then it finally catches hold, either because someone gives it a new twist or because a change in business conditions makes the problem important. A period of rapid growth follows. Consultants are called in freely because companies have not tooled up to deal with the new technique. This period may last three or four years. By that time every consultant in the country claims he is an expert in the field and the demand drops off because many companies have their own experts. During this maturity phase, consulting work is available but the competition is tough. You need an outstanding reputation or a very low overhead to make money at the business. Perhaps the maturity stage will last quite a period of time. Sooner or later, however, a decline occurs in the use of consultants to deal with that particular problem. We have seen it happen in budgetary control, job evaluation, and morale studies, and it is sure to happen with electronic data processing. We in Frederick & Frank should catch on to some consulting idea that is just starting its growth phase. We can't afford to dabble in every new thing that comes along, but if we picked a winner we could double our business within a year."

In line with this thinking, Mr. Pendleton suggests that the firm pick a growth industry and become recognized as experts in that field as it now is in the paper industry. "Frozen foods and plastic molding are possibilities, although specialized consultants already exist in both industries." Of course, the industry would have to be carefully examined to determine just what service Frederick & Frank might render. For example, pharmaceutical manufacturers are so predominantly concerned with discovering new products and getting them tested, patented, and on the market that they have relatively little interest in the kind of problems Frederick & Frank has traditionally dealt with. Production of television shows and movies clearly needs improved production and cost control, but producing a hit is so much more important that efficiency is pushed into the background. If there is an important role for management consultants in this industry, it has yet to be recognized.

Several years ago Frederick & Frank did give careful consideration to operations research. The conclusion was that few companies would be willing to pay consulting fees for "blue sky" projects. Large companies, it was predicted, might establish their own operations research staff and then use college professors as supplements on highly theoretical problems. (Frederick & Frank was particularly sensitive about the "unethical competition" of Case Institute professors in its home city. The feeling was that the operations research men at Case Institute were actually running a small consulting business while enjoying the tax benefits of a nonprofit educational institution.)

On the other hand, Frederick & Frank did anticipate that many of its clients would be interested in utilizing operations research techniques where they had proved to be of practical value. Consequently, Frederick & Frank has two men, a principal and a consultant, who follow closely the successful applications of operations research techniques to such problems as inventory control, production scheduling, and the like. These men are prepared to assist clients in using such tested techniques where significant savings appear likely. To date, these two men have not been overly busy with such engagements.

Another suggested field for expansion is the *management* of research and development. Many companies have increased their expenditures in this area but have not yet developed satisfactory means for planning and controlling such work. An informal check among clients about their interest in consulting services in this area showed a skepticism that much improvement could be made.

In talking about the various possibilities of new services, Mr. Buchele quipped: "If we set up a division for the management of R & D, maybe its first client should be Frederick & Frank."

5. Merger with public accounting firm. The most pressing question for the partners of Frederick & Frank regarding the future is an offer of a large public accounting company to buy out Frederick & Frank. The public accounting company already has a staff of 60 people in its various offices devoted to system analysis, installation of electronic data processing, and operations research. The company wishes to expand further into general management consulting and to hasten this process would like to buy a firm such as Frederick & Frank and also a market research organization. Hopefully, all the Frederick & Frank employees would continue with the larger organization where they could help train additional men to handle an expanded volume of business resulting from the wide contacts of the accounting comany. The partners of Frederick & Frank would be paid for their investment in the partnership (about $150,000 invested mostly in accounts receivable and a bank account) and would be given a five-year employment contract with a guaranteed minimum salary of $30,000 annually. As the business developed, presumably these men would get additional salary and bonuses. If for any reason they left the employ of the company, they would agree not to set up a competing consulting business for five years after they resigned.

The purchase offer had come unexpectedly to Mr. Buchele, Mr. Corbin, and Mr. Pendleton. They have always thought of Frederick & Frank as a separate enterprise and take pride in having risen to partnership and ownership positions in the firm. Mr. Buchele and Mr. Corbin have mixed reactions to the offer and wish to take time to assess the advantages and the disadvantages of such a move. Mr. Pendleton is afraid that he and others will be swallowed up by a "big organization." His preliminary comment was: "If we want to give up the idea of building the firm, another alternative is merely to keep ourselves busy—probably with one assistant each. The operating profit from the assistants should cover our reduced overhead, and each of us would have his own billings as clear income. Even if we worked only 150 days per year, that would be an income of $37,500—and lots of independence." Mr. Buchele and Mr. Corbin are not sure they are in as good a position as Mr. Pendleton to make such a scheme work.

QUESTIONS

Assessment of present situation:

1. Appraise the history of Frederick & Frank in terms of the product life cycle concept advanced by Mr. Corbin. Why do you think the firm developed as it has to date?

2. What are the crucial factors for future success of a management consulting firm in the United States? How does Frederick & Frank stand with respect to these factors?

Assuming the merger does not take place:

3. Would you like to work for Frederick & Frank? Why? What changes, if any, in personal policies—or other policies—do you recommend for attracting and holding competent men in the firm?

4. What are the short-range and the long-range advantages to Frederick & Frank of undertaking an aggressive promotion program? What are the disadvantages? What action do you recommend regarding this proposal?

5. What are the short-range and the long-range advantages to Frederick & Frank of becoming involved in management consulting in foreign countries? What are the disadvantages? To what extent, and how, do you recommend the firm move on this proposal?

6. What action do you recommend that Frederick & Frank take to expand the range of its services? In your answer, indicate who should do what, as well as areas of expansion.

7. How are your recommendations made in answer to Questions 3, 4, 5, and 6 interrelated? Do you have other recommendations for improving income from present practice? Can the firm carry out *all* of your proposals?

Decision regarding merger:

8. In considering the proposed merger, what obligations, if any, do you believe the partners of Frederick & Frank have toward their employees? Their clients? The management consulting profession? Do you think acceptance of the merger proposal would have an adverse effect on employees? Clients? The management consulting profession?

9. Do you recommend to Mr. Buchele, Mr. Corbin, and Mr. Pendleton that they accept the merger offer made by the public accounting company? Explain why.

Program of action:

10. Summarize the proposals you have made in answer to Questions 3 through 9 and then outline a program for the partners of Frederick & Frank to follow in carrying out these recommendations. Give particular attention to sequence and timing.

SELECTED BIBLIOGRAPHY

Chapter 1 • Approach to Central-Management Problems

DRUCKER, P. F. *The Practice of Management.* New York: Harper & Brothers, 1954, pp. 3-23 and 284-286.

FAYOL, H. *General and Industrial Management,* Storrs' translation. London: Isaac Pitman & Sons, 1949.

GORDON, R. A. *Business Leadership in the Large Corporation.* Washington: The Brookings Institution, 1944, Ch. III.

URWICK, L. *Elements of Administration.* New York: Harper & Brothers, 1944.

Chapter 2 • Dynamic Setting of Business

ALLEN, F. L. *The Big Change.* New York: Harper & Brothers, 1952.

BERLE, A. A. *The American Economic Republic.* New York: Harcourt, Brace & World, Inc., 1963.

GORDON, R. A. *Business Fluctuations,* 2nd ed. New York: Harper & Brothers, 1961, Part II.

HART, A. G., and P. B. KENEN. *Money, Debt and Economic Activity,* 3rd ed. Englewood Cliffs: Prentice-Hall, Inc., 1961, Ch. VIII, IX, and XX.

JONES, M. H. *Executive Decision Making,* rev. ed. Chicago: R. D. Irwin, Inc., 1962, Ch. 11-13.

LEWIS, J. P. *Business Conditions Analysis.* New York: McGraw-Hill Book Co., 1959, Ch. 12, 14, and 15.

Chapter 3 • Appraising the Outlook for a Company

ABRAMSON, A. G., and R. H. MACK (eds.). *Business Forecasting in Practice.* New York: John Wiley & Sons, 1956.

GORDON, R. A. *Business Fluctuations,* 2nd ed. New York: Harper & Brothers, 1961, Ch. 17.

LEWIS, J. P. *Business Conditions Analysis.* New York: McGraw-Hill Book Co., 1959, Ch. 16.

STEINER, G. A. *Managerial Long-Range Planning.* New York: McGraw-Hill Book Co., 1963, Ch. 2, 3, 8, and 13.

WRIGHT, W. *Forecasting for Profit, A Technique for Business Management.* New York: John Wiley & Sons, 1947.

Chapter 4 • Basic Company Objectives

CYERT, R. M. and J. G. MARCH. *A Behavioral Theory of the Firm.* Englewood Cliffs: Prentice-Hall, Inc., 1963, Ch. 3.

DAVIS, R. C. *Fundamentals of Top Management.* New York: Harper & Brothers, 1951, Ch. 4 and 6.

DRUCKER, P. F. *The Practice of Management.* New York: Harper & Brothers, 1954, Ch. 7 and 11.

EELLS, R., and C. WALTON. *Conceptual Foundations of Business.* Chicago: R. D. Irwin, Inc., 1961, Ch. 18, 19, and 20.

KOONTZ, H., and C. O'DONNELL. *Principles of Management.* New York: McGraw-Hill Book Co., 1964, Ch. 6.

Chapter 5 • Sales Policies—Products

BERG, T. L., and A. SHUCHMAN (eds.). *Product Strategy and Management.* New York: Holt, Rinehart and Winston, 1963.

COREY, R. *Industrial Marketing.* Englewood Cliffs: Prentice-Hall, Inc., 1962, pp. 145-160.

DEAN, J. P. "Product-Line Policy" in Britt and Boyd, *Marketing Management and Administrative Action.* New York: McGraw-Hill Book Co., 1963, pp. 204-216.

HOWARD, J. A. *Marketing Management,* rev. ed. Chicago: R. D. Irwin, Inc., 1963, Ch. 10.

Chapter 6 • Sales Policies—Customers

ALEXANDER, R. S., F. M. SURFACE, and W. ALDERSON. *Marketing,* 3rd ed. Boston: Ginn and Company, 1953, Ch. 5-13.

BLISS, P. (ed.). *Marketing and the Behavioral Sciences.* Boston: Allyn Bacon, 1963, pp. 41-74.

HOWARD, J. *Marketing Management,* rev. ed. Chicago: R. D. Irwin, Inc., 1963, Ch. 11.

PHELPS, D. M. *Sales Management.* Chicago: R. D. Irwin, Inc., 1951.

Chapter 7 • Sales Policies—Pricing

DEAN, J. P. *Managerial Economics.* New York: Prentice-Hall, Inc., 1951, Ch. 7-9.

KAPLAN, A. D. H., J. B. DIRLAN, and R. F. LANZILLOTTI. *Pricing in Big Business.* Washington: The Brookings Institution, 1958, Ch. 2 and 4.

OTTESON, S. F., W. G. PANSCHAR, and J. M. PATTERSON. *Marketing: The Firm's Viewpoint.* New York: The Macmillan Co., 1964, pp. 434-538.

OXENFELDT, A. R. *Industrial Pricing and Marketing Practices.* Englewood Cliffs: Prentice-Hall, Inc., 1951.

Chapter 8 • Sales Policies—Sales Promotion

HOWARD, J. A. *Marketing Management,* rev. ed. Chicago: R. D. Irwin, Inc., 1963, Ch. 1, 13, and 14.

KIRKPATRICK, C. A. *Advertising.* Boston: Houghton Mifflin Company, 1959, Ch. 1, 2, 19, and 24.

PHELPS, D. M. *Sales Management.* Chicago: R. D. Irwin, Inc., 1951, Ch. 14-16.

TOSDAL, H. R. *Introduction to Sales Management,* 4th ed. New York: McGraw-Hill Book Co., 1957, Ch. 6.

Chapter 9 • Production and Purchasing Policies

BUFFA, E. S. *Modern Production Management.* New York: John Wiley & Sons, 1961, Parts I and III.

FOLTS, F. E. *Introduction to Industrial Management,* 5th ed. New York: McGraw-Hill Book Co., 1963.

MOORE, F. G. *Manufacturing Management,* 3rd ed. Chicago: R. D. Irwin, Inc., 1961, Ch. 6, 7, 9, 10, and 16.

TIMMS, H. L. *The Production Function in Business.* Chicago: R. D. Irwin, Inc., 1962, Part II.

Chapter 10 • Production and Purchasing Policies (Concluded)

ALJIAN, G. W. (ed.). *Purchasing Handbook.* New York: McGraw-Hill Book Co., 1958.

CULLITON, J. W. *Make or Buy.* Cambridge: Harvard University Press, 1942.

ENGLAND, W. B. *Procurement, Principles and Cases,* 4th ed. Chicago: R. D. Irwin, Inc., 1962.

HODGES, H. G. *Procurement, The Modern Science of Purchasing.* New York: Harper & Brothers, 1961.

Chapter 11 • Personnel Policies—Selection and Training

JUCIUS, M. J. *Personnel Management,* 3rd ed. Chicago: R. D. Irwin, Inc., 1955, Ch. 5-16.

PIGORS, P., and C. A. MYERS. *Personnel Administration, A Point of View and a Method,* 4th ed. New York: McGraw-Hill Book Co., 1961, Ch. 14 and 15.

STRAUSS, G., and L. SAYLES. *Personnel.* Englewood Cliffs: Prentice-Hall, Inc. 1960.

WOLF, W. B. *The Management of Personnel.* San Francisco: Wadsworth Publishing Co., Inc., 1961.

Chapter 12 • Personnel Policies—Compensation and Arrangements for Work

ODIORNE, G. S. *Personnel Policy.* Columbus: Charles E. Merrill, 1963.

PIGORS, P., and C. A. MYERS. *Personnel Administration, A Point of View and a Method,* 4th ed. New York: McGraw-Hill Book Co., 1961, Ch. 20-24.

YODER, D. *Handbook of Personnel Management and Labor Relations.* New York: McGraw-Hill Book Co., 1958.

————. *Personnel Management and Industrial Relations,* 5th ed. Englewood Cliffs: Prentice-Hall, Inc., 1962.

Chapter 13 • Personnel Policies—Employee Services and Industrial Relations

CHAMBERLAIN, N. W. *Collective Bargaining.* New York: McGraw-Hill Book Co., 1951.

DUNLOP, J. T., and J. J. HEALY. *Collective Bargaining, Principles and Cases,* rev. ed. Chicago: R. D. Irwin, Inc., 1953.

SELEKMAN, B. M., et al. *Problems in Labor Relations.* New York: McGraw-Hill Book Co., 1958.

WHYTE, W. F. *Money and Motivation.* New York: Harper & Brothers, 1955, Part III.

Chapter 14 • Financial Policies—Uses of Capital

HUNT, P., C. M. WILLIAMS, and G. DONALDSON. *Basic Business Finance,* rev. ed. Chicago: R. D. Irwin, Inc., 1961, Ch. 3, 4, 5, 6, 9, and 18.

JOHNSON, R. W. *Financial Management,* 2nd ed. Boston: Allyn and Bacon, 1962.

LINDSAY, R., and A. W. SAMETZ. *Financial Management: An Analytical Approach.* Chicago: R. D. Irwin, Inc., 1963, Parts II and IV.

WESTON, J. F. *Managerial Finance.* New York: Holt, Rinehart & Winston, Inc., 1962, Ch. 6 and 19.

Chapter 15 • Financial Policies—Sources of Capital

DAUTEN, C. A. *Business Finance,* 2nd ed. Englewood Cliffs: Prentice-Hall, Inc., 1956, Part II.

GUTHMANN, H. G., and H. E. DOUGALL. *Corporate Financial Policy,* 4th ed. Englewood Cliffs: Prentice-Hall, Inc., 1962, Parts IV and VII.

HUSBAND, W. H., and J. C. DOCKERAY. *Modern Corporation Finance,* 5th ed. Chicago: R. D. Irwin, Inc., 1962.

LINDSAY, R., and A. W. SAMETZ. *Financial Management: An Analytical Approach.* Chicago: R. D. Irwin, Inc., 1963, Parts III and IV.

Chapter 16 • Financial Policies—Protection of Capital and Distribution of Earnings

BONNEVILLE, J. H., and L. E. DEWEY. *Organizing and Financing Business*, 6th ed. Englewood Cliffs: Prentice-Hall, Inc., 1959, Ch. 14 and 16.

GUTHMANN, H. G., and H. E. DOUGALL. *Corporate Financial Policy*, 4th ed. Englewood Cliffs: Prentice-Hall, Inc., 1962, Ch. 26 and 30.

HUNT, P., et al. *Basic Business Finance*, rev. ed. Chicago: R. D. Irwin, Inc., 1961, Ch. 15, 17, 19, and 28.

Chapter 17 • Grouping Activities for Effective Operations

BLAU, P. M., and W. R. SCOTT. *Formal Organizations*. San Francisco: Chandler Publishing Co., 1962, Ch. 1, 2, and 4.

GULICK, L., and L. URWICK (eds.). *Papers on the Science of Administration*. New York: Institute of Public Administration, 1937, pp. 1-130 and 173-187.

HOLDEN, P. E., L. S. FISH, and H. L. SMITH. *Top-Management Organization and Control*. New York: McGraw-Hill Book Co., 1948, pp. 30-58.

MOORE, F. G. *Management, Organization and Practice*. New York: Harper & Row, 1964, Ch. 21.

NEWMAN, W. H. *Administrative Action*, 2nd ed. Englewood Cliffs: Prentice-Hall, Inc., 1963, Ch. 9 and 10.

Chapter 18 • Organizational Relationships

BROWN, A. *Organization of Industry*. Englewood Cliffs: Prentice-Hall, Inc., 1947, Ch. 2-15.

LEARNED, E. P., D. N. ULRICH, and D. R. BOOZ. *Executive Action*. Boston: Harvard University Graduate School of Business Administration, 1951.

MARCH, J. G., and H. A. SIMON. *Organizations*. New York: John Wiley & Sons, 1952, Ch. 2 and 5.

McGREGOR, D. *The Human Side of Enterprise*. New York: McGraw-Hill Book Co., 1960, Ch. 5, 11, and 12.

Chapter 19 • Balancing the Organization Structure

DALE, E. *Planning and Developing the Company Organization Structure*, Research Report Number 20. New York: American Management Association, 1952.

HELMER, O. "The Prospects of a Unified Theory of Organization," *Management Science* (January, 1958), pp. 172-176.

HOLDEN, P. E., L. S. FISH, and H. L. SMITH. *Top-Management Organization and Control*. New York: McGraw-Hill Book Co., 1948, pp. 59-75 and 91-103.

MOORE, F. G. *Management, Organization and Practice.* New York: Harper & Row, 1964, Ch. 25, 26, 27, and 28.

NEWMAN, W. H. *Administrative Action,* 2nd ed. Englewood Cliffs: Prentice-Hall, Inc., 1963, Ch. 16 and 17.

Chapter 20 • Board of Directors and Central-Management Organization

BROWN, C. C. *The Director Looks at His Job.* New York: Columbia University Press, 1957.

COPELAND, M. T., and A. W. TOWL. *The Board of Directors and Business Management.* Boston: Harvard University Graduate School of Business Administration, 1947.

COPEMAN, G. *The Role of the Managing Director.* London: B. T. Batsford, Ltd., 1959.

GORDON, R. A. *Business Leadership in the Large Corporation.* Washington: The Brookings Institution, 1945, Ch. 5 and 6.

NEWMAN, W. H., and J. P. LOGAN. *Management of Expanding Enterprises.* New York: Columbia University Press, 1955, Ch. 3.

Chapter 21 • Executive Personnel

HOUSTON, G. C. *Manager Development.* Chicago: R. D. Irwin, Inc., 1961.

MACE, M. L. *The Growth and Development of Executives.* Boston: Harvard University Graduate School of Business Administration, 1950.

McGREGOR, D. *The Human Side of Enterprise.* New York: McGraw-Hill Book Co., 1960, Ch. 13-16.

RIEGEL, J. W. *Executive Development, A Survey of Experience in Fifty American Corporations.* Ann Arbor: University of Michigan Press, 1952.

WARNER, W. L., and N. H. MARTIN (eds.). *Industrial Man.* New York: Harper & Row, 1959, Part 3.

Chapter 22 • Facilities

IRESON, W. G., and E. L. GRANT (eds.). *Handbook of Industrial Engineering and Management.* Englewood Cliffs: Prentice-Hall, Inc.

MAYNARD, H. B. (ed.). *Industrial Engineering Handbook.* New York: McGraw-Hill Book Co., 1956.

MILLER, S., and D. C. D. ROGERS. *Manufacturing Policy,* rev. ed. Chicago: R. D. Irwin, Inc., 1964.

TIMMS, H. L. *The Production Function in Business.* Chicago: R. D. Irwin, Inc., 1962, Part III.

Chapter 23 • Short- and Long-Range Programming

BAUMACK, C. M., and L. J. KONOPA. "Inventory Control: How EOQ Can Help," in Madeheim, Mazze and Stein, *Readings in Organization and Management*. New York: Holt, Rinehart and Winston, 1963.

BOWMAN, E. H., and R. B. FETTER. *Analysis for Production Management*, rev. ed. Chicago: R. D. Irwin, Inc., 1961, Ch. 1-5.

EWING, D. *Long Range Planning for Management*, 2nd ed. New York: Harper & Row, 1964.

ROMAN, D. D. "The PERT System: An Appraisal of Program Evaluation Review Techniques" in Madeheim, et al., *ibid.*, 1963.

STEINER, G. A. (ed.). *Managerial Long-Range Planning*. New York: McGraw-Hill Book Co., 1963, Ch. 7, 9, and 16.

Chapter 24 • Activating

JONES, M. H. *Executive Decision Making*, rev. ed. Chicago: R. D. Irwin, Inc., 1962, Ch. 7 and 15.

KAPPEL, F. R. *Vitality in a Business Enterprise*, McKinsey Foundation Lecture Series. New York: McGraw-Hill Book Co., 1960.

McGREGOR, D. *The Human Side of Enterprise*. New York: McGraw-Hill Book Co., 1960, Ch. 2, 3, and 4.

RUBENSTEIN, A. H., and C. J. HABERSTROH. *Some Theories of Organization*. Homewood, Illinois: Dorsey Press, 1960, Ch. 16 and 17.

Chapter 25 • Controlling Operations

ANDERSON, D. R. *Practical Controllership*. Chicago: R. D. Irwin, Inc., 1947.

GOETZ, B. E. *Managerial Planning and Control*. New York: McGraw-Hill Book Co., 1949, Ch. 5 and 10.

KOONTZ, H., and C. O'DONNELL. *Principles of Management*, 3rd ed. New York: McGraw-Hill Book Co., 1964, Ch. 28-31.

RUBENSTEIN, A. H., and C. J. HABERSTROH. *Some Theories of Organization*. Homewood, Illinois: Dorsey Press, 1960, Ch. 27, 28, and 32.

Chapter 26 • Budgetary Control

BONINI, C. P., R. K. JAEDICKE, and H. M. WAGNER. *Management Controls*. New York: McGraw-Hill Book Co., 1964, Part III.

LEMKE, B. C., and J. D. EDWARDS. *Administrative Control and Executive Action*. Columbus: Chas. E. Merrill Books, Inc., 1961, Ch. 19, 20, 28, 43, 54, and 59.

THOMAS, W. E., JR. *Readings in Cost Accounting, Budgeting, and Control*, 2nd ed. Cincinnati: South-Western Publishing Co., 1960.

WELSCH, G. A. *Budgeting: Profit-Planning and Control*, 2nd ed. Englewood Cliffs: Prentice-Hall, Inc., 1964.

INDEX

A

A.B.C. Corporation, Case XIX, 497
Accounting reserves, 402
Acquisitions and mergers, 353
Activating, 639; goal-centered performance appraisals, 646; incentive structure in, 647; leadership tone, 639; man-to-man communication, 640
Activities, analysis of, 434; departmentation of, 435; grouping of, for effective operations, 431; limits on span of supervision of, 441
Administrative organization, integrated approach to, 741
Advertising, 182; assisting salesmen when calling on customers, 185; bringing customers to place where goods are sold, 183; building institutional goodwill, 185; media, 186; other problems of, 187; persuading customer to ask for specific product, 184; producing direct sales, 185; programming, 616
Agents, 144
Aggressiveness, 88
Analysis, critical path, 625
Analyst, financial, 514
Analytical framework, 3
Andersen Starch Company, Case VII, 173
Annual wage plans, 305
Appraisal of executives, 549; informal, 549; systematic, 550; uses of, 549
Appraisals, goal-centered performance, 646
Appraising, outlook for a company, 48; performance, 669
Arbitration of labor disputes, 315; by group bargaining, 315; government mediation and, 316; impartial, 315
Assets, fixed, see Fixed assets
Auberge Hotels, Inc., Case XXV, 678
Authority, control of delegation of, 462; decentralization of, 458; delegation of, to make decisions, 458; functional, 466; line, 455; to make exceptions, 461; when to delegate, 461
Automatic Lathe Company, Case X, 250

Automation, extent of, 216
Auxiliary departments, 483
Average unit costs, variations in, 161
Average rate of return on investment in fixed assets, 345

B

Balance sheet, estimated, 691
Baldwin Locomotive Company, 61
Banks, commercial, as source of capital, 375
Barber Ice Cream Company, comprehensive case, 787
Bargaining, group, 315; with unions, scope of, 313
Basic objectives, of a company, 81
Benefits, fringe, see Employees
Bell System, long-range program for, 628
Berry Company, William E., Case XXIII, 635
Blair Plastic Company, Case XXII, 595
Blakeman Textiles, Inc., Case XXI, 565
Blends Woven Label Company, Case XIII, 320
Blue Cross hospital insurance, 305
Blue Island Plating Company, Case XI, 274
Board of directors, and central-management organization, 500; duties for a, 509; inactive, 507; inside, 507; legal theory on, 506; membership of, 507; outside, 508; role of, 506
Bond indenture, 373
Bonds, as source of capital, 371; "calling," 375; collateral trust, 373; convertible, 375; debenture, 374; retirement of, 375; secured, 372; serial, 374; sinking fund for, 375; special provisions of, 374
Bonuses, as incentives, 650; executive, 560
Borrowing as a source of capital, 370
Branch, controller's relations with a, 466; sales, 143
Brokers, 144
Budgetary control, 685; essential features of, 685; in a business, 686

Budgets, 685; and coordination, 698; annual, approved by central management, 504; balance sheet, 691; capital, 344; cash, 688; central management use of, 696; comparison of actual results with, 691; control via, 698; effect of, on planning, 696; finished goods, 686; flexible, 695; materials purchases, 687; nonfinancial, 686; other expense, 688; personnel, 688; profit and loss, 691; sales, 686

Building construction, 579; cost of, 580; effect of, on operating costs, 580; provision for expansion of, 582; reducing risks by, 582

Buildings, appearance of, 583; depreciation of, 581; difficulties in selecting, 579; distinction between new and old, 579; interrelation of equipment, layout, and, 590; maintenance of, 581; problems of, requiring attention of manager, 579; service costs of, 581

Business, dynamic setting of, 21

Business economist, 514

Buying, see Purchasing

C

"Calling" bonds, 375

Capacity, backward taper of, 221; balancing, 222; how much, 220; maintenance and replacement of, 223; peak vs. normal load, 220; provision for growth of, 221

Capacity of the industry, 53; excess, 55; undercapacity, 53

Capital, adjusting sources of, to prevailing interest rate, 385; bonds as source of, 371; borrowing as source of, 370; budgeting, 344; circulating, see Circulating capital; collateral trust bonds as source of, 373; commercial banks as source of, 375; cost of, 384; debenture bonds as source of, 374; effect of distribution of earnings on, 405; effect of dividend policies on, 406; effect of profits and losses on requirements of, 338; fixed, 340; from common stock, 368; from new securities, rights granted with, 387; from owners, 367; from preferred stock, 368; long-term, notes as source of, 374; merchandise creditors as source of, 377; mortgages as source of, 372; other short-term credit as source of, 368; protection of, 396; raising new, 89; relation of other policies to use of, 341; return paid on new stock sold for additional, 385; secured bonds as source of, 372; selecting sources of, 383; short-term creditors as source of, 375; sources of, 367; underwriting and registration costs of, 384; use of, 338, 340, 383; use of stock rights as source of, 384; use of stock to raise, 369

Capital expenditures, approved by central management, 503; control of large, 666

Capitalization of disbursements, 403

Cash budgets, 688; monthly, 690

Cash flow, discounted, 345

Centralization vs. decentralization of decision-making, 95

Central management, annual budgets approved by, 504; capital expenditures and contracts approved by, 503; characteristics of problems of, 505; committee, 512; company objectives set by, 501; company-wide, integrated approach to, 735; compensation, see Executive compensation; control tasks of, 671; coordination and control by, 504; critical issues of, 500; distinctive tasks of, 500; insurance on, 399; key personnel selected by, 502; key points in integrated approach to, 743; long-range planning and strategy of, 502; major policies established by, 501; mergers and major agreements negotiated by, 503; officially representing the company, 504; organization of board of directors and, 500; organization structure changes by, 502; problems with buildings, 579; quality of, 96; relative ability of, 67; senior executives in, 510; staff, 513; use of budgets, 696; see also Executive personnel

Central-management problems, approach to, 3; intangibles in administration of, 10; major divisions of, 4; need for analytical framework for, 3; of a small business, 4; of a steel company, 6

Central Wire Company, integrating case, 423

Chain stores, decentralization of authority in, 459

Changes in American affairs, big government, 26; business corporations, 29; economic, 23; education, 22; forecasting, 31; income classes, 24; individual productivity, 25; institutional, 28; labor, 28; long-term, 21; migration, 22; new philosophy, 27; political, 26; population, 21; social, 21; stress and strain of, 30; technological, 25

Channel of distribution, 141; defined, 141; direct to consumers, 143; direct to retailers, 142; nature of problem of, 141; selecting, 144; through brokers or agents, 144; through jobbers, 141

Character of a company, 83; basic objectives that shape, 84

Chief executive, 511

Circulating capital, 340; extension of credit in use of, 349; financial, restrictions on inventory in use of, 348; miscellaneous investments of excess, 352; uses of, 348

Climate as factor in selecting location, 574

Cliques, 258

Closed shops, 312

Collateral trust bonds, 373

Collection policies, 351

Collective action vs. individual action, 493

Commercial banks as source of capital, 375

Commissions as incentives, 650

Committees, benefits of, 481; Community Chest campaign, 479; effective use of, 478; guides for successful operation of, 482; important factors in deciding when to use, 481; limitations of, 481; management, 512; management, in a small firm, 478; role of, in administrative organization, 477; salary, 478; situations where ineffective, 479

Common stock, 368

Communication, by consultative direction, 644; man-to-man, 640; of goal-centered performance appraisals, 646; of workable instructions, 640

Community relations, 90

Company, character of a, 83; comparative location of, 64; cost position of, 64; effect of increasing number of products on, 119; emphasis on stability vs. dynamics, 87; major function of a, 84; management philosophy of the, 95; market position of the, 60; place in industry sought by, 84; products, standing of, 62; relative ability of management of, 67; relative efficiency of equipment of, 65; relative financial strength of, 66; reputation of, in major markets, 63; social philosophy of the, 90; unique cost advantages of the, 66

Company objectives, basic, 81; hierarchy of, 82; relation of, to policies, 82; significance of, 81; that shape company character, 84

Compensation, administration of plan for, 284; amount of, 278; based on combined piece rates and time rates, 286; based on incentive rates, 286; based on profit-sharing plans, 288; based on results, 285; based on time spent, 285; executive, *see* Executive

compensation; high, 279; industry rates of, 280; low, 279; method of payment of, 285; personnel policies on, 278; recognizing differences in individual performance, 282; relation of, for different jobs within company, 280; relation of, to market, 278

Competitive conditions in the industry, 58

Competitors, contact with, 93; price agreements among, 158; reaction of, to pricing policy, 157

Composite, organization, 444; pricing policies, 165

Construction, *see* Building construction

Consultative direction, 644

Consumers, attitude of, toward style, 121; defined, 133; delimiting market area of, 140; direct channel of distribution to, 143; for consulting services, 135; for retail stores, 134; foreign, 139; from rural to urban, 139; location of, 137; market analysis of, 136; recognition of product differences by, 122; selection of, 134

Contracts, approved by central management, 503; hedging future, 401

Control, budgetary, 685; by appraising performance, 669; by central management, 504; by corrective action, 670; by standards of performance, 668; exercised by central management, 674; inventory, 665; nature of, 663; of delegation of authority, 462; of executive development, 667; of large capital expenditures, 666; of sales volume, 664; quality, in a food plant, 664; relation of, to decentralization, 671; relation of, to other phases of management, 674; reports, 669; representative problems of, 664; strictness of, 98; structure, chart for company, 672; structure, company, 671; tasks of central management, 671; through integrated data processing, 673; via budgets, 698; willingness to share ownership, 89

Controller, relation of, with a branch, 466

Convertible bonds, 375

Coordination, budgets and, 698; by central management, 504

Corporation, business, as an institution, 29

Cost advantages, unique, 66

Cost position of a company in the industry, 64

Costs, average unit, variations in, 161; effect of volume on, 161; incremental, 140; labor, 55; material, 56; of design change, 122; relation of, to pricing policies, 149; selling at a normal profit above, 159; selling below, 160; taxes and other, 57

Credit, collection policies for extension of, 351; extension of, 349; factors influencing policy on, 349; installment, 350; line, 376; short-term, as source of capital, 378

Creditors, merchandise, as source of capital, 377; long-term, as source of capital, 370; rights granted to, 387; short-term, as source of capital, 375

Critical path, definition of, 625

Critical path analysis, 625; chart showing, 626; general applicability of, 627; major features of, 625

Current ratio, 348

Customers, defined, 133; departments for various classes of, 439; large, 146; selection of, 134; service to, 92; size of, 145; small, 145

Cyclical fluctuations, 118; production based on, 244

D

Data processing, integrated, control through, 673

Debenture bonds, 374

Decentralization, of authority, 458; of operating units, 217; of operations, benefits of, 577; profit, 462; relation of controls to, 671; versus centralization in decision-making, 95

Decision-making, centralization vs. decentralization of, 95

Deconcentration of operations, 577

Delegation of authority, and the task of control, 462; to make decisions, 458; see also Decentralization

Demand for products or services of the industry, 49

Departmentation, 435; bases of, 435; basic factors in, 441; by customer, 439; by function, 440; by process, 437; by products, 435; by territory, 438; in a department store, 436; in packing companies, 435; parallel, 488

Departments, auxiliary, 483; customer, 439; exercising functional authority, 467; functional, 440; operating vs. service divisions, 483; process, 437; product, 435; territorial, 438

Department store organization, 436

Depreciation of buildings, 581

Design, use of, in selling, 180

Design change, costs of, 122; frequency of, 122, 124; pressures for, 123

Development of executives, 556; by training off the job, 558; by training on the job, 557; centered on individual, 556; programs for, 549; understudy method of, 557

Direct-line production, process versus, 588

Directors, board of, see Board of directors

Direct sales, advertising producing, 185

Discharge, of present employees, 263; reasons for, 264; seniority and, 264; transfer rather than, 263

Disciplinary action as motivation, 652

Discounted cash flow method of calculating rate of return on fixed assets, 345

Discounts, from established prices, 167; quantity, 168; trade, 167

Discrimination, racial, 256

Distress merchandise, buying, 235

Distribution, channels of, see Channels of distribution

Dividends, conclusion regarding policies for, 409; of Great Western Sugar Co., 408; policies on, 405; stable, 406

Diversification, dangers of unwise, 116; factors favoring, 117; spreading risks by, 119; versus specialization, 85, 114

Division-of-labor, extent of, 216

Dual executive, 512

Dual subordination, 457

Dynamics vs. stability, 87

E

Earnings, plowing back, 405; retained, need for adequate, 407; see also Compensation

Eastern States Iron and Steel Co., comprehensive case, 864

Economic, and government responsibility, 91; changes in American affairs, 23; education, 269

Economical sales unit, 118

Economic outlook, an approach to the, 32; for a company, 60; for an industry, 49; for general conditions, 31; long-range forecasting of, 32; short-range forecasting of, 36

Economist, business, 514

Education, changes, 22; economic, 269

Efficiency of equipment, relative, 65

Electro-Motive division of General Motors Corporation, 62

Employees, annual wage plans for, 305; compensation of, 278; fringe benefits for, 29; group life insurance for, 305; health programs for, 304; kinds of protection for, 304; medical care plans for, 304; pension plans for, 306; protection of, methods of financing, 306; regard for, 94; risks of, 303; security plans for, management of, 307; services for, 301; sick leave for, 304; social and recreational activities for, 301; supplementary unemployment benefits for, 305; unemployment insurance for, 305; *see also* Personnel policies

Employment Act of 1946, 27

Equipment, choice of new, 585; factors affecting choice of, 584; interrelation of buildings, layout, and, 590; layout of, 588; numerous kinds of, 583; replacing present, 586; selection of, 583; *see also* Fixed assets

Equity, trading on the, 372

Estimated balance sheet, 691

Evaluation of executives, 548

Exceptions, authority to make, 461

Execution, 4; by a small business, 5; by a steel company, 8; definition of, 613; interdependence of, 9

Executive compensation, 559; base salaries as, 559; bonuses as, 560; nonfinancial, 562; pensions as, 559; stock options as, 561

Executive development program, control of, 667; essentials of a sound, 545; formal, 544; informal, 544

Executive personnel, anticipating requirements for, 546; appraisal, 549; characteristics of, 547; development, 513; development of talents of, 556; development programs for, 544; importance of, 541; inventory of talent of, 548; jobs to be filled, 546; plans for progression of, 551; wide variation in company practice with regard to, 541

Executive progression, methods of selection for, 554; need for planned, 551; replacement table approach to, 551

Expansion, dangers of unwise, 116; of a product line, 115; program, 620

Expense budgets, 688

Expenses, out-of-pocket, pricing on basis of, 160

F

Facilities, 570; as part of business administration, 570; building, *see* Buildings; definition of, 570; equipment, *see* Equipment; location of, 571

Federal Reserve Board Index, 24

Federal Trade Commission, 58

Financial, analyst, 514; incentives, 650; security, as motivation, 648; strength, relative, 66

Financial policies, classification of, 339; integrated, approach to, 740;

on distribution of earnings, 405; on financial structure, 379; on mergers and acquisitions, 353; on protection of capital, 396; on selecting capital sources, 383; on sources of capital, 367; on uses of capital, 338; on uses of circulating capital, 348; regulating investment in fixed assets, 341; summary outline of, 411

Financial structure, meaning of, 379; of Long-Shot Printing Co., 381; of Red River Power Co., 381; of Schultz Electronic Controls, Inc., 380

Financing, a merger, 355; costs, changes in corporate, 386; of special equipment used by distributors, 342

Findlager & Sons, Inc., J., integrating case, 329

Finished goods budgets, 686

Firing employees, *see* Discharge

Fixed assets, capital budgeting for, 344; discounted cash flow computation for, 345; financing of special, used by distributors, 342; investment in, general restrictions on, 341; investment in, long-term outlook for, 343; leasing vs. purchase of, 347; minimum rate of return on, 343; regulating investment in, 341; *see also* Equipment

Fixed capital, 340

Flexible budgets, 695

Flexibility, in assignment of duties, 463; retention of, in organization, 492

Flow, discounted cash, 345

Fluctuations, seasonal or cyclical, 118; other ways of dealing with, 244; production based on, 243

Follow-up instructions, 643

Forecasting, approach to, 48; changes in environment, 31; competitive conditions in the industry, 58; cost position of a company, 64; demand for industry products or services, 49; long-range, 33; market position of a company, 60; outlook for industry and company, 48; role of, 37; short-range, 36; special competitive considerations, 66; supply of industry products or services, 53; use of GNP in, 33

Foreign markets, 139

Framework, analytical, 3

Frederick & Frank, comprehensive case, 914

Fringe benefits, *see* Employees

Functional authority, 466; composite, 468; other departments exercising, 467; reasons for cautious use of, 467; situations warranting use of, 466

Functional departments, 440
Fund, sinking, 374
Future contracts, hedging, 401

G

General Motors Corporation, Electro-Motive division, 62
GNP (gross national product), 32
Goal-centered performance appraisals, 646
Goals, company, *see* Company objectives
Goodwill, building institutional, by advertising, 185
Government, and economic responsibility, 91; big, 26; new philosophy of, 27; regulation of industry, 59
Grand Canyon hotel expansion, 620
Great Western Sugar Co., net profits and dividends of, 408
Gross national product (GNP), 32; in long-run forecasting, 33; national income and, accounts, 33
Group bargaining, 315
Group life insurance, 305

H

Hargrove, O'Donnell and Company, integrating case, 202
Health program for employees, 304
Hedging, 401; future contracts, 401; limitations on use of, 402; process, 401
Hiring, college students, 255; from within or outside the company, 259; nepotism and cliques in, 258; new employees from outside the company, 260; policies, classified, 258; racial discrimination in, 256; salesmen, 257; *see also* Personnel policies
Hoopes Ribbon Company, integrating case, 196
Horizontal, promotion, 262; strata in an organization structure, 455
Hours of work, 289; adjusting, to operations, 291; 35-hour week, 291
Human relations, and supervisory training, 268; in organization, 489

I

I.C.L.A. Construction Company, Case XVIII, 471
Impartial arbitration, 315
Incentive rates, 286; conditions affecting success of, 287; workers' attitude toward, 287
Incentives, attractive work, 649; disciplinary actions as, 652; financial, 650; financial security, 648; good treatment, 649; indirect, 647; influence and power, 651; positive, 650; psychological security, 648; respect by fellow men, 651; structure of, 647
Income, classes, changes in, 24; distribution, 23; personal, percent change in, 138; total, 23
Incremental costs, 140
Index, Federal Reserve Board, 24; of output and man-hours in the private economy, 1900-60, 27
Indirect motivation, 647
Individual, action vs. collective action, 493; adjustments to ability of, in business organization, 490; freedom within business organization, 494; in political organization, 493; productivity, 25
Induction, 266
Industrial relations, 308
Industrial Scale Company, Case XV, 391
Industry, capacity of the, 53; competitive conditions in the, 58; cost position of a company in the, 64; demand for products or services of the, 49; government regulation of, 59; labor costs for the, 55; material costs for the, 56; nature of companies in the, 58; organization of the, 59; place company seeks in the, 84; supply of products or services, 53; taxes and other costs for the, 57
Installment credit, 350
Institutional goodwill, building, by advertising, 185
Instructions, consultative, 644; follow-up, 643; tests of good, 642; workable, 640
Insurance, 397; company, selection of an, 400; nature of, 397; premium, 397; self-, 398; type and amount of, 398
Insurance for employees, annual wage plan, 305; Blue Cross, 305; group life, 305; major medical expenses, 305; supplementary unemployment, 305; unemployment, 305
Intangibles in administration, 10
Integrated approach, administrative organization, 741; execution of plans, 743; financial policies, 740; key points in, 743; need for, 735; outlook and basic objectives, 737; personnel policies, 739; production and purchasing policies, 738; resources 742; sales policies, 737; steps in, 735; to central management, 735; value of general survey to, 745
Integrated data processing, control through, 673
Integration, vertical, *see* Vertical integration

Interest rate, adjusting sources of capital to prevailing, 385

Inventory, control, 665; effect of valuation of, on profits, 404; financial restrictions on, 348; liquidation of, 160; minimum, 240; of executive talent, 548; speculation, the case against, 247

Investments, conservative policy for, 352; in fixed assets, 341; large bank balances as, 352; miscellaneous, 352; securities as, 352

Island Creek Coal Company, Case III, 70

J

Jobbers, 141

Job evaluation, 282

Jones Joints, Inc., comprehensive case, 823

Jurisdictional disputes, union, 313

K

Kaiser, Henry J., 88

Key personnel, quality of, 96; selection of, 502

Koch Electronics, Inc., Case XX, 517

L

Labor, as factor in selecting location, 574; changes in America, 28; costs, 55; division-of-, extent of, 216; unions, see Unions

Layout, 588; interrelation of buildings, equipment, and, 590; of retail store, 592; of woodworking shop, 591; process vs. direct-line production, 588; steps in improving, 591

Leaders, loss, 161

Leadership tone, 639; in contacts throughout the company, 640; in relations with immediate associates, 639

Leasing vs. purchase of fixed assets, 347

Level of operations, peak vs. normal, 220

Levels of maintenance, 223

Life insurance, group, 305

Line authority, 455; dual subordination in, 457; nature of, 456

Lining, price, 165

Liquidation of inventory, 160

Location, comparative, 64; deconcentration of, 577; factors affecting choice of, 573; narrowing choice of, 575; of buildings, 579; of facilities, 571; of hosiery mill, factors affecting, 571

Long-range forecasting, application of, 35; of changes in environment, 31; use of GNP in, 33

Long-range planning and strategy of central management, 502

Long-range programming, 628; applications of, 628; major benefits of, 630; nature of, 628; period covered by, 632; problems involved in, 632; revisions of, 633; topics covered by, 632; who prepares, 633

Long-Shot Printing Company, borrowing problem of, 370; financial structure of, 381

Long-term, changes in American affairs, 21; creditors as source of capital, 370; notes as source of capital, 374; outlook for investment in fixed assets, 343

Loss leaders, 161

M

Made-to-order policy, 239

Maintenance, 223; levels of, 223; of buildings, 581; preventive, 224

Major medical expenses insurance for employees, 305

Major Spectacle Corporation, Case XII, 296

Make-or-buy policies, for products, 210; for supplies and services, 231; guides to, 232; see also Production and purchasing policies

Management, see Central management

Management committee, 512; in a small firm, 478

Management philosophy of the company, 95

Management staff, 513

Managing a small business, 4

Man specifications, 547

Man-to-man communication, 640

Margins, effect of high profit, 159

Markdowns, 169

Market analysis, consumer, 133

Market position of the company, 60

Market prices, using accepted, 166

Markets, as factor in selecting location, 573; delimiting, 140; foreign, 139; relation of wages to, 278; sensitivity of, 157

Materials, as factor in selecting location, 573; costs, 56; purchase budget, 687

Mead Johnson Company, 62, 63

Mechanization, extent of, 216

Media, advertising, 186

Mediation of labor disputes, government, 316

Medical care plans for employees, 304

Membership in trade unions, 28

Merchandising programming, 615

Merger, alternative ways to finance a, 355; economic benefits of a, 354; financial expediency of a, 353; negotiated by central management,

503; problems of compatibility in a, 355; reasons for entering a, 353

Merit increases in base pay, 650

Metzger Chemical Company, Case V, 127

Middle States Steel Company, Case IX, 227

Migration, 22

Minimum rate of return on fixed assets, 343

Mortgages, 372

Motivation, attractive work as, 649; disciplinary action as, 652; financial, 650; financial security as, 648; good treatment as, 649; indirect, 647; of influence and power, 651; of respect by fellow men, 651; positive, 650; psychological security as, 648; *see also* Incentives

N

National Lumber and Plywood Company, Case II, 41

National Sponge Rubber Division of Nation-Wide Rubber and Chemical Corporation, integrating case, 533

Nepotism, 258

Net profit, *see* Profits

Network in critical path analysis, 625

Nonfinancial budgets, 686

Nonskid Tire Company, budgets for, 686-696

Normal load vs. peak capacity, 220

Normal profit, 159

Norris-LaGuardia Anti-Injunction Act, 28

Norris Paper Company, comprehensive case, 749

Notes, long-term, as source of capital, 374

Novins Wallpaper Company, comprehensive case, 888

O

Oates Co., The Silas, Case I, 13

Objectives, 4; basic company, 81; company, set by central management, 501; interdependence of, 9; of a small business, 5; of a steel company, 6

Occupational distribution of employed males in United States, 257

One-price policy, 167

Operating departments, relationships of, with service divisions, 485; versus service departments, 483

Operations, controlling, 663; deconcentration of, 577; grouping activities for effective, 431; level of, 220

Organization, 4; activity analysis, 434; adaption of, to crucial factors, 487; adding another executive to the, 491; adjustment of, to ability of individuals, 490; administrative, integrated approach to, 741; balanced structure of, 487; board of directors and central-management, 500; by customer departments, 439; by functional departments, 440; collective vs. individual action in, 493; composite, 444; departmentation in, 435; factors to be considered in establishing an, 433; freedom of individual within, 494; hierarchy in large concerns, 433; horizontal strata in structure of an, 455; interdependence of, 9; limits on span of supervision in departmentalized, 441; need for, in a growing business, 432; of a college, 431; of a dairy company, 438; of a department store, 436; of a manufacturing concern, 444; of a packing company, 435; of a small business, 5; of a steel company, 7; of the industry, 59; operating departments vs. service divisions in the, 483; parallel departmentation in, 488; personal side of, 489; planning staff, 513; political, individual in, 493; process departments in, 437; product departments in, 435; restricting scope of responsibility in, 490; retention of flexibility in, 492; revised plan of, 444; role of committees in administrative, 477; sales, 188; span of supervision factor in, 435; structure, changing, 502; suggested approach to, 434; territorial departments in, 438; too much emphasis on personalities in, 491; viewpoint of supervisor and supervised toward, 494

Organizational relationships, 455; decentralization of authority in, 458; functional authority in, 466; line authority in, 455; staff, 463

Organization chart, of a manufacturing concern before and after reorganization, 446, 447; of an electric clock company, 484

Orient Magnetics Company, integrating case, 325

Outlook, appraising the, for a company, 48; economic, an approach to the, 32; long-term, for investment in fixed assets, 343

Out-of-pocket expenses, 160

Output, total, 24

P

Parallel departmentation, 488

Parker Gear Company, integrating case, 721

Pay, *see* Compensation

Peak capacity vs. normal load, 220

Pensions, for executives, 559; old-age, 306

Performance, appraisals, goal-centered, 646; appraising, 669; standards of, 668

Personal, income, percent change in, 138; relations in organization, 489; solicitation, 187

Personnel, budgets, 688; development, 513; executive, *see* Executive personnel; key, quality of, 96; sales, 188; selection of key, 502

Personnel policies, 253; classification of, 254; integrated approach to, 738; new attitude toward, 254; on arrangements for work, 289; on compensation, 278; on discharge of present employees, 263; on employee services, 301; on hiring college students, 255; on hiring new employees from outside the company, 260; on hours of work, 289; on industrial relations, 308; on nepotism and cliques, 258; on promotion within the company, 262; on racial discrimination, 256; on selection, 255, 258; on selection from within or outside the company, 259; on selection of salesmen, 257; on training, 265; on vacations, 291; on working conditions, 293; summary outline of, 411

PERT (Program Evaluation and Review Technique), 625; development of, 625; general applicability of, 627; in actual situation, 626; major features of, 625

Philosophy, management, of the company, 95; social, of the company, 90

Phoenix Company, Case VI, 149

Piece rates, 286

Planning, advance, extent of, 97; *see also* Programming

Policies, 4, 113; bearing of, on organization, 434; customer, *see* Sales policies *and* Customers; establishing major, 501; financial, *see* Financial policies; interdependence of, 9; make-or-buy, *see* Make-or-buy policies; of a small business, 5; of a steel company, 6; personnel, *see* Personnel policies; pricing, *see* Pricing policies; production, *see* Production and purchasing policies; purchasing, *see* Purchasing policies; relation of objectives to, 82; sales, *see* Sales policies

Policy issues, major, in business enterprises, summary of, 410

Political, changes in American affairs, 26; organization, individual in, 493

Population changes, 21

Positive incentives, 650

Preferred stock, 368

Premier Paper Company, Case XVI, 414

Premium, insurance, 397

Present value of investment in fixed assets under discounted cash flow method, 345

Price, agreements among competitors, 158; changes, procurement adjusted to anticipated, 245; level, estimating profits for different, 163; lining, 165; protection, 169

Prices, changes in, 169; comparative quality and, 156; discounts from established, 167; effect of price agreements among competitors on, 158; influence of size of company quoting low, 158; of individual items, 165; reaction of competitors to, 157; relation of, to competing products, 156; response of volume to changes in, 164; role of, in selecting vendors, 237; sensitivity of markets to, 157; using accepted market, 166

Pricing policies, composite, 165; effect of volume on costs and profits under, 161; on basis of out-of-pocket expenses, 160; on comparative quality and price, 156; on different prices for different customers, 167; on discount from established prices, 167; one-price, 167; on highly standardized products, 156; on markdowns, 169; on price changes, 169; on regional differences, 168; on relation to competing products, 156; on selling at normal profit above cost, 159; on selling below cost, 160; need for, 155; price protection as part of, 169; reaction of competitors to, 157; regulating prices of individual items, 165; relation of competing products to, 156; relation of costs to, 159; sales, 155; using accepted market prices, 166; when there are differences in quality and services, 156

Process, departments, 437; production, 215; versus direct-line production, 588

Product, departments, 435; differentiation, 121; line, expansion of a, 115; policies, 114; quality, 121

Production, based on anticipated price changes, 245; based on seasonal and cyclical fluctuations, 243; coordination of purchasing, sales, and, 238; for stock or "to order," 239, 243; integrated approach to, 738; process vs. direct-line, 588; run, size of, 241; scheduling, 617; stabilization of, 242

Production and purchasing policies, 209, 231; capacity as factor in, 220;

coordination of sales with, 238; for maintenance and replacement, 223; for production processes, 215; for selection of vendors, 233; historical changes in, 209; integrated approach to, 738; requiring central-management attention, 210; summary outline of, 410; timing of, 247; to make-or-buy supplies and services, 231; vertical integration of, 210

Production processes, 215; capacity for, 220; choice of technology in, 215; division-of-labor in, 216; maintenance and replacement of, 223; mechanization and automation in, 216; research in, 218; size and decentralization of, 217

Productivity, individual, 25

Products, ability to pay for, 52; company, standing of, 62; competing, relation of prices to, 156; demand for industry, 49; diversification of, 114; durability of, 51; effect of increasing number of, 119; fluctuations in demand for, 51; industry supply of, 53; nature of use of, 52; pricing of highly standardized, 156; quality level of, 85; specialization of, 85; stability of desire for, 50; substitutes for, 50; technological and social changes in, 51; usefulness and desire for, 49; variety of, 116

Profit margins, effect of high, 159

Profits, calculation of, 402; decentralization of, 462; effect of accounting reserves on, 402; effect of capitalization of disbursements on, 403; effect of inventory valuation on, 404; effect of volume on, 161; estimating, for different price levels, 163; normal, 159; of Great Western Sugar Company, 408; plowing back, 405; policy issues in determination of, 404

Profit-sharing plans, 288

Program Evaluation and Review Technique, see PERT

Programming, 613; basic steps in, 621; company-wide, 614; critical path analysis of, 625; distinguished from scheduling, 614; for expansion, 620; for special purposes, 620; for tax revision, 621; long-range, see Long-range programming; nature of, 613; PERT analysis of, 625; short-range, see Short-range programming; see also Scheduling

Prometheus Steel Corporation, Case VIII, 193

Promotion, horizontal, 262; type of man for, 263; vertical, 262; within the company, 262

Psychological security as motivation, 648

Purchase order, size of, 241

Purchasing, conservative, 246; coordination of production, sales, and, 238; shrewd, 245

Purchasing policies, see Production and purchasing policies

Q

Quality, as a sales appeal, 180; comparative price and, 156; control in a food plant, 664; level, 85; of key personnel, 96; pricing when there are differences in, 156; what is, 121

Quality Watch Company, Case XIV, 359

Quantity discounts, 168

R

Racial discrimination, 256

Rate of return on fixed assets, computed by discounted cash flow method, 345; in capital budgeting, 344; minimum, 343

Ratio, current, 348

Reciprocity with vendors, 237

Recreational activities for employees, 301

Red River Power Company, borrowing power of, 370; financial structure of, 381

Registration cost of capital, 384

Reorganization of a manufacturing concern, 444

Replacement, of capacity, 223; scheduled, 224

Replacement table, 553; approach to executive progression, 552

Reputation, effect of, on sales, 181; of company in major markets, 63

Research, process, 218

Reserves, accounting, 402

Resources, 4; integrated approach to, 742; interdependence of, 9; of a small business, 5; of a steel company, 7

Retailers, direct channel of distribution to, 142

Retail store, layout, 592; markdowns in, 169; selecting consumers for a, 134; services offered by a, 178

Retained earnings, need for adequate, 407

Retirement of bonds, 375

Return on fixed assets, rate of, see Rate of return on fixed assets

Rights, granted to creditors, 387; granted to stockholders, 387; granted with new securities, 387; stock, use of, 384

Risks, business, 396; hedging of, 401; insurance against, 397; of employees, 303; reducing, by building construction, 582; reduction of, 396; spreading, by diversification, 119; willingness to take, 89

Robbins Lawn Mower Company, Inc., comprehensive case, 777

Rocklyn Corporation, comprehensive case, 844

S

St. Louis Blues, Inc., Case XVII, 453

Salaries, executive, 559

Salary, *see* Compensation

Salary committees, 478

Sales, branches, 143; budget, 686; coordination of production, purchasing, and, 238; direct, by advertising, 185; personnel, organization, and techniques, 188; relation of company, to industry and leading companies, 61; unit, economical, 118; volume, control of, 664

Sales appeals, 177; of salesmen, 181; of vendors, 237; other, 182; quality as, 180

Salesmen, differences in use of, 187; selection of, 257

Sales policies, classification of, 114; in relation to prices of competing products, 156; integrated approach to, 737; on advertising, 182; on channels of distribution, 141; on customers, 133; on different prices for different customers, 167; on diversification vs. specialization, 114; on location of consumers, 137; on frequency of design change, 122; on personal solicitation, 187; on price changes, 169; on pricing, 155; on product differentiation, 121; on products, 113; on sales appeals, 177; on sales promotion, 177; on size of customers, 145; regulating prices of individual items, 165; relation of, to costs, 159; summary outline of, 410

Sales promotion, 177; advertising, 182; appeals, 177; approach to problems of, 189; personal solicitation, 187; programming, 616

Scheduling, distinguished from programming, 614; nature of, 613; production, 617; selling and shipment of goods, 618; *see also* Programming

Schultz Electronic Controls, Inc., financial structure of, 380

Seasonal fluctuations, 118; production based on, 243

Secured bonds, 372

Securities, investment in, 352

Security, financial, as motivation, 648; psychological, as motivation, 648

Selection, of salesmen, 257; from within or outside the company, 259; of employees, 255; of new employees from outside the company, 260; policies classified, 258

Self-insurance, 398

Senior executives, 510; chief, 511; dual, 512; legal titles of, 510; tasks performed by, 511

Seniority and discharge, 264

Serial bonds, 374

Service divisions, drawbacks of separate, 486; need to distinguish, 483; operating departments versus, 483; relationships with operating departments, 485

Service Drug Wholesale, Inc., Case XXIV, 656

Services, ability to pay for, 52; consulting, consumers for, 135; customer, 92; demand for industry, 49; industry supply of, 53; make-or-buy, 231; offered by retail stores, 178; other customer, 180; pricing when there are differences in, 156; of vendors, 236

Short-range forecasting, of general economic conditions, 36

Short-range programming, 614; company-wide, 614; for merchandising, 615; for production scheduling, 617; for sales promotion, 616; for selling and shipment of goods, 618

Short-term, credit, other, as source of capital, 378; creditors as source of capital, 375

Sick leave for employees, 304

Silas Oates Company, Case I, 13

Sinking fund, 374

Slack time in critical path analysis, 625

Small business, managing a, 4

Social activities for employees, 301

Social changes, in American affairs, 21; in products, 51

Social philosophy of the company, 90

Solie Bakeries, Inc., integrating case, 713

Span of supervision, 441; factors restricting effective, 442; limits on, 441; other factors affecting optimum, 443; too narrow a, 442

Specialization vs. diversification, 85; of products, 114

Split, stock, 369

Stabilization of production, 242

Staff, assistants, general, 463; central-management, 513; chart used in company training manual, 464; relationships, 463; relationships, essential factors in good, 465; specialized, 464

Standardized products, pricing of highly, 156
Standards of performance, 668
State Telephone Company, Case XXVI, 702
Stock, common, 368; options as executive compensation, 561; preferred, 368; return paid on new, sold for additional capital, 385; rights, use of, 384; split, 369; use of, to raise capital, 369
Stockholders, rights granted to, 387
Style, consumer attitude toward, 121; use of, in selling, 180
Subordination, dual, 457
Substitutes for products, 50
Suburban Fuel Company, long-range program for, 629
Supervision, span of, *see* Span of supervision
Supplementary unemployment benefits, 305
Supplies, make-or-buy, 231

T

Taft-Hartley Act, 29
Tax revision program, 621
Taxes for an industry, 57
Technological changes, 25; in processes, 215; in products, 51
Territorial departments, 438
Textron Mills at Nashua, The, Case IV, 101
Time rates, combined piece rates and, 286; use of, 285
Total income, 23
Total output, 24
Town Shirt Company, integrating case, 522
Trade discounts, 167
Trading on the equity, 372
Training employees, basic issues in, 265; need for, 265; place of, in company management, 265; purposes of, 266; types of, 269
Triboro Textile Equipment Company, integrating case, 598
Trust bonds, collateral, 373

U

Undercapacity, 53
Understudy for an executive, 557
Underwriting cost of capital, 384
Unemployment insurance, plan for employees, 305; supplementary, 305
Unions, belligerent policy towards, 309; character of relations with, 309; follow the leader approach to, 310; horse-trading approach to, 310; management cooperation with, 311; membership in, 28; recourse to outside agencies in relations with, 315; scope of bargaining with, 313; straight business relationship with, 310; support of, 312
Union shop, 312
Unit costs, average, variations in, 161
United States Steel Corporation, price structure, 58; trends in hours and earnings, 290
Universal Company, 342

V

Vacations, 291
Vendors, reciprocity with, 237; role of price in selecting, 237; number of, 233; selection of, 233; services of, 236; summary regarding selection of, 237; types of, 235
Vertical integration, 210; in automobile industry, 211; in frozen food companies, 212; in publishing field, 211; key factors in, 212
Vertical promotion, 262
Volume, effect of, on costs and profits, 161; factors affecting response of, to changes in price, 164

W

Wage plans, annual, 305
Wages, *see* Compensation
Wagner Act, 28
Western Nadir Markets, Inc., integrating case, 606
Western Plywood Mills, Inc., integrating case, 418
Work, hours of, 289
Working conditions, 293